Sean Egan is a journalist, author and editor specializing in popular culture and sport. He has written for, among other outlets, *Billboard, Classic Rock, Death Ray, Goldmine, Guitar, Inside United, Record Collector, RollingStone.com, SFX, Tennis World, Uncut* and *Vox*. He is the author or editor of eleven books, including works on The Animals, Jimi Hendrix and The Rolling Stones. One of his books – *Jimi Hendrix and the Making of "Are You Experienced"* – was nominated for an Award for Excellence in Historical Recorded Sound Research by the Association for Recorded Sound Collections. His critically acclaimed novel *Sick Of Being Me* was published in 2003, while his 2008 collection of short stories, *Don't Mess With The Best*, carried cover endorsements from Booker Prize winners Stanley Middleton and David Storey.

The Mammoth Book of

The Beatles

Edited and with an Introduction by
Sean Egan

ROBINSON

RUNNING PRESS
PHILADELPHIA · LONDON

Constable & Robinson Ltd
3 The Lanchesters
162 Fulham Palace Road
London W6 9ER
www.constablerobinson.com

First published in the UK by Robinson,
an imprint of Constable & Robinson Ltd, 2009

A copy of the British Library Cataloguing in Publication
Data is available from the British Library

UK ISBN 978-1-84529-943-9

1 3 5 7 9 10 8 6 4 2

First published in the United States in 2009
by Running Press Book Publishers

9   8   7   6   5   4   3   2   1

Digit on the right indicates the number of this printing

US Library of Congress number: 2008942201
US ISBN 978-0-76243-627-9

Running Press Book Publishers
2300 Chestnut Street
Philadelphia, PA 19103-4371

Visit us on the web!
www.runningpress.com
Printed and bound in the UK by
CPI Mackays, Chatham ME5 8TD

CONTENTS

PART TWO: DISSENTERS

PART THREE: FILM AND TV

PART FOUR: BEATLE WOMEN

PART FIVE: INTERVIEWS

PART SIX: AND IN THE END . . .

APPENDIX

ACKNOWLEDGMENTS

"With The Beatles – Pre-Fame" © Antion Meredith, 2008
"Why The Beatles Create All That Frenzy"
  From *Evening Standard*, 2 February 1963
"How Does a Beatle Live? John Lennon Lives Like This"
  From *London Evening Standard*, 4 March 1966
  Reprinted by permission of Evening Standard/Associated News-
  papers Ltd.
"Beatles On TV Baffle Viewers"
  From *Daily Mail*, Wednesday 31 December 1967
  Reprinted by permission of Daily Mail/Associated News-
  papers Ltd.
"How They Changed And How They Changed Us"
  From *Daily Mail*, Saturday 11 April 1970
  Reprinted by permission of Daily Mail/Associated Newspapers
  Ltd.

"Paul Asks High Court: Break Up The Beatles"
  From *Evening News*, Thursday 31 December 1970
  Reprinted by permission of Evening News/Associated News-
  papers Ltd.

"BEATLEMANIA!"
  From *Daily Mirror*, Saturday 2 November 1963
"Yeah, Yeah, Yeah!"
  From *Daily Mirror*, Wednesday 6 November 1963
"MBE? You're Joking Of Course"

"Pattie Boyd: Something In The Way She Moved" © Ken Sharp, 2008

From *Goldmine* magazine in 2008.

Reprinted by permission of the author.

"That Old Gang Of Mine: John And Yoko" © Alan Clayson, 2008

"When Paul Met Linda" © Phil Sutcliffe, 2002

From Mojo special *1000 Days That Shook The World; The Psychedelic Beatles*

Reprinted by permission of the author.

"Masters Of Rock: The Beatles"

Extract from *Masters Of Rock* by Paul Gambaccini, British Broadcasting Corporation/Omnibus Press, 1982. © Paul Gambaccini, 1982

Reprinted by permission of the author.

Introduction; "Love Me Do b/w P.S. I Love You"; "Please Please Me b/w Ask Me Why"; *"Please Please Me";* "From Me To You b/w Thank You Girl"; "She Loves You b/w I'll Get You"; *"With The Beatles";* "I Want To Hold Your Hand b/w This Boy"; "Can't Buy Me Love b/w You Can't Do That"; *"Long Tall Sally";* "A Hard Day's Night b/w Things We Said Today"; *"A Hard Day's Night";* "I Feel Fine b/w She's A Woman"; *"Beatles For Sale";* "Ticket To Ride b/w Yes It Is"; "Help! b/w I'm Down"; *"Help!";* "Day Tripper/We Can Work It Out"; *"Rubber Soul";* "Paperback Writer b/w Rain"; "Eleanor Rigby/Yellow Submarine"; *"Revolver";* *"A Collection Of Beatles Oldies";* "Penny Lane/Strawberry Fields Forever"; "All You Need Is Love b/w Baby You're A Rich Man"; "Hello, Goodbye b/w I Am The Walrus"; *"Magical Mystery Tour";* "Lady Madonna b/w The Inner Light"; "Hey Jude b/w Revolution"; *"The Beatles";* *"Yellow Submarine";* "Get Back b/w Don't Let Me Down"; "The Ballad Of John And Yoko b/w Old Brown Shoe"; *"Abbey Road";* "Something b/w Come Together"; "Let It Be b/w You Know My Name (Look Up The Number)"; *"Let It Be";* "Solo Beatles"; "Life After The End: Posthumous Beatles Releases"; *"The Beatles At Shea Stadium";* *"Yellow Submarine";* "Interviews: Bill Harry" © Sean Egan, 2008

INTRODUCTION

"The four numbers on this EP have been selected from The Lennon and McCartney Songbook. If that description sounds a trifle pompous, perhaps I may suggest you preserve this sleeve for ten years, exhume it from your collection somewhere around the middle of 1973 and write me a very nasty letter if the pop people of the 1970s aren't talking about at least two of these titles as 'early examples of modern beat standards taken from The Lennon and McCartney Songbook'."

So read the sleevenotes to The Beatles' second EP, released in September 1963. Long before 1973, Tony Barrow, the author of those sleevenotes – who possibly didn't even mean them when he wrote them, hyperbole being the stock-in-trade of the sleevenote writer and publicist – had been unequivocally vindicated. In fact, his suggestion that Lennon and McCartney would be remembered as composers of "early examples of modern beat standards" was by now looking like not reckless projection but ultra-cautiousness. Had he said that Lennon and McCartney and their two colleagues would reshape the boundaries of popular music beyond recognition and that they would transpire to represent something profoundly greater than music – spokesmen for a generation's youth, figureheads for, even agents, of progressive social change – he might have been told by his editor to rewrite his copy on the grounds that such overstatement was too much even for adoring pop fans. However, he would have been right.

Paul McCartney (born 18 June 1942), John Lennon (born 9 October 1940), George Harrison (born 25 February 1943) and Richard Starkey (professionally known as Ringo Starr, born 7 July 1940) made up a musical ensemble which initially played genres of popular music called rock 'n' roll and rhythm 'n' blues. Their recording career lasted from January 1962 to May 1970. By 1967 – the apex of that career – one Timothy Leary was saying of them, "I declare that The Beatles are mutants. Prototypes of evolutionary agents sent by God, endowed with a mysterious power to create a new human species, a young race of laughing freemen."

It's easy to scoff at Leary – an advocate of swapping progress in one's career for drug-addled idleness – but, studying it objectively, his apparently outlandish prediction of The Beatles' influence sort of came true.

Leary, a psychologist and university professor, was by no means alone amongst the intelligentsia in his reverence for The Beatles. Kenneth Tynan, a famous theatre critic and journalist, wrote in *The Times* that The Beatles' 1967 album *Sgt. Pepper's Lonely Heart's Club Band* was "a decisive moment in the history of Western Civilization". Again it's easy to mock a man whose gleeful desire for the destruction of bourgeois convention can now seem embarrassingly dated and to possess the whiff of being bound up in his penchant for erotica and kinky sex, but this sort of statement was by no means unique. High-falutin' British establishment newspapers variously called The Beatles "distinctive and exhilarating" (*The Times*, 1963) and "the greatest songwriters since Schubert" (*Observer*, 1968).

In 1967, *Rolling Stone* journalist Langdon Winner wrote, "The closest Western Civilization has come to unity since the Congress of Vienna in 1815 was the week the *Sgt. Pepper* . . . album was released." During that week, Winner happened to be driving across the USA on Interstate 80. In each city where he made a stop for food or petrol, the tableau was the same: . . . *Pepper* . . . was omnipresent. He wrote, ". . . the melodies wafted in from some far-off transistor radio or portable hi-fi. It was the most amazing thing I've ever heard. For a brief while the irreparably fragmented consciousness of the West was unified, at least in the minds of the young."

October of 1967 marked the half-decade since The Beatles had released their first single under their own name. (A collaboration with Tony Sheridan had been released in January 1962 but is generally not considered a "real" Beatles record.) British music paper *Disc And Music Echo* celebrated the occasion with a series of articles about their impact. They polled various fellow musicians about the group that had become known as the Fab

Four. One of them, Ray Davies of The Kinks, noted, "It's funny we should be celebrating the fifth anniversary of The Beatles at the same time as the fiftieth anniversary of the Russian Revolution. For The Beatles changed people's images. Before them, art and films had been changing but they brought a change to pop. Previously, it had all been glossy, with people like Cliff Richard, so they did, in a way, start a revolution." Davies' near-namesake Spencer Davis uncannily echoed the Kinks man's comments: "It's ironic that the fifth anniversary of The Beatles should coincide with the Russian Revolution of 1917 . . . The Beatles really caused a social revolution. Musically and lyrically, The Beatles have broken through many conservative ideas . . . I regard them on par with the 'storm and stress' poetry movement in Germany at the turn of the eighteenth century."

None of these comments was considered particularly over-the-top at the time for a group who had issued just 107 original songs thus far. Neither were the comments the result of a mass delusion that dissipated once the group were no longer extant. Writing with the benefit of twenty-seven years' hindsight, respected journalist Ian Macdonald said, "Anyone unlucky enough not to have been aged between fourteen and thirty during 1966–7 will never know the excitement of those years in popular culture. A sunny optimism permeated everything and possibilities seemed limitless. Bestriding a British scene that embraced music, poetry, fashion and film, The Beatles were at their peak and were looked up to in awe as arbiters of a positive new age in which the dead customs of the older generation would be refreshed and remade through the creative energy of the classless young."

Such quotes simply will not be found in the archives about any other recording artists. Such quotes simply will not be found in the archives about any other recording artists. The Beatles genuinely were ". . . the biggest attraction the world has ever known" to repeat another quote from a Beatle aide, this time Derek Taylor writing in the sleevenotes to their 1964 album *Beatles For Sale*.

This book attempts, in a selection of writings on the group, both old and new to explain why this is so.

Sean Egan

PART ONE: LIFE AND ART

The Beatles' career told chronologically via contemporaneous press reports and retrospective evaluations of their music, with a couple of articles (one published, one new) that provide unusual perspectives on that career.

With The Beatles – Pre-Fame

by Antion Meredith

In the 1960s, Vic Briggs (today known as Antion Meredith) was a renowned guitarist performing with the likes of Brian Auger and Rod Stewart and playing on hits by Dusty Springfield, Johnny Halliday and Serge Gainsbourg. He went on to find a degree of fame and acclaim as lead guitarist and musical arranger with Eric Burdon & The Animals. When he first met The Beatles, however, he was a schoolboy just starting out on his career, while The Beatles were themselves still waiting for that elusive big break. In this previously unpublished extract from his forthcoming autobiography, Meredith tells of a band whose characters were noticeably edgier than the cheery moptop personas with which they would find fame.

In the summer of 1961 I was sixteen years old and on my summer holiday from Hampton Grammar School, located in a suburb of Greater London. At this point, despite my youth I had already been playing guitar in semi-pro bands for more than a year. Even though I dreamed of being a professional musician, I was glumly resigned to finishing the two years of school that lay ahead of me at the insistence of my mother.

Through my burgeoning musical career, I got to make the acquaintance of Big Jim Sullivan, quite a well-known guitarist in Britain at the time. One August day that year, I received a phone call from a man named Laurie Jay. "I got your number from Jim Sullivan," he said. "I play with a group called The Echoes. We need a guitarist and Jim tells me that you're pretty good." I was noncommittal at first but even though I was still at school (albeit on holiday), the chance of playing with a professional band was too much to resist and I had the unfortunate task of telling the band I was currently with that I was leaving them for greener pastures.

Shortly afterwards, when The Echoes were billeted in Chester for some gigs, one of my new colleagues, pianist Iain Hines, who had been working in Hamburg a short time previously, told us of some great bands from Liverpool that he had met in the German city, the best of which was called The Beetles. Their moniker alone was enough to leave us quite unimpressed ("What a stupid name! Who would want to hear a band called The *Beetles*?" I remember contemptuously thinking), but our snobbery would have done that job anyway. We were all from London and had the typical Londoners' attitude that there was nothing worthwhile north of Watford, except perhaps Stilton Cheese and Scotch whiskey.

"Liverpool's not far from here," said Iain. "I'm gonna call my mates and see if I can get them over."

Before our Wednesday night show, two characters showed up at the theatre. They both had black leather jackets and hair piled up in pompadours. One was peroxide blonde with a bit of a stutter. The other had dark hair, a bigger than normal nose and a ring on every finger. They had a slightly wild air about them. However, their outfits and hair seemed passé to my London eyes. As I was soon to discover, this was somewhat of a uniform for Liverpool musicians of the time. Iain introduced us: "This is Rory Storm. He's got a band called The Hurricanes in Liverpool. This is Ringo, his drummer." Unbeknownst to Ringo, within little over a year, this peculiarly named drummer would achieve fame with The Beatles. Unbeknownst to me, I was just about to meet his future colleagues.

In my limited experience of London musicians, I had already discovered that "attitude" was all too common. Despite their wild appearances, though, this pair of Liverpudlians were very friendly and seemingly without such affectations. They were easy to talk to and seemed to be genuinely delighted to meet us.

"Look, there's a club in Liverpool called The Cavern that has lunchtime sessions," Rory said in that distinctive thick, rich Liverpool accent. "Why don't you come over for a blow [English

for 'jam'] and you can get back in time for your evening performance?" I was intrigued. I had never heard of a rock club being
open for a lunchtime session.

The next day we got up a little earlier than usual, had breakfast
and caught a commuter train to Liverpool. The Cavern Club
was located on Matthew Street, which was in the middle of
Liverpool's fruit and vegetable wholesale market. Although the
market had long packed up by the time we arrived, we still had
to pick our way through cabbages and carrots lying in the street
to get to The Cavern. Rory Storm had let the management
know we were coming and we were welcomed at the door.

The Cavern, a basement venue, was no more than three
semi-circular tunnels connected by archways, with a tiny, low
stage situated in the centre tunnel. Even with a smallish crowd,
condensation was running down the bare bricks of the tunnel
walls and ceiling; one can only imagine what it would have been
like with a packed house for three or four hours. While The
Cavern might not have been physically very attractive, the ambience was welcoming and warm. Everyone we met was friendly
and seemed inexplicably delighted that we were there. This is,
I now realize, the Scouse hospitality that Liverpool is famous
for and was quite a contrast to the unyielding, harsh attitude
of post-war Britain in the part of the country that I grew up
in, one that I once described in an interview, profanely but
accurately, as "fucking heavy".

The lunchtime session had just started when we arrived. The
band that was playing had a drummer, a pianist and two guitar
players but no bassist. We found out that they were called Gerry
and The Pacemakers. Chirpy frontman Gerry Marsden turned
out to be as friendly as Rory and Ringo had been. We also met
now legendary Cavern DJ Bob Wooler, who welcomed us and
then introduced us onstage. When I'd first joined The Echoes,
I had been a little disheartened, as they played a weird mixture
of rock, pop and soft jazz, not really what I had expected.
However, our act seemed to be to the taste of the Cavern crowd:
we did our set and the kids loved us. One of the songs we
performed was "One Night", a smouldering Elvis song in 6/8
time. We would take the instrumental break down very low
and start to build it. As the intensity rose, as usual for our

performance, our drummer Laurie kicked his stool over and stood up at his kit, bassist Doug Reese jumped up on his speaker cabinet (which was big enough to support him) and Iain lay back on the floor, put his feet on the piano keyboard, made his body rigid so it was only supported by his shoulders and very convincingly writhed in ecstasy. (I was less extroverted than my colleagues so at this point would just wave my guitar around a little.) Pretty tame by the standards even of five years later, but in those days it was radical.

So enthusiastic was our reception that Laurie suggested, "Hey, let's come back tomorrow and bring Rolly with us." Rolly Daniels was a singer from India whom The Echoes were currently backing. I had taken an instant liking to Rolly when we met. He was a well-built, good looking young man with deep brown skin and curly hair. He had a fine voice and moved well on stage. Rolly introduced me to the delights of The Twist, which was popular in the States but had not caught on in the UK, where partnerless dancing was unheard of. I was quite impressed when Rolly told me that in India it was the custom to take two baths a day. At that time, most English people took one bath a week, whether (as the joke goes) they needed it or not. Rolly was also responsible for introducing me to Indian food, which is still a passion for me.

When we went back the next day, Rolly in tow, the band on stage turned out to be the celebrated Beetles that Iain had enthused over. Only, it turned out that the name was spelt "Beatles", the pun immediately making the name seem a little less stupid. The day before, Gerry Marsden and his band had come across as "nice guys", both in their good-time music and in their jocular rapport with the audience. There was something darker about The Beatles, in spite of an equally humorous stream of patter between songs. I think it was a certain cynicism, probably mainly from John Lennon, that set their rapport with the audience at a different level.

We chatted and exchanged pleasantries with The Beatles, but it was a brief conversation because we went on as soon as they finished their first set, then they went back on right after we finished ours. Although we had only met a few people on the Liverpool scene, without exception they had been friendly.

They had also been, well, slightly deferential to us. After all, we were professionals from London, then universally considered the entertainment capital of Britain. The Beatles, however, while friendly, were definitely not deferential. I didn't put it all together until years later, but now I can see that they considered themselves to be the top dogs on their scene and were not going to give any ground to another band, even if they were from London.

Frankly, I felt that deferential behaviour would have been in order. I had already picked up from Iain Hines and from Rory and Ringo that The Beatles were supposed to be the best of the Liverpool bunch. I thought they sounded okay: they were a tight band and clearly knew their material (mostly 1950s rock standards) well. Generally though, I was unimpressed with their music. Ditto their appearance. Their look – black leather suits – was not only unkempt but was considered a relic of the 1950s by us sophisticated types from the capital, although we did make allowances for the similarly clad original rock 'n' roll hero Gene Vincent. (Later when I went to Hamburg, I found out that leather clothing was very much a trophy for bands that had played in the city.) Their hair didn't make any particular impression on me, as it was not as long as it would be only a few months later. What I did find impressive about them, however, was their tremendous rapport with the audience (especially the girls) and the way they simply exuded confidence.

I was now beginning to realize that there was a quite different attitude about Liverpool audiences. In London, rock audiences were "cool", verging on flat-out hostile. It always felt like a battle of wills between the musicians and the audience to see if any applause could be wrung out. It was quite possible to play a gig in London and experience no – and I mean zero – applause from start to finish. This was true even for the top London acts. At The Cavern, the audience had no compunction about demonstrating that they were there to enjoy themselves, and were more than happy to show voluble appreciation to the bands if they pleased them.

We went on stage again and did our act with Rolly. Part of Rolly's shtick was that he would announce that he was going to sing an ancient Indian love song. He would start intoning a few words *a cappella* in Hindi – and then tear into Little Richard's "Long Tall Sally". It went down very well with the Scousers.

After we had finished, The Beatles went back on and we got another taste of the rather edgy nature of this ensemble. They proceeded to play their own version of "Long Tall Sally" and, as they did so, they mimicked Rolly's act using almost the same patter Rolly had – but not in homage. It was an out-and-out "piss-take", to use an English expression for ridicule. Perhaps it was driven by a sense of insecurity, for Rolly was very good and extremely professional, and females especially loved his act. I don't remember Rolly being angry, but then he – an all-round nice guy – wasn't the type to react. Laurie, though, was incensed about it and complained about The Beatles all the way back to Chester.

By the summer of 1963, I was an established professional musician. However, if I thought I had done well for myself, it was as nothing compared to what The Beatles had achieved in the two years since our paths had crossed. Their hairstyles and songs were the talk of the country. The three hits and number one album they had under their belts had partly been achieved by what was considered their cheery Scouse charm: they had toned down their edgy, cynical group personality a little in the cause of mainstream success. They had also traded in their leathers for Beno Dorn suits and ties. I spotted George Harrison's shaggy head (the group's hairstyles were now much longer, shock, horror) in a musical instrument store on London's Charing Cross Road, the heart of London's music scene. It so happened that my girlfriend of the time had worked with The Beatles in Hamburg and knew them well. She introduced me to Harrison.

"Hey George," I said, "Do you remember back in 1961, there was a band from London called The Echoes who came and did a guest session at one of your lunchtime Cavern gigs?"

He thought for a minute and said, "Oh yeah, I do remember that."

"Well, I was the guitar player in that band."

"You were? Oh yeah, I remember you had that Indian guy singing with you."

Of course, if this conversation had taken place a few years later, George would have probably been profoundly more interested in the memory, for by then he was deeply immersed in the Indian culture. I myself later became a Sikh and it would have been fascinating to sit down with George and chat about our mutual conversion to Indian religion and music.

It was not until April 1965 that I saw The Beatles onstage again. We were both appearing at the *New Musical Express* Poll Winners' Concert at Wembley Empire Pool, London, me in my capacity as Dusty Springfield's lead guitarist. They had by now piled success upon success: Beatlemania, an endless string of number one records, successful movies and a status almost of contemporary national treasures. Their act this night in front of a crowd of 10,000 may not have had that intimate rapport made possible by The Cavern but as they ran through "I Feel Fine", "She's A Woman", "Baby's In Black", "Ticket To Ride" and (irony of ironies) "Long Tall Sally", I could only be impressed. They looked and sounded fabulous and their stage presence, if now lacking that edginess I had noticed, was highly polished and professional. It was hard to believe it was the same band.

In July 1967, I was at a recording session with trad Dixieland bandleader Chris Barber. Paul McCartney had provided Chris with a song entitled "Catcall". (There is apparently a bootleg recording of The Beatles playing this instrumental.) Paul was present to help supervise the recording at Chappell Recording Studio on Maddox Street, my favourite studio in London and one where, incidentally, The Beatles recorded "Your Mother Should Know" the following month. After the session, some of us adjourned to the Speakeasy, a club favoured by the pop glitterati of those times. I was sitting talking to Paul and, as I had with George, reminded him of the time The Echoes had visited The Cavern.

"Oh yeah," he said. "I remember that."

It must have seemed several lifetimes ago to him. The difference in the stature of The Beatles now to where they were when I had run into George in '63, let alone when I had met them at the Cavern in '61, was almost beyond belief. The previous month, they had released *Sgt. Pepper's Lonely Hearts Club Band*

and were basking in the acclaim of that astonishing record. Almost every tune you heard on the airwaves bore some evidence of the way they had influenced the direction of pop music over the last five years, while the streets were full of men who had grown their hair in emulation of their hirsute heroes.

When I saw them on that day in 1961, I could never have imagined their extraordinary success or the effect they would have on the world. But while it is common knowledge how The Beatles changed the world, what I have never seen acknowledged in print is how much The Beatles changed the lives of countless aspiring musicians like myself. As a rock musician pre-Beatles, you were absolutely on the bottom of the music biz food chain. The Beatles' success brought musicians to a much higher standing. Suddenly, it seemed the world wanted to know rock musicians, and many of them became very wealthy as a result. Alas, I wasn't one of those musos who became rich, but I will always owe a debt of gratitude to those four young men who may not have shown me what I thought was due deference but who successfully insisted to the wider public that what rock musicians did actually mattered.

"Love Me Do" b/w "P.S. I Love You"

Released: 05/10/1962

by Sean Egan

In an alternate universe, The Beatles released "How Do You Do It" – written by Mitch Murray – as their first single, had a hit with it, followed it up with a few incrementally less successful records, made one album, and then disappeared from history. An unlikely scenario? Don't you believe it.

It was a small miracle that The Beatles introduced themselves to the wider world beyond their hometown Liverpool's Cavern club, their various places of occupation in Hamburg and the

101 other venues they had played in England with one of their own compositions at all. George Martin has said repeatedly down the years that he thought The Beatles – John Lennon (rhythm guitar, vocals), Paul McCartney (bass, vocals), George Harrison (lead guitar) and Pete Best (drums) – were no great shakes as musicians and songwriters when he signed them to EMI label Parlophone but that he was entranced by their personal qualities. It's therefore not in the least surprising that he should want them to record "How Do You Do It", a jaunty piece of Tin Pan Alley pop. The Beatles did lay down a version, but dismayed at its absolute lack of bluesiness and its distance from the material – both covers and originals – in their stage act, they pleaded with Martin to be allowed to do their own stuff on single.

Of course, had Martin put his foot down and resisted the band's insistence on issuing only their own songs on single, Epstein and The Beatles would have had to acquiesce. No one else had shown interest in signing the group and the power was therefore all with the producer. All credit, then, to Martin. Just as he decided not to make one of the band the "leader" – considered a prerequisite in pop at the time – but instead left alone the set-up of Lennon singing some numbers, McCartney others, so he went against the grain by giving the band their compositional head. He would be rewarded for this – artistically, anyway – beyond his wildest dreams.

Not quite from the beginning, though. It would be an astonishingly short time before The Beatles were recording classic records, but their debut was not one. "Paul started writing that when he was about fifteen and we finished it off over the years," John explained of "Love Me Do". "It was the first one that we'd dare do of our own," he added of its introduction into a live act full of their heroes' classics. This was a necessity, though, as bands all drawing from the same pool of material sometimes meant those on the same bill would find themselves virtually replicating each others' sets. Paul said, "We didn't have any finesse to be able to actually sound black, but 'Love Me Do' was probably the first bluesy thing we tried to do."

That George Martin should have decided that "Love Me Do" would be The Beatles' entrée is a mild surprise. There was better Lennon/McCartney material available. "Ask Me Why" was a sweet little number with mildly sophisticated vocal harmonies. The case can also be made for the pretty "P.S. I Love You" ("Love Me Do's" B-side), a song that would have impressed those who had never heard of The Beatles more. And what about their fine original rocker "I Saw Her Standing There"? Instead, the way The Beatles introduced themselves to the world was with a song that, to quote Philip Norman's description of its audition to Martin, ". . . was called 'Love Me Do'. That was its opening line. Its second was, 'You know I love you', its third was, 'I'll always be true'. George Martin listened, then asked to hear something else." It's actually worse than Norman suggests, for that verse is the only one, and is repeated over and over. It is also the chorus.

"Love Me Do" (from that embarrassing title down) is a teenager of a record: gauche, naive and self-conscious. The rhythm is utterly rinky-dink, whether it be played by Andy White, the top session drummer Martin had booked to fill in for Pete Best when he found the latter inadequate and whom he retained when the unknown quantity Ringo Starr unexpectedly appeared in the sacked Best's place (White appears on the album version and later pressings of the single) or Ringo (original single version). The verse-chorus meanwhile not only resounds with the banalities Norman sneeringly points out but its melody has a nursery rhyme ring.

Yet there is one thing that rescues "Love Me Do" and marks out its creators as people with potential: John's harmonica. Right from the get-go, when it propels the record out of the starting gate, it captures the attention and pleases the senses. Though Lennon had been playing harmonica since a child when his uncle George gave him one, his interest in the instrument was renewed in the first quarter of 1962 when Bruce Channel enjoyed a number two UK hit with "Hey! Baby", a record with a prominent harmonica part played by Nashville sessioner Delbert McClinton. The Beatles found themselves supporting Channel at a New Brighton gig in June of that year and Lennon took the opportunity to both befriend McClinton and get some tips from him on the instrument.

It's McCartney's recollection, though, that it was Martin's

idea for the record to feature harmonica and that Martin, when he made the suggestion, had no idea that Lennon played the instrument. If this is the case, it rather seems that fate was smiling on The Beatles. The harmonica runs throughout "Love Me Do" like a raspy, bluesy antidote to the general air of callowness and its technical dexterity provides a note of transcendence that is the very antithesis of the recording's general earthbound, clunky non-groove.

The new harmonica part meant that Lennon – who usually sang lead live despite the song being mainly Paul's – couldn't sing the climax to the verse because the harmonica crossed over the vocal. The band were assuming that the rising "ple-e-e-ease . . ." would simply peter out (overdubbing was still rare) but Martin thought it silly that the line hung suspended that way and suggested that Paul conclude it. McCartney was so nervous at his debut solo turn at the microphone that he swears to this day that he can hear his *a cappella* voice shaking.

While Martin was right to be a bit snooty about "Love Me Do", his failure to spot the potential of the far superior Lennon/McCartney track that was placed on the B-side is mystifying. "P.S. I Love You" has "hit" written all over it from its sweet sentiment of a man writing to the loved one he misses to the chiming, almost hypnotic quality of its verses to Paul's smooth crooning to the mesmerizing way John and George add emphasis by joining in with Paul every few words to the circular pattern created by the winding guitar figures and Ringo's ticktocking percussion and the way the bridge just repeats the first verse in a different key.

"Love Me Do" did not prove that all the record companies who had turned The Beatles down had been wrong, nor did it indicate that they would become the most celebrated entertainers of the twentieth century. It did indicate, though, that there was something interesting going on here. And while opinions are divided on whether its peak UK chart placing of number seventeen was manipulated by Epstein – who was able to order large numbers of copies through his family's North East Music Stores – it can be asserted with little fear of contradiction that it merited its place in the top twenty as much as any other single of the time.

The fact that it was the group's own composition was crucial. As their success grew with successive releases, it provided a point of press interest that – very unusually for British rockers – they wrote their own material, thus creating a virtuous circle of promotion. It also provided a greater intensity of affection amongst The Beatles' ever-growing fanbase. Though their collective, chirpy, irreverent, charming group image already gave them bags more personality than your average pop artists, writing their own songs gave their *music* character. Pop fans were treated to the novelty of something profoundly more than one of an interchangeable circle of artists singing the compositions of Tin Pan Alley hacks or scrambling to be the first to cover American hits. There was a reason to follow this group other than the normal shallow one of physical attractiveness.

Martin was convinced that "How Do You Do It" would make The Beatles "household names". In fact, it was the kind of pleasant but trite production-line song The Beatles would soon make redundant. It was eventually recorded by another of Martin and Epstein's charges, Gerry and the Pacemakers and became the first of that band's three successive number ones – the first time anyone had done this in Britain with their inaugural trio of releases. The Beatles at the time were genuinely worried about the competition that this chart feat indicated the Pacemakers were to them. That this anxiety seems from this distance absurd is down to one thing. Because they were self-reliant, The Beatles developed and mushroomed into an artistic phenomenon. The Pacemakers, meanwhile, enjoyed thirty-two months in the chart sun before fading away to the chicken-in-a-basket (and subsequently nostalgia) circuit. They left behind no classic records.

"Please Please Me" b/w "Ask Me Why"

Released: 11/01/1963

by Sean Egan

With a creditable debut single and a respectable chart placing
(even if the methods of its achievement might not have been
respectable) under their belts, The Beatles and George Martin
turned their minds to the issue of the record that would decide
whether the group were going to be a footnote in chart history
or something more substantial. The Beatles suggested "Please
Please Me", possibly to Martin's impatience. The producer had
heard the song before. He had rejected it as a candidate for
their debut because it was too dirge-like. Originally, they had
planned to put it on the flip of "Love Me Do" but had given
up on it because they couldn't seem to get it right that day.
Martin had suggested they save it for another time.

At some point in this process, Martin also suggested they
speed the arrangement up. Once this was done, and a guitar
hook from Harrison added, its potential became clear to the
producer, even if he did suggest improvements like repeating
a verse because it was too short. "I modified a little bit of the
ending and so on," the producer later said. It was during this
remoulding process that it seems to have been decided to add
harmonica, and that this was a calculated matter, as it was so
much a part of the attraction of "Love Me Do": the harmonica
would indeed be a Beatles trademark for their first few months
as a recording outfit.

This type of thing was how George Martin influenced The
Beatles' sound: not through direct composition but by nudging
them into tweaks in arrangement and structure. By Martin's

own admission, The Beatles came to be less inclined to take his advice as their own capabilities improved and as they acquired the confidence conferred by a global popularity that was unprecedented in showbusiness. Nonetheless, some will always harbour suspicions about how good The Beatles would have been had they done what so many other artists did and regularly changed producer. The Beatles took part in very few recording dates at which Martin was not present (mainly ones that occurred when Martin was on holiday). When Martin left EMI to set up as an independent producer in August 1965, The Beatles insisted that EMI rules dictating in-house production only be waived so that they could continue their successful association with him. For some, this would indicate fear, and the fact that the only protracted Beatles sessions on which George Martin was not completely in charge – the *Get Back* sessions, which resulted in the *Let It Be* album, where Glyn Johns called a lot of the shots – were something of a disaster suggests to those same people that the fear was a well-founded one. We'll never know of course, and some might say it doesn't matter (little art doesn't involve collaboration of some sort) but it would have at least been interesting to be able to compare and contrast the different results of different producers on The Beatles' product.

Indeed, one wonders whether a different producer would have recognized the qualities of "Ask Me Why", a Lennon/McCartney composition whose charms Martin inexplicably ignored in favour of "Love Me Do" for the first single and which ended up as the "Please Please Me" B-side. In this gossamer song of devotion's tenderness, adroit harmonies, delicious guitar cascades and intelligent arrangement, we get a glimpse of The Beatles' future greatness. Despite the many instances of Buddy Holly-like multi-syllable elongation of words, John's vocal approach is understated and in some places almost spoken word.

"I remember the day and the pink eyelets on the bed," said Lennon of the occasion he sat down to write "Please Please Me" in his aunt Mimi's house at 251 Menlove Avenue in Liverpool, a song which he also described as ". . . my song completely", a suggestion that Paul did not dispute. Like all self-written songs recorded by The Beatles apart from those of George and Ringo, it bore the publishing credit that would become the most famous in twentieth-century popular music: "Lennon/McCartney". Many of those songs would be solely the work of one or the other, Paul's "Yesterday" and John's "I Am The Walrus" being two of the most obvious examples. Though the two without question did contribute to each other's songs, and on some occasions even sat with guitars across their laps facing each other crafting a composition from scratch – which is what probably the majority originally assumed the joint composing credit meant – by early 1964, most "Lennon/McCartney" songs started out with and were mainly composed by one or the other, with the one who supplied the bulk usually ending up as the lead vocalist. Lennon/McCartney was as much pact as fact, and it was a good pact, for whatever the assumptions and motivations in their young heads when early in The Beatles' career they decided on this joint credit no matter what the respective contribution, they were laying the foundations of the strength of the partnership. If each was to receive fifty per cent remuneration and public credit regardless, there was no reason not to help the other as best they could, rather than hold back good riffs, hooks and ideas for their own work.

For "Please Please Me", John took his cue from what some would consider an unlikely source. "I was . . . always intrigued by the words . . . 'Please lend a little ear to my pleas'," he said of a line from "Please", a 1933 Bing Crosby recording. Crosby may seem a quaint taste now but as one of the first singers to master the microphone, his poised recording performances were, in fact, in contrast to the histrionics that had hitherto characterized song on record, at one point the apex of cool. In any case, Lennon's cue from Crosby was filtered through the style of someone with more rock 'n' roll cred. "I heard Roy Orbison doing 'Only The Lonely' . . . that's where that came from," Lennon revealed.

Sung by John and Paul in unison and propelled by a harmonica riff, albeit one far less pleasing than that of the debut single, the verses are naïve, lyrically and melodically and – like the bulk of "Love Me Do" – redeemed only by a freshness and exuberance. However, when in the chorus John engages in an insistent call-and-response pattern with George and Paul on the phrase "Come on", the world is given a glimpse of what would become two of The Beatles' exquisite trademarks: a knack for vocal arrangements and an air of communality, which were inextricably combined. Additionally, in the "Please Please Me" bridge, we get another taste of a nascent version of a vital component of The Beatles' future craftsmanship – as well as proof of what a fine drummer Ringo is. The bridge is the part of a song designed to prevent tedium setting in as a consequence of the verse and chorus melodies being repeated continuously. (Musicians often refer to it as the middle-eight, and do so even when it doesn't have eight bars.) Frequently, it is the best part of a song, providing a contrast to the verse and chorus melodies that is delightful, which in itself makes the song much better by increasing its artistic breadth. The Beatles would become masters of the art of a great bridge and their understanding of its importance in on full display on this record. Ringo effects the switch into the bridge – on his own – with a brisk little roll. The bridge is at a faster clip than the material that bookends it. Not significantly so, but because John – who sings it solo – invests so much passion in it, it feels positively breakneck. It also contains one of those little treats that embed affection for a song in the listener's heart, in this case the way John rhymes "complaining" with "rain in". We get another little treat at the close that has the bridge's qualities of contrast and impression of speed. Whereas "Love Me Do" faded out, "Please Please Me" has a "real" ending, and it's a great one: Ringo's drums engage in a call-and-response with the other instruments, executing brief, blurred tattoos that alternate with stabs of guitar before all instruments abruptly cease, leaving only a humming silence. We are left ever so slightly breathless.

George Martin seems to have been similarly affected. Though there had been a mild fluff in the band's first take of the song, he decided that its spirit wasn't going to be improved on. "Gentleman, you have just recorded your first number one," he said to them. At least, that's part of the legend. However, the fact that there is more than one version in existence suggests this is apocryphal.

Martin was correct about the chart position though. Some – brandishing their copy of *The Guinness Book Of Hit Singles* – will dispute this. They should take note of the fact that the whole of Britain, including The Beatles themselves, were under the impression that the record reached the pinnacle, which fact was a source of no little national pride and justification for media coverage. *Guinness . . .* has "Please Please Me" peaking at number two because its data for that period is taken from *Record Retailer* (later renamed *Music Week*), whose chart was the only one of the four competing charts of the era whose summit it did not scale. At the time, *Record Retailer* was by no means considered the definitive chart. If any was, it was that of the *New Musical Express,* as it was the oldest, although in fairness *Record Retailer*'s was the era's only independently audited chart. In any case, it all soon became moot, because such were The Beatles' record sales from here on, that their every release hit the top across the board, with only a couple of exceptions.

NATIONAL ATTENTION

Maureen Cleave is a name forever associated with The Beatles because of her infamous "We're more popular than Jesus" interview with John in 1966. However, the reason that Lennon was so indiscreet with her in that chat may have been due to the fact that he and his wife Cynthia were by this point fairly long-standing friends of Cleave, who had been one of the first non-pop, non-provincial journalists to write about the group. That and her and John's mutual love of the works of Richmal "Just William" Crompton. Cleave later revealed she had been alerted to the band by Liverpool-born journalist Gillian Reynolds. As a consequence, she spoke to the group just as "Please Please Me" was shooting up the charts and thereby caught a ride on the very first wave of Beatlemania, related below.

Though in no way dismissive of The Beatles' music, Cleave herein also pointed out the importance of their physical attractiveness, an element of their success that has perhaps been subsequently down-played by the group's admirers simply because of how discomforting it is. Phil McNeil – talking about the undisputed godliness the public attributed to them in the early years, something that went hand-in-hand with their handsomeness – astutely said in 1976, "Much as one would like to believe it, their musical genius was not particularly relevant."

Why The Beatles Create All That Frenzy

From *Evening Standard*, 2 February 1963
by Maureen Cleave

The Beatles are the darlings of Merseyside. The little girls of Merseyside are so fiercely possessive about their Beatles that they forced Granada to put them on television, and *they* wouldn't buy their first record in case they should become famous and go away to London and leave them.

Fortunately others did buy it, and now they are buying the second one, "Please Please Me", at the rate of 50,000 a week. They are a vocal-instrumental group, three guitars and drums, and they don't sound a bit like The Shadows, or anybody else for that matter.

But I think it's their *looks* that really get people going, that start the girls queuing outside the Liverpool Grafton at 5.30 for 8pm. Their average age is twenty and they have what their manager likes to call "exceptional taste in clothes". They look scruffy, but scruffy on purpose.

They wear bell-bottom suits of a rich Burgundy colour with black velvet collars. Boots of course. Shoes seem to have died out altogether. Their shirts are pink and their hairstyles are French. Liverpool lads of twelve and upwards now have small bouffant Beatle heads with the fringe brushed forwards.

On the stage, there's none of this humble bowing of the head, or self-effacing trips over the microphone leads. They stand there, bursting with self-confidence and professional polish – as well they might, for they have been at this game since 1958. They know exactly what they can get away with, and their inter-song patter is in the Max Miller-music hall tradition, with slightly bawdy schoolboy overtones.

John Lennon has an upper lip which is brutal in a devastating way. George Harrison is handsome, whimsical and untidy. Paul McCartney has a round baby face, while Ringo Starr is ugly but cute. (He's called Ringo because he wears two on each hand.)

"Their physical appearance," said my friend, who is a Liverpool housewife, "inspires frenzy. They look beat-up and depraved in the nicest possible way."

They are very friendly and charming. They like each other and everybody else, and are seen around a good deal. They also write their own songs.

They are considered intelligent, three of them went to grammar school, and John Lennon had more education at the Liverpool College of Art.

"It helps being intelligent, I suppose," he said, "though, mind you, I've met people in this business who aren't as thick as they look. On second thoughts, I'd rather be thick and rich, than bright and otherwise.

"We all want to get rich so we can retire. We don't want to go straight or get to be all-round entertainers.

"We'd like to have a bash at acting; not that we can do it but we'd like to see ourselves up there.

"People try to pin labels on to us. Now they say we're rhythm and blues, but ever since I read two years ago that calypso was taking England by storm, I've never believed a word I read. For us, this is just good fun.

"We don't really bother about what we do on the stage, or on television for that matter. We practise what we call 'grinnings at nothings'. One-two-three, and we all grin at nothing. When we go on tour with Helen Shapiro next week, I don't know how we'll manage. I thought I might lie down on the floor, like Al Jolson."

Paul McCartney said John was self-confident because he was

too blind to see all the nasty little faces in the audience not enjoying it.

"He can't see a thing," said Paul. "Can't tell how they're taking it. He develops these catch-phrases. You know what his latest one is? 'Thank you, folks, you're *too* kind.' Imagine that – 'Thank you, folks, you're *too* kind,' twenty times over. After a bit, the audience joins in. It drives us daft and we get him to change it.

"Actually, John has a great laugh about being blind. Our humour is based on anything other people don't laugh at – death, for instance, or disease. It sounds dreadful if you write it down, but it's the cruel stuff, the *cruellies,* that make us laugh. Not that we're unkind, or anything. We're just silly."

You can dance to The Beatles, but my Liverpool housewife says most people prefer to listen.

"They like to sit and throb," she said, "or stand and throb, and the walls stream with sweat. It's lovely."

It takes you back, doesn't it? To the early days of rock 'n' roll.

Please Please Me

Released: 22/03/1963

by Sean Egan

TRACKLISTING

Side one
1. "I Saw Her Standing There"
2. "Misery"
3. "Anna (Go to Him)"
4. "Chains"
5. "Boys"
6. "Ask Me Why"
7. "Please Please Me"

Side two
1. "Love Me Do"
2. "P.S. I Love You"
3. "Baby It's You"
4. "Do You Want to Know a Secret"
5. "A Taste of Honey"
6. "There's a Place"
7. "Twist and Shout"

Having secured one minor hit and one smash, George Martin felt justified in extending his label's contract with The Beatles to an album. This was the last album of this type that The Beatles would ever make. With their next album, they began revolutionizing the very concept of the LP, which at that point was merely a way to cash in on a pop act's hit singles. Here the fact that Parlophone were cleaving to the exploitation approach is underlined by the cover lettering, which under the band's name informs us of the album, "PLEASE PLEASE ME . . . with Love Me Do . . . and 12 other songs". The sheer dismissiveness of the "and 12 other songs" is something that you almost feel could be accompanied by a shrug of supreme corporate disinterest.

The Beatles weren't disinterested, though, putting their all into the record, even though they had precisely one day to record it. They even rehearsed through the lunch break of the ten-hour session, much to the documented amazement of engineer Richard Langham. The fact that Lennon audibly had a cold on that day was immaterial: George Martin was conscious of the small budget of the label of which he was head, though to be fair to Martin, he himself wasn't treating the material with contempt.

Naturally named after their smash single, The Beatles' debut long player is a truly sweet little album. It's gauche in places and clearly the work of people just beginning their proper recording career, and there's a sometimes suffocating callowness (contrived of course – their pre-fame residencies in Hamburg clubs had made men of these boys, musically, emotionally and sexually) but the band are always groping for excellence, never competence. The performances are crisp and tight, the instrumentation – apart from George's saggy guitar solos – good-to-very-good.

The fact that most of the songs here are originals was not unprecedented: The Beatles' fellow Scouser Billy Fury famously wrote all of his album masterpiece *The Sound Of Fury* (1960) before inexplicably being forced into a career of cover jobs by his record company. However, the ratio of originals-to-covers here is unusually high for an era where artists would usually be given the opportunity to include just one or two self-composed tracks purely as an egotistical and financial sop.

"Anna (Go To Him)" is a composition by Arthur Alexander, an R&B singer who was a particular favourite of Lennon's. You can hear clearly on this smouldering ballad that John has a cold but he still impressively gives notice of the ability he was going to display many times in The Beatles' career to make a song absolutely soar in the bridge. "Baby It's You" is in a similar smouldering vein, although this time the love affair is going well, ecstatically so. An early Bacharach/David (with the assistance of Barney Williams) song, its bridge is ready-made for John's wide-mouthed, closed-eyed quavering dramatics.

Scott/Marlow's "A Taste Of Honey" – theme tune to the 1961 kitchen sink movie – is one of those slightly silly elements of the band's then wildly eclectic live repertoire. A very un-rock 'n' roll and antediluvian-sounding track, it is nonetheless – courtesy of the band's slickness – a dark, almost elegant treat that acts as a nice contrast to the general giddiness of the rest of the material.

The weakest covers are both songs that illustrate the unusual degree of influence of girl vocal groups on The Beatles. "Chains" (written by US Tin Pan Alley king and queen Gerry Goffin and Carole King) is a jaunty tale of human bondage that was originally a hit for The Cookies and is here sung by George. It's passable but remarkable only for the steam-train whistle harmonica introduction. Pete Best's stage vocal showcase had been The Shirelles' "Boys" and Ringo inherited it. In more innocent times, the fact that Starr's vocal sees him render a girl group hit without changing the genders (except on the line about kissing his girl's lips) did not even attract much notice, let alone sniggers. Someone regularly screams somewhere in the mix to convince us that what we're hearing is exciting rather than perfunctory where it's not bizarre – although, curiously, this is actually one of the more assured vocal performances Ringo would turn in for The Beatles down the years.

The best cover present is the album closer "Twist And Shout", the first recorded example of the ability The Beatles had for taking already great songs by other artists into a different stratosphere. The last track recorded at the end of a long day, with John's cold-ravaged voice at the optimum state of rawness and necessarily captured in one take lest that optimum state spill over into complete voice-loss, this rendition of the Isley Brothers' sex-and-dance anthem is a berserk performance. John is ably assisted by George and Paul, whose call-and-response breaks delightfully into "Whoo-ooh"'s whenever the pair can find an excuse.

Technically, the versions of "Love Me Do" and "Please Please Me" are different to the single releases. For some reason, Andy White's version of the former is presented here, although it's not his drumming – indistinguishable from Ringo's – that makes it more agreeable in this context but the fact that it has found its true level as a moderately pleasing album track that never really deserved the status of single. Meanwhile, the title track, at least on the stereo version of the album, is noticeably different: faster, more exciting and with an amusing vocal fluff, although the harmonica overdub is the same as on the single. This version can be found on the 1973 compilation *The Beatles 1962–1966* (the "red" album).

In addition to those two singles and their B-sides, there are four other selections written by Lennon/McCartney (although it should be noted that the original songs on this album are credited – as had been the singles tracks thus far – to "McCartney/Lennon"). "There's A Place" is almost a precursor of Brian Wilson's later loner anthem "In My Room", though melodically clunkier, if mercifully less spiritually disturbed. "Misery" has a rather embarrassing mechanical descending bridge but is impressive in its knowing, almost post-modern self-pity. George's Liverpool accent slips through in parts of his second vocal showcase "Do You Want To Know A Secret" but that only adds to the charm – albeit modest – of this crooner.

The best original of the lot – and one that easily holds its place with any of the covers present – is the opener, "I Saw Her Standing There". This rocker is a fabulous start to the album, not only in its quality but the way that Paul gets it – and therefore the entire proceedings – going with the type of count-in usually edited out by a producer. It has of course become perceived as an integral part of the recording. The instrumental break sees the first instance of what would be a slightly embarrassing fixture of early Beatles records wherein Paul's scream of excitement/ enticement is followed by a somewhat lame solo from a still learning Harrison. Martin does his best to compensate for this by drenching the break in echo. However, that's about the only low point. The "You know what I mean" following the revelation of the titular girl's age as seventeen is in line with the track's streetwise lyrical tone and musical grittiness, one that sets it apart from the bland romance of the rest of the album's originals. The bridge is close to onomatopoeic, lifting (with the help of bullet-like beats from Ringo) as Paul tells us how his heart had gone *boom* as he approached his intended lover.

Please Please Me ascended effortlessly to the top of the charts. It stayed there for thirty weeks, deposed only by its follow-up, *With The Beatles*.

Though the stairwell at EMI's Manchester Square London HQ was a rather utilitarian backdrop for the cover shot, the pose The Beatles struck leaning over the handrail for photographer Angus McBean situated on the ground floor has been much parodied, including by The Beatles themselves.

"From Me To You" b/w "Thank You Girl"

Released: 12/04/1963

by Sean Egan

The origin of the A-side of The Beatles' third single lay with the *New Musical Express*, the British weekly music paper commonly referred to as the *NME*.

Today, it's the sole surviving UK music weekly, staggering along on a fraction of its former sales in an age where its demographic has been torn asunder first by glossy monthlies, then the internet. At the time, though, it was the most important of the music papers and – after a drop in influence – would cannily regain that position in the early 1970s by replacing its staid, old-school writers virtually overnight with scribes from the underground press (a change made necessary, of course, because of vast and swift social-political changes for which The Beatles were to a large extent responsible). In February 1963, however, the *NME* was still a paper that reflected the innocence of the time and its letters page had the greetings card-style name "From You To Us". Lennon and McCartney, travelling on a bus with the other Beatles and the rest of the artists on the package tour on which they played through February '63, decided to use the title as a jumping-off point for a song, it fitting in nicely with their penchant of the moment for the use of personal pronouns in song titles (a penchant that would be indulged on seven of their first eight singles before they grew bored with it). Naturally, "From You To Us" was a difficult title to turn to the requirements of romantic convention, so it became "From Me To You", a mid-tempo pledge of devotion in which the narrator promises his lover not only anything she wants but its delivery "with love from me to you".

The song, started and completed on 28 February 1963 as the tour bus made its way from York to Shrewsbury, was one of those compositions where John and Paul genuinely did sit crafting the song together. Once in Shrewsbury at the venue they were playing that evening, the pair asked tour headliner Helen Shapiro to listen to the song and another they'd written on the tour, "Thank You Girl". Paul played both on the venue's piano, John standing beside him singing with him. Shapiro said that she liked "From Me To You" best. The next day, the two sought the opinion of McCartney's father, who had made the trip to the Lancashire venue at which the tour was stopping because it was the closest one to Liverpool. When McCartney Snr – an amateur musician – declared "From Me To You" a "nice little tune" that was not, as they feared, too musically complicated to catch on with the fans, it reaffirmed their belief that it was the strongest of the two candidates for their next A-side.

"From Me To You" is another incremental step forward, show-ing The Beatles developing artistically even as the circumstances engendered by success – endless gigs and media appearances – made that task more difficult. Though they may have been trading in Moon-In-June romantic cliché – and would do for some time to come – and though they (on Martin's suggestion) fairly cynically made sure that their third single had a harmonica riff like their previous two, they were beginning to push at the boundaries of pop structure. McCartney has identified "From Me To You" as the first time The Beatles consciously did some-thing you weren't supposed to do in songwriting. The innovation he was referring to was the nature of the song's bridge, which modulated to an alternate key and therefore sounded – for pop – somewhat exotic. "That was a pivotal song," McCartney later reflected. "Our songwriting lifted a little with that song." However, as if understanding instinctively that the implied mordancy of the bridge was inappropriate, John, Paul and George climaxed it with a "Who-ohh!", a three-man yell of euphoria that would come to be considered a trademark of early Beatles material (even if they didn't do it on many songs). It was an example of the way the band's penchant for experimen-tation was not allowed to compromise their populism.

The "De-da-de-de-de-de-*daaa*" vocal phrase that opens the record in tandem with its introductory harmonica riff is a little soppy, but the staccato rhythm guitar that succeeds it is played with a real punch, even brutality. For the first time on a Beatles single, the lead vocal is solo, handled by John, although Paul and George frequently finish his lines with him, often in near falsetto.

B-side "Thank You Girl" has the same kind of lugubrious mechanical descending bridge that afflicted the debut album's "Misery". The melody is no great shakes either. While not exactly painful, it's one of the few Beatles flips that actually sounds like a B-side.

Ironically, though the A-side's harmonica riff may have been motivated by a desire to produce a recognizable Beatles motif, not only did this mark the last occasion on which it would appear on a Beatles single, the single marked the entrée of a tone and spirit that was hinted at on "Please Please Me", would reach its fulfilment on "She Loves You" and would remain the most important part of The Beatles musical DNA forever. It was manifested on this occasion in those giddy "Whoo-oo"s at the end of the twice-rendered bridge and in those falsetto line endings but would evolve into something more sophisticated – so much so that sometimes it couldn't even be isolated to specific musical elements. It was an air of happiness, an implication of vulnerability and a great capacity for love. In short, a huge, heart-warming humanity. It would explain why the world – not just that part of it that comprised their own generation – took The Beatles and their music to its heart. As if to demonstrate this, this was the first Beatles chart placing whose ascension to the UK top spot was disputed by no chart. And if the fact that Del Shannon made the lower reaches of the top 100 Stateside with it doesn't seem that impressive, this inaugural cover of a Beatles song by an American artist is noteworthy as being the first indicator of the global recognition of the group's craft that was soon to come.

"She Loves You" b/w "I'll Get You"

Released: 23/08/1963

by Sean Egan

Beatlemania starts here. As do the 1960s.

The Beatles had been successful hitherto, but how can one compare a number seventeen, a disputed number one, an undisputed number one, an EP ("Twist And Shout") that had made number two in the singles chart and a top-selling and acclaimed album with the release of a record that so encapsulates the *zeitgeist* and entrances the public that their commercial position became unassailable and their sociological status that of *de facto* leaders of the world's youth?

Not that John and Paul were thinking these would be the

consequences when they sat down to write "She Loves You" in a Newcastle-Upon-Tyne hotel room on 26 June 1963 or when they finished it at McCartney's childhood home. (This by the way was the first Beatles record of any description with the publishing credit rendered as "Lennon-McCartney" rather than the other way round.) "I thought of doing it first and thought of doing it as one of those answering songs," said McCartney. "You know the sort of thing the American singing groups keep doing. A couple of us would sing 'She loves you' and the others would do the 'Yeah yeah yeah' ones. Then John and I agreed it was a pretty crummy idea as it stood . . . but at least we had the basic idea of writing the song." It was decided that the lead singers – John and Paul harmonizing again – would append the "Yeah yeah yeah's" to the title phrase. It was a vital alteration. It's difficult to imagine "Yeah yeah yeah" becoming one of the most famous musical motifs of all time had it been cooed Shangri-Las style as an answering phrase.

Lennon and McCartney were employing the personal pronoun gimmick again, but as intelligent and imaginative people they chafed at the very restrictions they were setting themselves, so this time – at Paul's suggestion – they put a little twist on it: "She loves you", instead of the more obvious, infinitely more trite "I love you". Which in turn gives rise to a song that is very out of the ordinary: a man talking to another man, advising him on his love life, telling him he's out of order and needs to reciprocate the affection he's getting from his woman. Songs in the second person are rare enough. Songs in the rock 'n' roll canon evincing affection and emotional support between two men are – even to this day, let alone in 1963 – almost unknown. But the world would come to know and love this kind of tenderness in The Beatles, for though it may have started out as a compositional gimmick, what allowed The Beatles to pursue this idea whereas other groups – anxious about the unseemliness in such a unmanly sentiment – would have abandoned it, is that heartaching humanity referred to previously.

A hint of melancholy had been present in the group's three previous releases. It is entirely absent here. From the chorus (sung at the start) which consists simply of permutations of the words "She loves you" and "Yeah" and has the rousing effect of a cheerleader's chant, to the "Whooh!" with which Lennon, McCartney and Harrison jointly climax each verse, to the relentless fizzing of Ringo's hi-hat, to the delirious interjections of guitar arpeggios, we are hearing unadulterated, grinning euphoria. This is helped in no small measure by the record's breathlessness: it never lets up, careening relentlessly forward from the brisk drum roll that gets proceedings underway, to the clean ending two minutes and eighteen seconds later, with the final "Yeaaaah" hanging in the air. Nobody who heard it could help but be charmed.

The band were very aware of the way the record was stuffed with hooks and gimmicks, which also included enunciating the word "Yesterday" in Buddy Holly's hiccupping style. "We stuck everything in there," said Lennon later, "thinking when Elvis did 'All Shook Up', that was the first time I heard 'Uh huh', 'Oh yeah' and 'Yeah yeah' all in the same song."

But it was also something far more than a great pop record. When people discuss records that epitomized the 1960s, they rarely mention "She Loves You", or if they do, only in passing, as though such supposedly teenybopper fare is less crucial than, say, "Street Fighting Man". In fact, little has ever better summed up the revolutionary *zeitgeist* of that notable decade than this disc. In its informal tone (McCartney's father was slightly upset that the immortal refrain was "Yeah, yeah, yeah!" rather than "Yes, yes, yes" but it struck a chord with everyone who remembered being reprimanded by authoritarian teachers for not enunciating the word properly), its exuberance and optimism, its innovations in an era where newness was at a premium and its simple aura of freshness and youth, it was the product of a generation who were proud of the fact that their values and ambitions were not the same as their elders', and received as such, even if sometimes on a subliminal level.

The very structure of "She Loves You" appears designed by the band to underline their personal and visual appeal. British singer Kenny Lynch – another artist on the Helen Shapiro tour – has said, "I remember John and Paul saying they were thinking of running up to the microphone together and shaking their heads and singing, 'Whooooo!'" Lynch may be referring here to their writing of "From Me To You", which featured a primitive version of the effect. Lynch wasn't impressed by the plan ("I said, 'You can't do that. They'll think you're a bunch of poofs!'") but pretty soon one of the defining and best-loved sights of the era would be Paul and George shaking their noggins at the microphone they shared as they unleashed the "Whooh"'s in live renditions of "She Loves You". Meanwhile, Ringo was patently not unaware of the fact that the drum part gave opportunity for camera close-ups of his see-sawing, grinning head. That those heads were shaggy only added to the power of the image. The Beatles were not the talk of society merely because of the fact that they were a band who wrote their own songs or because they were a band whose every member – highly unusually – had a distinct personality or because their songs were often innovative. They were also a quite startling apparition. As Paul Du Noyer has observed of The Beatles' hirsuteness, "Their funny little Beatle haircuts were, in 1963, a genuinely strange sight, more shocking to see than even hippy weirdness was a few years later."

It's not going too far to state that also implicit in "She Loves You" were The Beatles' proletarian backgrounds and values. It was something that The Beatles clearly knew the currency of. Paul's younger brother Mike has recalled asking his sibling why he and his colleagues had been speaking in such broad Scouse on an early television appearance, to be told by Paul that it was something that would help get them noticed. Judging by that exchange – as well as The The Beatles' ostentatious cheeky and irreverent manner in an era when the public demeanour of pop stars was characterized by deference (even Elvis called people "sir" and "ma'am"), The Beatles were cognizant of the value of injecting in their art the air of change that – in Britain – was illustrated or vocalized by such anti-establishment plays as *Look Back In Anger* and such gritty novels as *Saturday Night And Sunday Morning*.

At the same time, though, The Beatles acted as a bridge between two generations who were pulling away from each other. "She Loves You" had the smack of the new and the young in an era where these went hand-in-hand with radicalism but at the same time the song was completely non-threatening. The record was so utterly charming that it was the sort of thing to put the minds of those parents worried about their children's modernism at rest: if the voice of the new age was so sweet, the younger generation and what they believed in couldn't be that bad.

As if all this weren't enough, "She Loves You" featured the first great Beatles B-side. From here on, Beatles 45s would have flips every bit as good as the charting side. Other groups were disinclined to "waste" good material on the obverse of a single and would stick on a discard or a cheesy cover version. This value-for-money was yet another thing that endeared the band to the public. "I'll Get You" is a song of intent to a prospective romantic partner, at once purposeful (the title phrase) and uncertain (the sweet opening line, "Imagine I'm in love with you", followed by the information from the narrator that such a task is perfectly easy because he's imagined it so many times before). It has a fine, undulating melody and a great swelling bridge.

"She Loves You" was a staggering sales phenomenon. After spending several weeks at the top of the charts, it simply wouldn't go away, hovering in the top three and then – incredibly – rising to number one again in late November '63, three months after its release. It remains the biggest-selling Beatles single to this day.

It was at this point that Beatles merchandise, official and unofficial, went into the stratosphere. Few fans would fail to purchase at least some Beatle product, whether it be kiddie/teenager fare like Beatle wigs, Beatle magazines, Beatle figurines, etc, or the more subtle stuff that was attractive to the older fans in the form of fashions such as the group's distinctive collarless jackets or a pair of the Cuban-heeled ankle boots they favoured, now suddenly collectively perceived as "Beatle boots". The world was awash with the Fab Four.

BEATLEMANIA

Inevitably, there are conflicting stories about the first use of the word "Beatlemania" to describe the screeching, hysterical adolescent frenzy that greeted the public appearances of the Fab Four.

A Scottish promoter named Andi Lothian claimed he devised it when promoting The Beatles' first Scottish tour in the first week of October 1963. Journalist Peter Reece says he came up with the word to describe the shrieking and screaming The Beatles generated at the Manchester Apollo. Although conceding that his freelance colleague, Bob Wrack of Salford and South Lancs News Service, may actually have come up with it, he said, "I 'phoned the copy Bob and I cobbled together to every Manchester office of the nationals, and as this event was the nearest thing we had ever witnessed to a city-centre riot, I'm sure the word Beatlemania was published." Yet he gives the date as sometime in 1962, which seems implausibly early. Meanwhile, some claim that Melody Maker's *news editor Ray Coleman devised the phrase (sometimes rendered as "Beatle Mania"). Many sources state that Britain's* Daily Mirror *was the first to use it in print on 14 October 1963 to describe the pandemonium following the group's appearance at the London Palladium but a search of the relevant issue turns up no such mention. Which might give credence to the claims for Sandy Gardiner, who used the word in* The Ottawa Journal *on 9 November 1963. Beatles scholar Mark Lewisohn says,* "I've checked this thoroughly. The first use of the word 'Beatlemania' in the national press was 21 October 1963, in the *Daily Mail*, as the headline for a piece written by Vincent Mulchrone."

Meanwhile, the Mirror's *first use of the word seems to have been on 2 November 1963 in the article printed below. The copy was accompanied by one large picture of a standing girl with her hands clutching her head, screaming, a police officer holding her back, another, smaller picture of seated Beatlemaniacs in various stages of ecstasy – and no pictures of The Beatles themselves.*

Beatlemania!

It's happening everywhere . . . even in sedate Cheltenham
The with-it bug bites so hard.

From *Daily Mirror*, Saturday 2 November 1963
(No byline)

Everyone, everywhere is catching it. IT is called Beatlemania.

Earlier this week it swept Sweden.

Last night it hit sedate Cheltenham – traditional home of retired brigadiers, colonels . . . and the Ladies' College.

And if you haven't got it yet, the fantastic pictures show just what Beatlemania can do.

Cheltenham loved it.

The four pop-singing Beatles took the stage of a cinema for two concerts – the start of a five-work British tour.

And 1,800 Beatlemaniacs squealed and screamed . . . right through the opening number.

Beatles leader John Lennon, 23, bawled for quiet. It just brought more squeals.

As Lennon and his fellow Beatles, Paul McCartney, Ringo Starr and George Harrison struggled manfully on, girls left their seats and rushed to the stage.

Two fans fell in the orchestra pit. The second-house reception was even more ecstatic.

Hundreds stood on their seats, waving coats and umbrellas.

Programmes were thrown on to the stage – with telephone numbers written on them in lipstick . . . .

BRITAIN IS ENCHANTED

The Beatles pinpointed their performance at the Royal Variety Show on 4 November 1963 as the moment when their status turned from rising stars to household names and darlings of the nation. They agreed to appear at the annual charity gala staged in front of royalty – on this occasion, the Queen Mother and Princess Margaret – under duress, feeling the plush setting of the Prince of Wales Theatre and its pampered clientele were inimical to their humble origins, disdain for stuffiness and rock 'n' roll orientation. However, Epstein – a man to whom tradition was important despite his unconventional sex life – was very keen and they acquiesced. When Lennon got his bit of revenge for this compromise by mocking the privilege of many of those present – "Would those in the cheap seats clap their hands? The rest of you can rattle your jewellery" – it made the moptops seem not surly but even more lovable.

This charming irreverence was integral to The Beatles' appeal. They clearly had no truck with many of the things that were wrong with their society – whose horrendous authoritarianism and class-consciousness aren't appreciated by many Britons today – but communicated this in a manner that was in no way threatening. They were not smashing down barriers to progress with a battering ram but politely knocking on them, an impish smile on their collective face. Even the starchiest elements of the Establishment – as represented by the media, politicians and royalty – were won over, or at the very least ostentatiously tolerant.

This editorial appeared in the Daily Mirror *two days after that triumphant royal command performance. In a self-consciously trendy leader column, the tabloid celebrated The Beatles' youth, freshness and clean hair. The only thing not conveyed in the editorial but implicit in it is the national pride in the group, who were proving even more than Cliff Richard – an indigenous rock star but one who, unlike them, didn't write songs – that these islands didn't have to submit to an endless wave of American imports.*

The column contains much that is unintentionally amusing in its fewer than 200 words. Not just its sigh of relief at the fact that the group's moptops are not lice-ridden, but the fact that it's written in a teen argot that hadn't been current since the late 1950s, not to mention the where-the-hell-did-that-come-from? reference to their disinclination to tell jokes about "homos". Nonetheless, it gives a sense of how willing the country was in 1963 to embrace The Beatles and all they were perceived to stand for.

Yeah, Yeah, Yeah!

From *Daily Mirror* Wednesday 6 November, 1963
(No byline)

You have to be a real sour square not to love the nutty, noisy, happy, handsome Beatles.

If they don't sweep your blues away – *brother, you're a lost cause.*

If they don't put a beat in your feet – *sister, you're not living.*

How refreshing to see these rumbustious young Beatles take a middle-aged Royal Variety Performance audience by the scruff of their necks and have them beatling like teenagers. Fact is that Beatle People are everywhere: From Wapping to Windsor. Aged seven to seventy. And it's plain to see why these four energetic, cheeky lads from Liverpool go down so big.

They're young, new. They're high-spirited, cheerful. What a change from the self-pitying moaners crooning their love-lorn tunes from the tortured shallows of lukewarm hearts. The Beatles are whacky. They wear their hair like a mop – but it's WASHED, it's super-clean. So is their fresh young act. They don't have to rely on off-colour jokes about homos for their fun.

Youngsters like the Beatles – and Cliff Richard and the Shadows – are doing a good turn for show business – and the rest of us – with their new sounds, new looks.

GOOD LUCK, BEATLES!

With The Beatles

Released: 22/11/1963

by Sean Egan

TRACKLISTING

Side one
1. "It Won't Be Long"
2. "All I've Got To Do"
3. "All My Loving"
4. "Don't Bother Me"
5. "Little Child"
6. "Till There Was You"
7. "Please Mr Postman"

Side two
1. "Roll Over Beethoven"
2. "Hold Me Tight"
3. "You've Really Got A Hold on Me"
4. "I Wanna Be Your Man"
5. "Devil In Her Heart"
6. "Not A Second Time"
7. "Money"

Though they were separated by just eight months, the contrast between The Beatles' first and second albums could not be greater.

One look at the cover demonstrated that. Whereas the sleeve of *Please Please Me* bore an unimaginative shot of four faces grinning like airheads for the camera, *With The Beatles* was adorned with a shot of four unsmiling faces shrouded in shadow. It was astonishingly moody imagery for the pop market. The photograph was taken by Robert Freeman but inspired by the pictures taken in Hamburg of the group by their friend Astrid Kirchherr (the woman also responsible for their moptop hairstyles, which a vast swathe of the male population of the Western world had either already adopted or was about to emulate).

The Beatles lived up to the impression given by the sleeve of serious artists with the record's contents. Any other recording act with hits like "From Me To You" and "She Loves You" behind them and with "I Want To Hold Your Hand" a week away from release would naturally have put some or all of them (especially the latter two) on their latest long player to maximize its sales. Instead, The Beatles issued an album with fourteen entirely new recordings, not a single one of which appeared on a single, before or afterwards. Some not fully conversant with how little control artists had in the 1960s might scoff at the idea of The Beatles as groundbreakers on this point but it is quite extraordinary how – with no reason for either them or EMI to think they weren't just another here-today, gone-tomorrow pop act with a couple of hits, despite the scale of their success – they were already successfully insisting on steering their own destinies.

This would not have counted for much if they hadn't matched the strides they had taken in artistic control with advances in their art. Though the ratio of originals-to-covers was the same as on the first album, the band's own compositions were markedly more sophisticated this time out. The production was also slicker, with double-tracking much in evidence, a result of the fact that the band were given several days over the course of a couple of months to record as opposed to the ten hours they had for the debut. We should pause here to acknowledge the trademark sound of George Martin, whose imprimatur may not have been instantly recognizable à *la* Phil Spector's style but who most certainly did have a distinctive soundscape. There is no known maladroit or muffled George Martin production job: his records are sheened, clean and characterized by exactly the delineation of instrumentation required for optimum listening pleasure, all the more impressive for the fact that he is not an engineer (i.e. he doesn't touch the controls).

This album marked the first time The Beatles had to write specifically for an album. Having used up their originals (or at least those they were prepared to have heard in public) on the debut album, John and Paul now had to devise a new group of originals, something their newly packed schedule was not conducive to. Consequently, they recorded the album's cover versions first.

"Till There Was You" is the first released indication of the McCartney philosophy that popular music is a broad church that encompasses tunes from musicals as much as rock 'n' roll.And so what? You wouldn't want all Beatles recordings to be like this Meredith Willson-written number from the Broadway show *The Music Man* but it's a perfectly acceptable couple of minutes of tumbling acoustic guitar and mildly exotic percussion (bongos), even if Paul's choir-boy vocal approaches the shockingly clean-cut at times.

John wasn't averse to commercialism either but this is manifested in a more credible way in the form of him choosing to execute a trilogy of songs of Tamla Motown (as it was then still called) origination. Written by a veritable committee of five composers, "Please Mr Postman" was a US number one for the Marvelettes but not a UK hit. John invests his usual lung-busting fervour in a song whose protagonist is convinced the titular mail delivery employee has made some kind of mistake in not bringing him a missive from his loved one but the track is slightly suffocating in its overly metallic qualities. Still, who can resist that strangely Latin-accented "Deeliver thee letter!" part. Smokey Robinson's "You've Really Got A Hold On Me" boasts a brilliant soulful lead vocal by John and some great call-and-response between him and Paul and George in the choruses. The combination of this, fine instrumentation (especially Ringo's rolls) and some elegant piano from George Martin makes this probably the best collective performance on the record. The album climaxes with "Money", a number co-written by no less than the Motown founder Berry Gordy when he was still primarily a composer (and in fact before Motown existed) with Janie Bradford. It's an obvious attempt to provide a climax as rousing as "Twist And Shout" had been on the first album and comes pretty close to the intensity and quality of that storming number.

Martin provides a snaking piano riff while John insists on his allegiance to mammon through clenched teeth and Paul and George heighten the drama with relentless backing chants of "That's what I want!"

George has his own trilogy, including his first released composition. (He'd already written the instrumental "Cry For A Shadow" and collaborated on "In Spite Of All The Danger" with Paul, but both were unreleased.) "Don't Bother Me" is no sop to Harrison but merits its place on this album as much as almost any of the Lennon/McCartney numbers. A song whose minor chord nature reflects the brooding title, it is impressively melodic and well structured. A taut band performance and adroit solo from George only enhance a track that makes one wonder why it took its writer another two albums to obtain space for more of his songs.

One of the George-sung covers, "Devil In Her Heart", was a girl group number, starting life as "Devil In His Heart", released by The Donays. This time round the genders are reversed, itself an indication that The Beatles aren't quite the naïfs they were when they rendered "Boys" almost exactly as The Shirelles had just months ago. The group do a good job on it, their instrumentation slick (nice arpeggios at the start) and George's unsophisticated voice bolstered by creamy harmonies. The other Harrison-sung cover, "Roll Over Beethoven" is, of course, one of many songs written and recorded by Chuck Berry that presciently mythologized rock and played on the disdain parents felt for the medium. Though George's vocal can't match the playfulness and always strangely clear diction of the author, he attacks it with likeable enthusiasm.

"I Wanna Be Your Man" was a John and Paul track given to The Rolling Stones to provide them with their second single at a time when the Jagger/Richards songwriting partnership had not established itself as the chief rival to that of Lennon/McCartney. Ringo sings The Beatles' version. For such a discard ("We weren't going to give them anything great, right?" John uncharitably observed later), it's actually a highly enjoyable recording. Not as heavy as the Stones' grimy rendition, it features an almost bossa nova beat, bobbing Vox organ from Martin and a persistent hi-hat.

The rest of the original numbers range from good to very good and most indicate a growing maturity of touch, both lyrically and musically. "It Won't Be Long" – a Lennon song – is a typical early Beatles play on words *a la* "Please Please Me" ("be long" and "belong") that sees the band try to inject a little of that "She Loves You" magic with a call-and-response based on the word "yeah". Almost nothing could match the excitement and novelty of that titanic latter record but the band turn in an enjoyable brisk and loving rocker.

John's "All I've Got to Do" is an endearingly tender ballad with a stop-start structure. Lennon gives it his all in the singing, and Martin ratchets up even that considerable power by giving us John-squared via the most noticeable example of double tracking herein. "Little Child" is another John vocal (with his harmonica in the background at the same time, indicating the increasing use of overdubs) on a throwaway number that is nonetheless rendered listenable by its professionalism. Paul provides a piano backbone.

"Hold Me Tight", a Paul vocal, is naive but catchy, although he does manage to slip in a daring reference to "making love". The bottom-heavy drive of the verses is let down (twice) by a bridge that feels like a motor stalling.

John's "Not a Second Time" is an impressively dark and understated refusal to succumb to the temptation of running back to the arms of the woman who hurt him.

The only major fault of the album is a lack of a real signature song. Even leaving aside "Love Me Do" and "Please Please Me", the first album could boast "I Saw Her Standing There". The closest this album comes to a Lennon/McCartney number of that iconic calibre is Paul's "All My Loving". It's not quite an evergreen but goes some way to living up to John's later estimation of it as "one of his first biggies". Very uptempo but somehow light-footed, it sees McCartney resurrect the S.W.A.L.K. letter-home concept of "P.S. I Love You". Paul's singing is a mixture of impressive (the falsetto ending) and out of his depth (parts of the melody line are beyond his range). Most impressive though is John's Ramones-like blurred, unceasing rhythm guitar, which can, surreally, have one imagining that punk was yet another thing The Beatles invented.

In his sleevenotes, Tony Barrow referred to the band as the Fabulous Foursome. The media's abbreviation of this – the Fab Four – caught on, giving The Beatles another nickname to go alongside The Moptops. The Moptops sobriquet became dated in '67, when the band changed their hairstyles, but the Fab Four has persisted in usage way past the context of the 1960s when "Fab" was contemporary rather than the comically anti-quated word it seems in any other context now.

This album naturally went straight to number one. That in itself would not have indicated anything other than that The Beatles were very successful recording artists. However, the fact that the album it deposed from the summit was their own *Please Please Me*, which had been sitting there since its release eight months back, underlined that there was something afoot here that was more in the realm of phenomenon.

"I Want To Hold Your Hand" b/w "This Boy"

Released: 29/11/1963

by Sean Egan

"I Want To Hold Your Hand", The Beatles' fifth single, is cere-brated as the record that broke the band in America. That is about the only thing it should be celebrated for. It's simply not very good.

It was written in the basement of the London house of the family of actress Jane Asher, into which McCartney had moved after beginning a relationship with her. Lennon memorably said of the method by which he and McCartney crafted the song that it was "one on one, eyeball to eyeball", a description McCartney agreed with. Paul was sitting at the piano – an instrument which both would become reasonably proficient on,

Paul having developed a lot of his ability on the instrument in Hamburg – and stumbled on a chord that made Lennon erupt, "That's it! Do it again." From the recollections of witnesses – including Gordon Waller, friend of Asher's brother Peter and later colleague with him in the singing duo Peter and Gordon – the song would appear to have been completed that day. (Waller also recalls Lennon playing the pedal organ.)

Not all Americans were entranced by the result. Future Jefferson Airplane frontwoman Grace Slick noted the band's pageboy haircuts and the sexless sentiments of their chart-topper and wondered if they were not a little old for this. Of course, the same could be said of every Beatles song of the era: The Beatles' romantic compositions rarely at this point reflected the group's personalities, forged in life experience that featured much swilling, fornicating, pill-popping and brawling. Curiously so, in a way, because they had been weaned on rock records far less inclined to tweeness, from Chuck Berry to early Elvis to Buddy Holly. But whereas one didn't have to be a part of their intended early teen demographic to enjoy "She Loves You", "I Want To Hold Your Hand" was the *reductio ad absurdam* of the suppression of their own personalities to the object of chart success.

It opens promisingly with some dramatic guitar chords. By the time of *Revolver*, these would have presaged a scorning dissection of human frailty from Harrison or wry, nasally observations on the vagaries of life from Lennon. Here, as soon as the vocal starts, the song sags into a mire of cliché, insincerity and embarrassingly virginal sentiments. Nobody really thought The Beatles were innocents – even in 1964, even in America – but the suspension of disbelief required for this particular song is absurd. Bob Dylan famously heard the last line of the bridge not as, "I can't hide" but "I get high" and wondered how they thought they could get away with it. If only the lyric genuinely did show even a flash of such imagination or subversion. After all, even "Please Please Me" could be interpreted as a complaint of sexual dissatisfaction. On "I Want To Hold Your Hand", John's lead vocal enunciates a lyric of no such ambiguity: it really is as shallow and callow as it sounds. Perhaps it would all be less cringe-making if it was borne on a tidal wave of musical wonder as "She Loves You" was, but the melody is jerky and the instrumentation, though pleasantly jagged, is such a raw contrast to the phoney ingénue sentiments of the words as to simply make them more irritating. The corny handclaps don't help either. By far the best component of the record is Ringo's thrilling, if brief, drum fills in the choruses.

Cynicism of motivation in no way precludes great art, *especially* in popular music, but here the note that is struck is totally false. There was probably no greater sincerity behind the creation of the B-side "This Boy". "Just my attempt at writing one of those three-part harmony Smokey Robinson songs," John later shrugged; Paul recalled they'd knocked it off in a couple of spare hours sitting on the twin beds of a hotel room. It is also no less teenage in its emotions than the A-side, right down to these grown men's use of the word "boy" to identify themselves in a lament for a girl lost to a love rival. But not only is it infinitely better than the hit side, it is one of the lesser-known classic Beatles songs. Delicately strummed guitars, understated drums and creamy John-Paul-George lead vocals take the song into a bridge which Lennon tackles on his own and in which he proves that he is as great a vocalist on ballads as he had already proved he was on rock songs with "Twist And Shout": his epic anguish is expressed in a performance that spirals to the heavens.

Having said all of that, this writer is in a minority. Most rock critics down the years have seemed to have no profound problem with "I Want To Hold Your Hand". The public certainly didn't. Though it could be argued it made number one in the UK on the basis of the brilliance of "She Loves You" – with advance orders of a million, it was destined to top the charts without anyone having heard it – it remained in the charts for more than five months, entering them when "She Loves You" was still number one in at least one of them – twelve weeks after its release – and deposing it. Unbelievably, this sort of all-conquering popularity would reach an even higher pitch in America.

There are different theories about why the USA took to The Beatles more even than they had the man who kicked off the whole rock 'n' roll phenomenon, Elvis Presley, when they had always turned their noses up at every previous attempt to sell them a British variant of their indigenous artform, unless you count Acker Bilk's 1962 US number one "Strangers On The Shore" and the Tornados' Stateside chart-topper of the same year, "Telstar". For many, the reason for The Beatles' selling coal to Newcastle/sand to the Arabs feat was a manifestation of national grief following the November 1963 assassination of John F. Kennedy. America wanted to take solace, and, in the opinion of many, four charming, handsome Englishmen playing a new-sounding, effervescent form of rock 'n' roll provided exactly the mixture of levity, warmth and good-time tunes that could act as a salve on a terrible wound. Nobody can ever prove or disprove this hypothesis of course, but the fact is that on 17 January 1964, "I Want To Hold Your Hand" was a US number one, following Capitol – EMI's American counterpart – agreeing to release Beatle product for the first time. Two and a half months later – 4 April 1964 – the fact that EMI had been forced to licence The Beatles' earlier material to various smaller US labels because of Capitol's initial disinterest led to a fairytale ending. In the wake of the Fabs' two appearances on *The Ed Sullivan Show* in February – the first of which broke all existing TV viewing records by attracting an audience of 73,000,000 – everyone with a right to issue and promote Beatles music in America did so. The flooding of the market this engendered gave The Beatles occasion to occupy the top five places on the *Billboard* chart. "I Want To Hold Your Hand" was number three, with "Can't Buy Me Love" occupying the top spot. They also had seven other placings in that week's Hot 100, which additionally contained two Beatles tribute records.

The Sound of the City

by Charlie Gillett

*Though intellectual book-length works on rock are now two a penny,
when Charlie Gillett's* The Sound Of The City *was first published
in 1970, they were virtually non-existent. Though Gillett's work had
been preceded by Nik Cohn's similarly acclaimed* Awopbopaloobop
Alopbamboom *(1969), the latter work's division of chapters by
artist gave it more of the flavour of Lillian Roxon's* Rock Encyclopedia *(1969) than the historical treatise* The Sound Of The
City *constituted.*

*Though his project naturally stemmed from his love of the genre,
Gillett wasn't interested in salivating over his subjects. Hence the
following section from the book – the major one in it on The Beatles
– having a flavour that could easily make it a candidate for this
book's "Dissenters" section.*

*In one brief section Gillett addresses things about The Beatles
that rarely concern biographers and historians: how The Beatles broke
the UK record industry's Southern hegemony, an analysis of why the
Fabs' vocal stylings seemed so novel to British ears and a discussion
of their socio-political import to the Angry Young Man/kitchen sink
drama generation. Credit is given where it's due but Gillett refrains
from succumbing to Beatlemania.*

*Those interested in more trenchant and dispassionate observation
like this, about both The Beatles and the history of rock itself, are
directed to the current, third edition of the book.*

Until The Beatles made their first record in the autumn of 1962,
it had been very difficult for any group based outside London
to gain access to the record companies. It had almost always

been necessary for ambitious musicians, singers, and groups to move to London and hope to attract the attention of somebody who mattered.

Without the reputations that came through records, groups outside London had to depend on the support of people who knew them through direct hearing, which meant that a group famous in Newcastle could be unknown thirty miles away on Tees-side, and that groups in south Lancashire had little demand in Yorkshire. Accordingly, Bristol, Birmingham, Glasgow and other cities each had its own local groups.

The equivalent situation in the United States would have meant that each city's groups had their own distinctive styles and that enterprising local businessmen in some of the cities would have formed record companies to exploit the inflexibility of the majors (the London-based companies), who usually rejected the few groups they did agree to audition, on the grounds that they were too noisy and lacked the control and technical proficiency expected of singers and musicians who made records. But in Britain there was little opportunity for such enterprise because there were no local radio stations to reach the local audiences. So with few exceptions, the groups remained unrecorded until The Beatles' manager, Brian Epstein, with more persistence than most, and a better group to promote, finally persuaded EMI to record the group in the autumn of 1962.

The success of "Love Me Do", which made the lower reaches of the top twenty, and "Please Please Me", which made second place, enabled Epstein to place several other south Lancashire groups he represented on EMI's roster, and a large proportion of them were successful. But apart from The Beatles, the south Lancashire groups had much less ability or individuality than their success suggested. Their important quality was a freshness which contrasted with the relatively characterless singers that audiences were accustomed to. But as singers, musicians, arrangers, and composers they were not only amateurs compared with the Americans they copied, but had little to say or express about their experience and feelings. They were pop music singers who lacked the kind of assurance that, for example, would allow one of them to improvise from an agreed arrangement without panicking the others.

The Beatles were different in several respects from groups with whom they were bracketed as part of "the Mersey Sound", both as musicians with a thorough understanding of the culture from which they drew their style, and as people who were unlike entertainers previously familiar to audiences and journalists.

The group's vocal style was a derivative of two American styles which had not previously been put together, the hard rock 'n' roll style of singers like Little Richard and Larry Williams, and the soft gospel call-and-response style of The Shirelles, The Drifters, and the rest of the singers produced by Leiber and Stoller, Luther Dixon, and Berry Gordy. Instrumentally The Beatles were at first less inventive, producing a harsh rhythm and shrill sound comparable to some of the better American "twist" records, including Bruce Channel's "Hey! Baby" and Buster Brown's "Fannie Mae".

Although the twist had been fairly successful (without the impact it had in America), the gospel-harmony groups had very little success in Britain, and the result for the British audience was a sound with a familiar rhythm and a novel vocal style. The way The Beatles echoed one another's phrases, dragged out words across several beats, shouted "yeah", and went into falsetto cries, was received in Britain as their own invention; it seemed that Britain had finally discovered an original, indigenous rock 'n' roll style.

The Beatles made no pretence that this was so and stressed how much they owed to Chuck Berry, The Miracles, and Buddy Holly and the Crickets. In an interview with the *New Musical Express* (February 1963) during the first flush of their popularity, they listed as their favourite singers Chuck Jackson and Ben E. King (given by both Lennon and McCartney), The Shirelles and Miracles (Lennon), Larry Williams (McCartney), and Little Richard (McCartney and Harrison). Harrison also mentioned Eartha Kitt, who was not evidently much of an inspiration to the sounds he made; Ringo Starr's choice of Brook Benton and Lightnin' Hopkins similarly had little bearing on his style (which more likely drew on Carl Perkins).

On their singles and albums through 1963, The Beatles continued to draw from their American influences, trying to realize their ambition to record a great raving dance song but invariably sounding better when they sang at a medium tempo, hitting the harmonies Lennon was interested in and doing so with precisely the confidence in themselves that the other British groups lacked, a confidence that enabled them to take risks, be unorthodox, and shrug off disasters.

Most Beatles covers of American hits broke new ground. Their LP tracks "You Really Got A Hold On Me" and "Baby It's You" transformed the innocence of the interpretations by The Miracles and the Shirelles into much stronger songs and created a sense of greater resilience behind the tender messages. In contrast to the expressiveness of these and other LP songs, the group's singles were more obviously concerned with effect, "Please Please Me", "From Me To You", and "She Loves You" successively using more devices calculated to excite and offering less complexity in their arrangements.

But for the audience at the time, it was the simplicity of The Beatles' arrangements that endeared them to their listeners. The first LP sleeve notes mentioned that only one track had any kind of double-tracking or other such studio tricks. The British audience valued authenticity, and despised the lush contrivances of contemporary American records. The Beatles re-established the singer's autonomy in the studio. They were able to do so because they played their own instruments, and were therefore less subject to their producer than a studio group would have been. They came to their recording sessions with their own songs, many of which they tried before live audiences on their tours. They listened attentively to the records that sold well in the United States and borrowed anything that seemed to fit what they were already doing. The Four Seasons, The Beach Boys, Phil Spector's sound were all saluted in their sounds, and the early rock 'n' roll singers continued to provide inspiration, though their performances were never transcended by The Beatles' versions of the songs.

Musically, The Beatles were exciting, inventive, and competent; lyrically, they were brilliant, able to work in precisely the right kind of simple images and memorable phrases that distinguished rhythm and blues from other kinds of popular music. They were also facile, so that some songs were words to sing and did not represent feelings the singers wanted to express – for example,

"It Won't Be Long" and "All I've Got To Do" on their second LP (called *With The Beatles* in England and *Meet The Beatles* in the United States). They had enough ability to endure as institutional hitmakers alongside Cliff Richard and the Shadows. But there was something else about them, and it was this that transformed the nature of the world's popular music as decisively as rock 'n' roll had done nine years before – their character as people.

The Beatles provided in meat and bone and a sharp glance across a room the spirit that several authors and playwrights had been trying to depict in fictional characters and the film industry subsequently tried to represent with actors. John Osborne drew Jimmy Porter in *Look Back In Anger*, and Richard Burton played Porter in the film. Alan Sillitoe created Arthur Seaton in *Saturday Night And Sunday Morning* and Colin Smith in *The Loneliness Of The Long Distance Runner*, who were played by Albert Finney and Tom Courtenay with much more authenticity than Burton had brought to Porter. But the characters as such still carried too much structured statement to be convincing. The authors had social messages to get across, and the characters inevitably came second, functioning as conduits for the writers' ideologies. In themselves, though, the films seemed much more real than the traditional product of British studios. They presented life in the working class as being more real, interesting and honest than in the middle class, a belief that middle-class socialists had had for some time but a novel theme for films.

The Beatles unwittingly exploded this image of working-class youth. In their first two years of fame, they did not make long structured criticisms of established society, but spoke briefly, obscurely, epigrammatically, in the same spirit that they wrote their best songs. Their social message was rarely expressed, but hung about their heads as an aura of impatience with convention and evident satisfaction with wealth and fame, and was expressed in their carefully chosen styles of bizarre clothes. Where authors had shown working-class youth as caged within a harsh physical world, resentful towards those they believed had made it that way, but resigned to their place in such a world, The Beatles presented working-class youth loose and free, glad to be out, unafraid to snub pretension, easily able to settle in comfortably where a rest could be found.

This image also turned out to be illusory, or at best only temporarily true. The Beatles ultimately settled for what they first pulled faces at, the luxuries of the wealthy, but not before they had significantly shifted the taste of audiences throughout the world. In contrast to the pained narcissism of most singers, The Beatles lightly mocked themselves as they sang, amused at the frenzy they aroused in their audiences. They were one of the few popular music acts to have more or less equal support from male and female admirers, and one of the few who were as interesting musically as they were visually.

In the United States, their success was not immediate. Their first four records were released in 1963 with little promotion or reaction. Capitol, who had first option for the American release of EMI's product, allowed other companies, including Vee Jay and Swan, to take up the group's records. The rest of the world took the British group more seriously, and at the end of 1963 Capitol conceded to the pressure of EMl, The Beatles' manager, and, in effect, world opinion, and itself put heavy promotion behind the next Beatle record, "I Want To Hold Your Hand". It went quickly to the top of the national charts, followed by several earlier Vee Jay releases and Swan's "She Loves You", so that in one week in March The Beatles had the top five records in the country, an unprecedented phenomenon. As in Britain, the extent of the group's impact was more visual and social than musical, and depended on the intensive coverage in the press and on television. America was no more accustomed than Britain had been to singers who were witty and intelligent and derisive of social conventions, who built out of this character a new kind of sex appeal, and who attracted the attention of both music critics and social critics.

And among the people who were most surprised by all the fuss were The Beatles themselves. For, as they kept telling anyone who would listen, there was nothing particularly new or startling in any of their records. For reasons that defied discovery, a large proportion of the Western world was determined to imbue The Beatles with all the qualities that could possibly be ascribed to any and all kinds of popular music. With stamina and versatility that were themselves worthy of admiration, The Beatles did their best to keep up with expectations.

THE SQUARES DIG THE BEATLES

This article proved that the conservative, broadsheet papers were no more immune to Beatlemania than the left-leaning tabloid Daily Mirror.

Though carrying no byline, it has since been established that it was written by The Times *music critic William Mann. Mann would transpire to be the sort of posh paper equivalent of the* Mirror's *Don Short. Whereas Short dogged The Beatles' steps for personal stories, Mann followed their musical journey, writing several well-known reviews of their key works.*

At first, this piece strikes one as being written curiously early in the band's career. The Fabs had already made some great records by the end of '63, but isn't it a little too soon for Mann to be waxing both enthusiastically and intellectually on their wares? There again, Mann doesn't strike one as being insincere: anxiety to be seen as with-it can be discounted as a motivating factor for his drawing attention to the "chains of pandiationic clusters" in "This Boy". Anyone who was inclined to laugh at the likes of his citing an Aeolian cadence in "Not A Second Time" (which by 1980 still included Lennon, who declared he had never found out what the term meant and thought it sounded like exotic birds) would not be having the last laugh. Mann was more prescient than premature. By the time Mann penned his review of Let It Be *in 1970, it was commonplace for rock music to be treated with the same reverence as classical music, and Mann's uncommon willingness way back at the start of The Beatles' career to take a mere pop group seriously must surely have contributed to this growing acceptance that popular music was a valid artform rather than pap for teenagers who would eventually grow out of it.*

What Songs The Beatles Sang . . .

From *The Times*, 23 December 1963
(Unsigned but since attributed to William Mann.)

The outstanding English composers of 1963 must seem to have been John Lennon and Paul McCartney, the talented young musicians from Liverpool whose songs have been sweeping the country since last Christmas, whether performed by their own group, The Beatles, or by the numerous other teams of English troubadours that they also supply with songs.

I am not concerned here with the social phenomenon of Beatlemania, which finds expression in handbags, balloons and other articles bearing the likenesses of the loved ones, or in the hysterical screaming of young girls whenever the Beatle Quartet performs in public, but with the musical phenomenon. For several decades, in fact since the decline of the music-hall, England has taken her popular songs from the United States, either directly or by mimicry. But the songs of Lennon and McCartney are distinctly indigenous in character, the most imaginative and inventive examples of a style that has been developing on Merseyside during the past few years. And there is a nice, rather flattering irony in the news that The Beatles have now become prime favourites in America, too.

The strength of character in pop songs seems, and quite understandably, to be determined usually by the number of composers involved; when three or four people are required to make the original tunesmith's work publicly presentable it is unlikely to retain much individuality or to wear very well. The virtue of The Beatles' repertory is that, apparently, they do it themselves; three of the four are composers, they are versatile instrumentalists, and when they do borrow a song from another repertory, their treatment is idiosyncratic – as when Paul McCartney sings "Till There Was You" from *The Music Man,* a cool, easy, tasteful version of this ballad, quite without artificial sentimentality.

Their noisy items are the ones that arouse teenagers' excitement. Glutinous crooning is generally out of fashion these days, and even a song, about "Misery" sounds fundamentally quite cheerful; the slow, sad song about "This Boy", which features prominently in Beatles programmes, is expressively unusual for its lugubrious music, but harmonically it is one of their most intriguing, with its chains of pandiationic clusters, and the sentiment is acceptable because voiced cleanly and crisply. But harmonic interest is typical of their quicker songs, too, and one gets the impression that they think simultaneously of harmony and melody, so firmly are the major tonic sevenths and ninths built into their tunes, and the flat submediant key switches, so natural is the Aeolian cadence at the end of "Not a Second Time" (the chord progression which ends Mahler's *Song of the Earth).*

Those submediant switches from C major into A-flat major, and to a lesser extent mediant ones (e.g., the octave ascent in the famous "I Want to Hold Your Hand") are a trademark of Lennon-McCartney songs – they do not figure much in other pop repertories, or in The Beatles' arrangements of borrowed material – and show signs of becoming a mannerism. The other trademark of their compositions is a firm and purposeful bass line with a musical life of its own; how Lennon and McCartney divide their creative responsibilities I have yet to discover, but it is perhaps significant that Paul is the bass guitarist of the group. It may also be significant that George Harrison's song "Don't Bother Me" is harmonically a good deal more primitive, though it is nicely enough presented.

I suppose it is the sheer loudness of the music that appeals to Beatle admirers (there is something to be heard even through the squeals) and many parents must have cursed the electric guitar's amplification this Christmas – how fresh and euphonious the ordinary guitars sound in The Beatles' version of "Till There Was You" – but parents who are still managing to survive the decibels and, after copious repetition over several months, still deriving some musical pleasure from the overhearing, do so because there is a good deal of variety – oh, so welcome in pop music – about what they sing.

The autocratic but not by any means ungrammatical attitude to tonality (closer to, say, Peter Maxwell Davies' carols in *0 Magnum Mysterium* than to Gershwin or Loewe or even Lionel Bart); the exhilarating and often quasi-instrumental vocal duetting, sometimes in scat or in falsetto, behind the melodic line; the melismas with altered vowels ("I saw her yesterday-ee-ay") which have not quite become mannered, and the discreet, sometimes subtle, varieties of instrumentation – a suspicion of piano or organ, a few bars of mouth-organ obbligato, an excursion on the claves or maracas; the translation of African Blues or American western idioms (in "Baby, It's You", the Magyar 8/8 metre, too) into tough, sensitive Merseyside.

These are some of the qualities that make one wonder with interest what The Beatles, and particularly Lennon and McCartney, will do next, and if America will spoil them or hold on to them, and if their next record will wear as well as the others. They have brought a distinctive and exhilarating flavour into a genre of music that was in danger of ceasing to be music at all.

"Can't Buy Me Love" b/w "You Can't Do That"

Released: 20/03/1964

by Sean Egan

While "I Want To Hold Your Hand" is massively underrated, The Beatles' sixth single is unjustly maligned. Philip Norman dismissively called "'Can't Buy Me Love' perhaps the least memorable of all Lennon and McCartney songs". Norman is not alone in thinking that the record is flimsy or a marking time exercise. Such disdain is perplexing.

It seems to have escaped the attention of the record's detractors that it's a lyrical development: the trite sentiments of romantic devotion that had characterized almost all their previous originals, even, to some extent, "She Loves You", had been replaced by something more sophisticated. Paul – in his first proper lead vocal on a Beatles single, which itself is the first Beatles single without harmonies – is still concerned with romance (The Beatles wouldn't break with that convention on a single until '66) but there is a new angle here, and a slight edge, as he tells his lover that he'll get her all the usual material expressions of affection like diamond rings but that the expressions of affection are for him somewhat less important than the affection itself. It's not Bertrand Russell, but already we are a quantum leap away from the nursery rhyme sentiments of "Love Me Do".

"Can't Buy Me Love" heralded a musical broadening too. It possesses a feeling of spaciousness and lightness, with acoustic rhythm guitar well to the fore. This and other components (the way Paul begins the title phrase at the start *a cappella*, the double-tracking and reverb on his voice, the easy-rolling rhythm, the way the electric guitar and the drums jointly bring the song to a close by lifting their knees higher and marching quicker) confer a certain elegance not evident on even the best of their previous releases. The instrumental break is excellent. George's electric guitar solo is no hard rock abandon but it is impressively spiky and raw in the context of this song. It's also unusually fluid for this stage of George's development. On top of this, there is just something indefinably lovely and warm about "Can't Buy Me Love".

What makes this all the more remarkable is that the timespan from the writing of the song to completion of recording was mere days. It was written in the last week of January 1964 in a Paris hotel room while the band saw through a miserable residency at the Paris Olympia – though Beatlemania was just about to sweep the world, first port of call France was snootily dismissive – and was finished, bizarrely enough, when they had an hour of studio time left over at an EMI Paris studio booked to record German language versions of "I Want To Hold Your Hand" and "She Loves You". That they could devise and complete a great pop record so effortlessly was another thing that set apart The Beatles from mere musician mortals. The Beatles were almost never diminished or depleted by workload, able to create great art on the run.

Whatever the under-appreciated qualities of the A-side, anyone who argues the merits of the record's flip has a valid point. "You Can't Do That" is a powerful, driving track whose lyric is informed by the green-eyed monster and whose music is powered by a clipped beat and a ringing, trebly guitar riff, played by Lennon in one of the first manifestations of his frustration with his rhythm guitar role. Though Ringo never needed assistance in making the percussion on Beatles records interesting, the cowbell and congas here add an intriguing extra layer.

Like "Can't Buy Me Love", this song takes us to unfamiliar, edgy Beatle territory. In "You Can't Do That" the narrator's state is one of sweaty anxiety as he angrily tells his lover not to talk to other boys, else he'll leave her flat. That Lennon's vocal is almost disturbingly convincing is merely a reflection of his true personality. The wider public were kept in blissful ignorance that The Beatles were anything other than the perennially good-natured boys they presented themselves as by a media who had yet to conclude that shattering their public image was more in their commercial interest than colluding in perpetuating it. The harsher side of Lennon's nature – known to people who had come into direct contact with him – gleams menacingly through on this track.

Long Tall Sally

Released: 19/06/64

by Sean Egan

TRACKLISTING

Side one:
1. "Long Tall Sally"
2. "I Call Your Name"

Side two:
1. "Slow Down"
2. "Matchbox"

EPs – four tracks on a seven-inch disc – were a big part of the
market in the 1960s. With albums costing so much money that
they would only come into the possession of many kids from
working-class backgrounds on birthdays and at Christmas,
Extended Play records – as opposed to Long Players – were a
useful halfway house. Selected tracks were taken from The
Beatles' first six albums and released in the EP format. (Other
EPs compiled their singles.) These EPs have rather been forgotten by history (rarely mentioned, for instance, in discographies),
but they are hugely integral to The Beatles' story insofar as they
were the place many Beatles fans from low-income families first
heard the group's album tracks. (The fact that the fidelity of
EPs was poor due to cramming two tracks on each side can
only have made the album – with the superior sonics conferred
by five-to-seven tracks spread across each twelve-inch side of
vinyl – seem even more of a luxury item.) The cover of one of

those EPs – the first one, *Twist and Shout* – even provided one of the iconic images of the band (leaping into the air, arms and legs splayed). That same EP effectively gave the title track the status of a Beatles single at the time: because the EP made number two in the singles chart and became the fourth biggest-selling non-LP record of 1963, beaten only by the singles "She Loves You", "I Want To Hold Your Hand" and The Dave Clark Five's "Glad All Over", it received as much radio play as any of the group's other hits at the time. It should also be pointed out that although McCartney has said The Beatles didn't allow the release of "Yesterday" on single in Britain while The Beatles were extant – unlike in America – because they were embarrassed about it not being rock 'n' roll enough, it was in fact the title track of a 1965 EP of selections from *Help!*, giving it wider exposure in the UK than a mere album cut.

Probably the reason for this neglect of The Beatles' EPs' place in history is that The Beatles tended only to use the EP format as another arm of the marketing machine. Other bands used the format more creatively. The Rolling Stones' three EPs, for instance, featured exclusive material. However, The Beatles did put out two EPs of material unavailable (originally at least) elsewhere themselves. One was *Magical Mystery Tour* (1967). The other was *Long Tall Sally*.

The least important tracks were both significantly placed on *Long Tall Sally*'s B-side. They were also both a little gristly for the sweet teeth of many Beatles fans. "Slow Down" was the first of three songs by American R&B artist Larry Williams that The Beatles would record. All three would feature Lennon on lead vocals. A mid-tempo schoolboy's lament that his playground crush is blanking him, it's not one of Williams' best. John provides his usual nicely abrasive vocal but George Martin's piano is by-numbers and George's guitar solo almost embarrassingly hesitant. "Matchbox" was recorded as a vehicle for Ringo. Both Ringo and John were big fans of its composer Carl Perkins, and Perkins actually watched this number being recorded. Again, it's not exactly the greatest creation of its composer (who was also responsible for the immortal "Blue Suede Shoes"). Twelve-bar blues like "Matchbox" require good singing and playing to relieve the monotony created by their repetitive structure. While

The Beatles' version of the song features a nice gritty tumbling riff from George and good brisk beat, with Ringo doing his usual enthusiastic but essentially flat singing job, it's the sort of track that would have only have been listened to repeatedly by those (of whom there were admittedly many) who tended to sport "I love Ringo" badges.

The tracks on the A-side are something else entirely. On the title track, Paul preserves for posterity his version of the berserker Little Richard signature song that had long been a staple of The Beatles' live set. The cause of the brilliance of Little Richard's 1956 hit ('57 in the UK) is to some extent embedded in the composer's demented DNA, so McCartney's take on his filthy, innuendo-laden tale is destined to be more pastiche than facsimile – something underlined by George Martin's piano work, which is too restrained – but it's nonetheless a valiant and not unexciting attempt to reach the stratosphere to which Richard soared. "I Call Your Name" was first recorded by Billy J. Kramer and the Dakotas, another Epstein-managed act, the previous year as the B-side of another Lennon/McCartney number, "Bad To Me", a pairing that was a UK number one. (The group had previously had a UK number two with John and Paul's "Do You Want To Know A Secret?"). The Fabs' version has a cool snaking riff, syncopated rhythm and a rich melody. In John's anguished vocal, he agonies over whether he has treated his departed lover badly. A bridge leaps intriguingly into a different time signature and tone. Also, intriguingly, it occurs after just one verse, an arrangement that results in a not-unpleasantly disorienting feel. The lyric is ambiguous: Lennon tells us that though he doesn't think he can make it without his lover, he doesn't weep over her.

In being comprised of three cover jobs and one Lennon/McCartney number that had already been recorded by another act, the artistic horizons of *Long Tall Sally* were some- what limited and even inimical to the position the group had now reached: it was released three weeks before the artistic triumph of *A Hard Day's Night*, the first Beatles album of all- original material. However retrograde a step, though, it remains a likeable entry in The Beatles' canon.

"A Hard Day's Night" b/w "Things We Said Today"

Released: 10/07/1964

by Sean Egan

The legend has always been that the title for "A Hard Day's Night" came from one of the wry asides Ringo was apt to make: after a long session that ended in the early hours of a morning, he quipped in his doleful Dingle accent, "That was a hard day's night, was that", or something similar. In fact, the phrase appeared in Lennon's first book, *In His Own Write*, published three days after the session in question, and therefore at the printers weeks before that, and of course in Lennon's head several months before that at the very least. Which is not to say that Lennon hadn't originally got it from Ringo. The Beatles were now living life at the thousand-miles-an-hour required to satisfy the public demand for them and memories could (and we know in some cases did) become conflated in such confused circumstances.

Whether originally Lennon's or Starr's, the phrase became the title of The Beatles' seventh UK single and of their first feature film. Director Richard Lester – tickled by the way the phrase summed up both the pandemonium of The Beatles' lifestyle (depicted, fairly accurately, in the film) and the wacky Beatles humour – said he intended to use the phrase as the title of the picture. The ever-competitive John wrote a song with that title overnight and brought it into the studio the next day where (underlining that thousand-miles-an-hour velocity) The Beatles immediately proceeded to record it. Journalist Maureen

Cleave – band friend and a key minor figure in their story – was there that day and told Lennon she found his intended second line ("I find my tiredness is through") weak. Lennon, who respected Cleave's opinion, came up with the alternative, and better, "I find the things that you do".

"It seemed a bit ridiculous writing a song called 'A Hard Day's Night' because it sounded a funny phrase at the time," Lennon later recalled. Indeed, though over-familiarity now means we think nothing of it, it is a title that seems to lend itself to nothing but a cheesy novelty song. But that's where Lennon's (and The Beatles' collective) genius kicked in. Though the title is humorous, the song that sprang from it is deadly serious. Not only is its music driving and bluesy, but its lyric is rooted in the modest backgrounds of three-quarters of the band in its discussion of the solace people take in their domestic life when the majority of their waking hours are spent doing (and travelling to and from) an unskilled or semi-skilled job that provides no deep satisfaction. As people who had either never or only briefly had proper jobs, Paul, George and Ringo couldn't relate to this first-hand. But as sons of, respectively, a cotton salesman (Paul's mother was, unusually, a higher earner than her husband through her job as a midwife), bus driver and divorced barmaid, they knew they didn't want to grow up to be what their parents had been, and certainly didn't want the same level of remuneration. Some might find it ironic, then, that it was Lennon who wrote the lyric, though frankly the depiction of him as middle class by some revisionist commentators is unconvincing. Though his aunt Mimi – who brought him up from the age of four following his parent's separation – seems to have lived a genteel, comfortable existence, it seems difficult to categorize Lennon's family as unequivocally bourgeois when it contained somebody like his father Fred, a real ne'er-do-well and classic example of a Gentleman of No Fixed Abode. Additionally, what kind of conventional career prospects would Lennon have had? Keith Richards once described his fellow Rolling Stone Brian Jones (a man from a genuinely posh background) as "unemployable", and one can't help but think the same applies to Lennon, who was simply too hot-headed, individualistic and knowing to have stuck to any course carved open for him on the career ladder by his razor sharp intelligence. Music wasn't merely a vocation – it was a life raft to which he was clinging, and this fact fully justified his description of himself in a post-Beatles song as a "working class hero".

Of course, none of this is overt in the lyric, which could just as easily be read as having no socio-political import. In some senses, the aching unhappiness implicit in the lyric is washed away by the music, which – bluesy base aside – is pure Beatles sunniness. Immediately after the opening downstroke on guitar (the most famous opening note of any recording), it positively hurtles along on a wave of what a surface reading would assume to be good cheer, propelled by bongos, which themselves add a tinge of the exotic, a cowbell and scrubbed acoustic guitar. There is real grit, though, in John's impassioned, sometimes groaning, lead vocal. Paul's comment that, "I might have been in on the middle eight" doesn't sound like an emphatic staking of a claim for having co-written the bridge but it's indisputable that he tackles the singing: Lennon couldn't reach its high notes.

Just as George shows off his new twelve-string Rickenbacker at the beginning, so he does so again at the end, this time with a figure that winds the song away into the void.

On the B-side, McCartney sings a low-key, intelligent ballad in which the narrator is able to step outside the moment even as he exults in the bliss of being with his lover and ruminates on the fact that this is such a happy occasion that they will later look back on it, and on the "Things We Said Today". Paul wrote it on a rare holiday following the completion of the filming of *A Hard Day's Night* whilst on a yacht with Ringo Starr, Ringo's wife Maureen and his own lady Jane Asher, who of course was the inspiration for the song.

"A Hard Day's Night" is spiritually brash, tender, frustrated, breathless and charming. Musically it is conventional in its populism but at the same time casually innovative (the non-sensically quippy title, the apropos of nothing guitar bookends). It was also everything the public had come to expect from The Beatles, partly because the public had come to expect the unexpected from these inventive young men.

Peter Sellers had a UK hit with a piss-take the following year in which he spoke the lyric as Richard III, the joke presumably being the contrast between the supposed triteness of the lyric and the dramatic Shakespearian style. Though he was way off on this score, one can't help but think that the irreverently witty Lennon probably found it funny.

A Hard Day's Night

Released: 10/07/1964

by Sean Egan

TRACKLISTING

Side one
1. "A Hard Day's Night"
2. "I Should Have Known Better"
3. "If I Fell"
4. "I'm Happy Just to Dance With You"
5. "And I Love Her"
6. "Tell Me Why"
7. "Can't Buy Me Love"

Side two
1. "Any Time at All"
2. "I'll Cry Instead"
3. "Things We Said Today"
4. "When I Get Home"
5. "You Can't Do That"
6. "I'll Be Back"

One really doesn't want to belabour the point of the ability of The Beatles to create great art out of the philistine motives of others, but it truly is amazing how superb is *A Hard Day's Night*, an album written and recorded in absurd haste (eight cumulative days) simply to provide the soundtrack for a film that was only made so that movie studio United Artists could exploit Capitol's lapse in not including soundtrack albums in their recording contract with The Beatles. That the band put together an album of Lennon/McCartney originals when the timeframe would have made it very tempting to pad out the LP with rock 'n' roll chestnuts from their Cavern repertoire, and that so much of the music with which they came up was imaginative, even innovative, were both considerable triumphs.

There again, perhaps if The Beatles had not been so rushed they would have striven for more sophisticated lyrics. The song-words here are as generic as the music is inspired. At the risk of demanding perfection instead of brilliance, it would have been nice if the well-read John and Paul had applied the full range of their joint intelligence to some of these sometimes banal songwords.

The main personal triumph, incidentally was John's. People who pose the question "John or Paul?" are barking up the wrong tree: the quality of the solo careers of each ex-Beatle surely proves beyond all doubt that Lennon and McCartney were geniuses together and merely very-good-to-great, at best, apart. However, it has to be noted that Lennon was the impetus for and chief writer of most of this album's songs. Even in McCartney's very-much-authorized biography *Many Years From Now*, author Barry Miles observes that "Tell Me Why", "I Should Have Known Better", "Any Time At All", "I'll Cry Instead", "When I Get Home" and "You Can't Do That" were exclusively Lennon compositions, with John also having written the majority of the other two tracks on which he sang lead ("If I Fell" and "I'll Be Back'), and collaborated with Paul on "I'm Happy Just To Dance With You". Never again would Lennon dominate a Beatles album to such an extent.

The original vinyl album (released on the same day as the title track appeared as a single) was divided between a first side that featured songs from the movie soundtrack and a second side of numbers that didn't make it to celluloid. No assumption should be made of discard status for the tracks on side two (tracks eight to thirteen in CD parlance), as director Richard Lester has explained they were only rejected because they couldn't be used to fit any scene's mood.

Some might argue that after the all-exclusive policy of *With The Beatles*, the inclusion of the title track and "Can't Buy Me Love" herein was an exploitative step backwards but – leaving aside arguments that the title track need not have been released as a single – not to include the film's title track would have been silly. Meanwhile, the use of "Can't Buy Me Love" in the now iconic film sequence where the band break out of a studio and romp like schoolboys on a field made its inclusion on the album inevitable. Nonetheless, including those singles' B-sides "You Can't Do That" and "Things We Said Today" as well seems a bit of a cheek. Meanwhile, that the album cover features four strips of simulated film reel with Beatle heads in different poses is either inspired in its playfulness and modernism or else shamelessly exploitative in its allusion to the parent movie.

On "I Should Have Known Better", John's calmly relentless acoustic rhythm guitar is mixed high and is almost as compelling as his great harmonica riff. If the lyric sometimes chases its own tail and is confused (why exactly could, as he claims, "this . . . only happen to me"?), it somehow makes sense conceptually, as it reflects the silliness and giddiness of being in love. "If I Fell" and side two's closer "I'll Be Back" are companion pieces, dreamy, almost supplicant ballads carried along on a frothy wave of three-part harmonies. You can hear that John is merely filling in melody line with random phrases but it's the blissful mood and the gorgeous tunes that count. (EMI, incidentally, pressed some singles of "If I Fell" for export with "Tell Me Why" on the flip. When import copies started coming back into the country at a premium price, the label pressed some for internal consumption. Some Beatles experts claim that this constitutes therefore an unacknowledged official UK release.)

"I'm Happy Just to Dance with You" is George's vocal showcase and – we can therefore assume as per McCartney's confessions to such – that it was a song that not much craft or interest was invested in. Yet not only is it perfectly serviceable but because it chooses to dwell on a prelude to romance (dancing) rather than the romance itself, constitutes a lateral angle on the album's romantic theme, thereby providing a nice variation of lyrical tone. It's fast, fresh and, in the bridge, has harmonies that gush like geysers.

Though one can make allowances for the banalities elsewhere, one can't help but be conscious of the fact that Paul's "And I Love Her" is a song that deserves a better lyric. A dark, exotic thing – the minor chord melody is decorated with Spanish-sounding guitar motifs and a rhythm track featuring bongos and claves – it labours under embarrassingly empty lines like "she gives me everything and tenderly", while the "and" in the title phrase makes no grammatical sense.

"Tell Me Why" is a galloping song of romantic discord featuring some strummed electric guitar parts that are almost punk-like in their blurred velocity and a line in its bridge where John, Paul and George hilariously parody their own trademark falsetto vocal harmonies by keening like The Shirelles after they've just been goosed.

As if to emphasize that the stuff on side two is in no way sub-standard, it starts with the magnificent rocker "Any Time At All', wherein John roars his willingness to please his love any which way required in choruses preceded by bullet-like snare drum shots from Ringo. He states the same sentiment more calmly in steady-rolling verses. It may well be the best track on the album, helped by what is one of Lennon's greatest ever vocal performances.

"I'll Cry Instead" sees the band take a trip down country road. It's not completely authentic-sounding, but country music filtered through the singular mind and style of The Beatles is no bad thing. And Lennon does capture perfectly the epic self-pitying tradition of the genre as he declares that, if he could, he would get himself locked up/get revenge on his departed lover/break girls' hearts all round the world, but that until that time he will content himself with his lachrymose activities. The band make their point in less than two minutes and then depart the stage, upon which you immediately wish the track was starting again.

"When I Get Home" is a pleasant piece of hackwork, seeing John lazily, and unintentionally comically, state he's gonna love his gal 'til the cows come home. But his vocals are of soul music intensity and the impatient verses in which he tells his companions to stop mithering him and make way so he can get back to his lover are great stuff.

Sonically, what is most striking on *A Hard Day's Night* is the group's leavening of their sound via the increased use of acoustic rhythm guitar. Though the Beatles had never been spiritually hard, there is also a softening of emotion in the lyrics. The overall tone is heart-melting. Tony Palmer once wrote a review of the White Album wherein he bizarrely claimed of that very emotionally varied record, "the extra-ordinary quality of the . . . songs is one of simple happiness". In fact that comment describes *A Hard Day's Night* more than any other album in The Beatles' canon. Even the sad numbers are informed by such sensitivity that they seem to resonate with bliss. One can imagine young people – boys *and* girls – being covered in an impressionistic wave of good feeling engendered by the record's tenderness and humanity. One can also imagine parents and grandparents experiencing pretty much the same sensation: love and good tunes are two things that span the generations. It's little wonder that the world fell in love with The Beatles. Following that first flush of success, this joyous album did more than anything else Beatle-related to absolutely embed them in the world's affections.

"I Feel Fine" b/w "She's A Woman"

Released: 27/11/1964

by Sean Egan

In the last week of November 1964, radio listeners swung their heads towards their radio sets in alarm or surprise as it emitted a peculiar humming sound that throbbed, then flared into an almost painful crescendo.

At a time when a lot of radios still had valves, it was easy for listeners to assume there was something wrong with their equipment. But when a sharp, bobbing guitar riff emerged from the speaker and the strange noise disappeared, they could return to their newspaper, or their enjoyment of the programme, with the hope that the fault was temporary. The next time they heard the strange effect, and it was again followed by the guitar lick, they realized it was not fault but design. The song to which the effect was attached was delightful, thus making what would be in any other circumstances an annoying noise a pleasing sound, for it – Pavlovian style – created a link with pleasure. The Beatles were cleaving to their primary principle of giving the public what they wanted at the very same time as they were providing the public with something they could never have imagined wanting, a neat balancing act that the Fab Four would execute more and more frequently over the coming years.

John's original comments about the origin of "I Feel Fine" were self-deprecating to the point of dismissiveness. "I tried to get that effect in practically every song on our new album but the others wouldn't have it," he explained of the weird noise, which, once this record was released, the general public learned was called "feedback". "I told them I'd write a song especially for the riff . . . We tried it . . . and it sounded like an A-side, so we decided to release it just like that." By 1980, though, speaking to *Playboy*, he was almost aggressive in his pride in the record: "That's me, including the guitar lick with the first feedback ever recorded. I defy anyone to find an earlier record – unless it's some old blues number from the twenties – with feedback on it."

That feedback was stated at the time to be a studio accident that The Beatles decided to leave in. McCartney has remembered – quite vividly, even though from a distance – a semi-acoustic Gibson John owned giving off a burst of feedback when he leaned it against an amp and started to walk off to listen to a take. Thrilled by the sound, the group asked George Martin if it could be put on the record. Martin acquiesced, though edited the start, which was too untidy even for a piece of distortion.

Yet this "found object" (to use McCartney's phrase) origin seems a little too pat. As musicians, The Beatles were all of course familiar with the phenomenon of feedback, the distorted sound that results if an electric guitar is moved too close to its amplifier. They were also almost certainly aware that some people were beginning to harness feedback and use it for artistic ends. The Beatles had recently played on the same bill as the High Numbers, soon to change their name to The Who, a band whose guitarist Pete Townshend was pioneering the creative use of feedback, though had yet to put it on a record. Eddie Phillips of the Mark Four (later The Creation) was doing the same thing, although The Beatles had not shared a bill with them. Basically, the use of feedback on record was something in the air, just waiting to be issued on a recording for the first time.

That riff John was so insistent on claiming seems to owe more than a little to that of "Watch Your Step", as done originally by Bobby Parker and covered by the John Barry Seven. The drumming also owed a debt to another record: Ringo plays what McCartney described as what The Beatles used to think of as "What'd I Say? drumming", in reference to the Latin-stylings of Ray Charles" drummer Milt Turner on that aforesaid classic hit. Yet whatever its nods to other artists, "I Feel Fine" was quintessentially Beatles, sunny and warm, and singable from the first exposure. Even its very title described the mood The Beatles' music put people in. The lyric is nothing more than a litany of phrases amounting to "I love her, she loves me and I'd dead chuffed about it", but somehow it feels nothing like as simplistic as the similarly themed "Love Me Do". Perhaps it's because of the way Lennon throws in the conversational "Y'know"s, or the almost defiantly proud tone of the line "She tells me all the time". There's also a nicely symmetrical pattern to the lyric, with the narrator starting out by telling us how good he feels because his baby loves him, then in the bridge how good his baby feels about him and how she tells the world about it, which bring us back to the first verse and why the narrator feels so good.

The track has a very good climbing guitar break. It also possesses the best Beatles harmonies on record so far. Paul and George chime in with John on the last line of each verse. In the bridge all three sing the first part of each line, then Paul and George provide a lush bed of "Oooh" as John finishes them. John's lead vocal is unusually powerful even for him, possessing a just-out-of-bed baritone quality.

"Eight Days A Week" had been earmarked as the song from the *Beatles For Sale* sessions to be the group's next single, but

"I Feel Fine" was considered better and, like *With The Beatles*, *Beatles For Sale* ended up having no UK singles pulled from it.

Paul considered his "She's A Woman", the flip of "I Feel Fine", to be something of a breakthrough for the band. Back in mid-October, he had told *Melody Maker*, "We spent a lot of time trying to write a real rocker. Something like 'Long Tall Sally'. It's very difficult. 'I Saw Her Standing There' was the nearest we got to it." By the beginning of November, McCartney evidently felt they were over that hump, for he told the same paper of "She's a Woman", "This is the first real rocker we've written, and we're glad."

Others have agreed with McCartney's diagnosis: the track has been posited in some quarters as a great neglected bluesy Beatles number and even somehow subversive because it features the phrase "turn me on". In fact, it's a slight and almost bizarre song, featuring a maddeningly repetitive stabbed Lennon riff and the quite fatuous rhyming of "presents" and "peasant".

Beatles For Sale

Released: 4/12/1964

by Sean Egan

TRACKLISTING

Side one
1. "No Reply"
2. "I'm a Loser"
3. "Baby's in Black"
4. "Rock And Roll Music"
5. "I'll Follow the Sun"
6. "Mr Moonlight"
7. "Kansas City/Hey, Hey, Hey, Hey"

Side two
1. "Eight Days a Week"
2. "Words Of Love"
3. "Honey Don't"
4. "Every Little Thing"
5. "I Don't Want to Spoil The Party"
6. "What You're Doing"
7. "Everybody's Trying to Be My Baby"

". . . the biggest attraction the world has ever known," says Epstein aide Derek Taylor in the sleevenotes to *Beatles For Sale*. Remarkably, this wasn't hyperbole.

For that reason, it was imperative from EMI's point of view that they release a new Beatles album in time for the lucrative Christmas market. The fact that The Beatles were exhausted after a year of recordings, gigs, interviews and television appearances was of no concern to them. Whereas The Beatles rose quite magnificently to the pressure of having to record *A Hard Day's Night* in the space of a week or so, the month over which they recorded – off and on – *Beatles For Sale* yielded less impressive results. In a big step backwards, there were six cover versions on the record and the rest of the material was generally not as good as the Lennon/McCartney originals on *A Hard Day's Night*, which makes another of Taylor's sleevenote assertions – "The best album yet" – a load of tripe. However, the idea that The Beatles' shattered and disillusioned state was reflected in both the music and their doleful appearance in Robert Fraser's photos on the deluxe gatefold jacket seems to be a matter of projection on the part of people who like to stick it to The Man. There don't seem to be any quotes in the archives from The Beatles complaining about this album being wrested from them against their will and the record is only a downer in its mood, not its quality.

The record would probably be better regarded were it not for the terrible sequencing. The circular "No Reply" is a most curious way to start an album, as is the triumvirate of minorchord brooding that constitutes the first three tracks. Modern kids will probably scrunch up their noses at such an observation but two or more generations of listeners without recourse to a

sequencing programme will have had their perceptions of the
record prejudiced by a disjointed running order over which they
had no ready control. And though it's a consolidation album
more than anything, *Beatles For Sale* demonstrates examples of
development: for instance the slightly richer sound courtesy of
incrementally more sophisticated production, the vaguely daring
decision to write a disproportionate number of sad songs and
the fade-in of "Eight Days A Week".

According to George at the time, the group only rehearsed
the album's originals. This is remarkable because the cover
versions are generally so good. One adds the caveat "generally",
because one of them is mediocre and another awful. Carl Perkins'
"Honey Don't" is a vocal showcase for Ringo (who had not
been given a track to sing on *A Hard Day's Night*). It's alright,
but if you're going to give a song to someone like Starr to sing,
it should be something whose structural and melodic qualities
can detract attention from the shortcomings of his voice and
the rhythmically plodding and lyrically whining "Honey Don't",
even if Ringo's guilelessness as a vocalist is quite endearing and
George's twangy guitar work is easy on the ear. Meanwhile,
"Mr Moonlight" is just stupid. A Dr Feelgood and the Interns
B-side, it was fairly well-known on Merseyside though being a
part of the repertoires of several groups, including The Beatles.
It's astonishingly old-fashioned, its personalizing the qualities
of the lunar luminescence that supposedly makes romance
more possible reminiscent of 1930s' pop songs. By the time of
the post-rock era, such sentiments seemed very formal and
chocolate-box stylized. The fact that it's the normally sarcastic
John singing only serves to make the song seem even more
preposterous. Not that a singer can't inhabit a character different
to his real self, but this is just a plausibility bridge too far. Almost
as though to prove how antiquated is the composition, The
Beatles' version includes an horrendous cheesy Hammond organ
break from Paul that one can imagine inspiring a shower of
peanuts if ever played on what sounds like its natural habitat,
a park bandstand. How The Beatles could include this on the
album while leaving off a glorious snarling version of Little
Willie John's "Leave My Kitten Alone" from the same sessions
defies understanding.

Of the cover versions that do pass muster, in the very good category comes "Words of Love", a song by Buddy Holly, the man whose "That'll Be the Day" was the first recording The Beatles ever made. While not one of Holly's better-known tracks, it's a nice "Everyday"-type croon. On the Fab Four's version, George provides a compelling continuous, winding guitar part while John and Paul sing a duet that eerily sounds like one person, double-tracked. The three great covers are "Rock And Roll Music", "Kansas City" and "Everybody's Trying To Be My Baby", sung by John, Paul and George respectively. "Rock And Roll Music" is another of Chuck Berry's mythologizations of rock and is probably the best of them. Lennon makes it even better, using his manic "Twist And Shout" commitment level to make the listener understand precisely what the visceral excitement was in rock that made his generation of fans slash seats and dance in cinema aisles. "Kansas City" was written by Leiber & Stoller and has been recorded by more people than can possibly be mentioned in this space. The Beatles were actually covering Little Richard's version, which contained a "Hey hey hey hey" refrain not actually present in the original song. Mike Stoller was amused that Richard took legal action to ensure that the track was credited as a medley on this album so as to obtain royalties, it being the case that Richard's tampering with the song in the first place was unauthorized. Paul sings the hell out of it, just as he did his previous Little Richard cover, "Long Tall Sally". His call-and-response with George and John in the closing stages is so infectious as to be the best part of the track. Some have dismissed George's take on Carl Perkins' tongue-in-cheek complaint about being the most desired male in sight, "Everybody's Trying To Be My Baby", as sub-standard. They have cloth ears. George's vocal prowess is not at this point in the same league of confidence and delivery as his colleagues' but it's a version that barrels along with the right amount of cheek and that bristles with a great guttural guitar part.

The Lennon/McCartney songs are accomplished but to a large extent strangely dejected. The exceptions are the euphoric "Eight Days A Week" (written when a chauffeur ferrying Paul to John's house for a writing session used the unfamiliar phrase to describe his onerous workload); the pretty song of imminent farewell "I'll Follow The Sun" (an old song by Paul given a re-tooled bridge by him and John) and the pulsing "What You're Doing" (which continues the Lennon/McCartney tradition of playing on words, i.e. "Whatcha doing"/"What you're doing").

The rest is despair. Even the supposedly happy love anthem "Every Little Thing" is weirdly melancholic. The opener "No Reply" sets the tone for the misery, a song of paranoia that sees the narrator standing outside his ex's house tormenting himself about whom she might be entertaining. This is immediately followed by "I'm A Loser", a self-pity anthem that is one part country and western and one part Bob Dylan (John's harmonica solo could have come off *The Times They Are A-Changin'* and his "My friend" off "Blowin' In The Wind"). The depressiveness then achieves a logical crescendo with "Baby's In Black", which would appear to be about a man hankering for a woman who is still grieving over the death of her partner. There is a pairing of similarly dark tracks on side two: the aforementioned "Every Little Thing" in which John (singing, unusually, a Paul compo-sition) rather mournfully celebrates the fact of his happiness and John's utterly despondent "I Don't Want To Spoil The Party", in which the narrator slinks away from a soiree after realizing his girl has decided not to be there. Not that this misery is not shot through with great pop craft and is not executed with fine playing and singing – it is: there is an attractiveness and sprightliness about this misery. However, The Beatles are here pushing at the limits of our capacity for sad songs. And notwithstanding the previous rejection of the idea of this as a forced-labour album, there seems the occasional example of sloppiness that might have been corrected had a little more time been available: for instance, in "Every Little Thing", Paul clunkily ends two consecutive lines with "for me" when there is a perfect rhyme going begging: "ecstasy".

These are, though, minor faults. *Beatles For Sale* might not be a masterpiece but it's all relative: who else was making albums as good as this in 1964? Few children, teenagers or indeed adults could have been disappointed to find it in their Yuletide stocking that year.

"Ticket To Ride" b/w "Yes It Is"

Released: 9/04/1965

by Sean Egan

Until McCartney's claim in *Many Years From Now* in 1997 that "Ticket To Ride" was a John song but only by 60:40, most had assumed that The Beatles' ninth UK single was Lennon all the way through. It should be pointed out, though, that this seems to have come more from the retrospective comments of Lennon, who by his own admission had a terrible memory. McCartney's recollection is given credence by a contemporaneous press comment from him: "We wrote the melody together, you can hear it on the record."

The pair had in mind a cousin of McCartney's who lived in the Isle of Wight town of Ryde and whom the two had once visited. There have also been suggestions that Lennon was making a sly reference to a phrase that was used to indicate that street girls in Hamburg had been given a clean bill of health, but this claim may just as easily have emanated from Lennon's mischievous sense of humour. The song was recorded in the middle of February 1965, a week before the band travelled to the Bahamas to begin shooting their second movie, *Help!*, for whose soundtrack it was chosen for inclusion.

Lennon remarked when "I Feel Fine" went straight to number one, ". . . we were ready to get to number five at first go, and I suppose if we'd have done that, we'd have been written off. Nobody would have remembered that The Beatles had had six number ones on the trot before 'I Feel Fine' . . . Coming in at number one was great because, well, we weren't sure we'd do it." The same nervousness applied to this record. Lennon has claimed that his colleagues were initially nervous about making

"Ticket To Ride" a single. Looking from this distance at their (undisputed) seventeen UK number ones from the twenty-one singles released in their home territory while they were extant, such insecurity seems absurd.. But longevity in pop had so far been confined to giants like Sinatra and Presley and, massively popular though The Beatles were, there was no reason yet to believe that they could make that jump from flash in the pan to immoveable fixture of the celebrity landscape. Maintaining their elevated level of success, therefore, was imperative. Yet, ironically it is precisely the innovative and non-populist aspects of "Ticket To Ride" that would assist in maintaining The Beatles' success rate.

The Beatles' ability to sustain a long career had not been suggested by their track record thus far of music that, no matter how pleasing, was oriented lyrically toward teen sensibilities. Sinatra and Presley had helped ensure their longevity by becoming entertainers in a wider sense, branching out in Presley's case into a movie career and in Sinatra's by that and hosting his own TV shows. The Beatles did not really have this option even if they wanted it, hampered by the logistics of being a group, not a single personality. It transpired that the way they were going to extend their shelf life was with records that ensured their continued relevance to their audience by evincing an increasing sophistication as their audiences grew up: recordings like "Ticket To Ride".

Even for a band who were almost unique in writing a goodly chunk of their popcraft in minor keys, and even for a band whose last album had been so maudlin, "Ticket To Ride" must have seemed an arrestingly disconsolate presence on the hit parade. This applies to both music and lyric. John's claim that this is "one of the earliest heavy metal records ever made" is pushing it a bit but it is true that there is none of the trademark Fab Four sprightliness here but instead a dense, lumbering rhythm. John's vocal is at times almost a groan. Admittedly, this seems partly in homage to the singing style of his current hero Bob Dylan, but it's also in synch with the song's relentless grimness as he tells the tale of a dying relationship and his imminent dumped status. That lyric begins in a quite startling way: few who heard its opening line for the first time can have been expecting it to end up being anything other than, "I think I'm gonna be sick". The melancholy persists even when in the bridge the track jumps into double-time.

There is nothing here of the puppy love in which The Beatles had previously dealt. This sombre song is clearly about a relationship between people somewhat older and more mature than that. It's also – daringly – clearly about pre-marital sex, still a fairly controversial topic in 1965. John refers to the woman who is about to throw him over as "living with me". That can only mean shacking up, because when John also refers to his love as a girl who's driving him mad, it hardly sounds like a reference to the settled domesticity of marriage. The air of substantiality lent the track by this is increased by the fact that this is the first-ever Beatles release of more than three minutes.

Yet melancholy though the tone and subject might be, there is an air of brightness over the proceedings. This is The Beatles – a group who even in studied misery mode can't help but be delightful. Meanwhile, individual elements are unquestionably Fab. The ringing, elongated guitar riff – played by Paul and their nod to The Byrds, who had just become huge by Beatle-ifying Dylan's "Mr Tambourine Man" in a record whose highlight was Jim McGuinn's distinctive twelve-string work – is close to hypnotic. The production – the most intricate yet – is thrilling: Lennon's voice is used to provide the harmonies that we normally expect from Paul and George: he joins in with himself on the last syllable-and-a-half of the first verse line, then the first part of the second verse lines, then on the last line of each chorus – and does so more like a chanting football supporter than backing vocalist. It is brilliantly astute colouring and mood enhancing. It is also – objectively – odd, but done with such conviction that the listener soon finds it natural.

Ringo's drumming, meanwhile, is magnificent. Starr has never been given proper credit for the inventiveness he displays on this record. It seems that the only time his playing on this track is ever mentioned is when it's noted that his "cross-beat" dragged style was the suggestion of McCartney. Kudos to Paul, no doubt, but are people deaf to the way Ringo provides such complicated, changing patterns throughout that his drumming can be listened to for pleasure on its own?

Right at the death, the band throw in one last delight, one of those moments that people listen to a record especially to hear. The record launches into double time and a double-tracked John repeats the song's motif about the girl not caring, but to a totally different melody and at a quite frantic pitch. He continues doing so to the fade.

The flip was another Lennon-dominated song, albeit that feeling of domination stemming from the bridge, which – just like "This Boy" – sees Lennon, after verses of lush three-part harmonizing, execute a soaring solo singing section with a jaw-droppingly towering crescendo. It strengthens the impression given by the A-side of The Beatles maturing, for that crescendo consists of Lennon admitting in a flash of self-knowledge not common in the young that he can't give his current partner the love she needs because his pig-headed pride won't let him get over the loss of a previous romance.

The aforementioned titans excepted, pop idols hitherto had experienced careers of a few years that withered on the vine when their fans outgrew their youth-targeted songs and new generations of fans proved more interested in fresher recording artists than in the subjects of the adoration of their older siblings. Though "Can't Buy Me Love" and, especially, "A Hard Day's Night" had seen The Beatles stepping away from teenybopper-pandering, "Ticket To Ride" was the real beginning of the process of them creating art to which people other than teenagers could readily relate. This doesn't seem to have been through calculation. Artistic restlessness, not sustaining the market, was the impetus for the unusualness of the song. But developing as artists as their fans grew physically and emotionally was turning The Beatles from a pop group to the voice of a generation.

"Help!" b/w "I'm Down"

Released: 23/07/1965

by Sean Egan

Maureen Cleave's very minor contribution to the lyric of "A Hard Day's Night" (*see p.67*) wouldn't have been quite enough to earn her a footnote in rock history, but she certainly deserves one for the stimulus she provided to the content of another title song of a Beatles movie, "Help!"

Cleave was puzzled by the way that little of Lennon's intelligence and wit – which the world was now familiar with not just through his often slightly edgy interviews but his published book of rhyme and doodles *In His Own Write* – made its way into his lyrics. Recalled Lennon, ". . . Maureen Cleave . . . said to me, 'Why don't you ever write songs with more than one syllable in the words?' I never considered it before, so after that I put a few three-syllable words in . . ."

This of course was not a failing unique to Lennon amongst rockers of the era. Pop or rock – or the combination of the two that The Beatles practised – had not yet proven itself to be a medium in which intellectualism could thrive. In short, few had tried to write about subjects other than romance, rock 'n' roll and bossy parents because there seemed no reason to believe teenagers would be interested in hearing about them, and the career of a chart act was fragile and uncertain enough without running the risk of alienating one's audience by getting clever on them. That being the case, it was also logical that in pandering to their audience with their subject matter, pop and rock artists should speak to them in their own language: monosyllables, double-negatives and contemporary catchphrases. Words and phrases like "self-assured", "independence" and "insecure", all of which feature in "Help!", were not part of the vocabulary of the hit parade. Nor did chart songs tend to feature themes like realization of youthful folly. In a medium that thrived on the generation gap, and in an era where the divisions between young and old were becoming chasms, writing lyrics like that of "Help!" – an admission that previous stances had been proven to be wrong in light of the knowledge and experience acquired through growing older – did not seem a logical or wise course of action. Lennon's hero and friend Bob Dylan didn't have these problems. His songs were chock-full of intellectual ideas, multi-syllabic words and adult themes. But Dylan was a folk, not a rock, artist at a time when an aesthetic, ideological and demographic Berlin Wall existed between the two genres.

Of course, Cleave didn't actually write any of the song. The number started life because it had been decided, seven weeks into shooting The Beatles' second feature film, that *Eight Arms To Hold You* – its original title – was a bugger to write a title theme for. As with "A Hard Day's Night", John used the title as a jumping-off point for a song far from the effervescent or comical number director Richard Lester – whose suggestion the title *Help!* was – was perhaps expecting. The song's lyric stemmed from the insecurities of what John later termed his "fat Elvis" period, in which he was putting on weight and realizing he was actually happier in his penniless Menlove Avenue days than he was as a wealthy and well-loved celebrity. And those Menlove Avenue days had been hardly bliss, spent desperately hiding the pain of the loss of his mother and his Uncle George (Mimi's husband, who died when John was twelve) behind his tough guy façade. In "Help!", he was saying that he had been wrong not to show that he needed other people's emotional sustenance. All of this led to Lennon claiming in 1970 that this and "Strawberry Fields Forever" were the only "true" – i.e. stemming from personal experience – Beatles songs he ever wrote.

The very fact that by his own admission John rushed to start the song before Paul could get in with a rival candidate for the title theme would seem to be itself a manifestation of his insecurity. The now usual finessing of the song with McCartney then took place. "I helped with the structure of it and put in little counter melodies," recalled McCartney.

Even if the fast, exhilarating pace of "Help!" was in Lennon's eyes a compromise after the band had baulked at his preferred slower arrangement ("The real feeling of the song was lost because it was a single; we did it too fast to try and be commercial"), "Help!" was a step forward for both popular music generally and The Beatles specifically. It built on "Ticket To Ride"'s achievement of beginning to make The Beatles sound like the adults they were. In the summer of 1965, the "Berlin Wall" that dictated that folk was for the intelligent and rock 'n' roll for the teenybopper, had several huge holes knocked through it. These holes occurred with the release – and more importantly – the success of The Rolling Stones' blast of streetwise bile "(I Can't Get No) Satisfaction" in June, Dylan's rock (not folk) "Like A Rolling Stone" – not only no less streetwise or bile-filled but also a revolutionary five-minute plus record – in August, and "Help!", released between those two platters in July.

The Beatles' record was less revolutionary than The Stones' and Dylan's, whose aforementioned hits were about hate, while The Beatles' number was, despite its disconsolate theme and big words, still a love song at heart. But The Beatles' audience was more vast than The Stones' or Dylan's combined and their influence on the course of the medium correspondingly greater. Not that The Beatles fans who did their usual thing of sending the song to number one on both sides of the Atlantic and all around the rest of the world gave a stuff about what barriers "Help!" was breaking down. They were doubtlessly far more interested in the fact that The Beatles had come up with another effervescent single bursting with love and humanity.

The record has an explosive opening with a three-man scream of "Help!". The tempo – propelled by acoustic rhythm guitar – remains deliciously frantic from there apart from a bridge that is probably a glimpse of the slow, Dylan-esque arrangement Lennon originally envisaged for the whole song. In the verses, The Beatles engage not in call-and-response but – delightfully – response-and-call, with George and Paul anticipating John's lead vocal lines (the counter-harmonies McCartney refers to), before joining in with him on the last line. In the choruses, George alternates impressively between lugubrious descending guitar lines and more trebly work.

The song ends as wonderfully as it began, with the three

Beatles frontmen crying out for help three times in incrementally more urgent tones before – with all instrumentation now halted – issuing a collective "Oooh!"

Paul gets the B-side with the nifty "I'm Down", which was by his own admission an attempt to write his own equivalent of the Little Richard numbers he had always loved singing live. Paul invests Richard-style passion in his whooping, hollering remonstration with his lover over her lack of appreciation and reciprocation, while John contributes an impressively wild Hammond organ part and George provides one of his most impressive guitar solos yet. It's not quite up to the standard of the best of the diminutive Mr Penniman but it is a significant counter-argument to the claims that were beginning to be aired now that the Stones were writing their own singles that, wonderful though The Beatles might be, they simply didn't have Jagger and co's rawness.

And Maureen Cleave's reaction to "Help!", the recording she had inspired that helped The Beatles go through artistic puberty? "She didn't think much when I played the song for her, anyway." Lennon confessed.

Help!

Released: 6/08/1965

TRACKLISTING

Side one
1. "Help!"
2. "The Night Before"
3. "You've Got to Hide Your Love Away"
4. "I Need You"
5. "Another Girl"
6. "You're Going to Lose That Girl"
7. "Ticket to Ride"

Side two
1. "Act Naturally"
2. "It's Only Love"
3. "You Like Me Too Much"
4. "Tell Me What You See"
5. "I've Just Seen A Face"
6. "Yesterday"
7. "Dizzy Miss Lizzy"

Help! features another striking Beatles LP cover, with the group's four figures draped in the blue costumes of the movie's skiing sequence set against a pure white backdrop. Though the group seem to be spelling out the album title in semaphore, in fact for aesthetic reasons it was decided to place them in such a way and give them such letters to render as to constitute gibberish.

This is the last thing that can be said about the contents of the album, yet it doesn't get the praise it merits. George Harrison once opined that *Rubber Soul* and *Revolver* were like parts one and two of the same album. Actually, that description more accurately applies to this album and *Rubber Soul*. Both saw The Beatles' music assume more and more of an acoustic flavour and both saw them employ lyrics that in almost all cases pointedly refused to trade in the banalities of their music hitherto. In 1965, the in-thing was folk-rock, a form created by the increasing number of covers of Dylan material in the pop charts, by hit pastiches of Dylan songs and by Dylan himself jumping ship and putting rock instrumentation behind his literate lyrics, heedless of the resulting disdain of some of his audience. (For a brief period, the avalanche of Dylan covers made him a rival for the crown of Lennon/McCartney as the songwriter whose compositions were perceived to guarantee a hit.) Though *Help!* was completed too early for it to be said to be influenced by the folk-rock explosion, it was a precursor to it, and perhaps that folk-rock explosion encouraged The Beatles to pursue the strain and develop it on its successor LP. (We should also acknowledge the possibility, naturally, that it was an influence on folk-rock itself.)

Once again, The Beatles were being worked like slaves, given from the 15–19 April '65 in the studio to record the tracks they would need to mime to in the film, with the title track added on 13 April. Between 14–17 June, they finished off side two, having already recorded "You Like Me Too Much", "Tell Me What You See" and "Dizzy Miss Lizzy". The latter song had been recorded at a reluctant session on 10 May when Capitol had asked for new material to enable them to put together another of their ragbag American Beatles LPs. Also recorded that day was another Larry Williams cover, "Bad Boy". Despite the pressure, The Beatles still triumphantly emerged with great product, and if there are a couple more instances of hackwork on this LP than on . . . *Night,* this is more than compensated for by the fact that rarely now do the lyrics make you wish they had spent more time or brain power on them.

Nonetheless, those who thought this soundtrack album was better value for money than their previous one because the B-sides of the title track and "Ticket To Ride" were left off were confusing cost with quality. "Yes It Is" and "I'm Down" would have been far more welcome presences than Paul's "Another Girl', a track whose musical laziness is not even redeemed by The Beatles' usual humanity, being as it is the rather mean-spirited song of a man telling his lover none too gently that she has been usurped. Nice squiggly, insolent guitar at the end though. Meanwhile, George's "I Need You" is rather stiff, although his colleagues' sympathetic vocal harmonies and the splashes of volume swell-pedal make it a perfectly acceptable way to pass two minutes twenty-eight seconds.

The other tracks on the first, soundtrack side bookended by the "Help!" and "Ticket to Ride" singles are all high-quality. The break-up song "The Night Before" is brisk, classy and achingly sad. It's also slightly daring when in the bridge Paul tells his absent lover that he wants to cry when he thinks of things they did the night before. John provides some ace electric piano. Lennon had made his admiration known for that man known to his mum as Robert Zimmerman before on "I'm a Loser", but "You've Got to Hide Your Love Away" is an even more blatant Dylan tribute, John's shouts of "Hey!" and his reference to "clowns" in this quasi-suicidal song of alienation being straight out of the rock poet's songbook. Pretty soon, the charts would be full of such pseudo-Dylan fare. Lennon is too clever to fall into the trap of subsuming his personality into Dylan's style in the manner of Sonny and Cher on "I Got You Babe" or Donovan on "Catch The Wind" (both also '65) but instead filters Dylan's style through his own. For instance, there is no harmonica on the track. Instead, an outside musician (i.e. not The Beatles or George Martin) appears for the first time on a Beatles recording as Johnnie Scott executes fluttering flute parts.

With its two electric guitars, "You're Going To Lose That Girl" is a sonic throwback to *Beatles For Sale*. It's adroitly done, and its bottom end is impressively cavernous, but its lyric of teenage romance in the context of the generally thoughtful songs on this album feels like The Beatles wearing an old suit that no longer really fits them. Having said that, it's mildly interesting for its variation on the "She Loves You" second-person approach: once again, John is lecturing an acquaintance on his neglect of his woman but unlike on the caring "She Loves You', he is bringing up his friend's neglect to issue a threat that he might well just take her away from him.

There had been no real difference in mood between the soundtrack and non-soundtrack sides of *A Hard Day's Night*. In contrast, the material on side two here is a notable contrast in tone. The exceptions are the covers that top and tail it. "Act Naturally" is a Buck Owens number that is perfect for Ringo in its style (Starr loved Country and Western) and its self-deprecating subject matter. The Beatles' version is sprightly and fun. The uninteresting cover of "Dizzy Miss Lizzy" is an appalling way to end an album, and a particularly appalling way to end a side that contains a jewel like "Yesterday". George's repetitive, ringing guitar lick has already outstayed its welcome by the second verse but it runs all the way through like some-body's car alarm outside your window on a public holiday. The cover of Williams' "Bad Boy" recorded on the same day would have been a far more preferable inclusion.

The five tracks sandwiched between "Act Naturally" and "Dizzy Miss Lizzy", though, are something else entirely. All boast a certain wistfulness and, with perhaps the exception of John's "It's Only Love", seem very consciously to step away from the conventions of the love song, some of them not even employing the words "baby" and "girl". In the case of "Tell Me What You See", it's not even certain that what we are hearing *is* a love song. With its talk of opening up one's eyes and its insistence on droningly sustained notes, the whole thing sounds like a baby, nascent version of the soon-to-come form of psychedelia.

The presence of "You Like Me Too Much" means two songs for George after a two-album gap since his first songwriting contribution. Unlike "I Need You", this one merits its place, not least in its affecting degree of self-criticism, even if Harrison also takes a measure of delight in the fact that his lover won't leave him "which is all that I deserve". John plays some interesting electric piano again and, though lightweight, the track is only really let down by a bridge whose melodic feebleness is hammered home by the fact that its lyric consists of the gauche words "I reeeeally do". "I've Just Seen A Face" is two minutes of cascading acoustic guitar parts and Paul relating the story of a romantic epiphany. The tumbling instrumentation and double-time tempo gives the whole thing the feeling of something Paul is relating out of breath and excited after running all the way here.

Considering the reams that have been written about it and the number of people who have sung it – it's the most covered song in history – it comes as almost a shock to realize how short "Yesterday" is: just five seconds over two minutes. Some have posited Paul's brooding lament for a departed female as a subconscious pining for his deceased mother. One always assumed that they could be dismissed until Paul gave quotes indicating he agreed with them. Oedipal or not, it's an accomplished little thing but one whose string quartet backing – the first use of classical strings on a Beatles recording and the suggestion of George Martin – provides a self-conscious grandeur that perhaps elevates it beyond its true merits.

However, it sounds a titanic masterpiece next to "Dizzy Miss Lizzy", which follows it (and is the second longest track on the album behind "Ticket To Ride"). It's disappointing that the album ends on such a poor note, not least because it provides ammunition to those who dismiss the record, which is actually the most underrated in The Beatles' canon.

"Day Tripper"/"We Can Work It Out"

Released: 3/12/1965

by Sean Egan

The Beatles' single of December 1965 did not feature a "b/w" sign in its advertisements. "We Can Work It Out" was not "backed with" "Day Tripper" nor vice versa because the band were so convinced the two songs were of equal worth that they decided to make the record the first Beatles double-A sided single. It was a disc of contrasts, American-style rock counterpointed by Euro-fare.

"We Can Work It Out" is an exercise in elegance. The music features a leisurely tempo, a French café tinge courtesy of accordion-like harmonium (provided by John) and a bridge in waltz time (George's suggestion). The presence of only the acoustic variety of guitar only adds to the chic feel. The lyric, meanwhile, sounds on first listen like a dialogue between lovers, but a careful examination reveals it to contain nothing that definitely categorizes it as a love song, something that adds to the feeling of sophistication. (For the record, it has been suggested that McCartney wrote it out of frustration with Jane Asher, who had decided to further her acting career by joining the Bristol Old Vic theatre company, which necessitated her moving out of London.)

The yin/yang of Lennon/McCartney – both as songwriters and as people – is demonstrated by "We Can Work It Out". Lennon was asked by *Playboy*'s David Sheff in 1980 about the differences in the pair's styles and pointed to this track as an example. "You've got Paul writing 'We can work it out'," Lennon explained, "Real optimistic, and me, impatient [with] 'Life is very short and there's no time for fussing and fighting my friend'." Lennon was referring to the contrast between the verses (written and sung by Paul) and the bridge (written by John and sung by the two together). It's significant that Paul's verses are conciliatory in nature, while Lennon's bridge is not: this is Paul the diplomat and Lennon the man who didn't suffer fools gladly writ large. The two parts don't clash though: we can easily believe that the narrator who is trying to tell his lover that they can overcome their differences is the same person as snarls the bridge; it's just that in the bridge, the strain of the narrators' diplomacy is wearing thin. This goes some way toward showing why Lennon and McCartney were never as good toiling apart as when they were complementing each other so well working together.

"Day Tripper" also sees the two co-operating, although in a different sense. Though it was predominately Lennon's song, McCartney's voice has equal prominence on it. Like the track on the obverse, one is free to read it as a song about romance (albeit a romance gone wrong) or not. The more streetwise members of The Beatles' audience would have made the connection between acid "trips" and the title phrase, and understood "Sunday driver" to be a contemptuous reference to a dabbler. However, one shouldn't – as many critics have – go overboard over the drug references, the similarity of the phrase "big teaser" to "prick teaser", the snaking guitar riff, the quasi-orgasmic build-up of the instrumental break or the general sinewy R&B nature of "Day Tripper". It's a good song but not, as often suggested, great, and the ambiguities of the lyric hardly support claims made for the band as great subversives.

More impressive is Ringo's shuffling drumming, and the fact that The Beatles were prepared to jeopardize sales by releasing the thing as a double-A in the first place: insanely, the sales of such a record were split. (Record shops at the time reported most customers asking for "We Can Work It Out".) However, the fact that it was the fastest-selling Beatles single since "Can't Buy Me Love" ensured it made number one in the UK as per.

Rubber Soul

Released: 3/12/1965

by Sean Egan

TRACKLISTING

Side one
1. "Drive My Car"
2. "Norwegian Wood (This Bird Has Flown)"
3. "You Won't See Me"
4. "Nowhere Man"
5. "Think for Yourself"
6. "The Word"
7. "Michelle"

Side two
1. "What Goes On"
2. "Girl"
3. "I'm Looking Through You"
4. "In My Life"
5. "Wait"
6. "If I Needed Someone"
7. "Run For Your Life"

That something was going on with The Beatles was immediately evident from the sleeve of *Rubber Soul,* their sixth UK album.

The cover – on which the group did not bother to put their name – featured The Beatles' faces distorted in a most peculiar way. The effect – similar to that of a fish-eyed lens – could almost have been a metaphor for the changes in The Beatles:

they were still the familiar and beloved mop-tops but their characters and their music were being pulled into new shapes by new experiences. The punning title was also strange: the world was used to their irreverent Scouse wit but this was a bit weird, as indeed were the bulbous, irregular letters in which said title was rendered. As for the music within, there was an absolutely shocking line in "Norwegian Wood": "And then she said its time for bed". There are also a couple of tracks that would have at the time sounded strangely philosophical, even spiritual, "Think For Yourself" and "The Word". Then there was the musical exotica: the use of sitar on one track, French words on another, a fuzztone bass on a third, a Greek chorus vocal effect on a fourth.

Marijuana and growing older informed the tone of the new songs, and the result was a new mature, sometimes even world-weary tone to add the usual – and naturally still present – Beatle strains of love and happiness. As a consequence, The Beatles – as if they had not entranced enough of the world already – added another layer of admirers and customers with this record: the hipsters and the folkies.

And all of this for an album recorded in a Christmas schedule-dictated rush. So much so that Paul rescued a French-style pastiche from the rejected-because-it's-too silly pile and John and Paul each hurriedly wrote a song on the night before the last day of recording. Those songs, respectively, were "Michelle" (one of the most beloved Beatles songs of all and a UK number one for The Overlanders), "You Won't See Me" (pretty good) and "Girl" (a timeless classic). This is a measure of how much greater was their inspiration compared to the previous year, which had also occasioned the hasty assembling of an album for the Christmas market and seen them turn in the nice but covers-padded *Beatles For Sale*. This time round, the results were an entirely self-written record.

Though it's in no way representative of what's to follow on the album, Paul's rocker "Drive My Car" is a great opener, totally "Swinging Sixties" London in its evocations of cool young dudes and their gear birds cruising in their motors via its streamlined guitars and cheery "Beep-beep!" refrains. There's some confusion as to who plays which guitar part but all are mighty fine: the slinky riff, the delightful solo and – most impressively – the growling rhythm work that makes the player sound like he's stuck at the traffic lights with his foot pressing the accelerator, impatient to go.

"You Won't See Me" is one of a number of songs on the record inspired by Paul's difficulties in his relationship with Jane Asher. "I wouldn't mind if I knew what I was missing" is a rather ungainly, even meaningless line, but overall the song is pretty impressive considering the brevity of its gestation period. It's Beatles-by-numbers but the corollary of that is that its effortlessly touching and melodic.

George's song "Think for Yourself" is interesting because it predates Harrison's immersion in Eastern philosophy. Though it must have been inspired merely by a marital tiff, he seems to be addressing not his wife but the unenlightened as he proceeds to denounce a "you" who is telling us we can have what we want if we close our eyes. Unless he really is accusing the missus of sacrificing spiritual wealth for material possessions? Paul provides a persistent buzzing bassline, produced by the fuzztone pedal, a new pop stars' toy that Keith Richards had made famous with The Rolling Stones' single "(I Can't Get No) Satisfaction" earlier in the year.

"The Word" that John is singing of in the track of that name is "love" and though Lennon no doubt intended this as merely an I-was-wrong piece of reflection like "Help!", it really is quite remarkable how completely this number seems to predict the Beautiful People and their viewpoint on life more than a year before San Francisco's first Human Be-In. A chugging, mid-tempo affair with a staccato riff and a snaking lead guitar part, it sees John making a now-rare return to harmonica in the closing stages.

Some have airily dismissed Paul's "Michelle" as typical McCartney mush, but if we're going to dismiss something because of a pretty tune and a heart-on-sleeve sentimentality, we may as well junk the entire Beatles canon. Such dismissiveness also ignores the innovation involved in the Continental ambience, the French phrases and an instrumental break that comes only behind John Entwistle's work on The Who's "My Generation" of two months previously in constituting the first ever bass solo on a pop record. The lush backing harmonies, by the way, are perfection.

Ringo gets a one-third writing credit for his vocal showcase "What Goes On" but that seems to be just John and Paul being generous: Ringo admitted he only wrote "about five words" and John stated that he had written its core years before. (It was tried at the "From Me To You" session.) It was used because Lennon disliked anything going to waste, Paul finishing it with him. Which means we can exonerate Ringo for everything except the flat singing on a track that is quite shockingly bad. Not only does it sound like a run-through, not only is George's country-esque guitar not even committed enough to warrant the adjective "perfunctory", but the chorus (which is supposed to be the highlight of a song) drones interminably. To add insult to injury, it's the second-longest song present.

"I'm Looking Through You" may be another song inspired by arguments with a certain Miss Asher. Its tone of complaint might be grating were it not for McCartney's fine melodic sensibilities and an extraordinary squiggly guitar blast that follows every instance of Paul's veritably growled accusation, "You're not the same!"

One feels that "Wait" gropes too often for weightiness and that the dramatic "I've been alone" ending demands a sensation of poignancy in the listener that the band haven't merited, but this revived *Help!* recording is undeniably catchy and has a structure that takes in multiple changes of tempo while managing a fine groove.

George Harrison churlishly criticized a cover version of "If I Needed Someone" that The Hollies issued in the same month as this album's release. He should have considered himself lucky that such a dreary tune and inauspicious lyric should have been mistaken as the free ticket into the charts that a Lennon/McCartney composition constituted, especially considering that the songwriting axis within The Hollies of Hicks/Clarke/Nash had already written far more songs then he, and of far better quality. Harrison's chiming guitar lick is worthy of a better track.

Lennon claimed that he wrote "Run For Your Life" to round off the album. While the recording and writing chronology doesn't back that up (it was actually the sessions' first recorded song, although it does appear last on the record, which may have been how John's notoriously patchy memory came upon the idea), he clearly considered it a "work" song. The track uses the line "I'd rather see you dead than to be with another man" from the Elvis Presley hit "Baby, Let's Play House" as a jumping-off point for another of his songs about jealously *à la* "You Can't Do That". Between Ringo's powerful, muscular drum-work and John's venomous vocals and above-average, often syncopated lyric ("sermon"/"determined"), it gets a powerful groove going, even though it's a little nasty. The one thing that truly gives away its hack-work status is the lazy way Lennon adds a superfluous "little girl" at the end of what would otherwise be nicely taut choruses.

The core of *Rubber Soul* is a quartet of four wondrous John Lennon songs. By which is meant four songs sung by Lennon. To use "Norwegian Wood", "Nowhere Man", "Girl" and "In My Life" to prove Lennon's superiority as a writer – as some McCartney detractors have tried – is absurd considering that Paul set the lyric of "In My life", contributed the crucial exotic elements of "Girl" and did his usual job of helping polish off the remaining two. However, it should also be acknowledged that these songs were certainly started by Lennon, that he wrote the majority of them and that they were therefore informed by his particular sensibilities, ones that were less conventional than those of McCartney, who largely spends the album throwing familiar pop shapes, albeit with impeccable craftsmanship. "Norwegian Wood (This Bird Has Flown)" became noteworthy for the fact of George's sitar, an instrument whose exoticness was so unknown in pop that its presence would have been remarkable no matter how good or bad George's playing was. For the record, his sitar work is lovely, but is no more pleasing on the ear than John's absolutely gorgeous acoustic guitar. The "It's time for bed" line, it turns out, is followed by a chickening out, as the lyric then has our protagonist not in sexual congress with the girl – a scenario the mores of the day made impossible in popular song – but sleeping alone in her bath. But that does provide the strange pay-off: like "Drive My Car", the song it succeeds in the running order, "Norwegian Wood" is a narrative with a resolution; whereas "Drive My Car" results in a romantic hook-up in lieu of a chauffeur's job, this one sees the spurned man setting the girl's bedsit ablaze. (Many assume Bob Dylan's melodically identical song "Fourth Time Around" from *Blonde On Blonde*, released the following year, is a parody of "Norwegian Wood". In fact, Lennon seems to have stolen the melody from Dylan, who had provided him with a tape of some of his unreleased songs – hence Dylan's sarcastic title.)

Lennon started writing "Nowhere Man" as a disparaging commentary on his inability to come up with a song one evening. By the time it was finished it had become an archetypal 1960s' blast against the square who couldn't understand the values of the new generation (see also The Kinks' "Mr Pleasant" and Dylan's "Ballad Of A Thin Man"). There's a note of ambiguity, though, for Lennon suggests that in his blinkered approach to life the Nowhere Man is a bit like you and me. (He couldn't apparently bring himself to say the ungrammatical "me and you", even though it would have made a rhyme with the preceding "going to"). The genius of The Beatles for harmony is nowhere better shown than in this track: lovely *a cappella* John-Paul-George vocalizing begins the song and swells the choruses, with Paul and George swinging into soft supporting la-la-las in the John-sung verses. The three voices switch places and positions as slickly and effectively as choreographed dancers. There is also a spangly, super-trebly electric guitar solo and quietly impressive drumming from Ringo.

"Girl" is exquisite. A love song sophisticated like no Beatles love song before, it throws in mentions of Catholic guilt and the kind of everyday spiteful behaviour of a warring couple that then rarely made it into popular song. The melody and lyric seem to fit together so totally as to make most other songs ever written seem contrived, and John's sighing vocal is faultless. The bridge sees a Greek chorus vocal backing and the last verse boasts mandolin-like guitar work. Building guitar parts and an incrementally more dazzling lyric spin out the ecstasy just when one assumes it can't get any better.

"In My Life" also involved a chickening out. The first verse is a most unusual one for mid-1960s pop, concerned not with romantic love but reflection, something the young – who are naturally peering ahead – are not too keen on. However, just when we feel we are in for a rock-era song almost unique in its contemplativeness and nostalgic bent, John switches the subject to the more conventional one of romance, using the places and faces he is reminiscing about in the first verse merely as a yardstick by which to judge his depth of feeling for his partner. Lennon once said the track started out as a, "What I Did On My Holidays bus trip song . . . mentioning every place I could remember." Though Lennon was disparaging about that original draft, it would have made for a very innovative song at the time and this listener would have liked to have seen McCartney set *that*. However, we can't complain too much about a heart-melting pledge of devotion with a fine melody and yet more flawless Lennon vocals.

Rubber Soul was released on the same day as "Day Tripper" /"We Can Work It Out". Only this group could resist the temptation to include such a pair of tracks and still be left with their best and most adventurous album yet. At the end of their third full year as a recording outfit, The Beatles were clearly as far from reaching the end of the conventional three-year shelf life of pop stars as it was possible to be. Their stature – in terms of artistry, popularity and socio-political import – was greater than ever.

BIGGER THAN JESUS

This is the article that became known as the "We're more popular than Jesus" story, the John Lennon interview from a London evening newspaper that caused a huge furore and threats on The Beatles' lives. (However, Sidney Bernstein, promoter of The Beatles' two Shea Stadium gigs has said that talk of the controversy causing 11,000 unsold seats at The Beatles second Shea Stadium concert a year after the first were erroneous, citing a mislaid shoebox of tickets as the real reason.)

The author was Maureen Cleave and her article was part of a series she was writing on the Fabs and Brian Epstein for the Evening

Standard. *Cleave was a friend of the Lennons, but it's probably not this that caused her to fail to take issue with John when he – paraphrasing* The Passover Plot *by Jewish historian Hugh Schonfield, which he had recently read – proclaimed his band to be more popular than Christ. More likely it was the fact that it was a palpable truth: as The Beatles became ever more embedded in the global public's affections, so church attendances were declining all over the world. It should be noted that part of the reason for the vehemence in Lennon's assertion was almost certainly the fact that religion had, while his generation was growing up, been somewhat intertwined with the rules and regulations of an unyielding society. Religious edicts and the rules of the classroom, the workplace and the home seemed cut from the same petty, censorious cloth.*

While it's not true to say that Britons didn't bat an eyelid over the article – journalist and broadcaster Gilbert Harding and actor James Robertson Justice were among the public figures to object to Lennon's comments – negative reaction was muted. However, when the following August US teen magazine Datebook *carried excerpts from the interview, the American response was less temperate, especially in the Bible Belt. Beatles records were publicly destroyed, the airwaves rang with posturing condemnations and – in a you-couldn't-make-it-up scenario – a high-ranking Ku Klux Klan member was interviewed on film explaining his moral objection.*

However, the piece deserves reproduction for more than being of historical interest for having started a furore. In a fine, leisurely pen portrait, Cleave captures superbly both how unprecedented was The Beatles' unassailable popularity and how Lennon, at the tender age of twenty-five, had been made staggeringly world-weary by Beatlemania.

How Does a Beatle Live?
John Lennon Lives Like This

From *London Evening Standard*, 4 March 1966
by Maureen Cleave

It was this time three years ago that The Beatles first grew famous. Ever since then, observers have anxiously tried to gauge whether their fame was on the wax or on the wane; they foretold the fall of the old Beatles, they searched diligently for the new Beatles (which was as pointless as looking for the new Big Ben).

At last they have given up; The Beatles' fame is beyond question. It has nothing to do with whether they are rude or polite, married or unmarried, 25 or 45; whether they appear on *Top of the Pops* or do not appear on *Top of the Pops*. They are well above any position even a Rolling Stone might jostle for. They are famous in the way the Queen is famous. When John Lennon's Rolls-Royce, with its black wheels and its black windows, goes past, people say: "It's the Queen," or "It's The Beatles." With her they share the security of a stable life at the top. They all tick over in the public esteem – she in Buckingham Palace, they in the Weybridge-Esher area. Only Paul remains in London.

The Weybridge community consists of the three married Beatles; they live there among the wooded hills and the stockbrokers. They have not worked since Christmas and their existence is secluded and curiously timeless. "What day is it?" John Lennon asks with interest when you ring up with news from outside. The fans are still at the gates but The Beatles see only each other. They are better friends than ever before.

Ringo and his wife, Maureen, may drop in on John and Cyn; John may drop in on Ringo; George and Pattie may drop in on John and Cyn and they might all go round to Ringo's, by car of course. Outdoors is for holidays.

They watch films, they play rowdy games of Buccaneer; they watch television till it goes off, often playing records at the same time. They while away the small hours of the morning making mad tapes. Bedtimes and mealtimes have no meaning as such. "We've never had time before to do anything but just be Beatles," John Lennon said.

He is much the same as he was before. He still peers down his nose, arrogant as an eagle, although contact lenses have righted the short sight that originally caused the expression. He looks more like Henry VIII than ever now that his face has filled out – he is just as imperious, just as unpredictable, indolent, dis-organized, childish, vague, charming and quick-witted. He is still easy-going, still tough as hell. "You never asked after Fred Lennon," he said, disappointed. (Fred is his father; he emerged after they got famous.) "He was here a few weeks ago. It was only the second time in my life I'd seen him – I showed him the door." He went on cheerfully: "I wasn't having *him* in the house."

His enthusiasm is undiminished and he insists on its being shared. George has put him on to this Indian music. "You're not listening, are you?" he shouts after twenty minutes of the record. "It's amazing this – so cool. Don't the Indians appear cool to you? Are you listening? This music is thousands of years old; it makes me laugh, the British going over there and telling them what to do. Quite amazing." And he switched on the television set.

Experience has sown few seeds of doubt in him: not that his mind is closed, but it's closed round whatever he believes at the time. "Christianity will go," he said. "It will vanish and shrink. I needn't argue about that; I'm right and I will be proved right. We're more popular than Jesus now; I don't know which will go first – rock 'n' roll or Christianity. Jesus was all right but his disciples were thick and ordinary. It's them twisting it that ruins it for me." He is reading extensively about religion.

He shops in lightning swoops on Asprey's these days and there is some fine wine in his cellar, but he is still quite unself-conscious. He is far too lazy to keep up appearances, even if he had worked out what the appearances should be – which he has not.

He is now 25. He lives in a large, heavily panelled, heavily carpeted, mock Tudor house set on a hill with his wife Cynthia and his son Julian. There is a cat called after his aunt Mimi, and a purple dining room. Julian is three; he may be sent to the Lycee in London. "Seems the only place for him in his position," said his father, surveying him dispassionately. "I feel sorry for him, though. I couldn't stand ugly people even when I was five. Lots of the ugly ones are foreign, aren't they?"

We did a speedy tour of the house, Julian panting along behind, clutching a large porcelain Siamese cat. John swept past the objects in which he had lost interest: "That's Sidney" (a suit of armour); "That's a hobby I had for a week" (a room full of model racing cars); "Cyn won't let me get rid of that" (a fruit machine). In the sitting room are eight little green boxes with winking red lights; he bought them as Christmas presents but never got round to giving them away. They wink for a year; one imagines him sitting there till next Christmas, surrounded by the little winking boxes.

He paused over objects he still fancies; a huge altar crucifix of a Roman Catholic nature with IHS on it; a pair of crutches, a present from George; an enormous Bible he bought in Chester; his gorilla suit.

"I thought I might need a gorilla suit," he said; he seemed sad about it. "I've only worn it twice. I thought I might pop it on in the summer and drive round in the Ferrari. We were all going to get them and drive round in them but I was the only one who did. I've been thinking about it and if I didn't wear the head it would make an amazing fur coat – with legs, you see. I would like a fur coat but I've never run into any."

One feels that his possessions – to which he adds daily – have got the upper hand; all the tape recorders, the five television sets, the cars, the telephones of which he knows not a single number. The moment he approaches a switch it fuses; six of the winking boxes, guaranteed to last till next Christmas, have gone funny already. His cars – the Rolls, the Mini-Cooper (black wheels, black windows), the Ferrari (being painted black) – puzzle him. Then there's the swimming pool, the trees sloping away beneath it. "Nothing like what I ordered," he said resignedly. He wanted the bottom to be a mirror. "It's an amazing household," he said. "None of my gadgets really work except the gorilla suit – that's the only suit that fits me."

He is very keen on books, will always ask what is good to read. He buys quantities of books and these are kept tidily in a special room. He has Swift, Tennyson, Huxley, Orwell, costly leather-bound editions of Tolstoy, Oscar Wilde. Then there's *Little Women*, all the William books from his childhood; and some unexpected volumes such as *41 Years In India*, by Field Marshal Lord Roberts, and *Curiosities of Natural History*, by Francis T. Buckland. This last – with its chapter headings "Earless Cats", "Wooden-Legged People", "The Immortal Harvey's Mother" – is right up his street.

He approaches reading with a lively interest untempered by too much formal education. "I've read millions of books," he said, "that's why I seem to know things." He is obsessed by Celts. "I have decided I am a Celt," he said. "I am on Boadicea's side – all those bloody blue-eyed blondes chopping people up. I have an awful feeling wishing I was there – not there with scabs and sores but there through *reading* about it. The books don't give you more than a paragraph about how they *lived*; I have to imagine that."

He can sleep almost indefinitely, is probably the laziest person in England. "*Physically* lazy," he said. "I don't mind writing or reading or watching or speaking, but sex is the only physical thing I can be bothered with any more." Occasionally he is driven to London in the Rolls by an ex-Welsh guardsman called Anthony; Anthony has a moustache that intrigues him.

The day I visited him he had been invited to lunch in London, about which he was rather excited. "Do you know how long lunch lasts?" he asked. "I've never been to lunch before. I went to a Lyons the other day and had egg and chips and a cup of tea. The waiters kept looking and saying: 'No, it *isn't* him, it *can't* be him'."

He settled himself into the car and demonstrated the television, the folding bed, the refrigerator, the writing desk, the telephone. He has spent many fruitless hours on that telephone. "I only once got through to a person," he said, "and they were out."

Anthony had spent the weekend in Wales. John asked if they'd kept a welcome for him in the hillside and Anthony said they had. They discussed the possibility of an extension for the telephone. We had to call at the doctor's because John had a bit of sea urchin in his toe. "Don't want to be like Dorothy Dandridge," he said, "dying of a splinter 50 years later." He added reassuringly that he had washed the foot in question.

We bowled along in a costly fashion through the countryside. "Famous and loaded" is how he describes himself now. "They keep telling me I'm all right for money but then I think I may have spent it all by the time I'm 40 so I keep going. That's why I started selling my cars; then I changed my mind and got them all back and a new one too.

"I want the money just to *be* rich. The only other way of getting it is to be born rich. If you have money, that's power without having to be powerful. I often think that it's all a big conspiracy, that the winners are the Government and people like us who've got the money. That joke about keeping the workers ignorant is still true; that's what they said about the Tories and the landowners and that; then Labour were meant to educate the workers but they don't seem to be doing that any more."

He has a morbid horror of stupid people: "Famous and loaded as I am, I still have to meet soft people. It often comes into my mind that I'm not really rich. There are *really* rich people but I don't know where they are."

He finds being famous quite easy, confirming one's suspicion that The Beatles had been leading up to this all their lives. "Everybody thinks they *would* have been famous if only they'd had the Latin and that. So when it happens it comes naturally. You remember your old grannie saying soft things like: 'You'll make it with that voice'." Not, he added, that he had any old grannies.

He got to the doctor two and-three-quarter hours early and to lunch on time but in the wrong place. He bought a giant compendium of games from Asprey's but having opened it he could not, of course, shut it again. He wondered what else he should buy. He went to Brian Epstein's office. "Any presents?" he asked eagerly; he observed that there was nothing like getting things free. He tried on the attractive Miss Hanson's spectacles.

The rumour came through that a Beatle had been sighted

walking down Oxford Street! He brightened. "One of the others must be out," he said, as though speaking of an escaped bear. "We only let them out one at a time," said the attractive Miss Hanson firmly.

He said that to live and have a laugh were the things to do; but was that enough for the restless spirit?

"Weybridge," he said, "won't do at all. I'm just stopping at it, like a bus stop. Bankers and stockbrokers live there; they can add figures and Weybridge is what they live in and they think it's the end, they really do. I think of it every day – me in my Hansel and Gretel house. I'll take my time; I'll get my *real* house when I know what I want.

"You see, there's something else I'm going to do, something I must do – only I don't know what it is. That's why I go round painting and taping and drawing and writing and that, because it may be one of them. All I know is, this isn't *it* for me."

Anthony got him and the compendium into the car and drove him home with the television flickering in the soothing darkness while the Londoners outside rushed home from work.

"Paperback Writer" b/w "Rain"

Released: 10/06/1966

by Sean Egan

". . . we're all, well, not worried exactly, but thinking and wondering which way everything's going to go for us . . . We've been lucky, so lucky. We've had some great experiences, and now it's something like a school-leaver wondering what career to choose, something new to break into."

These, amazingly, were the words of Paul McCartney in June 1966, speaking to *Disc And Music Echo*. From today's perspective, his patent fear that The Beatles were coming near to the end of their amazing run of success seems absurd. It must have seemed absurd to him and his colleagues in their heart of hearts as well, for though The Beatles were at that point just finishing their next album, that year had seen a significant slowing down in Beatles activity. That their stature at the end of 1965 in terms of artistry, popularity and socio-political import was greater than ever is what gave them the wherewithal – following the bonanza of the same-day release of *Rubber Soul* and "We Can Work It Out"/"Day Tripper" – not to release any further product for exactly six months and one week.

Today, that gap would be completely unremarkable but then was unprecedented for a top-ranking act. The Beatles had released two albums per year in addition to a minimum of three singles (whose contents were often not found on albums) in their three full recording years from 1963–65. This was normal. The only reason a pop artist would at that time not release a single in gaps of less than three or four months is because they were physically indisposed or because they were without a contract, the latter meaning that they were on the way down. Of course, it was normal because record companies thought that all pop acts were a flash in the pan and that their success should be exploited to the max before their popularity waned. It should also be noted that pop acts tended to share this opinion, and that The Beatles were no exception. Early interviews with the band reveal them to be fully cognizant of the fact that the vast majority of chart acts were quickly here and gone. Asked about this in one filmed interview, Paul was virtually predicting that in a few short years he and John would be Tin Pan Alley songsmiths.

But times were changing. Or rather, The Beatles were changing the times. There seems to have been a "never again" feeling amongst The Beatles after the recording of *Rubber Soul*. Notwithstanding that they had risen magnificently to the challenge of creating product for the Christmas market with that album, they were now determined that they would approach their work not as product but art. Art takes time. The Beatles had realized that being, to use Tony Barrow's phrase, "the biggest attraction the world has ever known" meant that they had power. This included the power to insist EMI vary the terms of their contract and allow them to dictate their release schedule. The corollary of this new arrangement was that both EMI and The Beatles were assuming that The Beatles' fans would not desert them in their absence, always the fear of the chart act before now. Though the band were "wondering which way everything's going to go for us", they were also clearly beginning to feel a certain amount of security.

It's doubtful that the public were under any impression that the hiatus spelt the end of The Beatles. The Fab Four were still omnipresent in the culture, both sides of the Atlantic. In February, they had another American smash hit single in the shape of "Nowhere Man", a track left off the US configuration of *Rubber Soul*. March saw the UK television broadcast of *The Beatles At Shea Stadium* documentary. March also saw the publication of the soon-to-be-famous Maureen Cleave Lennon interview in the London *Evening Standard*. The band played at the annual *NME* Poll Winners' Party on 1 May.

Even so, the gap in new records ensured something of a sense of a rebirth when their new single was released (on 30 May in America, eleven days afterwards in the home country). The title of the record was peculiar. "Paperback Writer" certainly didn't sound like it was going to be a love song. And indeed it wasn't – the first time a UK Beatle single had not addressed the subject of romance. (Technically, the US had the privilege of the first non-romantic Beatle 45 in the shape of "Nowhere Man".) The opening of the record was as arty as the title: a pretty succession of overlapping Beatle voices enunciating the title phrase as well as providing harmonies in such a way as to resemble the leaves of a fan being slowly opened. A guitar riff followed, a gritty one like that of "Day Tripper" but this one had a resounding thickness to it. There were also some extraordinary and prominent burbles of bass guitar. And the rhythm behind it was bolder than anything heard on a Beatle record before, almost brutal. Then the lyric started. Its first line was "Dear Sir or madam, will you read my book?" The record proceeded to be like what that line seemed to herald: a song in the form of a letter from an aspiring author to a publisher. Of course it wasn't completely wacky: the lyric was sung rather than spoken-word, and the lines rhymed. Further artistic licence was employed in the way that the song sort of double-backed on itself, as the aspiring writer revealed that the son of his protagonist is a man who, like him, wants to be a paperback writer. The music also followed a vaguely circular pattern (an impression helped by the fact that there is no bridge), with everything coming to a halt at regular intervals to make way for a repeat of that opening *a cappella* fan effect.

McCartney's memory of the song's creation only goes as far back as the drive to John's Weybridge house one morning for one of their regular songwriting sessions. Conscious of the fact that it would usually be straight to work, he was thinking of the letter format on arrival. He and Lennon sat down to compose, the lyric being written first – Paul doing the bulk of the writing with John's contributions constituting not much more than approving comments by the sound of it – before the two went upstairs to add the melody. However, then-Radio Luxembourg DJ Jimmy Savile recalled McCartney alighting on the idea prior to this, backstage at a TV show. Paul, he claimed, told him that one of his aunts had asked if he would ever write a single that wasn't about love. Paul noticed that Ringo was reading, and declared he would write a song about a book. Meanwhile poet Royston Ellis (the man who may have given The Beatles the spelling of their name) thinks that McCartney got the title phrase from him. Ellis had performed on stage with the band in 1960 and claims he would use the phrase to denote the extent of his authorial ambition (paperbacks selling in far greater quantities than hardbacks).

"Paperback Writer" was more a revolution for The Beatles than for pop. In fact, it was a catch-up exercise to some extent. Popular music had come on in leaps and bounds since The Beatles had created an explosion in the medium by virtue of their success and their small but telling innovations. The Stones, The Who, The Kinks, The Byrds and Dylan (the latter now unequivocally a rock artist) had already proven that writing about love was not a prerequisite for chart success. They had also proven that music that was far from conventionally pretty could be attractive to record purchasers (although of course that was merely a reiteration of the point that had been made by the very success of rock 'n' roll itself from 1955 onwards and which was lost to some extent in the "neutered" period of rock after its first flush of success when pompadoured balladeers proliferated). The only thing really novel about "Paperback Writer" was the letter form.

Some observers made much of the fact that "Paperback Writer" was the first Beatles single since "She Loves You" not to enter the charts at number one. However, the argument could be made that when it then proceeded to scale the summit, it meant correspondingly more because, unlike when a record entered in pole position, the public had actually now heard it. The success of the record confirmed the Fab Four's fans were prepared to grow up with them. This had never been so much of an issue with The Rolling Stones, who had a UK number one with a twelve-bar blues in 1964 and whose "(I Can't Get No) Satisfaction" was adult in both its monstrous riff, it's belligerent lyric and its innuendo-laden title. Nor of course with Bob Dylan, who had added the rock market to the folk market he already sat at the pinnacle of (the people who booed his electric backing band at his latest gigs being a vocal minority). But The Beatles had had an image virtually on the level of dolls for much of their career thus far and, though those dolls had incrementally been gaining a degree of sophistication, this record was the first one on which The Beatles weren't particularly lovable. Clever, maybe, or arty, and certainly not dislikable, but clearly not "the nutty, noisy, happy, handsome Beatles" the *Daily Mirror* had enthused over in 1963.

Some, though, were dismayed that popcraft was less in evidence here than what they felt to be artifice. Noted music critic and musician George Melly later remarked that he felt the song was "a poor thing, a falling off". It would have been interesting to see what the reaction would have been had the record's flip, "Rain", been released as the A-side. Predominantly John's, "Rain" was a stunning recording, the best thing The Beatles had released thus far (which is saying something). Though its lyric could be treated literally as a song about the folly of shallow people who didn't view rainy weather as being as good as sunshine, its scornful tone was perfectly in tune with an era where squares and their verities were increasingly and loudly being questioned and it's possible that – even if only subconsciously – the imagery is a metaphor. The track is distinctly un-Beatley in its disinterest in being ingratiating. Musically, "Rain" is phantasmagoric, a huge and brutal yet dazzling and beautiful soundscape. It is also the recording on which every Beatle – for the first time – operates as an equal. Lennon & McCartney's songcraft, John's sneering vocal and guitar arpeggios and Paul's bubbling basslines are thrilling, but no less so than George's serpentine, relentless guitar lick and definitely no less so than Ringo's drum performance, one of the greatest in the history of rock, then or now. Ringo simply never lets up, careening across his kit in a display of breathtaking virtuosity that any of his contemporaries more renowned for such proclivities – Moon, Baker, Mitchell – would have been proud to put their name to.

Even more than the A-side, "Rain" displayed the layered nature of The Beatles' new recording methods. Unable to get what they felt to be the right feel for the track, the band recorded it at a faster clip and then slowed the tape down for the desired effect. It's hard to imagine them doing that had they been obliged to clock-watch. Meanwhile, the last verse at first sounds like formless chanting but transpired to be what Lennon claimed for The Beatles as the first ever use of backward tape on a pop record.

WHY THE TOURING HAD TO END

Beatlemania was often draining for The Beatles. Lennon once made the observation that everybody they encountered wanted their attention, right down to hotel lift attendants. But sometimes the world's love for The Beatles could spill over into spite, whether it be an American politician getting The Beatles woken from their beds in order to meet his daughter on threat of telling the press about their supposed rudeness or more sinister episodes, the most extreme example of which – up to this point – is recounted in this news report. If anything, the Mirror's *story played down the seriousness of what happened at Manila airport in the summer of 1966. John Lennon – no shrinking violet – said the pushing, jostling, jeering and threats* the group encountered from a gauntlet of people indoctrinated by Philippines television into believing The Beatles had snubbed the country's dictators the Marcos, was "incredibly frightening". The requirement to declare their earnings the report mentions actually involved the confiscation of all monies they had made on the trip. Five weeks later, The Beatles would be touring America under the threat of death from fanatics outraged by Lennon's claim that The Beatles were bigger than Christ. The tour had started with death threats too, when The Beatles had dared to play the holy venue of the Budokan. Then there was the fact that a few days before the events in the Philippines, The Beatles had had to watch helplessly as fans were brutalized by the police at their German concerts. What with the lack of fulfilment involved in playing concerts where they couldn't even hear themselves above the screaming and the fact that they were financially secure, the Fab Four soon decided that they no longer needed the hassle of playing live. Their last performance before a paying public was at Candlestick Park, San Francisco, on 29 August 1966.

Beatles, Go Home!

That was the chant as an airport crowd jostled
and jeered the boys in "snub" row

From *Daily Mirror*, Wednesday 6 July 1966
(No byline)

Never before has anything remotely like this happened to The Beatles.

Up to yesterday they could be called the most feted young men in the world, acclaimed with frenzied enthusiasm wherever they went. Yesterday, there was frenzy . . . but of anger and hate. The Beatles were jostled, booed and jeered in a hectic airport scene at Manila, capital of the Philippines, as they left for their homeward trip by way of New Delhi.

Fists were shaken at them. Screwed-up pieces of paper were thrown at them. And there were shouts of "Beatles, Go Home!" . . . "Go to Hell!" . . . "Get out of our country!". . . and "We don't want you here!"

About 200 angry Filipinos – young and old – staged this unprecedented demonstration against The Beatles. They were smarting under an alleged snub to Senora Imelda Marcos, wife of their president. Many Filipinos, including the press, were upset when John, Ringo, Paul and George failed to appear as invited to meet Senora Marcos at the palace on Monday.

The Beatles said that they knew nothing about the invitation. And last night the president and his wife issued a statement regretting the airport incidents. They added, "There was no intention on the part of The Beatles to slight the first lady or the Government." But, earlier, the crowd at the airport had thought otherwise. After The Beatles' arrival at the airport, an angry crowd grew round them. Within minutes people were pushing them.

One of the party, Alf Bicknell, fell after being kicked in the leg. A radio reporter who got near The Beatles said that a Filipino swung a wild right at Ringo Starr – but missed. By contrast with their arrival, the departure of The Beatles was officially brusque and without any VIP treatment. The group had to carry their baggage up to the second floor themselves. The power for the airport escalator had been turned off. Almost all police protection and special arrangements were cancelled – and the tax office announced that The Beatles could not leave the Philippines until they had made a declaration of their earnings.

The Beatles themselves were bewildered. As they walked to their airliner, Paul McCartney exclaimed disconsolately, "Man, I don't understand." Consolation awaited The Beatles in a tumultuous and joyful welcome at New Delhi airport last night. Again, they were pushed, shoved and pelted – but with garlands.

"They treated us like animals where we just came from," Ringo Starr told 600 Indian fans. "We never meant to upset anybody by not attending the party. It was all fixed up for us to go – but the only thing was that nobody told us."

"Eleanor Rigby"/"Yellow Submarine"

Released: 5/08/1966

by Sean Egan

As with *Rubber Soul*, The Beatles released a double-A-sided single on the same day as their new album, although unlike that release, the tracks on the single were also on the LP. The impetus for this decision was Epstein, who was conscious of the fact that any Beatles song was pounced upon for an easy hit by cover merchants so it would be better for the band to have the hit versions themselves.

"Eleanor Rigby"/"Yellow Submarine" confirmed the impression given by "Paperback Writer" of a band who had left their lovable moptop image far behind, even if their heads still bore that world-sweeping coiffure in a more stylish, longer variant. Though the world had been familiarized with the idea of a Beatles track featuring nothing but Paul's vocal and classical strings with "Yesterday", "Eleanor Rigby" took that approach to a completely new level. The lyric, meanwhile, took commercial popular music places it had never been before. "Eleanor Rigby" was sheer bleakness, concerned with loneliness and, ultimately, death. The dispassionate recounting of the lonely lives of spinster Eleanor Rigby and solitary priest Father McKenzie – whose tales intertwine when the priest reads the service at Rigby's funeral to which "nobody came" – is unredeemed even by the sing-song qualities of The Kinks also grim life-on-the-dole hit of a couple of months before "Dead End Street".

Paul's recollection was that the title character's name was inspired by actress Eleanor Bron (who had appeared in the *Help!* movie) and a shop he passed in Bristol when visiting Jane Asher called Rigby & Evans. Though finished at John's house in Weybridge after McCartney had written the first verse, the number came not from the usual formal sit-down composition sessions with Lennon but more through a party atmosphere. So much so that various people could stake a claim in having helped develop it, with Ringo suggesting that Father McKenzie be depicted darning his socks, George suggesting the refrain about all the lonely people and ex-Quarryman Pete Shotton coming up with the idea of dove-tailing the characters via Rigby's funeral (much to Paul's initial disdain). Lennon's later claim to have written a goodly portion of the lyric seems to have been discounted by everybody present and must be attributed to the fact that there was plenty of wacky baccy being consumed. Of course, anybody can make suggestions, but weaving those ideas into a concise narrative is another thing entirely. Paul's unfussy and undemonstrative lyric led the celebrated British novelist A.S. Byatt to declare of "Eleanor Rigby" that it had "The minimalist perfection of a Beckett story."

Lovely though "Yesterday" was, there was something received about its arrangement, the feeling of an archetype. Although Martin's role as Fifth Beatle has been overplayed by some, his input here was crucial. The double string quartet arrangement he devised to back the song is absolutely appropriate in tone: sweeping, rapid-fire but utterly glacial. (Martin revealed that he devised his arrangement following a session at his home where Paul demonstrated what he wanted on piano.)

It's not true to suggest, as some have, that McCartney gives no impression of caring about these people's plights – what else is that wistful phrase wondering where all the lonely people come from if not compassion? – but at the same time there is an undeniable feeling of distance. The fact that the track ends cleanly with a brisk string flourish rather than fading out to contrive a sense of poignancy only intensifies the unsentimental, no-nonsense air, and this despite the fact that unlike on "Yester-day", John and George add decorative harmonies.

The fact that this record sees, unusually, one of the Lennon/McCartney duo predominately writing both sides of a single is disguised to an extent by the fact that Ringo takes the vocal on "Yellow Submarine". It's a silly-but-proud-of-it ditty about the titular seacraft that Paul mostly composed in bed one evening but which Dylan manqué-turned-flower child Donovan helped him polish off. The simple singalong chorus is perfect for a children's song. Also splendid are the sound effects and silly voices, the most prominent component of both of which is Lennon, no doubt exulting in the opportunity to inject some Goons-like humour into a recording. The only thing that prevents "Yellow Submarine" from being great is the lack of a bridge, which could have really lifted it into something special.

A couple of lyrical points: British demonstrators in recent years have taken to taunting police officers by singing, to the chorus of "Yellow Submarine", "We all live in a fascist regime . . ." Though Paul remembers distinctly where he got the idea for the name "Eleanor Rigby", St Peter's Church in Liverpool contains a gravestone in its grounds of an Eleanor Rigby who died aged 44 in 1939. Spookily, this is the church where Lennon and McCartney first met.

Naturally the record was a UK number one, although like "Paperback Writer", it did not enter the charts in that pole position. In America, the top spot wasn't such a big deal for the band, the proliferation of singles released from those Frankenstein monster American Beatles albums having so saturated the market that the sense of anticipation of a new Beatles release wasn't so great (or even the concept of a new release so well-defined.) Nonetheless, it's interesting that though hits Stateside, neither of the two sides (which, as was the custom in America, charted separately) made the top spot. However, mere sales figures can't measure the importance of the record. "Eleanor Rigby" quickly became one of the pop songs that even "only-like-classical-myself" types professed admiration for, just as The Beatles themselves had frequently been the one exception some made to their dislike of modern pop *per se*. Meanwhile, the existing pop fans were being educated, being taken places that they had never imagined they would want to go. Some had been sceptical about The Beatles' new-found artiness and lack of romanticism on "Paperback Writer", but ultimately, few could resist the chilly charms of "Eleanor Rigby".

Revolver

Released: 5/08/1966

by Sean Egan

TRACKLISTING

Side one
1. "Taxman"
2. "Eleanor Rigby"
3. "I'm Only Sleeping"
4. "Love You To"
5. "Here, There And Everywhere"
6. "Yellow Submarine"
7. "She Said She Said"

Side two
1. "Good Day Sunshine"
2. "And Your Bird Can Sing"
3. "For No One"
4. "Doctor Robert"
5. "I Want to Tell You"
6. "Got to Get You into My Life"
7. "Tomorrow Never Knows"

The Beatles' album *Revolver* was released in the UK on 5 August 1966. The *Help!* album had come out on 6 August 1965. *Rubber Soul*'s release had been sandwiched between the two. To release three acknowledged classic and epoch-marking albums in the space of one year comes close to showing off. Even Bob Dylan had taken fourteen months to complete his trio of consecutive masterpieces *Bringing It All Back Home, Highway 61 Revisited* and *Blonde On Blonde* (March 1965 to May 1966). There again, *Blonde On Blonde* was a double album. Perhaps it's best just to call it a draw on the issue of whether it was Dylan or The Beatles who most effectively combined productivity and artistry.

Revolver was the first Beatles album made as an album. Some have mistakenly given that significance to *Rubber Soul* but it was in 1966 that The Beatles' status as pop's aristocrats was confirmed by EMI tearing up the timesheet and allowing them unlimited time in the studio, free of charge. "We insisted on having the time to do what we wanted to do," Ringo told *Melody Maker* about the recording. "As we're quite big with EMI at the moment, they don't argue." This didn't just mean an unprecedentedly long two-and-a-half months recording period for their new album: recording was preceded by three months wherein The Beatles basked in an absolute, prolonged idleness they hadn't known since they were teenagers.

It was the very least the record company could do for an act that had ensured money had poured into their coffers over the last three years in quantities beyond their wildest dreams. It left the Fab Four to pursue their wildest dreams, musically. There was to be no "work" songs on their next album, no material rescued from the reject pile, no songs written in haste on the eve of the last day of recording. An indication of just where The Beatles' heads were as they prepared to embark on this record is provided by the fact that the first thing they recorded was something that pop had never heard the like of before: "Tomorrow Never Knows".

The band returned to a mostly electric sound here, with acoustic guitars less in evidence than at any time since *With The Beatles*. Not that this music sounded anything like the material on that album. The age of the studio-as-instrument was dawning and The Beatles were in the vanguard of it, using multiple overdubs, backward tapes and all manner of special effects to enhance and shade. There was also an explosion of the deployment of outside musicians: classical strings, Indian instruments, French horn, a brass section . . . The Beatles were no longer merely recording songs. They were rendering sound paintings. That the band were taking their musical adventures beyond far wilder shores than on *Rubber Soul* was signposted by a cover illustration from their Hamburg friend (and now Manfred Mann bass player) Klaus Voormann. It was bizarre indeed for the time, bizarre not only because of its monochrome hues in an age of ever-increasing technicolor but for its composition: line drawings of the four Beatles' heads with stuck-in photograph collage eyes (and in George's case lips) with a riot of Beatles photos occupying their hair. The Fab Four were still so instantly recognizable even in this strange depiction that once again it was decided that it was not necessary to print their name on the front cover.

Though *Revolver* marked the point at which McCartney started to develop into one of the greatest and most innovative bass players in rock history, the most extraordinary development on the record is that evinced by George Harrison. The man with the lip-bitten style and the embarrassing saggy solos of the first two albums is here transformed into a player of the highest calibre. His musicianship on *Revolver* is mellifluous and burnished and it is this that is largely responsible for the fact that the album sounds like it's rolling on castors.

Revolver starts with a triumvirate of songs that reveal the incredible breadth of writing talent now existing within The Beatles and, in its array of different styles, the band's astonishing span of musical ability. "Taxman" sees Harrison given the considerable accolade of leading off a Beatles LP. A burning hard rock cut (whose staccato riff owes a little to the riff of *Rubber Soul*'s "The Word"), it sees The Beatles dispense once and for all with the vestiges of their supinely cute image. First by dealing with subject matter in which teenagers were presumed simply not to be interested (the burden of taxation) and secondly, by biting the hand that fed them their MBEs, mocking Labour Prime Minister Harold Wilson (as well as Conservative opposition leader Ted Heath – The Beatles were never particularly party political). McCartney provides a searing guitar solo. Following that comes the complete contrast of the sweeping classicism of Paul's "Eleanor Rigby", which is succeeded by John's "I'm Only Sleeping", a wistful paean to the joys of turning the pillow over to the cool side boasting an utterly heart-melting melody.

No album could possibly maintain the quality of *Revolver*'s first few tracks, so we can't blame the Fabs for the way the record drops off after this point. We can, however, take issue with them over the glacial nature of the rest of the album – though few ever have. The passionless tone of "Eleanor Rigby" accurately reflects what is on its parent album, and, notwithstanding ". . . Rigby's" qualities, it was not an agreeable development. There had been two imprimaturs to The Beatles' sound throughout all their stylistic changes: harmonies and warmth. Often, those two things were intertwined, those communal, effusive three-part chants, yells and coos the perfect vocal accompaniment to the group's big-hearted songs. *Revolver* proves that the two can be separated. The harmonies are still present and correct, but the musical tone, and hence to a certain extent, the spiritual tone is cold. The music is airbrushed, gleaming and stunningly adroit, but none of that can disguise the chill in the air.

Take "Here, There and Everywhere", an appealing love song from Paul with spot-on backing harmonies built on the reasonable enough conceit of each verse using the different places in time and space specified in the title. It should come over as lovely. Instead, it feels sterile. "Got To Get You Into My Life", meanwhile, truly is the rubber soul to which their previous album title referred. A Stax pastiche from Paul, it manages the extraordinary trick of making soul, a form of music whose *raison d'être* is its passion, sound clinical. Its horn charts are sweeping, its pace frenetic, but it all feels mechanical. Like *Revolver* as a whole, it is something to admire, not to love.

George gets two more tracks, both of which indicate his increasing interest in Eastern philosophy. "Love You To" – which, barring Ringo on tambourine, none of the other Beatles appear on, the North London Asian Music Circle being responsible for the instrumentation – is impressive, pulsating raga rock. His "I Want To Tell You" is a more conventional rock piece. Both are charmlessly less profound than they are intended to be: Harrison's lyrics are inchoate but he seems to be demanding the Western world abandon its Godless, humility-lacking ways in judgmental terms that are lacking in humility themselves.

As a philosopher, Harrison may have had shortcomings but "She Said She Said" and "And Your Bird Can Sing" are the pair of tracks on which he truly proves his mettle as a guitarist. The former is a tale of an unsettling experience Lennon had while tripping. Harrison's fretwork is huge and blaring but completely melodic. "And Your Bird Can Sing" is one of a trio of tracks that open side two that comes fairly close to matching the brilliance of the first side's opening triumvirate. Its plucked riff is extraordinarily long and winding and accompanies a John lyric that is a close cousin to "Nowhere Man" in its put-down of a straight, though this one is more affectionate.

"And Your Bird Can Sing" is sandwiched between two beauties from Paul, one happy, one sad. In its rejoicing over good weather and good loving, "Good Day Sunshine" is quintessential Beatles. How could anybody not be touched by a tuneful romp that marvels "I'm in love and it's a sunny day!" George Martin contributes rumbling piano. "For No One" is as delicate and beautiful as fine porcelain, with Paul detailing the disintegration of a relationship by listing the minutiae of a couple's daily life and the pair's increasingly contrasting interests. Alan Civil adds the cherry on the cake in the form of a French horn solo.

John's "Doctor Robert" is a thinly-disguised ode to a drug dealer. At heart it's an uninteresting subject and an unremarkable melody but – as with "I Want To Tell You" – the band keep things at least listenable via the toning, shading and incremental build-up of components that was now second nature to them after several years' studio experience. Unremarkable is the very last thing that can be said about the closing track, "Tomorrow Never Knows", an epic, surreal musical collage featuring a droning, one-note melody, tapes tweaked to sound like seagull cries, mellotron, backward guitar and a vocal from John manipulated so that he sounds like the wisest man on earth delivering a message from a hilltop. The surreal lyric ("Turn off your mind, relax and float downstream") is lifted almost verbatim from the passages paraphrasing the Buddhist bible *The Tibetan Book Of The Dead* in the LSD primer *The Psychedelic Experience* by Timothy Leary. To those in the know, the whole thing was Lennon's attempt to covey in sound an "acid trip", druggie parlance for the results of ingesting lysergic acid diethylamide, thus instantly racheting up the band's hip factor. Whether "Tomorrow Never Knows" is an enjoyable recording is another

matter. Though undeniably atmospheric, it feels like if would
have served a much better function by being edited and used
as a middle section in a different song. Only Ringo saves
"Tomorrow Never Knows" from being an unbearable drone by
his hypnotic circular patterns. At the time, though, listenability
would have mattered less than it does today. "Tomorrow Never
Knows" and *Revolver* in general proved that The Beatles were
still Now.

'Sixty-six saw the three other acts who it was clear were the
only real contenders for The Beatles' pop crown – Dylan, The
Stones and The Beach Boys – also release albums that were
posited as masterpieces (thus far): *Blonde On Blonde*, *Aftermath*
and *Pet Sounds*. While *Revolver* is better than all those, it is
nowhere near as good as history has judged it to be. It has
retrospectively come to be seen as The Beatles' peak. It still
tops polls amongst critics to determine history's greatest album.
To this critic, though, large parts of it will always sound like
The Beatles as approximated by a computer.

COURTED BY THE INTELLECTUALS

*More than three years after The Beatles had begun conquering the
world, precious little serious journalism had been written about them.
While The Beatles did their best to give serious answers to intelligent
questions, they were seldom asked them by either news journalists
or pop paper staffers. In fact, early on, they were more apt to be
treated seriously in different mediums: the British TV documentary*
The Mersey Sound *(1963) and Michael Braun's book of life on
the road with the band,* Love Me Do *(1964) were respectful exam-
inations of their success. However, even those were wanting when it
came to analysis of their art. In fact, "analysis of their art" is a
phrase that would literally have been laughed at at the time: even
fans of pop and rock would not think of treating it so solemnly.*

Hunter Davies, a youngish columnist for the Sunday Times'

anonymous Atticus column was slightly frustrated by this. A Beatles fan, both because he came from the same type of Northern, working-class background as they and because he liked the music, he decided to write about them after being highly impressed by "Eleanor Rigby" and arranged an appointment to interview Paul at his London house. "It was pure self-indulgence," he later wrote. "I wanted to meet him, but I also wanted to hear the background to 'Eleanor Rigby' . . . I had never read any interview in which they had been asked seriously about how they composed."

The resulting 900-word article not only broke new ground in its insight into the group's working methods, it also led to bigger things for Davies, making the group amenable to him writing the first full-length and to this date only authorized biography (as opposed to autobiography) of the band, The Beatles, *published in 1968.*

Atticus: All Paul

From the *Sunday Times*, 18 September 1966
(No byline) but written by Hunter Davies

Paul McCartney was in his new mansion in St John's Wood. He lives alone. A Mr and Mrs Kelly look after him. Nothing so formal as housekeeper and butler. Their job, he says, is just to fit in.

The house has a huge wall and an electrically-operated black door to keep out non-Beatle life. Inside there is some carefully chosen elderly furniture. Nothing flash, affected or even expensive-looking. The dining room table was covered with a white lace tablecloth. Very working-class posh.

Mr McCartney, along with Mr Lennon, is the author of a song called "Eleanor Rigby". No pop song of the moment has better words or music.

"I was sitting at the piano when I thought of it. Just like

Jimmy Durante. The first few bars came to me. And I got this name in my head – Daisy Hawkins, picks up the rice in the church where a wedding has been. I don't know why.

"I can hear a whole song in one chord. In fact, I think you can hear a whole song in one note, if you listen hard enough. But nobody ever listens hard enough.

"Okay, so that's the Joan of Arc bit. I couldn't think of much more, so I put it away for a day. Then the name Father McCartney came to me – and all the lonely people. But I thought people would think it was supposed to be my Dad, sitting knitting his socks. Dad's a happy lad. So I went through the telephone book and I got the name McKenzie.

"I was in Bristol when I decided Daisy Hawkins wasn't a good name. I walked round looking at the shops and I saw the name Rigby. You got that? Quick pan to Bristol. I can just see this all as a Hollywood musical.

"Then I took it down to John's house in Weybridge. We sat around laughing, got stoned and finished it off. I thought of the backing but it was George Martin who finished it off. I just go bash, bash on the piano. He knows what I mean.

"All our songs come out of our imagination. There never was an Eleanor Rigby.

"One of us might think of a song completely, and the other just add a bit. Or we might write alternate lines. We never argue. If one of us says he doesn't like a bit, the other agrees. It just doesn't matter that much. I care about being a song writer. But I don't care passionately about each song.

"'Eleanor' is a big development as a composition. But that doesn't mean 'Yellow Submarine' is bad. It was written as a commercial song, a kid's song. People have said, 'Yellow submarine? What's the significance? What's behind it?' Nothing. Kids get it straight away. I was playing with my little stepsister the other day, looking through a book about Salvador Dali. She said, 'Oh look, a soft watch.' She accepted it. She wasn't frightened or worried. Kids have got it. It's only later they get messed up.

"I tried once to write a song under another name, just to see if it was the Lennon-McCartney bit that sold our songs. I called myself Bernard Webb – I was a student in Paris and very unavailable for interviews. The song was 'Woman' for Peter and Gordon.

They made it a big hit. Then it came out it was me. I realized that when I saw a banner at a concert, saying 'Long Live Bernard Webb'.

"We'd need a properly controlled experiment to find out how much our names really mean now, but I can't be bothered.

"I can't really play the piano, or read or write music. I've tried three times in my life to learn, but never kept it up for more than three weeks. The last bloke I went to was great. I'm sure he could teach me a lot. I might go back to him. It's just the notation – the way you write down notes, it doesn't look like music to me.

"John's now trying acting again, and George has got his passion for the sitar and all the Indian stuff. He's lucky. Like somebody's luck who's got religion. I'm just looking for something I enjoy doing. There's no hurry. I have the time and the money.

"People think we're not conceited, but we are. If you ask me if I wrote good or bad songs, I'd be thick to say bad, wouldn't I? It's true we're lucky, but we got where we are because of what we did.

"The girls waiting outside, I don't despise them. I don't think fans are humiliating themselves. I queued up at the Liverpool Empire for Wee Willie Harris' autograph. I wanted to do it. I don't think I was being stupid.

"I can go out and around more than people think, without being recognized. People never really believe it's you. They don't really expect to see you in the street, so you can get away with it.

"I think we can go on as The Beatles for as long as we want to, writing songs, making records. We're still developing. I've no ambitions, just to enjoy myself. We've had all the ego bit, all about wanting to be remembered. We couldn't do any better than we've done already, could we?"

WHATEVER HAPPENED TO
THE BEATLES?

In November 1966, with The Beatles having engaged in no collective activity since the Candlestick Park concert in August – gigs, media appearances or record releases – and with Epstein having announced there would be no new Beatles product this year, the general public were noticing a Beatle-sized hole in their lives. In a country with only two TV channels and one legal pop radio station, the absence of a quartet of faces and voices that had been a permanent part of the landscape for the last four years was conspicuous. Unthinkable in these low-productivity times but inevitable in a day and age where the assumption was that if pop stars did not work flat-out the public would forget about them, rumours were beginning to circulate about The Beatles' imminent demise. John and George spoke to journalist Don Short about an unforced hiatus the like of which was virtually unprecedented in showbusiness.

At The Crossroads

From *Daily Mirror*, Friday 11 November 1966
by Don Short

There's no great mystery, says John Lennon, about the long, long silence of The Beatles.

It's just what the others are making out of it, says George Harrison.

For weeks their marked absence from show business life has led to mounting predictions of a split-up of the world's most famous foursome. And now the Beatles have realized it's all gone beyond a joke.

But the answer, seems quite simple. They are at the crossroads. And it's something Paul, John, George and Ringo have got to sort out for themselves. They don't want to do any further tours at home or abroad because the value of such tours "is not progressive." The Beatles are exploring . . . trying to find their own new horizon. BUT THEY ARE NOT GOING TO SPLIT UP.

Endlessly they experiment with new sounds and they still haven't finally settled on a screen play for their next film – twice postponed because they've been cautious about choosing the right subject. Time has slipped by. But now, as questions press about their future, The Beatles are going to brush away the cobwebs. They plan a new single and another LP before their film. Said George Harrison: "We've been resting and thinking. It gave us a chance to reassess things. After all, we've had four years doing what everybody else wanted us to do. Now we're doing what we want to do . . . But whatever we do it has got to be real and progressive. Everything we've done so far has been rubbish as I see it today. Other people may like what we've done, but we're not kidding ourselves. It doesn't mean a thing to what we want to do now." George continued: "People live too easily in a plastic world. They think they are doing something, but when they peg out – they've done nothing."

John Lennon grinned. "George is being a bit blunt. You can always look back and say what you've done before was rubbish. Especially in comparison with what you're doing today. It was all vital at the time, even if it looks daft when you see things differently later on." Did this mean they were ashamed of their earlier songs like "She Loves You"? John shook his head: "I think of that particular song as a childhood memory."

Then the Beatles talked about the rumours. John told me: "We've no intention of splitting up. We're always going to be recording." And tours? "No one has said anything definite about them," said John, "but with the film and everything else on we're not going to have much chance for some time. We've got to give all our energy to the film. We've got to be tight, otherwise find ourselves doing *Help!* all over again."

Those splitting up rumours stemmed largely, The Beatles admit themselves, from their own independent interests. GEORGE has just returned from a six-week course on the sitar in India; JOHN has been playing a Soldier in a new Dick Lester comedy picture; PAUL has been scoring the theme music for Hayley Mills' next picture; RINGO has been busy – just being Ringo.

"From our independent experiences we've each got something more to offer," said John. And George added: "The thing is that we haven't been worrying ourselves. It's all the others who've been doing the worrying for us. It's a laugh."

"If we ever did split, we wouldn't split as people. We would still be good buddy pals," said John. "It isn't the money. They told us a bit back that we needn't work again if we didn't want to. But you can't really stop – it's all the interest and that kind of thing."

Has there been a row with their manager, Brian Epstein, as a lot of people are saying? "Row with Eppy? Not us," said George. Said Mr Epstein: "There have been no rows at all. We have always seen eye to eye." But he was obviously anxious over the growing rumours about The Beatles' future. Fans besieged Mr Epstein's Belgravia home last weekend demanding another Beatles tour, but he said: "I am not at all sure that personal appearances are in their best interests, but that doesn't mean they will never appear in person again. They will." He added: "I don't think they will split up because I'm certain that they will want to do things together for a long long time."

Which left Mr Lennon to joke with resignation: "I suppose that means we have got to be four mop-tops again!"

A Collection of Beatles Oldies

Released: 10/12/1966

by Sean Egan

TRACKLISTING

Side one
1. "She Loves You"
2. "From Me To You"
3. "We Can Work It Out"
4. "Help!"
5. "Michelle"
6. "Yesterday"
7. "I Feel Fine"
8. "Yellow Submarine"

Side two
1. "Can't Buy Me Love"
2. "Bad Boy"
3. "Day Tripper"
4. "A Hard Day's Night"
5. "Ticket To Ride"
6. "Paperback Writer"
7. "Eleanor Rigby"
8. "I Want To Hold Your Hand"

Because of The Beatles' new emphasis on art over commerce, Christmas 1966 was the first time since 1962 that there was no new Beatles album to exploit the lucrative Yuletide market. Parlophone plugged the gap by issuing a greatest hits, *A Collection Of Beatles Oldies* (the words "*But goldies!*" complete the title on the back of the sleeve). The first ever album-length Beatles compilation is now of only historical interest, rendered largely irrelevant by the issue of the "Red" and "Blue" compilation albums in 1976 and then deleted when the catalogue was issued on CD in 1987, jettisoned in favour of the *Past Masters* CDs that mopped up non-album Beatles tracks. At the time, though, it was an interesting stock-take of a remarkable career.

Having gone all arty on their last two album sleeves, it would have been a bit retrograde for the band to have put a cute moptops picture on this cover. Accordingly, they chose a design that was arty in the extreme. For the first time, The Beatles didn't appear on the front of one of their albums, usurped by a colour painting by David Christian which combined Swinging Sixties iconography with 1920s-style art deco and was dominated by a cool-looking, long-haired dude listening to his sound system (which, incongruously, is an old-fashioned gramophone with a horn). The photograph of The Beatles on the back, meanwhile, was semi-chaotic, with none of the group really looking at the camera and George with his back to it.

The album was arranged non-chronologically, those two titanic fixtures of Beatlemania "She Loves You" and "I Want To Hold Your Hand" topping and tailing the collection. It also wasn't strictly speaking the collection of singles many would have been expecting. "Love Me Do" and "Please Please Me" were ignored, while "Yesterday" (never a UK Beatles single but already the subject of many cover versions) and "Michelle" (again not a Beatles UK single but made famous through a hit version by The Overlanders) do gain inclusion. It was, however, a pretty accurate summary of a career – the musical part of it, anyway – that had gone through astonishing changes in a short space of time. Perhaps in a way it was a logical thing that "I Want To Hold Your Hand" closed the album, for the fact that it was preceded in the tracklisting by "Eleanor Rigby" demonstrated how the historically unprecedented success The Beatles had engineered with crowd-pleasing material like "I Want To Hold Your Hand" had given them the lofty position that enabled them to create material like "Eleanor Rigby", which pandered to no one.

Also of cultural interest is the fact that this album demonstrates that the strategy of including a previously unavailable track on a compilation in order to entice fans who already have the rest of the cuts is not the modern phenomenon we might imagine but was going on even in 1966. The enticement was "Bad Boy", another Lennon-sung Larry Williams cover, this one dating from the *Help!* sessions, which had been included on the 1965 American album *Beatles IV* but had not previously been issued in the UK. It would have been a mitigating factor if The Beatles/EMI had included the group's first two singles on the record: this would not have taken the album far over the forty-minute mark, so sound quality would not have been noticeably impaired. Still, many will have found it useful to have the collection's seven non-album singles on LP for the first time.

"Bad Boy", by the way, is fabulous. One hesitates to say that it was worth the price of admission, but the track is in the grand tradition of "Twist And Shout", "Rock And Roll Music", "Kansas City" and other standards that The Beatles improbably improved upon. Williams' song is a fairly common 1950s celebration of a rock 'n' roll-loving, teacher-baiting delinquent designed to appeal to every teen sick of their folks telling them to turn that garbage down and do their homework. In the hands of The Beatles, it assumes a roaring, high-octane power, George and John's growling guitars and Paul and Ringo's thrumming rhythm section perfectly complemented by John's powerful vocal, in which he invests so much belief that you can hear his voice catching.

If the band even registered that this was the first Beatles album not to make number one in the UK, they probably shrugged and returned to thoughts of the new project on which they were working, an album like no other.

"Penny Lane"/"Strawberry Fields Forever"

Released: 17/02/1967

by Sean Egan

"Penny Lane"/"Strawberry Fields Forever" was the first Beatles single since "Eleanor Rigby"/"Yellow Submarine", once again a gap of six months. Even then, it was released only reluctantly.

"Brian was frightened that The Beatles were slipping and wanted another single out that was a blockbuster," George Martin later said. The Beatles had three completed tracks from the sessions they had been working on since late November '66, these two and "When I'm Sixty-Four". Artistically, Martin made the right choice in the tracks he gave Epstein, creating a two-sided conceptual single inspired by landmarks of the band's Liverpool childhoods. Commercially, it brought about a mini-disaster.

The common assumption has been that The Beatles were hoist with their own petard with this record: that the strategy of a double-A-sided single that had worked so well with "Day Tripper"/"We Can Work It Out" and "Eleanor Rigby"/"Yellow Submarine" blew up in their faces when this record stalled at number two in the UK. It wouldn't have been so bad perhaps if a cast-iron rock classic kept them off the top spot that had been theirs for the asking since (arguably) "Please Please Me" and (inarguably) "From Me To You". But the record that broke the Fabs' sequence of eleven number one singles in their home country was "Release Me", a histrionic throwback to pre-rock

cheesiness by Englebert Humperdinck (born Reg Dorsey). That
they had been pipped by somebody with such a stupid name
– still unfamiliar to the public – only added fuel to the debate
about whether The Beatles after four years at the top were on
the way down. (Note: though it peaked at number two in the
other three charts, The Beatles' disc did scale the summit of
the *Melody Maker* chart.) The fact that there had been so many
unsold seats at the second Shea Stadium gig the previous year,
the fact that though "Paperback Writer", "Rain" and *Revolver*
had been technically impressive, they just didn't have that effervescent good nature that the world had come to love the group
for, the fact of their ever-declining productivity rate and the
issue of their retirement from touring (not formally announced
but obvious from their disinterested comments on live work),
combined with this new chart "catastrophe", for many did
genuinely add up to the smack of the beginning of the end for
The Beatles.

Subsequent evaluations from a perspective where such
debates have been consigned to the dustbin of history have
been more concerned with the aesthetic merits of the record.
Many consider it the apex of The Beatles' artistic achievements.
Some have even posited it as the greatest single of all time.
This critic gravitates towards the opinion that was broadly
expressed by the British public in receiving it fairly warmly
but not quite enthusiastically enough to make it a chart topper,
for – whisper it lightly – it's more likely that what kept it off
the top spot was not divided sales but the fact that it wasn't
that great.

Paul's "Penny Lane" takes its name from a real place in
Liverpool, which is both a street and the area around it, in
much the same way as Times Square in New York is not restricted
to the actual square that bears that name. "It's part fact, part
nostalgia for a great place," Paul later said. McCartney tells us
– to a very non-rock backing that includes flute, piccolo, cor
anglais, harmonium, oboe, flugelhorn and trumpet – of
characters that populate the titular locale. The song is bright
and pretty and peppy and a perfectly pleasant three minutes'
listen but it's also shallow. The characters depicted are so two-
dimensional and the observations made of them so facile that

they put one in mind of the roll call of characters in the BBC children's stop motion puppetry television show *Camberwick Green* (Police Constable McGarry, Windy Miller, Sgt Major Grout . . .). It's certainly hard to be impressed by the observation that the fireman's engine is "a clean machine" and difficult to understand how to take the claim that the barber has photographs of every head he has had the pleasure to have known on his walls (it can't be literally true, and doesn't seem a metaphor for anything). Meanwhile, that line about the nurse who thinks she's in a play and is anyway is the most cack-handed attempt at fourth-wall-smashing post-modernism imaginable. Some automatically assumed that a Beatles song not concerned with romance must be an advance, but "Penny Lane" is really not much less banal than "Love Me Do".

John's "Strawberry Fields Forever" works on a deeper spiritual and aesthetic level, although itself is far from the perfection many claim for it. The title comes from a Liverpool Salvation Army orphanage called Strawberry Field (no "s") in whose huge, wild gardens John used to play after bunking over the back wall. The lilting melody is lovely and its air of poignancy enhanced by John's unflashy, even mordant, singing. A peculiarity about the song is that it has the flavour of an anthem – John is revealing his perspective on life and inviting the listener to join him at the titular special place where he will share his enlightenment – but the lyric is also peppered with uncertainty, while the instrumentation is wistful in a very un-anthem-like way. Without the listener necessarily knowing why, this conflict creates quite a heart-tugging mood. Lennon himself said of the song, "'Nobody seems to be as hip as me', is what I'm saying. Therefore I must be crazy or a genius!"

"Strawberry Fields Forever" is even more lush than "Penny Lane", packed to the gills with instruments both familiar and obscure (one of which being something called a swordmandel, which apparently exists despite it sounding like a word from one of Lennon's lunatic poems). The Beatles recorded two versions: a pastoral affair dominated by the sound of flute (as reproduced by Paul on a mellotron) and a heavy, slightly menacing string arrangement. Lennon had been unable to make up his mind which he preferred and instructed a bemused Martin to split and splice them. Which brings to mind again the question of whether Lennon was crazy or a genius. Whatever the answer to that, it worked. Nevertheless "Strawberry Fields Forever", like "Penny Lane", is good but not great. In fact, both sound not like the bold, arresting statements required of singles but, more than anything, like good album tracks.

Whatever the merits or demerits of "Penny Lane"/"Strawberry Fields Forever", the single set the tone for the year of psychedelia and the summer of love. It was a record as flowery and ostentatious as the sartorial fashions of that year and the sonic template for the craze for the musically baroque and the exploitation of rapidly developing studio technology that took hold of just about every major pop act either side of the Atlantic in '67. ("Strawberry Fields . . ." alone took fifty-five hours to record – more than five times the time it took to record The Beatles' first album.)

It should also be noted that the record was important because of its Englishness. For almost the first time – there were antecedents like Gerry and the Pacemakers' "Ferry Cross The Mersey" and The Kinks' "Waterloo Sunset" – British places were being mythologized in a way that was commonplace with American landmarks and neighbourhoods. Hitherto, British rockers found it laughable that anybody would want to hear songs whose subjects were locales in their drizzly, grey and backward country. As if to emphasize the shrugging off of this inferiority complex (which was only logical, as The Beatles had reinvented and reinvigorated rock and sold it back to the Americans in a way that Dylan described as "bringing it all back home"), these two songs saw Lennon and McCartney use their own accents, John pronouncing "can't" with a long "a", Paul pointedly enunciating "customer" English northern-style.

The single was housed in The Beatles' first UK single picture sleeve, their adult selves on the front, pictures from their respective childhoods on the back. The single was promoted with arguably pop's first videos: two films involving outdoor shooting, jump-cuts, X-ray simulation, reverse footage and almost no lip-synching or instrument miming. The weird ambience was underlined by The Beatles' new image: all moustaches, candy stripes, loud colours and scarves.

George Martin had always complained that releasing these two tracks somewhat spoiled the album the band were working on (which, of course, was ultimately entitled *Sgt. Pepper's Lonely Hearts Club Band*), as – supposedly – the ethics of the time required that an album provide value for money, which meant all-new songs. This is a puzzling logic. The jacket of The Beatles' first album had made a virtue of the fact that the record contained the band's two chart hits thus far, and both *A Hard Day's Night* and *Help!* included two previously released 45s. While the prevailing ethos may have changed over the subsequent four years, it had not done so to such an extent that the band felt inhibited about releasing a double-A-sided single on the same day of the release of *Revolver*, an album containing both the single's songs.

. . . *Pepper* would have been enriched by "Penny Lane" and "Strawberry Fields Forever" – and if The Beatles had released "When I'm Sixty-Four" as a single (maybe not a bold, arresting statement but undeniably catchy and lovable), they would probably have won the tussle for the top spot with Englebert.

100 ALBUMS THAT CHANGED MUSIC

The article on Sgt. Pepper's Lonely Heart's Club Band *below was originally printed in the book* 100 Albums That Changed Music. *The article focuses on the effects of the album as much as its contents, as the book was designed to address not so much great albums as influential ones. The two things, of course, are usually very much intertwined, no more so than in the case of* Sgt. Pepper . . .

Sgt. Pepper's Lonely Heart's Club Band

Released: 1/06/1967

by Sean Egan

TRACKLISTING

Side one
1. "Sgt. Pepper's Lonely Hearts Club Band"
2. "With A Little Help From My Friends"
3. "Lucy In The Sky With Diamonds"
4. "Getting Better"
5. "Fixing A Hole"
6. "She's Leaving Home"
7. "Being For The Benefit Of Mr Kite!"

Side two
1. "Within You Without You"
2. "When I'm Sixty-Four"
3. "Lovely Rita"
4. "Good Morning, Good Morning"
5. "Sgt. Pepper's Lonely Hearts Club Band (Reprise)"
6. "A Day In The Life"

Upon its release, *Sgt. Pepper* was hailed as "a decisive moment in the history of western civilization". Not by some gushing pop paper pundit but London *Times* newspaper critic Kenneth Tynan.

Those people who weren't around upon the release of The Beatles' eighth (UK) album who sit down to listen to the record now will be puzzled, even contemptuous, of such – what seems like – hyperbole (especially if they listen to the watery stereo mix that is the only version available on CD). However, at the time such was the richness, inventiveness, colourfulness and exoticness of *Pepper* and such was its omnipresence that even years later such remarks do not seem too much like overkill to those who witnessed its unveiling first-hand. Though they would remain popular after this album – always perceived as being on a plateau above all other artists, artistically and commercially – its release was the crescendo of the world's love affair with The Beatles.

Revolver was the first Beatles album on which the Fab Four began to seem like something a little more than consummate pop craftsmen. Wonderful though their music had been hitherto, and despite their minor pieces of innovation in terms of such things as descending middle-eights and modest studio experimentation, it was only with the likes of that album's "Tomorrow Never Knows" that they began to profoundly question and explore the boundaries of modern popular music. In this sense, they lagged behind contemporaries like Bob Dylan and The Byrds (the latter had recorded a version of jazz-rock number 'Eight Miles High' as early as December 1965, though the song was unreleased until March '66). However, on *Sgt. Pepper* The Beatles made up for their previous relative conservatism with a vengeance. Rock and pop had never been so kaleidoscopic, dazzling and sophisticated.

This was partly because no rock artist had ever had the breathing space The Beatles had at this point. Having completed their final tour in August 1966, they now had nothing else to do, at least collectively, but to record. The four months and cumulative 700 hours that they took to complete *Pepper* is nothing by today's standards but then it was unprecedented. So much so that it alarmed their record company. The assumption was that fans would lose interest if new product was not available every three months. Hence Parlophone insisting on The Beatles delivering a stop-gap single: "Penny Lane"/"Strawberry Fields Forever", whose commercial release in February 1967 dismayed producer George Martin, who realized that this prohibited – as was then the tradition – the songs appearing on the subsequent album, which he felt weakened it. Hence also the sniffy article in the *News Of The World* newspaper in the months preceding *Pepper*'s release, which lambasted the band for their recent reclusiveness and rumours of their musical self-indulgence.

Pepper was essentially McCartney's idea. What if The Beatles weren't The Beatles but a completely new band and therefore able to do whatever they wanted musically because nobody had any prior expectations of them? They would need a new name. McCartney came up with the sobriquet "Sgt. Pepper's Lonely Hearts Club Band" after being inspired by the unwieldy and frequently official-sounding titles of bands in San Francisco's contemporaneous psychedelic scene (e.g. Quicksilver Messenger Service, Big Brother And The Holding Company, Jefferson Airplane). The antediluvian militaristic clothing fashions to be seen on the streets of London at the time may have also been an influence. Of course, everybody would know it was actually The Beatles so there would be no point trying to hide it – but if the music is anything to go by, psychologically it did the track. This record was the aural equivalent of the way that The Beatles at this juncture suddenly sprouted moustaches and adorned themselves in flower power finery: *Pepper* was still The Beatles but not as we had known them.

In fact, it is surprising in many ways that *Pepper* does sound like a Beatles album, rather than a McCartney solo project. Lennon contributes only four songs, one of which has a McCartney middle eight, and George Harrison – according to

McCartney – barely turned up for sessions. But The Beatles' imprimatur is present and correct: those unique, glorious three-part harmonies that had soundtracked so many people's journeys from adolescence to adulthood the past five years.

The album is nominally a performance by the titular show-band but only the segue between the opening anthem and "With A Little Help From My Friends" and the reprise of the anthem really conform to the concept. Though a showband might at a stretch be able to produce jaunty numbers like "When I'm Sixty-Four" and "Lovely Rita", are we really to believe they could replicate the shimmering, fish-eyed-lens soundscape of "Lucy In The Sky With Diamonds", the orchestral sweep of coming-of-age kitchen sink drama "She's Leaving Home", the carnival ambience of showbill-brought-to-life "Being For The Benefit Of Mr Kite!", the sitar-drenched philosophical musing "Within You Without You" or the growling hard rock of "Good Morning, Good Morning"? And where does "A Day In The Life" fit into all this, a haunting epic that comes *after* the Sgt. Pepper reprise and across which Lennon's chanted backing vocals and Starr's thunderous tom-toms drift quite eerily? The answer of course is that it doesn't matter: such is the brilliance of what we are hearing that nobody really cares that the conceit is sustained only by smoke and mirrors.

Pepper was not just exotic musically. Everything about the album felt weird and wonderful, from the fact that Englishness was a flavour running through it to the fact that that there were no pauses between the tracks, to its title – utterly bizarre until people got used to it – to the sumptuousness of it as an artifact: its cover simply bursting with colour, its back cover sporting song lyrics reminiscent of the libretto provided for people attending an opera, its unusual gatefold sleeve, its unashamedly silly cardboard cut-out inserts of things like the sergeant's moustache and (now long forgotten by most) the record's original psychedelically coloured inner sleeve. This very sump-tuousness was influential in itself: albums were very often henceforth things into whose design great thought went.

The underlying thread in this book is how the release of great and innovative music has inspired rock artists to make great and innovative music of their own. Though *Pepper* caused this process more than perhaps any album ever (and inspired a parody from the Mothers Of Invention called *We're Only In It For The Money*), it also saw the sad flipside of this virtuous circle. The Beach Boys' leader Brian Wilson instead of being inspired to make great music the way that he had by *Rubber Soul*, this time did not come up with a masterpiece like *Pet Sounds* but gave up the ghost and returned to his room, never to be the same talent again. Though his psychological condition at the time seems to be rather complicated – he had several other worries including conflicts with his Beach Boys colleagues, paranoia and mental problems caused by LSD – the forbidding magnificence of *Pepper* played its part in his *Smile* would-be opus failing to see the light of day for nearly forty years.

Though nobody suggests that *Pepper*'s brilliance was a completely illusory product of a heady time, the album has fallen down the esteem scale in recent years, both as a piece of art and as part of The Beatles *oeuvre*. Certainly, it possesses an emotional hole that almost no other Beatles album does: love songs are very thin on the ground. Nor does it have that punchiness that the no-frills *Revolver* boasts.

However, as a influential album its status can't be disputed. *Sgt. Pepper's Lonely Hearts Club Band* redrew all popular music boundaries forever.

"All You Need Is Love" b/w "Baby You're A Rich Man"

Released: 7/07/1967

by Sean Egan

Hurriedly put together and boasting a frequently trite and even meaningless lyric, "All You Need Is Love" is the ultimate example of what Paul has termed a "work song" – written for deadline reasons, not artistic ones. It was also an example (maybe the first) of The Beatles submitting to the *zeitgeist* rather than moulding it.

For Ian MacDonald, the late, acclaimed analyst of The Beatles' music, "All You Need Is Love", was a piece of hack work. "One of The Beatles' less deserving hits," he opined, accusing it of "comfortable self-indulgence." The Beatles meanwhile were so casual about the record's creation as to give the impression the song was intended more as a doodle than as the manifesto it was received as. To quote Paul from the time, ". . . a fellow from the BBC . . . asked us to get together a song for this . . . so we went away and we just played Monopoly for a bit and then the fellow said, 'Now where's the song?' . . . I wrote one and John wrote one . . . By the time that we had done the backing track for John's, we suddenly realized that this was the one." Hardly the tone of excitement one would expect for a commission for *Our World*, a landmark in television and satellite broadcasting which on 25 June 1967 would see the event of the first global live link.

The Summer of Love of 1967 saw the worldwide break-out of the fashions and philosophies of the hippies of San Francisco's Haight-Ashbury and the organizers of counter culture mass gatherings at Be-Ins, Love-Ins and the Monterey Festival. By writing a love-infused flower power anthem like "All You Need Is Love", The Beatles were jumping on that bandwagon, which you would expect of acts lesser-ranked than they. On one level, then, "All You Need Is Love" is an exploitation/gimmick record on a grandiose scale. However, such was the genius of The Beatles – and the public's love for them – that it was accepted as the Summer of Love's major anthem. Such was their further genius that unlike other celebrations of the spirit of that blissed-out season, it has not dated but instead assumed a wider significance.

That The Beatles were asked by the BBC to be the representatives of the United Kingdom on *Our World* as it broadcast to 26 countries simultaneously is an indication of the group's Godlike post-*Pepper* stature. (The album wasn't quite released when the offer was made but the media were *au fait* with how barrier-smashing it was via previews.) Perhaps the reason that neither John nor Paul attacked their proposed songs for the broadcast with any particular urgency (Epstein: "The time got nearer and nearer and they still hadn't written anything") was because few would have been expecting too much of a new composition on a live broadcast. In the event, on the evening the song (which saw The Beatles playing over a pre-recorded basic track) went over well. However, George Martin – like, presumably, The Beatles themselves – was under no illusions that the euphoria seen in the TV studio was due to musical excellence rather than the novelty of the occasion. Accordingly, now that it had been decided that The Beatles were indeed going to turn this casual creation into a single, he set about what he knew would be the hard work involved in polishing and embellishing it to bring it up to the high standards set by their previous 45s.

Yet for all that, "All You Need Is Love" is powerful. It's enjoyable and even absurdly moving. In a sense it's also quintessential Beatles, even if it could also be viewed as a cartoon version of that quintessence: that sunniness to their music, that life-affirming quality, that ability to make you feel glad to be alive after listening to them – what better (or more simplistic) way to sum it up than with the phrase "All You Need Is Love"?

In the 1960s, music was the most important thing in life for young people, serving not as the lifestyle accessory it is today but as a vital mirror to the ever more colourful and liberal society being (it was assumed) created daily from the ashes of the old, grey, censorious, authoritarian order. The Beatles seemed to be both the figureheads for popular music – they were the artists who kicked off the decade's entire musical revolution and were by common consent the greatest artists in the world – and the figureheads for change: society seemed somehow to be morphing to accommodate the informal, proletarian, unconventional, non-judgmental, adventurous values which The Beatles had in common with so many of their generation and for which they were the standard bearers by dint of being the four most famous people of that generation in the world. Thus, though The Beatles might have been joining sheep-like in the spirit of the Summer of Love, nobody was better qualified than them to provide the season's anthem. The events of the middle of 1967 – in which a beaded, head-banded, flower-bedecked youth throughout the West insisted that the world could be set to rights simply by everyone deciding to love each other – was like a socio-political manifestation of the very essence of the joyful music The Beatles had been purveying for the last four years. The philosophy was incredibly naive of course but, as with just about everything in life, you could only recognize its shortcomings by working your way through it in the first place.

The instrumentation on "All You Need Is Love" is wonderful, somehow reminiscent of the paisley shirts that were all the rage amongst the flower children: John's harpsichord (appropriately, an instrument whose sounds are like flowery piano), George's soaring electric guitar lines, and the almost choral chants of "Love, love, love" provide an ecstatic aural kaleidoscope. Meanwhile, George Martin's arrangements – racing strings and wack-wack-wack quasi-comedy brass – are sterling. Paul plays double bass and George Harrison violin on the record despite both being unfamiliar with the instruments. MacDonald sneered at that, feeling it a symptom of the relaxed temperature of the times when people mistook insistence on professionalism for being ungroovy, but bum notes don't seem to be in evidence.

The lyric only makes sense in fragments. When John says

that there is nothing you can know that isn't known, it feels like a piece of Confucian wisdom, but when he says there's nothing you can do but you can learn how to be you in time, it feels like an example of the fatuous pseudo-profundities that proliferated at that point amongst a generation whose rejection of their elders' wisdom meant they had to invent their own rules for the world, ones unencumbered by experience-gained knowledge. That and something to make the rhyme. Crucially, though, Lennon doesn't discriminate between the banal and the shrewd in his singing. His vocals are what ultimately make the record. He employs his mournful "Strawberry Fields" voice as he self-consciously creates the feeling of sad, aching happiness that The Beatles had hitherto generated probably without really trying or even knowing.

The deployment of outside material (Glenn Miller's "In The Mood" and "La Marseillaise", which, absurdly, starts the record, *apropos* nothing) is lazy (though Paul's singing of a snatch of "She Loves You" at the end is cute, the self-referentialism instantly recognizable as a comment on just how absurdly far these young men had come in such a short space of time).

We mustn't assume that sheer cynicism lay behind "All You Need Is Love". Many are the associates and friends of Lennon who have testified that he became a changed man over 1966 and 1967. The benevolence conferred by LSD, of which he was consuming vast quantities, had turned somebody with a hair-trigger temper and a penchant for using his fists into a man far mellower and more likeable. It seems safe to assume that Lennon was liking his new self. It also must have been quite an experience for him to find the world unexpectedly marching in step with him, suffused with exaggerated big-heartedness just as he was discovering the joys of kindness.

The general public certainly didn't see anything amiss about "All You Need Is Love". It soared to number one on both sides of the Atlantic and instantly became one of the group's most well-loved songs. To the fans, it was yet another example of The Beatles having their finger on the pulse of society. Interestingly, despite its contemporary relevance, it hasn't dated at all. While a song like "San Francisco (Be Sure To Wear Some Flowers In Your Hair)" by Scott McKenzie or "San Franciscan

Nights" by Eric Burdon & The Animals can now not really be understood and therefore properly enjoyed without a smattering of knowledge about their origins in the Summer of Love, it transpired that Lennon couched his own celebration of that season's spirit in a sufficiently universal way – there are no direct topical references in the lyric – that it retains a relevance. A young person coming to the song cold today can enjoy it as a generalized anthem of good spirit, or even a celebration of romance, and need know nothing about the atmosphere and events of 1967 at all.

The B-side is a very ornate piece of fluff. "Baby, You're a Rich Man" also has its roots in the climate of the time – its first line refers to the Beautiful People, another term for the Flower Children. The philosophy of its chorus (written by Paul) is fair enough (wealth is determined by spiritual, not material, riches) but the rhyming is so fatuous that it sounds like it's being made up on the spot. Lennon's verses aren't anything to write home about either. The song doesn't go anywhere and sounds half-formed, yet the aimlessness is of a lustrous kind because – this being the height of what we now know to be The Beatles' middle, baroque period – it is tarted up in exotic clothes, including a vibraphone from Eddie Kramer, who engineered at Olympic studios where this was – unusually – recorded. Lennon plays a clavioline, a synthesizer precursor which enabled him to produce a sound like an Arab-esque wind instrument. The track isn't unbearably awful – we *are* talking about The Beatles – but it's possibly the worst thing ever to make its way onto either side of a Beatles single.

"Hello, Goodbye" b/w "I Am The Walrus'

Released: 24/11/1967

by Sean Egan

"Smells a mile away, doesn't it?" John Lennon once said of The Beatles' sixteenth UK single.

Perhaps he was still smarting over the fact that his phantasmagoric "I Am The Walrus" was relegated to the single's B-side. Certainly, Lennon's flip displayed an adventurism and surrealism that can make – if you're in the right scornful mood – the simple popcraft of the hit side seem like it's all catchiness, no content. Nonetheless, "Hello, Goodbye" epitomizes the way The Beatles could turn the flimsiest of material into a very pleasant way to pass three-and-a-half minutes.

Ex-Beatles aide Alistair Taylor wrote an enjoyable memoir of his time spent working first for Epstein's company NEMS, then for Apple, entitled *Yesterday*. In this book – written in the form of letters to a fictional recipient called Michelle – he claimed to have directly inspired McCartney to write "Hello, Goodbye". Asking about the process of composition while at McCartney's house one day, he found himself marched to the living room where McCartney amiably proceeded to demonstrate how easy songwriting was – for him, anyway. Following McCartney's instruction to call out random words and hit notes on his harmonium, Taylor found Paul responding with notes and words himself. Before long, almost an entire skeletal structure of a song containing a quasi call-and-response pattern had emerged. While it's not a lyric dripping with profundity and while it hardly resounds with pathos, it does make sense: the narrator asks his lover why she wants to leave and insists that her attitude

should be in affirmative words like "hello", "yes", "go", not nega-
tives, like "goodbye", "no" and "stop". Paul has effectively
confirmed this story by allowing Barry Miles to include it in *Many
Years From Now*. Paul also said, ". . . it's a very easy song to write.
It's just a song of duality, with me advocating the positive."

The song has the smack of the kind of ditty McCartney
tended to write after The Beatles split. But where one suspects
that had Paul recorded this in his solo/Wings career, it would
have sounded like the glorified doodle it is, once McCartney
turned it over to his colleagues, their assured hands at arrangement and embellishment gave it that golden Beatles aura and
hence a feeling of substantiality. The finished record is chock-
full of delights: piano notes echoing into infinity, Paul's unusually
high vocal, the way that Lennon's backing vocals alternate
between a helium-like quality and sounding like they are coming
over the telephone, Ringo's nice, padding drumming behind the
chorus, George's keening echo-drenched lead guitar lines, the
instrumental break where Paul's treated "Why why why"s intertwine with some sweet violas and skittering drums, and finally
an inspired end section every bit as good – and unexpected –
as that strange outro to "Ticket To Ride", in this case one where
the band – after a false ending – launch into a mass chant and
a cha-cha rhythm that takes the song over the horizon. The only
thing that spoils the latter is that it's not the "aloha" (Hawaiian,
of course, for both "hello" and "goodbye") that it sounds like,
something that would have constituted the perfect end.

Fans flipping over to the B-side from this unambitious but
essentially highly agreeable concoction were to encounter a track
at the other end of the scale in terms of musical daring
and lyrical ingenuity. That the title was the utterly weird-looking
"I Am The Walrus" was a bit of a clue. The song itself was no
less bizarre. After a woozy, classical string introduction, a torrent
of the most surreal phrases and images follow involving sitting
on cornflakes, custard dripping from a dead dog's eye, a semolina
pilchard and a Hare Krishna-chanting penguin (the latter two
both kicking Edgar Allen Poe). The vocal melody lines are mainly
staccato but sometimes sag at the end in despair with the phrase
"I'm crying", a contrasting note to the actually quite venomous
and slightly unsettling tone to the song. There was also a reference

to dropped knickers that got the track banned by the BBC and a passing reference to "Lucy In The Sky With Diamonds", which was also an example of the self-referentialism that had started with "All You Need Is Love"'s quoting of "She Loves You" and would continue in other songs like "Lady Madonna" and (in the ultimate example) "Glass Onion". The recording also features what we would now call sampling, in this case a performance of *King Lear* recorded straight off the radio.

The immediate assumption was that LSD was the inspiration for the song, but, if so, this would have meant that Lewis Carroll and Edward Lear had been dropping tabs of acid well before Albert Hofman first synthesized the drug for Sandoz Laboratories: the more astute Beatle observer would have remembered that Lennon's two books had evinced his love for those writers, as well as other British surrealists. As Lennon himself explained, "I was just using the mind that wrote *In His Own Write* to write that song." Which of course makes it the culmination of the process that started when he was encouraged to develop his songwriting by friends who were amazed that none of his wild imaginings and keen intellect found their way into early Beatles songs. It doesn't follow, however, that the song means anything. Though there is a cockeyed Carroll allusion (the composer identified with the Walrus from "The Walrus And The Carpenter" in *Through the Looking-Glass*, not realizing that the author intended the Carpenter as the good guy), Lennon was actually mocking people who read stuff into song lyrics: "Dylan got away with murder. I thought, 'Well, I can write this crap too.' You know, you just stick a few images together, thread them together, and you call it poetry."

The track's radicalism has earned it greater kudos than it perhaps deserves, but in a year when the strange and the utterly arcane were proliferating in a form of music that was only ever supposed to have been about populism and therefore the commonplace, this one was up there with not only the strangest but also the most musically rich.

The yin and yang of Lennon & McCartney was on display again. As previously noted, wonderful though The Beatles' music had been since "Paperback Writer" saw them break with the romantic tradition, *Revolver*, *Sgt. Pepper* . . . – and indeed the

Magical Mystery Tour soundtrack that was just around the corner
– contained too much artifice and not enough soul. In other
words they needed leavening with love songs. The contrasting
sides of this single meant it was a Beatles record that struck
just the right balance between emotion and innovation.

Magical Mystery Tour

Released: 8/12/1967

by Sean Egan

TRACKLISTING

Side one
"Magical Mystery Tour"
"Your Mother Should Know"

Side two
"I Am the Walrus"

Side three
"The Fool On The Hill"
"Flying"

Side four
"Blue Jay Way"

After all the fuss The Beatles had made about setting their own
schedules, they found that they actually liked working hard.

Nineteen sixty-six turned out to be the only year in which The
Beatles did not record (though not necessarily release) the equivalent of two albums. Less than a month after the unprecedented

marathon recording process of *Sgt. Pepper* . . . , they were back in the studio working on the title theme to the soundtrack of *Magical Mystery Tour*, their proposed TV special. Even though work did not resume on the soundtrack – which would be a double-EP, equivalent to half an album – for another month (a single, two B-sides and material destined for the *Yellow Submarine* soundtrack were recorded in the interim), EMI must have been pleasantly surprised come December to find that they had Beatles product to market for Christmas just like the old days.

The title track to *Magical Mystery Tour* is enjoyable enough, with its anthemic qualities, its infectious Lennon-sung "Roll up" fairground barker vocals-refrain and its fluttering trumpets. However, it's really nothing but an aural advertising banner. It's also, in the context of the record, much ado about little: The Beatles are extolling the virtues of merely the following five songs, not all of which are that great. We should, however, concede that in the context of the film, the title theme is heralding nearly an hour of television.

Paul's "The Fool On The Hill" is by contrast a fully realized, proper song. If we are to take the attitude that love songs are necessarily less profound than socio-political compositions (which this writer doesn't), this number is probably as close to profound as McCartney was able to get. His lyric talks of an old eccentric who is laughed at by society. Paul, however, posits the question of whether it's society or the title character that is foolish. This is toytown philosophy compared to Lennon's observations on life and society of this period ("Strawberry Fields Forever", "I Am The Walrus", "A Day In The Life") but, at the same time, its plain language means we at least know precisely what the composer intended to convey and are not foolishly reading stuff into it that's not there. The music is lovely, a gossamer melody decorated with lilting flutes.

"Flying" is the only instrumental The Beatles released in their lifetime, leading to the most unfamiliar publishing credit of "Lennon-McCartney-Harrison-Starr". It's difficult to know what judgment to pass on this two-and-a-quarter minute fragment of music. It's pleasant enough, boasting some nicely surreal sound effects and a particularly interesting motif played on a mellotron set to sound like some sort of eastern reed instrument.

However, though it's perfectly agreeable to listen to on its own, it perhaps serves its purpose best as background to an interlude in the film. It would also have been interesting to hear the nine-and-a-half minute version that it is said the released version was cut down from.

"Blue Jay Way" was written by George as he sat forlornly waiting for ex-Beatles publicist Derek Taylor to find his way to a house he had rented on Blue Jay Way in California. Its refrain of "Don't be long" may have been heartfelt, but in repeating it *ad infinitum* Harrison makes the mistake of not merely conveying his boredom to the listener but inducing it in him. (Philip Norman has claimed that the line is repeated twenty-nine times. This writer has not verified this, on the grounds that life is too short.) A monotonous melody only compounds matters.

"Your Mother Should Know" is another song from Paul that displays his effortless way with catchy, sweet melody. Reminiscent of "When I'm Sixty-Four" it sees him putting both women and old-time values on a pedestal to the type of pop backing that was popular when he was a child, which had been made to seem helplessly antiquated by the rock revolution that The Beatles had been the most important component of.

"I Am The Walrus" is the last track in the package (and is actually listed on an inside pocket with the parenthesized addendum to its title: "No you're not!" said little Nicola). Though it had already been used as the B-side of "Hello, Goodbye", it was still an integral part of the project, with one of the most memorable and surreal sequences in the film built around the song (to which the bizarre cover shot, with The Beatles in animal costume, alludes). It should also be noted that the track is here presented in stereo, as opposed to the single's mono.

With its title theme, its baroque music and its track-segueing, *Magical Mystery Tour* feels very much like The Beatles' previous album, only not as good. One critic, brutally but accurately, labelled it a "poor man's *Pepper*". However, only "Blue Jay Way" is a song that The Beatles' catalogue would be better off without and only that and "Flying" aren't on balance an asset to it.

The *Magical Mystery Tour* double EP was quite a deluxe package, containing a gatefold sleeve and a colour booklet of thirty-two pages with stills from the film, lyrics and a strip cartoon. The

Extended Play format was dying out even as The Beatles released this, their last EP while extant: six days previously had seen the publication of the final *Record Retailer* EP chart. The EP reached number two in the singles chart, and was only kept off the top spot by "Hello, Goodbye", quite an achievement considering its expense. In the *Melody Maker* singles chart, it actually made the top spot, deposing "Hello Goodbye". In America, there was never any question of Capitol agreeing to the double EP format. Instead, Capitol issued, a week earlier than Britain got the EP, an album called *Magical Mystery Tour* containing the EP's contents on side one and the year's non-album Beatles singles and B-sides on the other ("Hello Goodbye", "Strawberry Fields Forever", "Penny Lane", "Baby You're A Rich Man" and "All You Need Is Love"). For once, a Stateside tampering with Beatles product seemed logical and useful rather than philistine and knuckleheaded and the album sold so well in Britain as an import than it became an official UK album in 1976 and subsequently made The Beatles-blessing dictated transfer over to CD.

THE FIRST CRITICAL DRUBBING

Though the Fab Four had been subjected to criticism for things they had done or were alleged to have done (the bigger-than-Jesus furore, the Marcos "snub", a confession by Paul in mid-June 1967 that he had taken LSD, etc), the broadcast of Magical Mystery Tour *on Boxing Day 1967 presented them with a very unfamiliar scenario: for the first time, their art was being universally panned.*

Of course the very fact that so many felt let down by the programme was in a sense a measure of the public's esteem for them. Why else would they care so much?

The film wasn't just a matter that television critics addressed themselves to. That The Beatles had done something that wasn't wonderful and charming was considered to be the stuff of front-page news. Hence the story below from the Daily Mail, *which was the joint-second lead story of that middle-market periodical the day after the broadcast.*

Beatles On TV Baffle Viewers

From *Daily Mail*, Wednesday 31 December 1967
(No byline)

Protests from viewers about The Beatles' *Magical Mystery Tour* jammed the switchboard at the BBC television centre last night. Mystified viewers also phoned the *Daily Mail*.

And Peter Black, the *Daily Mail* television critic who reviews the show on page three, gives this verdict: "Appalling."

BBC TV chiefs will almost certainly hold an inquest on the show at their next programme review meeting next Wednesday. But BBC executives emphasized last night as criticism poured in; "The Beatles made the film – not the BBC."

The 50-minute programme on BBC One received a huge pre-Christmas build up and was screened at peak viewing time last night. The film cost the Beatles more than £30,000 to make but is expected to bring in almost £1 million from overseas sales. It will be shown in America in colour in the new year.

But last night as the programme neared its end, the complaints started rolling in.

One caller to the *Daily Mail* said, "It was terrible. It was worse than terrible. I watched it in a room together with 23 other people and we were all stunned."

Mrs Iris Inglis of Richmond, Surrey said, "The Beatles' show was ridiculous. I tried hard to watch it but there was no beginning, no end and no sequence, only flashes of photographs. The only good thing was the strip-tease – and that was censored."

A spokesman for the Beatles said, "Like anything The Beatles do, there are elements about the film [that are] progressively different.

"There are some people who don't understand parts of it. Maybe they are looking for too much reality in sequences which are very intentionally unrealistic. That's where the magic and fantasy come in."

"Lady Madonna" b/w "The Inner Light"

Released: 15/03/1968

by Sean Egan

A new year, a new atmosphere, a new sound. Flower power philosophies were passé. So was baroque music. Who said so? Well, The Beatles first new record of 1968 was a driving, gritty and basic-sounding rock track and what The Beatles did, the music world copied.

The song itself, though, had all the humanity and tenderness of flower power anthems. It derived from McCartney's tendency to put women, especially mothers, on a pedestal. ("Your Mother Should Know" and a 1979 Wings B-side "Daytime Nighttime Suffering", one of his favourites among his compositions, are similarly themed.) Perhaps this derives from his own early loss of his mum. "I think women are very strong, they put up with a lot of shit . . . so I always want to pay a tribute to them," he has said.

McCartney saw a magazine cover photo of an African woman suckling her child that was captioned "Mountain Madonna" and took it from there. His lyric marvels at how a woman burdened with both poverty and children manages to hold everything together. There is an inter-verse pun about both children and stockings running, which itself seems like an allusion to the "See how they run" line in "I Am The Walrus". Paul goes through the days of the week as he documents the woman's incremental realization of her dire straits (although he inadvertently misses out Saturday).

Musically, the band take their cue from a Martin-produced 1956 Humphrey Lyttleton hit called "Bad Penny Blues". It is a quite blatant imitation, but Lyttleton was sanguine. "You can't copyright a rhythm, and rhythm was all that they had borrowed," he shrugged, admitting he had originally lifted the riff from Dan Burley. McCartney was also striving for something in the vein of Fats Domino, although frankly it's difficult to spot a link between the "Lady Madonna" uptempo shuffle and Domino's easy-rolling New Orleans style. Paul plays some pounding piano that is surprisingly mellifluous for someone of his standard on the instrument, and Ringo maintains a brisk tempo with brushes. The jazzy patina is added to by a four-man sax section that includes the legendary Ronnie Scott.

For all its good intentions, though, "Lady Madonna" remains a bit unimpressive. The brisk pace seems inappropriate to the bleak subject matter and the brass is incongruously jolly, which is compounded by John and Paul performing a parodic parping vocal impression of said brass section. The result is that we are not moved in the slightest by the poverty tableaux. It's catchy alright – especially that "See how they run" refrain – and the pulse does quicken every time Paul's solo piano introduction comes over the radio, but those two things are about the extent of its pleasures.

"The Inner Light" marks the first occasion George has been given either side of a Beatles' single. The achievement is thoroughly deserved, for "The Inner Light" is gorgeous, and if it's hardly a Beatles track – the instrumentation, recorded in Bombay, is provided by Indian musicians and there are no harmonies from his fellow Fabs – the same could be said of "Yesterday". In any case, it would have seemed logical to Beatles fans that an Indian-flavoured song featured on their latest record: upon its release, all of them except Ringo were still in Rishikesh, India, where they had gone to learn the joys of meditation at the feet of the Maharishi Mahesh Yogi. (Which is why a dispro-portionate number of the Beatle quotes in existence about "Lady Madonna" are Starr's – he did all the publicity for the record.)

George wrote the song after receiving a letter from Sanskrit scholar Juan Mascaro praising "Within You, Without You" and asking him to write a song containing the wisdom of Tao Teaching from a book called *Lamps of Fire*. Though Harrison can only take credit for the exquisite lilting melody – like a feather floating on a breeze – to which he set the poem "The Inner Light", extraordinarily the lyric feels identical in tone to and no less replete with nuggets of wisdom than another lyric of which he was the author, the aforesaid "Within You, Without You".

It's tempting to suggest that had The Beatles persevered with the number for which Lennon was agitating as the next single A-side – his beautiful "Across The Universe" – The Beatles would have had a far more commercial proposition on their hands. But Britons made "Lady Madonna" yet another chart-topper for The Beatles, and if it failed to make number one in either the *Cash Box* or *Billboard* charts in the States, it was still a big record.

Ultimately "Lady Madonna" seems significant mostly because it provided a litmus test for the world's enduring love affair with The Beatles: it showed that the public would automatically troop into the shops to buy even a relatively unremarkable record bearing their name.

APPLE

Don Short got the exclusive story on The Beatles' new business venture, Apple Corps, Limited. In a full-page story, the Daily Mirror man broke the news that the Fabs were about to set up a company that would produce films, electronics, clothes and, of course, records, although judging from his article he didn't seem to realize that the venture was essentially a tax avoidance project.

Which is not to say that The Beatles weren't genuinely excited by their new company and didn't have Utopian aims for it. However, though there was much activity at Apple over the next couple of years and though the organization did indeed put out a lot of product, almost all of it was music: the Apple boutique was short-lived, the Apple electronics division did not produce a single commercially available item and the Apple films division made only a handful of pictures.

The Dr Beeching referred to in the article was an infamous figure of the time, a man who ordered an inquiry into the nationalized rail industry service in Britain and concluded that a third of all railway stations should be shut down. The way that Apple was run turned out to be the very opposite of such ruthlessness, with money virtually disappearing out the door under the very gaze of the Apple employees who gave time to every crackpot and charlatan who demanded it. Ironically, when a Beeching figure – Allen Klein – did take the organization by the scruff of the neck and prune its branches, it was too late, and in any case he was a character that Paul hated.

The Big Business Beatles

With a bit of the Apple for all their old mates

From *Daily Mirror*, Wednesday 12 June 1968
by Don Short

A is for Apple. B is for Beatles and Big Business, a multi-million pound business the group is building from a fifth-floor office in Wigmore Street.

Soon to move to a quarter-million pound headquarters in Savile Row, and yesterday they revealed to me their plans for their new empire.

From behind a huge oak desk cluttered with coffee cups, sandwiches and sheets of paper, Paul McCartney told of The Beatles' four-pronged attack into the world of big business, and their bid to secure a Dr Beeching figure to run it all.

Apple Corps, Limited is the new company created by The Beatles with the spare half a million pounds left in the kitty after Beatlemania ended. It has branched into four major divisions – music, electronics, merchandise and films. Managing director is Neil Aspinall, the ex-road manager who used to carry The Beatles' bags. Aspinall has crossed the world three times making the contacts and forging the links for the organization to succeed. "He's really come right out of his shell. We always knew it was there but we didn't know he was going to develop with such tenacity," said George Harrison of Aspinall. "Mind, he should. He collected eight GCEs at school and that's more than the rest of us together, which makes him a lot brainier than us."

A lot of The Beatles' old friends have jobs in the organization, but Paul McCartney said: "In a year's time the organization will be so big that the friends we have will be immersed by friends we never dreamed of."

Each department has its own boss:

Denis O'Dell, 41, from Eire, associate. producer of The Beatles' first film *A Hard Day's Night*, has taken over as their film chief. As yet, Apple have got to get their first film off the ground. But O'Dell says: "We hope to have four major productions in the pipeline by the end of the year." And Apple plan to make The Beatles next picture. O'Dell told me: "Our first film is titled *The Jam* – the story of a traffic jam –and the love-hate, selfishness and greed it can cause." Also planned are the film versions of the two Lennon books, *In His Own Write* and *A Spaniard in the Works*.

Ronald Kass, 31, an American and once the whiz kid behind Liberty Records, is in charge of all the new artists and the sheet music as well as the records. "We're going away fast," said Kass. "Many people in the record industry are going to be stunned by the progress we make."

John Lyndon, who came to the attention of The Beatles after he promoted pop concerts is in charge of merchandise. He was once a Portobello Road stall keeper. He said: "Very soon we shall start a mail order catalogue, so the kids in the provinces who can't afford to come to London can get their garments and goods."

Surprising territory into which The Beatles move is electronics. John Lennon happened to meet bearded Greek research chemist and inventor Alexis Mardas, 26, who was tramping his way to Africa. The only people he knew in London were Lord Snowdon

and Prince Philip. But he got to know The Beatles as well –
and signed up with Apple. In the space of a few weeks he has
brought out over fifty new gadgets from radios to telephonic
equipment, and these are now being patented. In the new
building he will get a basement laboratory.

Yesterday in the Wigmore Street offices, there was a kind
of flurry which you might see in the City. There was a wiry-
haired singer from America hoping The Beatles or an Apple
executive would listen to a demonstration record. Wages
clerk Angela Walsh, 19, from Fulham making up the monthly
cheques for signature. There are forty-nine on the payroll. "I
know what everyone is earning in the organization apart
from The Beatles," she said. "But of course it is strictly
confidential."

The Beatles commute between the offices of the executives
they have appointed. John and Paul were in yesterday soon
after nine o'clock. They have decided to run the organization
themselves, although they haven't become directors or chair-
men, because they own it – and that's all they need to do.

"We've been looking for a Beeching figure to come in and
organize us," revealed John. "We had several of 'em in, but they
just didn't come up to scratch. The chaps we had in the interview
were bigoted. They thought they knew everything and that they
were just dealing with four clowns. But we saw through them
right away and felt we couldn't offer any one of them the
£20,000 a year we were prepared to pay. We could fall flat on
our faces – but, so what if we do? But at the moment we can
only see success," John said.

Apple is setting up a staff pension insurance scheme and
other facilities. Said Paul: "We're going to have our own brass
band."

There are six other key figures in the organization. Most
influential among them 25-year-old Stephen Maltz, who has
been accountant to The Beatles for the past three years. "I shall
be disappointed if Apple doesn't turn over £10m sterling within
the next three years," he said.

Brian Lewis, a solicitor who once worked on the James Bond
films, is assisting O'Dell on the picture-making front.

There's Derek Taylor, former Personal Assistant to Brian

Epstein. Peter Brown, who once managed Epstein's record shops in Liverpool, and Wendy Hanson, 31, publicity consultant. Another old Beatles' friend has an office in the Apple empire, 26-year-old Peter Shotton, former member of the Quarryman [*sic*] group of which The Beatles, apart from Ringo, were members. He was the washboard player of the group, but there was no place for him when The Beatles assembled as we know them today. Now he's personal assistant to John Lennon.

Today Apple is brushing aside the conventions of big business.

Tomorrow the Beatle bosses could be on their way to another fortune.

"Hey Jude" b/w "Revolution"

Released: 30/08/1968

by Sean Egan

"Hey Jude" was the first Beatles record to appear with an Apple label. As the band were still signed to EMI and Capitol, the label was purely for show. Nonetheless, as far as the public were concerned, it was the start of Apple, and it couldn't have been a better one.

It was a record that took the group's music more and more into adult territory. This mirrored their visual maturation. In a move that no doubt Grace Slick approved of, The Beatles were looking like grown men these days. Though the moustaches they were all sporting upon *Pepper*'s release made them look a bit more adult, the uniformity of those 'tashes was a variant on the conformity of their once-matching suits and moptops. Since then, however, they had shrugged off any instinct to look either clean-cut or even like a group. Beards, moustaches, hair whose length was constantly varying (and never synchronized with any other member's), John's almost defiant permanently spectacled appearance (his round-lensed glasses retained from his role in the 1967 movie *How I Won The War*) and outlandish and emphatically unmatching outfits: these were the new order of the day for The Beatles' appearance – and if the girls who had once swooned over their more conventional and cherubic looks weren't happy about it, too bad. The Beatles' decision to stand or fall on their music was helped immeasurably by the level of craftsmanship on this disc: the combination of quality on A- and B-sides make it possibly the greatest record ever made. No greater proof of The Beatles' breadth and depth could be provided than an artifact that boasted both one of the loveliest ballads ever recorded and a primal blast of dirty rock like no other.

There are three famous stories attached to "Hey Jude". The first is that Paul began writing it as "Hey Jules" when he was on his way up to see Cynthia Lennon after the news had broken that John was leaving her for Yoko Ono, "Jules" being his nickname for their son Julian, with whom Paul got on better than Lennon did in the days before John found his fatherly instincts with Sean. The story actually proves that McCartney – often portrayed as a sort of perfumed rattlesnake, outwardly avuncular but inwardly self-oriented – is essentially a considerate and compassionate individual. The second is that Ringo had nipped to the toilet when the tapes started rolling and only made it back to his kit in the nick of time to start his part. Which is eyebrow-raising because Ringo plays on the track like not a man who has just taken a pee but one who is dying to, those busy patterns putting one in mind of someone sitting with crossed legs, arms moving involuntarily manically as he prays for the session to end. Ballads are traditionally hard for drummers to play distinctively on, them fearful of spoiling the mood by bringing attention to their work, but Ringo pulls off that balancing act superbly here.

The third famous story is that John felt that Paul changed those dummy "Hey Jules" words into a subconscious message of goodwill to him and Yoko. Of course, when it comes to the subconscious it's impossible to know, but his belief is plausible. Either way, "Hey Jude" almost mathematically demonstrates just how far

The Beatles had come since "She Loves You", for the song is like a bookend to that number: both are compositions written in the second person in which a man tells a friend he should pursue the woman who is clearly destined to be the love of his life. Whereas "She Loves You" is giddy, though, "Hey Jude" is calm and reflective, as befitting the more advanced age of the writer.

Another difference created by the passage of five years between the records is that whereas "She Loves You" – whatever its air of newness at the time – essentially stuck to recognizable chart pop patterns, "Hey Jude" adheres to few known hit templates. Its lyric is often as opaque as that of "I Am The Walrus", its running time is a record of seven minutes and eleven seconds and its chanting coda is longer than the "proper" part of the song. Yet it became The Beatles' biggest-seller since (appropriately) "She Loves You". Nonetheless, while The Beatles may now have been in large part unrecognizable from the manufacturers of "She Loves You", two threads linking them to their earliest records – and helping maintain their perennial attraction – still existed: their unique stamp of humanity and those harmonies that somehow made you feel that they were your best friends. The former is evident right from the get-go – Paul's opening, quavering rendering of the title phrase is simply heart-breaking.

In fact, both sides of the single are shot through with the humanity that had made people love them in the first place: Paul's tenderness towards his friend on the A-side is no less considerate than John's concern about the innocent getting hurt in social protests on the flip, even though the aural assault of the B-side might initially disguise the fact. Almost all the quotes that exist from its author are concerned with the political impetus behind "Revolution" and his own ambivalence about aligning himself with civil disobedience. That and how he really wanted the original slow, acoustic version of "Revolution" to be an A-side before the suggestion was vetoed as too uncommercial by his colleagues and it was hived off to become "Revolution 1" on the White Album. What this all serves to distract attention from and prevent recognition of is the fact that "Revolution" is the greatest hard rock/heavy metal record ever made. Nothing has ever been louder or more gloriously distorted than this sonic blitzkrieg. You can actually hear the amplifiers into which the two fuzz-toned guitars are plugged distorting and coming perilously close to blowing. The brutality is added to by Ringo's cavernous bass drum sound. Yet the track is also tuneful, with a twisting, turning guitar lick and a fine melody. John's vocal is him at his scornful, nasal best as he enunciates a lyric of great directness and wit. His comment in response to being asked for a contribution to The Cause that, "We're all doing what we can," is genuinely funny. His switching to falsetto for the first line of the sections where he says things are going to be alright (effectively the chorus) shows the instinctive knack of a great singer for variation and shade. Somewhere in the middle of this maelstrom, famous session keyboardist Nicky Hopkins can be heard producing some boogie woogie piano. The gun blast of grimy guitar at the beginning of "Revolution" is one of the most exciting intros of any record.

"Revolution" is an early example of the form of heavy metal – so early and by such an influential act, that it helped define the form. Not that they were the first in this area: heaviosity was in the air that year, as bands took the principle of emphasizing rhythm and excitement over melody that was the defining attribute of rock 'n' roll to its logical conclusion. The Kinks' "You Really Got Me" came out in 1964 and may well be to metal what "Rocket 88" is to rock 'n' roll: a first entry in the form. The Jimmy Page-Jeff Beck line-up of The Yardbirds was approaching the pile-driving excess of metal in 1966. The Jimi Hendrix Experience provided the heaviest sounds yet heard in 1967 with "Purple Haze" and tracks like "Manic Depression" on *Are You Experienced*. Cream were approaching the same sound that year. However, 1968 was something of a watershed: Led Zeppelin were formed (their first album appeared in January '69), Iron Butterfly released their debut LP early in the year, August saw the emergence of Steppenwolf's first album and The Jeff Beck Group's *Truth*, and *Beggar's Banquet*, The Rolling Stones' album of December, included roaring cuts like "Sympathy For The Devil" and "Stray Cat Blues". But The Beatles – who two singles ago had been purveying the pretty, feather-light "Hello Goodbye" – out-heavied them all. And whereas most of the aforementioned acts made a career out of plumbing the genre, The Beatles moved on as soon as they had mastered it.

"Hey Jude" marked the end of what had been a slightly awkward period for the Beatles. A degree of disenchantment with them had rumbled through the press since Paul's LSD confession in June the previous year, and inevitably some of that disenchantment filtered through to the public (although it didn't stop them sending "Lady Madonna" to number one). With the release and overwhelming success of "Hey Jude", the LSD incident, the disappointment of *Magical Mystery Tour*, their semi-humiliating public distancing of themselves from the Maharishi, John's desertion of wife Cynthia for strange new love Yoko Ono and the fact that they had closed down their Apple Shop (a boutique) after a mere eight months of business were all washed away in the public's renewed appreciation of their brilliance. Additionally, the fact that an Apple single released at the same time – Mary Hopkin's "Those Were The Days", produced by Paul – also topped the charts helped renew their aura of musical leaders.

All of which was remarkable because, just as The Beatles' evolving image was reinventing the idea of what pop idols could look like, both sides of "Hey Jude" redefined what was possible in the hit parade. "Hey Jude" was quasi avant garde (which was another reason why Lennon – always a bit more musically adventurous than McCartney – loved it so much) but its titanic success made it by definition mainstream, which in turn gave permission for more daring from other acts. (We should, though, tip a hat in the direction of the Jimmy Webb-written epic Richard Harris summer 1968 hit "Macarthur Park", which "Hey Jude" – apparently pointedly – was precisely one second longer than.) You could make an argument that "Hey Jude" is a couple of minutes *too* long, but if you're of this opinion – and frankly this critic has never been able to listen to it without beginning to gaze out of the window well before the end of the "Na-Na-Nas" – you can always do what Paul recommended: ". . . the deejays can always fade it down if they want to – like a TV programme." Meanwhile, the B-side was slightly shocking for the fact that The Beatles, of all people, could make such an "ugly" sound and issue such an ostensibly harsh message.

The remainder of 1968 would see them continue the process of parading their pimples, both as people and in their art.

Chris Thomas On Recording The "White Album"

by John Tobler and Stuart Grundy

In 1968, Chris Thomas was a twenty-one-year-old at the beginning of his producing career when the chance of working with The Beatles on their latest album fell into his lap as a consequence of George Martin going on holiday. (A holiday, it has been suggested, that Martin abruptly chose to take because he was fed up with all the in-fighting at the sessions, but that's another story.) Thomas was working for Martin's Air London, the producing outfit he'd started a couple of years before, after going freelance. Thomas had applied for a job with him because he was "a loony fan of the Beatles". In this first extract from Tobler & Grundy's The Record Producers, *Thomas relates how a shy young novice made out with the biggest stars on the planet.*

The most significant record to which Chris contributed during this era was *The Beatles*, better known as The "White Album". "I did quite a lot of work on that when George [Martin] was away on holiday for a while, although it wouldn't be quite correct to call that my first production. What happened was that I came back from my holiday, and there was a note on my desk from George which said: 'Dear Chris, hope you had a nice holiday – I'm off on mine now. Make yourself available to The Beatles – Neil [Aspinall] and Mal [Evans] know you're coming down.' They'd been in there for three months by that time, and they'd done ten songs, starting in May, and now it was September. So I went down there, and it was very strange – I was sitting in the corner ready to throw up, so nervous with my suit and tie on, and Paul was the first one who came in. He obviously knew why I was there, but he said, 'What are you doing here then?' I thought, 'What the hell can I say to him?' I felt such an idiot sitting there, and I said, 'Didn't George tell you anything about this?' and he said, 'No,' which made me feel even worse. I said, 'Well, George asked me to come down to see if I can help you out,' and it seemed as though Paul was virtually questioning what I was saying, but he said, 'Oh well, if you want to produce us, you can produce us, but if you're no good, we'll just tell you to fuck off,' and he walked out. That was the encouragement, but it just destroyed me, and I couldn't speak after that.

"We started a track that day, and first of all, I just sat there and froze because I didn't know what to do, then at one point, they had a meeting – they used to have these sort of Apple meetings either at the beginning of a session, or halfway through, when they'd just be sitting on the floor for an hour and a half, talking about how they were running Apple and all the rest of it, so everybody else would turn the mikes off and go away and let them get on with it. At one point, I walked downstairs and I heard John say something about, 'He's not really doing his job, is he?' Now he could have been talking about an Apple employee. But I thought he was talking about me, because I'd been sitting there doing absolutely nothing all day. I thought, 'Right, that's it, I've got the sack, fine, that's all I wanted to know'. So I went back upstairs, and when they started recording again, I interrupted them halfway through a take. I pressed this buzzer that was like a klaxon in number two studio at Abbey Road, and said, 'Start again.' 'What do you mean, start again?' 'There was a mistake. Start again.' And they'd been doing this number for hours and hours and they went trooping up the stairs saying that there hadn't been a mistake. They listened to it, heard the mistake, walked back to the studio and carried on. I did take over a bit, simply because I thought I had nothing to lose, and I had about three hours left working there, so I'd do what I could. At the end of the day, I asked Paul if he wanted me to come back the next day, and he said, 'If you want,' and I was so glad it wasn't 'No,' and it started from there. I just got involved in a strange sort of way, and they actually involved me by telling me to play a piano part on one of the tracks, which was great fun."

The tracks from The "White Album" that Chris was involved in were: "Helter Skelter", "Glass Onion", "Happiness Is A Warm Gun", "Piggies" (on which he played harpsichord), "Savoy Truffle", "Long, Long, Long" – on both of which he played keyboards – "Bungalow Bill" and "Birthday".

The Beatles

Released: 22/11/1968

by Sean Egan

TRACKLISTING

Side one
1. "Back in the U.S.S.R."
2. "Dear Prudence"
3. "Glass Onion"
4. "Ob-La-Di, Ob-La-Da"
5. "Wild Honey Pie"
6. "The Continuing Story of Bungalow Bill"
7. "While My Guitar Gently Weeps"
8. "Happiness Is a Warm Gun"

Side two
1. "Martha My Dear"
2. "I'm So Tired"
3. "Blackbird"
4. "Piggies"
5. "Rocky Raccoon"
6. "Don't Pass Me By"
7. "Why Don't We Do It In The Road?"
8. "I Will"
9. "Julia"

Side three
1. "Birthday"
2. "Yer Blues"
3. "Mother Nature's Son"
4. "Everybody's Got Something to Hide Except Me and My Monkey"
5. "Sexy Sadie"
6. "Helter Skelter"
7. "Long, Long, Long"

Side four
1. "Revolution 1"
2. "Honey Pie"
3. "Savoy Truffle"
4. "Cry Baby Cry"
5. "Revolution 9"
6. "Good Night"

The jacket of *The Beatles* (instantly colloquially referred to as the "White Album" by the public) possessed a pure white gate-fold sleeve with no tracklisting on the back, a fake-stamped serial number and a title printed so discreetly as to be virtually Braille. It was the greatest contrast possible to the dazzling sleeve of *Pepper* . . . The public must have imagined that the album's contents were equally neat and decorous.

But the contents of The Beatles' eponymous ninth UK album were as sprawling, unordered and often impolite as the cover was simple and invitation-card correct. This was the record where the band finally broke free of any conventions and strictures, musical or sociological. The double-LP featured things that no Beatles record had ever contained. Though "Revolution" on the B-side of "Hey Jude" had conditioned the public to the fact that The Beatles could make music that was profoundly less than pretty (but still brilliant), nothing the band had done hitherto could have prepared their audience, musically, for the wall of noise of "Helter Skelter", the formless doodle of "Wild Honey Pie" or the lengthy avant garde sound collage "Revolution 9". And nothing could have prepared them spiritually for the emotional desolation of "Yer Blues", the irritableness of "I'm

So Tired", the smut of "Why Don't We Do It In The Road?" or the sheer venom of "Piggies". The Beatles were presenting themselves as they really were – people susceptible like all human beings to boredom, horniness, hatred, even suicidal depression – and the results were not necessarily pleasant to contemplate. They also must have been a bit of a shock to people still living in the emotional overhang of the Summer of Love and who thought that The Beatles' recent lengthy sojourn meditating in India had made them into more generous and temperate people. But at the same time that revelation of human flaw was liberating. The public were having reflected back at them their own reality when they were used to the media – with a few exceptions – giving them a chocolate-box, or at least a massively toned down, version of reality.

Having said that, the human flaws exposed in the lyrics were also manifested in the album's sessions in fractious and irritable behaviour that was often counter-productive to great art.

Many of the songs had been written in Rishikesh from February to April 1968. That these wealthy and pampered men were enduring the privations of camp life and a vegetarian diet as they humbly sought to find something in existence that even their money and privileges couldn't grant them made headlines all around the world, with some observing how it was all a long way from Lennon's Beatles-bigger-than-Jesus pronouncement. Also in the camp were The Beatles' wives/girlfriends, actress Mia Farrow and fellow pop stars Donovan and Beach Boy Mike Love. Ringo abandoned the quest for enlightenment after ten days and returned home with the droll explanation that it was just like Butlins, but in reality had found his temperamental stomach didn't agree with the food there. Paul departed after ten weeks. Harrison and Lennon (who had arrived first) came home in April; but would have stayed there longer had it not been for an incident in which the Maharishi was accused by Apple electronic wizard "Magic" Alex Mardas of coming on to a female in the camp and thus supposedly proving his elevated principles bogus.

John felt the album's songs' direction was influenced by the fact they were largely written on guitar, the only instruments to hand in Rishikesh. "They have a different feel about them," he said at the time. "I missed the piano a bit because you just write differently." The actual recordings were also different, although deliberately so. Paul said at the time of the album's release that the band didn't want to "go overboard" as they had on *Sgt. Pepper* . . . , adding, "And we've tried to play more like a band this time, only using instruments when we had to, instead of just using them for the fun of it."

Back in England at the end of May, The Beatles decided to make a preliminary recording of the songs they now had. The recording was done at Kinfauns, George's house in Surrey, on mostly acoustic instrumentation. The material that was released commercially began taking shape at Abbey Road studios on 30 May '68 and wasn't completed until 13 October. This was despite the fact that the sessions sometimes saw Beatles working separately in different studio rooms. There was a separateness about many of the songs as well, insofar as they were not Lennon/McCartney compositions but Lennon or McCartney compositions. As such, the album was a preview of post-Beatle work, and, as we now know, post-Beatle work was not always that great. The results of writing separately were grimly predictable: McCartney's songs often had all the melody in the word but lacked bite. John's had an emotional and intellectual depth absent in Paul's more whimsical exercises but were deficient melody-wise. Where once John and Paul had sought the other's valuable objective viewpoint on the songs they were developing, now each was presenting the other with a *fait accompli* and the opportunity to hone and improve was gone. To some extent, this method of writing would prevail throughout the rest of the band's career. When the band did engage in co-operation on this album, it was sometimes to worthless effect, i.e. jamming. Engineer Geoff Emerick was upset by the lack of fraternity and discipline and walked out on the sessions. George Martin temporarily did the same, suddenly going off on holiday. Ringo was also affected, partly because Paul was telling him how to play on "Back in the U.S.S.R.", and actually quit. After a week away, the sticksman was persuaded to come back but it was a harbinger of future discord that the most even-tempered Beatle had felt compelled to resign from the band.

Having said all that, none of these things would have been apparent if the group had released a single LP, for the best recordings here unquestionably befit the greatest recording artists of all time. By now, The Beatles were too powerful and too sure of their own talents to heed George Martin's advice to trim the fat and put out a single album of uniformly high quality. In fact, including material like "Wild Honey Pie" and "Revolution 9" suggests that quality, as such, was not their chief concern but rather indulging their artistic whims, whether the results be great or merely interesting – although such was their penchant for experimentalism and their hubris at this juncture that it's not guaranteed that they always understood which was which. (A second theory is that the band were trying to fulfil their contract with EMI more quickly with a double set.) Despite unloading a massive load of songs on the public, The Beatles didn't release any of them as a single.

The songs on the album fall into four categories, as detailed below:

EPHEMERA, DOODLES, SKETCHES AND RUBBISH

"Wild Honey Pie"

A discordant scrap of less than one minute of no artistic worth consisting of the words "Honey pie" and – climatically – "I love you" which bears no apparent relation to the other "Honey Pie" later on in the album. McCartney subsequently explained that it was an improvization, later embellished.

"The Continuing Story Of Bungalow Bill"

A Lennon composition about an American he met in Rishikesh who would alternate his search for enlightenment with tiger hunting. John himself described this as "a sort of teenage social comment song", presumably referring to the outraged simplicity of the lyric, but the melody is also one-dimensional, and you can't help feeling that if he and McCartney had been co-operating more on composition, Paul would have added a bridge that would have made all the difference.

"Don't Pass Me By"

Ringo's first sole songwriting credit. None of us begrudge him the royalties and its awfulness is as endearing as he is, but it truly is terrible, with a pedestrian melody, irritating instrumentation (monotonous piano and grating violin) and risible lyric (a man is upset at the lateness of his girlfriend and then remorseful when he finds out she has been in a car crash – and lost all her hair). The only good thing about this track is that it led to a priceless comment from John, who said Ringo ". . . composed it himself in a fit of lethargy."

"Revolution 1"

Considering that "Revolution" actually began life in this acoustic version, there seems no reason why this shouldn't constitute a perfectly enjoyable and intriguing alternate to the song's hard rock incarnation that we know and love from the B-side of "Hey Jude", but it's inexplicably boring. Meanwhile, its "Count me out/in" line may be John's honest attempt to reflect his ambivalence about violent uprising but it undermines the B-side version's worthwhile denunciation of irresponsible West-based revolutionists who were too enthusiastic about bathing the world in blood.

"Can You Take Me Back Where I Come From?"

A fragment of an unfinished McCartney song unlisted on the sleeve but tagged onto the end of "Cry Baby Cry". Essentially consisting of not much more than that line to acoustic backing, it's stupid and precious, both in nature and in the fact that McCartney couldn't be arsed to finish it but is still tickled enough about to present it to us for our listening "pleasure".

"Revolution 9"

Nominally related to the two other songs called "Revolution" bearing The Beatles' name (buried in its cacophony is what was originally the seven-minute fade-out of the version heard earlier on this album), "Revolution 9" is an unapologetic avant garde collage of disconnected sounds, the kind of which would have been impossible on any previous Beatles record, not just because of the extra space on a double album but because this is the first Beatles album recorded on eight-track. It feels like a recording of someone disinterestedly turning a dial on a radio and picking up snatches of music or speech before idly moving on to the next station. Lacking any apparent pattern – the only noticeable motif is a man with received pronunciation saying the words "Number nine" – it becomes random, at which point it ceases to be art. This goes on for nearly eight-and-a-half-minutes.

One wonders why Lennon didn't save this track for release on *Two Virgins*, the similarly avant garde and unmusical solo album he released a week after the White Album, especially as he admitted there was a lot of input into this cut from Yoko. It's not a Beatles track in any way shape or form. It was reasonably common knowledge now that "Lennon/ McCartney" was as much a gentleman's agreement as a reality but that publishing credit being applied to this piece was absurd.

FAILED EXPERIMENTS

"While My Guitar Gently Weeps"

One feels that one should like this evocatively titled Harrison rumination. It's got a nice melody, a good lyric (even if George is once again piously remarking on the shortcomings of the spiritually unenlightened), is well sung, boasts some wonderful rippling piano work from Paul and features a solo from one of the world's most celebrated guitars, Eric Clapton. Yet it's clunky, and Clapton's solo is unimpressive. The fact that this is a good song given the wrong arrangement is proven by the mellifluous, stark demo version released on *Anthology 3*.

"Helter Skelter"

Paul has said he wrote this track because he had heard Pete Townshend describe a Who song (thought to be "I Can See For Miles") as an attempt to come up with the dirtiest, loudest recording he could possibly muster. All power to that idea, but this frantic, rocking paean to riding down what Americans know as a spiral slide features what must be the only instance of terrible bass playing by Paul on record, and it detracts from the great harmonies, the blister-inducing drumming, the growling guitars and Paul's inspired vocal.

MATERIAL THAT IS QUITE ENJOYABLE BUT WHICH IN YOUR HEART OF HEARTS YOU KNOW IS NOT QUITE GOOD ENOUGH TO MERIT SPACE ON A BEATLES ALBUM IN NORMAL CIRCUMSTANCES

"Dear Prudence"
A John song that started life as an attempt to coax a reclusive Prudence Farrow – sister of actress Mia – out of her dwellings in Rishikesh. It has some good qualities, including thrumming bass and some freak-out drumming from Paul (on one of two tracks on which he played in Ringo's absence), but there's no escaping the fact that the tune is unremarkable.

"Blackbird"
Some have disputed Paul's claim that this song was partly based on black rights activist Angela Davis on the grounds that the chronology seems to prove his memory awry but if it is true, then it means that Davis has inspired two songs by rock giants, for the Rolling Stones' 1972 track "Sweet Black Angel" was written about her travails. The Stones' track is easily the superior, its cascading acoustic riff exposing Paul's solo acoustic work here as unexciting. The lyric meanwhile strives for a meaningfulness that is circumscribed by its vagueness.

"Piggies"
Since the death of Brian Epstein, The Beatles had become more and more politically outspoken. Before their manager's steadying (or suffocating, depending on your point of view) hand was lifted, the Fabs had restricted their political utterances to stating they thought the Vietnam War was wrong and criticizing the high level of taxation they were paying. Though it occurred before Epstein's death, John's remark about The Beatles being more popular than Christ was without question a political

statement – perhaps the most sensational that could possibly be made – but it was slightly spoiled by the fact that John withdrew it (sort of). In the post-Epstein era, apologizing for such a remark was increasingly becoming unthinkable, although it should also be acknowledged that The Beatles were responding to the climate of the time: who, come 1968, was not speaking their mind? In responding to this climate, they were also of course – by dint of their massive influence on the young – helping set it. "Piggies" is George Harrison's foray into political statement, a broadside against privilege which laments the sight of piggies living piggie lives and eating bacon when out to dinner with their piggie wives. The bile is impressive and the harpsichord pleasant but the message is inchoate and the tune merely a pleasant diversion.

"Rocky Raccoon"

This song contains the best line Paul ever wrote – "I'll be better, Doc, as soon as I am able" – but this Western populated by such people as the title character and a girl called McGill who called herself Lil though is known to everyone as Nancy is mere meandering whimsy. Though there's nothing inherently wrong with an empty song that goes nowhere, it has to be more scenic than this to make the circular journey feel worthwhile.

"Julia"

The knowledge that we have of John's titular beloved, prematurely deceased mother makes this song moving on a superficial level, but if we came to this "cold" – with Julia meaning nothing to us except as the name of the girl in the song – we would consider it a pretty-ish but flimsy acoustic noodle.

"Sexy Sadie"

It's just as well that what started as John's scathing kiss-off to the Maharishi had its lyric changed, considering the disputed facts that have emerged about the incident that led to Lennon and Harrison leaving Rishikesh: some witnesses have claimed the charges against the Maharishi were false and motivated by jealously on the part of Magic Alex. Unfortunately, that alteration makes for a less interesting song. There is some nicely treated McCartney piano and some of Lennon's barbed lyric has a power even in light of the transposed target but we are really left with a track that is just a vague complaint to and about the fictional titular female. (The mildly shocking fact of the word "Sexy" in a Beatles song title, incidentally, was another confirmation of the move away from their cute image.)

"Savoy Truffle"

A paean from Harrison to the glories of eating from a box of chocolate assortments whose chorus lists the individual flavours is the very definition of whimsy and the elaborate manner in which the song is dressed up – including a sweeping brass line and a dense rhythm section – can't disguise or compensate for that fact, even though it's not at all disagreeable.

"Cry Baby Cry"
"Good Night"

Two lullabies written by John, the first a quiet, fairy-tale-like song featuring kings, queens and duchesses, the second a lush affair with a Disney-esque orchestral arrangement given to Ringo to sing. Both are spiritually quite sweet, but musically mediocre.

THE VERY GOOD-TO-CLASSIC

"Back in the U.S.S.R."

Though this opening track proves that the jury is still out on whether McCartney was in order to tell Ringo how to play at these sessions – his drumming here is as flat and clumsy as it is imaginative on "Dear Prudence" – the song is a corker, a hard-rocking and hilarious romp in which Paul improbably suggests that a citizen of one of the grey states behind the Iron Curtain would celebrate its way of life the way that Chuck Berry did that of the States in "Back In The USA" and its females the way The Beach Boys did US womanhood in "California Girls".

"Glass Onion"

A track with the last vestiges of The Beatles' classicalism-drenched baroque period is employed to make fun of and string along those who read strange meanings into Beatles songs. (Its impetus was a letter from a schoolboy telling Lennon that his class teacher had analysed the words of "I Am The Walrus".) It's good fun, though Ringo's menacing drum track and Lennon's intense vocal make it of a dark kind.

"Ob-La-Di, Ob-La-Da"

This jolly ska number has attracted ridicule from many quarters, joining "Michelle" as a yardstick of Paul's alleged insubstantiality. Those who mock it simply don't understand The Beatles *per se*, for little sums up the qualities of the Fab Four as this breathless, sunny, good-natured and very tuneful tale of a market trader and a singer who fall in love. John provides a surprisingly adroit – for him – pumping piano and Paul's vocal has exactly the right amount of *joie de vivre*. Not for nothing did Marmalade score a UK number one with this luvverly composition.

"Happiness Is A Warm Gun"

A stunning concoction and possibly the best track on the album. A swing through more musical styles and tempos than anyone ever thought could be crammed into a song lasting less than three minutes sees John produce a parade of grotesqueries and perplexing but pleasing non sequiturs before the enunciation of that unforgettable, lamentable title phrase, which comes not from Lennon's surrealist brain but a real-life magazine advertisement. Lennon sings gloriously, especially in the misleadingly lovely opening bars and the operatic climax.

"Martha My Dear"

The first of a couple of tracks on the album in which Paul shows his facility with pastiches of 1930s pop, whether it be by the jolly era-correct brass arrangements or spot-on period phrases like "Though I spend my days in conversation". Delicious.

"I'm So Tired"

And in complete contrast, a scream of frustration from John, who was missing Yoko in Rishikesh and couldn't tell anyone about it, as he was still married. He shows the mark of a true artist by harnessing that wild rage to produce a melodic hard rock arrangement, a funny lyric (Sir Walter Raleigh was a "stupid get" for discovering the tobacco that John alleviates his frustration by partaking of) and a singing performance that gets incrementally more desperate.

"Why Don't We Do It In The Road?"

Made by Paul with Ringo in a separate studio room while Lennon and Harrison were otherwise occupied, to the later publicly-aired hurt of John. It being the case that the song has minimal backing and lyrically consists merely of the title phrase and the reassurance "No one will be watching us", this little ditty is the epitome of self-indulgence, but the track itself is a textbook example of how to make a pointless ride sufficiently interesting as to ensure the listener is glad he has been taken on it. Paul screams the words with increasingly greater hysteria until it ultimately becomes hilarious and the track is sufficiently short that it doesn't run the risk of trying to make too much of its irrefutable but slender charms.

"I Will"

If "Why Don't We Do It In The Road?" is – as Paul has pointed out – a McCartney song that sounds like one of Lennon's, there's little mistaking the imprimatur on "I Will". Though John was capable of this kind of tenderness, only Paul would offer almost generic lines about loving someone "forever and forever" and loving them with all his heart, and only he could really get away with them courtesy of his incredible knack for a lovely tune.

"Birthday"

Great hard rock very often relies on nothing but a good guitar riff and a compelling (even nonsensical) lyrical motif. So it is the case with the rip-roaring "Birthday", one of several tracks on the album which proves, in the wake of *Sgt. Pepper* . . . and *Magical Mystery Tour*, that The Beatles were still the great, raw rock 'n' roll band they had been back in Hamburg. It also proves that improvization could yield far better results than "Wild Honey Pie": the band roughed out a simple sketch for the backing track because they wanted to bomb it over to Paul's house to watch the Little Richard movie *The Girl Can't Help It!* They added the lyric after they'd seen the movie. The delightfully apropos of nothing choral decoration may be where The Stones got the idea to embellish "You Can't Always Get What You Want" with a choir the following year.

"Yer Blues"

One is sorely tempted to put this in the Noble Failure category because it has a sloppiness that by definition was absent from the greatest Beatles music. However, if this would be the worst track on this author's fantasy single White Album, it's a hell of a far cry from the likes of other albums' makeweights like "Dizzy Miss Lizzy" or "What Goes On". The only blues released by The Beatles in their lifetime, (the "yer" is a self-deprecating English Northern expression), it's a sibling of "I'm So Tired" in being an outpouring of misery from Lennon over his separation from Yoko. If the repetitive structure of the blues isn't done any favours by the band's slightly ramshackle playing, one can't claim that the subject matter isn't compelling: "I'm lonely, wanna die" is a lapel-grabber of an opening line if ever there was one.

"Mother Nature's Son"

Written by Paul after a lecture by the Maharishi about the joys of communion with nature. Though Paul has explained that the horns are a sonic reference to the brass bands that once proliferated in English Northern rural towns, this clash of the rustic and the industrial still strikes a jarring note. However, we can forgive this because of an exquisite melody and tremulous singing.

"Everybody's Got Something To Hide Except Me And My Monkey"

Another song inspired by the emergence of Ono into Lennon's life, this one rejoiceful. The only bad point is some occasional contrived whooping, as though we need somebody to point out to us that this is a hard rock recording so exciting as to almost be excruciating.

"Long, Long, Long"

A moving and almost spooky song by George, which he cleverly makes feel like a love song when he has himself admitted it's a tribute to God. If it sometimes feels more like a song's middle section than a song itself (though it does have its own bridge), the quiet passion, Paul's spectral organ and Ringo's tension-building drums (John doesn't appear) more than compensates. It ends with a wonderful shivering sound effect.

"Honey Pie"

Another example of what Lennon disparagingly referred to as "Granny music" and which Paul, its composer, called "fruity old songs". It's great fun, with Paul's voice given at one point a scratchy effect as though we are hearing it on an old 78 rpm vinyl record that someone has rescued from an attic. The 1920s/30s ambience is continued on a song in which Paul adopts the absurdly posh voice considered *de rigueur* on British pop songs of that vintage to relate the tale of a working girl who crosses the Atlantic to find the big time and leaves a distraught lover in her wake. The authenticity is flawless. In recreating the music of the era concerned, McCartney reaches the heights of the very best writers of that era, not the average ones. Some might dismiss the ability for perfect pastiche on the grounds that they don't like the type of music being pastiched, but such ability comes pretty close to genius. Despite his contempt, Lennon plays an unusually fine solo, which George later compared to Django Reinhardt.

This writer finds it interesting that his list of the very good-to-great material happens to constitute fourteen tracks (The Beatles' policy pre-*Pepper* had been to include that number of tracks on their albums, seven per side) and that the running time of this fantasy White Album would amount to thirty-six-and-a-half minutes, around about standard for a single vinyl LP. To which Paul's response (probably representative of his colleagues) would no doubt be what he said to the a-single-album-would-have-been-better brigade in *Anthology*: "It's The Beatles' White Album – shut up!"

Yellow Submarine

Released: 17/01/1969

by Sean Egan

TRACKLISTING

Side one
1. "Yellow Submarine"
2. "Only a Northern Song"
3. "All Together Now"
4. "Hey Bulldog"
5. "It's All Too Much"
6. "All You Need Is Love"

Side two
1. "Pepperland"
2. "Pepperland"
3. "Sea Of Time"
4. "Sea Of Holes"
5. "Sea Of Monsters"
6. "March Of The Meanies"
7. "Pepperland Laid Waste"
8. "Yellow Submarine in Pepperland"

The soundtrack to the third Beatles movie is the bastard of The Beatles' album catalogue. Half of it isn't even comprised of Beatles music at all, two of the tracks of Beatles origination had been previously released, three of the four new Beatles tracks were discards considered too insubstantial for a "real" Beatles LP and the sleevenotes by Derek Taylor championed not the current album but the White Album by lazily reproducing an *Observer* rave review. That George Harrison gets as many songs on the record as Lennon/McCartney is a yardstick for how disinterested the band were in a project for which they were contractually obliged to provide at least three original songs. ("Baby You're A Rich Man" had been intended for the project but was used on the B-side of "All You Need Is Love" instead.) That one of those Harrison tracks was dismissively titled "Only A Northern Song" (a reference to the group's song publishing company) indicates that Harrison himself was not exactly overwhelmed by his unprecedented equality nor with his own composition. The album appeared on Parlophone, rather than The Beatles' new Apple label. In what feels like a final gesture of contempt, the album was not even released until six months after the film hit the cinemas because The Beatles didn't want it to detract from sales of the White Album. The album seemed no less mercenary than the avalanche of licensed *Yellow Submarine* merchandise – including toys, figurines and books – that appeared on the market to coincide with the film.

It would have made a lot more sense to release an EP of the new songs to accompany the film, *a la Magical Mystery Tour*. However, Brian Epstein had agreed a contract with George Martin whereby he would receive equal billing on a Beatles album as a thank-you for all he'd done for the group, thus restricting the group's room for manoeuvre. The group did in fact prepare a *Yellow Submarine* double EP in Spring 1969 with the then-unreleased "Across The Universe" included as a bonus, but it was never released, possibly because they realized those who had already shelled out for the album would be upset.

So how bad is *Yellow Submarine*? Well as a listening experience, it's not that disgraceful at all. To run the risk of repetition, this *is* The Beatles we are talking about. The title track (whose omission would have been a bit strange) and "All You Need Is Love" are quality songs. It should be noted that the "All You Need Is Love" included here is markedly different to the single. The latter was in mono, this is stereo.

George Martin's incidental music on side two is actually rather good, as one would expect of a classically trained musician whose professional experience meant he understood both classical and popular idioms. It may be only tangentially connected to The Beatles, but anyone weaned on the Fab Four's melodic sense couldn't possibly resist his sweeping "Pepperland" and his raga-Disney hybrid "Sea of Time".

George's "Only A Northern Song" may have been composed in a mood of bitterness – he wrote it to fulfil his contractual obligation to the publishing company Northern Songs, which he was anxious to get away from because of what he felt was the low level of remuneration it brought him – but it's actually a pretty cool, post-modern and funny track. He doesn't mention his unhappiness with the finances but does suggest to the listener that any deficiency in the sound is not due to them but to the inefficiency of him and his colleagues. In one extraordinary segment, he talks of being out of key in a section that indeed does seem to have veered off-tune. Despite the couldn't-give-a-shit ambience, the track is actually quite rich and features some pleasantly demented trumpet work.

"It's All Too Much", Harrison's other song herein, is a lengthy track (6:23) that has its adherents as a psychedelic freak-out but for this listener is a featureless affair that comes perilously close to being as interminable as "Blue Jay Way". It's somewhat unwise for George to sing a snatch – for no apparent reason – of The Merseys' hit "Sorrow", because when he does one can't help thinking that one would much rather be listening to that.

McCartney's "All Together Now" demonstrates Paul's philosophy of "If in doubt, resort to a refrain of 'I love you'" (a policy he later parodied on Wing's "Silly Love Songs"). Its mild hands-across-the-water feel has led some to speculate that this was the song Paul was working on for the *One World* global broadcast until John trumped him with something even more giddily fraternal. It's so slight that it feels like a children's song but it's sweet enough and its countdown components and chant-like qualities led to it being sung on British soccer terraces for a few seasons.

John's "Hey Bulldog" is the only really substantial new song, and it's a corker. Boasting an undulating piano riff from Lennon, a fine, dark melody, a menacing atmosphere, a memorable chorus in which John insists to someone they can talk to him if they're lonely, and a changing verse line that is even hookier than the chorus (e.g., "Some kind of innocence is measured out in years"), it is up there with the best Beatles tracks of the period. John later claimed that its lyric is meaningless, but the picture he paints in verse two of a man who no one understands bearing a grudge toward society and the means to exercise that grudge (child-like/jack-knife/sweaty hands) is chilling. "Hey Bulldog", incidentally, did not originally feature in the prints of the movie distributed in the USA.

The *Yellow Submarine* album was released to a less than expectant public. Those who did shell out for it were not as great in number as for other Beatles LPs. Though it went into the top three, excepting *A Collection Of Beatles Oldies* . . . , this was the only Beatles album released while the band were extant not to top the UK charts. But by the time of its release, the band were known to have embarked on another movie project, and the sense of vitality around the group was in no way diminished.

"Get Back" b/w "Don't Let Me Down"

Released: 11/04/1969

by Sean Egan

On 22 January 1969, The Beatles started making an album that was intended to get them back to where they had been when making the *Please Please Me* LP: a rock 'n' roll band banging out their material and committing it to tape without overdubs. Ringo has said that the White Album was his favourite Beatles recording experience because the group had played as a band – rather than recording piecemeal – on so many of the sessions. It's this logic that was partly the motivation for the decision to rehearse for a new album (originally to be called *Get Back*) that would be recorded at a live gig, with London's Roundhouse initially pencilled in as the venue. There would be a TV documentary of the band rehearsing the new songs and a film of the concert. This would be the first-ever Beatles live album, and of course a rather unusual one. George Martin was very enthused by this idea of an LP of unheard material recorded live. (By a quirk of fate, American proto-punks The MC5 had had the same idea and February '69 would see the release of their debut, *Kick Out The Jams*, an in-concert recording.)

Though there were certainly no plans to go back to touring, the news of a live gig would have been exciting to Beatles fans. The Fabs hadn't performed to a paying public for close to two-and-a-half years. They weren't completely unusual anymore: drug busts and internal problems meant that The Rolling Stones had played one gig since April 1967, while Bob Dylan was more concerned with raising a family than picking up the thread of the touring life he had abandoned in 1966. Nonetheless, that the Fab Four were talking of reviving Beatlemania even for just one night was a notable piece of news.

However, the decision to film this process necessitated the band working in a film studio in Twickenham in union-dictated social hours, which rock 'n' roll bands of The Beatles' stature are not used to or comfortable with. George Harrison walked out on these sessions. While his statement to his colleagues that he was leaving the group permanently was no doubt heartfelt, it lasted as long as Ringo's resignation had at the White Album sessions and he returned on condition that the idea of a concert (which had now become a Tripoli appearance after having gone through a period when a Roman amphitheatre was mooted) be abandoned and the recording be relocated to the studio in the basement of the Apple headquarters in Savile Row. It has long been the assumption that Harrison (who didn't need much provocation to be grumpy anyway) walked because of what he felt to be McCartney's insufferable bossiness but more recent suggestions have been made that in fact George was infuriated by the fact that Lennon seemed more interested in his wife than the band. A fistfight is said to have erupted between Harrison and Lennon. Also a source of grievance for George was the way his songs continued to be overlooked or discarded after a few run-throughs.

Lennon later characterized the album's recording as "the most miserable session on earth". While that may be accurate, he seemed oblivious to his own part in this process. Compounding the taboo that Lennon had broken by bringing Yoko into the White Album sessions when outsiders had always been banned from Beatles' recordings, Lennon was constantly in the company of Yoko again and on one occasion failed to attend a band meeting. Ono proceeded to endear herself to the group by making detrimental pronouncements on their music and by speaking on behalf of John at meetings, albeit with the increasingly withdrawn Lennon's permission. The sessions didn't get too much better at Savile Row. Recording live means that everything – vocal, instrumentation, vibe – has to be optimum all at the same time: a fluffed vocal line or bum note can't be fixed afterwards if you have made up your mind, as The Beatles had, that overdubs would be cheating. This resulted in the band having to perform take after take after take, which tedium rather works against the principle of rediscovering the joys of rawness and spontaneity.

Then there was the problem of material. The Beatles were embarking on another album project only three months after having exhausted their well of material with a double album. The group had always been superb at writing fast and making great recordings at short notice but the dynamic of the band had changed since they'd jumped off the two-albums-per-year treadmill that had forced them to be so inspired. Lennon and McCartney were no longer writing together, with the inevitable increase in the time it took each to write songs. Additionally, while the quality of Paul's songs seemed undiminished as a result of this process, in John's case the writing seemed to suffer from the lack of outside input: apart from "Don't Let Me Down" he certainly came up with no classics at this juncture.

Little of this, of course, filtered through to the general public at the time. The first publicly released fruits of the *Get Back* sessions in the form of this title theme, as it were, gave the public nothing but hope for it.

The song originated in a wry McCartney take on the anti-immigration feeling prevalent in Britain at the time. Fearing, however, that the public would think that he was endorsing the

"Get back" views of TV comedy show bigot Alf Garnett rather than mocking them, Paul changed the words so that the song became an uptempo cousin of the White Album's "Rocky Raccoon" in its whimsical Americana.

As if not content with being a great songwriter and an excellent singer (and indeed a fine harmonica player), John Lennon laboured under the delusion that he was a hot guitarist ("Ask Eric Clapton, he thinks I can play, ask him" he anxiously told *Rolling Stone* in 1971). However, in elbowing Harrison aside on this record in pursuit of his deluded belief that he could play lead, he inadvertently did the track a favour, for George's rhythm guitar on "Get Back" is sublime, keeping it simply skimming along. Also making for a nice, slinky groove is Ringo's clipped, brisk drumming and the percolating electric piano of Billy Preston, an old friend from Hamburg days who had been brought in by George because when Clapton appeared on the White Album Harrison had noticed how well the usually fractious "household" behaved when they had a guest in. Lennon's lead guitar lines, by contrast, are watery and unimpressive, weakening the track slightly. Meanwhile, Paul strains for some of the notes, making one wish a little that the band had persevered with an abandoned Lennon vocal take that resides on bootlegs.

The label of this record credited it to "The Beatles with Billy Preston". Though the presence of an outside musician might be regarded as weakening the notion of The Beatles playing together without embellishment, the Texas-born keyboardist played wonderfully and certainly deserved his unprecedented, for a Beatles record, equal billing. This especially applies to the B-side. "Don't Let Me Down" is one of the many songs John, in the first flush of his relationship with Yoko Ono, wrote about her. Whatever one's feelings about Ono – and many Beatles fans of the time were showing considerable hostility to her – it can't be denied that she was a good muse. "Don't Let Me Down" is a thing of sumptuous beauty and tenderness with a perfect melody, heart-breakingly sweet lyric and *simpatico* gentle instrumentation. Amongst the most impressive things about the recording is that despite the no-overdubs rule, "Don't Let Me Down" sounds almost impossibly slick. From its beautiful opening descending chord to the naked disbelieving passion of the way Lennon sings – or more accurately yells – the title phrase, to the way George's flecks of lead guitar sound like bluebirds fluttering over dew-kissed grass, to the way Paul movingly joins in with his friend on the choruses, to the way Paul throws in endlessly interesting, quicksilver bass patterns, to the way Billy Preston helps bring the song to a soft, sweet close via some gorgeous tickling of the electric ivories, The Beatles manage to give us a taste of the bliss John is euphorically asserting he has found with his new woman. That the track has a mere three chords and the lyric sometimes strays towards gibberish ("I guess nobody ever really done me . . ."), simply goes to show that making a great record can be as much about great performance as great material.

Though *Top Of The Pops* ran a clip of The Beatles performing "Get Back" on the Apple rooftop in the famous impromptu concert of 30 January 1969 and though John in promotional interviews at the time suggested the version of "Don't Let Me Down" might have been recorded on the rooftop (he wasn't sure), in fact both sides of the single were studio recordings. The headline of the advert for the record stated, "THE BEATLES AS NATURE INTENDED".

"The Ballad Of John And Yoko"
b/w "Old Brown Shoe"

Released: 30/05/1969

by Sean Egan

On 20 March 1969, John Lennon and Yoko Ono were married. The Beatles' single "The Ballad Of John And Yoko" was a song about the tribulations the couple had faced in trying to do this and the ridicule that came their way over their subsequent public stunt for peace whereby they spent their honeymoon holding court in their pyjamas to the world's press at the Amsterdam Hilton.

It was a song torn from the day's newspapers, so stuffed full of topical references as to seem the last thing that, even a year hence, anybody would understand and therefore be listening to. Not only that, but the indignation of the lyric was absurd. The Lennon's tribulations were rather minor, and mostly their own fault, due to trying to travel to France without passports and chartering a private jet to get wed in Gibraltar after finding out that the British protectorate wouldn't have the temerity to demand to see passports. Meanwhile, though well-intentioned, the Bed-In for peace (as they styled it) was preposterous (as though governments were going to announce the cessation of wars as a consequence) and involved the issuing pearls of wisdom like, "We must bury our own monsters and stop condemning people. We are all Christ and all Hitler."

Lennon could have elected to put this song out on Apple's adjunct label for experimental music Zapple, as he had his and

Yoko's *Unfinished Music No. 2 – Life With The Lions* earlier in the month. He could also have elected to put it out under his own name. Indeed, five weeks after the release of ". . . Ballad . . .", he issued "Give Peace A Chance" – which also addressed public reaction to his and Yoko's public stunts for peace – under the sobriquet the Plastic Ono Band. Yet Lennon decided to use The Beatles' trading name for "The Ballad Of John And Yoko", perhaps because he knew it would sell far more if attached to their name, or perhaps because even at this juncture in time he still viewed the band as his primary artistic outlet.

When John came round to his house and told him of his new creation, Paul could have been forgiven for being hesitant. Not just because of the tension that existed between him and John because of the irritable *Get Back* sessions and the fact that they were now on opposite sides of a dispute revolving around the retention of Allen Klein as Beatles manager (John, George and Ringo wanted the brash, no-nonsense American who was currently busy cleaning up Apple by firing everyone in sight, Paul preferred Linda's father, attorney Lee Eastman). The new song's refrain was "Christ you know it ain't easy" and featured another line in which Lennon claimed that the world wanted to crucify him. It was only three years previously that "God Only Knows" by The Beach Boys had achieved a landmark by being the first hit record with the deity's name in the title. This song however was a totally different proposition. Although people used Christ's name as an epithet in their everyday lives, it was then so rarely heard on television and so unprecedented in chart records as to be shocking. Meanwhile, one didn't have to feel particularly religious to find repugnant the self-aggrandisement of Lennon comparing himself to a man dying in agony in a crucifixion simply because he'd not been waved through French customs like a potentate and had been mocked by a few newspapers. The song actually marked a period in which Lennon became increasingly pompous and egotistical, as illustrated by his solemn announcement at an Apple board meeting that he was the reincarnation of Jesus and culminating in his infamous 1971 *Rolling Stone* interview that saw him falsely assert that he and McCartney had stopped writing together in 1962. For somebody who had recently found the love of his life, he seemed a somewhat disgruntled individual.

However, McCartney turned out to be game ("John was in an impatient mood so I was happy to help") and the two went across the road to the Abbey Road studios to commit the creation to tape. On Paul's part, perhaps he felt a certain solidarity with his old friend over their recent marriages. He had wed Linda Eastman at a London registry office just ten days before Lennon and Ono had pledged their vows: the public had not taken to either bride. Eastman was hated by Beatles fans almost as much as Ono. In both bride's cases, the shattered delusions of the young women who imagined they still stood a chance if their favourite Beatle was single was compounded by their bewilderment that, literally able to have any women in the world they wanted, Paul and John chose the supposedly charmless and unattractive creatures they did. This dislike wasn't restricted to deluded fans. People as varied as Keith Richards' bodyguard and drug procurer Tony Sanchez and strait-laced Beatles aide Alistair Taylor have recorded with horror Linda accusing them on the basis of no evidence whatsoever of being out to swindle Paul not long after she hooked up with McCartney. Similar outraged comments have been directed at Yoko, who has been accused in the early part of her relationship with John, by people whose word is considered reliable, of yanking the hair of car drivers if she felt they were going the wrong way and imperiously threatening to have people sacked for complaining about her daughter Kyoto pulling the plugs out of the Apple offices switchboard.

Ringo was away, filming *The Magic Christian*, and George on holiday, so it would only be the two of them on the track. Paul handled bass, drums, piano and maracas and John the guitar parts and lead vocals. The pubic were *au fait* with the fact of this record boasting only half the Beatles (albeit the most important half) as it was announced at the time. Said public probably didn't have any problem with that but must have groaned with contempt and disbelief when they heard that the new Beatles single was to be called "The Ballad Of John And Yoko". Having helped Lennon repeatedly make a fool of himself, Ono was now contaminating Beatles product? Yet the record – released less than seven weeks after the previous Beatles single, testament to its newspaper-like status – went to number one in the UK (and stayed there a fortnight) and even made number eight in America despite a broadcasting ban in some areas over the "Christ" epithet and crucifixion reference, which was a red rag to a bull for those sections of America who still hadn't forgiven Lennon for the Maureen Cleave bigger-than-Jesus interview. Ostensibly more surprising is that, despite its topicality and hence its potential impermanence, the record is still listened to and enjoyed four decades on. This is a testament to its power. It takes a lot to make people be prepared to listen to you compare yourself to Christ, even if the combination of Lennon's brown hair being currently to his shoulders and his sporting a full beard did disconcertingly make him visually resemble the Messiah. But Lennon, with McCartney's able help, pulls it off, courtesy of chutzpah and craft.

Despite the ultra-modern sacrilege and the fact of it being the first Beatles single mixed in stereo, the track is actually quite retro, a Fifties-style rockabilly number at bottom (so much so that it ends with a guitar flourish that's a direct quote from Johnny Burnette's "Lonesome Tears In My Eyes"), with the electric guitar riff John plays over his own acoustic rhythm part quite generic in nature. Paul's drumming is merely serviceable and his high-pitched vocals on the last verse probably the first time ever that harmonies weakened a Beatles track. However, the track has a raw power, a good structure and the benefit of a lead singer who actually believes in the preposterous claims of persecution in the lyric, which allows him to render it with impressive – even infectious – fury.

George gets another B-side in the shape of "Old Brown Shoe". Like the A-side, it's not technically The Beatles in that Lennon plays no instrument in a period where he would find a reason to be absent when The Beatles were recording songs written by Harrison. However, unlike the A-side – brilliant but betraying its skeleton crew in its quasi-ramshackle sound – nobody would know the group was undermanned from the flip's sound, which is wonderfully slick, befitting one of Harrison's greatest ever compositions. It's a spiritual song addressing the usual Harrison concerns of suppressing the ego, but is dressed up like a love song in much the same way as The Who's "Bargain" can either be viewed as Pete Townshend's tribute to

Mehr Baba or a message of devotion to a lover. The structure shows that the awkward period Lennon had spoken of, where space was having to be made on Beatles albums for Harrison songs that they were too polite to point out weren't up to snuff, was now over. (As does the fact that George demoed "Old Brown Shoe" on the same day as he demoed two other soon-to-be classics, "Something" and "All Things Must Pass".) Here Harrison shows all the hallmarks of having had the best apprenticeship any rock songwriter could have in working alongside and observing the modus operandi of Lennon and McCartney. It wouldn't even be right to say that the verse-chorus-verse-chorus-bridge design is textbook, because Harrison goes one further, altering the second and fourth lines of the chorus and thereby making the song correspondingly more interesting. The way the bridge gallops into an instrumental break that sees George play a searing solo (proving George's quantum leap in that department too) increases the excitement at a point where the listener feels that that's not actually possible. To cap it all, the lyric is excellent, literate and playful. The part about how the narrator will become a singer if he grows up is disarmingly self-deprecating, while lines like, "I want a love that's right, but right is only half of what's wrong" are worthy of Harrison's good friend Bob Dylan, to whose "To Ramona" he nods at one point.

Abbey Road

Released: 26/09/1969

by Sean Egan

TRACKLISTING

Side one
1. "Come Together"
2. "Something"
3. "Maxwell's Silver Hammer"
4. "Oh! Darling"
5. "Octopus's Garden"
6. "I Want You (She's So Heavy)"

Side two
1. "Here Comes the Sun"
2. "Because"
3. "You Never Give Me Your Money"
4. "Sun King"
5. "Mean Mr Mustard"
6. "Polythene Pam"
7. "She Came In Through the Bathroom Window"
8. "Golden Slumbers"
9. "Carry That Weight"
10. "The End"
11. "Her Majesty"

Various release dates were set for the *Get Back* album and all were missed. Eventually, it was decided that the album and movie would be released simultaneously. The Beatles therefore put the project aside and concentrated on other activities.

They were busy men. They all had duties at Apple, super-
vising, producing, accompanying in the studio or merely just
encouraging the label's artists. In the case of John and George,
they were continuing their solo careers.

Paul had actually been the first Beatle to have an album
released when his soundtrack to the working-class film drama
The Family Way appeared in January 1967, though Paul didn't
play or sing on the album. Similarly, George wrote but did not
appear on his soundtrack to the movie *Wonderwall* in November
'68, which album beat John and Yoko's *Two Virgins* to the shops
by twenty-eight days. The latter, because Lennon performed on
it, must go down as technically the first commercially released
Beatles solo work. John and Yoko put out a follow-up to *Two
Virgins* in May '69 called *Unfinished Music No. 2 – Life With
The Lions*, the same day as George released his own second
album, *Electronic Sound*. Whereas *Wonderwall Music* was
comprised of Indian-influenced pieces, George's second album
consisted of two lengthy instrumentals created by him via the
then-new Moog synthesizer. As with Lennon's albums
(comprising sound effects and primitive, minimalist song), they
didn't seem like "real" music and hence it's difficult to imagine
the public thinking this heralded The Beatles splitting up. Even
the flimsy *Yellow Submarine* album released in January seemed
profoundly more substantial.

The public may have thought slightly differently of "Give
Peace A Chance", a second song to emerge from the Lennons'
somewhat confused and inchoate attempts to bring attention to
the cause of ending war. Though as per the old agreement its
publishing credit read "Lennon/McCartney", the record was
attributed to "Plastic Ono Band", another move guaranteed to
create contempt in a general public who were gaining the impression that Lennon had lost his mind. (Not long after his wedding,
Lennon generated a global tidal wave of tuts by announcing he
had changed his name to John Ono Lennon.) It was, though,
undeniably a real song, and a catchy one, making number two
in his home country and number fourteen in the States.

John and Paul recorded "The Ballad Of John And Yoko" on
14 April '69. There were sporadic Beatles sessions after that
but it was only from 1 July that the group's recording activities

had a specific objective, the next Beatles album, one that would ultimately be titled *Abbey Road*. Some have assumed that the reason The Beatles recorded *Abbey Road* is that they knew they weren't long for this world and that they wanted that world to remember them as polished and accomplished artists instead of the flawed human beings and musicians that *Get Back* would eventually reveal them as. This isn't unambiguously borne out by the facts. George Martin remembers it that way, for instance but not Ringo. Moreover, though the new album was completed on 25 August, it wasn't until 20 September (six days before the album's release) that Lennon amazed his colleagues at an Apple board meeting by telling them he was leaving The Beatles. He hadn't come to his decision to leave until experiencing the excitement of leading a band at the Live Peace In Toronto concert on 13 September. Perhaps one of the reasons that The Beatles decided to record together again at this point is simply because of the company they ran. Unlike other bands who dispersed when recording was over, the four Apple directors saw each other every day. Differences, instead of becoming embedded by distance, sorted themselves out as they interacted on a regular basis.

Though naturally there were some newly written songs, most of the compositions for *Abbey Road* had been around for a few months. The band knew they couldn't touch the *Get Back* material that had been earmarked for the album, but there was still plenty of material left over from those sessions: the majority of tracks on *Abbey Road* were rehearsed to at least some degree at Twickenham/Savile Row. (There were also tracks that didn't make it onto *Abbey Road* or *Let It Be* but saw life beyond The Beatles, such as "Teddy Boy", which appeared on Paul's first solo album.) And if some of the songs were mere scraps and doodles, the idea that someone had to turn them into a suite was a masterstroke, like turning leftovers into a gourmet meal. (Paul and George Martin have both claimed credit, and John seemed enthusiastic enough in a music paper interview while it was being done as to suggest he had a hand in the concept.)

It was Paul's decision to call the new album *Abbey Road*. It was a sort of joke: *Everest* – the name of Geoff Emerick's favourite cigarettes – had been mooted as the title but when talk turned to shooting a group photo session at that mountain for the cover, it didn't seem such a good idea and the name of the very street they were recording on was the logical, extreme alternative title. Additionally, perhaps subconsciously the switch from exotic place name to local one was also due to the fact that the band had felt relieved to be back in the familiar environs of Abbey Road studios after their unhappy experiences at Twickenham and Savile Row. The design they chose for the front cover depicting them walking in file over the zebra crossing outside the studio had effects both predictable (much imitation and parody, hordes of tourists getting their pictures taken there) and unpredictable (clues being read into the cover supposedly confirming the recent Paul-is-dead silly season news story, the sleuth's focusing on things ranging from The Beatles' attire to the number plate of the Volkswagen car in shot). For the first and only time, both artist name and album title were left off a Beatles album cover. Also for the first time, there was no mono version of a Beatles LP.

The album opens strongly with Lennon's moody swamp rock "Come Together", followed by Harrison's beautiful "Something". The tracks were subsequently released as either side of a single, so are discussed later. Paul's "Maxwell's Silver Hammer" is hated by some. An example of McCartney's penchant for whimsy, only with an added offensive dimension in being the jolly tale of a serial killer, it's certainly not substantial, despite the massive amount of work that went into it. Nonetheless, it has its own cartoonish charm, although it features – as do parts of the rest of the album – a taste of musical horrors to come in the shape of the Moog synthesizer, a most unwelcome synthetic-sounding presence in The Beatles' normally warm and natural soundscapes. Paul's "Oh! Darling" is a number that crosses Fifties-style doo-wop with modern rock to engaging effect. The lyric and melody are fairly generic but McCartney's nigh-hysterical vocal indicates he's mocking the whole affair anyway.

With "Octopus's Garden", after six years of trying, Ringo finally manages to write a good song, even if the footage of George helping him in the *Let It Be* movie and subsequent comments from John indicate that his colleagues assisted him more than a little with the music. Written by the drummer when on holiday with actor Peter Sellers after he had fled the White Album sessions before a telegram from his colleagues telling him he was the best drummer in the world brought him back home, the song is based on the genuine fact that octopi pick up brightly coloured objects they find on the ocean floor – including man-made items – and place them outside their caves. No doubt there is an unromantic evolutionary reason for this fact, but the anthropomorphic rationale is that they want a nice little front garden just like Mr and Mrs Suburbia, which idea Ringo ran with to create a charming declaration that he would like to take his love down under the ocean waves and sit basking in such a garden. It's actually a superior track to that other aquatic Beatles children's song "Yellow Submarine".

Towards the end of his time with The Beatles, Lennon started rediscovering the merits of the old-time rock 'n' roll music that had made him want to be a musician in the first place. In an example of the absolutism he was prone to, he virtually decided that the changes to rock since the Fifties – which of course he and his Beatles colleagues had been in the vanguard of – had been a retrograde step and that the simplicity of his original heroes like Chuck Berry was what he wanted to aspire to. "I Want You (She's So Heavy)" was a consequence of this philosophy. Its structure is over-simple and its lyric doesn't extend much beyond the words in its title. What John had overlooked was the fact that while Chuck Berry's music may have been simple (to such an extent that many have complained that most of it sounds the same), his lyrics – wonderful, witty, simile-packed vignettes of street life – never were. A pared-down version of this track could have been an interesting part of the second side's suite but what at first is a fairly enjoyable mantra and basic rock groove soon becomes tedious, not least because of some suffocatingly dark over-production. Eventually it becomes unbearably repetitive, way before its abrupt end as it approaches the eight-minute mark.

Harrison leads off side two with another song that, like "Something", indicates he is now the equal of Lennon & McCartney. It's the same sort of celebration of good weather and good lovin' that inspired Paul's "Good Day Sunshine" three years before and just as irresistible, not least because of George's superb winding acoustic guitar work.

Following that, we are into the suite that takes up the rest of the side. It starts with John's "Because", which features some lovely three-part harmonies from John, Paul and George, hip poetry ("Because the world is round it turns me on") and a touching faith in love. Paul's "You Never Give Me Your Money" is a song whose opening lines about getting funny papers instead of promised moolah are directed at Allen Klein, more in sorrow than in anger. However, it then develops into a highly enjoyable and high-spirited song about a boy out of college exulting in the "magic feeling" of having nowhere to go.

"Sun King" is initially dismaying because its guitar figures are a blatant rip-off of the recent Fleetwood Mac instrumental hit "Albatross" (as rock Gods, one really feels The Beatles are simply too elevated to plagiarize) and disorienting, because it's opening line "Here comes the Sun King" is so similar to the title and lyrical refrain of the Harrison track we have just heard. But some nice backing harmonies and some lovely lead vocals from John soon dispel our disquiet. The rhythmic "Mean Mr Mustard" is a brief, funny number from John featuring a grotesque character who could have come from one of his books. It segues into another mini-song about a character from the *demi-monde* in Lennon's head, "Polythene Pam", which is equally catchy and amusing. John's call of "Look out!" to herald Paul's "She Came In Through the Bathroom Window" is a well-judged move, helping give a sense of momentum and coherence to these forcibly jammed together fragments (as does the fact that the band recorded the basic tracks of the suite as one, rather than splicing). ". . . Bathroom..", like "You Never Give Me Your Money" and like many numbers from Paul's solo career, is the song-as-novel, populated by characters and vignettes that sound like they can't possibly have come from the author's personal experience. It's outrageously catchy.

"Golden Slumbers" sees Paul add a melody to a lyric that had been public domain for several centuries. It's a lovely and – thanks to his raw singing – soulful lullaby. All three Beatles frontmen sing the "Carry That Weight" admonition, which segues into a return to the theme of "Bathroom Window" and out again, which is succeeded by a reprise of "You Never Give Me Your Money".

The climatic track "The End" is magnificent. It's also in retrospect rather moving. Though the band may or may not have known this would be their last album when they recorded it, this closer feels very much like they did. As if saying farewell, each Beatle is giving a turn in the spotlight. Ringo performs a solo, then rousing chants of "Love you!" (a message to the fans?) herald Paul, George and John (in that order) taking it in turns to provide examples of guitar virtuosity that are quite stunning in their technique and growling distortion. With the four having each taken a bow, a sweet couplet brings matters to a close just like they do in Shakespeare plays, with John, Paul and George singing and harmonizing in a final moment of togetherness.

But not so fast. Unlisted on the original vinyl album's sleeve, "Her Majesty" appears after a gap of twenty seconds. It's a discard from the suite, one that sees Paul prove he can be just as funny and irreverent as John as he tells us – accompanied by just his acoustic guitar – that he loves the Queen and would make her his if only his alcohol dependency didn't prohibit it, a message delivered in a concise twenty-one seconds. It either spoils the drama of the climatic couplet or else undercuts its pseudo-pathos with its humour, depending on your mood.

But then *Abbey Road* is in some ways a mood album. If it catches you in the wrong one, its ambiguous qualities – the over-the-top production, "Maxwell's Silver Hammer", "I Want You/She's So Heavy", the washes of synthesizer, the way we're being presented with the suite as though it's a grand *meisterwerk* instead of the compromise of an exhausted and compositionally uncreative group – can be irritating. Celebrated rock critic Robert Christgau (such a Beatle fan that he would give a favourable review to the *Let It Be* album that many found scrappy) said it gave him a headache. But if one is in a generous mood, *Abbey Road* seems fine stuff and that cobbled-together suite assumes a sweeping majesty.

It's an album that for the first time in The Beatles' career – with the one exception of *Beatles For Sale* – doesn't feel like a progression over its predecessor. The Beatles had spent the decade shedding skins, adopting new styles either in response to outside influence or of their own volition. Each LP and, often, single had sounded different – either subtly or profoundly – from the one before and at the same time had pushed the boundaries of popular music. With *Abbey Road*, it was as though they had realized there was nowhere further to go. Having done R&B, minor chord pop, folk-rock, psychedelia, the concept album, the double album, the longest single ever, heavy metal, noise collage and various other explorations and innovations, what else was there to do? The music on *Abbey Road* was "rock", the style that had developed (mainly because of them) from the rock 'n' roll of the Fifties. This genre included ballads like "Something" and "You Never Give Me Your Money", for by now rock had come to mean not so much a fast tempo or heavy rhythm but a form of popular music informed by a philosophical informality that would best be described (in the parlance of the day) as hipness.

You could argue that punk, post-punk and electro-pop were new forms of rock rather than the old form just dressed up in the latest attitude or technology. You could posit stuff like hip-hop and dance music as an evolutionary step in rock rather than completely new forms that have little in common with rock. But the fact is that what people conceive of as rock today is pretty much the style of music to be found on *Abbey Road* nearly four decades ago. Compare that with the way that by 1969 rock/rock 'n' roll had changed beyond recognition since it hit the world in 1955. The Beatles had been chiefly responsible for that metamorphosis, helping the then still developing music grow and mature to its full potential. The romantic in you likes to think of *Abbey Road* as a statement of where they had taken the music that had inspired them and brought them together in the first instance, and as a public acknowledgment of the fact that they could do no more for it: having taken it as far it could go, The Beatles bowed out.

"Something" b/w "Come Together"

Released: 31/10/1969

by Sean Egan

The release of "Something" more than a month after the appearance of *Abbey Road* marked a lamentable milestone in The Beatles' career. It was the first time that tracks released on a single had already appeared on a Beatles album. The closest they had come to this previously was when "Eleanor Rigby" and "Yellow Submarine" were released on 45 simultaneously with *Revolver*. For many at the time, this mercenaryism must have been part of the whiff of decay that hung over a band whose individual members were all bringing into question their commitment to or interest in the group via solo projects and who were arguing in the press about the merits and demerits of Allen Klein and Lee Eastman as possible Beatles managers. This impression was added to by the fact that the single only got to number four, a shockingly low UK chart placing for The Beatles, making it their least successful single since "Love Me Do".

Yet it also marked for George a somewhat happier milestone: his first Beatles A-side. According to Allen Klein, the two landmarks were related. The former manager of the band (or three-quarters of it) later said, "It was done on purpose, not to make money but to help the guy." Referring to the fact that Lennon had told his colleagues in the 20 September Apple board meeting that he was leaving the group, Klein claimed, ". . . for a period of time they weren't going to be working together anymore . . . It was really to point out George as a writer, and give him courage to go in and do his own LP." In the coming decade, of course, releasing singles from an album that was already in the stores would become the norm.

"Something" was an astounding achievement for Harrison, both artistic and financial. The fact that "Something" got as high as it did in the charts despite nobody who had already sent *Abbey Road* to number one needing to buy it is almost certainly indicative of its crossover appeal. The kids who had been purchasing Beatles 45s in 1963 were now grown up and in jobs, so there wasn't a large number of people buying Beatles singles because an album was out of their reach. Instead, "Something" was being bought by people who would not normally buy records by rock artists *per se*. An instant evergreen, it appealed to the sentimental old as much to the hip young. It is now second only to "Yesterday" in the stakes of most covered Beatles song.

The composer seems to have picked up the title of a track by Apple signing James Taylor, "Something In The Way She Moves". He used that as a jumping-off point for a beautiful tribute to his wife, model Patti Boyd, in a song featuring a wonderful winding melody. The performance boasts several peaks of intensity and has an arrangement in which George's excellent guitar work is well to the fore, including a classy, stately riff and a fine, clipped solo. Moreover, the track has that undeniable pop magic: it features bits that people look forward to and/or love singing along to, notably the way George renders the word "moves" as multi-syllable epics and the bridge in which he is asked by a friend whether his love will grow and he responds that he doesn't know but he should stick around and maybe it will show, while behind him the band go into a wonderful bobbing descent.

The music, like all of *Abbey Road*, is super-slick and curiously cushioned. A Morse-code organ, flecks of wah-wah guitar and discreet but telling strings add layers to what is even at its base a sumptuous song. Though it wasn't the first song Harrison had written about Patti, it was the greatest. Boyd would act as muse for other remarkable love songs. Unfortunately for Harrison, they were songs written by his close friend Eric Clapton, who fell in love with Boyd while her marriage to George was very much still active. At first, it seemed that Clapton's and

Boyd's affair would be just a fling, something that caused Clapton such anguish that he wrote the classic bereft anthem "Layla" (released in 1970) about his feelings. Eventually, Boyd did indeed leave Harrison for Clapton. Clapton subsequently wrote the tender "Wonderful Tonight' about Boyd, a song whose domestic notes are so well-observed that they will be recognized by any long-established couple. Clapton and Harrison, incidentally, remained friends.

As was now the norm, The Beatles produced a promotional film for their new single in lieu of any willingness on their part to visit TV studios to mime to it or play it. It was a film that underlined their separateness, as they were also unwilling to be filmed with each other. Nonetheless, it was rather sweet, depicting the band and their respective partners frolicking and making love-struck eyes at each other. One can't really imagine any other top-ranked rock act pulling this off. The Stones or Dylan doing the same thing would have come across as soft, yet somehow it seemed perfectly in keeping with the nature of The Beatles and their art.

A week before the release of "Something", Lennon issued the second Plastic Ono Band single, "Cold Turkey". It pointedly bore the publishing credit "Lennon", thus breaking a pact with Paul going back to the early 1960s which had survived the *A Hard Day's Night* album (which had largely been comprised of John solo compositions), the likes of "Yesterday" and "Eleanor Rigby" (which bore little or no Lennon involvement) and "Give Peace A Chance" (which Paul was involved in at no stage). Though McCartney had received sole credit for his soundtrack to the 1966 movie *The Family Way* (which sort of didn't count anyway, as it wasn't a rock record), when John realized he still stood to receive fifty per cent of the royalties, he suggested that Paul should keep the money for himself, only to be told by his friend and partner "Don't be soft." The deep bonds of friendship and understanding revealed by that latter anecdote were now unravelling. It was another crack in the façade of The Beatles, another clue that this story was not going to have a happy ending. It has been said that Lennon was prompted to instigate this end of a publishing era by McCartney indicating he did not want "Cold Turkey", a dissection of the miseries of withdrawal from heroin (which both Lennons had direct, recent knowledge of), on a Beatles record.

The Plastic Ono Band would never be a fixed, permanent group (the first record credited to them had featured only Lennon, percussion and a crowd chanting the choruses), but on this occasion consisted of Lennon, Eric Clapton on guitar, Klaus Voormann on bass and Ringo on drums. Though this is a pretty nifty line-up, and though the song was important to Lennon (it was actually recorded when he was going through turkey), this doesn't mean the record is very good: in particular, the chorus is a limping dog. To make matters worse, when Lennon returned his MBE to the Queen in November 1969 for the noble reason of protesting against Britain's involvement in the war in Biafra/Nigeria, he destroyed his point – and made a fool of himself in a way the public was now getting used, though not inured, to – by adding a flippant line about his gesture also constituting a protest about "Cold Turkey" slipping down the UK charts (from its peak of fourteen).

Perhaps the affair was symptomatic of a problem. The B-side of "Something" – "Come Together" – is one of John's few substantial contributions to *Abbey Road*, and even that caused Lennon to have to later settle out of court with Morris Levy, publisher of Chuck Berry's "You Can't Catch Me", over alleged similarities between the two songs. Lennon began writing it when LSD guru Timothy Leary visited him at his first Bed-In and asked if he would provide him with a campaign anthem of that title because he was planning to stand for political office. There were a couple of connections between Leary and The Beatles. Lennon had used Leary's interpretation of *The Tibetan Book Of The Dead* to write "Tomorrow Never Knows", while in 1967 Leary made that comment reproduced in this book's introduction about The Beatles being prototypes of evolutionary agents sent by God to create a new human species. When Leary was imprisoned on drugs charges, his plans for public office were scuppered but Lennon persevered with the song, adding lines about the subject holding you in his arms and you feeling his disease which even an iconoclast like Leary would not have wanted to use to sell himself to the public.

The backing is rich, subdued and dark. Ringo creates a slinky rhythm, alternating between padded circular patterns and a clipped beat, while Paul's bass throbs exquisitely. John adds to the vague air of menace with a vocal issued between gritted teeth.

"Let It Be" b/w "You Know My Name (Look Up The Number)"

Released: 06/03/1970

by Sean Egan

The Lennons and the Plastic Ono Band released an album each in the space of just over a month at the end of 1969. John and Yoko's *The Wedding Album* was more experimental weirdness destined never to be listened to again after the first hearing, while *Live Peace in Toronto 1969* was an aural document of the Plastic Ono Band's recent performance in Canada split between a worthwhile side (John's tracks: some of his solo stuff and some covers of oldies) and an atrocious one (Ono's caterwauling contributions).

February 1970, though, saw the release of a truly excellent Plastic Ono Band single. "Instant Karma" fulfilled an ambition of its composer to write, record and release a record in as short a time as feasible, which turned out to be ten days. A rumination on the penchant of fate to seek quick retribution, it has a fine melody and a catchy chorus ("We all shine on"). The most outstanding contribution in a stellar band line-up that includes George Harrison, Klaus Voormann and Billy Preston is that of drummer Alan White, playing hyperactively to a completely different tempo to the rest of the group with arresting results. The record also had a star producer, Phil Spector, a name that would loom large in the brief remainder of The Beatles' career. Lennon must have felt that his bringing that career to a halt with his notice to quit in September the previous year had been vindicated by the number five UK chart placing he secured for this record.

Meanwhile, the pretence that The Beatles had a future was still going on. Exactly a month after "Instant Karma" came the release of "Let It Be', the last Beatles single released before it became publicly known that the band were to split. It is a thing of beauty inspired by, of all people, Allen Klein.

Sort of. The Beatles' legal wrangles were getting McCartney down when he wrote the song. His mother, Mary, whom he had lost to breast cancer when he was fourteen appeared to him in a dream and told him not to get worked up about matters, to "let it be". The meaning of the entreaty changes in the context of a song that moves from Paul's vision of "mother Mary" to visions of world peace. At first, it is used to mean "Let it lie", but when the subject matter turns to the objective of peace on earth instead of peace of mind, McCartney brilliantly turns it into a leitmotif with a more universal application which can be roughly defined as "Let it come to pass".

Even though we now know that those making the understandable assumption that the mother Mary being referred to was the Virgin Mary were mistaken, the track still feels like a hymn. "Let it be" is one of those phrases that has the smack of ancient wisdom and feels like we have heard it all our lives. Also in common with hymns, the song has a gently anthemic flavour. Other numbers in the rock canon with those same qualities are the traditional "We Shall Overcome", Dylan's "Blowin' In The Wind" and "The Times They Are A-Changin'" and Simon and Garfunkel's "Bridge Over Troubled Water". Despite sounding like hymns, like "Let It Be", they are secular and address not a deity but a cause. The cause is rather scattershot, even opaque in all of them, but all the songs create a feeling of solidarity in the listener.

As per "Hey Jude", Paul handles a slow, simple piano part without virtuosity but with enough competence as to be pleasing. We know that all traces of *Get Back*'s intended back-to-roots approach have disappeared when his voice receives choral accompaniment. This mix, however, is a lot less ornate than the mix that would appear on the album.

Also, as with "Hey Jude", a one-man-and-piano introduction gradually becomes a full band arrangement. On his last Beatles single (at least while the group was extant), George pulls off a distinctive fluid solo that demonstrates how far he had come as a musician in the last eight years.

Its title phrase also gave "Let It Be" the flavour of a valedictory in the wake of the realization a month after its release – when many radio stations were still playing it, what with the movie and album of the same name hitting the market – that The Beatles would not be recording again.

That the record's B-side was a revived discard from four years previously was an indication of the lethargy and decay now surrounding the band. "You Know My Name (Look Up The Number)" had actually been announced in the press in late '69 as a Plastic Ono Band single and it was even given a provisional Apple catalogue number, with "What's The New Mary Jane" its intended B-side. It was then revealed that the decision had been reversed. The assumption is that the other Beatles resented John hijacking what were both Beatles recordings and attributing them to his other band, even if they were in the vein of the Plastic Ono Band's more edgy, experimental style. The track's long and tortuous recording process had started in May 1967. After a period in mothballs, it was given vocal overdubs by John and Paul in April 1969. The Plastic Ono Band version was to be a four-minute edit of the six-minute track done by Lennon in November 1969, four months after the death of the alto saxophonist on the record, Brian Jones of The Rolling Stones. This version is the one that ended up on the flip of "Let It Be".

It's an essentially lightweight track but in no way terrible. The "song" consists of the title phrase repeated over and over to different tunes, in different keys and tempi against fake nightclub background noise. It gets more comedic as it progresses, and the funny voices give it a Goon-like humour. Paul plays some nice supper club piano and Jones' sax work is also pleasant, if brief.

For the second time in a row, a Beatles single did not top

the UK charts, "Let It Be" peaking at number two. It was beaten to the top by, interestingly enough, Simon and Garfunkel's quite similar "Bridge Over Troubled Water", which is presumably where John got his mistaken memory that Paul had been trying to emulate that song with "Let It Be". The assumption has always been that the public didn't buy the record in sufficient numbers to take it to the top because they knew that it was the title track of their forthcoming album. However, lost in the wrinkles of history is the fact that in the week of its release, up to 500 shops in the northwest were boycotting EMI product in protest about changes to the company's returns policy – a dispute that may have robbed The Beatles of the honour of ending their singles career on a high.

THE REVELATION OF THE END

"The Beatle thing is over. It has been exploded, partly by what we have done, and partly by other people. We are individuals – all different. John married Yoko, I married Linda. We didn't marry the same girl."

This quote was given by Paul McCartney to Life *magazine, appearing in its issue dated 7 November 1969. Amazingly, its significance was not widely picked up on, mainly because* Life*'s London correspondent seemed to have made his way uninvited to Paul's Scottish farm – where Paul had secluded himself and his family following John's September bombshell about quitting the band – primarily to ask him about the Paul is Dead rumours circulating at the time.*

As far as the media and therefore the public were concerned, The Beatles were still operational, an illusion it was possible to believe in because the quartet were bound together by the fully functioning operation that was Apple. However, when a press release consisting of a self-interview was distributed with review copies of Paul's debut solo album McCartney *on 10 April 1970, seven days before the album's official UK release, few were able to accept any more that The Beatles were going to continue. McCartney didn't want to do press about the record because it would mean difficult-to-handle questions about The Beatles. Instead, he asked Beatles aide Peter Brown to give him a questionnaire to fill out so that the newspapers and music press could have some comments to print about the album. Paul later said of Brown's questionnaire, "Peter Brown realized that the big question was The Beatles so he put in a couple of loaded questions and rather than just say, 'I don't want to answer these', I thought, 'Fuck it. If that's what he wants to know I'll tell him.' I felt I'd never be able to start a new life until I'd told people." McCartney's bloody-mindedness was also possibly partly due to a perfectly understandable irritation with the fact that such were the ways in which the Apple contract to which all the Beatles were now obligated was drawn up, he had to ask permission of the other Beatles to release the album. Additionally, he had also been extremely unhappy when his three colleagues decided to renege on the originally agreed release date for McCartney, stating that this was when Let It Be should be issued instead – an action that may have been a "Screw you" to McCartney for refusing to accept that Allen Klein was the best man to manage The Beatles' affairs.*

The questionnaire didn't definitively say The Beatles were dead – when specifically asked in it if the break from The Beatles was temporary or permanent, McCartney said he didn't know – but his terse "No" to the question of whether Lennon-McCartney would ever be an active songwriting team again and his not-quite-civil comments about not missing The Beatles, having a better time with his family than with the group and not planning a new Beatles single or album were as far from The Beatles' normal image of four men bonded by hair, unprecedented success and common purpose as it was possible to be and was interpreted as a burning of bridges. All of which was ironic, of course, because it was John who had broken up the band, and Paul has subsequently admitted he was devastated by Lennon's decision, descending into a crippling depression. Lennon meanwhile admitted that he wished he had done what Paul did and got the "credit" for breaking up The Beatles.

Also included in the press pack was an information sheet about the album. The questionnaire consisted of four typed pages, single-spaced, with an Apple logo in the top left corner. It was untitled and dated simply "April 1970". This innocuous-looking document would unleash tidal waves across the world.

The 1970 McCartney Self-Interview

Q: Why did you decide to make a solo album?
A: Because I got a Studer four-track recording machine at home
– practised on it (playing all instruments) – liked the results,
and decided to make it into an album.

Q: Were you influenced by John's adventures with the Plastic
Ono Band, and Ringo's solo LP?
A: Sort of, but not really.

Q: Are all songs by Paul McCartney alone?
A: Yes sir.

Q: Will they be so credited: McCartney?
A: It's a bit daft for them to be Lennon/McCartney credited,
so "McCartney" it is.

Q: Did you enjoy working as a solo?
A: Very much. I only had me to ask for a decision, and I agreed
with me. Remember Linda's on it too, so it's really a double
act.

Q: What is Linda's contribution?
A: Strictly speaking she harmonizes, but of course it's more
than that because she's a shoulder to lean on, a second opinion,
and a photographer of renown. More than all this, she believes
in me – constantly.

Q: Where was the album recorded?
A: At home, at EMI (no. 2 studio) and at Morgan Studios
(Willesden!)

Q: What is your home equipment (in some detail)?
A: Studer four-track machine. I only had, however, one mike, and as Mr Pender, Mr Sweatenham and others only managed to take six months or so (slight delay) I worked without VU meters or a mixer, which meant that everything had to be listened to first (for distortion etc . . .) then recorded. So the answer – Studer, one mike, and nerve.

Q: Why did you choose to work in the studios you chose?
A: They were available. EMI is technically very good and Morgan is cozy.

Q: The album was not known about until it was nearly completed. Was this deliberate?
A: Yes, because normally an album is old before it even comes out. (aside) Witness GET BACK.

Q: Why?
A: I've always wanted to buy a Beatles album like people do and be as surprised as they must be. So this was the next best thing. Linda and I are the only two who will be sick of it by the release date. We love it really.

Q: Are you able to describe the texture or the feel of the album in a few words?
A: Home, family, love.

Q: How long did it take to complete?
A: From just before (I think) Xmas, until now. THE LOVELY LINDA was the first thing I recorded at home, and was originally to test the equipment. That was around Xmas.

Q: Assuming all the songs are new to the public, how new are they to you? Are they recent?
A: One was from 1959 (HOT AS SUN). Two are from India – JUNK and TEDDY BOY, and the rest are pretty recent. VALENTINE DAY, MOMMA MISS AMERICA and OO YOU were ad-libbed on the spot.

Q: Which instruments have you played on the album?
A: Bass, drums, acoustic guitar, lead guitar, piano and organ-mellotron, toy xylophone, bow and arrow.

Q: Have you played all these instruments on earlier recordings?
A: Yes, drums being the one that I normally wouldn't do.

Q: Why did you do all the instruments yourself?
A: I think I'm pretty good.

Q: Will Linda be heard on all future records?
A: Could be. We love singing together and have plenty of opportunity for practice.

Q: Will Paul and Linda become a John and Yoko?
A: No, they will become Paul and Linda.

Q: What has recording alone taught you?
A: That to make your own decisions about what you do is easy, and playing with yourself is very difficult, but satisfying.

Q: Who has done the artwork?
A: Linda has taken all the photos, and she and I designed the package.

Q: Is it true that neither Allen Klein nor ABKCO have been nor will be in any way involved with the production, manufacturing, distribution or promotion of this new album?
A: Not if I can help it.

Q: Did you miss the other Beatles and George Martin? Was there a moment when you thought: "Wish Ringo was here for this break?"
A: No.

Q: Assuming this is a very big hit album, will you do another?
A: Even if it isn't, I will continue to do what I want, when I want to.

Q: Are you planning a new album or single with The Beatles?
A: No.

Q: Is this album a rest away from the Beatles or the start of a solo career?
A: Time will tell. Being a solo album means it's "the start of a solo career . . ." and not being done with the Beatles means it's just a rest. So it's both.

Q: Is your break with the Beatles temporary or permanent, due to personal differences or musical ones?
A: Personal differences, business differences, musical differences, but most of all because I have a better time with my family. Temporary or permanent? I don't really know.

Q: Do you foresee a time when Lennon-McCartney becomes an active songwriting partnership again?
A: No.

Q: What do you feel about John's peace effort? The Plastic Ono Band? Giving back the MBE? Yoko's influence? Yoko?
A: I love John, and respect what he does – it doesn't really give me any pleasure.

Q: Were any of the songs on the album originally written with The Beatles in mind?
A: The older ones were. JUNK was intended for ABBEY ROAD, but something happened. TEDDY BOY was for GET BACK but something happened.

Q: Were you pleased with ABBEY ROAD? Was it musically restricting?
A: It was a good album. (No. 1 for a long time.)

Q: What is your relationship with Klein?
A: It isn't. I am not in contact with him, and he does not represent me in ANY way.

Q: What is your relationship with Apple?
A: It is the office of a company which I part own with the other three Beatles. I don't go there because I don't like offices or business, especially when I am on holiday.

Q: Have you any plans to set up an independent production company?
A: McCartney Productions.

Q: What sort of music has influenced you on this album?
A: Light and loose.

Q: Are you writing more prolifically now? Or less so?
A: About the same. I have a queue waiting to be recorded.

Q: What are your plans now? A holiday? A musical? A movie? Retirement?
A: My only plan is to grow up!

THE SCOOP ON THE SPLIT

Journalist Don Short had been there just about every step of the way on The Beatles' amazing journey from provincial musicians to global stars, his byline appearing on just about every Daily Mirror *story covering another of their incremental steps toward becoming the most significant entertainers in human history. It's somehow apposite that he secured the exclusive of all exclusives about the band when a copy of the promotional questionnaire for Paul's first album came into his hands and he realized the ramifications of the blunt, undiplomatic answers to the questions provided for Paul by Beatles aide Pete Brown.*

The inevitable consequence was a Mirror *front page news story that, once picked up by the rest of the media, shocked the world. Curiously, though the questionnaire carried quite a few explosive comments, Short used none of them, with even the one quote that purported to be from the questionnaire actually Short's not completely accurate paraphrasing of McCartney's simple "No" responses to the questions of whether he had any plans to record with The Beatles or write with John.*

Though shocked, the world wouldn't have been completely surprised. Whether The Beatles were on the point of breaking up was an issue in the public domain to some extent already. Although the public didn't know that Lennon had told the others at an Apple board meeting in September '69 that he was leaving, both the fact that in January 1970 the New Musical Express *asked Lennon whether The Beatles would record together again and that John's answer was ambiguous indeed ("It just depends how much we all want to record together again. I don't know if I want to record together again. I go off and on it . . .") proves that the band's lack of activity and tense public comments about each other was an issue in the air.*

However, the press statement was as close to a formal confirmation that the band were no more as there could be. It was clear that an era was about to end, poetically just as the 1960s – the expansive, explosive decade that The Beatles either fashioned in their image or else rode the mood of – were giving way to a decade that would be marked by considerably less optimism and love.

Paul Is Quitting The Beatles

Lennon-McCartney song team splits up
Clash over the running of Apple

From *Daily Mirror*, Friday 10 April 1970
by Don Short

Paul McCartney has quit The Beatles.

The shock news must mean the end of Britain's most famous pop group, which has been idolized by millions the world over for nearly ten years.

Today, 27-year-old McCartney will announce his decision, and the reasons for it, in a no-holds-barred statement.

It follows months of strife over policy in Apple, The Beatles' controlling organization, and an ever-growing rift between McCartney and his songwriting partner John Lennon.

In his statement, which consists of a series of answers to questions, McCartney says: "I have no future plans to record or appear with The Beatles again. Or to write any more music with John."

Last night the statement was locked up in a safe at Apple headquarters in Savile Row, Mayfair – in the very rooms where The Beatles' break-up began. The Beatles decided to appoint a business adviser. Eventually they settled for American Allen Klein. His appointment was strongly resisted by Paul, who sought the job for his father-in-law, American attorney Lee Eastman. After a meeting in London, Paul was outvoted 3-1 by John and the other Beatles, George Harrison and Ringo Starr. Since the Klein appointment, Paul has refused to go to the Apple offices to work daily.

He kept silent and stayed at his St John's Wood home with

his photographer wife Linda, her daughter Heather and their own baby, Mary. Close friends tried to pacify John and Paul. But August last year was the last time they were to work together – when they collaborated on the *Abbey Road* album.

There were other elements that hastened Paul's decision to quit. John Lennon on his marriage to Yoko Ono set out on projects of his own. Ringo went into films, and George stepped in as a record producer.

Today McCartney will reveal his own plans for a solo programme. Early today an Apple spokesman denied that Paul McCartney had left The Beatles.

But he said that there were no plans "at the moment" for any more recordings.

AN OBITUARY

The day after the Daily Mirror *scoop about Paul's press release interview, the* Daily Mail *devoted most of an entire page (in the days when their pages were broadsheet-sized) to the story. Two pictures accompanied a pair of articles, the photographs contrasting their cute days via a picture from the moptop era with their appearance in later years by way of a picture from their final photo session at John's Tittenhurst Park home on 22 August '69. A news report by Brian Dean and Richard Herd entitled "As the Beatles sing their swan song . . ." summarized the press statement that Short had leaked with some new quotes, including one from Allen Klein which may possibly even have sparked Paul's idea to sue to break up Apple ("It's never pleasant when someone appears not to like you. Paul's reasons are his own personal problem. Unfortunately he is committed to Apple for a number of years. His dissociation from me has no effect").*

Alongside this news story, Pearson Phillips attempted to encapsulate what The Beatles had meant over the past seven-and-a-half years. Perhaps revealingly he wrote about what effect The Beatles had had on the culture rather than on music: the Mail *was (and remains) a conservative, middle-of-the-road paper and its readers (at least then) would generally not have had much interest in popular music. However, the fact that he chose to focus on what he did does not mean Phillips was wrong. Music being less important than society as a whole, perhaps The Beatles' effect on the culture was the primary issue, and – though he was writing in the shorthand necessitated by a limited number of column inches and newspapers' overnight deadlines – Phillips summed up that effect pretty well . . .*

How They Changed and How They Changed Us

From *Daily Mail*, Saturday 11 April 1970
by Pearson Phillips

Before them there was God Save The Queen at the cinema and a password to conformity which went: "Just a short, back and sides please."

After them there were Union Jack shopping bags and a quarter of a million people at a pop music concert in Hyde Park.

Heaven knows what they meant, what they symbolized or whether they were anything more than children of their times. Future historians will explains that in a footnote.

From here all we know is that when they arrived things changed. Music changed, show business changed, society changed.

Didn't love change? That word lurv. Before them there were

things called romance and glamour. They injected sincerity, realism, sex. They picked up a pass from D. H. Lawrence, and they ran the whole length of the field. They put the sugar on The Pill.

Your Royal Family changed. The Middle Class got hip. The working classes disappeared in a flurry of silk neckerchiefs.

Footballers changed. The collar-stud industry collapsed. The Times changed. Liverpool arrived. The North invaded the South. Youth crystallized into an entity of its own. Nobody wanted to be grown up anymore, even the grown-ups. Especially not the grown-ups. Votes came at eighteen.

Possibly it would have all happened without them. Discothèques would have pounded away, the King's Road, Carnaby Street. But it would not, could not, have happened with the same style.

They brought irreverence, humour, carefully nurtured individuality to it all. They pricked many wrinkled balloons.

And now, in the way of all the best meteorites, they have disintegrated.

Glyn Johns:
On Recording the *Let It Be* Album

by John Tobler and Stuart Grundy

Though he never got a producer's credit on a Beatles record, Glyn Johns was the producer of the Get Back *sessions in all but name – at least judging by the fascinating account he gives of those recording dates below in an extract from the book* The Record Producers.

"There was a television show of The Beatles called *Around The Beatles* which was done by Jack Good, with Terry Johnson doing the engineering, and me as assistant, but that was years ago – the only time I worked with The Beatles thereafter was on *Let It Be*. For that, I was approached in December 1968 by Paul McCartney to go and work with The Beatles. He rang me up and said they were going to do a television show that they were going to produce themselves, and they were going to make a documentary film of them making the show; from that, an album would be released of all new material which they were writing for the show which would be recorded live. They were to rehearse for this whole episode at Twickenham Film Studios on a sound stage, and he wanted me to go along for the rehearsals, and pretty much become involved from Day One, which I did.

"It was obviously a fascinating experience. I was a Beatles fan, everybody was, and felt The Beatles were wonderful, but having been so incredibly busy at the period of time up to then, I didn't really know any Beatle records, although I'd obviously heard them on the radio from time to time – I don't think I'd actually bought one, although I may have bought *Rubber Soul*, but anyway . . . The point is that I admired them . . . but they weren't necessarily my cup of tea as far as what I wanted to do, although I was extremely flattered that they should ask me to work with them, and so I did. The point I'm trying to make with all this preamble was that by the time I actually got into a room with them, although I was quite used to working with famous people, and was very rarely phased by anyone I met, no matter how much I admired them, actually being in a room with The Beatles for the first time – all four of them with nobody else there – was pretty weird, and I suddenly realized how extraordinary the whole situation was, having never given it a lot of thought before.

"The time I worked with them was at the end of their career, obviously, and the *Let It Be* thing was something of a fiasco. It proved, however, to be an extraordinarily educational period for me – it obviously couldn't have been anything else, but that was why I wanted to do it, because I knew I'd learn something. The extraordinary thing is that they proved up to that point that they were the masters of the 'Produced Record', yet the stuff I did with them wasn't 'produced' in that way at all, it was all recorded live in rehearsal, in a room, in a rehearsal situation. And for that, I think it has great value, because for the album, I originally put together an album of rehearsals, with chat and jokes and bits of general conversation in between the tracks, which was the way I wanted *Let It Be* to be – breakdowns, false starts. Really the idea was that at the time, they were viewed as being the be-all-and-end-all, sort of up on a pedestal, beyond touch, just Gods, completely Gods, and what I witnessed going on at these rehearsals was that, in fact, they were hysterically funny, but very ordinary people in many *ways*, and they were capable of playing as a band, which everybody was beginning to wonder about at that point, because they hadn't done so for some time – everything had been prepared in advance, everything had been overdubbed and everything, and they proved in that rehearsal that they could still sing and play at the same time, and they could make records without all those weird and wonderful sounds on them.

"That became an obsession with me, and I got the bit between my teeth about it, and one night, I mixed a bunch of stuff that they didn't even know I'd recorded half the time – I just whacked the recorder on for a lot of stuff that they did, and gave them an acetate the following morning of what I'd done, as a rough idea of what an album could be like, released as it was. There was one thing that only happened once, a song that Paul played to the others, which I believe he later used on one of his ensuing albums, called 'Teddy Boy', and I have a tape of Paul actually teaching the others this song. I loved it, and I was hoping they'd finish it and do it, because I thought it was really good. But my version does go on a bit, and they're just going round and round, trying to get the chord sequence right, I suppose, and the best bit is where John Lennon gets bored – he obviously doesn't want to play it any more, and starts doing his interjections.

"They came back and said they didn't like it, or each individual bloke came in and said he didn't like it, and that was the end of that. A period of time went by and I went to America to work with Steve Miller, and when I came back, I got a call from John and Paul asking me to meet them at EMI, which I duly did. They pointed to a big pile of tapes in the corner, and said, 'Remember that idea you had about putting together an album?' and I said, 'Yes'. They said, 'Well, there are the tapes – go and do it'. So I was absolutely petrified – you can imagine. I was actually being asked to put together a Beatle album on my own. So I did – I went off and locked myself away for a week or so and pieced an album together out of these rehearsed tapes, which they then all liked, really liked. This was some months after the thing had actually been recorded, and we'd actually started work on *Abbey Road* about the same time. I did a bit of *Abbey Road,* not all of it, and I don't really know now how much I did do of it, because I can't remember, but it was probably about a third or a half of it that I recorded. We worked on most of the tunes together – well, I was there. You know this business about who produced them and who didn't, and all the rest of it – I was never given a producer's credit with The Beatles. Anyway, we had an extraordinarily good working relationship, and I got on really well with them all and found them all, as individuals, to be most interesting people. One of the things that came out of it for me, which I think needs to be said because it's rarely said, is what an amazing drummer Ringo Starr is – very few people have ever caught on to that, and I don't ever hear anybody talking about what a great drummer he is, but I think he's absolutely amazing and has the most incredible feel. I know people use him on sessions now, and perhaps those that use him do it because of his ability, but I think a lot of people imagine that the reason he's used on sessions is because of his name. That isn't it – he's an incredible drummer, and it's a shame in a way that he's never been recognized more, simply because he was a Beatle, which is really weird.

"There was a lot of friction in the band when I worked with them, although that's all gossip really, and I suppose has little to do with what we're supposed to be talking about . . . Being more specific, the recording which took place on the roof of Apple was actually my idea. The TV show idea had been shelved, because they couldn't find anywhere to do it – Paul wanted it to be like a barn dance sort of thing originally. Then they wanted to do something with a lot of their fan club there, and they wanted to do it outside, but since it was during the winter months, we couldn't really do it in a park or anything like that. Then they thought about hiring an ocean liner and putting all the fans on it, playing for them on the way to wherever we were going, some island with an open amphitheatre where they could play for the fans again, then put them all back on the liner and go home again. It was a great idea, but unfortunately it never came off – I think I'd have quite enjoyed that . . . Ideas were being thrown around, but in the end, everything got so dissipated that they decided to shelve the television thing totally, after about four or five weeks, I think.

"So then I suggested that we went into the studio to record the material in a finished form, since there was already a documentary about the songs being written and rehearsed, and if a film was made of them recording, playing the songs properly, it would provide an end to the film – here's them rehearsing, and here's them actually finishing it – and they agreed to that, so we went to Apple. They'd just finished building their studio in the basement of Apple, which was a total disaster area, so I borrowed some mobile equipment from EMI which we used to do the recording. Then the conversation came round to how they could play to more people than just playing in the studio. We were having lunch one day, and someone was talking about the roof of the building and what could be done with it, like turn it into a garden area or something. So I said, 'Well, let's have a look at this roof,' and Michael Lindsay-Hogg and I, and I think, Ringo went up on the roof and looked at it, and sure enough, you could play to the whole of London from up there – we thought. So they set it up, and it worked very well. It brought Savile Row to a grand halt, anyway, and as was shown in the film, the police came and stopped it all, and my version of the album actually starts with 'One After 909', which was recorded on the roof. I don't know if that ever got on Phil Spector's version of the album."

Perhaps a word of explanation would not go amiss at this point: *Let It Be*, as has already been explained, was conceived as some kind of multi-media documentary. Although recording was started at the end of 1968, the album of *Let It Be* did not emerge until May 1970, while another Beatle LP, *Abbey Road,* was begun and completed during the fifteen-month hiatus, so that although *Let It Be* was not the final album recorded by The Beatles, it was the last original LP by the group to be released. The delay was apparently caused by arguments between members of the group, the result being that the tapes which Glyn had recorded under the aegis of George Martin were at some point entrusted to Phil Spector, who was given the job of mixing the album.

Glyn: "I cannot bring myself to listen to the Phil Spector version of the album – I heard a few bars of it once, and was totally disgusted, and I think it's an absolute load of garbage. Obviously I'm biased, because they didn't use my version, which upset me, but I wouldn't have minded so much if things hadn't happened in the way they did. First of all, after The Beatles had broken up, John Lennon, as an individual, took the tapes and gave them to Phil Spector, without the others even being aware of it, which was extraordinary. I think Spector did the most atrocious job, just utter puke, and it was raw and unbuggered about with and done without any nonsense, any overdubbing or anything.

"Mind you, the film's even worse – it was atrocious. I was there when it was being shot, and there was some amazing stuff – their humour got to me as much as the music, and I didn't stop laughing for six weeks. John Lennon only had to walk in a room, and I'd just crack up. Their whole mood was wonderful, and that was the thing, and there was all this nonsense going on at the time about the problems surrounding the group, and the Press being at them, and in fact, there they were, just doing it, having a wonderful time and being incredibly funny, and none of that's in the film. The film was taken over by Allen Klein, who actually got The Beatles much later, after *Let It Be* was all recorded, and that was when the rot set in. Klein saw a rough-cut of it and said he didn't want anyone else in the film but The Beatles, so everyone else who was in any shot at any time was taken out, the net result being that it got a bit difficult to watch after a while. Also, some of the stuff that I know was in there originally, and was extremely interesting, was conversations with other people, members of the film crew, people who were just around, people visiting, like Billy Preston – but Klein said that only The Beatles could be in the film, and that was it.

"So what was originally going on was a rehearsal, and there was an interchange, and you saw how things happened, you saw a song grow, and you saw conversations between people – that was all taken out, and hence it was ruined. And then, of course, the Spector thing ruined the record as well, so everyone might as well have not bothered . . . Fortunately, of course, two of my tracks from those sessions got released as singles, 'Let It Be' and 'Get Back', and obviously I'm incredibly proud of them, although I didn't get a credit on them as producer. (In fact, 'Get Back' contains no producer's credit, while 'Let It Be' bears George Martin's name as producer.) I think that if my version of the album had come out, they'd all agreed to give me a producer's credit. Lennon was the only one who questioned it – I sat each of them down, and said, 'Look, I know you originally employed me to be engineer on these sessions, but I consider that as there was no producer, and as I was the only one there and I've actually put it together on my own, I'd really appreciate a producer's credit. I don't want any royalties or any money, just the credit.' All the others said that was perfectly all right, but Lennon couldn't understand why I didn't want any money, so I had to explain that if it was me there, or Joe Bloggs there, The Beatles would sell three billion zillion records anyway, so I didn't deserve a royalty on their records, but obviously, if my name was there as producer, and I was only asking for credit for what I'd done, then clearly I would benefit from it in other ways, and it would assist my career, to say the least. I think he finally understood, and anyway, my version of the album never did come out, so there was nothing in contention anyway."

Let It Be

Released: 08/05/1970

by Sean Egan

TRACKLISTING

Side one
1. "Two Of Us"
2. "Dig a Pony"
3. "Across The Universe"
4. "I Me Mine"
5. "Dig It"
6. "Let It Be"
7. "Maggie Mae"

Side two
1. "I've Got A Feeling"
2. "One After 909"
3. "The Long and Winding Road"
4. "For You Blue"
5. "Get Back"

The album which Paul was still referring to as *Get Back* in his April 1970 self-interview for the *McCartney* album finally saw the light of day in May 1970 under the title *Let It Be*.

Though The Beatles had not formally announced a split upon the release of the *Let It Be* album, it was by now blindingly obvious that they were finished as a working group. The I-don't-envisage-working-with-The-Beatles-again press release bombshell that Paul had dropped a month previously was just the culmination of disputes that had been rumbling through the press for a year. The fact that not a single Beatle turned up for the long-awaited premiere of the *Let It Be* movie in Liverpool on 20 May bespoke a disinterest so total as to leave little room for ambiguity about what the future held for them. Meanwhile, the black border around the four Beatle photographs of this album's cover (once again, no band name in evidence) plus the album's very title (which had assumed a significance not intended when the song was written) screamed out "In Memoriam".

Paul was distancing himself from the album, unhappy about what had been done to it behind his back by Phil Spector, especially on "The Long And Winding Road". The Beatles had rejected two separate versions of *Get Back* material compiled by Glyn Johns. In the absence of any willingness on the part of The Beatles to undertake the chore of sitting and listening through up to several dozen versions of songs – all uncatalogued – to decide which was the best, the legendary American producer was appointed by Lennon (whose "Instant Karma" single, of course, he had recently helmed) without McCartney's permission to salvage something from the endless hours of tape the *Get Back* sessions had produced.

The two versions of *Get Back* assembled at The Beatles' behest by Glyn Johns in May 1969 and January 1970 are widely available on bootleg. Johns includes false starts, studio chatter, break-downs and warm-up burbles of instrumentation. The albums – apart from "The Long And Winding Road" and "Let It Be", classy compositions whatever the circumstances – are frequently raggedy, hesitant and sloppy, but that is not unrepresentative of the sessions. Spector had no intention of making such an honest album. The American was famous for his "Wall Of Sound" grandiose production technique, one at the opposite end of the scale to what The Beatles had been trying to do with *Get Back*. Overdubbing an epic string arrangement, harps and a female choir on Paul's relatively spartan piano ballad "The Long And Winding Road", for instance, was exactly the kind of thing anyone with a knowledge of Spector's records – which describes all of The Beatles – would expect him to do. McCartney was appalled. In contrast, Lennon's opinion of that and the entire Spector album was, "He was given the shittiest load of badly-recorded shit with a lousy feeling to it ever, and he made something of it."

Yet while Spector has been pilloried for making a nonsense by his overdubs of the sleevenotes where it is stated that "this is a new-phase Beatles album . . . In comes the warmth and freshness of a live performance . . .", in other ways he sticks quite faithfully to his remit of providing a soundtrack album and a snapshot of the sessions rather than a conventional Beatles LP, putting in snippets of dialogue, song and whimsy that give a flavour of the loose nature of the recording dates. An argument could be made that he should have included some of the many cover versions of hits from the group's younger days that they recorded at these sessions but the only really black mark is the unforgiveable omission of the beautiful "Don't Let Me Down".

This album was preceded by the release of "The Long And Winding Road" as an American single, which was the first Beatles product to be issued after it had become public knowledge that the band were history. It may have been the case that the issuing of "Something" as a single after it had already seen release on the parent *Abbey Road* album was not done for purely mercenary reasons but not even The Beatles could dispute that this move was a money-making one. Such naked avarice was the kind of thing that had supposedly been left behind when The Beatles wrested control of their career from the record company back in 1966. It seems significant that "The Long And Winding Road" was not issued on single in Britain, a country in which such financial chutzpah did not go down so well.

Speaking of which, originally, if you wanted to buy *Let It Be* you had no option but to also purchase *The Beatles Get Back*, a 164-page, 11" x 8" book containing photographs and dialogue mostly (but not all) from the movie in a deluxe package housed in a slipcase. It wasn't until six months later that a more budget-friendly version of the album in the traditional simple card sleeve appeared in shops. Though they may have panned it anyway, it's difficult to imagine the leftish *NME* being as scathing as they were about the *Let It Be* album ("a cheapskate epitaph, a cardboard tombstone") had it not offended their VFM sensibilities.

Though decades of disputes over Phil Spector's overdubs, voluble McCartney criticism and the 2003 release of the second-time-lucky *Let It Be . . . Naked* might give the impression that the *NME*'s viewpoint was representative, this is by no means the case. While not being unaware of the fact that Spector had done a salvage/demolition job (delete according to which Beatle's viewpoint you're discussing), many critics concluded that, on balance, *Let It Be* was a pretty good album. This applied to both establishment writers (e.g. William Mann, who declared in *The Times*, "Let us attend the funeral when life is pronounced extinct; at the moment the corporate vitality of The Beatles, to judge from *Let It Be*, is pulsating as strongly as ever") and counter-culture (Robert Christgau awarded it an A-minus grade in *Village Voice*, saying, "Though this is a little lightweight, it makes up in charm what it lacks in dramatic brilliance"). Another accolade which seems to have barely impinged on the public consciousness is that the film's music won The Beatles an Oscar: Best Original Song Score.

Had it been issued by any other rock artists, *Let It Be* would have been regarded as great-to-classic. And had Paul kept his gob shut about "The Long And Winding Road", we would have been able to enjoy the harp and choir without worrying that we might be knuckleheads easily impressed by manipulative schmaltz.

In the spirit of the *Get Back* sessions, Spector included a jam and a non-original on the album, though both are snippets of less than a minute. "Dig It" is a stream-of-consciousness from John using the blues song "Rollin' Stone" as a jumping-off point for a disconnected litany of celebrities' names as he and his colleagues extemporize musically. It's tolerable at around forty seconds but one suspects the recording of twelve-and-a-half minutes from which it was cut down would be close to unbearable. The track bears the publishing credit of all four Beatles, as does "Maggie Mae", which also notes that it is a traditional song. A so-so number about a Liverpool prostitute sung in thick Scouse, some suspect the hand of Lennon in the latter's placing after "Let It Be". (Lennon certainly lets his derision show in his mocking, Goon-like introduction to the latter in which he refers to it as "'Ark The Angels Come".) One feels compelled to place George's "For You Blue" in the same bracket as those two snippets. Though a fully-fledged song, it's also very insubstantial: a generic blues with a less-than-profound lyric ("Because you're sweet and lovely, girl, I love you"). George's acoustic guitar work, though, is excellent and his spoken-word praise for Lennon's slide playing is amusing and even affecting, considering what we know went down between the two men at these sessions.

The versions of "Let It Be" and "Get Back" on the album are different to their single incarnations. "Let It Be" uses the same master as the single but is a lot more orchestral and has a different guitar solo. "Get Back" is also the single master but with some amusing chatter from John in which he rewrites the lyric dubbed onto the start and some Apple rooftop dialogue appended to the finish.

Because of its American single status, "The Long And Winding Road" has a far greater recognition level in the US than the UK. McCartney was famously appalled at what he felt to be the saccharine harp and choir overdubbed by Spector without, he claims, his permission (the first-ever example of female group voices on a Beatles album, excepting the amateurish fans' accompaniment on the first version of "Across The Universe"). Maybe he's right but the impartial listener will be distracted by Richard Hewson's sweeping string arrangement, which, even though it makes a nonsense of the back-to-basics concept, is actually stunning, a thousand times more imaginative and complementary to the music than Mike Leander's dreary string arrangement on *Sgt. Pepper . . .* 's "She's Leaving Home". Paul's lyric, which reflects on past hiccups in his love life and on his present bliss, is vulnerable and touching and the melody as delightfully serpentine as the titular road.

Paul's "Two Of Us" is an acoustic affair with a heart-wrenching melody and clever, almost syncopated lyric that is lifted beyond even its considerable qualities as a song by its performance. In a masterstroke, John and Paul sing it together, thus giving the touching impression that the tribute to a partnership that has created "memories longer than the road that stretches out ahead" is a reference to Lennon/McCartney, an impression that can't help but sustain even when one reads interviews with Paul where he reveals the song was another inspired by his love for Linda.

John's "Across the Universe" and George's "I Me Mine" are both songs that really have no business on this album. Both were technically part of the *Get Back* sessions in that they were played at them, albeit briefly, and the decision to include the footage of such in the movie motivated The Beatles to include the songs on the accompanying album. However, neither of the songs appeared on the album in the form seen in the movie, in the case of "I Me Mine" because a group recording didn't exist. Nonetheless, it would be unwise to quibble, as both are great tracks.

The version of "Across The Universe" included here is actually the same master recording already released a month before John played it at the *Get Back* sessions, specifically on a wildlife charity album called *No One's Gonna Change Our World* (December 1969). Presumably it was John's love of The Goons that caused Spike Milligan, ex-member of that comedy ensemble, to score the astonishing commercial coup of being given a brand new Beatles recording for the project. The song originated, of course, way back in early 1968. For a creation with a beautiful melody and dazzling lyric ("Words are flowing out like endless rain into a paper cup" – and that's just the first line), it's remarkable how much "Across The Universe" has been buggered about with. Lennon retrospectively accused McCartney of engaging in unconscious sabotage of his songs by suggesting that two teenage Beatle fans be invited in off the street to sing harmonies on it but he himself allowed the song to be artificially sped up to virtually chipmunk speed for the charity album and allowed it to be artificially slowed down and plastered with strings for the version here. (There would be two further official releases of "Across The Universe", one an early master, one another example of the familiar master buggered about.) Through all the tampering, though, "Across The Universe" retains its charms and is so conducive to making one at peace with the cosmos that it could serve as a mantra every bit as effective (or more so) than the one John uses –

"Jai guru deva" and "Om" – in what constitutes the song's chorus.

"I Me Mine" was the last-ever Beatles recording, laid down on 3 January 1970, although Lennon didn't participate because he was on holiday. (The last time the four Beatles were in a studio together was 20 August 1969, working on finalizing "I Want You (She's So Heavy)" and the running order of *Abbey Road*.) Paul, George and Ringo may only have been knocking off the recording to synchronize the *Let It Be* film and album products but the result is a powerful track and one in fact that sounds almost shockingly polished compared to the rather raggedy nature of most of the rest of *Let It Be*, with some particularly fine guitar work – soaring lead lines and growling rhythm – from George. Organ from Paul gives the track an extra sleekness. George's disdain for selfishness and materialism is the subject once again but there is little piety in what is actually an engaging and clever lyric. Symptomatic, though, of the bitty feel of the whole album and the ramshackle nature of its entire recording is the fact that Spector felt compelled to splice the opening part of the song onto the back of it because it was only a minute-and-a-half long.

Spector decided to use three songs from the 30 January '69 Apple rooftop concert, "Dig a Pony", "I've Got A Feeling" and "One After 909". (Johns had only used one on his albums.) These three tracks give us the closest approximation of what the original concept of a new Beatles album played live would have sounded like. From this evidence, the conclusion must be that it would have sounded pretty good. Though the sonics were affected by the blustery wind and by the cold that had Lennon complaining that he was finding it difficult to form chords with his numb fingers, the concert was a triumphant vindication for Paul, who had been the one most enthused about a live performance. The Beatles clearly enjoyed themselves as they went through "Get Back" (three times), "Don't Let Me Down" (twice), "I've Got A Feeling" (twice), "The One After 909", "Dig A Pony" and the national anthem, their knowledge of what a "great little rock 'n' roll band" (to use McCartney's phrase) they were evident as they swapped vocals and helped each other on harmonies and generally put on a tight performance that saw the bitterness of the last few weeks evaporate in the winter air. "Dig a Pony" sees John revisit the profound meaninglessness of the verses of "All You Need Is Love", replacing talk of you being able to learn how to be you in time with equally grand-sounding but empty announcements like, "You can syndicate any boat you row". As with ". . . Love", though, he invests everything he has in the lyric and has us half-believing him to be speaking sense. We are, in any case, inclined to be charitable towards the song's sentiments because the band performance – especially Paul's harmonizing – is rousing stuff, while the bridge in which John tells someone, presumably Yoko, that all he wants is them, is moving. John and Paul collaborate on the playful "I've Got A Feeling", with Lennon providing a non sequitur of a middle section to McCartney's song in a reverse of the way Paul gave the "Woke up, got out of bed" bit to John for inclusion in his "A Day In The Life". "One After 909" is a vintage Lennon/McCartney song resuscitated for this project. (They had tried recording it back in '63 on the "From Me To You" session.) A number in the tradition of train songs like "Midnight Special" and "Rock Island Line", it has a highly serviceable melody and a toe-tappingly brisk pace but it's the performance that really makes it, with fine, tight playing, percolating keyboards from Billy Preston and great understanding by John and Paul in their mostly joint lead vocal. When the latter pair swing together into a "Weeeell . . ." halfway through the number as seamless and brotherly as an Everlys joint vocal, it's enough to bring tears to the eyes, a reminder of the golden days of a partnership once so harmonious and which begat so much pleasure for so many millions and is about to disappear into history.

Phil Spector's adding John's "Hope we passed the audition" rooftop *ad lib* at the close of the final track, "Get Back" – replicating the ending of the film – may be a dishonest splice (the Apple rooftop version of "Get Back" not appearing on the album), but it's a neat move, leaving us with a smile on our faces and warm feelings toward the artists, for the answer can only be "Yes".

NO WAY BACK

Though it occupied the lead space in the Night Special edition of London's Evening News, *the story that confirmed the final nail in the coffin for the hopes of those who thought there was a possibility that The Beatles as an entity would continue was brief.*

That number of hopefuls seemed to include some, possibly all, of the non-Paul members of The Beatles themselves. In late April 1970, George Harrison had implied in an American radio interview that more Beatles albums were not beyond the realms of possibility. Speaking just over a fortnight after Paul's inflammatory self-interview press release, he said in response to a Beatles reformation question, "I'll certainly try my best to do something with them again . . . I think it's the least we could do is to sacrifice three months of the year at least, you know just to do an album or two. I think it's very selfish if The Beatles don't record together." Others close to The Beatles have said that their impression was that joint work under the Beatles banner was likely in 1971.

The writ that Paul McCartney served on the last day of 1970 to legally terminate The Beatles' partnership – a partnership that required him to stay on Apple and to seek permission of the other three ex-Beatles when he wished to release a record – put paid to that, and was (intentionally or not) the checkmate response to George Harrison's alleged statement to him that, "You're staying on the fucking label. Hare Krishna."

There would be further details of the case printed in later editions of the Evening News – *and of course, the minute details of the legal wrangling would be splashed all over the papers the following year – but in a sense they don't bear repeating. What followed was the antithesis of the brotherhood and communality of the 1960s, a decade whose spirit The Beatles had either created or epitomized. As journalist* Johnny Black *sadly put it of The Beatles' public divorce, which began in the High Court on 19 January 1971, "It would be long, messy, humiliating and final."*

Paul Asks High Court: Break Up The Beatles

McCartney writ against John, George and Ringo

From *Evening News*, Thursday 31 December 1970
(No byline)

Paul McCartney began High Court proceedings today to end his partnership with The Beatles.

His writ asked for the appointment of a receiver to deal with the assets of the pop group. He also sought a court order winding up the affairs of "The Beatles and co.", and for accounts and inquiries of partnership dealings.

The defendants to the writ are Beatles John Lennon, George Harrison, Richard Starkey (Ringo Starr) and Apple Corps, Ltd. The writ was issued in the Chancery division.

They are currently said to be earning together about £7 million a year.

Solo Beatles

by Sean Egan

Imagine . . . a 1971 Beatles album.

If we are to assume that like *Let It Be*, it would consist of ten (full-length) tracks, it could conceivably include "My Sweet Lord", "All Things Must Pass" and "What Is Life", classic songs from George Harrison's November 1970 album *All Things Must Pass*, Ringo's fine single of April 1971 "It Don't Come Easy", "Smile Away", "Heart Of The Country" and "Back Seat Of My Car" – highlights of Paul's May 1971 LP *Ram* – and "Imagine", "Jealous Guy" and "Give Me Some Truth", titanic tracks on John Lennon's *Imagine* (October '71). (Lennon's December 1970 *Plastic Ono Band* is not taken into consideration here because so many of its songs are a reaction to no longer being a Beatle, thus creating a plausibility problem insurmountable even for a fantasy.) Such an album is a mouth-watering prospect and would surely have constituted the greatest Beatles album ever.

Instead, of course, what we got in that eleven-month period was three fair-to-very-good albums by John, Paul and George (Ringo released two covers albums in 1970), the consequence of the fact that four people contributing their three or four best songs of the moment to a project is a situation guaranteed to create better product than four separate projects in which each individual has to come up with all nine or ten (or more) tracks on his own.

There must even have been some amongst the public who were assuming that The Beatles' split might be good news:

instead of one album per year by The Beatles, they would have the pleasure of one each by John, Paul, George and Ringo. Of course, that sort of thinking is at the wild end of the scale of logic. Even so, many sober-minded people were shocked at just how far short The Beatles fell in terms of aesthetic brilliance as they proceeded to pursue their careers as four separate entities. After all, it was widely known even when the group was still extant that John and Paul were writing together increasingly less often. Meanwhile, the evidence of his songs on *Abbey Road* indicated that George was fast catching up with them as composers. While few can have been expecting much of the solo work of Ringo, surely Messrs Harrison, Lennon and McCartney would – with the help of the top sidemen that their legends and money could obtain them – be able to make music almost as good as the work they had crafted together?

Evidence that this would never be the case came pretty quickly. Nobody expected too much of Paul's 1970 debut *McCartney*, first, because it was technically issued while he was still a Beatle so wasn't intended as an entrée to a post-Beatles career, secondly because it was what it was: a low-fi, homely collection. Follow-up *Ram* (1971), and credited to "Paul and Linda McCartney" in a move that indicated that Paul had – like John before him – merged his musical and private personas, was a nice record but not much less low-key than its predecessor. When McCartney set up his new group, Wings, it would have been assumed that he would try to make a spectacular entrée with them but the only notable thing about *Wildlife* (also 1971) for people used to the songcraft and polish of Beatles fare was how shockingly slovenly and underwhelming it was. Not everything – or perhaps anything – he released afterwards was as bad as that, but frankly The Beatles would never have put their name to it. Paul's masterpiece remains the third Wings album (credited to "Paul McCartney and Wings"), *Band On The Run* (1973). When it came out, some were half-heartedly proclaiming it a return to past glories but, though a quality piece of work, it so happened that the nature of its contents made for an easy comparison to The Beatles' peaks, and the comparison was not flattering to Paul the solo artist. The opening, title track was a suite complete with reprise. It was instantly obvious that this cartoonish jailbreak tale with lazy rhymes was as close as he was capable of getting to the conceptual majesty of *Sgt. Pepper* ... or the *Abbey Road* suite, just as the pleasant but empty 1971 character study single "Another Day" was the closest he could get to the acute observation of "Eleanor Rigby". And while his penchant for competent but lesser-known musicians might have diminished his craft a little, it was clear that all the superstar sidekicks in the world wouldn't be able to transform any of his songs into classic records.

Lennon's music, meanwhile, had all the grit and soul that McCartney's lacked but little of the gloss and melodicisim that came some easily to his former songwriting partner. His December 1970 release *Plastic Ono Band* was one of the most curious mainstream records ever released by a major rock artist. It was a musical essay on the pain he had experienced in his life shot through with his recent experiences with psychotherapist Arthur Janov, who encouraged screaming as therapy. "Mother" and "My Mummy's Dead" explored his devastation at the loss of his mother which he had hidden with a macho exterior he was now disowning, "Working Class Hero" was a broadside against the conservative and authoritarian culture he had grown up in (with the shocking line "You're still fucking peasants as far as I can see" finally shattering whatever vestiges there remained of The Beatles as four loveable, sweet moptops), "Isolation" tore into those who ridiculed Yoko and the love he had for her and – climactically, although the brief "My Mummy's Dead" followed it – "God" was a myth-busting litany the final entry of which declared that he didn't believe in The Beatles. "The dream is over," Lennon sang of the belief that The Beatles were going to change the world. (His spoken equivalent to that sentiment was expressed in 1971's *Rolling Stone* interview wherein he said of The Beatles' sociological legacy, "The people who are in control and in power, and the class system and the whole bullshit bourgeoisie is exactly the same, except there is a lot of fag middle class kids with long, long hair walking around London in trendy clothes . . . Apart from that, nothing happened.") It might be easy to scorn Lennon's self-indulgence and self-pity from today's perspective – after all, whatever the undoubted difficulties in his formative years, he was a vastly privileged and wealthy man whose job involved him doing something he loved – but it was revolutionary: in those days, celebrities simply did not come out with such naked, self-excoriating artistic statements, nor did male rock stars show such vulnerability as in those songs' lyrics or the dependence on a female partner Lennon revealed (or confirmed) when he said at the end of "God" that he only believed in Yoko and he. Trouble was, that however powerful and groundbreaking this statement was, it wasn't much cop musically. The tunes were very reminiscent of some of his White Album work: somewhat opaque. Just as he wasn't around any more to knock the sentiment and whimsy out of Paul's songs, so Paul was no longer a handy presence to inject a bit more melodic imagination into *his* creations. Not for nothing had Lennon & McCartney been the foremost composers of the twentieth century. They had complemented each other perfectly and the qualities each brought to the table were lost to their art forever when they seemed no longer inspiring each other, whether that inspiration took the form of direct collaboration or even the benefits that close proximity engenders (helpful advice, worry about incurring the others' ridicule, anxiety to out-do the other). Even had they began collaborating with others – which neither ever did for any prolonged period – the slack could not have been taken up: only once in your career do you encounter the perfect partner.

Imagine (1971) was Lennon's high-water mark as a solo artist. John himself described it as a "sugar-coated *Plastic Ono Band*", in reference to the fact that it saw the cutting-edge approach of that previous album wrapped up in prettier melodies and in a production on which Phil Spector's grandiose tendencies were given full rein. The title track was no less hands-across-the-water than Paul's "Let It Be", (which, of course, John had ridiculed) and became an instant classic, just as "Let It Be" did. "Jealous Guy" is even better, while at the opposite end of the scale to that track's musical delicacy and emotional vulnerability is the ferocious hard rock anti-square anthem "Give Me Some Truth". However, the fact that John's masterpiece also contains such banal dreck as "Oh My Love", "Love" and "Oh Yoko!" is an illustration of how far he had fallen.

At the close of The Beatles' career, it seemed logical to assume that George Harrison would soon be the equal of Lennon & McCartney, if he wasn't already: the last album recorded by The Beatles featured his "Something" and "Here Comes The Sun', which were as good as anything else on that fine record. At first, it seemed that that assumption was going to be proven correct. His solo career got off to a spectacular start with *All Things Must Pass*. That his debut LP was a massive triple set may or may not have been a fuck-you to the Lennon-McCartney songwriting axis that he had latterly felt was keeping his songs off Beatles albums. The third disc was dispensable in the way that all recorded jams are, but the first two discs were choc-full of classy melodic rock that sounded far more Beatles-esque than the initial post-Beatles solo efforts by Messrs Lennon and McCartney. Highlights were the title track – which the Fabs insanely spurned the chance of issuing – "What Is Life" and "My Sweet Lord". Though the gloss of the latter's globe-spanning success (a number one in both the UK and US) has been slightly tarnished by a 1976 court ruling that it inadvertently plagiarized The Chiffons' "He's So Fine" (the fault, in the reckoning of some, of Billy Preston, who suggested a melody amendment when it was recorded), it remains a great song (and better than the one it supposedly ripped off). It also proved George's religiosity was not inconsistent with commercial success. Harrison consolidated his status as most successful ex-Beatle with the two Concerts For Bangla Desh that took place on 1 August 1971. Though his place in the rock firmament would have been the last thing on his mind as he set about putting together a concert to help stricken Asian earthquake victims that set the template for the charity rock event, the fact that it was George who orchestrated this noble affair and sensationally persuaded Bob Dylan out of concert retirement for it only added to the impression of a man truly coming into his own. The album of the concert topped the charts. Again, Harrison will have had more elevated things on his mind than the fact that what transpired to be his only UK number one LP was actually not credited to him. (The 2005 CD remaster has turned this Various Artists record into one by "George Harrison and Friends").

Harrison's period of triumph was to be startlingly short-lived.

Though he had another US number one in the shape of "Give Me Love – (Give Me Peace On Earth)" (1973), he proved surprisingly unable to sustain the quality of *All Things Must Pass*.

Ringo would ultimately have the sort of career one would expect of a man who could neither write melody nor sing very well. He got by with a little help from his friends, whether it be the Beatles fans who loyally bought his records or his ex-Beatles colleagues who were happy to furnish him with songs. Having said that, had his career ended in 1974, he would have been remembered as a man whose catalogue was comprised of some unexpectedly brilliant singles. The powerful "It Don't Come Easy", the T. Rex-alike "Back Off Boogaloo", the plaintive collaboration with Harrison "Photograph" and the jolly Johnny Burnette revival "You're Sixteen" – UK hits, one a year, from 1972 to 1974 – were better records than anybody had expected from him. The B-side of "It Don't Come Easy", "Early 1970", was a Ringo original that constituted his contribution to the musical dialogue that took place between The Beatles in the early 1970s and easily stood its artistic grounds against the entries of John (the scathingly anti-McCartney "How Do You Sleep?"), George (the detailing of the Apple court case impasse, "Sue Me Sue You Blues") and Paul (the sorrowful reply to John, "Let Me Roll It").

Ringo's first two solo albums, *Sentimental Journey* and *Beaucoups Of Blues*, both appeared in 1970, the first a selection of old-time pop standards, the second a selection of country covers. The second was substantially the better album but neither was destined to be a classic: cover jobs require a strong, interpretative voice, which Starr will never have. *Ringo* (1973) was much, much better. Featuring an all-star cast, good songs (including ones from all three of his ex-Beatles colleagues) and a fine Richard Perry production, it bequeathed two hits in the shape of "Photograph" and "You're Sixteen" that – added to the chart placings of his two previous hit parade entries – temporarily and bizarrely made him the most successful ex-Beatle hit merchant. The following year's *Goodnight Vienna* repeated the same formula of superstar mates providing songs and music and Perry the production, but with less successful results. And, extracting the Perry production part, much the same can be said about the whole of the rest of his career. You don't need to lose sleep about what you're missing by not investigating any of his other albums. Declining sales meant that *Old Wave* (1983) was released outside of the UK and US only, and presumably had something to do with the fact that there was a nine-year gap between that album and his next studio effort, *Time Takes Time*.

For a while Starr had a pretty successful acting career, appearing in *Candy* (1968), *The Magic Christian* (1969), *Blindman* (1971), *200 Motels* (1971), *Son of Dracula* (1974), *Lisztomania* (1975), *Caveman* (1981) and *Give My Regards To Broad Street* (1984). He also directed a documentary about T. Rex, *Born To Boogie* (1972). Most of his acting roles had the smack of gimmick casting but his portrayal of a malevolent greaser in the rock 'n' roll flick *That'll Be The Day* (1973) was critically acclaimed. Ringo also provided the voiceovers for the 1980s TV cartoon series *Thomas The Tank Engine*, where he made canny and knowing use of his distinctive, doleful tones.

But he seemed to lose either interest or opportunity in pursuing acting. Which didn't leave him much to do. He had a record company and a furniture design company, but neither lasted long. Lennon, probably mindful of an easy-going attitude on Starr's part that sometimes bordered on the comatose, had once said that he worried about what was going to happen to Ringo when The Beatles' career was over. As if living down to Lennon's worst fears, during a period in the 1980s, Ringo succumbed to alcoholism and cocaine use. He said he was bored rather than unhappy – having found married bliss with actress Barbara Bach, whom he married in April 1981, after his marriage to Maureen of "Thanks Mo" fame on *Let It Be* ended in 1976 – and now appears to have emerged from the darkest depths.

Since 1989, he has exploited the willingness of the same people who will no longer buy his records to revisit their youth on a night out by touring regularly with the All-Starr Band, a group whose rotating stellar membership has included Billy Preston, Clarence Clemons, members of The Band, Nils Lofgren, Todd Rundgren, Dave Edmunds, John Entwistle and

Jack Bruce, amongst others. Another former member of the All-Starr Band is one Zak Starkey, his son, born in 1965. After a difficult start in the business when he seemed destined to always be known as "Son of Ringo", Zak is now a genuinely respected drummer, the first-choice sticksman of both Oasis and The Who (who sometimes vie for his services).

Liverpool 8, Ringo's 2008 album, saw him reflect on his humble origins and marked something of a return to form – although that is not saying much. Starr remains impossible to dislike (even if he did upset some Liverpudlians by saying in a 2008 television interview that he didn't miss the city of his birth), though those who admire his drumming can't help but feel a little impatient at the way he allowed his post-Fabs career to develop along the lines it did. He was never going to be able to sustain the living legend status conferred on him by membership of The Beatles – if Lennon, McCartney and Harrison couldn't, there was no way the drummer could – so a full-blown solo career was an unwise move. Instead, he should have become a grandiose version of a session musician, earning a living by regularly lending his services to his superstar friends (of whom he has many) and thus improving their product at the same time as maintaining his own reputation. Because he didn't, the nonsense that he was a passenger in The Beatles – inadvertently started by his own self-deprecation in the 1960s and perpetuated by comedians and scriptwriters seeking a cheap, easy laugh – has taken hold. Starr is now the most underrated musician in the history of rock.

Because of his tragic murder, John's catalogue is as easy to summarize as Ringo's. Following *Imagine*, he took a bizarre detour into radical politics with *Some Time in New York City* (1972), the type of which he had presaged with the fist-pumping 1971 single "Power To The People". Admirable though it may have been for Lennon to use the platform he had to try to help others – his support for John Sinclair seems to have got the White Panther Party leader released from his brutal prison sentence of ten years for supplying two joints – simplistic sloganeering seemed a little beneath his talents. He was on far more comfortable territory with that year's single "Happy Xmas (War Is Over)" which though equally simplistic in its belief that

"War is over if you want it" had a warmth and humanism that has made it an alternative to more traditional Yuletide fare like "White Christmas".

November '73 saw Lennon issue the far more conventional album *Mind Games*. It was so-so, although the title track showed he could still pull off a great song. Far better was the October 1974 effort *Walls And Bridges*. It was a fine album with good, catchy songs (especially "Whatever Gets You Thru The Night" – a US number one – and "#9 Dream") and a lush production. Lennon later dismissed the record, but that may have been because it was written when he was romantically involved with a woman called May Pang during a separation from Yoko.

The largely disappointing oldies collection Rock 'N' Roll (1975) had started life because Lennon promised music publisher Morris Levy that he would record three songs in his catalogue to avoid being sued over the supposed resemblance of "Come Together" to the Levy-owned "You Can't Catch Me". After that, with Lennon's recording contract lapsed, he left music behind and concentrated on starting a family with Yoko, with whom he had been reunited. When he next emerged in 1980, it was with an album credited to both he and Ono called *Double Fantasy*, on which the couple explored their bliss on alternate tracks. The fact that the album was platitude-ridden and musically soporific was virtually expunged from the public consciousness when Lennon was shot dead by an ex-fan on 8 December that year, at which point tracks like "Woman" (an ode to Ono he posited as a grown-up version of The Beatles' "Girl") and "Beautiful Boy" (in which he exulted in the joy brought him by his son Sean) were instantly and permanently transformed from banal into poignant.

The work-in-progress version of the planned follow-up to *Double Fantasy* was released in 1984 under the title *Milk And Honey*. Unexpectedly, it contained an absolute gem in the shape of "Nobody Told Me". It should be pointed out that the nature of the track – an uptempo cry of uncertainty – seems rather more truthful to the real nature of the Lennons' marriage than the contented-househusband-baking-bread scenario Lennon depicted in interviews at the time: employees of the Lennons spoke of distant and frosty relations and even violence between the couple.

Though Lennon's post-Beatles catalogue is the most meagre in volume of all The Beatles, he provided us with enough to adjudge his solo abilities. Essentially, he was good-to-very good, with flashes of greatness, though susceptible to allowing an absolutist streak in his personality to cloud his artistic judgment (e.g. the self-conscious radicalism and posturing of *Some Time In New York City*, the surrender to marital bliss – or at least the idea of it – detailed on *Double Fantasy*).

Harrison's post-Beatles legacy was also unexpectedly depleted. In his case, it was because he spent a lot of time financing and producing movies. Though he naturally remained an excellent guitarist and retained a great degree of craftsmanship, the quality of his songs did not blossom in the way that *Abbey Road* and *All Things Must Pass* had suggested. *Living In The Material World* (1973) was a well-made and often highly agreeable album but by the time of the following year's *Dark Horse*, his spiritual concerns were turning increasingly into disagreeable piousness and judgmentalness. Additionally, some of the songs were plain stinkers. *Extra Texture* ('75) was a bit better but not much. *Thirty-Three And A Third* (1976) has a neat title, it being both the speed the LP played at and Harrison's age at the time of its intended original release but that was almost the only notable thing about a curiously substandard way to mark his first album on his own Dark Horse label. It was also curious that it took him two-and-a-quarter years to release its follow-up (the standard gap between albums at the time was less than half that) but to some extent the eponymous album was worth the wait, containing a *joie de vivre* not often found on George's records, some cracking tunes and plenty of his always slick guitar work. It also saw him dust off White Album reject "Not Guilty" for a much-belated but deserved public airing. There was an identical time lag before the next album, *Somewhere In England*. This one turned out to be less enjoyable, but it did contain George's moving tribute to the slain Lennon, "All Those Years Ago", although Harrison blotted his copybook slightly by shoehorning in a religious reference that was not only distasteful but also ironic in light of the fact that Lennon had once revealed in an interview that he got fed up with collaborating on songs with George because his former

Beatle colleague insisted on putting into every song what John termed "the God verse".

Though 1982's *Gone Troppo* materialized only fifteen months after its predecessor and was decent enough, Harrison seemed casual about its fortunes (which turned out to be not great) and the fact they he subsequently disappeared off the recording radar for five years somehow didn't seem surprising. What was surprising was that when he did return in late 1987 with *Cloud Nine*, it was in a pretty big way. "Got My Mind Set On You" – written by James Ray – climbed to number two in the UK charts and was a US number one. Those who detected a desperation in the fact that this lead-off single was the only track on the album not written by the artist were wrong: there were several fine numbers present, including a wry tribute to his former life, "When We Was Fab". The only major fault was the stupid, bombastic production by Jeff Lynne.

Nonetheless, Lynne was now a big part of Harrison's life, both as friend and colleague. The two, with fellow rock legends Bob Dylan, Tom Petty and Roy Orbison, formed the supergroup The Traveling Wilburys, whose 1988 debut album *Volume 1* was a twinkle-eyed, good-time listen. Orbison died before the 1990 follow-up *Volume 3* [sic]. This would transpire to be Harrison's last studio album before his own death. (The above-average in-concert document *Live In Japan* appeared in 1992).

Harrison made a speedy and good-humoured recovery from an attempt on his life by a deranged knife-wielding fan in December 1999, but the cancer that he had been battling with since 1997 finally got the better of him on 29 November 2001. Though he had found happiness with new wife Olivia, his last decade had been somewhat blighted by business issues. He successfully sued his Handmade Films partner Denis O'Brien over losses the company had mysteriously made but it was an unhappy denouement to a film production career that had seen Handmade bring into existence well-regarded movies such as *Life Of Brian*, *The Long Good Friday* and *Withnail And I*.

The album on which he was working prior to his death was released as *Brainwashed* in November 2002. It had some good moments but as with all such projects that rely on the producers

(Lynne, with Harrison's son Dhani) second-guessing the artist's final intentions, it's difficult to reach a conclusion on its merits.

Paul McCartney's solo career is more difficult to encapsulate than those of any of his ex-colleagues. Alone among them, he has recorded consistently, seeing no need to take sabbaticals for the purpose of raising his family (even though he had more children than any of the others) or to pursue other interests (although he has dabbled in movie-making and maintained a very successful sideline as a song publisher). Though from the late 1980s onwards, his productivity level slowed down to modern industry standards of a studio album at three- or four-year intervals, the fact that he has been making solo albums for a period that is now nearly five times longer than The Beatles' recording career means he is responsible for a quite vast non-Fabs back catalogue.

Though he was slow out of the blocks – initially his records were less artistically and commercially successful than those of John, George or Ringo – he became one of the most successful recording artists of the 1970s. *Red Rose Speedway* (1973) had seen him recover some of his pop smarts and penchant for gloss, while that year's fine standalone single comprising the powerful, horny rocker "Hi Hi Hi" and the slinky reggae number "C Moon" were his two best songs since The Beatles' split. Additionally, the banning of "Hi Hi Hi" by the BBC for possible drug references enhanced some unlikely rebel credentials he was then acquiring: the Beeb had also banned his naïve but heartfelt response to the Northern Ireland Bloody Sunday massacre "Give Ireland Back To The Irish" (for which he pulled his scheduled next single, "Love Is Strange"), and 1972 had seen him experience a couple of drug busts. Nineteen seventy-two had also seen McCartney achieve the coup of writing and performing the theme tune to the latest James Bond movie, *Live And Let Die*. It managed to assimilate the Bond theme characteristics while maintaining a certain cool (it had a reggae bridge, for instance), to such an extent that those bad-boy rockers Guns N' Roses covered it in 1991.

The accomplished *Band On The Run* was greeted with some relief by those who must have wondered what had happened to the gifts of the man who had always seemed the most musically talented Beatle. Its track "Jet" made a great single, although the lovely "Bluebird" was the album's true highpoint. McCartney released two singles in '74. One was "Juniors Farm" by "Paul McCartney and Wings", the other was also Wings (albeit augmented by Chet Atkins and Floyd Cramer) but was credited to "The Country Hams": called "Walking In The Park With Eloise", it was a sentimental journey for Macca, as it was a song that had been written a long time before by his Dad. *Venus And Mars* (1975) saw a return to the simple Wings name under which *Wildlife* had been issued but which "Paul McCartney and" had been put in front of on the previous two albums. This was despite the fact that, guitarist Denny Laine excepted, this was a completely new line-up of the band. Laine and the McCartneys would be the only mainstays of the Wings personnel, whose revolving membership would at various times feature quire significant talents like guitarist Jimmy McCulloch and drummer Joe English. *Venus And Mars* was again marked by serious intent, melodic and production lushness, lack of bite and an overabundance of whimsy, but that ambiguous mixture was proving increasingly palatable to Joe and Jo Public.

Though far from their best album, *Wings At The Speed Of Sound* (1976) marked a certain peak for the band, coinciding as it did with a very high public profile courtesy of top quality hit singles "Silly Love Songs" and "Let 'Em In" and successful tours that year. By now, the days of the newly-formed band playing unannounced gigs in British pubs and universities were long over as they rocked arenas in both Europe and America. It would have been gratifying to McCartney, who at that point was volubly trying to lay the ghost of The Beatles, that many of the kids who came to the shows were clearly too young to have any living memory of The Beatles – although after initially resisting McCartney was now prepared to include some Beatles songs in the sets.

Between *Wings At The Speed Of Sound* and 1978's *London Town*, McCartney released the single "Mull Of Kintyre". Though he had had US chart-toppers in the shape of the twee "Uncle Albert/Admiral Halsey", the grandiose ballad "My Love", "Band on The Run", "Listen To What The Man Said" and "Silly Love Songs", "Mull of Kintyre" was – amazingly – his first number one single in his home country. Even more amazingly, this pleasant Caledonian-flavoured paean to a Scottish beauty spot proceeded to become the biggest-selling UK single of all time, deposing "She Loves You" from that position. (Its B-side "Girls' School" was chosen as the single in the States.) Much to EMI's displeasure, McCartney declined to put "Mull of Kintyre" on *London Town* on the grounds that it didn't fit in. Nineteen seventy-seven also saw McCartney anonymously arrange the release of the album *Thrillington*, an orchestral version of *Ram* that he had commissioned in 1971.

London Town and 1979's *Back To The Egg* were lacklustre and the following year Wings were torn asunder by McCartney's January drug bust. His attempt to smuggle marijuana though Japanese customs saw him spend nine nights in prison before he was released and deported. In the aftermath of the incident, Paul's disinclination to go on the road led Denny Laine finally to desert the Wings ship. From hereon, all McCartney's records – unless he was collaborating with another name artist or recording incognito, as with the records he releases occasionally under the *nom de guerre* The Fireman – would be credited to him alone.

The first such record was *McCartney II*, a sequel to his first eponymous album exactly ten years on and informed by the same DIY sensibilities. It was very flimsy, though "Coming Up" was an inexplicable hit, with a live version actually making number one in the ever-McCartney-receptive States. *Tug Of War* (1982) was at the opposite end of the spectrum. Its use of George Martin as producer – barely employed by any of The Beatles after the split, with them favouring the likes of Phil Spector and often self-producing – seemed pointed, a declaration of a new determination to ratchet up the declining quality of McCartney product. It sort of worked, although its pleasant but not profound quality once again confirmed McCartney's post-Beatles narrowed artistic horizons. The slushy but well-intentioned collaboration with Stevie Wonder on the call for racial tolerance "Ebony And Ivory" (a Transatlantic number one) got all the attention but the gossamer "Wanderlust" and the high-velocity "Take It Away" were the true highlights.

McCartney collaborated with another black American artist

that year on "The Girl Is Mine" a saccharine co-written hit for him and Michael Jackson. They repeated the trick the following year with slightly less embarrassing results in the shape of "Say Say Say".

Pipes Of Peace (1983) comprised offcuts from the *Tug Of War* sessions, so by definition was similar but not as good, though its title track gave Paul his third UK number one. The following year's *Give My Regards To Broad Street* was the sound-track to McCartney's feature film of the same name. Some of the album consisted of re-imaginings of Beatles (as well as solo) recordings. His prerogative of course, but the inevitable unflattering comparisons were drawn. Still, the album bequeathed a Transatlantic hit in the shape of "No More Lonely Nights". The supporting cartoon feature for . . . *Broad Street* featured the amusing "We All Stand Together" – a song in large part rendered in frog's croaks – which became a UK top three. Much derided, its critics should loosen up. Lennon would have found it amusing.

Press To Play (1986) was unusual in that it saw McCartney collaborate in writing most of it with his partner ex-10cc man Eric Stewart. Two heads unfortunately turned out to be worse than one and the record was an artistic letdown. There was another even more unexpected writing collaboration on some of follow-up *Flowers In The Dirt* (1989), which featured some tracks co-written with new-waver Elvis Costello. A good album, it was followed by the disappointing *Off The Ground* (1993). Considering the dread hand of Jeff Lynne was at the producer's controls for half of 1997's *Flaming Pie*, the result is not too bad at all. And, yes, the album title is a reference to John's humorous explanation in *Mersey Beat* way back when of the origin of The Beatles' name.

Nineteen ninety-seven was the year that McCartney became Sir Paul. "Rude not to", he observed of his decision to accept when the knighthood was offered him. Still, it probably made him no more chuffed than the fact that the previous year had seen the opening of the Fame Academy-like Liverpool Institute for Performing Arts on the site of his old school, Liverpool Institute. McCartney – who had helped finance and fundraise for the project – said at the opening ceremony (also attended by the Queen) that he'd better not start talking about how proud his mum and dad would have been to see this occasion because he might start crying.

The death of Linda McCartney from cancer in 1998 created another eerie parallel between the lives of McCartney and Lennon. Just as the world had wondered in 1980 how on earth Yoko would be able to survive the loss of the man to whom she seemed joined at the hip, so it seemed inconceivable of a life for Paul McCartney without the woman from whom he had only spent nine nights apart – those nine spent in a Japanese prison cell. An understandable hiatus in McCartney's recording activities followed. He felt his way back in via the second Fireman album, *Rushes* (1998), the 1999 1950s covers album *Run Devil Run* (his equivalent of John's *Rock 'N' Roll*) and the latest of his classical works *Working Classical* (also '99). *Driving Rain* – released in 2001 – was his first rock outing since the tragedy and was a decent effort.

However, Nigel Godrich thought that decent (and the musicians on *Driving Rain*) wouldn't quite do when he was given the task of producing McCartney's next album. McCartney – who more than one close observer has noted is transparently a man used to being listened to, as might be expected of someone who employs, directly and indirectly, many people – had to deal with the unfamiliar situation of having some of his songs rejected as not up to scratch. He responded not by sacking Godrich but by accepting his criticism and issuing not only his best album for many a long year but one which stripped away all that McCartney gloss to reveal a vulnerability that was the result not of the pop craftsman's adroit and knowledgeable choice of stock phrases and chord progressions but of pulling material from a profoundly deeper place than normal. Perhaps he was uncomfortably aware that though his ability to pack stadiums remains undiminished, *Driving Rain* had spent one week in the UK album charts, making a mere number 46, before dropping out.

McCartney has issued five live albums, the most interesting of which are Wings' 1976 triple set *Wings At The Speed Of Sound* and his 1991 limited edition *Unplugged* album. If one includes his 1967 soundtrack for *The Family Way*, he has released four collections of classical music, usually relying on outside help/collaboration. *Liverpool Oratorio* (1991), *Standing Stone – A Symphonic Poem* (1997) and *Working Classical* have been reasonably well received, as has "Nova", his contribution to *A Garland For Linda* (2000). McCartney clearly enjoys this work, so maybe it would be churlish to point out that he will never be able to catch up in ability with people who compose classical music full-time. Ditto his excursions into techno with his Fireman releases – collaborations with Youth – the first of which came in 1994.

McCartney thought he'd found true love again in the shape of Heather Mills, whom he wed in 2002. Though the marriage produced daughter Beatrice (born in 2003), it lasted only until 2008.

McCartney remains alert to the best ways to reach his audience. In 2007, he amazed many with the announcement that his new studio album *Memory Almost Full* would be available not on Parlophone but Hearmusic, the label owned by the Starbucks coffee chain. That audience – consisting of both original Beatles fans and people he has picked up down the years – is still there for him, despite hiccups like *Driving Rain* and despite a fact that has been apparent for three decades or more to everybody (including, surely, McCartney himself): that his product is not, and has never been, as good as that of The Beatles.

The same of course goes for his three former colleagues. Yet the solo careers of The Beatles were always destined to be a disappointment. What shocked even those who understood the mathematical equation detailed previously that dictated that solo albums would never be as good as Beatles group efforts was the drastic reduction in the ex-Beatles' socio-political significance. Though it would have been silly to expect the individual Beatles to continue to have the same significance for their audience as previously – as people get older, the intensity of their feelings for pop groups diminishes, no matter how good or important – it only took one or two albums by each of the ex-Fabs for them to assume wildly reduced places in not only the rock firmament but the wider world. Lennon, McCartney, Harrison and Starr became very quickly merely just another quartet of artists. Very big-selling maybe, but of no profound significance to the rock audience beyond their own fans, and certainly – unlike The Beatles – of no significance to those not interested in popular music. As public figures, the allure of the fragmented Beatles was shockingly diluted.

The Beatles power and allure stemmed from them being a group. Though Lennon and McCartney were indisputably the most talented Beatles, the assumption that, had the two of them recorded The Beatles' canon with session musicians, they could have been either a cultural phenomenon or that that canon would have been as good as the music they made with George and Ringo is nonsense.

The world fell in love with The Beatles as people because they were a package, a goodie bag of personality. Their four distinct and contrasting personalities were summed up by Charles Shaar Murray, who said, "Ringo was the big nose, Paul the big eyes and John the big mouth. George chose to remain the big mystery." That's obviously a form of shorthand – he could also have said that Ringo was loveably plain and self-effacing next to his handsome and cocksure colleagues, Paul beautiful and a diplomat, John thrillingly less diplomatic and so clearly on a different intellectual plane that a 1964 magazine article about him was called *The Beatle With A Future*, and George a changeling who went from grinning, gushing baby of the band to somebody soberly spiritual.

"I love Ringo badges" far outsold any of those of the other three in America, but the importance of The Beatles as a *group* on every level is far deeper than banal facts like that. Those trademark three-part harmonies that graced so many Beatles choruses, verses and bridges would probably not have been recorded by a duo working with hired hands, yet it is the air of communality and co-operation provided by those harmonies – as well as their aesthetic qualities – that gave The Beatles' music such warmth. That warmth was a huge part of their unprecedented and unequalled appeal.

Then there is the musical chemistry of the group. Some might be inclined to dismiss the notion as cliché. But how else does one explain why groups of infinitely greater musical ability – The Yardbirds, Cream, Jethro Tull, The Grateful Dead, to choose some names at random – were simply incapable of making records in the same league as The Beatles, at least consistently? For the same reason that when Jimi Hendrix used bassists in his bands far superior to the slenderly talented Noel Redding, the records simply did not have the crackle and quality of those of The Jimi Hendrix Experience, even though two-thirds of the group was the same. The way a band interacts musically – the indefinable, unpredictable alchemy of person-alities, styles, habits and tastes – is more important to the sound of a band than virtuosity. The Beatles *meshed*. And the world meshed with them.

Throughout the first decade following The Beatles' split, every single solo ex-Beatle record had a ghost hovering in the back-ground: namely, the notion that it would be better if the four just stopped pretending that they could be as good apart as they were together and re-form. Only with Lennon's death did that ghost depart the stage. All four expressed public impatience and/or irritation at the endless talk of a reunion. Two of the more famous comments on the subject were, "You can't re-heat a soufflé" (Paul) and "Why should The Beatles give more? Didn't they give everything on God's earth for ten years?" (John). Both would seem a little disingenuous, given Paul's 1979 CBS contract which he ensured contained a clause allowing him to record with The Beatles should the possibility arise and suggestions from people who knew Lennon that he was contem-plating the possibility of working with The Beatles just before his death. Additionally, in May 2008, May Pang claimed in a radio interview that in early 1974 The Beatles were discussing a one-off reunion gig in upstate New York, with Harry Nilsson guesting. (Incidentally, forgotten by history is a comment Paul made as early as December 1973: "The only thing that has prevented us from getting together again has been Klein's contractual hold over The Beatles' name; when he is out of the way, there is no real reason why we shouldn't get together again.")

Though The Beatles had always displayed an intelligence and thoughtfulness about their art that suggested that any reunion would at least be handled with sufficient care and hard work as to scupper any possibility of the sort of disappointment that attended the reunions of, for example, The Byrds and the Small

Faces, ultimately we should be grateful that they split up when they did. An example of why was provided by a correspondent to the *New Musical Express* upon the 1982 announcement that The Jam were to bow out at their peak. The letter writer thanked The Jam for being his generation's Beatles, and not being his generation's Rolling Stones. Though The Beatles' ending wasn't perfect or tidy, it took place at the right time, both in world chronology and their own lives. The juncture in history at which they split is poetic: they bowed out in the first year of the 1970s, after having moulded the previous decade in their own image. Additionally, it has subsequently been proven that, for whatever reason, rock musicians do their best work in their twenties and that any career that lasts beyond that is marked by a long, slow decline. Though The Beatles stood head and shoulders above their contemporaries in popularity and significance, The Stones were the closest anybody came to The Beatles' feat of combining great art with a position as figureheads for the young and symbols of the new world order they wanted to build. (Dylan was incredibly important in terms of influence on other artists but didn't have the profile of those bands: in other words, society beyond the rock consumer was only vaguely aware of him, and it's difficult to be a figurehead in a vacuum.) The Stones' first decade as recording artists was magnificent, the second very good. Since then they have become an ever more embarrassing joke.

The Beatles as an entity lived fast, died young and left a beautiful corpse. Their reputation is unsullied by music that is a grotesque parody of their former glories. For that mercy, we can bear all the mediocre and disappointing solo albums in the world.

Life After The End:
Posthumous Beatles Releases

by Sean Egan

For a group who split up in 1970, there has been an extraordinary amount of Beatles cataloguc activity subsequently, and it is certainly not restricted to reissues. For a full list of UK Beatles releases – including every picture disc, coloured disc, reissue, box-set and corporate rip-off – consult this book's discography by Graham Calkin (*see p.555*). The releases mentioned in this chapter are the most important or noteworthy posthumous UK Beatles product.

FROM THEN TO YOU
Released: 18/12/1970

As Christmas 1970 came round, another sign of the end of an era materialized in the form of The Beatles' fan club Christmas record. Each and every Yuletide since 1963 had been marked by the appearance of a flexi-disc mailed out to members and containing banter, singing and sometimes instrumentation from the Fab Four. With the first Christmas of the 1970s approaching and John, Paul, George and Ringo embroiled in Apple crumble and immersed in their post-Beatles lives and careers, the fan club had to make do. Fairly ingeniously, cognisant of the fact that a whole generation had come of age since The Beatles hit the world, as well as the fact that such discs got lost easily, the club compiled all the previous Christmas flexis on an album that, though it was not commercially released, had an Apple label. The front cover depicted, in colour, the cover of the first-ever fan club flexi and the monochrome back cover featured the front cover of the other six previous flexis. It would be nice to see this item released on CD but so far we've had to be content with the release of parts of the '66 and '67 flexis as a bonus track on the CD single of "Free As A Bird".

1962–66
1967–70
Released: 19/04/1973

The first Beatles product following the court case that confirmed their final dissolution was this pair of double compilation albums, colloquially referred to as the Red and the Blue albums. They were probably issued as a response to a 1972 American bootleg compilation called *Alpha-Omega*, which – amazingly – had actually been advertised in the mainstream media. (There was doubt for a while whether it was actually illegal because it was designed to exploit a loophole in a new copyright law.)

They were excellently packaged, with the Red album featuring a picture from the same session on the EMI stairwell that produced the cover of the *Please Please Me* album and the Blue having the cover originally intended for the *Get Back* album: The Beatles replicating the stairwell pose six years later, their now hirsute, weathered, outlandishly garbed forms acting as a highly effective form of shorthand for the way they, their music and the world had changed in the intervening six years. Legend has it that Allen Klein was responsible for the albums' track-listings, which raised some eyebrows by including the likes of "Old Brown Shoe", "Across The Universe" and "Octopus's Garden", all great songs but hardly hits or better-known Beatles numbers. (The US version of the Red album even included a snatch of a James Bond-ish Ken Thorne instrumental passage at the start of "Help!" because that's how it appeared on the US *Help!* soundtrack album.) Also eyebrow-raising was the decision to remix some original mono tracks into simulated stereo (it was widely assumed at the time that the public would tolerate nothing less), thus stripping them of their original power. This record company obsession with stereo would become an increasing problem with Beatles product, one that persists to this day.

The albums might have the feel of accessories designed for those only casually interested in music, but in those days they served as a useful mopping up of single A-sides when the alternative was going out and buying multiple seven-inch records which you had to get up and change frequently on your turntable. They were also a good introduction to The Beatles for those people who thought that popular music had started with glam rock. They were followed unfortunately by a slew of compilations that were often worthless.

"Yesterday"
Released: 8/03/1976

On 6 February 1976, The Beatles' recording contracts came to an end. With that date having passed with a Beatles reunion having not occurred, this meant that should such a rock fans' fantasy actually ever come to pass, EMI would be in competition with any other label for The Beatles' signatures. Perhaps because they no longer needed to keep the Fabs sweet, EMI duly embarked on an often philistine exploitation of their back catalogue. This would become a significant bone of contention between The Beatles and EMI, one only resolved in 1987 when as a condition of the group acquiescing to the belated release of their work in CD format – five years after the compact disc's first appearance and at least two years after the CD had gone mainstream – the group regained full artistic control and ensured everything they considered non-canon was deleted.

The first measure taken by EMI in milking their cash cow was reasonable enough. On 6 March 1976, they began re-promoting The Beatles' twenty-two original UK singles. Contrary to popular belief, they weren't technically reissues, as none had ever been deleted, but they were now made available in green card sleeves, featuring different colour photographs on the back relevant to the period of the original record's release. Shops were provided with "point-of-sale" counter boxes for the records, encouraging impulse purchases. However, the fact that two days later came an augmentation to this re-promotion was a harbinger. The Beatles had deliberately not issued "Yesterday" on 45 in their home country for reasons of rock 'n' roll credibility. Now EMI made it available as a UK single, putting the unrelated "I Should Have Known Better" – a track from two albums prior to "Yesterday" – on the flip.

In mitigation, EMI would no doubt point to the fact that "Yesterday" made number eight, nestling cheek-by-jowl with Brotherhood Of Man, Barry White, The Glitter Band, 10 C.C., Abba and other chart creatures undreamt of in 1965. All twenty-two past singles charted too. On 4 April 1976, all twenty-three Beatles singles were in the UK top 100, a feat possibly even more impressive than the group's domination of the *Billboard* chart in 1964 – considering that they were a defunct unit who were playing no part in advertising the records in question.

The revival gathered pace in May when Sean O'Mahoney brought back to life *The Beatles Book*, the official band magazine that he had run from almost the first moment of Beatlemania (August 1963) to the last (December 1970). Initially, O'Mahoney simply reprinted the original magazines with eight pages of new material wrapped around them. When all seventy-seven of the original series had come out for a second time, it was September 1982 and another Beatles chart revival was about to take place as EMI began re-issuing The Beatles singles on the twentieth anniversary of each original release date. Consequently, O'Mahoney kept the magazine going, switching over to all-new material. He only pulled the curtain on the magazine in 2003.

The '76 new wave of Beatlemania was understandable. That the public still hankered for the magic created by McCartney, Lennon, Harrison and Starr together was illustrated by the fact that January '76 had seen concert promoter Bill Sargent publicly offer the four $30 million for a single concert under the name The Beatles – a mind-boggling sum even for today, let alone then. The fact that the music scene had become soporific and boring in the band's absence and the world (but particularly Britain) was in the grip of an economic and political malaise only added to the sense of nostalgia of those who had lived through every musical and societal change the Fab Four brought about (or at least seemed to). Rather excitingly, The Beatles did not dismiss the offer out of hand. Paul said at the time, "It's a positive maybe at the moment," without any apparent sarcasm. Also in 1976, Sid Bernstein – who made history by putting The Beatles in Shea Stadium – took out a full-page advertisement in the *New York Herald Tribune* asking The Beatles to stage a concert for charity. Though George was a little more caustic than Paul about all these pleadings for a reunion ("That was a sick offer. It's putting pressure on us in a way and I don't like it"), even he conceded, "It's not beyond the bounds of possibility . . ."

It was not to be. In the four years before the assassination of Lennon made a live reunion a moot point, neither Sargent's or anybody else's entreaties – including a plea from United Nations secretary general Kurt Waldheim for a concert to raise money for the Vietnamese boat people – yielded fruit. However, reunions seem to have come closer than people realize. Bernstein, who would have put on the boat people concert, said, "John called me for more details in 1979 and my secretary hand-delivered the details over to their offices at the Dakota." He added, "The reaction that appeared in the *Palace Herald Tribune* by Paul stated something to the effect that 'It's more weight than our shoulders can carry'." Although Paul was dismissive about the boat people concert, when negotiating an American record deal with CBS in 1979, he insisted on a clause that would allow him to make records with his former colleagues in The Beatles under that name if the chance arose. Lennon, meanwhile, in his (then secret) sworn disposition in 1980 in The Beatles' court case against the producers of *Beatlemania!* – a Broadway show that was like a version of the tribute bands that proliferate today, only with a narrative – said, "I and the three other former Beatles have plans to stage a reunion concert". This concert was supposedly to be filmed and included as the finale to *The Long and Winding Road*, a Beatles autobiographical documentary that work had begun on back in 1970.

ROCK 'N' ROLL MUSIC
Released: 10/06/1976

Now forgotten – although the low-rent cover depicting a pair of hands holding the mock-translucent sleeve lingers disagreeably in the memory of some – but this album was the recipient of a massive promotional budget and was many 1970s kids' introduction to The Beatles. It was also a valuable riposte to those (actually quite numerous at the time) who portrayed The Beatles as soft compared to The Stones. It was clearly compiled by a fan, rescuing "I'm Down" from its then obscure B-side status, extracting "Hey Bulldog" from the wastelands of the *Yellow Submarine* album and reeling in the forgotten-by-many content of the *Long Tall Sally* EP in its entirety. "Back In The U.S.S.R." was released as a single in the UK the following month to promote the set and made number nineteen.

MAGICAL MYSTERY TOUR
Released: 19/11/76

The British release of this American album, this was effectively made part of the official UK canon in 1987 when the Beatles allowed it to be kept in print on CD and took the attitude that the UK singles and B-sides it rounded up on its second side were available on album and thus didn't require inclusion on the *Past Masters* mop-up CDs.

LIVE! AT THE STAR-CLUB IN HAMBURG, GERMANY; 1962
Released: 2/05/1977

This double album was the first release of a Beatles Hamburg live performance that would subsequently be repackaged and reissued by many different labels.

What at first sounds like profoundly interesting material turns out to be disappointing on two counts, one being the appalling sound quality – to quote Robert Christgau, ". . . nothing I had read prepared me for the abysmal sound quality of this record, especially how far down (and away) the voices are" – the other being the fact that what one assumed (and was claimed) was a snapshot of The Beatles before they were signed to a record company was nothing of the kind. In the excellent reference tome *The Beatles Encyclopedia*, Bill Harry claimed that the recording was made by Adrian Barber, a former member of Cass & the Cassanovas and the Big Three, when he was stage manager at the Star-Club. Brian Epstein offered a derisory sum for the material when it was offered to him. It was self-styled first Beatles manager Allan Williams who put the tapes on the market when he obtained the rights to them in the 1970s. "Spring 1962" was the vague date usually given for when the recording was made, and "Ringo sitting in for Pete Best" was the explanation provided for the fact that The Beatles' regular sticks-man of this period was not present. It later transpired that had the real recording date been revealed – 31 December 1962 – it would prove that the recording was the property of EMI, to whom the band were by now signed. That date means of course that the historical interest is much reduced, and indeed means the performance is lacklustre: instead of a band with everything to aim for, they are a disinterested ensemble with their mind on bigger things than fulfilling a contractual obligation.

Nonetheless, the band's last-ever Hamburg club perform-ance is of some historical value. Artistically, though, it's next to worthless, and not just because of the sound quality and the fact that club owner Horst Fascher appears on at least one track on lead vocals. *Goldmine* contributor Gillian G. Gaar said of the album, "Though the band rushes through their set at a breakneck pace (a clear indication of their desire to hurry through the engagement in order to rush back to England in order to promote their next single), the range of material – from 'Falling In Love Again' to 'Twist And Shout' – is fascinating, and a last look at the band's vast catalogue of cover songs."

In 1998, at the second time of asking, The Beatles got a court to declare all discs with Star-Club material illegal and the record-ings can now currently only be found on second-hand releases and bootlegs.

LIVE AT THE HOLLYWOOD BOWL
Released: 6/05/1977

Curiously, appearing in the UK in the same month as the Star-Club album was a live album of The Beatles in profoundly different circumstances, namely when they were the greatest attraction on earth. Three appearances at the titular venue – 23 August 1964 and 29 and 30 August 1965 – were spliced by George Martin to create one artificial concert. This was done of course at the behest of an EMI who were keen to exploit the new wave of Beatlemania they had unleashed (so keen that the album was advertised on TV, then reasonably rare in Britain for music). In some cases, sections of songs performed a year apart were married up to obtain uniform sound and performance quality. The wall of screams created by 17,000 teenagers may be historically accurate but hardly presents The Beatles' music in optimum conditions. Nonetheless, some discern charm and musical efficiency here (critic Robert Christgau gave it a grading of "A" in his *Consumer Guide*). Those who felt short-changed by a running time of less than half an hour should note that this was the usual length of a Beatles concert. The Beatles' opinion of this release can be discerned in the fact that it has never been released on CD.

LOVE SONGS
Released: 19/11/1977

The flip side, as it were, to the *Rock 'N' Roll Music* compilation and one that many fans of Johnny Mathis and Barry Manilow were no doubt delighted to find in their Christmas stockings that year. Nothing wrong with the music, of course, and the compilers get a house point for including little-known B-side ballad gems "This Boy" and "Yes It Is". The packaging is quite classy as well, with a fake leather cover effect and the inclusion of a poster taken by famous photographer Richard Avedon.

"Sgt. Pepper's Lonely Hearts Club Band"/"With A Little Help From My Friends"
Released: 30/09/1978

A single issued to coincide with the feature film named after The Beatles' 1967 opus, with the Ringo "Billy Shears" showcase that it segued into on the album retained because otherwise the disc would have been embarrassingly short. The feature film, starring The Bee Gees and over which The Beatles had no control, was atrocious.

THE BEATLES COLLECTION
Released: 2/12/1978

All The Beatles official UK studio albums in a box. *Magical Mystery Tour* is excluded but *A Collection Of Beatles Oldies* is not. Rounding out the set is *Rarities*, an album of B-sides, EP tracks, foreign language tracks, etc, a sort of precursor to the *Past Masters* albums. *Rarities* was released separately the following October, which no doubt pleased those who had shelled out for material they already had just to get that bonus album. The American version of *Rarities* had a different tracklisting to reflect the rarity status of different tracks in the States. For instance, the American version included the endless, gibberish material found in the run-off groove of *Sgt. Pepper* . . . , which was not included on . . . *Pepper* . . . Stateside.

HEY JUDE
Released: 11/05/1979

A UK release for the compilation released in the US in 1970. Though it comprised songs from as far apart as 1964 and 1969, it was useful to Americans because none of the tracks had appeared on LP in the country hitherto. This was the case for many tracks in the UK too. The fidelity of "Hey Jude" improved on a twelve-inch album as opposed to its seven-plus minutes being squeezed onto seven inches of vinyl.

THE BEATLES BALLADS
Released: 13/10/1980

Another Beatles ballads album release for the Christmas market. Doubly pointless: as well as the usual caveat that one should buy the original Beatles records if you want to hear them, this replicates most of the contents of *Love Songs*. Nicely surreal *Alice In Wonderland*-like cover though.

ROCK 'N' ROLL MUSIC VOL. 1
ROCK 'N' ROLL MUSIC VOL. 2
Released: 24/10/1980

The *Rock 'N' Roll Music* double issued as two separate albums on EMI's budget Music for Pleasure label, much to The Beatles' alleged disgust. The two records are collectors' items however because they include re-mixes by George Martin done to clean up the recordings for modern, stereo-attuned ears which EMI in the UK originally nixed because they were worried such tampering might constitute a breach of contract.

THE BEATLES BOX
Released: 3/11/1980

Available only through EMI's mail order division, this collection is a grandiose best-of, 126 tracks across eight albums selected by World Records. It's a misbegotten package. The running order is chronologically by release date, except on the final disc, where *Abbey Road* songs sits where *Let It Be* tracks should. It also accidentally includes some rare alternate mixes of songs. Thrilling no doubt as it is to have, for example, the version of "All My Loving" with an intro consisting of five taps on the hi-hat and "And I Love Her" from a German album with the final riff repeated six times instead of four, such things hardly justified the exorbitant cost.

REEL MUSIC
Released: 29/03/1982

A pointless compilation of songs from Beatles movies.

"Movie Medley"
Released: 24/05/1982

This single jumped on the medley craze of the time started by the "Stars On 45" hit by Starsound. A beat was added to extracts from seven songs from Beatles movies to create surely the nadir of Beatles reissues. However, such was the popularity of such McNugget-type servings of music at the time that the record went top ten.

THE COMPLETE SILVER BEATLES
Released: 10/09/1982

This was the first official release of The Beatles' audition for Decca on New Year's Day 1962 that saw them turned down in favour of Brian Poole and the Tremeloes. There's no record of the Tremeloes' demo available for comparison, but it wouldn't have been difficult for them to be better that day than The Beatles (The Silver Beatles artist credit is wrong: they hadn't been called that since August 1960), who, here, are generally anonymous and play a weird combination of material (Chuck Berry and Buddy Holly nestling cheek-by-jowl with cornball fare like "Besame Mucho" and "Sheik Of Araby"). There were three Lennon/McCartney songs performed ("Hello Little Girl", "Loved Of The Loved" and "Like Dreamers Do"), but this album, like all subsequent legal releases of this material on various labels, has omitted those tracks for fear of court action. The collection made it into the CD age (*The Silver Beatles* on the Overseas label in 1986 was the first compact disc release, beating the band's official canon to the medium) but only just: those legal fears have prevented any release since the late 1980s, except those tracks from it that the Fabs decided to include on *Anthology 1*. Dick Rowe, the Decca employee who in conjunction with Mike Smith turned The Beatles down, has always angrily denied Brian Epstein's claim that he told him guitar groups were on the way out, although the other reason given for Decca going with The Tremeloes (they lived nearer and therefore it would cost them less to get them down for recording) is perhaps even more hilarious.

"Love Me Do"
Released: 4/10/1982
Reissued to coincide with the twentieth anniversary of the release of "Love Me Do", The Beatles' debut single improved its original chart placing by reaching number four (in a chart, by the way, that was now standardized as a consequence of the BBC and *Record Retailer* – which was later re-titled *Music Week* – deciding in 1969 to both use a chart compiled by the British Market Research Bureau, a chart that came to be seen by the media and public as "official"). EMI actually messed up by putting out the version featuring Andy White that had originally been on the debut album but rectified matters by including the real, Ringo original on a twelve-inch version. The rest of The Beatles' singles catalogue was also subsequently reissued on the twentieth anniversary of the original release, with incrementally diminishing chart returns.

20 GREATEST HITS
Released: 18/10/1982
Though the title seems too low-rent for The Beatles, this could have been a useful enough release had EMI stuck with their original plans to make it a double set. The single album format

required the jettisoning of "Please Please Me", "Penny Lane", "Strawberry Fields Forever", "Something" and "Let It Be". Even so, the album ran to nearly an hour. Unfortunately, this was well past the forty-minute mark at which vinyl sound quality began to deteriorate. In a word, worthless. Although perhaps less so than the American version whose slightly different tracklisting included – outrageously – a "Hey Jude" forcibly truncated by two minutes.

COMPACT DISCS
Released: from 26/02/1987

In February 1987, the first ever Beatles CDs were released, comprising the first four UK albums. The rest of the group's album catalogue was released on CD in batches throughout the rest of the year. It had taken a long time because The Beatles – whose sales figures gave them the greatest bargaining power in the business – had a series of demands they wanted met before they would countenance agreeing to sign anything to do with a medium that didn't exist when their recording career began. The Fabs wanted full control over what was and was not released and licensed. No doubt they also had steep demands about the royalties they expected in future, something that would go some way towards compensating them for the pathetically low remuneration they had received prior to the new contract Allen Klein had secured for them in 1969, the naivety which led Brian Epstein to negotiate laughably low remuneration for Beatles merchandizing and licensing, and the dishonest (according to Lennon and several writers) behaviour of Epstein towards the end of his life when he might have been assuming The Beatles would not renew their contract, which was due to expire two months after his death from an accidental overdose of the prescription drug Carbitol on 27 August 1967.

With the record company champing at the bit to take advantage of a new invention that was causing people to go out and buy their record collections all over again and cognisant of the lost millions that each year's delay constituted – and unhappily aware that The Beatles, as individuals with no shareholders to chivvy them along, were able to hold out longer than them –

EMI had no option but to agree to the demands of Messrs Harrison, McCartney and Starkey and Mr Lennon's widow. After this point, there would be no more worthless compilations, and no more abominations like the *Sgt. Pepper . . .* movie. There would also be a uniform worldwide catalogue: the American albums that had long prompted public expressions of dismay by The Beatles were all deleted and the British albums became the only versions available. (It's a depressing thought that EMI might have gone on exploiting and cheapening The Beatles' catalogue forever had the invention of this new medium not given the Fabs leverage.)

Which is not to say that The Beatles always showed astute judgment in what they now chose to release or the way they presented it. Things began going awry with the second and third tranches of CD releases. Though the CDs of the albums *Please Please Me* through *Beatles For Sale* were issued only in mono, it was decided that the albums *Help!* through *Sgt. Pepper . . .* would be made available in the CD medium only in stereo. It was an absurd decision, dictated by the presumption that people in the modern age would be put off buying an album if it didn't have "stereo" written on it. Up until around 1968, the main mix for pop records was the mono one. The stereo mix was something often knocked together in a couple of hours and was intended only for the well-off minority who had the relevant equipment. In short, the mono mixes were the way the music was *intended* to be heard. Anybody who has heard both mono and stereo versions of records made before 1968 will be able to confirm that the mono version is simply bolder, more powerful and a better listening experience. What with EMI having tended from the 1970s to make Beatles albums from *Help!* onwards only available in stereo, the band's own decision to continue this policy in the CD age means that two generations of listeners have never heard the middle period of the band's career properly. Happily, at the time of writing, the rumour is that when The Beatles' catalogue becomes available as digital downloads in 2009, The Beatles will rectify this fault at least to the extent of giving people the option of which version they want to purchase.

Something that is not really The Beatles' fault is that with the advent of the CD, some of their records' meticulously planned packaging has been lost to history. For instance, the medium of the compact disc presented problems with the "White Album"'s embossed title. The current CD edition simply features the title in grey. (It also presents a tracklisting on the back.) Having said that, EMI had always shown a tendency to dilute the original packaging of albums long before CD was thought of. The psychedelically coloured inner sleeve of *Sgt. Pepper* . . . had been replaced by standard white bags after a while and the numbered covers of the "White Album" had been gradually phased out, as were the unusual top-opening inner sleeves of the "White Album"'s original issue.

Something else that is not The Beatles' fault, is that their CD catalogue now sounds rather dated. It's astonishing to think of it, but George Martin's remastering of the band's output for compact disc took place nearly a quarter of a century ago now. The remastering technology has made massive strides since, so much so that people complain that even those Beatles CDs not afflicted by stereo mixes sound rather bright and harsh compared to modern remasters. The time is ripe for the planned overhaul.

PAST MASTERS VOLUME ONE
PAST MASTERS VOLUME TWO
Released: 8/03/1988

VOLUME ONE

TRACKLISTING

1. "Love Me Do" (single version)
2. "From Me To You"
3. "Thank You Girl"
4. "She Loves You"
5. "I'll Get You"
6. "I Want To Hold Your Hand"
7. "This Boy"
8. "Komm, Gib Mir Deine Hand"
9. "Sie Liebt Dich"
10. "Long Tall Sally"
11. "I Call Your Name"

12. "Slow Down"
13. "Matchbox"
14. "I Feel Fine"
15. "She's A Woman"
16. "Bad Boy"
17. "Yes It Is"
18. "I'm Down"

VOLUME TWO

TRACKLISTING

1. "Day Tripper"
2. "We Can Work It Out"
3. "Paperback Writer"
4. "Rain"
5. "Lady Madonna"
6. "The Inner Light"
7. "Hey Jude"
8. "Revolution"
9. "Get Back"
10. "Don't Let Me Down"
11. "The Ballad Of John And Yoko"
12. "Old Brown Shoe"
13. "Across The Universe"
14. "Let It Be"
15. "You Know My Name(Look Up The Number)"

With the release of these two albums, the entire Beatles catalogue (excepting the airbrushed-from-history *Hollywood Bowl* album) was now available on compact disc. *Past Masters* volumes one and two are superb mopping up exercises, collating all Beatles tracks of any description that did not make it onto a UK album (taking into account that the UK album catalogue now formally includes the American *Magical Mystery Tour* album). Singles, B-sides, unique EP tracks, rarities like the wildlife album version of "Across The Universe", the alternative mixes of "Get Back" and "Let It Be" that appeared as singles and even The Fabs' two German language recordings are rounded up by compiler

Mark Lewisohn, author of several excellent books on the group. The only black mark against the collections is that Lewisohn could have opted to be more literal in rounding up non-LP tracks and given us stuff like the single versions of "Please Please Me" and "Help!" with their slightly different vocal tracks. He has also, depressingly, opted for stereo, not mono, versions from "I Want To Hold Your Hand" onwards.

To their credit, EMI agreed to a classy title and packaging job when the temptation must have been to call the albums something like "Greatest Hits", which title would not have been too much of a misnomer: "She Loves You", "I Want To Hold Your Hand", "I Feel Fine", "We Can Work It Out", "Paperback Writer", "Hey Jude" and "The Ballad Of John And Yoko" are indeed some of The Beatles' most famous and biggest selling records. It's a testament to the brilliance of the Fab Four that such titanic songs were standalone records, not originally included on albums. It's also a testament to their brilliance that the B-sides were often just as good: "I'll Get You, "This Boy", "Yes It Is", "I'm Down", "Rain", "The Inner Light", "Revolution", "Don't Let Me Down" and "Old Brown Shoe" is a dazzling litany of brilliance that would have constituted any other group's greatest hits, let alone flipsides. For this listener, *Past Masters Volume Two* constitutes the greatest collection of music ever assembled.

LIVE AT THE BBC
Released: 30/11/1994

TRACKLISTING

Disc one
1. "Beatle Greetings"
2. "From Us to You"
3. "Riding on a Bus"
4. "I Got a Woman"
5. "Too Much Monkey Business"
6. "Keep Your Hands Off My Baby"
7. "I'll Be on My Way"
8. "Young Blood"
9. "A Shot of Rhythm and Blues"

10. "Sure to Fall (In Love with You)"
11. "Some Other Guy"
12. "Thank You Girl"
13. "Sha La La La La!"
14. "Baby It's You"
15. "That's All Right (Mama)"
16. "Carol"
17. "Soldier Of Love"
18. "A Little Rhyme"
19. "Clarabella"
20. "I'm Gonna Sit Right Down and Cry (Over You)"
21. "Crying, Waiting, Hoping"
22. "Dear Wack!"
23. "You've Really Got A Hold On Me"
24. "To Know Her Is To Love Her"
25. "A Taste Of Honey"
26. "Long Tall Sally"
27. "I Saw Her Standing There"
28. "The Honeymoon Song"
29. "Johnny B. Goode"
30. "Memphis, Tennessee"
31. "Lucille"
32. "Can't Buy Me Love"
33. "From Fluff to You"
34. "Till There Was You"

Disc two
1. "Crinsk Dee Night"
2. "A Hard Day's Night"
3. "Have a Banana!"
4. "I Wanna Be Your Man"
5. "Just a Rumour"
6. "Roll Over Beethoven"
7. "All My Loving"
8. "Things We Said Today"
9. "She's A Woman"
10. "Sweet Little Sixteen"
11. "1822!"
12. "Lonesome Tears in My Eyes"

13. "Nothin" Shakin'"
14. "The Hippy Hippy Shake"
15. "Glad All Over"
16. "I Just Don't Understand"
17. "So How Come (No One Loves Me)"
18. "I Feel Fine"
19. "I'm a Loser"
20. "Everybody's Trying To Be My Baby"
21. "Rock and Roll Music"
22. "Ticket to Ride"
23. "Dizzy Miss Lizzy"
24. "Medley: Kansas City/Hey! Hey! Hey! Hey!"
25. "Set Fire to That Lot!"
26. "Matchbox"
27. "I Forgot To Remember to Forget"
28. "Love These Goon Shows!"
29. "I Got To Find My Baby"
30. "Ooh! My Soul"
31. "Ooh! My Arms"
32. "Don't Ever Change"
33. "Slow Down"
34. "Honey Don't"
35. "Love Me Do"

In the last three months of 1988, BBC's Radio 1 broadcast a series called *The Beeb's Lost Beatles Tapes* containing a selection of the live-in-the-studio performances The Beatles recorded for the British Broadcasting Corporation between March 1962 and June 1965. It was a veritable wet dream for fans of the Fabs, featuring not only alternate versions of familiar Beatles songs but songs never issued commercially by the group. Some of the cover versions included were broadcast long before they made their appearance on a Beatle record. Also included was much of the unique witty banter that had made the band so interesting as people.

Even as late as the early- to mid-1960s, radio was still actively listened to by millions, as opposed to being employed as background. Appearing on BBC radio in those days was therefore of incalculable importance. Brian Matthews' *Saturday Club* attracted a staggering audience of nine million, around a sixth of the entire population of Britain. Programmes like *Easy Beat* and *Steppin' Out* and others were less popular but the BBC had a monopoly on domestic radio and music was scarce on TV, so even those lesser-ranking programmes constituted the kind of advertisement for one's records that money literally could not buy. Epstein must have been beside himself when in 1963, The Beatles were offered their own teatime radio series, *Pop Go The Beatles*. However, by the time they laid down their final studio performances for the Beeb three-and-a-quarter years after their first, their phenomenal success meant The Beatles no longer needed to spend their time in BBC studios to drum up interest in their wares.

Inevitably, following *The Beeb's Lost Beatles Tapes* there was a clamour for a record release of the material, but for six years fans had to be content with recordings of the programme taped off the radio or bootlegs. (It has been said that bootlegs were also the original source of the music heard on the programme, as the BBC had, in an example of the kind of housekeeping then common in British broadcasting, destroyed the lot.) Finally, along came *Live At The BBC*. Some of the material was recorded before a live audience, but is mercifully devoid of the screaming that ruined just about all other in-concert Beatles recordings even if it is of naturally lower fidelity than the studio tracks. The whole collection is sensibly left as mono. The Beatles' jokey banter with DJs is preserved, and indeed given track titles.

Though this two-CD collection of material is the equivalent of a vinyl triple album, it comes nowhere near to constituting everything The Beatles broadcast on the Beeb. With the band having recorded multiple versions of several songs down the years for the Corporation (for instance, the version of Chuck Berry's "Too Much Monkey Business" included here was the fourth, and they ultimately did "Love Me Do" nine times for the BBC mics), a comprehensive collection would have been tediously repetitious. (For those who doubt it, there are some multi-CD sets of the whole shebang on bootleg.) However, even those who are not anally completist might question compiler George Martin's decision not to include material from the group's very first, pre-EMI-signing BBC broadcast (a perform-ance in front of an audience) from March 1962: surely the presence of Pete Best on drums on those tracks makes for historical interest that renders totally irrelevant the fact that "no quality recording exists", as sleevenote writer Kevin Howlett puts it. Newsflash, George and Kev: better recorded the material on here may be, but most of it is also only of interest for historical reasons anyway.

It has to be conceded that the set is by and large flat and disappointing. Nothing wrong with the decision to release it: with the material already on the market in lavish illicit sets from which The Beatles received nothing in the way of royalties, it was their perfect right to get a little of the action, and no doubt part of their motivation was also a genuine sentimentality (Lennon particularly was said to have fond memories of days spent at BBC studios). But would an alien know from these recordings that The Beatles were the greatest recording artists in history? The answer is empathically no. There were plenty of reviews which went out of their way to make allowances for the material on this set: though professional, the recordings were circumscribed by the conditions in what were studios primarily designed for broadcasting, not recording; overdubs weren't possible, so the material has an inevitable lacklustre feel compared to their post-*Please Please Me* records; a performance that was presumed to be something that disappeared into the ether as soon as broadcast is hardly going to display the same passion invested by the band in making a record, especially by a lead vocalist conscious of preserving his voice. Not intended for posterity . . . BBC a staid institution . . . Beatles were always overworked . . . Etc, etc. However, a listen to The Who's similar collection *BBC Sessions* – a stunning CD – shows that none of these things ruled out great performances. Whisper it lightly, but maybe The Beatles just weren't very good at radio sessions.

"From Us to You" is a very brief piece of music that sees The Beatles customize their third hit to give their radio show a theme. The Ray Charles song "I Got a Woman" is given quite a good treatment, the acoustic rhythm guitar making it less lumpen than the famous version by Elvis, whom John sometimes resembles in his vocal. George's solo is primitive. "Too Much Monkey Business" is a number by Chuck Berry, and one of nine Berry covers here. Lennon doesn't inject the required fury into this litany of the aggravation of proletarian life but the manic blur of guitars behind him goes some way to making up for that. "Keep Your Hands Off My Baby" is a strangely low-fi but competent rendition of the Little Eva record written by the phenomenally successful Brill Building team of Goffin & King. "I'll Be on My Way" is the sole Lennon-McCartney song here not previously released on a Beatles record. Billy J. Kramer had put it on a B-side but it deserved better. Similar in tone and subject matter to "I'll Follow The Sun", it also sounds uncannily like a latter-day Buddy Holly composition and would have made an enjoyable track on *Please Please Me*, increasing that album's sonic breadth.

The Beatles don't really have the range of comedy voices that The Coasters displayed on their original version of the Leiber–Stoller–Pomus composition "Young Blood" and the result is a flat affair. "A Shot of Rhythm and Blues" was a B-side of one of John's favourites, Arthur Alexander. It's an immutable fact of popular music that anyone trying to write an anthem celebrating the virtues of rock (or R&B) ends up with an oxymoronic creation that doesn't convey the qualities the song is speaking of, and this composition was no exception. The Beatles don't salvage it in any way. Lennon once said that the only album he'd ever thought was good all the way through was the first LP by Carl Perkins. "Sure to Fall (In Love With You)" is a cover of a song from that very album. This rather plodding and country-ish track – John and Paul swapping vocals – doesn't live up to that incredible recommendation but has some nice spangly guitar work.

The Leiber–Stoller–Barrett "Some Other Guy" song was one of those being performed by The Beatles in the earliest existing footage of them, shot at The Cavern. This version too was recorded in front of a live audience. It's average, as is the following rendition of their own self-written B-side "Thank You Girl", also recorded live.

"Baby It's You" is rendered close to as smoothly as it was on *Please Please Me*, including creamy harmonies and sonorous guitar break, but Lennon reins back on the vocals. Though they were huge Elvis fans, the Fabs never released a song made famous by Presley during their career, so their version of the

King's debut record "That's All Right (Mama)" has a high interest value at the very least. Unfortunately, they take it at a stroll, not a gallop, Paul's vocal is too restrained and the recording is muffled. So associated is the Chuck Berry number "Carol" with The Rolling Stones due to it being featured on their 1964 debut album that it's strange to contemplate The Beatles doing a version. Yet Lennon yielded to no man in his love of Berry and this version predates the one the Stones issued by nine months. The Stones' version, however, leaves this tame, half-interested version standing.

"Soldier of Love" is another Arthur Alexander song, written by Cason & Moon. John can't really go wrong with a rich, winding, mordant melody and interesting militaristic metaphor for romantic devotion, and his colleagues back him up adroitly on one of the set's superior efforts. "Clarabella" is a little-known song by ex-members of Bill Haley's Comets. This tame exercise doesn't convey the fact that the band had been performing it since 1960, nor does it justify Paul's occasional whoops. "I'm Gonna Sit Right Down And Cry (Over You)" is another number made famous by Elvis, the artist third behind only Chuck Berry and Carl Perkins in representation on this set. Sung jointly by John and Paul, it's merely adequate but interesting to the extent that it has some Beatles falsettos grafted onto the Presley imprimatur, as well as some fairly frenetic drumming by Ringo.

"Crying, Waiting, Hoping" was a component of the so-called Apartment Tapes recorded by Buddy Holly in his New York home but unreleased until after his death. A good cut, and George's mellifluous lead guitar is enjoyable and very Holly-ish. "You've Really Got A Hold On Me" sees The Beatles operating at about seventy-five per cent of the commitment they achieved when performing this number on *With The Beatles*, which means it's pretty good rather than excellent. "To Know Her Is To Love Her" is Phil Spector's song for The Teddy Bears, given a gender change and sung sensitively by John. Paul and George trill sweetly behind him and the whole thing is disarming and pleasant. "A Taste Of Honey" is fairly good but doesn't quite have the onomatopoeically thick, rich texture of the version on the debut album. "Long Tall Sally" is a foot-dragging version of the Little Richard classic that's not even worth mentioning in the same breath as the Fabs' later version from the *Long Tall Sally* EP. When Paul insists that "We'll have some fun tonight", it seems wildly optimistic. "I Saw Her Standing There" is an anonymous rendition of the *Please Please Me* highlight. It doesn't say so in the sleevenotes but it seems to be recorded live, which probably accounts for the sonic murkiness.

"The Honeymoon Song" is one of Paul's middle-of-the-road excursions, *a la* "Till There Was You". It's efficiently done but as corny and quasi-laughable as you would expect, something that was the theme to the movie *Honeymoon* to be. "Johnny B. Goode" was never a UK hit for its author but became Chuck Berry's signature song. John's listless singing and his colleagues' bored playing makes one yearn for their version of the composer's "Rock 'N' Roll Music". This is immediately followed by another Berry song, "Memphis, Tennessee", a rather contrasting, downbeat story of a man separated from what we presume to be his lover but which turns out in a twist in the tale to be his daughter. The version is uninteresting and makes one yearn for the later Faces' version, where Rod Stewart proves that being low-key doesn't mean devoid of passion. John seems to say "Mum" instead of "Mom".

"Lucille" is a nondescript version of the Little Richard classic. The version of "Can't Buy Me Love" that follows sounds like a rehearsal, and George's solo – so great on the record – is a damp squib. "Till There Was You" once again strikes one as a track that just shouldn't work but which is undeniably pleasing on the ear, if less so than on the more layered *With The Beatles* version.

George Martin's piano, which acted as a bed for George's guitar solo on the record, was overdubbed on "A Hard Day's Night" here (very unusual for a radio session), but lest anyone think this proved the band couldn't match their studio performances, Ringo impressively manages to almost replicate the frantic tempo of the original. The version of "I Wanna Be Your Man" comes out better than some of the considerably more worthy Lennon-McCartney originals herein. On a good, bluesy rendition, Ringo sings with impressive soul while maintaining the beat. "Roll Over Beethoven" features some good singing by George but the band are on autopilot behind him. The biscuit tin drumming by Ringo detracts from an otherwise adequate version of "All My Loving". A nondescript version of "Things We Said Today" follows. "She's a Woman" was never a great Beatles song but this version is not too bad, with the rhythm guitar far less clanking and irritating than on the original record.

The Beatles finally do Chuck Berry justice with a very good performance of "Sweet Little Sixteen", which has a Lennon vocal with real bite, plus a good chunky guitar solo. "Lonesome Tears In My Eyes" is the Johnny Burnette song whose riff inspired the closing guitar part of "The Ballad Of John And Yoko". On this version six years before the then-unimaginable position and conditions from which The Beatles recorded that latter single, they execute an enjoyable rendition with a nice Latin groove, circular drum work and mellifluously strummed electric guitar. George takes the lead vocal for an enjoyable and alert cover of a Johnny Fontaine rockabilly number "Nothin' Shakin'".

It's interesting that the Fabs cover Chan Romero's dance anthem "The Hippy Hippy Shake", because the raucous UK hit version by The Swinging Blue Jeans sounded, mood- and vocal-wise, almost spookily like The Beatles' version of "Twist And Shout". This version predates The Swinging Blue Jeans' hit by five months but is far less exciting, principally because a chance was missed: a song tailor-made for a searing Lennon vocal is rendered by Paul. Also, the rhythm section is leaden. Not to be confused with the Dave Clark Five hit of the same title, "Glad All Over" is a number made famous by Carl Perkins, this one sung by George. Merely okay, and the rockabilly guitar parts are cheesily generic. "I Just Don't Understand" was a 1961 hit for movie star Ann Margaret. You would imagine this would be the kind of thing Paul would alight on to put in The Beatles' set but it's John who tackles this smouldering lament for the thoughtlessness of a lover, and does so with passion. The band back him well, especially the oohing harmonies. "So How Come (No One Loves Me)" is an Everly Brothers song of self-pity, rendered efficiently by John and Paul (and possibly George).

The guitars are limper and the rhythm less sprightly than on the original when the band tackle "I Feel Fine" but the opening feedback is replicated surprisingly well, the harmonies are faultless and even Ringo's Latin-tinged drumming replicated accurately. "I'm A Loser" is an unexcited canter through the *Beatles For Sale* track. John seems to laugh at his "popping" the microphone at one point but that's about the only moment of interest.

"Everybody's Trying To Be My Baby" is another track from the supposedly uniquely flawless Carl Perkins debut LP. This version is an unremarkable, more acoustic variant of the *Beatles For Sale* cover. A highlight of *Beatles For Sale* of course was "Rock And Roll Music". Nothing could match Lennon's rendition therein but this version – draggy, instrumentally clunky, even if vocally John tries – is awful. "Ticket To Ride" is rather limp and like an out of focus picture of the original. "Dizzy Miss Lizzy" – that atrocious Larry Williams cover that ensured a fine album, *Help!*, ended on a whimper – here mercifully boasts a less irritating guitar lick. It seems to feature electric piano.

One is truly running out of alternatives for adjectives like "tame" and "nondescript" when it comes to covers of "Medley: Kansas City"/"Hey! Hey! Hey! Hey!" and "Matchbox". Paul sings "I Forgot To Remember To Forget", another cover of a song made famous by Elvis. It has a charm that may be related to its musty recording quality and a nice delicate guitar break. "I Got To Find My Baby" is a lesser-known but high quality Chuck Berry song. There's good singing from John, who also plays mouth harp, which he points out in the introductory dialogue is not the same as a harmonica, which he played on "Love Me Do". "Ooh! My Soul" is a Little Richard number sung, of course, by Paul. Merely okay. The Goffin & King composition "Don't Ever Change" was a post-Buddy Holly hit for The Crickets. Three-part harmonies and tidy instrumentation do justice to this sweet number.

"Slow Down" is perfunctory. "Honey Don't" – once again from that Carl Perkins LP entrée – was recorded more than a year before the version on *Beatles For Sale*. This version is inevitably superior because Lennon (as he did on stage at this point) takes the vocal. Ringo, though, impresses with his hi-hat work, which gives it a good groove. The album ends with "Love Me Do". That no better version of their debut could be found amongst the nine The Beatles performed for the BBC than the dreary one included here sums up the underwhelming nature of *Live At The BBC*.

"Baby It's You"
Released: 20/03/1995

TRACKLISTING

1. "Baby It's You"
2. "I'll Follow The Sun"
3. "Devil In Her Heart"
4. "Boys"

In The Beatles' day, a single was a seven-inch piece of vinyl with one track either side. By the time "Baby It's You" – the first official UK Beatles single since 1970's "Let It Be" – hit the shops, things had changed a little. The compact disc had revolutionized the music world from the mid-1980s onwards, its Perfect Sound Forever (supposedly), handy size (though it destroyed the art of the album cover) and single-sided nature consigning those who favoured the vinyl format to the status of Luddite laughing stocks. The smugness of those who embraced the future in the 1980s was not to last long. Within considerably less than two decades the consumers who had gleefully re-bought their entire record collections on CD were finding themselves bewildered by the fact that the compact disc was well on its way to being made obsolete itself by internet downloads.

The first official Beatles CD singles were reissues of their original twenty-two "45s" (as they were no longer called) in 1989, individually and then later in a box set. On these discs, of course, the B-sides nestled against the A-sides on the same face of the disc. "Baby It's You" was a single released in the UK (there was no American release) three months after *Live At The BBC* designed to boost the album's sales. Though it appeared in cassette and vinyl formats too, by now those formats were only being retained to cater to a small rump of specialist buyers.

The CD single of "Baby It's You" featured four songs in total. The title track had appeared on *Live At The BBC* but the remaining three hadn't, although had been recorded at BBC sessions. It was of course a ploy to get people who already had the album to buy the single as well, something that served to demolish at a stroke the work done in mopping up all the loose ends of The Beatles' catalogue with the *Past Masters* compilations. "I'll Follow The Sun" is a pretty good version of the pastoral *Beatles For Sale* track. "Devil In Her Heart" was recorded for the BBC two days before the Fabs laid down a superior version for *With The Beatles*. The nondescript "Boys" herein is one of seven versions of the gender-confused cover The Beatles recorded for the BBC.

The record's cover was a pastiche of a 1960s record sleeve. Like the *Live At The BBC* album, it featured a black-and-white picture of the group outside a BBC studio. "Baby It's You" made number seven in the UK.

ANTHOLOGY 1
Released: 21/11/1995

TRACKLISTING

Disc one
1. "Free As A Bird"
2. "Speech: John Lennon"
3. "That'll Be the Day"
4. "In Spite of All the Danger"
5. "Speech: Paul McCartney"
6. "Hallelujah, I Love Her So"
7. "You'll Be Mine"
8. "Cayenne"
9. "Speech: Paul"
10. "My Bonnie"
11. "Ain't She Sweet"
12. "Cry For A Shadow"
13. "Speech: John"
14. "Speech: Brian Epstein"
15. "Searchin'"
16. "Three Cool Cats"
17. "The Sheik of Araby"

18. "Like Dreamers Do"
19. "Hello Little Girl"
20. "Speech: Brian Epstein"
21. "Besame Mucho"
22. "Love Me Do"
23. "How Do You Do It"
24. "Please Please Me"
25. "One After 909" (Sequence)
26. "One After 909"
27. "Lend Me Your Comb"
28. "I'll Get You"
29. "Speech: John"
30. "I Saw Her Standing There"
31. "From Me to You"
32. "Money (That's What I Want)"
33. "You Really Got A Hold On Me"
34. "Roll Over Beethoven"

Disc two

1. "She Loves You"
2. "Till There Was You"
3. "Twist and Shout"
4. "This Boy"
5. "I Want to Hold Your Hand"
6. "Speech: Eric Morecambe And Ernie Wise"
7. "Moonlight Bay"
8. "Can't Buy Me Love"
9. "All My Loving"
10. "You Can't Do That"
11. "And I Love Her"
12. "A Hard Day's Night"
13. "I Wanna Be Your Man"
14. "Long Tall Sally"
15. "Boys"
16. "Shout"
17. "I'll Be Back (Take 2)"
18. "I'll Be Back (Take 3)"
19. "You Know What to Do"
20. "No Reply (Demo)"

21. "Mr Moonlight"
22. "Leave My Kitten Alone"
23. "No Reply"
24. "Eight Days a Week (Sequence)"
25. "Eight Days a Week (Complete)"
26. "Kansas City/Hey-Hey-Hey-Hey!"

Boxed sets have been around in concept if not name as far back as the 1978 MCA six vinyl album collection *The Complete Buddy Holly*. However, the handy size and the extra running time of the CD turned it from a luxury, cumbersome item into something far more accessible and commonplace.

With record companies needing a way to entice purchasers who already had most of the contents of a multi-CD compilation on vinyl, it soon became a tradition for box sets to feature plenty of previously unreleased material. As with the original release of their back catalogue on CD, it took a while for The Beatles to put their name to a box set. When they did, it was with a box set – or rather series of them – to end all box sets, ones that were part of a multi-media extravaganza encompassing a TV series, a lavish, lovely book (albeit one not released until five years after the TV series' broadcast) and three double-CD sets of never previously released material, all of these strands of the project titled *Anthology*. Only Bob Dylan's never-ending *Bootleg Series* releases bear comparison, and even those are essentially a cult affair whose sales don't even come close to the chart-topping feats of the *Anthology* CDs.

Lennon once said that Glyn Johns' versions of the *Get Back* album were The Beatles with their trousers off; that description actually better fits these collections. The *Anthology* series are of course legal bootlegs: collections of the kind of out-takes, alternate takes, live recordings and radio session material that crop up on illicit releases. In a way it's brave of The Beatles to have put these sets out at all: it wouldn't be possible to discern from them that they were history's all-time greatest. These ones really were for the fans. When challenged about the *Anthology* series by a journalist when the first CD's release was imminent, McCartney made an analogy with an Egyptian pot: people didn't want to see Egyptian pots in museums because they were the greatest examples of Egyptian pottery but because of their rarity value and historical interest. He's essentially correct. Although there is plenty on the *Anthology* CDs that merited release in the first place, most of it would not be of interest unless we knew who the artists were and what their significance was to popular music. As with *Live At The BBC*, the *Anthology* releases are certainly not the place for those new to The Beatles to start.

All three *Anthology* CD sets boast sleeve designs by Klaus Voormann. Though Voormann had to submit ideas like other people, it somehow seems unthinkable that the man who was The Beatles' Hamburg friend, who gave The Beatles the idea for the moptop hairstyle, and who designed the *Revolver* cover should not have gotten the gig. His designs turned out to be excellent, composed of peeling, torn bill posters whose every rip revealed a different iconic Beatle image below, each album's art representing the era the contents covered.

Anthology 1 encompasses 1958 to 1964. Although there is juvenilia aplenty here, a real criticism that could be made of *Anthology 1* is what it leaves out. Where the hell is the sound recording of John Lennon playing with his schoolboy skiffle group the Quarry Men at the Woolton Village Fete on 6 July 1957, the day he met Paul McCartney? It's astonishing enough that such a recording exists but even more astonishing that The Beatles or EMI or both decided not to put it on this release, especially as the record company had shelled out £78,500 for it at auction. And why no recordings from the Star-Club or The Cavern? There are several other frustrating omissions that defy logic, discussed below.

On *Anthology 1*, there is actually an attempt to give the CDs an historical context via a narrative created by archive interview extracts between the music. Though this works well, it is half-hearted and was abandoned for volumes two and three.

The historical interest of the first archive track on *Anthology 1* is beyond belief. "That'll Be The Day" was the first recording made by the group that would become The Beatles. It was 1958 and they were still called The Quarry Men and John Lowe was on piano and Colin Hanton on drums, but the central trio of Lennon, McCartney and Harrison was already there. In those days, there were plenty of small-scale studios that enabled groups to cut a single copy of a disc of themselves playing, which in a sense was better than the later equivalent, the demo tape, because it left them with an artifact that looked like something they might buy that bore their musical heroes' names on the label. For one side of their disc, The Quarry Men recorded the signature song of Buddy Holly, a decision so poetic as to be unreal. Holly was the man who gave so much – name, sound, group format – to the band that would become The Beatles that it could be argued that The Beatles were really an English version of The Crickets, the group of which Holly was the lead singer, guitarist and principal songwriter and whose records were issued under the alternating names "Buddy Holly" and "The Crickets" (but never, contrary to popular misconception, "Buddy Holly *and* The Crickets"). The name The Beatles was arrived at because the group were looking for an insect alternative to The Crickets. The Beatles – like The Crickets unusually had – generated their own material. Like The Crickets too, The Beatles wrote in the rock 'n' roll idiom with an unusual classiness, spurning twanging rockabilly motifs and generic rock 'n' roll-progressions for more streamlined instrumentation and melodic constructions (both The Crickets and The Beatles were unusual for insisting on bridges in their songs) without sacrificing excitement.

"That'll Be The Day" – a song in which a man joshes his lover that she will never carry out her threats to leave him via a line from John Wayne to a highly catchy tune that is punctuated by one of the all-time classic guitar riffs – had been a UK number one in late 1957. John takes the lead vocal on The Quarry Men's version. The un-rock 'n' roll way that John insists on pronouncing the last "t" of "that'll" is peculiar but otherwise the track is an assured and high-spirited romp through the song. George and Paul can just about be heard executing backing harmonies over the constant hiss that not even digital technology could remove from the 78rpm shellac ten-inch disc.

On the flip of said disc was something even more intriguing: "In Spite Of All The Danger", the first recorded Beatles original, furthermore one that carries a unique writing credit: "McCartney/Harrison", although John sings lead. The historical significance of this being so incalculable, then, why on earth has the decision been made to edit it? Bootlegs reveal that the original recording was forty-one seconds longer than what we are presented with here. Presumably this was done for artistic reasons but it's absurd to bring aesthetic considerations into the equation with material like this. That caveat out of the way, one could imagine people thinking these boys were going to be stars from this track even then. The three-part harmonies that would become so familiar to billions within five years are present on a slightly country-esque number that actually sounds not too dissimilar to The Crickets. It's a genuinely good track, with a pop-savvy structure, a nifty solo from George and twinkle-eyed, almost comedic backing vocals.

"Hallelujah, I Love Her So" is the first of a trio of demos recorded at Paul's house which constitute the only record of Stuart Sutcliffe's tenure as bassist. (The band had no drummer at this point in 1960.) The sound quality doesn't allow any insight into whether Sutcliffe was any good, as it's worse than on the tracks from the shellac disc. Paul sings lead on this passable version of the Ray Charles classic. "You'll Be Mine" becomes the earliest recording of a Lennon/McCartney song to gain commercial release. It's something of a comedy number with booming, spoken-word Lennon sections sandwiched by McCartney singing parts. "Cayenne" is a McCartney instrumental whose title alludes to The Shadows' hit instrumental "Apache", a UK number one that year. It's difficult to judge its worth not only because of the sound quality but because it's faded out rather quickly.

This home demo trio is followed by a triumvirate of Hamburg tracks, material recorded in Germany through the aegis of one Bert Kaempfert in June 1961. The sessions were done in conjunction with Tony Sheridan, a rock 'n' roll journeyman whom The Beatles sometimes backed on stage in Germany. "My Bonnie" sees Sheridan take the lead vocal. There might conceivably be said to be some wit in the way the song starts as a respectful rendering of the out-of-copyright traditional number before lurching rudely into a rocked-up arrangement, but tackling such a hoary old chestnut displays a distinct lack of imagination. As detailed elsewhere in this book, even the recording's one saving grace – that when in January 1962 it was released as a single by "Tony Sheridan and the Beat Brothers" it brought the band to the attention of Brian Epstein – is in dispute. Pete Best's drumming, by the way, sounds perfectly good. "Ain't She Sweet" features John on lead vocals on a cover of a 1920s pop standard, probably picked up by The Beatles from the Gene Vincent version. It's alright but a little staccato. "Cry For A Shadow" is the most worthwhile of the trio. It's an instrumental with another unique composing credit: "Harrison/ Lennon". The two guitarists create quite a professional concoction, George's keening lead lines counter-pointed with John's rattling rhythm work. The title of course is another allusion to the band who when they weren't backing Cliff Richard were the pre-eminent British instrumental group.

Five songs from The Beatles' audition for Decca Records in January 1962 follow, including a couple of the Lennon/ McCartney originals that legal complications have made so hard to find. (It's a motif of the senseless editing and omissions attending this CD set though that, frustratingly, the third original is missing.) "Searchin'" sees Paul sing a version of a Coasters' hit and once again the contrast between this and The Coasters' cartoon vocals indicates that this type of singing is not The Beatles' forte. Having said that, the track that follows – "Three Cool Cats", another Coasters record – is not half bad, with George singing competent lead, the band playing the slinky instrumentation well and John performing some amusing ethnic backing vocals. "The Sheik Of Araby" was a song so old – written in the 1940s, it alluded to silent movie star Rudolph Valentino – that only a comedy treatment would work at this stage, and that's what the band provided, with backing chants of "Not 'arf!" and an introductory Arab-esque motif. George sings lead. It's alright, but who did they imagine would be interested in such material should they ever get that elusive recording contract?

The Lennon/McCartney numbers included from the Decca audition are "Like Dreamers Do" and "Hello Little Girl". The first – sung by Paul – is a peculiarly old-fashioned crooner. It also features lumpen drumming that in contrast to the Hamburg material makes one wonder whether there was, in fact, some credibility to the claims of incompetence on the part of Best by his colleagues. The latter number – the first song ever written by John – features somewhat over-enthusiastic backing vocals but is a likeable if lightweight pop number.

"Besame Mucho" and "Love Me Do" are the only surviving tracks of the four committed to tape when The Beatles performed those and probably several other tracks for George Martin in June 1962. The young head of Parlophone Records – a division of EMI – had agreed to give Epstein and The Beatles some of his time after feeling sorry for the manager when he looked crestfallen after he told him he didn't think much of the Decca audition recordings he played him. "Besame Mucho" is another song in the vein of "The Sheik of Araby" in the sense that it's so old-fashioned, middle-aged and *faux* exotic that it would seem only a comedy treatment is applicable. Yet The Beatles play it straight. Meanwhile, we have a Pete Best version of "Love Me Do" to add to the Ringo Starr and Andy White versions. It's slower and longer. John's harmonica is not as good as on the record, Best's drumming is notably poor – lurching from tempo to tempo and executing clumsy rolls – and the whole thing has a ramshackle feel. Not very good, but again of incredible historical interest.

Such interest reaches something of a crescendo with the inclusion of "How Do You Do It?", The Beatles' version of the song that George Martin wanted to release as their first record once he had granted them that elusive recording contract on the strength of not so much their performance at the Parlophone audition but the compelling and likeable collective personality he found they had in the flesh. The group resisted the release as their first record of this Mitch Murray Tin Pan Alley number with history-making consequences, but there is no trace of contempt for the material he is singing in John's lead vocal as he and his colleagues perform a perfectly creditable version of a perfectly creditable, if Toytown, pop number. Never has history adjudged a decision to be more right than The Beatles' refusal to put it out as their entrée, but it would have made a worthy inclusion on the *Please Please Me* album.

Speaking of which, the version of the title track of that LP included herein is a fairly good early pass, but with harmonica completely absent. The previously unissued 1963 incarnation of "One After 909" is represented as both a "sequence" (bits of different renditions that break down, punctuated by the band arguing over why things aren't working) and as a composite, a complete version assembled for the CD from the good parts of the breakdowns. You could argue either that this is tampering with history or that it is no more dishonest than normal recording techniques, in which sections are bolted together all the time (albeit not normally at such a chronological remove). Either way, it's clear that "One After 909" could have added a bit of grit to the debut album.

By the time of the recording of "Lend Me Your Comb" in July 1963, The Beatles were chart toppers and had their own radio show, from which this average version of a track made famous but not written by band favourite Carl Perkins was taken. "I'll Get You" is an October 1963 performance on the family TV viewing staple *Sunday Night At The London Palladium.* The audience add their own handclap beat, and screams, to a competent Beatles performance of their quality B-side.

Five further live tracks follow, these ones recorded in the same month in Stockholm. They make for a lovely surprise, proving that there are high quality in-concert tracks in existence of the band from the Beatlemania days. The sleevenotes imply that they are included to show that The Beatles were a good live act until the screaming got too soul-destroying for them to care. As does the Lennon interview extract that precedes it where he talks of the fact that in the pre-EMI days the band were brilliant on stage and "there was no one to touch us". The tracks are more raw and energetic than you would expect. They are also clearer, no doubt helped by the fact that Swedes are too polite to wail until the song's over. A powerful version of "I Saw Her Standing There" starts the proceedings. "From Me To You" is given an oomph (and faster tempo) not heard on the record. The preview of "Money" from *With The Beatles* naturally has no piano, but the band do perfectly well with guitars that at some points are raucous indeed and John gives it his all vocally. John is just as impassioned in his singing – but in a different, more tender way – in another *With The Beatles* preview, "You Really Got A Hold On Me". "Roll Over Beethoven" follows and is a better version – both in terms of

George's singing and the frantic tempo – than either the *With The Beatles* or *Live At The BBC* versions. It almost goes without saying that there were two other songs performed at this broadcast Swedish concert and that they are not included here.

Performances follow from the 1963 Royal Variety performance that sealed The Beatles' reputation as the pop group that even the oldies could love, even though they were so cheeky as to make a reference to the royalty and posh people present being able to rattle their jewellery in time rather than clap their hands. Four numbers were performed by the Fabs that day. How many does this set include? Three, naturally. The first, "She Loves You" is a fine energetic performance of what was fast becoming the national anthem for teenagers. No doubt the jewellery-rattling dignitaries that John was referring to would have been among the few in the venue who knew "Till There Was You" from their set. (*With The Beatles* wouldn't be released for a couple of weeks.) It's an okay rendition but with three versions now available on official Beatles product, its novelty value is fast becoming diminished. The "Twist And Shout" finale – introduced with the jewellery-rattling comment – follows. As with "She Loves You", it's energetic but not as impressive as those surprisingly fiery Stockholm performances.

Competent performances of "This Boy" and "I Want To Hold Your Hand" from the British television comedy programme *The Morecambe And Wise Show* follow. The latter has a pleasant rawness to it. A sketch with the titular hosts follows wherein following some banter (which will make sense to UK listeners but will probably be largely incomprehensible to Americans not weaned on Eric Morecambe's gags about Ernie Wise's short, fat, hairy legs), the band gamely join their hosts in a rendition of old-time show tune "Moonlight Bay". Not much of a listen aesthetically but as a part of the documentary mosaic of the set, a fair enough inclusion.

"Can't Buy Me Love" is take two from the song's original session. Though it has some horrendously out of kilter lead guitar and only a guide vocal from Paul, it too would have documentary value if its guitar solo had not been "flown in" (added in modern times) from take one. This sort of thing is justified with a track like "One After 909", of which a finished master didn't exist, but is senseless tampering with history if applied to an already commercially released song like this.

It would have been unthinkable not to include in a project of this kind The Beatles singing on *The Ed Sullivan Show* on Sunday 9 February 1964: the audience of 73 million was the highest in television history up to that point, and partly as a consequence of this first major exposure to the American public of The Beatles (even if this was not the group's first time on US TV), they were soon to dominate the culture. To this day, The Beatles are actually more famous and popular in the States than they are in their homeland – which is going some. It's actually a little surprising that only one number is represented, "All My Loving". Having said that, had the other four songs they performed been presented to us, a certain weariness would probably have set in, not just at the meant-for-TV-not-CD-audio quality but also at the repetition of material: "She Loves You", "I Saw Her Standing There", "I Want To Hold Your Hand" and – Gawd 'elp us – "Till There Was You".

Some early versions of tracks from *A Hard Day's Night* follow. "You Can't Do That" is take six, as opposed to the take nine that was the master version. As you'd kind of expect, it's nearly there but not quite. An early "And I Love Her", though, is a different beast entirely. This version – take two – is a full band version with electric instrumentation and therefore very different to the familiar intimate acoustic one. Some vocal fluffs and a certain roughness that you would expect from only the second take of a track that took two subsequent re-makes to perfect prevent it from being a fully realized alternate version but it's close. With "A Hard Day's Night", we are presented with the first-ever take of the song. It's slightly slower than its finished incarnation. Three hours and eight more takes later they had a classic in the bag. This is a promising version, whose guitar solo is not too dissimilar to the piano break George Martin played on the finished track, for those who believe that Martin had all the good ideas.

The Beatles got their own 1964 television show in the shape of *The Beatles In The Round*. It would be very interesting as a cultural artifact to see that show released on DVD but there's little to be gained from the raw audio versions of "I Wanna Be

Your Man", "Long Tall Sally" and "Boys" (not actually part of the TV show in the end, so a real rarity) presented here, although their version of the Isley Brothers' hit "Shout" fares better, partly because we have nothing to compare it to: the band never put a version of this part of their live repertoire on disc. It's a frenetic version with – uniquely – all four Beatles taking turns to sing lead vocals. Only poor sound quality prevents it from making the journey from interesting to fascinating.

"I'll Be Back" takes two and three display The Beatles quickly realizing that the waltz-time that John had originally envisaged for his lovely song from *A Hard Day's Night* was not going to work. After take two breaks down, they do it in conventional 4/4 and immediately it starts working. An interesting window on the Fabs' adaptability and musical intelligence.

A couple of Ringo-less tracks follow from the point in June 1964 at which the drummer was hospitalized with tonsillitis. Jimmy Nicol deputized on live dates while he was absent, though absolutely no one seems to know who the mystery drummer was on the demo of "No Reply" here. More uptempo, sprightly and far more jaunty ("You dirty liar!" Paul sings in response to the line "That's a lie!") than the mordant, round-in-circles *Beatles For Sale* version, it would have been interesting to see this arrangement develop from the laughter-punctuated run-through here. "No Reply" is preceded by a George Harrison song that never made it beyond the demo stage, "You Know What To Do". It's actually quite impressive, with a proper structure, including a bridge, competent melody and understated tone. On the basis of this evidence, it deserved to be fleshed out and achieve the status of Harrison's second song on a Beatles album.

Ringo was back on the drum stool by August when The Beatles were finishing *Beatles For Sale*. The version of "Mr Moonlight" here is preferable to the awful familiar version from that album, mainly because there is a guitar solo present which, though it has a peculiar scraping quality, is preferable – as would be just about anything – to Paul's atrocious organ solo on the album rendition. The following out-take from *Beatles For Sale* is a real treat, a storming cover of the Little Willie John/Johnny Preston hit "Leave My Kitten Alone" with a fearsome Lennon vocal and a bridge in which Ringo sounds like he is working a pile-driver rather than a kick drum. Why the band abandoned it after adding the overdubs necessary for a finished master is unfathomable.

A version of "No Reply" from the following month is actually sort of depressing, for it shows the band continuing down a wrong turning they had taken with the song that would culminate in the *Beatles For Sale* version, shedding the jauntiness of the first take for the over-sombre master. The development of the same album's "Eight Days A Week" is shown in a sequence (takes one, two and four) that breaks down in the usual series of mild expletives and banter but shows them groping for the final arrangement from an initial girl group-type arrangement and a differing melody in the title line. A complete take – take five – then follows. There's no fade-in like on the familiar version and the melody still differs. Most bands (and this listener) would have settled for this rendition, but The Beatles clearly realized that the title line needed to be more plaintive and that some of the burbles of instrumentation were just too rough for public consumption.

The Beatles only recorded two takes of "Kansas City"/"Hey-Hey-Hey-Hey!" The one that features on *Beatles For Sale* was take one. *Anthology 1* closes with the other take, which is almost just as corking as the first one, although the backing vocals could be mixed up higher.

"Free As A Bird"
Released: 04/12/1995

TRACKLISTING:

1. "Free As A Bird"
2. "I Saw Her Standing There"
3. "This Boy"
4. "Christmas Time (Is Here Again)"

When the news first came through, it seemed in the realms of those "Beatles-to-reform" stories that had appeared so frequently in the newspapers since 1970 but had begun to seem increasingly preposterous even when John was still alive. But the surviving members of The Beatles and Yoko confirmed it: there was going to be a new Beatles record, the first in a quarter of a century, and it was going to be constructed by the surviving band members playing over the top of a previously unissued John Lennon recording. It was all being done in the name of *Anthology*, The Beatles' TV autobiography and multi-volume CD project.

Some found it absurd, and it was certainly an idea that took a lot of getting used to at first, especially as originally the talk had only been of the remaining Beatles reuniting to provide some soundtrack music for the *Anthology* programme. Even those appalled by the idea, of course, only felt that way because of their love for the group, and therefore inevitably were intrigued to at least hear the results – as was the entire world. When the single "Free As A Bird" was released from its armed guard on 20 November 1995 and made available to the media, television channels gave over time to live reaction to the historic moment. Curiously, though, the track wasn't issued as a single until a fortnight after its parent album, *Anthology 1*, hit the stores.

"Free As A Bird" was written by John Lennon in 1977 as a direct reaction to his winning his court battle to remain in the United States, whose New York citizens he found refreshingly disinclined to mob him despite the fact that their country contained the most intense Beatles fans in the world. It is exultant in an exhausted rather than giddy way. Lennon recorded three versions of voice-and-piano demos of the song on cassette at his Dakota apartment. When a version was chosen by the surviving Beatles, many hours had to be spent cleaning up the hiss on the tape and getting it in time to make it ready for public consumption. Meanwhile, giving Lennon's voice and his piano separate tracks was out of the question given the circumstances of the original recording. In none of his three demos did Lennon finish the bridge: the furthest he got was its first two lines. This gave McCartney an opportunity to revive his old songwriting partnership with Lennon – which he has publicly mentioned would often involve him devising parts, or all, of a bridge for a composition for which Lennon had only so far worked out the verses and choruses.

Though Harrison, McCartney and Starr retained the services of their trusty old studio engineer Geoff Emerick on the recording, many were shocked to find out that George Martin was not the designated producer. The official story was that the hearing of Martin, now in his late sixties, wasn't as acute as it had once been and that he had nobly stepped aside from the project for that reason. Some have postulated that Martin's hearing was perfectly adequate to the task and that Harrison – ever wary of McCartney's alleged propensity to boss Beatles sessions – had insisted on having his man on board, namely Jeff Lynne, former frontman of Electric Light Orchestra-turned-record producer, a man with whom Harrison had recorded and co-produced when he, Bob Dylan, Tom Petty and Roy Orbison had formed the supergroup The Traveling Wilburys. Some found Lynne's producer role for the new Beatles record amusing on the grounds that ELO had been formed to take up where "I Am The Walrus" and other orchestral Beatles tracks left off: the man who had always been a Beatles wannabe was now in a position beyond his wildest fantasies.

Whether or not Martin really was aurally challenged, the decision to recruit Lynne was a disaster. "Free As A Bird" opens shockingly and dismayingly with cacophonous, monotonous drumming. Lynne was using a production technique that was not only anachronistic for Beatles fare but wasn't even modern: this was a throwback to the 1980s, which had seen the arrival of the click track, the archetypal invention for which there had never been any need, as proven by the fact that so many records from that decade are now unlistenable. The warmth and inspiration of 1960s and 1970s drumming were replaced by rigid, tedious, unimaginative drumming – all for the sake of keeping time slightly more efficiently. In an utterly perverse development, this failing had attention brought to it by a production fashion for putting an inordinate amount of echo on the snare drum and mixing it well forward. And shame on the critics and media pundits for engaging in an Emperor's New Clothes syndrome by failing to point out the idiocy of this development at the time. Even more awful is the fact that Ringo inevitably received a lot of the blame for the disappointment that "Free As A Bird" was to many. It compounded the reputation he had lately acquired among the public courtesy of barbs from the musically pig-ignorant of a man whose name was a byword for rock group passenger.

Having said all that, "Free As A Bird" is not a complete disaster. The so-happy-it's-sad nature of the song is very fitting, such a feeling having always been a huge component of The Beatles' sound. George's keening guitar figures add to that feeling. John's vocal is moving, even without the dramatic resonance. Naturally, his voice is markedly more low-fi than the rest of the record but somehow that mustiness is appropriate for someone effectively speaking from beyond the grave. Paul's bridge doesn't quite make sense, him attempting to shoehorn in something that alludes to his and John's former songwriting partnership in a lyric that was never meant to be about that – "Can we really live without each other?" – but the sound of his voice counterpointed with Lennon's (George sings the second, shorter bridge) can't help but create a little *frisson*.

There is a half-hearted attempt to provide a Beatles imprimatur in the shape of harmonies but they sound more like ELO harmonies, partly because John isn't there, partly because Lynne throws himself into the vocal mix. Lynne compounds the shortcomings of the drum track by putting some phasing – a favoured ELO technique – on it at the end.

The record doesn't besmirch The Beatles' legend any more than, say, the return of Björn Borg to competitive tennis after his retirement makes people remember him as a past-it thirty-three-year-old embarrassment rather than one of history's great players. However, the record could have been so much more than this. Courtesy of Lynne, it has already dated in a way that The Beatles' 1960s canon has not.

The CD version of the "Free As A Bird" single had three additional tracks not to be found on the parent album. "I Saw Her Standing There" is take nine of the *Please Please Me* song, the take that actually bequeathed that immortal "One-two-three-*four*!" opening but which we now learn was spliced onto the first take when that one was chosen for inclusion on the album. Always nice to hear this track and it's about as good as the familiar version – but that's to say the differences are almost imperceptible. "This Boy" is presented in two incomplete takes, a bit of banter on the first one (take twelve) giving us a ringside view of the partnership Paul was talking of in "Free As A Bird". The second, take thirteen, is almost perfect but has to be abandoned because – still in the days where overdubbing the vocals wasn't considered an option – the words get mangled. The merriment and good nature with which John, Paul and George greet the prospect of yet another take, as opposed to the more understandable irritation, is endearing. "Christmas Time (Is Here Again)" is a Beatles original that was used – cut up and interspersed by dialogue – on The Beatles' 1967 fan club flexidisc. This is the first time the uninterrupted recording has been issued. It's hardly of overwhelming artistic stature but naturally a real rarity. Tagged on at the end are The Beatles' individual seasonal greetings from the previous year's flexidisc, with some Lennon Highland-flavoured gobbledegook following that.

The cover artwork was a drawing by Lennon from *In His Own Write* that had a convenient ornithological theme. The single sold well but, disappointingly, failed to make the top spot either side of the Atlantic. One wonders how Paul felt about the fact that the record that kept "Free As A Bird" at number two in his homeland was "Earth Song" by Michael Jackson, a man who had infuriated him by buying The Beatles' song catalogue, which Lennon and McCartney had lost control of in the 1960s. In the States, the *Billboard* chart – now that country's sole recognized chart, its competitor magazine *Cash Box* having fallen by the wayside in 1996 but its charts out of credibility long before that – registered it scoring a peak of number six.

"Real Love"
Released: 04/03/1996

TRACKLISTING

1. "Real Love"
2. "Baby's In Black"
3. "Yellow Submarine"
4. "Here, There And Everywhere"

In The Beatles' home country, headlines were made by the decision of Radio 1 not to playlist "Real Love", the second "new"

Beatles recording after "Free As A Bird". The measure was even condemned in Parliament by a MP who wanted the Prime Minister to intervene.

It was to some extent a phoney controversy – not only did the track get some plays on the station, but Radio 1 in the 1990s couldn't be expected to be the Beatles-championing station it was in the 1960s. (It was still called the Light Programme when The Beatles started.) In recent years, the station had purposely sought to make itself more relevant to the young in order to justify the Corporation's licence fee and a record by men in their fifties from a band extinct for a quarter-century was, it was reasonable to expect, not going to be of much interest to its demographic. Only the newsworthiness of "Free As A Bird" had got that record exposure on the station. Radio 2 is now the natural home of those who grew up on the Fab Four.

However, it can't be denied that there might have been reasons other than demographic reach dictating the decision. First, unlike "Free As A Bird", this disc does not have the *frisson* of a never-before (legally) heard Lennon composition. Judging by their public comments on it, the surviving Beatles were under the impression that "Real Love" was indeed that but in fact, it had appeared on the soundtrack album to the 1988 film *Imagine*. Additionally, it didn't have the bigger-than-life qualities (or at least ambitions) of "Free As A Bird".

As before, the home-recorded basic track (Lennon vocal and piano) provides a musty, ghostly contrast to the slick present-day studio work of Harrison, McCartney and Starr, although, curiously, right at the beginning it is the modern instruments that sound faded and archaic and – when it is brought in – John's voice that sounds fresh and now. "Real Love" is the sort of song that Lennon often wrote after he met Yoko Ono, containing an attitude of almost supplication to the inevitability and joy of romantic love. Recorded circa 1979 according to the sleevenotes (although some sources claim it started life two years previously as "Real Life"), it mercifully avoids the banalities Lennon could sometimes be guilty of in this lovestruck mode, banalities which did not start, contrary to popular opinion, with the *Double Fantasy* album but were present as far back as the supposedly edgy album *Plastic Ono Band* (check out "Love", with its profound advice that "Love is feeling, feeling love").

Though the song doesn't have the anthemic flavour that made "Free As A Bird" so appropriate as The Beatles' "comeback" single and for Paul's superimposition of his thoughts on Lennon-McCartney, its narrower horizons don't prevent it from being rather nice. This time round, by necessity because of the song's complete state, Paul is in the background, restricting himself to bass and (presumably) backing vocal contributions. George is also subdued compared to ". . . Bird", although his flecks of guitar work and restrained solo are impressive enough. Once again, Lynne can't resist giving the drum track more wallop than necessary, although in keeping with the understated ambience Ringo's work is not rendered as in-your-face as on "Free As A Bird". Nonetheless, while one can make the argument that "Free As A Bird" just about had the requisite grand attributes that made a Beatles 45 in the 1960s, there's no deluding oneself that "Real Love" would have made the cut as a single back then.

"Baby's In Black" is from one of the August '65 Hollywood Bowl concerts. Considering how short *The Beatles At The Hollywood Bowl* album was, it's surprising that this wasn't included. It's also surprising that this track was included on this single, as The Beatles have made their disapproval known of the . . . *Hollywood Bowl* album by refusing to sanction its release on CD. Perhaps they were disgruntled by the splicing of performances from different nights, which would be a bloody cheek considering all the splicing they allowed of studio tracks on the three *Anthology* CD sets. The only splicing the sleevenotes admit to here is John's introduction from the first night being tacked onto the front of the performance of the second, a performance which is pretty good, if entirely dispensable.

Not quite as dispensable though as "Yellow Submarine", which is a new mix of the song that gives a new prominence to the sound effects and has an unused Ringo spoken word introduction. Still, one can't quite escape the nagging feeling that had this busy mix (which is nothing to do with The Beatles) been used back in '66, it would have made the track less monotonous.

Take seven of "Here, There And Everywhere" with a guide vocal from Paul and no backing harmonies except a sample overdubbed near the end in 1995 for the purposes of this CD sounds like the very recipe for dispensability. But this listener isn't sure that this isn't actually better than the *Revolver* master. It's somehow less self-consciously tender than the familiar one, partly because of the absence of those delicate harmonies, partly because Ringo's drumming is slightly more energetic, partly because Paul's flawed vocal is more soulful.

The cover of the single featured – *apropos* of nothing – a photograph of the band in the mid-1960s in the period in which they were beginning to dispense with suits for casual-but-smart mod gear. The record made number four in the UK but stalled just outside the top ten in the States.

ANTHOLOGY 2
Released: 18/03/1996

TRACKLISTING

Disc one
1. "Real Love"
2. "Yes It Is"
3. "I'm Down"
4. "You've Got to Hide Your Love Away"
5. "If You've Got Trouble"
6. "That Means a Lot"
7. "Yesterday"
8. "It's Only Love"
9. "I Feel Fine"
10. "Ticket to Ride"
11. "Yesterday"
12. "Help!"
13. "Everybody's Trying to Be My Baby"
14. "Norwegian Wood (This Bird Has Flown)"
15. "I'm Looking Through You"
16. "12-Bar Original"
17. "Tomorrow Never Knows"
18. "Got to Get You Into My Life"
19. "And Your Bird Can Sing"
20. "Taxman"

21. "Eleanor Rigby (Strings Only)"
22. "I'm Only Sleeping (Rehearsal)"
23. "I'm Only Sleeping (Take 1)"
24. "Rock And Roll Music"
25. "She's A Woman"

Disc two
 1. "Strawberry Fields Forever (Demo Sequence)"
 2. "Strawberry Fields Forever (Take 1)"
 3. "Strawberry Fields Forever (Take 7 & Edit Piece)"
 4. "Penny Lane"
 5. "A Day in the Life"
 6. "Good Morning Good Morning"
 7. "Only A Northern Song"
 8. "Being For The Benefit of Mr Kite! (Takes 1 And 2)"
 9. "Being For The Benefit of Mr Kite! (Take 7)"
10. "Lucy In The Sky with Diamonds"
11. "Within You Without You (Instrumental)"
12. "Sgt. Pepper's Lonely Hearts Club Band (Reprise)"
13. "You Know My Name (Look Up the Number)"
14. "I Am The Walrus"
15. "The Fool On The Hill (Demo)"
16. "Your Mother Should Know"
17. "The Fool On The Hill (Take 4)"
18. "Hello, Goodbye"
19. "Lady Madonna"
20. "Across The Universe"

As with the first *Anthology* CD set, *Anthology 2* begins with a
"Threetles" record – "Real Love" – before diving back into the
archives. This time round, as a matter of necessity, there are
fewer live renditions and alternate versions of songs, the former
because, of course, the band stopped touring halfway through
the February 1965–February 1968 period covered herein, the
latter because the days were now well and truly over (at least
until the *Get Back* sessions) of The Beatles knocking out tracks
on which they all played and sang at once.

  By this point, creating masters meant deciding on a best basic
track and then spending time overdubbing extra elements, which

involved the "bounce-down" process. Though such was The Beatles' perfectionism, there are a smattering of such alternate, abandoned masters in existence, they are inevitably fewer and further between than either discarded complete takes with no overdubs from the very early days or the complete takes with minimal overdubs of the period immediately thereafter. Because of this, the compilers have frequently decided to create their own alternate masters, by flying in different parts from different takes or making composites of out-takes. It is of course tampering with history (albeit with The Beatles' permission) and the results possess a value not much beyond a novelty. Though *Anthology 1* just about deserved to be a double-CD and *Anthology 3* would cover a period where there were plenty of live-in-the-studio out-takes and discarded versions, it occurs that more space was given to *Anthology 2* than it merits.

Things get off to a dodgy start with the archive stuff in the shape of "Yes It Is": this is take two with a guide vocal by John segueing into the master that created the finished track, although not the master in the form with which we are familiar but an edited part and one furthermore remixed. In short, a real Frankenstein monster of a piece designed, we are told, to demonstrate just how quickly the group turned a track they had never played collectively before into that great B-side of "Ticket To Ride" (five hours). That statistic is indeed impressive but the track neither constitutes a great listen nor has that incredible rarity value possessed by so many cuts on *Anthology 1*.

Another alternate of a great B-side follows in the shape of take one of "I'm Down". Paul, singing live, leaves gaps for the overdubbing of backing vocals. Paul dismisses it as "plastic soul" at the end but it's nigh indistinguishable from the basic track of the finished master (which was take seven). "You've Got To Hide Your Love Away" is represented by the only other complete take of the *Help!* highlight. The guitar work at the close indicates the group may not yet have been thinking of the flute that occupied this space on the finished track. "If You've Got Trouble" is a never-before-released Lennon-McCartney original from the *Help!* sessions, sung by Ringo, and a finished master too. Considering that Paul has admitted that he and John would not invest all of their songcraft in tracks destined for George or Ringo vocals, this mid-tempo anthem of callousness (the spite leavened by Ringo's good-natured voice) is actually pretty good and this listener would have preferred it to occupy space on *Help!* in preference to "Another Girl" or "Dizzy Miss Lizzy". Ringo's indifferent call before the instrumental break – "Rock on . . . anybody!" – is inadvertently hilarious. "That Means A Lot" is another *Help!* out-take, and, though not a classic, a puzzling omission from an album that had its *longeurs*. Paul's voice is drenched in echo as he delivers a discourse on how happy his lover's little displays of affection make him and the track overall has a massive and cavernous sound. PJ Proby later had a minor UK hit with the song.

The only existing alternate version of "Yesterday" follows, actually take one. The master was take two, and that of course had a string quartet overdubbed. This is just Paul and guitar. It's good, but lacking something. I know! A string quartet. "It's Only Love" is take two of the underrated *Help!* cut. Taken at a faster clip than the familiar one, with John's vocal perhaps less soulful, it's still a worthwhile listen.

Four songs (of six performed) follow from the now forgotten live TV show *Blackpool Night Out*, the titular English coastal town being one of the few places British people could afford to go on their holidays at that point in history. "I Feel Fine" is feedback-less and perfunctory. "Ticket To Ride" is better, well played and full-hearted. The following first-ever live performance of "Yesterday" is of historical interest. Paul's voice and guitar are accompanied on stage by a string quartet and the composer delivers his song with a professionalism that temporarily silences the screamers. George and John top and tail the performance with good-natured ridicule. The first-ever stage performance of "Help!" follows that. In a strong rendition, Ringo makes up for a vocal fluff from John by frantic drumming that increases the usual tempo and by a relentless in-your-face hi-hat.

"Everybody's Trying To Be My Baby" is the sole song chosen to represent The Beatles' historic performance at Shea Stadium on 15 August 1965. What seems a peculiar choice of song is actually justified by the fact that it didn't make it onto the TV special of the concert, so has been unheard ever since.

Surprisingly, considering the wind-tunnel scream conditions, it's not too bad, with George's lead guitar robust throughout, although towards the end there are a few wince-making lurches into tunelessness. Still, great art was on no one's mind that day.

"Norwegian Wood" is an early master of the *Rubber Soul* track, built on the very first take of the song and marked "best" in the manner in which recording artists indicate the version intended for release. Nine days later, they changed their minds and set about recording it all over again. This earlier version is rougher around the edges and has more of an Eastern ambience than the familiar version, as well as busier sitar. How extraordinary that with The Beatles pressurized for the third Christmas in a row to record their second album of the year, they should exhibit a perfectionism totally at odds with their workload. "I'm Looking Through You" is a version of the *Rubber Soul* track that, like the previous "Norwegian Wood", was considered to be finished after a basic track was laid down and overdubs added, but after a gap of a couple of weeks The Beatles re-recorded it not once but twice and discarded this original "best". This is a slower but wilder version, with some quasi-experiential monotonous keyboards and prominent percussion. It's difficult to hear it cold – putting out of one's head the warmer, more mellifluous familiar version – but it's certainly an interesting lateral angle on the song.

"12-Bar Original" is a most un-Beatle-like track. This recording dating from the *Rubber Soul* sessions would have been the band's first released instrumental had it made it to that LP. It's vaguely Booker T & The MG's in nature. This edit of just under three minutes was cut-down from a version lasting more than six-and-a-half minutes. It's not at all awful but it lacks the vigour, character and compelling motifs that made the vocal-less records of the MGs and The Shadows so memorable.

"Tomorrow Never Knows" is take one of the track that would close *Revolver*. The muffled, Eastern-ish guitar sound running throughout is a new element. The tape loops are absent and Ringo's drumming is less hypnotic and it feels exactly like the primitive version of the finished track it is. "Got To Get You Into My Life" is a version of another track that was remade although, as space had been left for more overdubbing, was probably not considered a finished master. We don't know whether horns would have been added to the version, but even if they had, it would still sound very different to the version that was released: it's slow, has a stop-start structure, features a prominent, one-note organ part, an "I need your love" three-part vocal refrain and backing harmonies. It also possesses an intimacy the *Revolver* version doesn't. It feels a bit bare but one suspects that had horn charts filled those vacant spaces, it would have been preferable to that Cold Soul familiar rendition.

"And Your Bird Can Sing" is an early version. Though it's clearly inferior musically to the rebuilt one we know – George's stunning super-long guitar lick is here just a hesitant chiming sound – The Beatles themselves clearly thought it was fine for a period of just under a week, hence their attempt to overdub vocals. Said vocals repeatedly collapse into giggles, possibly because of the presence of marijuana, well documented as a big part of the band's life at the time. It's sort of endearing but aesthetically worthless.

As the version of "Taxman" here is take eleven as opposed to the finished version's take twelve, the differences are understandably slight. The references to Messrs Heath and Wilson are replaced by less topical "Anybody got a bit of money?" chants and the song has a clean ending, not a fade.

It's easy to ridicule the inclusion of the backing string arrangement for "Eleanor Rigby" (as *Mojo* magazine did: "Strings only! No Paul! Erm . . .") but the track, remarkably, has a genuine pathos even without that lyric. It would have been nice though if after a lifetime where Martin was paid the scale rates for helming the most successful records of all time, he could have been given a publishing credit instead of the track's composition bizarrely going the usual Lennon/McCartney route.

The out-take of "I'm Only Sleeping" presented here features John and Paul duetting and a very simple acoustic arrangement. It's also faster than the one we know and some of the vocal inflections are quite jazzy. Bizarrely, it's one of five takes recorded *after* the eleven takes that produced the master for the *Revolver* album, which just shows that The Beatles weren't always right when they decided to rebuild a track. This version is nice but not as heart-melting as the *Revolver* one. However, it's in a different universe to the following two tracks, recorded live at Budokan in Japan days after *Revolver*'s completion. Having laid down an astonishing and sophisticated album as well as stunning non-album tracks "Paperback Writer" and "Rain", and further- more done so at their own leisurely pace, the group now had to endure once more Beatlemania and inadequate live facilities. The whole of the show that these two tracks – "Rock And Roll Music" and "She's A Woman" – came from was recorded, as was another of the five gigs the group played at the Hall. On the basis of this evidence, only the tone deaf would petition for the full release of those recordings.

CD disc two opens with no fewer than three versions of "Strawberry Fields Forever". The first is a home demo. In this low-fi affair, Lennon talks of taking the listener "back", not "down", to Strawberry Fields, which would actually make more sense. Take one is the first recorded studio version of the pastoral variant, featuring some swooping electric guitar. We are then treated to the full version of the pastoral variant of the song, the one that on the finished record gave way to the heavy, orchestrated version after a minute. It features an entire verse that was later dropped. The only thing that spoils the purity of this treasure is the fact that grafted on to the end of it is an extended version of the coda (backward cymbals and wild drumming) to be found at the end of the finished master. We don't know whether The Beatles would have included this coda – in either long or unedited form – had they merely released the pastoral version. It certainly seems at odds with this version's tranquillity in a way it doesn't with the pastoral/heavy spliced master version. Nonetheless, it does give us a chance to be reminded of what a good drummer Ringo is.

"Penny Lane" is presented in what can only be described as an artificial alternate take (the compilers refer to it as "a unique combination of the many different takes and sounds that comprised that original master, broken down . . . and remixed anew"). The fact that Paul's vocal is not double-tracked here makes for a negligible difference but the instrumental break – giving the focus to cor anglais – is noticeably dissimilar. The drums are mixed to the fore, or rather mixed badly (what is it about modern engineers and in-your-face drums?) and the track doesn't have the suppleness and the brightness that even the overrated famous one does. "A Day In The Life" goes even further down this "unique combination" path by welding together different parts of out-takes of the track to create a "What If?" alternate universe reject version. Of course it's entirely fatuous on one level – it's the version The Beatles might have made had their decisions implausibly coincided with every single one of the many micro decisions the compilers have made and had they been possessed of little musical judgment (i.e. not realized the out-take stuff was inferior). However, it's moderately interesting.

"Good Morning, Good Morning" is the same track as we hear on *Sgt. Pepper*, including vocals, only without the horn overdubs, guitar solo and unforgettable speaker-panning animal noises at the end. The overdubs were there for a reason, of course, but this bare hard rock version is powerful.

One *Pepper* session George did of course attend was that for "Only A Northern Song". The version presented here seems to be one of the two takes that was combined for the version that appears on *Yellow Submarine* plus an alternate lead vocal that was discarded but superimposed for the CD – although one can't really care enough about this slight song to try to fathom if that is what the tortuously worded notes in the *Anthology 2* booklet are in fact explaining.

"Being For The Benefit Of Mr Kite!" is represented in break-downs and a full version, take seven. More tampering with history occurs with a "cross-fade" at the end of take seven to introduce some of the effects from the final master, only helpfully given a greater clarity. Things are beginning to get a bit much by the time we are presented with a Frankenstein's monster of "Lucy In The Sky With Diamonds". For those who might be fascinated by a track that features take six in the form of a basic track and guide vocal by Lennon, a tamboura from take seven and chorus vocals from take eight, this must be heaven on earth.

"Within You Without You": backing track only! No George! Erm . . . Seriously, Harrison's *Sgt. Pepper* . . . track is underrated. Though the sitar as an instrument can be as greasy and repellent as a badly-made curry, it can – like a well-made curry – be rich and tasty and the instrumentation on "Within You Without You" (entirely Indian and non-Beatle) was always highly impressive. It's also quite a journey: George plinking away on "Norwegian Wood" or Brian Jones strumming the sitar on The Stones' "Paint It Black" is one thing, but at five-and-a-half minutes "Within You Without You" was a truly prolonged immersion in the musical values of a faraway land that was even further away culturally in 1967. Though one misses Harrison's lyric – one of the most cogent and persuasive of his spiritual songs – this is good, heady stuff.

"Sgt. Pepper's Lonely Heart's Club Band (Reprise)" is an early take with a guide vocal and though it features an ending different to the familiar version is only remarkable for the way Ringo's drums are mixed well to the fore, and enjoyably so. Notice to Jeff Lynne and to modern engineers: this is how you do it. And "You Know My Name (Look Up The Number)" as presented here is how you do archive releases properly. It's the same version as appeared on the B-side of "Let It Be", only in stereo and with the two minutes excised by Lennon (presumably not to damage sound quality on a seven-inch record) now restored. Though not the greatest Beatles song ever, this is a genuinely worthwhile track, one requiring no tampering with history or absurd second-guessing of Beatle decisions.

"I Am The Walrus" is the basic track with an apparently different (sometimes stumbling) vocal but not yet containing sound effects and the string arrangement that appear on the final master. Interesting mainly to note Ringo's intelligent and sensitive work, especially on cymbals. "The Fool On The Hill (Demo)" is just Paul and piano. The tune's all there but the lyric is still under construction. Take twenty-seven is the one we hear of "Your Mother Should Know" here. It has quite an irritating harmonium part that was mercifully excised from the final arrangement and almost militaristic drumming in places. "The Fool On The Hill (Take 4)" is a slightly more muscular version than the *Magical Mystery Tour* cut. That recorder, drums and lead vocals were dubbed on indicates that Paul thought he had it in the bag here. The next day, he scrapped the whole thing and started again.

The version of "Hello, Goodbye" shares a lot of its DNA with the familiar version courtesy of the mix-and-match ethos of the reduction/bounce-down process necessary to add different elements in the day before eight-track (and subsequently sixteen-track, thirty-two-track and the current digital situation of infinite number of tracks). Consequently, slightly more raw guitar parts are the only real differences that truly jump out at the listener, regardless of the "many differences" the sleevenotes trumpet.

"A unique remix of some of the different takes and sounds that comprised the master" of "Lady Madonna" follows, and by now we know the negligible interest factor associated with that. "Across The Universe" though is on the face of it something else altogether, a completely different master to the one heard on the *No One's Gonna Change Our World* and *Let It Be* albums. It being the case that this alternate completed master has not been subjected to fatuous teenage girl vocal overdubs, wildlife effects, appended string parts or vari-speeding, one feels one should prefer it to the aforementioned versions as a matter of course. Somehow, though, it doesn't gel, and the way that John gasps in lungfuls of air between lines works to spoil the intended transcendent mood more than somewhat.

And that's it. After sitting through this bizarre collection, one wonders whether one should withdraw the caveat stated in the *Anthology 1* review that this is not the place for the uninitiated to start with Beatles fare: surely only those not familiar with Beatles music would be able to sit through this parallel universe history of the years concerned without recurring feelings of dismay and irritation at the way the greatest catalogue in history is being cheapened?

ANTHOLOGY 3
Released: 28/10/1996

TRACKLISTING

Disc one
1. "A Beginning"
2. "Happiness Is A Warm Gun"
3. "Helter Skelter"
4. "Mean Mr Mustard"
5. "Polythene Pam"

6. "Glass Onion"
7. "Junk"
8. "Piggies"
9. "Honey Pie"
10. "Don't Pass Me By"
11. "Ob-La-Di, Ob-La-Da"
12. "Good Night"
13. "Cry Baby Cry"
14. "Blackbird"
15. "Sexy Sadie"
16. "While My Guitar Gently Weeps"
17. "Hey Jude"
18. "Not Guilty"
19. "Mother Nature's Son"
20. "Glass Onion"
21. "Rocky Raccoon"
22. "What's The New Mary Jane"
23. "Step Inside Love"/"Los Paranoias"
24. "I'm So Tired"
25. "I Will"
26. "Why Don't We Do It In The Road"
27. "Julia"

Disc two
1. "I've Got A Feeling"
2. "She Came In Through The Bathroom Window"
3. "Dig A Pony"
4. "Two Of Us"
5. "For You Blue"
6. "Teddy Boy"
7. Medley: "Rip It Up"/"Shake, Rattle and Roll"/"Blue Suede Shoes"
8. "The Long And Winding Road"
9. "Oh! Darling"
10. "All Things Must Pass"
11. "Mailman, Bring Me No More Blues"
12. "Get Back"
13. "Old Brown Shoe"
14. "Octopus's Garden"

15. "Maxwell's Silver Hammer"
16. "Something"
17. "Come Together"
18. "Come And Get It"
19. "Ain't She Sweet"
20. "Because"
21. "Let It Be"
22. "I Me Mine"
23. "The End"

For the third *Anthology* album, there was no new Threetles track leading off the proceedings. The reason for this omission was that the third Lennon demo on which the surviving Beatles worked, "All For Love", was abandoned due to Harrison deciding Lennon's songcraft had been going off the boil towards the end of his life, a pronouncement that didn't go down well with Paul. Some, of course, might suggest that this was a blessing and that any further Threetles track would have made the incremental decline in interest level and artistic quality from "Free As A Bird" embarrassingly evident; others might suggest the absence creates a certain lop-sidedness. Still others, of course, will have decided after the somewhat underwhelming *Anthology 2* that they didn't give a damn one way or the other – although the UK chart stats for the three albums don't indicate declining public interest as the series progressed.

Instead we have as an opener "A Beginning". This is an orchestral piece of less than a minute originally designed to introduce Ringo's White Album track "Don't Pass Me By". It would have made a quite incongruous opener indeed for that rinky-dink number. As it employs the same musicians as rendered the orchestration on the same album's other Ringo-sung track "Good Night", it understandably has the same Disney-esque, wistful feel. It's nothing remarkable and one gets the impression is included merely to make a bookend with the set's concluding "The End" but only the curmudgeonly would begrudge George Martin getting – *Yellow Submarine* aside – his first composing credit on a Beatles record.

For many years, an acoustic version of the White Album and offcuts from it has been doing the rounds in bootleg circles.

Comprising tracks laid down by John, Paul and George in May 1968 at Kinfauns, George's house in Esher, they would make a very welcome official release in their entirety. (*The White Album Unplugged*?) For the time being, we'll have to make do with the inclusion of seven of these tracks on *Anthology 3*. The first here is "Happiness Is A Warm Gun". Although this solo-John-with-guitar snippet doesn't yet have the title refrain, it does have a section wherein the composer enunciates the immortal line, "Yoko Ono, Oh No, Yoko Ono, Oh yes", a perfect encapsulation of how being in love with Yoko seemed to turn his faculties to mush. Of negligible interest. For some reason, between this track and the rest of the Kinfauns cuts is an early full-band version of "Helter Skelter" from July '68. It's slow, deliberate and clean-sounding, in other words all the things you wouldn't expect to find in a track supposed to out-dirty "I Can See For Miles" and manifestly not "Hell for leather", to employ a line used by Paul in this rendition that didn't make it to the final master. This four-and-a-half minute track was originally twelve-minutes-plus, as it marked a point where the band were extemporizing on the idea. There are two other such lengthy "Helter Skelter" jams in existence, both presumably less interesting than this one – no mean feat. Back at Kinfauns, John is working on "Mean Mr Mustard", which wouldn't see the light of day until *Abbey Road*. Mustard's sister at this point is Shelley, not Pam, and the song has a chorus that was later jettisoned. "Polythene Pam" is another song that would end up on the *Abbey Road* suite. As with ". . . Mustard", there are minor differences but it's essentially the song we know. "Glass Onion" did make it to the "White Album" not long after the recording of the moderately interesting acoustic demo here. "Junk" would have to wait until Paul's first solo album in 1970. The melody is pretty and the mood lovely but the unfinished lyric is blocked in with humming. "Piggies" has a whistling instrumental section and though the song has nothing that's not to be found on the finished master, apart from a mention of "pork chops" instead of bacon, it's an enjoyable maquette. The last of the Kinfauns tracks is "Honey Pie" in a percussive and surprisingly effective bare version of the number that had quite a production on the "White Album".

A "variation" of "Don't Pass Me By" is an eyebrow-raising prospect, it being the case that the master is something that sounds like it deserved to be left on the cutting room floor. However, shorn of that irritating violin, it actually proves to have a ramshackle charm – even if it's something that you don't care if you ever hear again.

"Ob-La-Di, Ob-La-Da" is legendarily a song that Paul's colleagues were heartily sick of by the time a finished master was achieved via a moment of improvization wherein John began pumping out a music hall piano part that changed its nature. The nature it possessed hitherto can be heard on this out-take, which must have been considered the basis for a master, even a finished master, as it features congas and three saxophones. It's a softer version than the familiar one. There's absolutely nothing wrong with it, but the "White Album" version not only benefits from that barrelhouse Lennon piano but has a life-affirming quality that somehow just isn't resident here.

Ringo was the only Beatle on the "White Album"'s "Good Night". All Fabs seem to be present on this version, even if only in the form of them discussing the song at the start of the track. This recorded rehearsal (which is cross-faded into the final master because it's incomplete) is lovely, Ringo's vocals accompanied by bobbing piano. The presence of strings – brought in by the CD's compilers at the two-minute mark (of 02:35) as a final flourish – is how they should have been deployed on the finished master, rather than the Disney-fied drenching to which we were subjected.

The version of "Cry Baby Cry" here is take one, with John's vocal, Ringo's drums and discreet bass. John is overly sibilant, but this is actually a superior version. Ringo's drum patterns are ace. "Blackbird" here is take four as opposed to the master's take thirty-two. Apart from the absence of the bird whistling overdubs, the differences – lyric in slightly different order – are negligible. "Sexy Sadie" lacks the reverbed piano of the master that was recorded a month later, which this listener found about the only interesting part. Here, Sadie is only the greatest of them all rather than latest and greatest. As with the original, you just can't help thinking everything would have fallen into place with this song if only John had stuck to the original

"Maharishi" title and lyric. "While My Guitar Gently Weeps" features just George on voice and acoustic guitar and Paul on discreet washes of organ. This demo is profoundly better than the finished master, not only because it features an additional verse but because Harrison's lovely mellifluous acoustic work is far preferable to Clapton's electric histrionics on the remake. A great track and, unknown to its composer, the definitive version.

The studio run-through of "Hey Jude" is lacking the orchestration of the master version. At 04:18, it's also lacking three minutes, which this listener frankly doesn't miss, although he does miss the busy drumming style Ringo used on the familiar version. "Not Guilty" is a real treat. This Harrison song was left off the "White Album" despite a massive amount of work (this is a mind-boggling take 102 and – the presence of a vocal track and instrumental overdubs attests – a finished master). A quiet but scathing song whose target may be a lover or the kind of person he lambastes in "Piggies", it's better than any of the four other tracks George did manage to obtain on the "White Album".

"Mother Nature's Son" is an acoustic take. Not much more to be said. "Glass Onion" is the same as on the "White Album" except for the fact that while George Martin was on holiday, stand-in producer Chris Thomas employed sound effects such as smashing glass, a telephone and a soccer commentator. Martin suggested the orchestral score we hear on the master, so this mix was discarded, although the bareness of it allows us to hear a barrel-chested rock power. "Rocky Racoon" is take eight of a song of which take ten was chosen for public consumption. It has a slightly different lyric. The track almost breaks down when Paul says "sminking" instead of "stinking" of gin. There's no piano but the only thing you'll miss is that great line about Rocky being better as soon as he is able.

A legendary out-take, "What's The New Mary Jane" was a lengthy avant garde Lennon piece recorded for the "White Album". George is the only other Beatle present, although Mal Evans and Yoko lend a hand. Though it doesn't live up to its myth, "What's The New Mary Jane" deserved to make the album's final cut more than its kindred-spirit track "Revolution 9", not only because it bears some resemblance to music (it has a tune and a lyric, albeit primitive) but because its sound effects are interesting and occasionally unsettling, thus making for – unlike "Revolution 9" – a creation that engages the listener even if the form is not his cup of tea.

Anthology 3 descends into real bootleg territory by including "Step Inside Love" and "Los Paranoias", a segue of The Beatles larking around on a casual version of a song Paul wrote for former Cavern coat-check girl turned pop star and television host Cilla Black and a spur-of-the-moment jam based on a Lennon wisecrack. It brings a smile to your face the first time you hear it but compulsion to revisit it there will be none. Worse than bootleg material is "I'm So Tired". No bootlegger would have the technical wherewithal to present such a thing as the "amalgam" of different parts of out-takes of this song. Once more, worthless tampering with history. No messing is possible on "I Will" – it's just Paul on guitar and vocals and John and Ringo on percussion – but the fact that this is take one whereas the finished master was take sixty-seven will probably tell you all you need to know about the quality.

"Why Don't We Do It In The Road" is an early take that demonstrates the song's unlikely acoustic origins. Though Paul's vocals alternate between soft and hard, the song is lacking the incremental build up of hysteria that made the master so funny. "Julia" follows. As with the finished master (which emanated from the next take), one feels almost guilty about dismissing a song mainly about the mother John lost in traumatic circumstances but honesty compels one to note that this take is less good than the finished one, and that one wasn't all that.

CD 2 starts with nine never-before-heard tracks from the *Get Back* sessions at Apple Studios in the basement of the Apple building in Savile Row, where recording had relocated in January 1969 after George had refused to participate in any further work at Twickenham Film Studios. Like a lot of the *Get Back* sessions material, "I've Got A Feeling" has a slightly scraggly feel (apart from the slick work of Billy Preston), but it's also got passion and a sense of fun, as well as a feeling of co-operation (especially between John and Paul) that was a little lacking on the "White Album". It breaks down because John "cocked it up trying to get loud" by his own admission but before that we have enough (about 02:43) to make it an enjoyable alternate to the version on *Let It Be*.

"She Came In Through The Bathroom Window" is a rehearsal of the song that would end up in the suite of *Abbey Road*. It's slow and a bit boring. "Dig A Pony" is presented in its unadulterated state, boasting the "All I want" bookends edited out by Spector on *Let It Be*. Apart from that, this early version is nothing remarkable. "Two of Us" is punctuated by feedback but it's always nice to hear this gorgeous song. This one is more gentle than the *Let It Be* version. "For You Blue" is made very different by the presence of a honky tonk piano from Paul, one that makes it preferable to the familiar version. "Teddy Boy" never made it onto a Beatles record but ended up on *McCartney*. This is a splice of two run-throughs. Though Paul fluffs the vocals, the song never ended up much better than this: it's a meandering and somehow pointless composition.

A trio of the many oldies The Beatles played at the *Get Back* sessions follows. The medley of "Rip It Up", "Shake, Rattle and Roll" and "Blue Suede Shoes" is enjoyable enough but one is uncomfortably aware that the quality is – Billy Preston's blurred-fingered organ on "Blue Suede Shoes" aside – not too great. Yes, this is informal jamming and possibly of songs the band haven't played for years, but surely The Beatles are supposed to sound a little better than a pub band?

"The Long And Winding Road" meanwhile gives the public the chance to make up their minds about what Paul had been moaning about for a quarter-century (and whose scars were so deep that it led McCartney to storm out of the 1997 *Q* awards in disgust when he realized that Phil Spector was being given a bauble). This is the *Let It Be* version without Spector's orchestration and angelic backing vocals. One appreciates the presence of this in The Beatles' catalogue at long last but at the end of the day and with all due respect to the principle of the need for the artist's vision to be observed, frankly the Spector version sounds better. I'll get me coat.

"Oh! Darling" is a rehearsal *sans* the piano of the *Abbey Road* version but with Preston on organ. John engages in call-and-response. In one sense it's better than the one we know already, lacking the slightly sledgehammer approach found on the *Abbey Road* track. A unique addendum comes when John reveals he's just heard Yoko is now free to marry him following the arrival of her *decree nisi* and the band – quite touchingly – start jamming on his celebratory cry.

Three demos of songs recorded by George in February 1969 on the day of his 26th birthday appear on *Anthology 3*. The first is "All Things Must Pass", which would never be released by The Beatles but would become the title track of his first post-Fabs album. The spiritual nature of the song is revealed in its title. Though comprising only a basic track of vocal and guitar with another guitar overdubbed, it's lovely and would have been an asset to either *Let It Be* or *Abbey Road*.

It's back to the Apple Studio for a cover of "Mailman, Bring Me No More Blues", a number made famous by Buddy Holly. Though musty, it's got a slick feel that most of the *Get Back* sessions tracks lack. "Get Back" is the last of three versions of the song the Fabs performed on the Apple rooftop. The police arrived part of the way through and consequently we lose sound from John and George before the end but it's still a muscular performance and would be worth its place even if it weren't for the historical interest involved in the song constituting the last-ever public performance by The Beatles.

"Old Brown Shoe" is another of George's birthday demos. Unlike with "All Things Must Pass", we have a Beatles version – and a brilliant one – with which to compare it, so despite its relatively intricate construction for a demo it can't help but come off worse against that.

"Octopus's Garden" is take two of a song whose master came from take thirty-two but is surprisingly already well developed. Ringo's drumming is excellent – and, amazingly, performed at the same time as he sings competently. It's impressive enough – even without the finished track's sound effects – to have become the master itself.

If an out-take of the already out-take-like "Don't Pass Me By" is strange, what are we to make of a not-as-good-as-the-one-we-know version of "Maxwell's Silver Hammer"? The track doesn't have the anvil sound effects of the *Abbey Road* version and Paul – who sang on every take to preserve the feel – sings the harmonies and synth parts himself. His vocal descends into laughter as he fluffs the lines. There's nothing more to say about it apart from the fact that the "One more" Paul insists on at the end must have placed his colleagues on the point of murder.

"Something" is the last of George's three birthday demos. It's just the composer's voice and electric guitar, although a segment of the song present here was dropped for the final version. It's alright, but such was Harrison's facility on the instrument it would have been nice to hear an acoustic guitar demo. Take one of "Come Together" has a live vocal because John liked recording that way at this point, although he sometimes descends into giggles. The swamp rock feel of the *Abbey Road* master is absent and the lyric would change but Paul's bass is possibly even better here than it would be on that.

"Come And Get It" is the demo of the pleasant and catchy song Paul donated to Badfinger, who had a hit with it in 1970. As it's a Paul solo demo of a song that was never intended for The Beatles, you could make the point that it has no place on this collection, but it's nice to have a McCartney version out there.

"Ain't She Sweet" was of course a track on *Anthology 1* in the form of a pre-fame German recording. Here we have a version from eight years on. The older one is more fresh-faced but on the newer recording the band is hugely more proficient, especially Paul's bass playing.

The instrumentation of "Because" is stripped away to highlight in isolation the three-part harmonies (recorded three times) of that *Abbey Road* track. Okay, point taken that these kids could sing, but we'd already gleaned that from the "proper" version. "Let It Be" is an early version of the song with a still unfinished lyric. Quite interesting, but the dialogue that tops and tails the track is stupid because it's spliced: it relates to takes of the song other than this one.

"I Me Mine" is the pure version of a track that Spector artificially lengthened by adding the front end to its back end. Pointless you might think, but it does have historical value as the product of the last Beatles full recording session, even if John buggering off to Denmark on holiday spoils that historical import a little.

"The End" is "a new remix . . . embracing numerous elements omitted during the mix sessions . . ." This principally means more guitar sparring and more orchestration.

And there it is. After all the hullabaloo, and after sitting through three double set CDs of wildly varying quality, one can't help but feel that this whole exercise could have been profoundly truncated. The *Anthology* CD series is like a grandiose "White Album", something that in no way justifies its length and which almost immediately has people compiling their own edited, fantasy version (a project far more easy in the age of the programmable CD). A double- or at most triple-set CD would have sufficed, one containing the juvenilia and the pre-fame demos (of which there could actually have been more), the never-before-released songs, the better alternate versions and the better live cuts.

In 1985, EMI planned an album of unreleased Beatles material called *Sessions* before protests from The Fabs stayed their hand. It's sobering to glance at that abandoned release's tracklisting:

1. "Come And Get It" (McCartney demo)
2. "Leave My Kitten Alone"
3. "Not Guilty"
4. "I'm Looking Through You" (alternate version)
5. "What's The New Mary Jane"
6. "How Do You Do It?"
7. "Besame Mucho" (From first EMI session)
8. "One After 909"
9. "If You've Got Trouble"
10. "That Means a Lot"
11. "While My Guitar Gently Weeps" (early take)
12. "Mailman, Bring Me No More Blues" (From the *Get Back* sessions)
13. "Christmas Time (Is Here Again)"

Though there was some controversy over the ham-fisted way EMI engineers had decided to edit, even reshuffle, the sections of individual tracks on the proposed LP, it's pretty much the type of material found on *Anthologies 1–3* but without the chaff.

It instantly strikes one as something that would have been a valuable addition to the canon in a way the *Anthology* CDs – bloated both as a series and individually – do not.

YELLOW SUBMARINE SONGTRACK
Released: 13/09/1999

To coincide with MGM's thirtieth anniversary release of the *Yellow Submarine* movie on DVD and video, Apple prepared a CD which would rectify some of the alleged faults of the original soundtrack album by including almost all of the Beatles songs heard in the movie while excluding the George Martin material. The new album was called *Songtrack* to differentiate it from the original soundtrack, which remained in print. Almost as though trying to compensate for the fact that even with this alteration, it still remained the case that there were only four Beatles songs here not available elsewhere (apart from the original soundtrack, of course), The Beatles made the eyebrow-raising decision to remix – as opposed to remaster – the contents. This must have presented them with a problem, because there was nothing wrong with the mixes in the first place, despite the talk you will hear of the sonic compromises that had to be made when recording more than four elements (later with eight-track, eight elements). Some reviewers syco-phantically hailed this as an advance which polished The Beatles' music for the more sophisticated palette developed by the public in the age of the compact disc. In fact, the results are dreadful, which is predictable considering that the only thing one can do to create an alternate mix of what was previously an optimum mix is to weaken it. Remixers Peter Cobbin, Paul Hicks and Mirek Stiles present clinical, artificial-sounding versions of the warm, natural-sounding Beatles tracks we have known for so many years. As well as this, in some cases – notably "Hey Bulldog" – the results are either incompe-tent or deliberately provocative: for instance, why on earth are they artificially bringing forward the occasional slap of a drum in the soundscape, as though trying to jolt us out of whatever reverie we can manage? Those who object to the remixing here are not Luddites. *Yellow Submarine Songtrack* manages a feat that previously seemed impossible: making the original *Yellow Submarine* album sound like a masterpiece. Incidentally, for the record, the George Martin material could have fitted onto the CD as well.

1
Released: 13/11/2000

Some have suggested that the astronomical sales figures for this compilation will eventually make it the biggest-selling CD of all time – and that's even despite the fact that so many people get their music these days through downloads, both legal and illegal, and CDs burnt for them by others. It in no way deserves such a status. Released to fill a gap in the market for a single-CD Beatles best-of, like the wretched *20 Greatest Hits,* it ended up being a compromise for running length reasons. Apple spun a story about the album containing songs that got to number one in either the UK or US (hence the title). Most would have been able to swallow that line – and the consequent loss of "Please Please Me" and "Strawberry Fields Forever" – had the set not also included "Something", which failed to climb to the summit either side of the Atlantic. The sleevenotes dishonestly claim that the latter song made number one in the *Billboard* chart but in fact the other side of the single it resided on, "Come Together", achieved that feat and the peak chart placing of "Something" was number four. "Something" was clearly included as a royalty-related sop to George Harrison, who no doubt would have vetoed the project without it, just as (it is said) he vetoed "The Long And Winding Road" as the title of what became the TV programme *Anthology* and made sure that his friend Jeff Lynne produced "Free As A Bird", a childish and horrendous decision respectively.

LET IT BE . . . NAKED
Released: 17/11/2003

"By stripping away the decorative layers applied to some of the tracks, this special edition reveals *Let It Be* as it was meant to be," states Kevin Howlett in the sleevenotes to *Let It Be . . . Naked.* The same sleevenotes carry a comment from Paul McCartney: "If we'd had today's technology then, it would sound like this because that was the noise we made in the studio. It's all exactly as it was in the room . . ." The CD case came adorned with a sticker that declared the contents to be "*Let It Be* . . . as it was meant to be. The band's cut from the original sessions." All three claims are as absurd and inaccurate as the comment on the back of the original Spector-ized *Let It Be* album that ". . . essential to the content of the film LET IT BE was that they performed live for many of the tracks; in comes the warmth and the freshness of a live performance . . ."

McCartney had been talking for years of putting out the *Let It Be* album as it was first intended (i.e., without the Spector overdubs that had made a nonsense of the original live-in-the-studio concept) and had publicly lamented the unrelated legal in-fighting among The Beatles and the Lennon estate that prevented this from coming to pass. When finally, after thirty-three years, the opportunity came for the project he had been dreaming of for so long, what resulted was a botch that made utterly no sense. Perhaps because the release of the "real" version of "The Long And Winding Road" on *Anthology 3* – the *Let It Be* version without Spector's embellishments – had got something off his chest, he took no active part in this project.

The people to whom the project was handed over were Paul Hicks, Guy Massey and Allan Rouse, one of which trinity (Hicks) had worked on the abomination that was *Yellow Submarine Songtrack*. One can accept their decision to remix and clean-up the master tapes to give us a twenty-first century Beatles – using the magic of ProTools to remove tape hiss, mic pops and the wind on the Apple rooftop and bringing forward buried interesting elements is fine as long as the original *Let It Be* album remains in print (as it does) for purposes of historical fealty – but the three went much further than that, not only artificially altering incorrect vocal pitches but stitching together different takes and flying in solos from version to version for optimum listening "pleasure". Even in The Beatles' day, musicians did the latter all the time of course, but the whole point of the *Get Back* sessions was that this is explicitly what The Beatles decided they weren't going to do. Therefore, it makes the whole exercise unnecessary: rather than *Let It Be* as it was meant to be heard, *Let It Be* . . . *Naked* is just *another* version of how it *wasn't* meant to be heard. For the record, Hicks, Massey and Rouse have stated that there was a logic and integrity to their version of the album insofar as, sonic tampering and the mix-and-match approach aside, they stripped everything back to only The Beatles and Preston.

The sleevenotes didn't mention the fact that so much tampering had been done: only magazine articles carrying interviews with the participants and the internet observations of keen-eared Beatles fans brought it to the public's attention and it was only through them that we know the following: "Get Back", "Dig A Pony" and "Two Of Us" are the same takes as used by Spector (although "Get Back" loses the "Hope we passed the audition" vocal splice). On the new mix of "For You Blue" (which sounds a lot sharper than the *Let It Be* version), George's live vocal has been replaced by another because the live one was considered by the compilers to be a guide vocal only. "The Long And Winding Road" is a totally different take, with a differing lyric, to the one chosen by Spector. As it was recorded five days after the familiar one, Hicks, Massey and Rouse decided it was closer to being definitive, musically and lyrically. "I've Got A Feeling" is a composite of two different takes recorded on the Apple rooftop, as is "Don't Let Me Down". "I Me Mine" is the same as the Spector version, including the artificial lengthening but without Spector's orchestration. The fourth variation of "Across The Universe" to be made commercially available uses the master employed on *No One's Gonna Change Our World* and *Let It Be* but strips it down to just The Beatles, so no wildlife sound effects or teenage girl vocals (George Martin version) and no orchestration (Phil Spector version). The trio have added a building echo. "Let It Be" uses the same master as the single and album but has a few bits brought in from other takes of the song, most notably a guitar solo from the version of the song heard in the movie that was considered to be of greater quality. "One After 909" is the same rooftop version as used by Spector but with the "Danny boy" bit at the end cut.

So will you want to rip the CD from your player and hurl it across the room? Of course not. Stop me if you've heard this one, but this *is* The Beatles. Though there is the nagging issue that the decisions about which bits to stitch together made by Hicks, Massey and Rouse would not necessarily have been the ones made by The Beatles – creating a problem about artistic credibility and integrity of vision – once those familiar opening bars of "Get Back" punch from the speakers, it's difficult not to get swept up in the brilliance of what one is hearing. These are great songs. And if the group *had* decided to produce the record the way all their post-*Please Please Me* product had been produced, this must be at least a fair approximation of what it would have sounded like. The absence of that tinny, scraggly, quasi-exhausted sound that runs through the two Glyn Johns versions of the album and parts of the official original version may be dishonest but it's also a relief. Leaving off the studio chatter and snippets of songs ("Maggie Mae" and "Dig It" are jettisoned from the reshuffled running order) is also less representative of what went down at the *Get Back* sessions but also beneficial, giving the album the feel of a considered artistic statement that it never previously had. Additionally, the trio get kudos for including "Don't Let Me Down".

Perhaps ingeniously, where the trio do make an effort to retain the original album's attempt to convey the *Get Back* sessions' *ad hoc* nature and the concept of a soundtrack, they hive it off to a separate disc. The bonus disc, titled *Fly On The Wall*, features studio chatter and snippets of songs both original and traditional from the *Get Back* sessions, most of it never heard on disc before. There's a lovely piano piece by Paul and a charming and very Northern original called "Fancy My Chances With You". However, the fact that the thirty-five tracks on the bonus disc (compiled by Howlett) run to just under twenty-two minutes will convey how bitty and disjointed the sum total is. It would have been nice if the second disc had instead been occupied by both Glyn Johns' versions of the album. Failing that, an audio record – un-tampered with – of the entirety of The Beatles' final public performance on the Apple rooftop.

The album's cover featured photo negative images of The Beatles using the same pictures (except in the case of George) as on the cover of the original *Let It Be* album.

THE CAPITOL ALBUMS VOL. 1
Released: 15/11/04
THE CAPITOL ALBUMS VOL. 2
Released: 03/04/06

Could there possibly be anyone in the world hankering for the American configurations of Beatles albums that were swept into the dustbin of history when the release of the Fabs' catalogue on CD standardized Beatles albums worldwide in their British configurations? American Beatles albums were, up until . . . *Pepper* . . . , shorter than their UK counterparts because the greater the number of songs on a US album, the higher were the royalties payable. But the tampering didn't stop there: American record companies were utterly philistine, throwing together tracks from UK singles, EPs and albums and even the two German language Beatle recordings willy-nilly. The *A Hard Day's Night* and *Help!* soundtracks were exactly that, featuring only the new Beatles songs heard in the film, not the second sides of the British albums, plus the movie incidental music that had nothing to do with the Fabs. However, it can't be denied that millions of Americans grew up on these packages and that they were the "real" Beatles albums to them. It's presumably this that motivated the release of the above two collections of the first eight Capitol Beatles albums. (The first American Beatles LP was the Vee Jay label's *Introducing The Beatles* in 1963, but all of its contents eventually appeared on Capitol LPs.) The *A Hard Day's Night* soundtrack album is missing from the second set, as it was a United Artists release. Buy if you're prepared to shell out what is quite an exorbitant sum for the privilege of owning mono mixes of some tracks from *Help!* and *Rubber Soul* that are not currently available on CD, if you're interested in hearing the CD debut of four dozen 1960s wide-separation stereo mixes, if you're American and nostalgic, or if you're not American but curious about the way the world's biggest Beatles lovers heard them at the time.

LOVE
Released: 20/11/2006

So, after *Live At The BBC*, the three *Anthology* sets, the *1* compilation, *Yellow Submarine Songtrack*, *Let It Be . . . Naked* and the *Capitol Albums* box sets, what other way is there to sell the music of The Beatles to the public again? With a grand version of the "Movie Medley" single that was earlier in this chapter cited as the nadir of Beatles product. Try to keep up.

Love is the soundtrack of the Cirque du Soleil show of the same name whose gala opening was on 30 June 2006 at the Mirage Theatre in Las Vegas. The show uses circus and athletic routines to tell the story of The Beatles, albeit in very broad brush strokes and with the aid of fictional characters like Sgt. Pepper, Eleanor Rigby and Mr Kite. The Beatles' music comprises pre-recorded material, the material heard on this soundtrack album.

The only new music the album contains is a George Martin orchestral piece designed to accompany an early take of "While My Guitar Gently Weeps". The rest of the material is a mosaic of previously released Beatles music put together by Martin (miraculously recovered from the hearing problems that made him excuse himself from the "Free As A Bird"/"Real Love" recordings) and his son Giles. With Martin and Martin *fils* helming the project, one is naturally inclined to expect a greater reverence than displayed by the teams that oversaw *Yellow Submarine Songtrack* and *Let It Be . . . Naked* but *Love* is in some ways just as cavalier with The Beatles' legacy and just as presumptuous in its treatment of Beatles music as those projects.

To give an example of what it contains, take track seven. It starts with "Drive My Car" as heard on *Rubber Soul*, except that it has a horn section dubbed in from what sounds like "Savoy Truffle" and the guitar break flown in from "Taxman". It then segues into *Beatles For Sale*'s "What You're Doing", although maintains the same beat courtesy of a loop of Ringo's drumming from "Drive My Car". Then we're taken into a snatch of *Rubber Soul*'s "The Word" before the "beep-beep-yeah" bit of "Drive My Car" takes us into the fade. Although some tracks are presented relatively straight and complete, rarely is the temptation resisted to pimp the ride in at least some way: for instance "Help!" is given a bit of rising echo at the close – precisely what its unimprovable "Help me-ee-oooh!" ending did not need. We also get such delights as "Nus Gnik", which is – yes! – *Abbey Road*'s "Sun King" backwards. Also present in backwards form is the crashing end piano note of "A Day In The Life". "I guess we thought that as it made such a great ending, turned around it was bound to make a great beginning," states Giles with singular logic in the sleevenotes. The rest of that opening consists of the three-part harmonies of "Because" *a cappella* and the bow-taking part of "The End" on *Abbey Road* (Ringo's drum solo and the three guitar solos) which segues into "Get Back" on the grounds that "Get Back" was at the same speed, with the opening chord of "A Hard Day's Night" employed to paper over the edit. This kind of thing goes on for an hour and twenty minutes. In the context of such manic meaninglessness, Paul's unlisted White Album doodle "Brother Can You Take Me Back?" – an artificially lengthened version of which is dropped in – actually begins to assume a stature of some sort, which just goes to show how insubstantial the whole thing is. Some might get a kick out of trying to identify parts of Beatles tracks flown into other Beatles tracks for no other reason except the tempi allow it, but how long can that trainspotterish pleasure last?

The alternate universe composite mixes of out-takes on the *Anthology* CDs were one thing but this takes fatuousness to new depths. Occasionally, the fact of the original brilliance of the music from which this is constructed has your toes tapping and pleasure synapses firing, but then one is reminded of the overall meaningless again by another absurd edit or the very illogic of the fact that these songs (especially the *Pepper* material) have been isolated from their proper contexts. It differs from a jukebox or a random programme on your CD player only in the unfamiliar intrusions.

Love has only two things going for it. One is its title, which is a perfect and succinct summation of the spirit of The Beatles' music. The other is that it keeps The Beatles in the headlines and on the radio waves and consequently under the noses of new generations of music listeners who might otherwise think that the metronomic, soulless, soporific garbage that increasingly pours out of their radios and TV sets is all there is to popular music. However, the fact that the whole thing reduces The Beatles' music to iconography and Pavlovian responses is underlined by the cover artwork which uses silhouettes of the group leaping into the air that are designedly instantly recognizable as the shapes the boys are throwing on the cover of the *Twist and Shout* EP.

PART TWO: DISSENTERS

Not everybody thought the Four were particularly Fab. Some even despised them. A sometimes sobering selection of writing from the 1960s and subsequently giving the points of view of Beatle agnostics.

PART TWO: DISSENTERS

THE MENACE OF BEATLISM

Paul Johnson is known to most people under fifty or so as a harrumphing right-wing journalist. However, at one point in his life, he was a very different beast: a harrumphing left-wing journalist. This denunciation of The Beatles appeared in the New Statesman *– then as now the pre-eminent journal of the British Left – shortly after William Deedes, a minister in the Conservative cabinet, had tried to butter up a group of Young Conservatives (and presumably the floating voters aged under thirty in the wider public) by waxing lyrical on the qualities of the Fab Four. Johnson had a good point about the cynicism involved in the gesture. Time, though, has made a mockery of his disdain for Deedes' claim that, "They herald a cultural movement among the young which may become part of the history of our time . . ."*

The Menace of Beatlism

From *New Statesman*, 28 February 1964
by Paul Johnson

Mr William Deedes is an Old Harrovian, a member of the cabinet and the minister in charge of the government's information services. Mr Deedes, it will be remembered, was one of those five ministers who interviewed Mr Profumo on that fateful night and were convinced by him that he had not slept with Miss Keeler. Now any public relations man, even a grand one who sits in the cabinet, can use a touch of credulity; but even so I remember thinking at the time: "If Deedes can believe that, he'll believe anything." And indeed he does! Listen to him on the subject of The Beatles:

"They herald a cultural movement among the young which may become part of the history of our time . . . For those with eyes to see it, something important and heartening is happening here. The young are rejecting some of the sloppy standards of their elders, by which far too much of our output has been governed in recent years . . . they have discerned dimly that in a world of automation, declining craftsmanship and increased leisure, something of this kind is essential to restore the human instinct to excel at something and the human faculty of discrimination."

Incredible as it may seem, this was not an elaborate attempt at whimsy, but a serious address, delivered to a meeting of the City of London Young Conservatives, and heard in respectful silence. Not a voice was raised to point out that the Emperor wasn't wearing a stitch. The Beatles phenomenon, in fact, illustrates one of my favourite maxims: that if something becomes big enough *and* popular enough – and especially commercially profitable enough – solemn men will not be lacking to invest it with virtues. So long as The Beatles were just another successful showbiz team the pillars of society could afford to ignore them, beyond bestowing the indulgent accolade of a slot in the Royal Variety Performance. But then came the shock announcement that they were earning £6,250,000 a year – and, almost simultaneously, they got the stamp of approval from America.

This was quite a different matter: at once they became not only part of the export trade but an electorally valuable property. Sir Alec Home promptly claimed credit for them, and was as promptly accused by Mr Wilson of political clothes-stealing. Conservative candidates have been officially advised to mention them whenever possible in their speeches. The Queen expressed concern about the length of Ringo's hair. Young diplomats at our Washington embassy fought for their autographs. A reporter described them as "superb ambassadors for Britain". It is true that the Bishop of Woolwich has not yet asked them to participate in one of his services, but the invitation cannot be long delayed. And, while waiting for the definitive analysis of their cultural significance by Messrs Raymond Williams and Richard Hoggart we have Mr Deedes' contribution on behalf of the cabinet.

Of course, our society has long been brainwashed in preparation for this apotheosis of inanity. For more than two decades now, more and more intellectuals have turned their backs on their trade and begun to worship at the shrine of "pop culture". Nowadays, if you confess that you don't know the difference between Dizzy Gillespie and Fats Waller (and, what is more, don't care) you are liable to be accused of being a fascist.

To buttress their intellectual self-esteem, these treasonable clerks have evolved an elaborate cultural mythology about jazz, which purports to distinguish between various periods, tendencies and schools. The subject has been smeared with a respectable veneer of academic scholarship, so that now you can overhear grown men, who have been expensively educated, engage in heated argument on the respective techniques of Charlie Parker and Duke Ellington. You can see writers of distinction, whose grey hairs testify to years spent in the cultural vineyard, squatting on the bare boards of malodorous caverns, while through the haze of smoke, sweat and cheap cosmetics comes the monotonous braying of savage instruments.

One might, I suppose, attribute such intellectual treachery to the fact that, in jazz circles, morals are easy, sex is cheap and there is a permissive attitude to the horrors of narcotics. Men are, alas, sometimes willing to debauch their intellects for such rewards. But I doubt if this is the real reason. The growing public approval of anti-culture is itself I think, a reflection of the new cult of youth. Bewildered by a rapidly changing society, excessively fearful of becoming out of date, our leaders are increasingly turning to young people as guides and mentors – or, to vary the metaphor, as Geiger counters to guard them against the perils of mental obsolescence. If youth likes jazz, then it must be good, and clever men must rationalize this preference in intellectually respectable language. Indeed, whatever youth likes must be good: the supreme crime, in politics and culture alike, is not to be "with it". Even the most unlikely mascots of the Establishment are now drifting with the current: Mr Henry Brooke, for instance, finds himself appointing to the latest Home Office committee the indispensable teenager, who has, what is more, the additional merit of being a delinquent.

Before I am denounced as a reactionary fuddy-duddy, let us pause an instant and see exactly what we mean by this "youth". Both TV channels now run weekly programmes in which popular records are played to teenagers and judged. While the music is performed, the cameras linger savagely over the faces of the audience. What a bottomless chasm of vacuity they reveal! The huge faces, bloated with cheap confectionery and smeared with chain-store makeup, the open, sagging mouths and glazed eyes, the hands mindlessly drumming in time to the music, the broken stiletto heels, the shoddy, stereotyped, "with-it" clothes: here, apparently, is a collective portrait of a generation enslaved by a commercial machine. Leaving a TV studio recently, I stumbled into the exodus from one of these sessions. How pathetic and listless they seemed: young girls, hardly any more than sixteen, dressed as adults and already lined up as fodder for exploitation. Their eyes came to life only when one of their grotesque idols – scarcely older than they – made a brief appearance, before a man in a camel-hair coat hustled him into a car. Behind this image of "youth", there are, evidently, some shrewd older folk at work.

And what of the "culture" which is served up to these pitiable victims? According to Mr Deedes, "the aim of The Beatles and their rivals is first class of its kind. Failure to attain it is spotted and criticized ruthlessly by their many highly-discriminating critics." I wonder if Mr Deedes has ever taken the trouble to listen to any of this music? On the Saturday TV shows, the merits of the new records are discussed by panels of "experts", many of whom seem barely more literate or articulate than the moronic ranks facing them. They are asked to judge each record a "hit" or a "miss", but seem incapable of explaining why they have reached their verdict. Occasionally one of the "experts" betrays some slight acquaintance with the elementals of music and makes what is awesomely described as a "technical" point: but when such merit is identified in a record, this is usually found to be a reason for its certain commercial failure.

In any case, merit has nothing to do with it. The teenager comes not to hear but to participate in a ritual, a collective grovelling to gods who are themselves blind and empty. "Throughout the performance," wrote one observer, "it was impossible to hear anything above the squealing except the beat of Ringo's drums." Here, indeed, is "a new cultural movement": music which not only cannot be heard but does not need to be heard. As such I have no doubt that it is, in truth, "first class of its kind".

If The Beatles and their like were in fact what the youth of Britain wanted, one might well despair. I refuse to believe it – and so I think will any other intelligent person who casts his or her mind back far enough. What were we doing at sixteen? I remember the drudgery of Greek prose and the calculus, but I can also remember reading the whole of Shakespeare and Marlowe, writing poems and plays and stories. It is a marvellous age, an age of intense mental energy and discovery. Almost every week one found a fresh idol – Milton, Wagner, Debussy, Matisse, El Greco, Proust – some, indeed, to be subsequently toppled from the pantheon, but all springing from the mainstream of European culture. At sixteen, I and my friends heard our first performance of Beethoven's Ninth Symphony; I can remember the excitement even today. We would not have wasted thirty seconds of our precious time on The Beatles and their ilk.

Are teenagers different today? Of course not. Those who flock round The Beatles, who scream themselves into hysteria, whose vacant faces flicker over the TV screen, are the least fortunate of their generation, the dull, the idle, the failures: their existence, in such large numbers, far from being a cause for ministerial congratulation, is a fearful indictment of our education system, which in ten years of schooling can scarcely raise them to literacy. What Mr Deedes fails to perceive is that the core of the teenage group – the boys and girls who will be the real leaders and creators of society tomorrow – never go near a pop concert. They are, to put it simply, too busy. They are educating themselves. They are in the process of inheriting the culture which, despite Beatlism or any other mass-produced mental opiate, will continue to shape our civilization. To use Mr Deedes' own phrase, though not in the sense he meant it, they are indeed "rejecting some of the sloppy standards of their elders". Of course, if many of these elders in responsible positions surrender to the Gadarene Complex and seek to elevate the worst things in our society into the best, their task will be made more difficult. But I believe that, despite the antics of cabinet ministers with election nerves, they will succeed.

MBE? YOU'RE JOKING OF COURSE

Left-leaning British tabloid the Daily Mirror *made the announcement that The Beatles had been made Members of the British Empire in the Queen's birthday honours list their front page lead. That story shared space on the cover with another MBE-related piece titled "How did the lads earn this gong?" and an item about a gun siege at a London flat.*

The story was genuinely big news, for awards in the Queen's birthday honours list had hitherto been made almost exclusively to soldiers, members of the establishment and people who had provided what was considered to be a form of public service. The 1965 awards had a self-consciously trendy tinge to them, with stars of television dramas and The Beatles' fellow recording artist (albeit of an older vintage) Frankie Vaughan also benefiting. It was another sign – in an era when there was a plethora of them – that times were changing. The principal reason for those changing times – for the way that popular culture was being granted a validity by people in power in both politics and the media – was The Beatles.

Though the MBE is the lowest honour that the Queen is able to bestow, giving it to The Beatles was seen by many as a gimmick and by some as an insult to people who had earned the award by public service. In defence of such naysayers, the suspicion lingers that it was an award engineered by Labour Prime Minister Harold Wilson to put himself in the good books of the youth not too long before he lowered the voting age from twenty-one to eighteen. Though it has latterly become the common wisdom that the award was for services to exports, when originally asked what it was for, a spokesman at the Prime Minister's office, where the Honours List recommendations were drawn up, said, "We don't have to say, and we don't always say", and a "source" in the Prime Minister's office could only feebly offer, "Well, The Beatles are leaders in their particular art."

Some previous medal recipients returned their awards in horrified protest at The Beatles' impending investiture. Beatles biographer Philip Norman caustically pointed out in 1981 that while sometimes the award was hard-won in war, it was also doled out to sub-postmasters on a Buggin's turn basis. Mirror writer Donald Zec had a viewpoint more akin to those of the medal returners. He expressed it in the article below, which appeared on an inside page of the paper on the same day of the announcement. Peter Noone is still waiting for his OBE but some of Zec's other fears about where it would all end detailed near the close of the piece have come true.

MBE? You're Joking Of Course

From *Daily Mirror*, Saturday 12 June 1965
by Donald Zec

Hilarious bordering on the absurd – at any rate this is the way I view today's astonishing announcement giving The Beatles the MBE.

No doubt the fans, the record companies and the gleeful impresarios will regard this royal "come hither" as being timely and well-earned. But there will be others who will see it as the most preposterous piece of whimsy ever to chuckle its way out of Buckingham Palace.

I have to say at once that I belong to the second group – unequivocally, unreservedly, unrepentantly. "You're joking, of course," was my startled reaction to the news. YES – I think The Beatles are a nice bunch of chaps and I like them. YES – they are as agreeable a group of self-made millionaires that ever warbled their way around the world. YES – they're a showbiz phenomenon that has earned a fortune in dollars, started a cult, brought out riot squads and made the front pages.

So does this mean that Her Majesty the Queen should be

"graciously pleased" to make them Ordinary Members of the Civil Division of the Most Excellent Order of the British Empire? NO. Not in my book. Not if the aim of this important award is to reward "those who have rendered services of a conspicuous character" to the Nation.

John, Paul, George and Ringo may have rendered conspicuous services to "pop", the telly, the record companies, Mr Epstein, Mr Ed Sullivan and all. And in the process, the services they have rendered unto themselves have been equally gigantic – and good luck to them. That's show business and if they've earned a faster buck than the rest of the yammering entertainers from the Merseyside to Manhattan then it's because they can belt it out better than the rest. But in the name of all that's sane if not sacred isn't pinning a royal medal on to a Beatle jacket – four Beatle jackets – just too darned much?

What criterion can there be for this chummy leap by the royalty – or its advisers – on to the screeching long-haired bandwagon? Are we measuring the services to the nation by John, George, Paul and Ringo merely in terms of the dollars their records have earned? If so this confers precious little distinction upon the Membership of this Most Excellent Order of the British Empire. The lads swept in on a craze, cashed in on a mood, brilliantly exploited a trend. They became idols overnight, but sooner or later the worshipping will stop as tomorrow's phenomenon elbows them out of the way, The pop world, in spite of the lush pickings to be made from it, is a freak world nourished by stunts, sustained by gimmicks. Today's frenzy may be tomorrow's flop. The road from the Golden Disc to the dole can be much shorter than you think. Is the award then for services to music? If so then a few kind words should be said for the Electricity Board without whose energy (and alternating current) the Mersey Sound would be timid stuff indeed.

Will the raucous, lively compositions of Mr John Lennon, MBE, and Mr Paul McCartney, MBE, echo through the corridors of history?

You tell me.

The award to Frankie Vaughan who has sung, cadged, and toiled in aid of the National Association of Boys' Clubs, makes better sense. It does because it recognizes that kids need centres where they can assert their individuality, learn proper values. But the Beatle cult, for all the ear-splitting enthusiasm that shrieks in its wake, the yelping and the "yeah yeahs," is too shaky a pinnacle for young kids to aim at. This shifting, superficial world, propped up by the charts or the Top Twenty rating, is not a world which Her Majesty or her advisers should dignify with royal awards. And where will it end? Dame Marianne Faithfull? Sir Rolling Stones? Herm (of the Hermits) OBE?

No, John, George, Paul and Ringo. You've earned the millions – but the medals, I think, have come a shade too soon.

DANDELIONS IN STILL AIR:
THE WITHERING AWAY
OF THE BEATLES

Any article that describes Ringo Starr as "beneath contempt" is clearly and knowingly over-the-top, but then that description applies to most of the work of the late American music journalist Lester Bangs. It was part of its incendiary charm.

Bangs had high standards for his heroes, to such an extent that most of them seemed to rather quickly become ex-heroes, as illustrated by this extract from a review of The Rolling Stones' album Goat's Head Soup *in 1973: "Just because The Stones have abdicated their responsibilities is no reason we have to sit still for this shit! . . . Unless we get The Rolling Stones off their asses IT'S THE END OF ROCK 'N' ROLL!"*

Similar disillusion with another set of 1960s titans informs the article reproduced below, first published in the low-circulation The Real Paper *in April 1975 and quickly reprinted two months later in the glossy rock magazine* Creem. *The titans in question of course were The Beatles. Bangs, in a lengthy and quintessentially rambling and semi-colloquial essay, was observing how un-Fab they now seemed to him at what was the half-decade mark of their dissolution. He would prove to be wrong about the quality of Beatles records diminishing with time – they are as well regarded now by the vast majority of their original admirers as they ever were – but Bangs also accurately reflected the disappointment and surprise of many at the way The Beatles' socio-political import was fading, not to mention dismay at the way their solo records fell so far short of what they had achieved collectively.*

As usual, Bangs' copy was full of unexplained contemporary references which today's reader might need enlightenment on: Richard Goldstein was a New York Times *critic who aroused much*

*controversy by daring to dissent on the brilliance of . . . Pepper . . . ,
while* Helter Skelter *was the title of a Los Angeles prosecuting attorney's book on the Manson murders that were supposedly inspired by parts of the White Album.*

The article also reveals that for all his coolness, Bangs even at this late stage still thought The Beatles sang "I get high" in "I Want To Hold Your Hand" rather than "I can't hide".

Dandelions In Still Air:
The Withering Away of the Beatles

From *The Real Paper* 23 April, 1975
by Lester Bangs

Name me one 1960s superstar who hasn't become a zombie. Dylan doesn't count, because he's been revivified, at least in terms of being a hot contender, *by Blood on the Tracks.* And Lou Reed is a professional zombie who can cackle in the grooves instead of up his sleeve. But Mick Jagger, Joe Cocker, Steve Stills . . . they're all washed-up, moribund, self-pitying, self-parodying has-beens. And the more I thought about it, the more it seemed to me that the four splintered Beatles may well have weathered the pall and decay of the 1970s the worst.

One by one, in order of descending credibility: Paul McCartney makes lovely boutique tapes, resolute upon being as inconsequential as The Carpenters which in itself may be as much a reaction to John's opposite excesses as a simple case of vacuity. You could hardly call him burnt out – *Band On The Run* was, in its rather vapid way, a masterful album. Muzak's finest hour. Of course he is about as committed to the notion of subject matter as Hanna-Barbera, and his cuteness can be incredibly annoying at times. If he was just a little more gutsy, he might almost be Elton John.

Lennon, as ever, seems Paul's antithesis. He'll do *anything*, reach for any cheap trick, jump on any bandwagon, to make himself look like a Significant Artist. His marriage to Yoko was culture-climbing that revealed a severe and totally unexpected inferiority complex. Of course, John's been staying drunk a lot, making a public spectacle of himself with such shameless élan that Lou Reed is gonna have to hustle his ass or lose the crown: Kotexes on the forehead, standing on tables in night-clubs screaming "I'm John Lennon! I'm John Lennon!", disrupting the stage acts of his peers in a manner more befitting Iggy Pop or perhaps the famous Lenny Bruce-Pearl Bailey incident in Vegas.

Somehow you have to feel affection and even a curious admiration for John as he engages in these escapades. In spite of the fact that they amount to a stance that might best be summed up as I Am Pathetic, Therefore I Am Charismatic (lifestyle is Art, said John and Yoko, so now he's Fatty Arbuckle, having left his Coke bottle on the train in *A Hard Day's Night*), which itself has become trite in these dunced-out and depleted times, there is a curious mangled echo of the Olden Spirit of Beatle Mischief in all this public idiocy.

His records, of course, are something else again. Paradoxically in spite of his lurching stabs at social significance, he moves closer to Paul's mode of technically clean, spiritually piddling hackwork with each album. He sings about scars in his face on the barroom floor, but without much conviction any more, and his instrumental surroundings are more blandly competent every time out. *Walls and Bridges* constituted a schlocky parody of the tortured artist writhing in a sterile sanitorium of his own design, and the fact that it reached Number One and spawned hit singles is disheartening in that it will certainly not encourage him to strive for anything that might be transcendent in the way that the "Mother"–"Working Class Hero" album, for all of its embarrassing infantilism and freelance spite, had a certain gauche and wretched majesty.

George Harrison belongs in a daycare centre for counter-culture casualties, another of those children cancelled not (so much?) by drugs this time but something perhaps far more insidious. His position seems to be I'm Pathetic, But I Believe in Krishna, which apparently absolves him from any position of leadership while enabling him to assume a totally preachy arrogance toward his audience which would be monumental chutzpah if it weren't coming from such a self-certified nebbish.

Ringo is beneath contempt. He used to be loveable because he was inept and knew it and turned the whole thing into a good-natured game. Now he is marketing that lameness in a slick Richard Perry-produced package, and getting hits via the stratagem, but the whole thing reeks. It is a bit as if Peter Max were designing stage sets for *Hee Haw's* Archie Campbell.

So the moptops have ended up mopping the floor of the supermarket, which is keeping them from bankruptcy and no doubt reassuring them that they still Matter on some level, but they do not and never will again give off a glint of the magic they used to radiate with such seeming effortlessness. That magic is currently one of the hottest items in the Woolworth's where 1960s nostalgia is peddled like bric-a-brac – in spite of the *Sgt. Pepper* Broadway bomb. Elton John was characteristically shrewd in releasing a cover looking back at "Lucy in the Sky with Diamonds".

On the other hand, I am constantly hearing people say, with minor perplexity, that they can still play early Stones albums, but old Beatle records (like old Dylan records), and particularly *Sgt. Pepper,* gather dust on the shelves. As with Dylan singing about Hattie Carroll, The Beatles celebrating the explosion of Love as a Way of Life amounts now to an artifact, just as today's Heavy Statements will prove to be just about as ephemeral. Somebody told me the other night that people would still be listening to Led Zeppelin's "Stairway To Heaven" a hundred years from today, and *Sgt. Pepper* as well. He's full of shit, of course, because "Stairway To Heaven" is not for the ages in the sense that Duke Ellington, say, might be, and as previously stated there aren't that many here among us who listen to *Sgt. Pepper* even eight years after it exploded on the pop world and, as prophesied by Richard Goldstein, proceeded to all but ruin the rock of the next few seasons by making rank-and-file musical artisans even more self-conscious and pretentious than dope already had.

The centre of any pop aesthetic has even less chance of holding than the last administration of this country had. rock 'n' roll will *not* necessarily stand; currently it seems to be jaywalking on its knees. But maybe that's a good reason to dig out all those musty Beatles albums and see if we perhaps can find in them, if not the bouncy mysticism that once seemed our staff of life, at least a good time. And perhaps in doing this we can discover the roots of the four separate styles of disintegration we're currently witnessing.

I have this theory, which has gotten me into minor fracases on a couple of occasions, that The Beatles' initial explosion was intimately tied up with the assassination of President John F. Kennedy. In fact, I have been known to say that JFK's killing was a *good* thing, historically speaking. A man died in an ugly fashion, he happened to be a man that people who didn't know anything about corporate politics considered the leader of the "free world", it was a national tragedy, etc. But on another level it was good because it opened a lot of things up. When Kennedy was in office we were living in a national dream world, the New Frontier as panacea, the illusion of unity. Underneath it all things were just as shitty as ever, but patriotism in those days seemed viable even for many of the avant-deviant-opposition fringes of our society. That misconception was shattered with the president's skull: the dream was over, and we were left with fragmentation, disillusionment ("I don't believe in Jesus, I don't believe in Elvis," etc.), cynicism, hostile factions.

All of which was fine. People began to look inside themselves, instead of toward a popstar of a president, for their definition of America. Out of this forcible introspection erupted the New Left, acid, all those alternative lifestyles which by now have of course become even more oppressive than the delusions of the Kennedy era. So in that sense it was healthy for the body politic that we lost that mythological leader; it forced us to contemplate a whole new set of options.

It also left us with a gnawing void which forced us to find

new leaders, of a new kind or any kind at all, and fast. Thus The Beatles, exploding across America from Ed Sullivan's stage and several different record companies, just weeks after the shot was fired. They were perfect medicine: a sigh of relief at their cheeky charm and a welcome frenzy to obliterate the grief with a tidal wave of Fun for its own sake which ultimately was to translate into a whole new hedonist dialectic.

I can remember the first time I ever heard The Beatles as distinctly as, I suppose, everyone else in the Western world. Walking home from school, I stopped off at the local record shop to check on the latest jazz, and there they were, "I Want to Hold Your Hand" spinning around and engulfing that shop with warm swelling waves of something powerfully attractive yet not quite comprehended, not yet. I wasn't much of a rock fan at the time, but there was some unmistakeable stunning blare to that record that set it completely apart from what had come before in spite of its seemingly rudimentary form. It was that high droning scream they hit you with on "Iwannahold-your–*haaaaaaaaaand*" and "I get *hiigh*," something that connected with broader concepts and idioms than any previous rock, like a muezzin's cry almost, and I stood in awe and thought: "The Beatles in the sky." That was where that cry, on the last brilliantly resonant syllable of each of those lines, seemed to be coming from.

Celestial and the boys next door all in one cheery, impudent package – Jesus, no wonder they were lapped up so greedily. Even better, there were four of them, filling the leadership gap with a new kind of junior (and equally illusory) democracy that gave the phrase "rock 'n' roll group" a whole new meaning and inspired a whole generation, blah blah blah. But the point is that in spite of the fact that each had his fanatical adherents, they were never John, Paul, George, and Ringo half so much as they were The Beatles, and *that* stood for something that they never could achieve apart, or even separately within the band. To search for the roots of their current degeneration in those early records is probably fruitless, in spite of odd parallels and contradictions: cosmic peace 'n' love George used to write (at least for the band) almost nothing but bitter put-downs like "Don't Bother Me" and "Think For Yourself". John could be as hateful then as now (from "You Can't Do That" to "How Do You Sleep" is not so far), and Paul was always a closet schmaltzmeister ("Michelle").

But the main thing that emerges from the career of The Beatles is the rise and fall of the concept of the *group,* which began to give way in rock to the ascendance of the solo artist at about the time they released their White Album, which has often been criticized for being a collection of songs by four separate individuals instead of a unified statement. Not to get too pretentious, but The Beatles' decline also parallels the decline of the youth culture's faith in itself as a homogenous group, for the proof of which we need look no further than the very corniness of a phrase like "youth culture" when you encounter it upon the page. That ain't no fuckin' culture no mo', the blacks even started imitating whites imitating blacks, and the adjourned Beatles, like most of their peers and contemporaries, have by now finally settled for imitating themselves.

To listen to early Beatles albums, or any Beatles albums up to the White Album, is to listen to collective enterprise, and of course the banality of the early songs becomes doubly ironic when you consider that "love" in the "I Want To Hold Your Hand" sense became transposed into "LOVE" as in flowers and beads grubbily handed to you on street corners and all you need is a little crystalline surcease of sorrow, the whole confused mess driving you crazy as John Lennon yelps out "Gimme Some Truth" and Paul responds from suburbia with "Another Day", perhaps his most topical solo venture ever. Impotent flailings vs. the celebration of the mundane.

Maybe that's why those old Beatle albums are so irritating today that just now, as I was playing *Rubber Soul* while writing this article, I took it off to type in silence, and my friend working nearby agreed that what once was ecstasy, the heart's rush of being in love for the first time, had through some curious process become a mere annoyance. The Beatles today are out of time, out of place, out of synch with a present reality that isn't particularly grim (from this chair, anyway) but neither is it exactly amenable to certain types of artifacts.

But the real artifact, of course, is not the record. It's the mood. It's the innocence, it's the unconscious sense of intimacy and community which automatically self-destructed the instant it became self-conscious, i.e. the very day we opened up *Sgt. Pepper* and saw those four smiling moustached faces assuring us with a slightly patronizing benevolence that all was well. There was of course a kind of smugness about it all, which led to such successive artifacts as Manson and John Denver. I don't particularly feel like reading Bugliosi's *Helter Skelter* either, not because I've OD'd on gore and outrage – it took the movies to do that – but *because it's in the past, it's boring, its old hat even, I've been there and I just don't care any more.*

What made The Beatles initially so exciting and sustained them for so long was that they seemed to carry themselves with a good-humoured sense of style which was (or appeared to be) almost totally unselfconscious. They didn't seem to realize that they were in the process of becoming institutionalized, and that was refreshing. By the time they realized it the ball game was over. In this sense, *Rubber Soul* (in packaging) and *Revolver* (in content as well) can be seen as the transitional albums. They doped it up and widened their scopes through the various other tools they had access to at the time just like everybody else down to the lowliest fringe-dripping cowlicked doughboy in the Oh Wow regiment, and the result was that they saw their clear responsibility as cultural avatars in what started out as a virtual vacuum (nice and clean, though), which of course ruined them. And possibly, indirectly, us.

But it's okay. Because, while I would not indulge in the kind of ten-year-cycle Frank Sinatra–Elvis Presley–The Beatles who's-next-now's-the-time theories that have been so popular and so easy lately, I do think that, like the assassination of JFK, the withering away of The Beatles has had its positive effects. Acidheads can (could?) be unbearable in their arrogant suppositions of omniscience, but if there's one thing good you can say about downs it's that nobody could get pretentious about them. The spell and its bonds are broken.

The death of The Beatles as a symbol or signification of anything can only be good, because like the New Frontier their LOVE nirvana was a stimulating but ridiculous, ephemeral and ultimately impracticable mass delusion in the first place. If The Beatles *stood* for anything besides the rock 'n' roll band as a communal unit suggesting the possibility of mass youth power, which proved to be a totally fatuous concept in short order, I'd like to know what I have missed by not missing The Beatles. They certainly didn't stand for peace or love or true liberation or the brotherhood of humankind, any more than John Denver stands for the preservation of our natural resources. On the other hand, like Davy Crockett hats, zoot suits, marathon dances, and bootleg alcohol, they may well have stood for an era, so well as to stand out from that era, totally exhumed from it in fact, floating, light as dandelions, to rest at last on the mantle where, neighbouring your dead uncle's framed army picture, they can be dusted off at appropriate intervals, depending on the needs of Capitol's ledgers and our own inability to cope with the present.

PENNY LAME

Some may consider this attack on the Fabs a week after they appeared on the front cover of the New Musical Express *almost exactly forty years after their first appearance in that music paper to be wilfully ill-informed about the groups' history and catalogue in places, but the truth the article conveys – that (unthinkable in the 1960s) they are not held in particularly high regard by large bulks of the generations born after The Beatles were in their pomp – is certainly arresting.*

Dave Simpson is a Guardian *music writer and the author of* The Fallen – Searching For The Missing Members Of The Fall *(Canongate). He says, "The Fall are much better than The Beatles ... Much bigger body of work, more experimental, more creative use of language, better tunes. Surely no one in their right mind would prefer 'Maxwell's Silver Hammer' to 'Container Drivers' or 'Mollusc In Tyrol'?"*

Penny Lame

From the *Guardian*, 18 November 2003
by Dave Simpson

I've never liked the Beatles. There. I've said it.

I was part of the lucky generation born between The Beatles' world-conquering existence and the now endless wave of CD repackages, anniversary collections and retrospectives that force-feeds secondhand Beatlemania to modern generations of unsuspecting youth. When I was a kid discovering Showaddywaddy and Wizzard (who I still prefer to the Fabs), The Beatles were just a fading throwback loitering in secondhand shops. My mum reminisced, horrifyingly, about their "nice suits". One school trip took us to a museum which had cardboard cutouts of John, Paul, Ringo and The Other One. Maybe it was the fact that they were bigger than me, didn't smile, and smelt musty, but there was something about them I found very scary.

I never bought the myth – all that thumbs aloft, wacky Scousers, lovely boys, world peace stuff which we now know to be nonsense because they were in fact either taking heroin, fighting among themselves or dreaming up the Frog Chorus all that time. Even at my early age, something in McCartney's eye said: "Sshh, in thirty years I'll be asking my lawyers to get the credits reversed to McCartney-Lennon and presiding over a de-Spectorized version of *Let It Be* which will show how much we relied on top producers."

Even when I outgrew Slade, The Beatles remained thoroughly uninteresting. A mate of mine – troubled that I was a Non-Believer – lent me *The Beatles Live At The Hollywood Bowl*. It sounded like a bootleg of Gerry and the Pacemakers and a lot of girls screaming. I pushed it aside in favour of the UK Subs.

Lennon's death triggered national Beatle worship all over again, but for me rock's most significant loss of 1980 was Joy Division's Ian Curtis.

Of course, even this Beatlephobe cannot deny their incalculable cultural significance: they wrote their own songs before The Stones did and gave the world the bowl cut. They are feted for their lyrics. But for every "In My Life", there's "I Am The Walrus": "You've been a naughty girl, you've let yer knickers down". Poetry? Not really. When I think of the great moments of pop history, the Drab Four were not around. They didn't turn up at Live Aid or on the Anarchy Tour, and their chief influence on acid house was to provide a toe-curling hit for Candyflip. They did, however, pen a number one hit for Gareth Gates in 2002.

The Beatles are what they always were – the safe, money-spinning, housewives' choice. Their albums are easy listening (fine for fifty-somethings, but The Beatles were cardigan-wearing duffers in their twenties). *Sgt. Pepper*, their much-trumpeted "psychedelic" album was as mindbending as an Asda mushroom pie. Give or take "Helter Skelter", they never even rocked, really. Next to The Stones, The Who or The Troggs, The Beatles are the low alcohol lager of the 1960s.

Of course, you're not supposed to say this. Do and they'll burn you in the street. When I once casually mentioned in a feature for *Melody Maker* that Oasis were better than The Beatles, the postbag bulged for months. Karl Wallinger – who penned the Fab-alike "She's The One" for Robbie Williams – howled on Radio One in outrage. Like Michael Jackson worshippers and Cliff stalkers, Beatles fans refuse to confront the notion that their heroes could be flawed. But is the fact that their fanbase includes Mark Chapman, Michael Jackson and Mike Read not enough to put anyone off?

Like Christmas, Beatlemania is now a vast and increasingly meaningless business run by ageing Fab fans. The record industry is in such trouble that it relies on endless repackages of "Eleanor Rigby". *Let It Be . . . Naked* might not be the end. Next could be *Rubber Soul . . . Naked*. One day, we might even be confronted with Paul McCartney naked. To move on, pop must rid itself of this whistling, thumb-raising cancer. Oasis and The Rutles aside, the list of great bands inspired by The Beatles is not long, yet they continue to exert a stranglehold, pumped out of taxis, covered on *Pop Idol*, even appearing on the cover of last week's *NME*.

The line we're always pummelled with is that they set the standard for great songwriting. Yes, "Strawberry Fields Forever" and "Hey Jude" are marvellous. But if I ponder the rest – especially "Yellow Submarine" or "Maxwell's Silver Hammer" – all I think is "Help!"

LIVING LIFE WITHOUT
LOVING THE BEATLES

As a native of Liverpool, Gary Hall committed one of the worst sins any Scouse son could by deciding he didn't like the music of The Beatles. He explained his dislike of the (for him) un-Fab Four in a self-published book, Living Life Without Loving The Beatles *(2003), in which he graded Beatles fans (Culture Vulture, Nostalgic Impolitic, Latecomer, Musician, American and – the most severe form of Beatles fan known to man – Beatle Head.)*

His book created a sufficient stir that it was sold to mainstream publisher Equinox, who in 2006 put out a revised, expanded edition, from which this section about the most harmless form of Beatles fan – a Grade One – is taken.

Living Life Without Loving The Beatles

by Gary Hall

Of all the different Beatles fans you'll meet, the easiest to deal with by far will be the *Grade One*. A *Grade One is* the type of Fab Four fan that doesn't really like music! Don't get me wrong, if there's something on the radio at work with a catchy tune, they'll sing along at the top of their lungs, or if they're going out with their mates at the weekend, they will of course have a good boogie after a skinful. But if you were to ask them, for example, the title of Springsteen's first album or who was the bass player in The Clash, they'd be knackered. As a rule this lot are sitting ducks. But how do you spot the buggers? That's the problem. It's not as if they're going to be wearing a placard round their necks saying "Musically Retarded" when you meet them. Which means you'll have to dig deeper into their shallow depths for clues.

Let's assume a scenario. Your partner rings you last minute at work; you've been invited to Jill and Tony's that evening for dinner; can you be ready by eight? Not wanting to disappoint, you dash home, make a few calls, put on side one of *Dusty In Memphis* or *Otis Blue* (it's your scenario, you choose), jump in the shower and make yourself respectable. By eight o'clock you're standing at Jill and Tony's door.

Obviously you've had no time to build a profile of these people. In fact, you've got no background on them whatsoever; for all you know they may go line dancing or sing karaoke. On the other hand, they may be fine, but forewarned is forearmed. Therefore, in order to establish, as soon as possible, if your hosts are *Grade Ones* or not, you'll need to look for clues the moment you arrive. However, marching over to their hi-fi system within seconds of walking through the door and ransacking through their CD collection for evidence, whilst rolling your eyes and snorting in disgust as you conduct your enquiries, is not the way we like to do things in this book. Try to be nice. Shake hands. Say hello. Hand over that bottle of wine you've brought. Sit down, and quietly observe.

Check out their clothes. Can you see the brand name without squinting? Is there a Monet on the wall? Is it the *Poppy Field?* (Obviously if it's the original, this small matter can be over-looked.) Is there a poster from Ikea of the New York skyline, with the words *New York* emblazoned across the bottom, just in case you should get confused and have a skyline relapse? Look carefully on tops of cupboards, under chairs and tables. Can you see a box of Trivial Pursuit? Is it out on the table already? If your hosts for this evening are the kind of people who would wear those garments, choose such safe and easy images to adorn their walls, and find it hard to summon up the concentration to converse with you for the duration without resorting to board games, then it is possible that you are indeed in a household inhabited by *Grade Ones*.

The biggest clue of all, of course, will be the hi-fi system. If it blends in amongst the furniture with old oak speakers draped in foliage, with an amplifier like the dashboard of a classic car, a discreet CD player and a turntable with stories to tell, then it's unlikely your hosts are *Grade Ones* – trust me. However, if it's an all-singing, all-dancing high-tech digital boom box that looks like it's ready for lift off, that's not a good sign; you may need to examine their CD collection for conclusive confirmation. But not yet. Have a glass of wine first and help yourself to Twiglets. Settle in, and let the evening unfold. When the time feels right, seize the moment.

"Do you mind if I take a look at your CDs, Tony?"

"No, go ahead mate, I haven't bought much over the last few years," he says, as he gets up from his chair and kneels down in front of the cabinet so you can't see a bloody thing. "Most of my stuff's on vinyl at my mum's – Human League, Meatloaf, Madness, loads of Queen and Bowie. I used to love that George Michael as well until I found out he was batting for the other side. I had a couple of albums by this really obscure Irish folk singer that you'll probably never have heard of called Enya. She had a bloody belting voice, I'll tell you that. Oh, and I've got a load of old Beatles records too. One of the singles I've got must be worth a bob or two, I reckon, because it's mono, right, but the music still comes out of both speakers when you play it."

As Tony awaits your combined reaction of admiration and envy, his trip down memory lane is thankfully cut short by voices from the kitchen.

"Come and get it fellas, it's on the table."

As you amble into the dining room, Tony continues to dig himself in deeper by informing you that he's now replaced most of his Fab Four catalogue on CD since he's moved in with Jill. Don't react in any way to his confession. Now you know where you stand, you can plan your defence in advance. For now though, just smile, sit down, tell Jill how good the food looks and immediately change the subject to holiday plans.

Whilst you're eating dinner and trying to remain conscious as Tony regales you with tales of his days as a Weekend Warrior in the TA, the Starship Enterprise is flashing away in the lounge in neon heaven to the temporary tones of Toploader, this week's safe bet. Not your ideal choice I'm sure, but make the most of the ambience that Eastbourne's rock giants have to offer, because I've got a funny feeling that things may soon take a turn for the worse.

I was right. Dinner consumed, the girls happily engrossed in work gossip, all of a sudden, without warning, Tony gets up and staggers over to the Starship Enterprise. Before you have time to think of a hundred reasons why The Stones are better than The Beatles, Toploader are history and the opening bars of "Come Together" have already started polluting the atmosphere. Then a few minutes later, just as you're starting to come to terms with the noise pollution, Tony, whose only demand on you up until this point has been trying to get you to commit to doing this bloody parachute jump with him for charity, suddenly wants to further spoil your evening by "having the talk" with you about The Beatles.

"They're the greatest, aren't they?" he cries out during the guitar solo on "Something", still playing his air guitar, with his eyes shut tight, drifting in and out of halfwit heaven.

Okay, your turn, off you go. "Who are?"

"The Beatles, of course."

Okay, try to be diplomatic. Barring a miracle, this is the first and last evening you'll ever spend in Tony's company and he's just a simple guy, so give him a chance.

"Well Tony, you've got to hand it to the lads, they worked hard and they sold millions of records."

Good response, well done. Unfortunately, it doesn't look like this is going to bring the conversation to a natural close as you'd maybe hoped it would. "Yeah, they did mate, and let me tell you why, because they're the best bloody band of all time."

Oh dear, red rag to a bull I'm afraid. Ah well, at least you've tried. You might as well let him have it. "What makes you think they're the best band of all time, Tony?"

He's totally mystified now. You've just answered your own question in his mind by stating that they've sold millions of records. He lurches towards you, so close now that you can make out the remains of dinner in his moustache and smell the Diamond White on his breath as he raises his voice even louder than before in order to make himself absolutely clear.

"Because pal, as you've just said, they've sold millions and millions of records and wherever you go in the world today, Ibiza, Corfu, Orlando, Torremolinos, even Lanzarote, and that's a bloody island in the middle of nowhere, everybody, everywhere, knows at least a few Beatles songs."

Now I know most people in this situation would try to steer the conversation to different matters a.s.a.p. But remember you're here to learn how to live your life without loving The Beatles and survive, so if like me, you're not one to leave such outrageous perceptions unchallenged, here's how to knock *a Grade One* out with just one punch. You'll need to alter the dish, time and place name to suit your own individual circumstances.

(The following parable is also recommended for use with any strain of Fab Four fan [apart from the Beatle Head] when you feel that he or she may be confusing the value of art with the power of commerce.)

"Tony, in June 1990, I was sitting in a small trattoria across the road from the train station in Milan. It was late Saturday evening; I hadn't eaten since I'd left my hotel in Mantova around 9 a.m. that morning. Even with the beautiful warm night breeze still blowing in through the door as the last of the evening's caffeine addicts rolled in for one last shot, the heat did little to tame my hunger. I was starving. When eventually the food arrived it looked like it had been created by Leonardo da Vinci. It sat there on the table before me still sizzling with the heat, too hot to taste but too fragrant to ignore. I watched the tomatoes, such an intense red, as if plucked from a rustic Cezanne still life, bursting through the crust of the golden cheese sauce like an Arizona sunset. To simply describe this as lasagne would be like describing Bob Dylan's *Blood On The Tracks* as a twelve-inch disc of black plastic with a small hole in the middle. It was the most delicious food I've ever eaten. Once I'd finished, I asked the waiter if I could meet the person responsible for this masterpiece. A wonderful old lady came out from the kitchen. She spoke no English. I spoke very little Italian. But I think she realized that by the time I'd hugged her, wiped the tears from my eyes and stopped pointing at the plate whilst repeating 'bella, bella' until it no longer sounded like a word, that she had touched my soul and taste buds at a very deep level.

"Marks and Spencer also make a lasagne, Tony. I've had one several times. They're actually quite nice. But if you were in the mood for a lasagne right now, which do you think you'd prefer?"

"Well, it's obvious mate," he says, without even thinking about it. "The one you told me about in that café in Italy."

Okay, so far so good, now for the second part of the question.

"Marks and Spencer is a multinational company with many stores dotted around the globe. The trattoria in Italy is a small family-run business with seating for perhaps thirty max. Tell me Tony, who do you think sells the most lasagne?"

Okay, that's it. He's out for the count. His time's up. Well done. But, before you get too smug, remember that Tony is only a *Grade One*. He doesn't really like music; he's only trying to fit in and be one of the gang by playing it safe. He's not going to fight his corner like some of the other strains of Beatles fan that you're going to meet in later chapters, and why should he? It's only music, for Christ sake. It's not as if you've cast aspersions on the road handling of his Ford Mondeo!

For more writing by Gary Hall see: www.freespeechbooks.com

PART THREE: FILM AND TV

As four photogenic young men, The Beatles were a group tailor-made for the big and silver screens. Herein, discussion of all the official Beatle-related movies and television programmes.

A Hard Day's Night

Premiered: 6 July 1964

Bob Neaverson is one of the UK's leading experts on The Beatles' films, and author of two authoritative books on the subject, The Beatles Movies, *first published in 1997, and* At The Apple's Core *(2002), which was co-written with Denis O'Dell, the former head of Apple Films and producer of many of The Beatles' films and promotional clips.* The Beatles Movies *was highly acclaimed as the first in-depth critical analysis of The Beatles' film output, and the first to place them within their cultural context. Below is printed an adaptation of the chapter from the book on the group's first film* A Hard Day's Night.

A Hard Day's Night

by Bob Neaverson

Although shooting for the film began in March 1964, its preparation commenced some six months earlier, in October 1963, when Beatles manager Brian Epstein met with the independent American producer, Walter Shenson, who had been appointed by United Artists' European production head, George H. Ornstein. At this point in their career, The Beatles, although an enormous phenomenon in Britain, had yet fully to establish themselves within the American market. The group had not yet attained the superstar status which followed their groundbreaking television appearance on *The Ed Sullivan Show* in February 1964. So the project was initially envisaged by the American-owned company as little more than another low-budget exploitation picture which would capitalize on the group's fleeting success with the teenage market and, most importantly, provide its record label with a lucrative tie-in soundtrack album. Indeed, as Shenson later revealed, the company was only interested in making a Beatles film "for the express purpose of having a soundtrack album", and he was given no other guidelines apart from an instruction to make a film with "enough new songs by The Beatles for a new album."

For their part, The Beatles were initially sceptical about appearing in pop musicals, and not without good reason. After all, not only did they lack any formal acting experience, they had, according to former press officer Tony Barrow, also seen their former hero, Elvis Presley, throw his "beautiful image as a pop superman clean out of the window" by forsaking his more obvious talents to undertake a career in movies.

Worse still, they were unimpressed by the flimsy, contrived B-movie quality of British pop films, and felt that theirs would be no different. As Lennon said to Epstein prior to shooting, "We don't fancy being Bill Haley and the Bellhops, Brian. We're not going to walk in and out of endless studios bumping into Helen Shapiro and Mark Wynter and saying 'Hi there' to Alan Freeman." More importantly, things were going extraordinarily well as they were, so why put their heads on the chopping block by interacting with a world of which they knew nothing? Did they really need to risk making fools of themselves and destroying their hitherto impeccable track record?

Because of their initial lack of confidence in the film's prof-itability, United Artists' budget for *A Hard Day's Night* was set at a modest £200,000, with The Beatles receiving £20,000, plus seven per cent of the profits. According to Tony Barrow, United Artists had expected to pay up to three times this percentage, but because of their initial scepticism over the film's success, they "weren't particularly overjoyed at their good fortune". Having drawn up the agreement, and arranged for the group to write and record six new songs for the soundtrack, Shenson had to decide what kind of film to make. On meeting The Beatles, he had tentatively decided that the film should be a musical comedy and, with their agreement, hired American expatriate Richard Lester as director.

In many ways, Lester was an obvious choice both for The Beatles and for Shenson. He had already worked with Shenson on the comedy *The Mouse on the Moon* (1963), and as a former musician and director of the trad boom musical, *It's Trad Dad* (1962), was well attuned to contemporary pop sensibilities. Indeed, Lester had heard The Beatles' music some time before they achieved mass popularity, on a live bootleg tape from the Cavern Club which he had heard through friends working at ABC studios, near Manchester. More importantly for The Beatles, he had worked with their favourite comedians, The Goons, on a number of television and film projects. The Beatles greatly admired the surreal and anarchic humour of The Goons, and in the BBC series on 1960s British cinema, *Hollywood UK*, Shenson revealed that the main reason The Beatles had accepted Lester as the film's director was that he had worked with the comedy group on various projects.

Having hired the director, Shenson needed a screenwriter. Although a number of screenplays were submitted for the project, none was considered appropriate. At the suggestion of Lester, Shenson hired Alun Owen, a scriptwriter whose previous television credits included *Z Cars* and *No Trams to Lime Street*. Like Lester, Owen was well suited to both the film-makers and its stars. He had already worked with Lester on the comedy pilot *Dick Lester Show*, and was, in the words of Alexander Walker, already a "*persona grata* with The Beatles", having had a similar upbringing in Merseyside. As Joe McGrath, who contributed some script ideas to the film, remembers, "He knew where those boys were, as they say in America, coming from." Shenson briefed Owen that the script should be an "exaggerated 'day in the life'" of the group and on 7 November 1963 sent Owen to Dublin to observe The Beatles' chaotic touring routine. By spring 1964 Owen's script was complete and The Beatles, on their triumphant return from America, were the most famous entertainers on earth. However, this did not affect the film's production schedule or budget, and despite the fact that the group's enormous bankability could easily have justified far greater production costs, it was decided by all parties not to drastically alter any existing agreements. However, a three-picture agreement was drawn up between United Artists and Epstein (with increasingly lucrative terms for The Beatles), and the group's profit percentage was raised.

On 25 February, just two days after their return from America (and just six days before the start of shooting), The Beatles returned to Abbey Road to begin recording the songs which would comprise the soundtrack of the film: "Can't Buy Me Love", "Tell Me Why", "If I Fell", "You Can't Do That", "I Should Have Known Better", "I'm Happy Just to Dance With You", and "And I Love Her". However, there were some changes made to this line-up. "You Can't Do That" was dropped from the film, and the opening title song, "A Hard Day's Night," was recorded some weeks later, in April, shortly before the completion of shooting. This song was added because the film lacked an original title and on hearing the phrase (initially a "Ringo-ism") in a conversation with Lennon, Shenson decided that it perfectly captured the film's "feel" and immediately instructed Lennon and McCartney to write the film's title song around it. Although this was the first time the group had been asked to write in a lyrically contrived manner (Shenson had given no lyrical or thematic guidelines for the other songs on the sound-track), Lennon wrote the song in one evening and played it to the producer the following day.

In keeping with the film's modest budget, the production schedule was extremely tight, with shooting taking place at various London locations and at Twickenham studios over an eight-week period. The decision to shoot at real locations created nightmarish logistical problems for Denis O'Dell, the film's associate producer. Having arranged for British Railways to provide a special route for The Beatles' train, O'Dell discovered that information would leak out to fans who would then attempt to besiege the train. As he remembers, "Kids would be jumping in front of the bloody train, so every day we would change the route because we couldn't get The Beatles on the train, never mind get to shoot." For The Beatles, the speed of the shoot created a back-breaking workload. Whilst shooting the film they also had to keep abreast of a number of other commitments, including completing the soundtrack album, attending a number of awards ceremonies, and making several appearances on British television.

Yet despite the speed and frugality of its production *A Hard Day's Night* remains, for many writers and film critics, the most accomplished and important pop musical in film history. It was described by Andrew Sarris as the "*Citizen Kane* of juke box movies" and American critic Roger Ebert has commented that he would have no hesitation in placing it in the top five musicals of all time. Twenty-three years after its release, a poll conducted by *Beatles Monthly Book* revealed it to be the most popular film release amongst fans, polling twice as many votes as *Help!*, the runner-up. While it is not my intention to enter into puerile debate about what should constitute a film's "classic" status, it seems that the underlying reason for the film's critical reverence rests with the originality and complexity of its stylistic and ideological properties, properties which were conspicuously absent from previous pop films. With *A Hard Day's Night,* the pop musical "came of age", making the vehicles of Cliff Richard and Elvis Presley seem, like their music, to be hopelessly naive and outdated.

The formal style of the film was vastly different from that of The Beatles' contemporaries, both in its extraordinary eclecticism and in its daring rejection of traditional Hollywood aesthetics. Most strikingly, the film included sequences that rejected the Hollywood "performance" oriented aesthetic. By integrating scenes (such as the "Can't Buy Me Love" sequence) in which music is used in an "illustrative", conceptual capacity, Lester set a precedent that would come to influence many of the pop films which followed it, and ultimately form an important visual touchstone for music video, a format pioneered by The Beatles themselves from the mid-1960s onwards.

Moreover, unlike the vehicles of Tommy Steele and the later musicals of Cliff Richard, *A Hard Day's Night* was not hell-bent on merely imitating the conventional narrative structure and film style of the Hollywood musical. Instead it opted for a reactionary, and seemingly self-conscious amalgamation of formal techniques derived from a range of styles and genres, including various strands of film and television documentary, the films of the British and French "New Wave," television advertising and early US silent slapstick comedy.

Perhaps the most striking formal difference between the film and its predecessors is its illusion of documentary-style realism, which is achieved in a number of ways. From the outset, the notion of producing a film based on real characters set within (for The Beatles) realistic situations goes against the artificiality of, say, the Elvis cycle, in which Presley plays fictitious characters in overtly contrived scenarios. Although clearly "acting", the group effectively play themselves in a narrative which, despite its fictionalized plot, accurately depicts a slice of their chaotic routine at the height of Beatlemania. As Owen stated in an interview with Alexander Walker, "What Shenson and I want to avoid is a 'slick' movie; a rough-cast look is the aim, a documentary feel. This may seem apostasy but I want a film that can stand on its own without The Beatles."

In keeping with this realist aesthetic are many of Lester's formal techniques, which are culled from a number of different realist genres, most notably drama-documentary and "direct cinema" documentary. Indeed, despite his use of breakneck editing (possibly derived from his advertising background), the regular use of real locations, hand-held sequences and naturalistic lighting frequently imbue the action with a sense of overpowering actuality which, at times, becomes so stylistically similar to documentary or newsreel footage that it becomes impossible to differentiate fact from fiction. The opening "chase" sequence, for example, is, although dramatized, formally consistent with contemporary direct cinema, its grainy black-and-white transparency and hand-held camerawork making it almost indistinguishable from the Maysles Brothers' documentary film of the group in America, *Yeah, Yeah, Yeah* (1964). In a similar manner, Owen's script, based on direct observation and populated by Spoonerisms, colloquialisms and Liverpool slang, lends the action such a unique sense of naturalism that it also creates a convincing illusion of actuality (or at least improvization), despite the fact that only a minimal number of genuinely "ad-libbed" lines were employed in the final cut. Asked about the number of improvizations, cast member Victor Spinetti remembers that "there were a hell of a lot, but they were all cut out. We kept to the script. They [The Beatles] didn't!"

While realism had, of course, already been absorbed into commercial British film style through New Wave "kitchen sink" dramas such as A *Kind of Loving* (1962) and *This Sporting Life* (1963), *A Hard Day's Night* was undoubtedly the first pop musical to adopt this aesthetic so freely and wholeheartedly into its discourse.

For further information on Bob Neaverson's writing, visit: www.beatlesmovies.co.uk

HELP!

Premiered: 29 July 1965

Help! *was the second Beatles feature film. To some extent, its produc-tion found The Beatles at a decadent stage of their career.*

Lennon was bored by it and in the middle of what he would call his "Fat Elvis" period, overweight and unhappy at what he had found upon his ascent to the mountaintop of success. Shooting loca-tions were decided on for reasons other than necessity: the sections shot in the Bahamas meant that the band could look into the area's tax-saving benefits, while Paul has admitted that the only reason Help! *contained a skiing sequence is because the Fabs fancied going on the piste. Additionally, during shooting, the band were, by all accounts, having joints for breakfast, dinner and tea. And while one doesn't want to be boringly PC, the reference by Lennon in the script to an Indian girl's filthy eastern ways does raise an eyebrow.*

Help! *wasn't received as warmly by the critics as* A Hard Day's Night *and is now held in even lesser regard. Even the fact that it was shot in colour and had exotic locations is held against it by some enamoured of the cinema verite and monochrome of* A Hard Day's Night. *However, like the* Help! *album, the film is underrated. It's very easy on the eye, its Technicolour made to seem all the more sumptuous by the exotic settings, which as well as Alpine ski slopes and the Bahamas, also include stately English home Cliveden standing in for Buckingham Palace and spitting-distance-of-Stonehenge Salisbury Plain. Nor do you have to be a Beatlemaniac to appreciate that the Fabs look like a million dollars. The humour is American zany but also British dry and if the script sometimes tries too hard for laughs or to portray The Beatles as the cool antidote to the fuddy-duddies who control the world, the pace is too fast for any scene to drag.*

Ringo's mordant performance in A Hard Day's Night *made him the unexpected star of the first film. Consequently, this movie places him at the centre, with all the action stemming from the fact that he has been sent a ring by an Indian fan to join the others on his laden fingers. The religious cult which owns the ring is horrified to find this out and sets out to kill the hapless sticksman. A reasonable degree of merriment ensues – the best joke is a recurring gag involving a skin diver (a cameo for Beatle employee Mal Evans) popping up out of the water wherever in the world The Beatles find themselves to ask the right way to England – and where it flags there is, of course, a Beatles tune to keep one preoccupied.*

The standards of a lot of the fans of course were far less stringent than the critics and they lapped up a work that consolidated the image of the Beatles as a nutty, noisy, happy, handsome band of men, epitomized by the scene that shows the group all living in one long house with a separate front door for each.

It's interesting that the legend has always been that the television show The Monkees *was originally commissioned to be an American equivalent of the way the Fabs were portrayed in* A Hard Day's Night. *Both the evidence of one's eyes and the timeline (*The Monkees *didn't hit the airwaves until September 1966) suggests that* Help! *was the bigger influence on the "Pre-fab Four".*

Though it's over the top, British journalist Kenneth Tynan's review of the film was perhaps closer to the truth of the quality of Help! *than the current revisionism which virtually dismisses it, a viewpoint to which Lennon ("bullshit") and McCartney ("pretty higgledy-piggledy") adhered. Though born in 1927 and very well educated (it's a fair bet that only he quoted Coleridge in his review of the picture), Tynan was a man absolutely in the forefront of what would soon come to be termed the counter-culture. He was one of the first to champion John Osborne's Angry Young Man anti-establishment play* Look Back In Anger, *ensured he became the first person to say "fuck" on British television and battled censorship and conservatism at every turn. Reading his review – written in the journalistic equivalent of* Help's *comic book visual vernacular – one is put in mind of a part of another famous review of* Look Back In Anger, *this one by John Barber, who exulted in a redeeming quality of that flawed play that* Help! *– for all its faults – also possessed: ". . . it is young young, young."*

Help!

by Kenneth Tynan

THIS this THIS this THIS is the kind of THING (from outer SPACE?) you can expect from *Help!*, the new (and BAM!! it's new or never) film directed by focus-pulling, prize-winning, gag-spawning, zoom-loving Richard (The KNACK) Lester, shot (POWWW!) in Eastmancolour but influenced by *Observer*-colour and suggesting whole libraries of colourmags sprung BOING! to instant obsolescent life, complete with COOL gaudy consumer-tailored featurettes (one Lester missed: "Tread Softly: The Dream-World of Wall-to-Wall Carpeting") and genuine only-connecting ADS (another Lester missed: "Why not fly to the Aleutians in your custom-built Hammond Organ?"), not to mention FOUR EXPENSIVE TWO-DIMENSIONAL OBJECTS – namely John Lennon, the snickering heavyweight punster; surly, bejewelled Ringo Starr; George Harrison, the twelve-string narcissist; and Paul McCartney, the boy next fibre-glass-electric-eye-operated door (under that wig he's really – GASP! – Anne Rutherford) who are flung about (URGGHH!), battered (SPLAT!!) and flattened (KERPLUNK!!!) in a comic-strip chase through tourist-enticing London, the whiter-than-white Austrian Alps and selected sunsoaked Bahamas, pursued by Oriental goodness-gracious villains ("It's a Sellers' market," quips writer Charles Wood) and guaranteed mad scientists, all plotting to slice (EEK!) a magic ring from surly Ringo's bejew-elled finger, while off-beat Lester movie garners harvest of heady hosannas ("LOFTY GROSSES LOOM FOR MOPHEADS' LATEST – Flicker's Total Sexlessness Augurs Wham Family

Fare') from notoriously hard-to-please CRITICS (ECCHH!!) in American trade press . . .

In other words, *Help!* is a brilliant, unboring but ferociously ephemeral movie. Richard Lester's direction is a high-speed compendium of many lessons learned from Blake Edwards, Frank Tashlin, Goon comedy, fashion photography and MGM cartoons. The Beatles themselves are not natural actors, nor are they exuberant extroverts; their mode is dry and laconic, as befits the flat and sceptical Liverpool accent. Realizing this, Lester leaves it to his cameraman (David Watkin) to create the exuberance, confining The Beatles to deadpan comments and never asking them to react to events with anything approaching emotion. He capitalizes on their wary, guarded detachment. "There's something been in this soup," says John, having calmly removed from the plate a season ticket and a pair of spectacles.

The script (by Marc Behm and Charles Wood) is chopped into fragments; hundreds of half-heard gags zip by, of which we are given time to laugh at about two dozen. The best-sustained sequence is the one where Ringo is trapped by an escaped tiger that can be tamed only by a full choral rendering of Beethoven's Ninth. The musical items are superbly shot, and the title song is the most haunting Beatle composition to date.

To sum up *Help!* I must go to Coleridge, who said that whereas a scientist investigates a thing for the sheer pleasure of knowing, the non-scientist only wants to find out whether it will "furnish him with food, or shelter, or weapons, or tools, or ornaments, or *play-withs*." *Help!* is a shiny forgettable toy; an ideal play-with.

THE BEATLES CARTOON TELEVISION SERIES

Though inveterate TV fan and admirer of surrealist humour John Lennon was fairly predictably a fan of The Beatles *cartoon TV show, it would seem his former colleagues were not. The series was never networked in Britain (though did get a regional broadcast in the area covered by the Granada TV franchise area long after The Beatles were defunct). In the mid-1990s, Apple Corps bought the rights to the series and it promptly disappeared from the face of the earth, possibly never to be seen again except on the videos and DVDs circulating amongst collectors.*

Though unknown to Britons, the show was hugely popular in the United States, originally airing on Saturday mornings for three seasons from September 1965 and then being re-run extensively. The very first weekly series in animation history to feature cartoon versions of real people, it no doubt strengthened the American image of the band as loveable moptops that Lennon would later lament, but it can also only have increased The Beatles' popularity, not least by the shop window it constituted for the individual shows' featured songs. In that sense, it is possibly just as important as the movie A Hard Day's Night. *It's also important in a wider sense: subsequent animated TV programmes about pop groups both real (The Osmonds, The Jackson 5) and imagined (The Archies, Josie And The Pussycats, The Brady Kids) would surely not have happened without this precedent.*

Falling ratings led to the series' cancellation. The fact that "Tomorrow Never Knows" and "Strawberry Fields Forever" were among the featured songs in the final series provides a clue as to the reason for those falling ratings: The Beatles simply weren't the moptops the cartoon still portrayed them as (albeit with occasional nods to new developments like sideburns and glasses), and while their growing fans may still have bought their records, they were now too busy dating and engaging in other more adult activities to sit down in front of the TV on Saturday mornings. Meanwhile, a new trend towards superheroes was being ushered in with the live action Batman *show and an animated* Superman *programme.*

Mitchell Axelrod was just two when he saw his first Beatles cartoon at the time of the series' original transmission. His happy memories of the show led him in 1999 to write Beatletoons, *which gave due prominence to a part of The Beatles' story which The Beatles themselves seem keen to suppress.*

Beatletoons

by Mitchell Axelrod

"Ladies and gentlemen . . . The Beatles."

Millions of people know that those five words spoken by Ed Sullivan on the night of 9 February, 1964 began The Beatles' historic conquest of America and the world. Yet very few know that it was during the same week of that history-making performance, that the initial stages were being set for The Beatles to conquer a world of a different kind, the cartoon world.

Saturday morning cartoon viewers were about to be rocked and rolled by the four lads from Liverpool. On 25 September 1965, at 10:30 a.m. Eastern Standard Time, *The Beatles* cartoon show premiered on ABC Television in the United States. Each half-hour show consisted of two five-and-one-half-minute episodes. The moptops would be placed in such "usual" situations as being chased by girls, or such "unusual" ones as going to museums, amusement parks, or to the movies. "Unusual" ones because as we now know, it was virtually impossible for the "real" Beatles to venture out in public without being besieged by fans or the media. Most features would place the Fab Four in different locales such as Africa, Japan, America or their native England, and each episode was loosely based on the lyrics of a Beatle song, which was included in each adventure. Sand-wiched between the two episodes were two sing-a-long segments in which John, Paul or George would encourage the viewing audience to sing-a-long with some of their latest tunes. Ringo would always provide the comic relief (filling in for the ever vacationing or ill prop man), by trying to put the audience in the "proper mood". Often with funny, if not silly, results. Mini Beatles adventures would be the background as the words to classic and not so classic Beatles songs were shown on the screen, minus the white bouncing ball. Tying the whole program together were assorted Beatle bits which usually involved the boys getting into some sort of mischief which would lead to "a word from our sponsor". In total, for the three-and-a-half years they were on ABC-TV, there were thirty-nine shows that featured seventy-eight episodes and some seventy-five sing-a-longs. Ratings for the first season went through the roof, and a hit program had been created.

Al Brodax had already been very established in the world of animation when the idea of a Beatles cartoon came about. At King Features Syndicate, he was the head of the motion picture television department. Along with his associate, Mary Ellen Stewart, and his production manager, Abe Goodman, Al had already been responsible for giving the world a new batch of *Popeye* cartoons. Al recalls, "We did 220 *Popeye* pictures in eighteen months. Paramount Pictures did 235 *Popeye* pictures in thirty-five years." The Brodax team proved that they could produce mass quantities in a limited amount of time, while maintaining a high standard of quality. This unique ability would prove to be useful during the process of creating the Beatles cartoons.

Contrary to public belief, the idea for The Beatles in cartoon form did not come from Al Brodax, but it took the creative mind and business sense of Brodax to nurture the idea and bring it to fruition. It happened with the new Popeyes, and the Brodax Midas touch was about to be cast upon The Beatles. In late 1963, a man came to King Feature's carrying very bad caricatures of The Beatles. He approached the editor of cartoons at King Features, a man named Sylban Byck. Sylban didn't know or care who The Beatles were. Being a very kind and gentle man, he very politely said, "I'm not interested." Al picks up the story.

"I ventured into the Beatle thing because originally somebody came up to King with the rights to make a comic strip. This man starts to wander down the hall towards the men's room. He looked distraught, so I followed him down the hall. I asked him what was the matter. He told me he had these drawings and said he had gotten the rights to use The Beatles as cartoons. I asked him if it was just for print use, and he wasn't sure. So I jumped at the opportunity and I said, yes and I'd also like to have the right to make them move and he didn't know what I was talking about. I said I'd like to animate them. So he followed me into the men's room and I got the name of his lawyer, very nice guy from New York named Hofer. Through Mr Hofer, I was able to secure the rights to do a television show. [Author's note: Mr Hofer is rumoured to be Walter Hofer, the man who had the credit of publisher on The Beatles song, 'I Want To Hold Your Hand'.] The Beatles' management weren't very strict about approvals of anything at that time. It was too early in the game."

Having secured the rights to animate The Beatles for television, Al went out to California to have a bunch of artists do caricatures of The Beatles, but unfortunately, "I never got any that I was happy with." Nonetheless, *Variety*, the Bible of the entertainment business, announced in its 11 November 1964 issue that King Features had indeed secured the rights to The Beatles cartoons and that the series was being developed for night-time network airing in the next season. Now it was coming to the end of 1964 and Al knew that The Beatles were very hot. He also knew that the new season was quickly approaching and he needed a network and some funding for his idea. With only the preliminary drawings, and a schedule of what he wanted to do with the cartoons, Al called Anson Isaacson, the President of the A.C. Gilbert Company, a toy manufacturer, to try to get some funding. A meeting was set up in Chicago, where the company was based. "Anson was a wonderful, but busy man who kept making excuses and kept me sitting in the lobby for about twenty minutes. He would send out his secretary to say how sorry he was that he couldn't meet with me yet. After a while, he came out and asked me what I had. I showed him the pictures and the plans I had and he said, 'I'll buy it'. I never even got into his office."

Anson Isaacson proceeded to call Mr James E. Duffy, Vice President in charge of Sales at ABC Television. Isaacson told Al that he had a deal and that ABC-TV would air the show. Ed Vane, director of daytime programs in 1965, recalls that the network bought what was considered the industry standard of shows. "I think the standard buy was seventeen original shows with a right of repeat of two plays for each of them and that would fill out a fifty-two week cycle. We always assumed there would be at least one pre-emption on Saturday mornings for a golf tournament or some event that would knock the schedule off." The A.C. Gilbert Company bought half of all the allotted commercial time for the entire fifty-two-week season. Not only did Brodax now have a sponsor for his show, but he also had a network to air it. With only rough sketches and an idea, Al Brodax and his team were now ready produce the Beatles cartoons.

The formidable task of forming the characters of the animated Beatles was given to Peter Sander, a twenty-one-year-old from Bromley, Kent in England. His job was to design the characters for the series that was being done all over the world. He based his designs on photographs that he had of the group. According to Norman Kauffman of TV Cartoons Studio, "Peter formed simple characters so that we could animate them in a simple way, in the style of the 1960s. Sander saw John (as most did) as the leader of the group and in control of all situations, Paul as the most poised and stylish Beatle, George was portrayed as loose-limbed and angular, while Ringo was seen as the nice, gentle, but always rather sad-looking Beatle." Al Brodax remembers that Peter Sander had long hair and looked like a Beatle. Al recalls, "Peter was good and he was quick. Even The Beatles liked his caricatures of them."

The designs that Peter Sander came up with were compiled on what are called model sheets. Model sheets are what the storyboard artists and studios are supposed to use to create the cartoon fun. They include the basic features, gestures and tendencies of the characters to be animated. Usually the model sheets are to be used by many animators in one studio, but again, the Beatles series was far from usual. The model sheets would have to be sent to the other studios around the world that were chosen to animate the Beatles series. This created a degree of unevenness when watching the different episodes from different studios. Many of the studio people I spoke with told me that their inspiration for the movement of The Beatles in the series was The Beatles' first film, *A Hard Day's Night*. This fact is very evident when watching some of the episodes as certain scenes look as if they were copied straight from the film. Animator Dennis Hunt recalls, "We studied the movie and films of The Beatles performing. We would run the films backwards and forwards on the moviola. Videos hadn't taken over yet. We observed that John stood face-on to the audience and bobbed up and down. George and Paul swung their guitars up high and leaned towards each other. Ringo shook his hair all over as he played his drums."

Finding the scriptwriters for the show would turn out to be one of the easier tasks for the Brodax team. They called upon the talents of four people to provide the verbal actions of the characters. They were Dennis Marks, Jack Mendelsohn, Heywood (Woody) Kling and Bruce Howard. Al must have been extremely happy with his writers because the four men were the only writers of all seventy-eight Beatle episodes.

Al came up with the format of the show. He had the foresight to think about syndication when the series was in the development stages. "It was just an idea to have strong pieces that we could mix and match later on for syndication. We did a lot of theme things about subjects such as ghosts, cowboys, ships at sea, Transylvania and things of that nature." Brodax gave the writers storylines. "We had ten-minute meetings about the stories, and that was it." It was then up to the writers to write the stories and turn them into scripts.

Al would give the writers a list of songs and a list of countries and locales to work with. Jack Mendelsohn remembers that Al would send him a Beatles album and mark off the songs that they were given the rights to use in the show. "Sometimes, some of the songs that we were not allowed to use were better suited for writing an episode."

There were between two and four half-hour shows to be written for each country/locale. The two featured episodes on each weekly show would usually take place in the same country/locale. The writers would choose a country or locale, and then choose songs that they thought would fit into the story. Dennis Marks recalls that "I Want to Hold Your Hand" was a perfect example. "The song immediately suggested a love-sick octopus to me. I could see a lot of fun in animating all the 'hands' and there would be peril in the obvious underwater setting, so I suggested a shipboard setting." But could Dennis come up with three or four more shipboard stories? "I was sure I could, so Brodax gave the go-ahead for the '. . . Hand' story-line." Another shipboard story of Marks' was for the song "She Loves You". It featured a zany knife-thrower.

As far as what the writers would use to model The Beatles' characters and personalities after, both writers recall that they were provided with the Style Sheet provided by Peter Sander. The "style sheet" (often called the model sheet) is a set of rough drawings of what the characters look like, with one or two lines of character descriptions, such as "always slouches" or "laid back". As for the uniformity of scripts with four different writers involved, Ed Vane of ABC responds, "Al did explain to us that he was going to parcel out stories to a number of writers all at the same time. This meant that ABC was going to get a number of mediocre rapport writers as well as those who were good at this very unusual form of writing, the six-minute Saturday morning story. At the time, there weren't too many who were experienced, or good at it, and we were going to have to get four sets of them. That made us churn. But we did think the heat of The Beatles at the time and the appeal of the music would conquer whatever story shortcomings there would be."

Stories had to be approved by Al Brodax, sent to ABC-TV for approval, then back to the writers to write the scripts. Script approval went the same route, "sometimes with suggested changes, sometimes with definite changes ordered, and sometimes with no changes," recalls Dennis Marks. "ABC had right of approval on virtually everything," remembers Ed Vane. "Contractually, we had total control, but it was an illusion because if we were to make the air dates that were set, there could not be an awful lot of quarrelling about a sentence in a script. While we were battling about a word, the war would be lost and there would be no film to show on a Saturday morning." There was the occasional rejected storyline, but no rejected scripts.

Having found a studio to produce the cartoons, it was now time to find the "Beatle" voices. There had been rumours The Beatles themselves would provide the voices. "Never," recalls Al Brodax. "The thing that attracted them most to the series was all they had to do was sign a piece of paper and no work was involved. However, Ringo liked animation and he did come to the studio now and then to see what was happening."

Al already knew that he wanted to use Paul Frees to do some voices. Paul was a giant in the animation industry. Throughout his many years in show business, Paul Frees would provide some of the most recognizable cartoon voices in history, including such favourites as Boris Badenov from *Rocky And Bullwinkle*, Inspector Fenwick from the *Dudley Do-Right* show and Ignatz Mouse on the *Krazy Kat* cartoon.

Lance Percival was already in the entertainment business when he was cast to do voices for the Beatles series. Lance tells the story: "I knew The Beatles in the 1960s because I was in a hot television show called *That Was the Week That Was* when the series got going. I did a couple of TV slots with them in the early days and then I made a few records with their producer, George Martin. All this had nothing to do with being cast in the cartoon, as they had no say in it." Lance remembers being sent down to audition for the part. "I got the job through my agent, who sent me for an audition with Big Al Brodax. The fact that I knew The Beatles *may* have helped, but I auditioned, as did many others, and I was asked to play the parts of Paul McCartney and Ringo Starr." It was also decided that Paul Frees would provide the voices of John Lennon and George Harrison.

Any parts that were to be spoken by a female were provided by Englishwoman Jackie Newman. All other incidental characters were voiced by Paul Frees as well. Ed Vane of ABC says, "I think it was either May or June of 1965 when I went to London with Al Brodax and Paul Frees. We met Lance Percival there. Since ABC had right of approval of what the voices should sound like, we had to listen to their various attempts at coming up with proper voices for each of the four. There was never any attempt to do an impression of The Beatles. These had to be cartoon voices. After many experiments, and a lot of trial and error, four voices were selected. They were approved by Al and me and whatever clearances were necessary with The Beatles management." Lance played Paul McCartney "bright and cheerful," and Ringo Starr was portrayed as "the low-voiced fall guy for the humour." "I made the Ringo voice a little more Birmingham, and more slow," recalls Lance (slipping easily into the exact voice of the Ringo character). "Ringo probably thought, what the hell was that? But it was an accent that could be easily understood in America." George Dunning of TVC was quoted as saying that, "Paul Frees portrayed John Lennon in a Rex Harrison voice, which he thought was quite good." Scriptwriter Jack Mendelsohn recalls that when Frees did the voice of Inspector Fenwick on the *Dudley Do-Right* show, he was essentially "doing his Eric Blore impersonation." Eric Blore was a character actor in the 1930s and 1940s. "He loved doing that voice and used a modified version for the voice of John Lennon. While it was perfect for the Inspector, it was just not right for a twenty-five-year-old character."

In selecting the voices, another decision was made which turned out to be very controversial. It was decided by all that the voices to be spoken by the cartoon Beatles would be "Americanized". Brodax recalls that the reason for this is because he didn't think the kids in the United States would understand The Beatles' hometown language of Liverpudlian. "That's why I used the American, Paul Frees," recalls Al. Lance Percival recalls "pulling back" on the accent a bit for American television. "I've been in movies where the same thing happens. The producers had to sell it to a big market, so the solution was to put in just enough accent to make them sound English.

When Paul finally saw the cartoons, he didn't recognize his character's voice. But they all had to understand that King Features was not looking for a genuine Liverpudlian accent." Jack Stokes, director for the series at TVC, says that the voices sounded nothing like The Beatles' own Liverpool accent: "Just some daft idea of how we English sound to Americans. The Beatles hated them." In fact, not many people over in England liked the voice characterizations that were used for the series. "That's true, as far as the English were concerned," remembers Brodax. "But here in America, people understood them. They would never have gotten the ratings they got if we would have used Liverpudlian voices. In the beginning, The Beatles loved the series, as I remember it, because of the high ratings we got. As the years went by, more recently, they weren't all that crazy about it because they didn't really like the voices I used." John Coates recalls that, "It was because of the voices picked that The Beatles cartoons were not allowed to be shown in England. The decision was made by none other than Brian Epstein himself."

Amidst the controversy, the soundtracks for the series were recorded at a studio located at 18 Rodmarton Street. "It was parallel to Baker Street," as Lance recalls, "which must have given Sherlock Holmes something to chew over!" Generally, the actors stuck to the scripts except for the odd word change here and there. "We never strayed from the scripts," recalls Percival. "I put in ideas all the time. Some of them were kept in the soundtrack in the end but some were edited out." In fact, one of the most memorable aspects of the cartoon is the infectious laugh that Ringo would usually do in each of the cartoons. It was sort of a "huh huh huh huh, yeah." That laugh was a complete accident. Lance Percival remembers that the laugh was his experiment that was kept in the soundtrack only to become a staple of the series.

Lance recalls the first time The Beatles saw the cartoons, "We [who did the voices] went to see it at a small cinema in Soho for a first showing, which The Beatles attended. [Author's note: It was actually shown at TVC Cartoons' animation studio.] They arrived in a big black limousine. They rushed up the stairs and sat down to watch. They were naturally very curious to know who played which voices. Paul McCartney in particular was very enthusiastic. I think they really enjoyed it all."

Come that 25 September '65 TV premiere, the two cartoons shown on the morning were "I Want to Hold Your Hand" and "A Hard Day's Night". But would the popularity of the real-life Beatles translate into ratings for the animated Beatles? This was a huge risk on the part of ABC television. This was the first time in the history of television that real life entertainers were being portrayed as cartoon characters, and ABC was well aware of that. "Yes, of course it was a gamble," recalls Ed Vane. "The conventional wisdom at that time was that real people don't animate well and if you're going to animate real people, why don't you just go out and get the real people themselves. We figured that was well worth the challenge because The Beatles were so big. I had four kids and The Beatles' music was playing morning, noon and night." With fingers crossed, everyone involved awaited the ratings for the first show.

The ratings did not come in until a couple of weeks after the premiere, but when they did, there was much to celebrate. The ratings showed that *The Beatles* series opened with an almost unprecedented fifty-two share (actually 51.9) of the viewing audience. "Fred Silverman was going crazy because of it," recalls Al Brodax, referring to the Vice President of Daytime for rival network CBS. "He was standing on his head because we made a dent in CBS' morning line-up. And they thought ABC would never do that."

The Beatles at Shea Stadium

by Sean Egan

The Beatles At Shea Stadium has rather been ignored even by those who have set out to chronicle only The Beatles' movie and TV *oeuvre*.

That it is a legitimate part of that oeuvre cannot be in doubt, even though The Beatles' company Subafilms Ltd and Epstein's NEMS Enterprises Ltd co-produced it with Sullivan Productions, Inc, a company owned by Ed Sullivan, the TV show host whose programme had been such a big part of The Beatles' conquest of America. The film was first shown in the UK on the BBC (when it still only had one TV channel) on 1 March 1966. The States had to wait until 10 January 1967 before ABC gave it its American premiere, although at least it was in colour: the BBC transmission and its repeat on 27 August '66 were in black-and-white – colour broadcasts wouldn't arrive in the group's home country until '69.

It made sense to create a record for posterity of what was a high-water mark in both The Beatles' career so far and in entertainment *per se*. Never before had there been such a public demand for entertainers that it merited – even necessitated – the throwing open of a sports stadium to accommodate it. There would be attendances for concerts subsequently that dwarfed the estimated 55,600 that crammed into Queens' William A. Shea Municipal Stadium, home of the New York Mets baseball team, on Sunday 15 August 1965 to see the Fab Four. But it was the Shea concert that paved the way for those later, bigger gigs. And those gigs couldn't hope to match the cultural impact or capture the public imagination of a concert that witnessed the very apotheosis of Beatlemania: a wall of screaming, hysterical (mostly) females drowning out the very sound they had ostensibly come to hear. For the night's work, The Beatles picked up the staggering sum of $160,000.

The documentary starts with The Beatles' voices talking about the scale of the concert over shots of the stadium, first empty, then full. Though they provide plenty of commentary, all of which seems exclusive to the film, the visuals of the band members are restricted to the gig and events leading up to it: there is no depiction of them talking because The Beatles are clearly considered so famous at this point that no explanation is required of whether it is John, Paul, George or Ringo speaking. A jump cut then occurs showing the group performing the last song of the evening, "I'm Down". John by now is fully into what Ringo called his "cracked up" state of the night, playing the electric piano with his elbows. Both he and George are noticeably on top of the world, grinning wildly as they share a microphone to sing the backing vocals. The four sweat-drenched men then take a bow and depart the stage. This is followed by the title, and the caption "Filmed and recorded as it happened on a summer's evening in New York City".

Not quite. Though the presence of no fewer than twelve cameras meant that the visuals would certainly be up to par, the sound quality of this concert was never going to be good. Though there are dirty great speakers beside the band, the Fabs could still hardly be heard above the screaming. McCartney has even suggested that The Beatles were plugged into the PA system that was normally reserved for announcements about people's lost property and the like, although there seems to be dispute over this. Though poor audio quality would do on the night, it was hardly the kind of thing that would sound good coming out of television speakers. In January 1966 therefore, The Beatles did some doctoring work at a London studio that specialized in dubbing films.

We are indebted to the scholarly work of Beatles expert Mark Lewisohn for the knowledge that Paul put new bass parts on "Dizzy Miss Lizzy", "Can't Buy Me Love", "Baby's In Black" and "I'm Down", that John overdubbed new organ on to "I'm

Down" and that the group re-recorded "I Feel Fine" and "Help!" from scratch. Meanwhile, the version of "Act Naturally" heard in the film is simply the studio version from *Help!* dubbed in, while "Twist And Shout" actually originates not from Shea but the Hollywood Bowl concert that took place fifteen days later. The Beatles realized that they couldn't make the two new recordings too good: though the quality is not disgraceful, they cannily produced versions of "I Feel Fine" and "Help!" scruffy enough to be plausible as being from Shea. An apparently deliberate clue to the doctoring is inserted into the documentary in the form of a shot where Ringo is heard singing despite the fact that he has his mouth closed.

The documentary shows us DJ Murray the K introducing support act the King Curtis Band fronted by a troupe called the Discotheque Dancers, through whose act the girls in the audience – with only one act on their mind – scream throughout. We also see performances by Brenda Holloway and Sounds Incorporated, though not sadly from the most interesting additional entertainment, The Young Rascals. The milling of the audiences and the work of the many police officers on duty then occupy the cameras as the unseen Beatles talk about their fans, the gig and America. We then get some backstage Beatles footage: flying in on their helicopter, then smoking and jamming in their dressing room. It is revealed that the set-list was drawn up at virtually the last moment.

"Great American" Ed Sullivan is introduced and in turn introduces the band: "Honoured by their country, decorated by their Queen and loved here in America – here are The Beatles!" Holding their instruments, the group trot across the pitch to the stage at second base, dressed in stylish militaristic outfits – khaki jackets and black trousers – and shake hands with Sullivan. They tune up and deliver some "Hello's" into the mics before launching into "Twist And Shout". For the record, the full set-list of the concert comprised a mere dozen songs: "Twist And Shout", "She's A Woman", "I Feel Fine", "Dizzy Miss Lizzy", "Ticket to Ride", "Everybody's Trying To Be My Baby", "Can't Buy Me Love", "Baby's In Black", "Act Naturally", "A Hard Day's Night", "Help!" and "I'm Down". Even "Twist And Shout" was a truncated version. For some reason, the vast majority of these songs are Lennon vocals, with Paul getting three, plus his duet with John, "Baby's In Black", and George and Ringo one apiece. Ultimately George fared worst. His rendering of "Everybody's Trying To Be My Baby" was excluded from the film completely.

Paul announces the next number, "I Feel Fine". John makes a sarcastic reference to the American Frankenstein albums as he announces "Dizzy Miss Lizzy". This version, by the way, however doctored and low-fi, is preferable to the *Help!* version, that irritating ringing guitar lick played down in favour of Paul's newly dubbed propulsive bass riff. The performance is intercut with the sort of shots of girls fainting, screaming and becoming distraught at their own happiness that proliferate throughout the film.

At one point in the performance of "Ticket To Ride", George seems to be chatting to Ringo. Starr turns out to be up next – at least in the documentary: his "Act Naturally" displaces George's excised vocal showcase. The first Paul vocal of the documentary follows, "Can't Buy Me Love". In the introduction to "Baby's In Black" John begins to waffle a little, once again referring to the American *Beatles VI* album ("I 'aven't gorrit"), then pointing at a girl vainly trying to elude the cops in a sprint in the direction of the stage ("Ahh! Look at 'er!"). In the introduction to "A Hard Day's Night" (which song was actually preceded by "Act Naturally" on the night), John babbles in mock foreign. For the first time in the documentary, the music is interrupted, with The Beatles philosophizing about their success and music over the song. Epstein – to be seen in this segment standing proprietarily beside the stage, chewing gum – is also heard. In the lead-up to "Help!", Paul provokes the crowd to boo the police as they round up another stray Beatlemaniac. Lennon stares into his face in mock amazement as he does.

A recurrence of the "I'm Down" footage follows, with commentary over the top this time. An aerial shot zooms away from the stadium and the end credits roll.

We shouldn't have a problem with the overdubbing of the instrumentation in this film. Live albums – even if not tampered with via studio re-recording (the norm) – are always guilty of dishonesty. Even on the rare occasions when musicians can forebear from improving live recordings by correcting bum notes and out-of-tune passages in the studio, the very act of bringing up to optimum levels various elements of the multi-tracks (standard) means that what is heard on the record is not usually what was heard by the audience on the night. Even with the "corrections", *The Beatles At Shea Stadium* is a serviceable and interesting snapshot of the time and of the nature of Beatlemania.

If anything, it could be longer. At forty-eight minutes – tailor-made for an American TV slot of an hour, including commercials – it doesn't even feature all twelve of The Beatles' numbers ("She's A Woman" is the other cutting room casualty), so the over-representation of the support acts – even if Cannibal and the Headhunters and the Young Rascals don't make the cut – is irritating. More space should have been devoted to footage of the group in their leisure time: the offstage material here is simply too fleeting and unrevealing.

What one is most struck by about *The Beatles At Shea Stadium* is that the events captured on it are a depiction of a time that is gone forever. Young girls still like pop groups, of course, but their reaction to them today is far more knowing and composed than seen here. Partly this is due to the changing nature of the female sex following the emancipation created by the Pill, partly it's because people today are far more cognizant of the fact that their idols have feet of clay due to no aspect of their professional or private lives being considered beyond media coverage.

The Beatles At Shea Stadium is currently not commercially available, one of many items on Beatles fan wishlists (which a DVD of *Let It Be* and mono CDs of the albums from *Help!* through to *Sgt. Pepper* . . . usually top) for future release by Apple Corps.

MAGICAL MYSTERY TOUR

The appraisal of The Beatles' 1967 TV film Magical Mystery Tour *below comes from Chris Ingham's* The Rough Guide To The Beatles, *a book that constitutes a thoroughly enjoyable primer on the group. It is a somewhat more considered assessment of the reason for the film's overall aesthetic failure than the sentiments conveyed in the* Daily Mail's *front page story reproduced earlier (see p.156).*

Magical Mystery Tour

by Chris Ingham

After they made the decision to stop touring, The Beatles discussed other ways to reach their public when they weren't releasing records. The obvious answer appeared to be television. Specials by entertainers like Frank Sinatra were commonplace in the 1960s and The Beatles saw a chance to gatecrash the medium and do something unusual at the same time.

Paul had been visiting Jane Asher in the US. In a park in Denver, with Mal Evans, he came up with the idea of a charabanc trip peopled by a motley bunch of character actors, comics, musicians and freaks, a Magical Mystery Tour where the participants would create the film: they'd plan a few activities en route, write a few songs, just let things happen organically and shoot the ensuing fun. There was possibly an element of Ken Kesey and his Merry Pranksters about the idea, too. Kesey, famously, had been wandering around America with a bus full of hippies compiling a movie (that never appeared) called *The Merry Pranksters Search For A Cool Place*. Paul, who'd just been hanging with Jefferson Airplane in San Francisco, would undoubtedly have heard of it.

On the plane back to the UK, Paul and Mal drew up a pie-chart of what might take place in an hour-long film – a song here, a dream-sequence there – and each Beatle would be given a scene to write or a song slot to fill. Shot in colour, the project would eventually also yield an unusual six-song double EP with a lavish book of pictures, cartoons and lyrics, making a pricey but delightful Christmas bonanza from the Fabs to their fans.

Planning began under Brian Epstein. Budgets were approved and the title song was recorded in April. After Brian's sudden death, The Beatles decided to continue, with much of the organizing, directing and editing left to Paul. But the hiring of crew and talent was a skill none of The Beatles possessed and it was rather haphazardly done. Little thought was given to whether the cast would mix or even understand the concept, let alone whether anybody would generate the kind of footage they needed.

Nevertheless, there were some good ideas in the mix and The Beatles attacked the project with gusto. Shooting took place in Devon, Cornwall and on an abandoned airbase near Maidstone, Kent. The cast included Scottish poet Ivor Cutler, music hall comic Nat Jackley, and absurdist rockers The Bonzo Dog Doo Dah Band. The budget was £40,000, but the anticipated two-week edit ended up taking eleven weeks and Paul approached the BBC with little time to make the Christmas slot he was after. They got Boxing Night (and a second, colour show on BBC2 on 5 January) although, because of the unusual nature of the film, they were paid only £9,000 by the BBC. (It was subsequently sold all round the world, however, and was shown in cinemas in the US, generating millions of dollars in rentals.)

When it premiered on BBC1 it was shown in black and white, which rendered sequences like the psychedelic cloud ballet that accompanies "Flying" utterly pointless, but its main failing was its inappropriateness for its slot. More French New Wave than family Christmas viewing, it baffled a British public expecting easily digestible light entertainment from the loveable moptops. Reviews panned it for being a giant home movie, self-indulgent and embarrassing. Seen now, in colour, and judged in the avant garde, stoned spirit in which it was made, it fares slightly better, but is undoubtedly flabby and, generally, dull.

Certain sequences remain entertaining, though. John's cameo as a waiter serving Ringo's corpulent Aunt Jessie a wheelbarrow full of spaghetti is one. Paul's "Fool On The Hill" interlude (shot in late October in Nice, France while editing was well underway) has a sweet trippiness to it, and the closing big production job on "Your Mother Should Know", where The

Fab Four turn Fred Astaire and high-kick dressed in white tuxedos, is cute. Less engaging today are the "I Am The Walrus" segment, which looks like an amateurish video, and the boys' capering about as wizards in the clouds, controlling the tour.

But Paul and John remained proud of the results. "I enjoyed the fish and chip quality," said John, "the fact that we went out with a load of freaks and tried to make a film is great, you know?"

"I really had to carry the can when it got bad reviews," says Paul. "But by the same argument I can now take credit for the cool little film I still think it is."

Yellow Submarine

Premiered: 17 July 1968

by Sean Egan with Donald Sauter

Yellow Submarine is the movie The Beatles started out being uninterested in – even resentful of – but were ultimately won over to by the quality of what was produced. A question remains, however, as to who was responsible for that quality.

The movie contract signed by The Beatles with United Artists in 1963 called for the production of three feature-length pictures. But though *A Hard Day's Night* and (to a lesser extent) *Help!* had been critical and commercial successes, the group had begun to lose interest in making movies. Edgy playwright Joe Orton had written them a screenplay called *Up Against It* to which their largely still clean-cut image was not suited. They also went so far as to buy the rights to Richard Condon's Wild West novel *A Talent For Loving* before deciding they weren't happy with the script. Progress on fulfilling the last part of their UA contract dragged on so much that before long they were so immersed in the making of what was intended as their masterpiece, *Sgt. Pepper ...*, that a new film was the last of The Beatles' priorities. Eventually someone – perhaps reminded of the American Beatles cartoon series, which had only recently ceased production – hit upon the idea of an animated Beatles movie and *Yellow Submarine* was born as an ingenious way of fulfilling the film contract hanging over the Fabs' heads without the group having to do much actual work themselves.

Logically enough, the producer was Al Brodax, the man behind that Beatles cartoon series. As with the TV programme, on *Yellow Submarine* Brodax collaborated with UK animation house TVC. Also as per the TV series, he had to fly by the seat of his pants somewhat: he was given only eleven months and a budget of $1m to deliver the final product. It's said that up to forty writers contributed to the script, but the credited ones are "Lee Minoff and Al Brodax; Jack Mendelsohn and Erich Segal", with Lee Minoff acknowledged as providing the "original story". Erich Segal was later to become famous for the novel *Love Story*. Czech Heinz Edelmann provided the designs for the movie, which a massive team of up to 200 animators used as their template. Those designs recognized the fact that The Beatles were no longer clean-shaven moptops in suits and reflected the beards, moustaches, glasses and outlandish clothes that now came with The Beatles' image package.

Though The Beatles initially pledged to provide the voices to their animated selves, they hummed and hawed to such an extent (initially for good reason, traumatized by Epstein's death) that actors had to be brought in to do the dialogue. John Clive rendered John, Geoffrey Hughes Paul, and Paul Angelis George and Ringo. Apart from the intangible benefits of their name and their blessing, the one thing The Beatles did give the makers of the film was songs: four new ones and their pick of the oldies. (The producers chose mainly latter-day Beatles fare: there was nothing used from the days before *Rubber Soul*.)

So it would seem cut-and-dried that though it was critically well-received (notoriously hard-to-please movie critic Pauline Kael was impressed) and reasonably commercially successful (although not being given a full release by Rank after the distributor erroneously concluded its opening three weeks had not generated good business hampered its chances in The Beatles' home country), *Yellow Submarine* was a Beatles movie in name only.

And yet the story immediately seems more complex than that. One is immediately struck by the fact that the tone of a lot of the movie feels like it comes straight out of John Lennon's singular brain, or at least one of his books. For example, take the lines at the beginning, "Once upon a time, or maybe twice" and "80,000 leagues beneath the sea it lay. Or lie, I'm not too sure." Visually too, Pepperland – a strange place whose landscape is littered with iconography rather than buildings (busts, profiles, statues, Sgt. Pepper drum skins) – also puts one in mind of both wacky Beatles humour and the drawings in Lennon's two books of verse and doodle, *In His Own Write* (1964) and *A Spaniard In The Works* (1965). This could be coincidence of course, or even the result of deliberate immersion on the part of the creators in the humour of the Fabs (Alun Owen, scriptwriter of *A Hard Day's Night*, famously followed the band around on their public engagements to get a handle on them). There was also the fact that Segal would seem to be cut from the same cloth as Lennon. When Brodax tried to persuade the reluctant Segal to come on board, he pointed out the recent astronomical sales of *Sgt. Pepper's Lonely Hearts Club Band*. When Segal dryly replied, "Mrs Pepper must be pleased", Brodax thought that this was exactly the sort of thing that Lennon himself might say.

Certainly conventional wisdom has it that any similarity to The Beatles' humour and vision in this movie is coincidental. For instance, *Beatles Book Monthly*, June 1988, (p. 4) claims that after paying little attention to what was happening with the film and providing the four new numbers virtually under duress, when The Beatles actually saw *Yellow Submarine* they were shocked that Epstein had written off the project so casually. The piece said, "In separate conversations with me at the time, both John and Paul expressed belated disappointment that they hadn't involved themselves far more actively in the production . . . John was particularly taken with Minoff's original creation of 'Pepperland'. One could easily imagine Lennon himself creating belligerent 'blue meanies' and menacing 'apple bonkers'."

In *The Love You Make*, the memoir of Apple director, Peter Brown, the author states, "The Beatles had virtually nothing to do with this animated film, aside from composing a few songs for it when it was almost completed." *The Beatles A To Z*, a handy reference book by Friede, Titone and Weiner, says (p. 233): "Though The Beatles were not actively involved with the production, they did make an appearance in the final sequence."

Bob Hieronimus is a *Yellow Submarine* expert and author of

the book *Inside The "Yellow Submarine":The Making Of The Beatles' Animated Classic* (2002). A newspaper article about him appearing in the *The Baltimore Sun* on 26 September 1999 says: "One of the first things [Hieronimus] discovered is that the success of *Yellow Submarine* really has little to do with The Beatles themselves, except as a source of inspiration . . ." Their permission for United Artists to make *Yellow Submarine* the third of their movies was given, the article said "grudgingly". It added, "They wouldn't work on the film . . . fearing the worst."

Yet the 1999 documentary *The Yellow Submarine Sails Again* – made as an infomercial to publicize the release of the film on video that year – tells a very different story: "John Lennon and Paul McCartney would sometimes call up producer Al Brodax with script suggestions. One morning at 3 a.m., John called and said, 'Wouldn't it be great if Ringo was followed down the street by a yellow submarine?' And the suggestion made it into the script."

The same anecdote is to be found in Nicholas Schaffner's *The Beatles Forever*, first published in 1978, subsequently revised. It even goes a little further, actually giving John credit for the basic plot of the movie: "According to producer Al Brodax, the plot was inspired by a three a.m. phone call from John Lennon, who said: "Wouldn't it great if Ringo was followed down the street by a yellow submarine?" Additionally, what are we to make of the fact that the movie contains what seems curiously like a reference to the first time John Lennon and Yoko Ono met: the elevation to the sky where the film's characters are met with the giant word "Yes" recalls Lennon's first meeting with Ono at the Indica Gallery in November 1966 where he was charmed by a Yoko exhibit called *Ceiling Painting* wherein someone climbing to the top of a ladder was met by the word "Yes", a positivism he found refreshing. This incident was not yet public knowledge – nor was Lennon's burgeoning relationship with Ono – at the time the *Yellow Submarine* movie was being made, so we are once again left with a scenario of either remarkable coincidence or direct Lennon input.

Lennon himself laid claim to significant swathes of the ideas to be found in the movie. In a 1971 interview with Peter McCabe and Robert D. Schonfeld, recorded in the book *John Lennon:*

For The Record, he said, "Brodax got half the *Yellow Submarine* out of my mouth. You know the idea for the Hoover? The machine that sucks people up? All those were my ideas. They used to come to the studio and sort of chat . . . 'Hi, John, old bean. Got any ideas for the film?' And I'd just spout out all this stuff, and they went off and did it."

John's bitterness hadn't noticeably faded by 1980 when he talked with David Sheff of *Playboy.* Asked about the song "Hey Bulldog", Lennon replied, "That's me, cuz of the *Yellow Submarine* people, who were gross animals apart from the guy who drew the paintings for the movie. They lifted all the ideas for the movie out of our heads and didn't give us any credit."

Sheff's original interview tapes, as aired on the massive BBC radio series *The Lost Lennon Tapes* (broadcast from 1988–92) provide even more detail. Here, Lennon talks of "Erich Segal writing Lennonesque lines straight from *In His Own Write* style" and says, "But they got all the ideas for the glove in the sky and the thing that sucks people up was my idea. They said, have you got any monsters? I said, yeah, there's Horace the vacuum cleaner in the swimming pool which was a thing you could buy, and it went round the pool sucking up the things, you know. And I said that could be a monster that sucks . . . And all things like that, they just took them and never credited."

Given Lennon's propensity for over-dramatizing things in interviews (the 1971 *Rolling Stone* interview being the most famous example), as well as his notoriously bad memory, it would seem safe to assume that he was going a little overboard when he claimed, "Brodax got *half* the *Yellow Submarine* out of my mouth," and that they lifted "*all* the ideas for the movie from out of our heads." (This writer's italics.) Still, the fact that he had so much resentment twelve years after the fact certainly makes one wonder if The Beatles were so dissociated from the movie as we have often been led to believe.

Anyone who's interested can see John's pool vacuum – actually called Percy, not Horace – in *Beatles Book Monthly,* No. 52, November 1967, p. 12. It accompanies an article called "John At Home, part two". There is even a paragraph devoted to "Horace". Discussing the Lennons' swimming pool, it says, that a certain Percy was the only one in it at the time: "Percy is the machine that keeps the pool clean, and slowly travels around the surface, trailing long plastic tubes which twitch around the bottom of the pool. If you don't have a Percy, apparently, that horrible green slime grows on the bottom and sides and dirt floats on the top."

Whatever the provenance of the ideas and visions in *Yellow Submarine*, Lennon did concede, "I liked the movie." All of the group eventually decided they liked the cartoon enough to give it their overt blessing by appearing at the end in a section that is less than a minute long but is good-spirited and makes sufficient references to the film we've just seen to make us think they give a damn about it. It also seems to indicate that the bitterness Lennon felt in the aforementioned later interviews was not present at the time, another thing that leads one to conclude that Lennon might have been exaggerating a tad in his claims of ideas harvesting.

The makers of the movie had the luxury of being more or less completely self-indulgent. With success in some form guaranteed by The Beatles' name, songs and images being attached to the project, they could engage in the equivalent of a giant doodling exercise. While there was a narrative – the blue meanies take over Pepperland, Old Fred (voiced by Lance Percival, who was Paul and Ringo in the cartoon series) is sent to get help, enlists The Beatles, whose uncanny similarity to Pepperland's imprisoned musical heroes Sgt. Pepper's Lonely Hearts Club Band is felt to be something that can rouse the oppressed masses – it is wafer thin, thus enabling (or necessitating) all sorts of divergences and non sequiturs as it leisurely makes its way to its denouement. Thus we are treated to a stream of utterly surreal imagery and scenarios, such as corridors with endless doors stretching into the distance in Ringo's house, seas of time, science, monsters, holes, etc, banks of television screens sitting on plains with no apparent source of energy, holes that you can pick up and put in your pocket, etc etc. Some have posited that nobody could come up with such imagery if they hadn't been on an acid trip, and certainly such surrealism and weirdness were in the air in the form of album cover art, advertising and the like in the acid-drenched year in which the movie was started, yet the imagery is not much more far-out than that to be found in

Disney's *Fantasia* (1940, by which time it is true that LSD had been synthesized for the first time, but one assumes that it hadn't made its way to the Disney animators). Beatles references are regularly shoehorned into the script (Fred says to Ringo, "Won't you please, please help me", the sea of holes prompts a mention of the song "Fixing A Hole", and so on), as are Beatles songs. Mostly, this seems contrived, as when "When I'm Sixty-Four" is used in a sequence where The Beatles artificially age, while Nowhere Man becomes a Pepperland character. However, "Eleanor Rigby" is used as a backdrop for a powerful and quasi-poignant section set in our world, and the use of a "Within You Without You"-like piece of Indian music as a sort of signature theme for George is funny. The new songs actually feel more substantial when set against and synchronized with the imagery (and George's "It's All Too Much" is far more bearable at its truncated length in the film). The fictional Beatles' voices by the way are quite good, with Paul's especially true to the original.

Critic Pauline Kael said of *Yellow Submarine* that it was "charming." Alexander Walker, a film critic almost as well-known in his native UK as Kael is in her native US, said, "Its inventiveness never flags." Others might be more inclined to the view of the newspaper reporter who snapped at McCartney after the film's premiere, "What a boring waste of time." One can see his point: the endless parade of surreal imagery becomes wearying, the humour is droll rather than laugh-out-loud hilarious and the film feels essentially soulless.

Whatever your opinion of the aesthetics involved, the objective observer will surely come to the conclusion that The Beatles – or even possibly just John Lennon – deserved some sort of acknowledgment for creative input.

The film incidentally did not fulfil The Beatles' contract with United Artists: though the studio was happy enough to release it, it pointed out to the group that they were still owed a film on the grounds that the contract called for The Beatles to appear themselves in pictures, not their cartoon equivalents.

Based on an original article by Donald Sauter, first published on: *www.geocities.com/donaldsauter/index.html#beatles*

LET IT BE

Premiered: 13 May 1970

Let It Be, *The Beatles' final movie, could not have been a greater contrast to their debut film,* A Hard Day's Night, *which for all its revolutionary pretend-realism presented the group as moptopped moppets. As The Beatles and the world left behind the 1960s, it was to enter an era that was far less tolerant of artifice or shallowness than the world into which* A Hard Day's Night *had been released.* Let It Be *fitted right into this new mood of realism. It might be far less celebrated a film, but it is even more revolutionary than the* "Citizen Kane *of juke box movies": what other artists would dare sanction release of a movie that was a merciless, unsentimental document of them tearing themselves apart?* Let It Be *showed The Beatles trying to make an album but demonstrating in their raggedy playing, John's greater interest in his ever-present old lady than the band – manifested by he and Yoko contemptuously waltzing around the studio while the others played "I Me Mine" – George's seething resentment of what he felt to be Paul's bossiness ("I'll play whatever you want me to play. Or I won't play at all. Whatever it is that will please you, I'll do it") not a band giving vent to creativity but trying to hold themselves together in vain. Perhaps they only allowed release of* Let It Be *because they knew the end was now determined, but even so the integrity they had shown throughout their career shone through in the decision.*

In this extract from Bob Neaverson's acclaimed book The Beatles Movies, *we present a history and analysis of the film.*

Let It Be

by Bob Neaverson

The historical development of the *Let It Be* movie is nothing if not unconventional, not least because it evolved from far humbler origins, as a short television documentary film initially intended to detail The Beatles' rehearsals for a separate and more elaborate television special which never came into fruition. To understand the genesis of the film, one has to return to 1968 and the awkward and disagreeable atmosphere which pervaded the recording sessions for *The Beatles*. The lack of collaboration and increasing reliance on studio technology (and quite possibly evolving personal differences) had convinced McCartney (by now the prime mover in The Beatles' projects) that the flagging group needed to unite and energize itself by returning to their rock 'n' roll roots, producing songs which, bereft of the studio trickery of old, could be performed live. With this in mind, McCartney proposed that The Beatles should work towards putting together a live performance of new material; not a live tour (none of the group could face returning to the rigours of the stadium circuit), but a recorded "one-off" live performance of new songs which could then be broadcast worldwide as a television special and released as an album. The underlying concept of making a film of a live performance was not new to The Beatles, who had already invested in a concert film for television, *The Beatles at Shea Stadium* (1965). But where would this new live perform-ance take place? In the spirit of underground "happenings", suggestions were made for suitably "far-out" locations, but no single venue could be decided upon by the increasingly individually-minded Beatles. One of the first suggestions, which originated from Apple Films' chief Denis O'Dell, was that the group should play at a disused flour mill near the Thames, but this idea was eventually rejected. Another of his ideas was for the group to play on board an ocean liner, but this was vetoed for practical reasons. By far the most interesting idea was that the group should play in a Roman amphitheatre in North Africa. As chance would have it, O'Dell had seen an Italian opera company performing *Orestes* in Tripoli, and came up with the fascinating idea of getting The Beatles to perform a live set in front of an Arab audience. As O'Dell recalls, "It was a wonderful, open-air amphitheatre, right by the sea, with the most incredible acoustic sound . . . John flipped. He thought it would be incredible . . . but you could never get all four of them to agree."

Getting agreement on film projects was something that had been difficult with The Beatles for some time. As O'Dell remembers, "What I wanted to do dearly, and more than anything else, was a major feature film with The Beatles." In 1968, he had hit upon an intriguing idea for a third Beatles feature film, that they should make a filmed version of the Tolkein classic, *Lord of the Rings,* for which he attempted to secure the rights and the services of a major director. One possibility was David Lean, who found the idea fascinating but was unavailable. He also approached Stanley Kubrick. Meanwhile he managed to get The Beatles interested whilst on their trip to visit the Maharishi in Rishikesh, India. "John was really excited about doing the music for it," and the group began to earmark parts for themselves. However, having read the books and met with both Lennon and McCartney over lunch at MGM studios, Kubrick maintained that he felt the film was unmakeable, and eventually the project fell through.

When, in late 1968, it was finally agreed to begin rehearsals for the live performance television special (to be shot at an unspecified location), O'Dell suggested that the preparations should be filmed for a separate half-hour television documentary showing The Beatles at work. "I thought it would be an awful waste not to put everything on film." With this in mind, it was decided that Twickenham film studios would provide an ideal location for the rehearsals and Michael Lindsay-Hogg (who had worked on several Beatles promos) was hired, to document the sessions by impassively capturing The Beatles "*au naturel*". There were to be few concessions to classical documentary techniques, the idea being that merely showing The Beatles rehearsing and interacting would hold the audience's interest and provide insight into the group's relationships and activities. Lindsay-Hogg explained later: "I didn't want to make a straight documentary. I figured if we just showed them working, we'd learn quite a bit about them." In keeping with this premise, "staged" visual concessions would be kept to a minimum (a few coloured lights to provide ambience) and the rehearsals would be shot in their totality, complete with the talking, rapping and humorous banter that went on between songs.

Filming (on 16mm), began at Twickenham studios, on the first day of rehearsals 2 January 1969. However, the sessions got off to a terrible start, with The Beatles struggling desperately to find a new musical direction. After a week of bickering, boredom and apathy, George Harrison snapped. Following an argument with McCartney he quit the stage and, with a non-committal parting shot of "See you round the clubs", he returned to his bungalow in Esher.

Harrison's disappearance inevitably created something of a dilemma for the film-makers. However, Denis O'Dell wisely recognized the importance of "keeping the remains of [the project] together", and instructed Lindsay-Hogg to spend the next few days on close-shots of McCartney, Lennon and Starr which could later be edited into the film. Accordingly, in the days following Harrison's departure, the remaining members of the group returned to Twickenham and went about their business in much the same fashion as when Starr had "left" during the White Album sessions, with the cameras still rolling. But when, on 15 January, Harrison returned to the fold, he did so on condition that the live concert should be axed and that The Beatles should instead make an album of the songs which they had been working on in the newly-built recording studio at their Apple headquarters. Mark Lewisohn claims: "It was at this point, and this point only, that the footage shot at Twickenham for a 'Beatles at Work' television production turned instead into the start of a feature film idea, to be called – like the album they'd now be making – *Get Back*." The Beatles may have felt that, since the idea for the live concert had been jettisoned, they should instead appease their audience with something more substantial than a thirty-minute television documentary. Not only that, producing the film through Apple (Denis O'Dell and Neil Aspinall would helm the production and The Beatles would retain the role of executive producers) meant that they had ultimate control of the film's style and content. Moreover, they still owed, or possibly felt they owed, United Artists a final film. *Yellow Submarine* had been rejected by UA on the grounds that their contract required films starring the group rather than cartoon representations of them.

Although the group had given in to Harrison's demand to abandon live performance, there was a kind of compromise; the album would still be recorded with a quasi-live aesthetic and the new Beatles album and film would employ, as the working title implied, a "back to basics" approach. There would be none of the high-tech studio trickery so prevalent since *Revolver,* the recordings would not be overdubbed at all, any mistakes would remain intact, and the emphasis would be on resummoning the rock 'n' roll spirit of their formative years. However, relationships were still strained. Working on the principle that people behave better in company, Harrison drafted in another musician, the soul singer and pianist Billy Preston, to help relieve the tension and provide inspiration for the tired Beatles. According to Harrison, when Preston was brought in there was a "one hundred per cent improvement" in the strained atmosphere.

However, despite the seductiveness of its alluring premise, and Harrison's subtle attempt to temper the hostilities, both shooting and recording were initially hampered by practical problems. The Beatles had planned to restart the project on Monday 20 January in the basement studio newly-constructed for the group by the Greek electronics "expert", "magic" Alexis Mardas of Apple's electronic division. Although the studio was due to be ready for the group's use on this day, it became patently apparent upon their arrival that Mardas' bizarre designs were unable to live up to their inventor's claims, and filming and recording were delayed by two days while the ever-reliable

George Martin negotiated the use of mobile recording equipment from Abbey Road. When the necessary technology did arrive, the sessions were infinitely more enjoyable and productive than they had been at Twickenham and, while it would be inaccurate to suggest that they were totally successful in harnessing the group's true live potential, the group refined and recorded a number of new and inspired songs (including Harrison's "For You Blue" and McCartney's wonderful "Get Back"). However, progress was still somewhat slow, and sessions would often take a similar manifestation as they had at Twickenham, with productivity giving way to impromptu jamming and mainly insipid covers.

This was of little help to Lindsay-Hogg. Despite having shot hours of fascinating, if sombre footage of The Beatles jamming and recording (interspersed with all the extra-musical footage of the group clowning around, arguing, telling jokes, and soberly discussing their future plans between songs), the director's material still lacked an adequate resolution or suitably professional musical "climax". Indeed, despite having shot a total of three weeks' rehearsal/recording footage, the film still lacked enough suitably polished or completed performances and, since Beatles albums had been known to take months to complete, the idea of merely continuing in the same vein seemed both impractical and inadequate for all parties.

Out of this frustration, on 26 January came the suggestion that the group should play an impromptu live performance on the rooftop of Apple's Savile Row headquarters, to be filmed by Lindsay-Hogg as the climax of the movie. Harrison was apparently still hesitant about the idea but eventually gave in to pressure from the others, and on 30 January 1969 The Beatles played spirited versions of "Get Back", "I've Got a Feeling", "Dig a Pony", "Don't Let Me Down" and "One After 909" to the cameras and the bewildered crowd of office workers who were milling around Savile Row in their lunch hour. The concert "happening" was a triumph. After three weeks of apathy, indecision and slow progress, The Beatles had finally managed to rekindle their ability to generate the excitement of their spellbinding live performances, and once again they proved that when they put their personal and artistic differences behind them, they were consummate ensemble players.

However, the rooftop performance was not, as has been frequently documented, the end of the *Get Back* shoot. Perhaps realizing that they still needed more polished numbers for a commercial film release (be it for television or cinema), they completed shooting the following day at the Apple basement studio, with note-perfect live performances of the finished versions of "Let It Be", "The Long and Winding Road" and "Two of Us".

Although shooting for the film was completed in January 1969, it would be another sixteen months before it was released, largely because of delays and disagreements in the preparation of the accompanying album. The film, now significantly retitled *Let It Be,* received its world premiere in New York on 13 May 1970, by which time The Beatles were no more. Unsurprisingly, none of The Beatles attended.

ANTHOLOGY

by Sean Egan

The review below of the DVD version of The Beatles' long-awaited film autobiography Anthology *was first published in* Discoveries *magazine cover-dated December 2003.*

The 1996 home video version of *Anthology* – the sumptuous but often strangely bland video autobiography of history's finest pop artists, first broadcast the previous year – massively expanded the project, from four and a half hours without commercials to ten hours. This constituted a profound improvement on the original TV programmes, especially for Americans: Beatles songs were almost always played in full, not presented in extracts. (TV viewers in the UK – where it was broadcast in one-hour segments across two months – had that privilege from the beginning.) Unbeknownst to many, though, the video version also lost material from the TV version: because the entire project was re-edited from scratch for the VCR market, there were minor discrepancies and omissions. These omissions are not restored for this five-disc DVD version and the DVD version is itself subtly different again to the video version (different Apple rooftop footage, for instance). The fifth disc, meanwhile, is mostly all-new material.

Disc five starts with a Threetles group interview/jam session sequence. The most interesting moment comes when Ringo reveals that he was treated as something of an outsider when he joined the group, at which point George chips in with the fact that he himself wasn't inclined to pally up with the newcomer because he was insecure about his own position in the pecking order and felt it might be further undermined if he was too welcoming. Ringo is responsible for another sit-up-in-seat moment, this one far more pleasurable: when George and Paul start playing an early McCartney song called "Thinking Of Linking" on acoustic guitars, Ringo – arms folded – is taken by surprise. Quickly recovering, he whips up the brushes he is employing for the session and effortlessly falls into rhythm with the pair, putting one immediately in mind of that story about how he recovered brilliantly after a bathroom visit almost made him miss his entry on "Hey Jude".

The second section sees Paul, George, Ringo and Beatles producer George Martin at Abbey Road studios playing some key tracks, in the process of which they employ that by now familiar rockumentary technique of fading out different elements of the multi-track masters to comment on how wondrous specific parts are. Unfortunately, any insights into Ringo's indeed extraordinary drums on "Tomorrow Never Knows" are doomed to non-appearance by the jokey, bantering atmosphere. Martin is at least a bit more insightful in the section he has to himself where he proceeds to play the original two-track demo of "A Day In The Life". This track, although it features only vocal, guitar and piano and lacks Paul's middle section, transpires, startlingly, to be almost as spectral and haunting as the finished version.

There are also mini-docs on the compiling of the *Anthology* albums, the recording of the "Free As A Bird" single and the making of the video of that latter "comeback" disc, a video whose stunning nature in all the brouhaha over the fact of the single itself got rather lost. Director Joe Pytka explains the rationale behind a promotional film that saw the camera swooping like the titular bird over scenes from The Beatles' career and lives. The effect of the mixture of the song's contemplative sentiments, the video's own reflective nature and the dazzling camera work and FX made for what is quite simply one of the most emotionally affecting and technically staggering pop videos of all time. Having originally moved us with that video, Pytka moves us a little more by revealing that he refused George Harrison's request to mime the George Formby pastiche at the song's end, unaware that Harrison had played it on the record: now that Harrison is gone, Pytka could kick himself. The video itself is used as a fitting closure to The Beatles' story on disc four, nicely linked by Paul who – discussing with his colleagues those perennial "Are The Beatles To Re-form" questions that dogged the group for so many years – points out that with "Free As A Bird", they, in a way, did (even if he does wink at Ringo after he says it).

The video for "Real Love" – that second Threetles single – is also included on disc five. It's a nice enough song but both the reflectiveness and the scenes-from-Beatles-life promo film feel like ersatz "Free As A Bird". Interviews with the people behind the making of the *Anthology* series round out the package. They are of negligible interest and little insight: are we really supposed to be impressed that interviewer Jools Holland asked the kind of questions an ordinary journalist wouldn't when such questions are on the level of what clothes Priscilla was wearing at the Fabs' meeting with The King? However, at least the section gives backroom staff their deserved turn in the spotlight.

Although this set costs less in real terms than the shorter video version did, it's still a little ungenerous time-wise. Discs one-to-four clock in at about two and a half hours each, which leaves plenty of unused space into which could have been inserted some of the missing singles promo films, which would have made a refreshing contrast to the low-fi, low-res live

versions of apparently arbitrarily selected songs that predomi-
nate. Perhaps it's naive to have hoped that the documentary
The Beatles At Shea Stadium could have been included in its
entirety – no doubt another money-spinning DVD is planned
of that – but there would certainly have been space. The running
time of disc five, meanwhile, is a paltry one hour, twenty minutes:
just think of how many goodies could have been included on
the acres of empty space there.

The re-mixing (for, let's call a spade a spade, that's what it
is) on this DVD release of Beatles tracks into 5.1 Surroundsound
is no doubt exciting for those who don't care if history is
tampered with, but let's hope it's restricted to this medium and
that a reverse process will take place on CD, where proper (i.e.
mono) CD versions of (UK albums) *Help* through *Sgt. Pepper's*
. . . are long overdue. Incidentally, the music sequences are at
considerably louder volume than the interview passages, necessitating irritating constant recourse to the remote control.

It would be easy to be swept up by the brilliance of the music
and the engaging nature of the interviewees herein (it doesn't
get said enough that The Beatles were four of the more agreeable
personas celebrity has known) but this package has major faults
and those faults are mostly tied in with the way that The Beatles
as an entity have milked their assets in the modern age. There's
nothing wrong with exploiting your catalogue but from their
premium-priced, no-bonus-track CDs to their parsimonious no-
liner-notes CD packaging to the unnecessary two-CD format
of the Red and Blue compilations, The Beatles have seemed to
be taking their fans for granted, aware that their legend and the
quality of the music will dispel misgivings about inattention to
value for money.

So is it worth buying the *Anthology* series in this format if
one already has the video version? The answer is yes, but for
rather underwhelming reasons. First, because it can now be
seen that the video tape – that innovation that ruled the world
for three decades – was a crummy piece of interim technology
whose cumbersome retrieval methods and perishability we
would have laughed at had it appeared at the same time as that
little ol' versatile disc. Additionally, although sensuality shouldn't
really be a consideration, this set *feels* lovely. It's a little bit like

a magic box: all those great tunes, great memories and historical interest squeezed into a tidy oblong barely bigger than one's hand.

The Beatles almost certainly would not have sold any more of this package if they had included more material on it. But as Mary McCartney undoubtedly told Paul and as Aunt Mimi surely said to John, "It's nice to be nice." Wouldn't it be cool if, just once, that colossal corporation that The Beatles now seem to constitute, ignored the fact that – because they are so loved – nothing they do will stop them selling CDs and DVDs, and instead gave their fans – simply because they wanted to – a package bursting at the seams with material and graced with worthwhile annotation?

PART FOUR: BEATLE WOMEN

Women were always important to The Beatles, whether as muses, career catalysts or alleged sources of conflict between the group members. Some writing on the major females in The Beatles' lives.

ASTRID KIRCHHERR

She may have been the other half of the man destined to leave The Beatles before they hit the big time, but Astrid Kirchherr's importance in The Beatles' story is indisputable. Eyewitness to The Beatles' development from gauche young novices to grizzled stage veterans in Hamburg, originator of the half-shadow Beatles imagery made iconic by the With The Beatles *sleeve, provider of The Beatles' world-sweeping hairstyle, she has a fascinating tale to tell, both about the Fab Four and about Stuart Sutcliffe, the so-called Fifth Beatle. Ken Sharp spoke to her in 1996 upon the publication of her book of photographs* Liverpool Days.

Astrid Kirchherr

by Ken Sharp

George Harrison once said, "The Beatles were never better as a live band than in Hamburg." One of the lucky witnesses to The Beatles' burgeoning sound during that golden time was Astrid Kirchherr. Her life inexorably changed in October of 1960 when fate led Astrid, accompanied by then-boyfriend, Klaus Voormann, who later designed The Beatles' *Revolver* and *Anthology* albums and was bassist for Manfred Mann, to a seedy club called the Kaiserkeller in Hamburg's St Pauli district where she first saw The Beatles perform. Not surprisingly, she was instantly won over by their raw, visceral music, cheeky humour, engaging personalities and striking image. Kirchherr was particularly smitten with Stuart Sutcliffe, the group's bass player. They were soon a couple and their romantic and mutually artistic relationship flourished until Sutcliffe's tragic death of a brain haemorrhage on 10 April, 1961. Stuart wasn't the only Beatle who adored Astrid: the other Beatles were equally enamoured of her existentialist philosophies and style.

Despite many factual inaccuracies and a considerable stretching of the truth, the motion-picture *Backbeat* vividly captures Astrid and Stuart's relationship and The Beatles' formative days in Hamburg. Astrid's brilliant photographs of The Beatles during their formative years in Hamburg still stand as perhaps the most memorable images of the group. Her classic half-shadow portraits of The Beatles inspired noted shutterbug Robert Freeman when shooting the photograph used on the

With The Beatles album cover. She is also credited as helping to create "The Beatles haircut".

After The Beatles conquered the world, Astrid remained close friends with the group, visiting them in Liverpool and London in the mid-1960s and continuing a warm friendship that exists to this day. *Liverpool Days*, a Genesis Publications limited edition tome, chronicles Kirchherr's photographs and memories of those halcyon days. A future *Hamburg Days* book is in the works. Most recently, Kirchherr has contributed a wealth of photographs and the introduction to the exceptional new book *Stuart: The Life And Art Of Stuart Sutcliffe*, another Genesis Publications limited edition book.

Q: *What has been your involvement with the new Stuart Sutcliffe book,* Stuart: The Life And Art Of Stuart Sutcliffe*?*
Astrid Kirchherr: "Well Pauline [Sutcliffe, Stuart's sister] is in charge of all of Stuart's paintings. Because we are quite friendly with one another and we meet whenever there's a chance, she asked me if I would do the introduction for the book. And of course I was delighted to do so. I'm ever so proud that there is a book out about Stuart's work and about Stuart as a person not only as the "fifth" Beatle because I think he was a very, very gifted young man, when you see his pictures and think about how old he was when he did them. So I wrote an introduction and all the pictures of Stuart when he was in Hamburg I did. On the front cover of the book will be my favourite picture of Stuart. I don't know if you remember it. It's a portrait and it's very black and white and he's got all these freckles and you can't stop looking at his eyes. The thing about Stuart was he was a big actor as well. When he did one step on that stage when he used to do music with The Beatles he changed. He became the big rock 'n' roll star and he did all his poses which he knew looked great."

Q: *Stuart Sutcliffe passed away when he was twenty-one. If he had lived, do you feel Stuart would have found great success. as an artist despite his "fifth" Beatle tag?*
"I'm positive of it. Even though he would have always had a hard time being known as the 'fifth' Beatle because now people

start to realize his talent. But a couple of years ago they just said 'Oh, that's the fifth Beatle'."

Q: *You were involved with the* Backbeat *film . . .*
"I was pleased with the film. I had to learn to make compromises. It was a low budget film. I loved the way all these people were so enthusiastic about it. They were all very young, the whole crew. The actors were nineteen, twenty, twenty-one. It was a joy working with them."

Q: *Do you think Stuart would have liked the film* Backbeat?
"Yes, I think he would. He would have liked the people who did the film because they were very, very young, all of them. Very enthusiastic and he liked people like that very much."

Q: *How did you come to first see The Beatles?*
"Klaus Voormann took me to see them at The Kaiserkeller. Klaus just heard the noise, the music, and he didn't know who was playing at the club. He just followed the noise. They had the teddy boy haircuts combed back with grease and little tight jeans and very, very pointed shoes. And very tiny little jackets with velvet collars. I met them some nights later because this club that they played in was in an area in Hamburg called The Reeperbahn. The exact name of the street is Grosse Freiheit. The Kaiserkeller was just a tiny little dirty place. It was badly decorated with fisherman's nets, the real awful stuff. And they had a little stage made out of bricks but when I saw the Beatles for the first time it was unbelievable – the personalities, the charm and the enormous gift of them."

Q: *Could you sense there was a leader in The Beatles?*
"Of course. It was John."

Q: *After you met Stuart how quickly did it develop into a romantic relationship?*
"It sounds so over romantic, like in books from Barbara Cartland. When I saw Stuart for the first time, I thought 'Oh my God!' Then when I spoke to him for the first time to hear his voice. He spoke very, very high educated English. He also

put on the Liverpool dialect. He was so charming and so sexy. He knew exactly what was going on. He felt exactly the same, if you might call it, love at first sight or attraction, let's put it like that. It sounds so unreal but it was right, it was like that. We just fell in love. My boyfriend was Klaus, which for both of us was very hard. Stuart became very, very friendly with Klaus and liked Klaus a lot because he was an artist and very intelligent and had a lot of humour and he looked absolutely great. So Stuart loved Klaus as well."

Q: *What were your impressions of John Lennon, Paul McCartney, George Harrison and Pete Best when you first met them?*
"Well they were very, very friendly, very good mannered which people don't believe me somehow [laughs]. They were just sweet young guys who looked great and who looked very wild. You never expected them to be so well mannered and so warm and tender."

Q: *Your Hamburg friends were nicknamed The Exis. Where did that nickname originate?*
"At the time around 1960 and even before that when art schools just started to grow again, we didn't have the opportunity to get our influences from all over the world. We didn't have any television. We couldn't get any magazines like *Vogue, Harpers Bazaar.* Or any interesting books from America or England. So we got hold of the nearest and the closest things we could get which was from France. That includes all the writers at the time, that means Sartre, Marquis De Sade, Baudelaire. And also the film-makers, Cocteau. And the whole French scene was called the existentialists. So because we all had this French influence wearing black clothes and looking moody, they called us 'The Exis'."

Q: *Could you take us back to what sights one would encounter taking a walk down the Reeperbahn and what one would encounter while The Beatles were in Hamburg?*
"Well it is still very colourful, but it had much more atmosphere then because there were just bars, one after another where girls were dancing and prostitutes standing in the road. And little

bars where sailors used to go and get drunk. And little places where then, which was amazing, was transvestites standing outside looking for men. So the whole atmosphere was absolutely fascinating. If you imagine four little boys from Liverpool walking down that road, it was unbelievable for them."

Q: *Did you ever witness The Beatles abominable living conditions when they were playing The Bambi Kino?*
"I never went in there but they told me about it. They had to sleep behind the screen of the cinema. It was absolutely filthy. Did you see the *Backbeat* film?"

Q: *Yes.*
"It looked like that."

Q: *George Harrison has said The Beatles were never better than during their performing days in Hamburg.*
"No, they weren't. The thing is, they had to play every night. They didn't have a night off or a day off. They played about eight hours every night. I would see them every night [laughs]. John mentioned that a few times that that was the best practice they could ever have. Stuart used to sing "Love Me Tender" for me. It was very charming. Stuart used to sing some more songs. He used to sing "Twenty Flight Rock" which he did absolutely great. He loved Eddie Cochran so Eddie Cochran songs were done by Stuart.

"He didn't sing so often but you can quite imagine when John and Paul who sang the most then and George then came in slowly with a couple of songs, their voices were sometimes so strained so all of them had to have a go. Pete Best didn't sing at all but Ringo did. They also used to play "One After 909", one of the first songs that John and Paul wrote together.

"I always requested that song from John because I liked it so very much. John wasn't quite sure it was good. Whenever I asked him to play it, he said, 'No, don't give me that shit. I don't want to.' But he did it in the end every time I requested it."

Q: *It's been reported that Stuart could barely play the bass. But Klaus Voormann has said Stu was a very good bass player.*

"That was the thing, I don't play an instrument myself. I can only believe what Klaus is saying and Klaus adored Stuart's bass playing because it was so simple. Klaus said he always tried to copy Stuart later on but he couldn't because his playing is too complicated. So I know that Stuart could only play a couple of notes but he made such a great show of it."

Q: *The Beatles took Preludin, known as "prellies" to keep energized during their eight-hour live sessions.*
"They were actually pills to make slimming easier for you. We used to take them with a couple of beers. They made you just a little speedy. But you can't compare it to speed from today or cocaine or anything. Its just baby food compared to that."

Q: *Set the record straight. Did you or did you not cut The Beatles' hair thus creating the famous Beatles haircut?*
"Well the story is that all my friends were influenced by the French. Because of me loving all the French stuff and seeing people wearing that style but only shorter, I wanted Klaus to have that cut but longer so I told Klaus to let his hair grow and I gave him a longer haircut.

"So when Stuart met all my other friends including Jurgen Vollmer they all had this haircut which we adopted from the French people. When Stuart met Klaus he wanted this haircut. So I cut it for him and got all the grease out and he looked fantastic with it. John didn't like it at all if you can imagine that. After a couple of weeks I went to England to see them and George came round and asked me if I could do the haircut for him and I said 'yes, of course'.

"They had quite long hair then but because it was greased back you couldn't see it. But still Paul and John didn't feel like getting their haircut like that. And then Paul and John went to France to see this friend of mine who's also a photographer named Jurgen Vollmer who also did the John Lennon *Rock & Roll* cover. He then lived in France and worked there. They thought they had a good opportunity to visit Jurgen and have him show them around Paris. So he talked John and Paul into having their hair cut like that."

Q: *What would The Beatles do when they weren't playing?*
"They used to come to my house a lot because my mother used to make them real English breakfasts with bacon and egg or she did steaks for them with mashed potatoes. They really missed English cooking. They used to hang around in my room which they found pretty amazing because it was all black and trees hanging down from the ceiling.

"I had a great collection of classical music and jazz. I had hundreds of books. So they listened to all the classical music and jazz and looked through all my books and they had a wonderful time."

Q: *Can you give us background on the famous shot of The Beatles done on the fairground?*
"That was the first session I ever did with The Beatles. I asked them if I could take their pictures. They were absolutely delighted that a professional photographer asked them if I could take their pictures. I said, 'Well, if you let me take your pictures, you get nice pictures of each one of you. You will get quite a nice collection.'

"So they were more than willing to do so. The photos were taken in Hamburg at a place where we usually have a fairground twice a year with all the big trains to put up the carousel. It's called Heilegen Geistfeld. Ken, I can't tell you how professional they acted. I just told them what I would like, my idea of them looking so rough and somehow so full of wisdom. They knew exactly what I wanted. They loved the photos. When I did the prints and I came along at night to see them, I gave each one of them about four or five different ones. They had never seen a print bigger than a postcard and my prints were quite big so they were absolutely delighted."

Q: *Many of your photos from the time employed the half-shadow look which Robert Freeman adopted for the cover of* With The Beatles. *Were you flattered by that?*
"No, because I have the idea that The Beatles wanted Robert to do so. Robert is a very, very good photographer and I love his work. I presume The Beatles asked him to do that."

Q: *Was there ever any talk of you shooting any photos of The Beatles once they made it?*

"Well I did some photos of George for his LP *Wonderwall*. George phoned me and said, 'Will you please do me a favour and take these pictures of me?' I said, 'All right because it's you, love but I really don't feel like it.' So that's the only time I ever said yes."

Q: *Why were The Beatles deported from Hamburg?*

"There were two clubs, one called The Kaiserkeller which was owned by Bruno Koschmider and The Top Ten which was owned by Peter Eckhorn. In The Top Ten club was another English young boy playing who was Tony Sheridan. He was pretty famous in England already. The Beatles used to go round whenever they had an hour off to The Top Ten to see Tony Sheridan because they admired him so much. Sometimes one of them used to go up and play with him. Then they came to know Peter Eckhorn.

"The club was much nicer and Peter Eckhorn was a very, very nice man. Koschmider wasn't nice at all. So Peter said, 'Why don't you play here?' And they said, 'Yeah, okay. We'd love to, that would be great.' Somehow the rumours got round to Mr Koschmider and he just accused them of putting fire to his dirty old Bambi Kino which wasn't true. So of course the police came around and arrested them. I drove them to the rail-road station."

Q: *Did you think they would return?*

"Yes, of course because Mr Eckhorn was such a nice man. He said, 'Don't worry, I'll get that in order.' And another horrible thing was George was only seventeen which this Koschmider man knew but he pretended when he got them arrested that he didn't."

Q: *How long was Stuart away from you?*

"I can't really remember. When they were deported, I went to see them about four weeks later in Liverpool. When they went back to Liverpool they used to play a different ballroom every night. They had a little van and a driver which was Neil Aspinall, who's now the head of Apple. He used to drive this little van. We used to be all stuck in the back."

Q: *Was there a difference seeing The Beatles in Liverpool as opposed to Hamburg?*
"When they came back from Hamburg they were all dressed in leather and all the Liverpudlians thought they were German. So they were immediately quite successful there. Don't forget they had a hell of a lot of practice in Hamburg so they were absolutely fabulous, instrumentally and singing."

Q: *Was there a rivalry between Paul and Stuart as reported in several Beatle books?*
"Not really. Even when Paul was that tiny, when he was 19, he was a perfectionist, as far as music was concerned. He was always on time, a real professional. And because Stuart's first love was painting, he didn't, excuse the expression, give a shit. He just played his note and he was sure that John adored him because of the way he looked.

"Of course Paul was angry sometimes when he didn't play the right notes and he didn't bother to practice. John had a very close relationship to Paul on a different level than Stuart. His relationship to Paul was music. He admired and loved Paul.

"From Stuart, he got the other side, the artistic side, the love for painting, for writers, the whole artistic world and lifestyle. Another thing about John and Stuart is that they had an extremely similar sense of humour. They'd just throw the ball to one another as we express. They were so quick in their mind. It was a joy to watch them and listen to them talking."

Q: *Why do you feel John was only able to open himself up to Stuart?*
"I don't know. I think they were soul brothers in a way as far as art was concerned, life as being an artist. John admired Stuart for his strength wanting to be an artist. Stuart knew from the very beginning that all he wanted was painting. And John had so many gifts, it was hard for him. He was a great musician and a great artist as well."

Q: *There's a lot of wild stories about John in Hamburg where he's come out on stage wearing a toilet seat over his head or yelling out to the German audiences. 'Heil Hitler!' Any truth to these stories?"*

"Yeah, that's all true. It was funny. It was just a big laugh. Everybody loved John in Hamburg. He wore the toilet seat over his head once for a joke. He would never repeat himself. John was far too clever."

Q: *Were you there the night the stage broke at the Kaiserkeller?*

"Yes. Well the stage broke, they just jumped and the stage broke. It was made out of all bricks."

Q: *How do you think The Beatles changed as performers moving from the Kaiserkeller to the Top Ten club and the Star-Club?*

"They were the best playing in the Top Ten and the Kaiserkeller. They loved to be in Hamburg. They loved the Star-Club. They got on well with the owner of the Star Club, who was a great guy. His name was Manfred Weissleder. He's dead. He got the Star-Club going. Peter Eckhorn is dead too but I think Koschmider is still alive."

Q: *Could you sense when Stuart began drifting away from playing with The Beatles to concentrate on his art?*

"Yeah, yeah because it was clear from the beginning that he only did it as a joke because John talked him into it. When Stuart left the band they also left the Top Ten club. They still kept in contact. After he had left the band, whenever Stuart would go to England he would go to see them."

Q: *When were you and Stuart planning to get married, did you have a date picked?*

"No, not really because Stuart was still in art college then in Hamburg."

Q: *What did Eduardo Paollazzi mean to Stuart as a mentor and art instructor?*

"When The Beatles played at the Top Ten, the whole club was filled with art students then: Stuart, and John and all of them were quite friendly with the art students They told Mr Paollozzi about it who was a professor in Hamburg art schools. They asked him to come along and see this English band who were great and he did one night. And then Stuart talked to him and Mr Paollozzi said, 'Okay. come along and show me some of your work.' Stuart went to see Mr Paollozzi at the art school and he said, 'Let me see what I can do for you. I'd like you to be in my class.' He somehow managed to get Stuart a scholarship for The Hamburg College Of Art."

Q: *Is it true Stuart fell down the steps of your attic art studio and this accident may have exacerbated his chronic headaches?*
"No. That's absolutely silly. You see, I knew that he was ill and had these severe headaches but you must imagine, when you're that young, death is so far away from you. You don't think about it. If somebody says 'I've got this terrible headache', well it's a shame and I felt so sorry for him.

"I went to the doctors with him and everywhere. But it never crossed my mind that I would lose him. The last fourteen days of his life he stayed in bed most of the time and doctors X-rayed him and they did the whole treatment. One mustn't forget that in '62 medical technology wasn't as good as today."

Q: *You were with Stuart when he died.*
"They took him in an ambulance when he was already unconscious and in the ambulance he died. I was by his side."

Q: *It's been said when John was told about Stuart's death he kept his emotions hidden, perhaps because he couldn't face another tragic loss like the death of his mother.*
"John took it in John's way. When I met him at the airport and I told him that Stuart died he just collapsed laughing. It was just an hysterical fit. That was his way to deal with it."

Q: *While The Beatles included Stuart's photo on the cover of their* Sgt. Pepper . . . *album, John never really spoke about Stu after he died. Why?*
"I think because it was so very private for him, so intimate, his

relationship with Stu; that that belonged to John and not to the public."

Q: *Do you think Stuart would have felt honoured to be one of the faces on the* Sgt. Pepper . . . *album?*
"Probably, yes he would."

Q: *Your days with The Beatles didn't end with Stuart's tragic death but you visited them in London later on.*
"They used to invite me to London. They talked to me on the phone so it was just a great friendship where I had three great friends who looked after me."

Q: *What was your relationship like with Pete Best?*
"I loved Pete. He's a great guy, a lovely man. But he was always the loner. He wanted to be left on his own. He had his own thing going. He never quite mixed up with them. But Pete is very, very well mannered, very sweet and lovely. But he just didn't fit in."

Q: *Do you have any recollections of when The Beatles came to Hamburg in 1966?*
"The were completely different live than from the early days in Hamburg. It was a completely different band. But I really enjoyed it. The Beatles were staying in a little castle outside of Hamburg and after the show we all drove to the castle and had a party."

Q: *What was your relationship like with the band after they broke up?*
"The most close contact I have with them is with George. George came to Hamburg to see me. He just came to see me and he stayed in my house. That was in the 1970s. I went to see him when I was in London.

"Today it's a great friendship. That doesn't mean we see each other daily but whenever we see one another it's the same warmth and love. I'm grateful and thankful that I had the opportunity to know those wonderful people.

"George I last saw two years ago. He came to Hamburg to

see a concert and he wanted to take me there but I couldn't because I had the flu. So he came to my house and made me some tea. We just had a long talk and then he had to go.

"When Paul did his world tour, he sent his chauffeur to pick me up and I went to the concert. The last time 1 saw him was when he had the premiere of his film *Get Back* in Hamburg. I've never been as close to Ringo as I was to George or Paul."

Q: *Lastly did you enjoy The Beatles'* Anthology *CDs and TV show?*
"Yes. I think it's wonderful, I wish Beethoven had a chance to do something like that because maybe we would understand more about him."

CYNTHIA LENNON

In 1995, Alan Clayson spoke to John Lennon's first wife and mother of his first son Julian (by now a recording artist himself) upon the occasion of Cynthia releasing a record, "Those Were The Days".

Cynthia Powell, as was, met John at art college and though she got married to John in August 1962 because he had made her pregnant, has insisted that in the beginning the two were very much in love. She has sometimes come across as muddled: her condemnation of the Anthology *project as a money-grubbing exercise was a little rich (as her long-standing friend Paul McCartney has noted) considering the existence of her "Lennon's" restaurant. But she has always emerged as a likeable figure and one who deserves sympathy for the way she was humiliated in the eyes of the world when John left her for Yoko.*

Here, as well as discussing her single, she reveals fascinating titbits of information that only someone intimately involved with the story of The Beatles could be privy to.

Cynthia Lennon

by Alan Clayson

The eyes indicate that Cynthia's journey to middle life hasn't been peaceful, but otherwise she retains the same blonde, timorous beauty of the girl sucked by affinity into the vortex of Beatlemania. The soft, flat north-west vowels still peeped out during our conversation in Kensington's Cafe Rouge when I was but one of many media appointments arranged by Cynthia's agent to promote her debut single, a remarkably assured revival of Mary Hopkin's "Those Were The Days", the Apple 45 that knocked another Apple 45, "Hey Jude", from Number One in 1968.

As a graduate from the same establishment (Liverpool Regional College of Art), what was your impression of Stuart-Sutcliffe-as-artist?
"If you'd seen his early drawings, his basic art, he was head and shoulders above everybody at college. He was the star pupil, an inspiration to all of us. Then, at the end of his life, he went into abstract painting – a progression for him. Stuart was never really part of The Beatles. He was a friend of ours, which is why we wanted him along. Stuart didn't play [bass] guitar until John and he became friends. John taught him, and he practised until his fingers bled."

In Backbeat, *the bio-pic of Stuart, how accurate was that portrayal of you by [actress] Jennifer Ehle?*
"Not exactly how I was, let's put it that way. *Backbeat* had me as a very simple girl from Liverpool who wore tweed coats and

head scarves, and that the only thing I ever wanted in life was to have a baby and a house and get married – which was totally untrue. I was at art college for five years, training to be an art teacher, and I had no dreams of marriages or babies or anything like that when I met John. However, because it wasn't a film about John and I, but Astrid and Stuart, I enjoyed the feel, the essence of the film intensely. In that way, it didn't really matter to me if I was portrayed properly or not."

You've come across very well on your new record. The song itself always seemed better suited to someone more worldly than Mary Hopkin, who was only a teenager at the time . . .
"My voice has gone down about two octaves since I was Mary Hopkin's age – probably because of all the cigarettes I smoke, all the whiskeys, all the wines. When he heard my voice, my producer Chris [Norman, ex-Smokie] thought that 'Those Were The Days' would be perfect for me. It's very commercial. It's also *very* pertinent, looking back. It is a good song for a person of my age, a good singalong. When Mary sang it, it was beautiful, but the lyrics are more for an older person. Chris wrote another verse that was more relevant to me than to Mary, but the publisher said straightaway that there was no way in which we could possibly change the lyric."

How did the single come about?
"Last November, a fax came through from a record company who wanted to get in touch with my son Julian [who had his first hit in 1984]. My partner Jim and I both got very miffed because it's not on to go through the back door of the mother to get to the son. You have to go through the record company or Julian's management. Jim called them back and said sarcastically, 'There's no way you're going to have Julian, but you can have his mother' – and they got back to us, and said, 'That's a very good idea, but we can't do anything with Cynthia unless we know whether she can sing or not.'

"We went round all our village in the Isle of Man, trying to find equipment to do it on. It was our fun for that weekend. We borrowed the ghetto-blaster and microphone off Chris Norman and his business associate Kenny Brough. I did 'If I

Fell' to a backing track. It was so high and so belting for my voice, and I was killing myself with this microphone in the kitchen with a glass of wine, singing to myself. Jim went out to commit suicide, so I did my own selection of songs to which I knew the words without accompaniment. We took the equipment back to Kenny and Chris, who were inquisitive enough to ask to hear it. They said, 'Let's give it a whirl'. Within three weeks, I was in the studio, but before that, I was doing a Beatles convention in America – so to get it done, hopefully, before Christmas, they did the backing track first so that when I came back, I could go straight into the studio. I was terrified, but I did have my duty-free Glenfiddich, and that helped.

"For the B-side, 'Walking In The Rain', I suggested that one part should have a man's voice talking to the woman – and it worked really well when Chris sang it, but Polydor, his German record label, said, 'No way can you sing on somebody else's record' – so we had to bring a session singer in. Nevertheless, I really enjoyed making the record. I was on cloud nine for weeks afterwards.

"Julian was so amazed after I sent him the first mix, just to give him an idea. He didn't even know I could sing – because I hadn't told him that I'd been a soloist in a church choir when I was young, because it had never cropped up. He thought I'd done really well, considering that my last performance to any kind of public audience was singing 'Who Is Sylvia?' when I was fourteen.

"I also went to piano lessons, ballet – all the things that little girls love to do, but the one thing that was important to me was painting and drawing, so that really took over from singing and dancing. I still paint when I get the chance. I like painting cats. I did have five cats, but now I'm down to one. I'm illustrative rather than abstract. For commercial reasons – to pay the bills – I did textile design in 1984 for a big firm in England, a three-year contract."

You are also an author [of A Twist Of Lennon, W.H. Allen, 1978].
There are many sides to your talent, most of them hitherto unpub-
licized. Have you ever tried composing?
"I had a go at songwriting when I lived in North Wales in the 1970s. It was very child-like. I've written poetry, very deep and

serious for me, but I found in the transition from writing poetry to music that, every time I came to the middle eight, I'd get thrown. I couldn't understand it. I couldn't align the words and the music."

If it picks on airplay, 'Those Were The Days' might enter the charts. Have you any plans to take the show on the road?
"It's a one-day-at-a-time situation. One thing usually leads to another thing. There's been talk about an album."

As Julian has found out, a famous surname certainly opens doors, but it can give a career both the best and worst start . . .
"It's a double-edged sword. You have to prove yourself even harder, but it's difficult for outsiders to understand, if you want to be a hermit and live on an island, then that's fine. If you actually want to move into the marketplace and earn a living, than you have to be prepared for all the flak that will be thrown your way.

"I was living in a very nice house in Cumbria which Jim and I brought cheap because it didn't have a kitchen or a bathroom. We did it up. It got a bit scary in Cumbria, however, because I was doing interviews and opening garden fetes, and they printed my address in the local newspaper. I got all kinds of ragtails and bobtails knocking at the door, off their heads on marijuana or acid. We don't like security or alarms. We prefer a free existence, so we both thought it might be a very good time to step off the mainland and pull the drawbridge up."

You still speak at Beatle Conventions, though. I've done a few too, and I reckon they're a more socially acceptable form of obsession than, say, collecting information about swimming pool lockers.
"The first one I ever visited was in 1982 on Long Island, I had an exhibition of cartoons that I'd been invited to exhibit. There were so many John lookalikes there that it freaked me out. It was two years after John died, and I couldn't get out quick enough. Now it's a different matter. Wounds heal, and it's not so obvious now. The fans that I have met have been absolutely lovely. That's the best part for me: meeting the fans and talking to them.

"I appreciate that there are still people who are fascinated with and love The Beatles. Though I love the music, I'm not fascinated because I still think of them as students and school-boys. Even when I see them now, I see them as they were when they were little."

PATTIE BOYD

Ken Sharp got to speak to George Harrison's ex-wife in 2008 upon the publication of her autobiography.

Pattie Boyd: Something in the Way She Moved

by Ken Sharp

In her new book, *Wonderful Tonight: George Harrison, Eric Clapton and Me*, for the very first time, Pattie Boyd unravels her extraordinary life serving as both wife and muse to two of rock's most formidable icons.

A former model, Boyd landed a minor acting role in The Beatles' 1964 film, *A Hard Day's Night*. Harrison was instantly enamoured by her beauty and charm and soon they were an item. Less than two years later, in January of 1966, they were married.

During her marriage to George, Pattie willingly took a back-seat in the relationship, enjoying what appeared to be a picture-perfect life with a Beatle, living in a spacious mansion in Esher that was painted in day-glo psychedelic colours.

"Something" is inarguably one of the treasures in The Beatles' musical canon. Written by George about his lovely wife, it would later be heralded by none other than Frank Sinatra as one of the greatest love songs of the twentieth century. But life behind the towering fortress walls of their new home, the enormous "Friar Park" castle was anything but sweet and their marriage was starting to crumble.

And here's where the story takes a surprising turn better suited for a trashy soap opera. As her marriage was going through the paces, Pattie was being aggressively pursued by a new romantic rival, George's close friend, Eric Clapton. Pattie wisely kept him at bay for several years. (The guitarist once demanded that she leave Harrison to pursue a relationship with him or he'd willingly succumb to the black spell of heroin. The result, Heroin: 1, Clapton: 0.) Besotted by raw, all-consuming love, Clapton wrote his signature classic, "Layla", a tortuous display of fiery passion for his best friend's wife. Eventually leaving Harrison for Clapton (they divorced in 1977), the couple would marry in March of 1979 and later divorce in 1988. Patti would also go on to inspire one of Clapton's most beautiful love songs, "Wonderful Tonight".

The press-shy Boyd has never told her story before. Within the pages of *Wonderful Tonight,* she paints a compelling "warts and all" story, an equally tender and tough portrait of both fun-filled and dark days with two of music's most talented members of rock royalty.

Share your memories first meeting The Beatles on the set of A Hard Day's Night.
"I was working as a model and my agent called me one day to tell me that there was a casting audition to go to. When I arrived there I recognized the director because I'd done some TV commercials with him. He told me this wasn't an audition for a commercial. Then I went home afterwards and I heard from my agent that I got a part in a Beatles film, which was *A Hard Day's Night.* I was a bit stunned by this. I had no desire or ambition to be an actress.

"They said, 'Oh don't worry, it's just a walk on part.' In the film I had to be a schoolgirl. So I turned up at the appointed place, a train station, caught the train and then a little way out of Paddington Station the train stopped. I looked out and saw these four very recognizable people were standing on a platform. It was The Beatles. There was nobody else there. They jumped on to the train and came into our carriage and introduced themselves as [if] we didn't know who they were [laughs]. And they were so charming. We shook their hands and then they went off and filming began. I just thought George was so unbelievably good-looking and adorable. They were all so funny and humorous and seemed to be mucking about all of the time. George and I just hit it off. I don't know whether it was by design or deliberation but we ended up sitting next to each other for lunch. I remember feeling so silly because I was still dressed in a stupid schoolgirl uniform. To me, it felt like it hadn't been that long since I'd actually been in school. Anyway, we were both really shy but we [were] enjoying sitting next to each other and talking a bit. Then at the end of the day of filming, the train was headed back to London and George looked at me and said, 'Will you marry me?' And because they'd all been so amusing and funny throughout the day I just laughed as if he were joking. I really felt it was a joke. Then he said, 'Can I take you out to dinner tonight?' I said, 'Well, actually I'm going out with my boyfriend [Eric Swayne] but you can come along too.' He said, 'No, that wasn't the idea at all.'"

You eventually broke up with that boyfriend and began to go out with George.
"Yeah. But how lucky it was that I was called back for more filming. This wasn't the original plan. I was only supposed to be there for that one day of filming."

What were the qualities about George that made you realize he was the one for you?
"I think it was his absolute charm and endearment. He was very endearing. He seemed to really love my family and got on very well with all my brothers and sisters. He was just eternally sweet to everybody. He was very easy to be with. He was very soft and lovely."

George was labelled by the press as "The Quiet Beatle". How off the mark was that?
"Well, when we first started going out together he was very quiet. As time went on and he gained more confidence he wasn't quite as quiet. And then there were times it was difficult to stop him from talking. Thankfully we had a lot to talk about." [Laughs].

Did you get a chance to visit many Beatle recording sessions?
"No, because really and truly we weren't really allowed to. We weren't encouraged to go to the studio. I remember once going through the studio to meet George Martin; I think they might

have been recording Mary Hopkin. But I never saw a Beatles recording session. That wasn't encouraged at all. When Yoko came on the scene she was allowed to but otherwise none of the wives were allowed to."

In terms of the Beatle wives' involvement in the band's activities, was there an unwritten code that wives were forbidden to visit the studio or go on the road?
"Yeah. If we were there while they were on tour it would have been an added security issue. When they went into the studio it was far better that there were no distractions from us. I mean, girls can be distracting, let's face it. So they really didn't want any of that distraction. They wanted to totally focus on their work."

Bring us back to the first time you saw The Beatles in concert.
"I saw The Beatles in concert for the first time when they played at the Hammersmith Odeon in London in 1964. George and I had met and it seemed this show must have happened a few months after that when The Beatles played. I was given a few seats right near the front and it was wonderful. It was fantastic! The audience were screaming all of the time. To me, that was odd because I didn't realize that was what happened during their shows. The noise was huge but The Beatles' performance [was] really great."

Was it a different George onstage than off?
"Absolutely. He was himself in his professional role of being a musician. Whereas I just knew him as my boyfriend, someone who was great to hang out with and loved my family and really enjoyed hanging out with my friends. So this was very clearly another role that I didn't really recognize him in."

Did he feel more comfortable off stage?
"Yes. I always felt he was never very comfortable onstage. I think it made him nervous. He was much more comfortable offstage and being in the company of friends and family and people that he loved."

Through the years, George expressed how he grew tired of Beatle-mania fairly early on in the band's career.
"After he and I met, we would have such a great time together and I don't want to be boastful about it but I think he really preferred hanging out with me and actually enjoying life. Touring got in the way and he didn't really enjoy it. He didn't really see the point of touring because just as soon as they walked toward the stage the people would start screaming so loudly. And when they started playing the screaming got even louder to the point where nobody possibly could have heard anything. He saw it all as a bit of a waste of time."

But when you watch The Beatles film showing them performing at Shea Stadium, it does seem like they're having a blast.
"Yeah. With Shea Stadium, of course, that was one of their big conquests in America. I remember George talking to me about the show. He said he couldn't believe how enormous it was and how many people were there. He was overawed by that and did enjoy playing that show."

You write in your book that The Beatles were "fearful" of their fans.
"I didn't mean to say they were *fearful* of their fans. They weren't really fearful of them. But their fans followed them everywhere they went. The fans were really demanding of their time. Obviously they couldn't exist without their fans. Before we had a gate put up outside of our house in Esher, fans would come to the house all the time. On a couple of occasions some of my things were stolen. I had the most beautiful watch. George and I went to London and while we were out somebody must have came in and stolen my watch and a few other items. Depending on his mood, more often than not if fans came to the door he would shoo them away. But if he was in a good mood and they were nice people he would be charming and sign autographs and have a few words than them. But it was an intrusion. He'd rather be getting on with his life than dealing with that and whatever else we were doing."

Unlike many groups of today, there was a real bond of friendship and camaraderie among The Beatles.

"The Beatles were very close and tight and would hang out together. They all grew up in the same area of Liverpool. Automatically when you grow up with somebody from the same sort of background and experiences, you have a bond. At a very young age, they were sent to Germany to work in Hamburg for very, very long hours and little sleep and little money. They took loads of pills to keep them up all night. That unites people. It's very bonding. Their language to each other was so fast, almost encoded. It was almost a secret language. They were very tight, very tight."

From your perspective, who was George closest to in The Beatles?
[*Long pause.*] "I don't know. It would change all the time. I mean, John and Cynthia and George and I went on a couple of holidays together. We went to Tahiti and had a great time. There was some bonding there and we had great fun together. Other times he'd hang out with Ringo and other times he'd go visit Paul."

Paul was the best man at your wedding.
"That's right, yeah. That was really nice of Paul to be the best man. John and Ringo weren't at the wedding. They must have been doing something else, I can't think of what, but they weren't around."

In the book you state that "The Beatles lived an unreal life and never had to grow up".
"Everything was always taken care of for them. I think they realized they had to start growing up when Brian Epstein died. He was a father figure for them. He enjoyed looking after them and taking care of all their needs. He would anticipate what they would like, when they'd like to go on holidays, this, that or the other. Brian taught them the niceties of life, introduced them to fine wines. Brian introduced them to London and theatre. When he died there was a period where they felt lost but then I think after that they gained their feet and realized they had to take control of their lives. And that's when they had to grow up. The boys had to disappear and put on long trousers."

After The Beatles played their last show in San Francisco, George said that now he was no longer a Beatle. When he came home from that last tour of America did he express his relief that the touring days were over?

"Yes, he was very happy he didn't have to go on tour anymore. He really didn't like it. He felt they'd done it. He was happy that they'd now be able to solely concentrate on working in the studio, which he preferred. He loved being in the studio. That's where he was happiest."

George truly came to the fore as a songwriter in the late 1960s, penning numbers that stood proud alongside the Lennon and McCartney songbook. Did he express to you his frustration of getting his songs recorded?

"Yes, he did. It was very difficult for him. George was in a difficult position. In any three-way partnership there's always going to be one person who feels left out. Ringo didn't really come into the equation, he was mainly a drummer, not a songwriter. John and Paul wrote most of the songs and I know George felt frustrated that he wasn't contributing as much as he felt he could and should."

With the magnificent love song, "Something", he proved himself on a par with John Lennon and Paul McCartney.

"Yes, that's true. I don't think George knew it was a great song but it was clearly a very beautiful song he'd written and he was very happy that it was going to be a single. He was thrilled. He played it for me and I remember him being so happy about it."

Knowing it was written about you, how did that make you feel?

"Oh, I thought it was the sweetest thing he could have done. I loved it. It's a wonderful song."

There's a funny story in your book about your cleaner, Margaret.

[*Laughs.*] "Margaret was so funny. She was our cleaner and she was just adorable. She was almost like an older sister/mother figure for George and I. She was a bit radical as well. Whenever John came over she would ask him, 'Oh John, can you give me one of those lovely pills?' [*Laughs.*] They were uppers. I always knew when she got one from John [*laughs*] because she'd suddenly start vacuuming like mad, vacuuming the whole house and dusting everywhere." [*Laughs.*]

Bring us back to the dinner party where the dentist, John Riley secretly dosed you, George, John and Cynthia with LSD.
"At about nine or ten o'clock at night we were dosed. We were furious! I thought I'd be like this for the rest of my life [*laughing*] and maybe I am. It was awful. That trip lasted about eight hours. It was terribly surreal. People started looking like animals and they would grow ten times their height. It was like being in a movie where things come in and out at you."

How did acid change George?
"I think it affected him in a positive way. He enjoyed the mind expansion part of it but then he grew out of it and didn't want to do it any more."

Not many people may know this but you were the one who pointed the way toward transcendental meditation.
"I think they were on tour somewhere and a friend of mine, Marie-Lise, saw a little ad about learning how to meditate. So off we went to London and took these lessons in transcendental mediation. We had our mantra and now we were off meditating. When George came back I told him about it. Then shortly after that I think it was Paul who suggested we all go see a lecture in London being done by the Maharishi. I was thrilled because it was his form of meditation that I'd been studying. So we all went and listened to his lecture. The Maharishi couldn't figure out why suddenly after he'd been coming to England for years doing his lectures that all the press were there. He couldn't think what had happened because he'd never heard of The Beatles. So there we are and he was very flattered by the press being there and he quickly realized that The Beatles were important people. So he invited us all to go to Wales where he could teach us privately about meditation."

Ironically, it was in Wales where The Beatles heard the terrible news that their manager, Brian Epstein had died.

"Strangely enough, isn't life so amazing that Brian would die at a time that they would all learn spirituality from the Maharishi? It was like they were replacing a father figure with a spiritual father figure in a way. That's how I saw it. It was the saddest day. None of us could believe that Brian had died. All of them were just ashen with shock with the news of Brian dying. The Maharishi helped them cope with it. Thank God he was there. At least we all had the comfort of him to help us deal with our grief."

What are your memories of The Beatles' trip to India to study with the Maharishi Mahesh Yogi?
"It was very nice to be a part of that enclosed life that we lived there. There were probably about eighty people living there. George was very serious about meditation as was John. But Paul and Ringo . . . not so much. Ringo had a bad time there, especially with Maureen because she couldn't stand flies. And those flies really irritated her. But for us, every day was glorious. There was nothing nicer than being in a very nice and calm environment. Everybody was being very gentle and sweet. John, Paul and George would play the guitar and write songs. It was absolutely the most lovely atmosphere. We'd meditate for hours on end. The food was delicious. These kids from Australia came along and said they were good chefs. So they enrolled in the ashram and they cooked. We were on the banks of the Ganges River. It was lovely to go down to the Ganges when it started getting warmer. It was just a very nice time."

When George returned from India, there was a change in his personality.
"Yes, he became more serious. After he returned from India the reality for George and the rest of The Beatles was that they now had to be businessmen and handle everything to do with The Beatles' slowly-growing empire. They had to look after everything. With Apple, they had to find business partners and then they were all arguing over who should handle them, should it be Allen Klein or Paul's relatives. It was really difficult then. From being musicians they had to wear the hat of being businessmen as well and intrinsically that's not in their nature.

They're musicians. They're artists. They're creators. So they had to play another role and it proved very difficult for them.

"George didn't like to have to make these business decisions and play that kind of role. So then he started staying in the office or in the studio quite a lot and recording various artists like Billy Preston, Doris Troy and Jackie Lomax. People like that. After a few years George and I grew apart. He wanted to hang on to his spirituality. He started chanting a lot. I think he was desperately trying to reach a nice calm space in his head. But it was so pressurizing and difficult for him. On top of everything else, The Beatles all started arguing with each other on creative levels as well. It was tough times."

During the recording of Let It Be, *George left The Beatles. What did he share with you about his disenchantment after he came home?*
"He came home and told me how he'd left the band. He was in a really bad mood. He said the vibes were so ghastly and that The Beatles were going to split up. I didn't really know what to say to him. I think in a way it was a slow break-up. They all saw it as they were all divorcing each other. I remember one time Ringo came to our house and said he was leaving The Beatles. We were like, 'No, you can't do that!' Gradually they all kind of let go of being in the band. It was too difficult to sustain."

Paul and John's relationships with their wives, Linda and Yoko, endured long after your marriage to George and Maureen's to Ringo ended. Can you explain why?
"At the time, I thought American girls were so cool and so together. I think perhaps Linda and Yoko were much more aware of their needs and wants and they were much more in control whereas I wasn't. I tended to go along with whatever George wanted to do and Maureen did as well with Ringo."

Discuss the duality of George. On one hand, he was a seeker of enlightenment and spirituality and the other he was having affairs on the side.
"George was a human being. He was human, terribly good-looking and very famous. He had his ups and down. Temptations

were thrown at him continually. If you're gonna decide that you're gonna be a priest it's very difficult. I think George was far more aware than other people of the continual battle of one's demons. We all have demons inside of us. We're all full of black and white. He struggled with it. He always wanted to be a good man and do the right thing."

It was surprising to read in your book that George had an affair with Ringo's wife. How did Ringo react to his good friend having an affair with his wife?
"I don't remember. Obviously Ringo was seriously pissed off. But I don't know whether his anger was directed more to Maureen than to George. Remember, I was going through my own hell at the time. I wasn't really noting everyone's pain and anguish. I was going through my own struggles. It was a pretty heavy time for all of us."

Bring us back to when you and George visited Frank Sinatra for the "My Way" recording session.
"We were in L.A. I think maybe George was finishing an album. Then we got a message that Frank Sinatra invited us to a recording session. So we turned up with Mal Evans and we were led into the control room. From the control room we could look through the glass panel and see this very large studio with a full orchestra. Then Frank walked into the studio and I was riveted. Here's the famous Frank Sinatra. He walked in, took the mic and he sang 'My Way'. He was absolutely stunning. All of us in the control room were silenced. Then Frank came into the control room, heard it back again and said, 'That's it!' He did it in one take. Then he said, 'Let's all go out for dinner.' All these limos kind of appeared and we all went to some restaurant on Sunset Boulevard. There was this huge table and everybody sat down. George and I tried to sit next to Frank but his best friends had to sit next to him so we were shoved down the table. [*Laughs.*] George and Frank had a good conversation in the control room and then they spoke at the dinner as well. I think Frank was probably quite curious about George and wanted to hear about The Beatles."

In 1972, you and George met another legend, Elvis Presley, backstage at Madison Square Garden.

"George had total respect for Elvis, he loved him. We were sitting in the audience and suddenly someone came up and said, 'Elvis wants to meet you.' We obeyed like little lambs and went down into his dressing room. We went in and asked where Elvis was and they said, 'He's in the bathroom.' Then he came out and he was wearing his white suit. In my mind's eye he was about ten foot tall. [*Laughs.*] He was magnificent! He shook George's hand and they spoke a few words and that was it. We were then ushered out and went back to our seats.

"I later met Elvis again with Eric [Clapton]. We were in Memphis and Eric's manager, Roger Forrester, said that Elvis invited us to the cinema to see a movie with him. This was just a stunning invitation and we would have to be churlish to have said no. Off we went and we were dropped off at the cinema. We walked into the empty theatre and there was Elvis sitting a few rows from the front surrounded by a few people. So we said hi to Elvis and then we went to sit in the row behind him but his minders said, 'No, no, no, you can't sit there.' We had to sit a few rows back. [*Laughs.*] But Elvis knew Eric was in town so it was very sweet of him to invite us to the cinema."

Being a muse for both George Harrison with "Something" and later with Eric Clapton for "Layla" and "Wonderful Tonight", discuss how it put tremendous pressure on you to be perfect and live up to that ideal.

"Yes, that's true. There is an automatic self-imposed pressure. You can't help but think that people will look at you and go, 'Oh my God, what is it about her that's so special that a song is being written for her?' That's quite pressurizing really. But like I said, it was mainly me assuming the mantle of pressure and trying to live up to it. But I mean, what a great, great compliment. Maybe I never thought about the joys of it at the time because it was such a beautiful and flattering place to be in."

Bring us back to being at the kitchen table when George wrote "My Sweet Lord".
"I remember it very, very clearly. It's a beautiful song and he was so proud of it. It was absolutely stunning. I know he wrote it. He didn't copy it from The Chiffons. It was deeply upsetting and really hurtful when he was called into court in America for supposedly plagiarizing one of The Chiffons' songs. That song became a bit tainted when we were told he'd have to go to court and defend himself with his guitar. George stopped listening to the radio after that so he wouldn't be influenced by any music. There was no possibility of anything else influencing him when he wrote songs."

Can you recount when Eric first played you "Layla"?
"Yes, of course. Eric played it for me on cassette. It was so beautiful. He kept looking at me for my reaction. He wanted me to realize that he had written it for me. It was inspired by a book that we'd both been given by a mutual friend called *The Story of Layla and Manjun*. It was written by a Persian poet and it's a beautiful love story. We were both very familiar with the book and story and the song was based on that story. I was totally mesmerized by the song. It was the most unbelievable music I'd ever heard. Great lyrics, wonderful sentiment and so heartfelt. I still love it."

Eric pursued you for quite some time but you kept pushing him off.
"It may have been two or three years before we became involved. Things were going so bad at home, my relationship with George was collapsing. I thought it was best to go off and visit with my sister who was living in L.A. at the time. I just wanted to get away and work out what I was going to do next. Eric phoned up and said, 'Come join me on tour and see what it's like.' I'd never been on a tour before. It's really exhilarating and sexy and great fun. I had a great time. I thought, 'This is the life, this is wonderful.' I think that was it. I'd made that choice. But I was still not sure if I'd made the right decision."

The normal reaction when one man admits love for another is that friendship is over. Can you explain how George and Eric were able to maintain their friendship?

"Their friendship was mainly based on music. There was a great respect for each other's music. I suppose that was stronger than the other parts of their lives. I'm sure most people would think it's surprising that they were civil about it. I mean, what can I say? That's how it was."

Any regrets today about your relationships with George and Eric?
"No. I accept it. There's no point in wishing and regretting. Frankly, I think that holds you back from life and progressing. You just have to accept it. There were many things involved around making important decisions in my life. I can't think that I made mistakes. Whatever's done is done."

From all accounts, your wedding reception in 1979 was a star-studded event, which featured the likes of Eric, three Beatles (George, Paul and Ringo), Mick Jagger, Robert Plant, Jeff Beck, Ronnie Wood, Jack Bruce, Bill Wyman and others jamming.
"It was fantastic. It was an all-star band. It was a moving feast. The line-up kept changing. Everyone you mentioned played and more. There was a constant turnover of players. If a drummer left someone else was waiting in the wings to pick up the drum sticks. It was wonderful."

Recount your last meeting with George at your cottage a few months before his death. Had he come terms with his imminent passing?
"I don't know if George fully realized that. But on reflection I think maybe that was why he did come over to visit me. He was really sweet. He brought me two little gifts and a plant. He had initially gone to see Ringo who lives near me and then just on the off-chance phoned to see if I was in too. We had a lovely time."

In the book you cite how you felt George's near-fatal stabbing incident may have weakened his defences to the cancer that later claimed his life.
"I think that is true. To have experienced that sort of seriously vicious attack would freak anybody out forever and then your defences are down and one can become vulnerable."

In describing your two husbands, you describe Eric as your "play-mate" and George as your "soulmate".
"It was always great fun to hang out with Eric. It was always playtime. But this was when he was drinking and when someone is drinking they just think of the most mad things to do and the most childish things to do. And it's all great fun. We were in a lucky position because there were always people to pick up the pieces and look after us and cushion the fall. So that was great fun. But then with George he was a true spiritual seeker. We had a very special friendship/relationship that would last all our lives. I knew that. George was always there for me. He was a sweet and gentle person. So what if he had demons. He'd been trying so hard to be good and spiritual."

Lastly, apart from "Something," "Layla" and "Wonderful Tonight", can you select a favourite George and Eric song?
[*Long pause.*] "That's a difficult question. For George, I have to say that I loved a lot of the stuff that he did with The Traveling Wilburys. I loved that music."

And Eric?
"Oh gosh, that's a hard one. [*Long pause.*] How about 'Bell Bottom Blues?'"

"Bell Bottom Blues" is a surprising choice. Why did you select that one?"
[*Laughing.*] "Because I think it might have been about me."

YOKO ONO

In what he describes as a "a composite re-write and development of various books and articles I have written", Alan Clayson explains the nature of John Lennon and Yoko Ono's love and how, in the final full year of The Beatles' existence, it transformed John – temporarily at least – into a sort of cosmic dingbat.

That Old Gang Of Mine: John And Yoko

by Alan Clayson

"That old gang of mine was over the moment I met Yoko"
– John Lennon.

Long before Messrs Harrison, Lennon, McCartney and Starr were disassociated formally as a business enterprise in 1971, each Beatle, however reluctantly or unknowingly, was well into his solo career. Not long after they'd ceased touring in 1966, John's role as Private Gripweed in *How I won The War,* a curate's egg of a film satire, say, or George's safari to India to study sitar had been among factors hinting that professional bonds were loosening.

As they'd been within earshot of each other for every working day since God knows when, it was refreshing, noted Ringo, "to choose when we're together instead of being forced together – and you need to break up a bit to relax, man." Both the media and the lads themselves felt that the separateness of individual projects Enriched The Group As A Whole – to coin a publicist's cliché.

If not as united in play as they once were either, John, George, Paul and Ringo still tended to keep pace with each other's caprices: being photographed at the same premieres, covering the same exhibitions, sampling the same stimulants. They were all sporting moustaches on the *Sgt. Pepper* ... montage. Moreover, marital fetters counted for less than the Beatle brotherhood then – and, so it was assumed, for always. Ringo's Maureen, Cynthia Lennon, Pattie Harrison and Paul's fiancée, Jane Asher were all pale blonde by then, but "the men have a stranglehold on each other" continued Starr. "At one time, we never went out, even with our own wives and girlfriends, unless another Beatle went along too."

That's how he explained it – as much to himself as anyone else – in the *New Musical Express* when he was the first of the four to return home from the Maharishi's encampment in the Himalayas at the beginning of 1968's cold, dry spring. Within months, however, it had become "Lennon and McCartney" rather than "Lennon-McCartney", and, like children of parents who stay together just because neither has yet quite sufficient activation to leave, Ringo – who'd quit briefly already – and George were waiting for John or Paul to marshall his words and dare the speech that everyone knew had to be made.

Just as Billy Shepherd's *The True Story Of The Beatles* ascribed the foundation of the group to John Lennon forming a skiffle combo with fellow schoolboys in the late 1950s, so most later Beatles biographies trace the disbandment to his peculiar behaviour in 1968. By the end of that year, Lennon was regarded by Joe Average as being as mad as a hatter. In restaurants that fame hadn't prevented him from frequenting, strangers on other tables would speak in low voices and glance towards him. Some insisted they could sense an aura of insanity effusing from him as others might the "evil" from child murderer Myra Hindley's eyes. Was he really off his head? Had he – like Friedrich Nietzsche, philosopher of irrationalism – lost his mind during the interminable contemplation of his own genius and glory?

In the moptop era, he'd been not so much mad as merely "zany" in the eyes of the world. In all respects, he appeared sane to Cynthia, even if she'd viewed the trip to India as a final opportunity to revive their marriage. Neither of them were infatuated teenagers any more, holding hands round Liverpool. Before they even tied the knot, all such pretty fondnesses had long gone. Pregnancy had obliged him to marry her – though, had he been reading Nietzsche in 1962, Lennon may have agreed with the German philosopher's personal credo: that marriage and family are incompatible with a life of constant creativity. For him and Cynthia, therefore, there may have never been much hope.

That isn't to say he didn't care about the mother of his child – for all the confusion there still was between Lennon the husband-and-father and Lennon the "available" pop star. Neither was he immune to twinges of conscience as the enormity of what he was about to do sank in – but by 1968, he had no apparent option but to burn his boats as far as he was able, and either instigate a new beginning or anticipate a fall from grace by destroying himself. In the death, he did both.

To a journalist's tape recorder, he had confided his love for a Japanese-American "concept artist" named Yoko Ono, who had captured his heart during a period when, according to Barry Miles, Paul McCartney's biographer, a vulnerable John was in the throes of a nervous breakdown, informing Miles later that "I was still in a real big depression in . . . *Pepper* . . . I was going through murder."

Yoko – who'd said she was "very fond" of John – was a most unlikely Morgan le Fay-esque figure. Small, bossy and seven years his senior, she had arrived in London two years earlier with her second husband and their daughter, having accepted an invitation to take part in a symposium on Deconstruction In Art. She made an easy decision to remain, following overtures from galleries for her to exhibit and, apparently, from Island, a label that went in for oddball ethnic material, for her to submit demos – as she had found a niche already in the distant reaches of the avant garde through vocal gymnastics that owed much to the choral babbling and odd tone clusters of Schoenberg and Penderecki. Back in New York, she had used her voice like a front-line horn in the company of free jazzers like Ornette Coleman, and was seeking similar work in what was for the time being her adopted country.

One's principal source of income, however, came through writing articles for *Art And Artists* and *IT,* and running an art course at the Anti-University, an "alternative" seat of learning in Shoreditch. Her students grew fond of her for her slangy turn of phrase, her Japanese accent from which a strong *Noo Yawk* twang protruded – and, crucially, her infectious enthusiasm for her subject.

Yet perceptible mainstream press interest surfaced via her staging of "happenings" that followed a British stage debut at the Roundhouse. It featured audience participation antics with titles like "Line" (you had to draw one and erase it), "Wall Piece" (joining Yoko in banging your head against one) and the finale, and a sort of word-association game in which Ono yelled something at the paying customers, who responded by bawling back whatever flashed across their collective mind for five minutes.

Free of charge was an event in Trafalgar Square where, recounts record sleeve designer Gene Mahon, "Yoko wanted to be in a black bag, and she called upon a guy called Ed Klein and myself to be 'bodyguards'. Another escapade at the same landmark was wrapping its lion statues in brown paper, attracting roughly the same attention as ex-civil servant Stanley Green, who paced daily back and forth along Oxford Street in a sandwich board that blazoned his creed of "Less Lust From Less Protein" to the few who stopped to read it.

Ono, however, was "cool", and Green wasn't at the dawning of the age of Aquarius. Quarter-page notices heralding her activities surfaced as regularly as rocks in the stream in the fortnightly *International Times* – *IT* – London's, and, by implication, Britain's, foremost underground organ.

The newspaper was sped on its way with a knees-up on a cold October night in 1966 at the Roundhouse where proto-hippies milled about with celebrities like Paul McCartney and other powerful friends of *IT*'s editor, Barry Miles. Thousands more than can have actually have been there were to reminisce about the free sugar-cubes that may or may not have contained LSD; the huge bathtub of jelly; the ectoplasmic light-shows that were part of the act for The Pink Floyd and The Soft Machine – and the latter's recital being interrupted halfway through when the stage was plunged into darkness apart from tiny amplifier bulbs, and Yoko Ono's miked-up voice intoned, "Touch the person next to you". Then the lights came back on, and The Soft Machine carried on as normal.

There she was again the following April at another *IT* benefit, Fourteen Hour Technicolor Dream at Alexandra Palace where she presented promenading onlookers with a female, rendered supine by some narcotic or other, seated on a step-ladder with a blazing spotlight shining on her. Volunteers were handed a pair of scissors each, outfitted with a microphone plugged into the sound system, and directed by the ubiquitous Yoko to cut away the woman's garments. Not everyone was impressed, far from it. "Yoko Ono's happenings were boring," grimaced another *IT* associate, John Hopkins. "She was the most boring artist I'd ever met."

Bitter division remains about Ono's cultural impact during this period. Was she a Tracey Emin *du jour* – or to Art what the late Screaming Lord Sutch was to British politics? Food for such thoughts was digested during an expedition to Liverpool's Blue-coat Chambers in 1967 where she'd had a crowd innocent of the capital's *sang froid* picking up pieces of a jug she'd just smashed. It was an Art Statement, like. She also brushed the stage, ate sandwiches – and wrapped herself in bandages. When she was thus covered, John Garman of multi-media aggregation Scaffold shouted out, "You're wanted on the telephone." Everybody laughed.

The previous November, some found nothing amusing about, for instance, an all-white chess set, an apple with a £200 price tag and further puzzling "Unfinished Paintings And Objects" by Yoko Ono, who, at the preview, had been on the look-out for a mug with a pocketful of money.

That evening, she was introduced to John Lennon. Not quite two years later, she had replaced McCartney as his artistic collaborator as she had Cynthia in his bed. A perturbed *Beatles Monthly* had passed her off as "John's guest of honour" after he brazened it out by escorting her to London's Old Vic theatre on 18 June 1968 to catch an adaptation of his slim 1964 volume, *In His Own Write. Two Virgins*, the Bed-ins and further "happenings" were to follow swiftly.

One of them took place on a Sunday in March 1969 at the University of Cambridge. With his back to the audience, Lennon pushed an electric guitar against a speaker – causing ear-splitting spasms of feedback – and twiddled with some electronic device to create bleeps, flurries, woofings and tweetings to complement peep-parps from Danish saxophonist John Tchikai, the clatterings of drummer John Stevens and Yoko's screeches, wails and nanny-goat jabberings.

John's hand in such far-out music had been one in the eye

for McCartney in the game of hipper-than-thou one-upmanship that had persisted since time immemorial, but nowhere as much as Lennon and Ono's *Unfinished Music No. 1: Two Virgins*, not least for its macabre cover photographs of the pair naked, back and front, that pledged John to Yoko more symbolically than a mere engagement ring ever could – and a magnification of the gap between "us two and you lot" which would soon embrace Paul, George and Ringo too.

When auditioning to join what became Rory Storm and the Hurricanes in 1957, fourteen-year-old George had played and sung Gene Vincent's arrangement of a 1920s song, "Wedding Bells". Its hookline ran, "Those wedding bells are breaking up that old gang of mine."

"The old gang of mine was over the moment I met Yoko," smiled John Lennon. "It was like when you meet your first woman, and you leave the guys at the bar and you don't play snooker and billiards anymore. Maybe some guys like to continue that relationship with the boys, but once I'd found *the* woman, the boys became of no interest whatsoever, other than they were like old friends – but it so happened that the boys were well known and not just the local guys at the bar."

As well as an expression of this, *Two Virgins* was also, so he and Yoko explained, another Art Statement. The man-in-the-street was too bewildered to give an Art Reply. More comprehensible than *Two Virgins* was *Oh Calcutta!*, a post-*Hair* revue then running at the Roundhouse, embracing nakedness in clear white light – and, incidentally, an apposite sketch about schoolboys masturbating together penned by John Lennon, whose career summary in the printed programme ran: "Born 9 October, 1940, Lived. Met Yoko 1966". In London's underground stations at the same time, a poster promoting a newly-released flick, *Till Death Us Do Part* – based on the BBC comedy series – featured a naked Warren Mitchell-as-Alf Garnett – albeit covering up his genitalia with hands and tobacco-pipe – and a caution thanking "John Lennon for pioneering this form of publicity".

It resonated too at the reception following Cilla Black's wedding reception in 1969. Reading a congratulatory telegram from John and Yoko, the bride got a ripple of polite laughter by adding the addenda "Stay nude" (the same scansion as "Hey Jude": get it?). Lennon's intimates had not associated penis display with one who, only three years earlier, had seethed "You don't do that in front of the birds!" when he, Cynthia and the Harrisons had been confronted by an unclothed Allen Ginsberg at a London soiree held on the beatnik bard's birthday.

Most likely, his penchant for such exposure was because of too many acid trips triggering onsets of self-imposed humiliations. He and Yoko had also started on heroin, now a more popular muse for certain songwriters than hallucinogenics.

It was feasible that, as well as consumption of hard drugs, John Lennon's conduct had something to do with St Francis of Assisi's self-abasing habit of preaching the gospel in the nude. Conversely, a few months prior to the cloak-and-dagger release of *Two Virgins* – and the day before he consummated his friendship with Yoko – it was said that Lennon had summoned McCartney, Harrison and Starr behind closed doors in an Apple boardroom in order to proclaim himself the Messiah. He wasn't being funny ha-ha either.

Of all the other Beatle couples, Ringo Starr and his wife Maureen swooped most unquestioningly to Lennon's defence. *Two Virgins* was, concluded Ringo, "just John being John. It's very clean." Yoko became "incredible". No one doubted it either. "We'd be pleased when people realize that she's not trying to be the fifth Beatle," added Starr – though, when waiting to console Yoko before Lennon's cremation twelve years later, he was overheard to mutter, "It was her who started all this." This indicated an adjustment of his previously stated opinion, as late as 1971, that her and John's *amour* had not taken priority over group commitments. "Ringo was a little confused," deduced Klaus Voormann, a friend from Hamburg, "because John's closeness to Yoko was sad to him. John and Yoko were one person, which was difficult for him to accept."

George Harrison, however, wasn't confused at all. One day, he could no longer contain his resentment, particularly as Yoko was now taking an active hand in the running of Apple Corps, The Beatles' crumbling business empire. George burst into the office the couple had commandeered, and came straight to the point. Naming Bob Dylan among those with a low opinion of Yoko, Harrison went on to complain about the present "bad vibes" within The Beatles' circle that were interrelated with her coming. "We both sat through it," sighed John. "I don't know why, but I was always hoping they would come around."

Soon, John's extreme broadness of gesture was an embarrassment to the world outside the protective bubble of The Beatles too. Perhaps the media got wind of the "Messiah" business – because, early in December 1969, it was reported in the *Daily Express* and then several other domestic newspapers that John was "considering" an offer to play the title role in a forthcoming musical, *Jesus Christ Superstar*, but only on condition that Yoko star too as "Mary Magdalene". This was a surprise to composer Andrew Lloyd-Webber and his lyricist, an EMI production assistant named Tim Rice, who issued a terrified denial straightaway.

The *Express* item was, allegedly, the first John heard of the matter, but he didn't mind. It gilded the image. In reciprocation, someone had shouted, "You are a very holy man" when he and Yoko had emerged from Marylebone Magistrates Court on 28 November 1968, when he had been fined after pleading guilty to possession of substances contrary to the provisions of the 1966 Dangerous Drugs Act, section 42.

The rip tide of this latest drama was to wash over Lennon's attempts in the next decade to settle permanently in the United States, but in 1968, he accepted it as part of life's small change – and he didn't find the fuss completely distasteful. Indeed, he seemed so bound up in himself – and Yoko – that every occurrence and emotion was worth broadcasting to as wide an audience as possible, just as, in microcosm, Rory Storm had been prone to do in the dear, dead Merseybeat days, ensuring that his birthday celebrations were public events, and spray-painting "I Love Rory" on a wall at Bootle railway station.

With the means to go infinitely further, John Lennon ordered the issue on Zapple, Apple's short-lived subsidiary record label, of his second LP with Yoko. *Unfinished Music No. 2: Life With The Lions.* The back cover was a *Daily Mirror* shot of him with his arm round a distressed Yoko in the midst of policemen and morbid inquisitiveness outside Marylebone Magistrates. The disc's content, however, was concerned principally with Yoko's subsequent miscarriage – and included the dying foetus' heart-beat, which was offered to and rejected by *Student* magazine as a giveaway flexidisc.

Most self-obsessed of all was autumn 1969's *Wedding Album*. One side of this feast of entertainment was the two's repeated utterances of each other's name suspended over pounding heart-beats – though there was a shadowy link, I suppose, with Marcel Duchamp's "ready-made" art and the provocation of Dada just after the Great War.

If that was the case, then *Self-Portrait* paralleled Duchamp's *Fountain,* a urinal with "R Mutt 1917" painted on it, This forty-two-minute movie starring Lennon's now-famous cock – and some fluid that dribbled from it – was screened at London's Institute of Contemporary Arts in September 1969 as one of several British premieres of Warhol-esque films of similar non-events made by John and the more seasoned movie director, Yoko. Like other of Ono and Lennon's collaborations during this period, most of them were laboured, inconsequential and generally misconstrued comedy. The chief exception was *Rape,* a disturbing hour or so of an obtrusive cameraman following an increasingly more alarmed foreign student around London. *Rape* aside, however, some viewers tried to fool themselves that Yoko and John's celluloid ventures were quite absorbing in parts, even as others fidgeted in their seats.

Rape, the least tedious of all, was broadcast on Austrian tele-vision on 31 March 1969, just as Yoko and John, on a very public honeymoon at the Amsterdam Hilton, were undertaking a "Bed-In for Peace". Now bearded to the cheekbones, John had dragged on a cigarette during a quiet, white-costumed wedding in Gibraltar on 20 March. It was followed at the Amsterdam Hilton's honeymoon suite by this first Bed-In for world peace in hopes that lying about for a week whilst enter-taining the press would stop the atrocities in Vietnam and Biafra more effectively than any protest march or student sit-in.

Both the ceremony and the event were mentioned in "The Ballad Of John And Yoko", The Beatles' final British number one. That each chorus began with the interjection "Christ" restricted airplay, and the entire narrative confirmed the Lennons' status as a Scandalous Couple on a par with Serge

Gainsbourg and Jane Birkin, makers of that summer's "Je T'Aime . . . Moi Non Plus", on which an easy-listening arrangement seeped incongruously beneath their coital grunts, moans and whispers.

John – who was about to change his middle name by deed-poll from "Winston" to "Ono" – and the second Mrs Lennon's canoodling went beyond the bounds of generally acceptable ickiness too. Moreover, to say things most people didn't want to hear or understand, John and Yoko had made their headline-hogging lives an open and ludicrous book with further eye-stretching pranks such as press conferences from inside kingsize sacks, the slapdash letter that would accompany John's renouncement of his MBE, nailing acorns to world leaders, his scrawly lithographs of themselves having sex, and ordering the plastering of billboards proclaiming "War Is Over!" all over eleven city centres. The Ancient Greeks had a word for such conduct: "hubris", which defies adequate translation, but alludes to a heroically foolish defiance rooted in the notion that one is beyond the reaches of authority and convention.

This was reciprocated when a lot of the "War Is Over!" signs were defaced within a day of their appearing. However, something those who did so could grasp more readily, if not sympathize with, had emerged from another crowded "Bed-In" – this time in Toronto – where Lennon's "Give Peace A Chance" was taped. Though "Lennon-McCartney" was given as the composing credit on the record label, this was to be his first smash without Paul, George and Ringo, attributed as it was to the *ad hoc* "Plastic Ono Band". The subsequent full-page advertisement in the music papers assured readers "*You* are The Plastic Ono Band!". Yet, over thirty years later, I still haven't received any royalties for "Give Peace A Chance". Have you?

Never mind, it was a catchy effort – certainly more so than "Revolution 9", the longest track on The Beatles' "White Album". Included at the insistence of Lennon – who created almost all of it with Yoko – only the recurring "Number nine" utterance lends "Revolution 9" even shadowy orthodox form. Nonetheless, it was lauded by Barry Miles in *IT* as a send-up of John Cage's "Fontana Mix", an eleven-minute "chance operation" tape collage from 1958, and a classic of its kind.

Thus, the outlines between The Beatles and Lennon's activities with Ono were fast dissolving and yet widening the chasm between him and his old comrades. "I don't think you could have broken up four very strong people like that," countered Yoko. "There must have been something that happened within them – not an outside force at all."

With all pretensions of The Beatles' four-man brotherhood now gone, Yoko's constant and baleful adherence to John at Abbey Road entitled Paul McCartney to bring along girlfriend Linda Eastman, who was from a family of US showbusiness attorneys. While Linda and the older Yoko had both attended school in the same smart New York suburb, they didn't have much in common, although they were both to marry their respective English *beaux* during the same month.

That there were moments of congeniality, but generally lukewarm rapport between the chief Beatles' immovable women was one of Ringo's "little niggly things" – one of them – that cropped up as the group worked through the "White Album" and then *Let It Be* ("the most miserable session on Earth", scowled John).

While they rallied for the subsequent *Abbey Read*, it was, as Debussy said of Wagner's *Das Rheingold*, "a glorious sunset mistaken for a dawn" – for, when it was hot off the press, John was approached to compere an open-air pop festival in Canada. Instead, he, Yoko and some hastily-rehearsed accompanists – Eric Clapton, drummer Alan White (from The Alan Price Set) and, on bass, Klaus Voormann – performed at midnight on Saturday 13 September 1969. Issued as *Live Peace In Toronto 1969*, their ragged set consisted mainly of olde-tyme rock 'n' roll, Yoko's screech-singing – and a nascent arrangement of "Cold Turkey", a forthcoming new Plastic Ono Band single.

It penetrated most international Top Twenties by the New Year. Its B-side was Yoko's "Don't Worry Kyoko (Mummy's Only Looking For Her Hand In The Snow)", which her spouse found as potent as he had Little Richard's "Tutti Frutti". Interminable work-outs of "Don't Worry Kyoko" and "Cold Turkey" filled John's last stage appearance in Britain when he led a "Plastic Ono Supergroup" – with George Harrison in its ranks – at London's Lyceum ballroom in December 1969.

Along with George and Ringo, John had melted into the managerial caress of Allen Klein, the US "Robin Hood of pop", whose reputation stood on his extracting fortunes for his clients from seemingly ironclad record company budgets and percentages. They applauded too his purge at Apple that curbed embezzlements and fiddles, and discontinued sinecures and unviable ventures like Zapple. Yet Klein's streamlining of Apple was nothing compared to his re-negotiation of a royalty rate with US outlet, Capitol, that amassed millions for The Beatles – albeit a Beatles who couldn't care less any more.

Paul favoured his own father-in-law to bring order to Apple and The Beatles' increasingly more tangled threads. With his maiden solo album on the way, Paul had been preparing a press release that, in April 1970, almost-but-not-quite proclaimed, his departure from the group. Yet John had slipped a teasing ". . . when I was a Beatle" into an interview with *Disc & Music Echo* in November 1969, and had tendered privately his own resignation well before Paul.

Having said it at last, much of the tension that had accumulated during the emotional and vocational millennia that had passed since he'd first encountered Yoko had flowed from John Lennon. An unsettled chapter in his life had just ended. If a lot of his problems had been self-inflicted, it had been a demanding and stressful time that he wouldn't wish on anyone else. Now he could get on with the rest of his life. How could he have known then that he had only ten years left?

Alan Clayson is the author of The Quiet One: A Life Of George Harrison, *(Sidgwick and Jackson),* Ringo Starr: Straight Man Or Joker? *(Sanctuary),* Backbeat: Stuart Sutcliffe: The Lost Beatle *(with Pauline Sutcliffe, Pan Macmillan),* Hamburg: The Cradle Of British Rock *(Sanctuary),* John Lennon *(Sanctuary),* The Walrus Was Ringo: 101 Beatles Myths Debunked *(with Spencer Leigh, Chrome Dreams),* Paul McCartney *(Sanctuary) and* Woman: The Incredible Life Of Yoko Ono *(with Barb Jungr and Robb Johnston, 2004).*

LINDA McCARTNEY

*". . . a lovely couple . . . all the same, I wouldn't let my old lady play
the piano," derisively remarked Mick Jagger in an interview in reference
to the fact that Linda McCartney, née Eastman, was an integral part
of Paul's post-Beatles band Wings. Mick was the model of restraint,
however, compared to some of the British tabloids (one headline was,
"Who the hell does Linda McCartney think she is?").*

*There is a valid point to be made about the wisdom of bringing
a non-musician into a rock group, but it was going to be no other
way: Paul fell for Linda as completely and overwhelmingly as John
did Yoko and until Linda's death from cancer in 1998, only Paul's
incarceration in a Japanese prison could separate them. And though
Paul may have put a spanner in the works of Wings ever being a
truly great group by employing someone who was a talented photographer but not a trained musician, the upside to that situation was
that she was the muse for many fine songs, "Two Of Us", "The Long
And Winding Road", "Maybe I'm Amazed", "My Love" and "Silly
Love Songs" amongst them.*

*Phil Sutcliffe traces the beginnings of what is indubitably one of
the love affairs of the twentieth century.*

When Paul Met Linda

by Phil Sutcliffe

"The Bag O'Nails was a soul club really, but when the hippies started coming down it was like having a hundred Quasimodos in, you couldn't hear the band for all the fucking bells," avers John Gunnell, co-owner of the Kingly Street watering-hole-to-the-stars – the place where Paul McCartney met Linda Eastman.

So Gunnell banned the bells: "These people would come jangling up to the door and we'd say, 'Sorry, no bells,' and, nice as you like, they'd go back to their cars and put their normal gear on."

By November 1966, when Gunnell and his partners bought "the Bag", Swinging London was shading into Psychedelic London. But rather tentatively. Although the Beat Boom bands had embraced flowery shirts and the antiseptic reek of patchouli, in off-duty hours they sought the members-only haven of what long-time Beatles staffer Tony Bramwell calls "these gentlemen's youth clubs", sanctuaries they shared with well-heeled business-men, tourists and footballers (the Bag O'Nails became Frank McLintock era Arsenal's hang-out). In turn, these "straights" remained unruffled because no conspicuous consumption of psychedelics occurred in front of them – fear of US visa depri-vation ensured that most drug use, even pot smoking, remained ultra-covert at the time.

Before Gunnell bought the place, since Victorian times it had been an upper-class "hostess" joint. He retained the long, narrow cellar room's harem-style silk drapes, flock wallpaper and booths along the walls, cleared a small dancefloor and installed a bandstand and DJ turntables. For some months, former account customers would ring for "a bottle of Dom and a couple of dolly birds" to be home delivered.

But there again *plus ça change*. In Barry Miles' *Many Years From Now*, Paul McCartney said that, basically, he went to his "favourite club" on the pull – as he would tell John Lennon, he wasn't married to Jane Asher and, anyway, that winter she toured America for six months with the Bristol Old Vic company. "We were young, we were looking pretty good and we had all this power and fame and it was difficult to resist playing with it," he said. "Now I recall, I might have got asked for money one night after pulling some bird. I wouldn't pay, though."

A regular, he came for DJ Al Needles' choice soul selections and live acts including Sam & Dave, Junior Walker and John Lee Hooker. Plus the crack, of course. Always friendly with the staff, from manager Joe Van Duyts to Spanish cook Manuel, no matter what time of night he arrived he could always whistle up one of his Scouse favourites, a chip buttie or a Spam sandwich (this predated by a few months what 1960s scenesman Jeff Dexter dubbed the "macroneurotic" movement).

With work on *Sgt. Pepper's Lonely Hearts Club Band* finished, on 15 May 1967 he took off on one of his solo club crawl nights, maybe taking in The Cromwellian and The Crazy Elephant before ending up at the Bag O'Nails. He joined Bramwell, already ensconced, for his usual, Scotch and Coke. A booth or two nearer the band – Georgie Fame, that night – sat Linda Eastman with Eric Burdon and Chas Chandler from The Animals, whom she'd photographed several times in America.

Nobody noticed if the Earth moved, but some snapshot memories of the quietly fateful occasion remain. Linda recalled an "our eyes met" moment. Bramwell says McCartney went over to her table. The late Chandler always insisted he made the introduction. Conversely, McCartney says she was actually leaving when he "accidentally" stepped in front of her and delivered his "big pulling line", asking her to come on to The Speakeasy with him. They both remembered what Georgie Fame was playing as they spoke: a Billy Stewart song, "Sitting In The Park".

With Burdon, Chandler and Bramwell, they drove the half-mile to Margaret Street where they enjoyed the house staple, plates of peppersteak and chips with chef Enzo's special mushy peas *alla* fried onion. But for Paul and Linda the more abiding memory was the DJ's pre-release unveiling of "A Whiter Shade Of Pale". They thought it was wonderful and it must be Traffic. In remarkably delayed-action fashion, it became "their song".

They met again at Brian Epstein's house four days later – Linda establishing her professional credentials by shooting the *Sgt. Pepper's Lonely Hearts Club Band* press launch. After that, they didn't see each other again for almost a year while McCartney helter-skeltered through his internationally scandalous LSD confession to *Life* magazine, Brian Epstein's death, the Maharishi, *Magical Mystery Tour* and a forlorn last try of an engagement to Jane Asher.

Then, in May and June 1968, he met Linda for an hour in New York and three days in Los Angeles. Another three months on, he rang and asked her to come over and stay with him. She arrived on the night The Beatles finished recording "Happiness Is A Warm Gun", 25 September.

John Gunnell says the day before they married, 12 March 1969, McCartney came down to the Bag O'Nails and invited the entire staff to the wedding (which none of the other Beatles attended).

But, the night they met, did Paul pull after all? Well, he drove Linda back to his house in Cavendish Avenue. And Linda, with either enduring American innocence or acquired British relish for the double entendre, later reported, "I was impressed to see his Magrittes".

Thanks to interviewees: Keith Altham, Tony Bramwell, Jeff Dexter, Georgie Fame, John Gunnell. Other sources: *1960s: Portrait Of An Era* by Linda McCartney (Pyramid); *Paul McCartney: Many Years From Now* by Barry Miles (Vintage); *The Beatles: A Diary* by Barry Miles; *Days In The Life: Voices From The English Underground 1961–1971* by Jonathon Green (Pimlico).

PART FIVE: INTERVIEWS

Verbatim or semi-verbatim interview transcripts are sometimes rambling affairs but they often provide much greater detail on a subject than articles which feature their edited highlights, as illustrated by the following interviews, new and old, with Beatle people.

PETE BEST

Pete Best is the most famous rock 'n' roll cast-off in history. The man who was given the boot from The Beatles on the very cusp of their recording career proper has become a byword for shattered pop dreams.

Best was in a skiffle group at school but caught what he calls "the bug" when he saw the nascent Beatles performing at the Casbah Club, the live music venue run from the basement of his family home by his mother Mona. The Silver Beatles recruited Best in August 1960, dropping the "Silver" part of their name on the way over to Hamburg on their first trip there. Why The Beatles decided to replace him on drums with Ringo Starr in August 1962 after two years' service remains in dispute but when he was – for whatever reason – sacked after George Martin had supposedly brought into question his abilities, Best's first reaction to the shock was to pick himself up, dust himself down and try to obtain stardom himself. As the best-looking Beatle and a man with a huge following in Liverpool, he probably imagined that the prospects were good. But stints in Lee Curtis And The All-Stars and then his own band didn't work out. By 1965, he was attempting suicide.

The release of Anthology 1 *in 1995 marked something of a healing process for Best, who by the close of the 1960s had abandoned his quest for showbusiness success, going first into bakery and then the civil service. The retrospective included several tracks featuring his drumming. He was reportedly offered the choice of a flat fee or royalties. Cannily, he opted for the latter and became wealthy.*

This author spoke to him in 2002 when he was promoting The Beatles: The True Beginnings, *a book by his brother Roag about the Casbah Club. A pleasant man – with his Liverpool accent much broader than those of any of his former colleagues, as one would expect of someone who never left the city – he still seemed a little bewildered by his ejection from the group who would become entertainment's greatest phenomenon.*

Interview with Pete Best

by Sean Egan

Why is it that Liverpool of all the cities in Britain had so many bands?
"I think it was part of the heritage. Liverpool's always been a vibrant stronghold for musicians, even dating back to jazz, big band. There was always eminent musicians came out of Liverpool and then when the skiffle/rock/Mersey pop – whichever name you want to put on it – evolved, it seemed a natural thing for the kids in Liverpool to be doing. There were musicians behind every door and when it actually became possible to actually play music without spending an awful lot of money – tea chest basses and all the rest of it – every other kid wanted to either grab a tin box, a set of drums . . . They just wanted to play."

Would it be fair to say that only a dozen or so were really top quality?
"No, I think that'd be hard. There were twelve or fifteen bands which played regularly 'cos they were crowd pleasers. The promoters realized if they put those bands on, the crowds would be there. But there were a lot of other bands in Liverpool which didn't get the break. They were good and possibly with a little bit more exposure, a little bit more belief by the promoters, they would have been up there. But it's tough business and there's only so many bands which promoters will book."

When you started playing drums, was there any thought in your mind of doing it as a long-term proper career?
"Far from it. I was doing it because I was sucked into this rock 'n' roll idiom. I initially started off tinkering around on a guitar and I found that wasn't to my liking and then I was influenced by watching the old films of Gene Kupra and it was like, 'That's me'. I was always one who had itchy feet and fingers, I was always tapping things. People said I had natural rhythm. I just thought the drums would be the avenue. We formed The Blackjacks as a result of The Quarry Men not continuing to play at the Casbah – Ken Brown who was in The Quarry Men asked me to form a band and I did with school friends who'd been through the skiffle era before that, so they were seasoned musicians even though they weren't professionals and I was just going to do it for fun. I had no inclination to become a professional, but life plays funny tricks on you. At that stage my intentions were to go to teacher training college. I was going to become a language master because I'd studied that in school. [The Beatles] had the offer for a month in Germany and it turned out to be five months and it turned out to be two years. Once I'd tasted the long hours and the adrenalin was flowing, I wasn't going to go back to teacher training college. I was going to be a drummer."

What bands had you played in before The Beatles?
"I'd played in a skiffle group at school."

When did your mum come up with the idea of the Casbah Club?
"Early 1959. She saw a programme on the television about the Two I's coffee club in London and that was so prolific. People were getting discovered there. She just turned round after seeing this programme and said, 'Be a good idea to open a coffee club in the basement'. We were totally overjoyed with this. They were the in-thing. She set a date in stone as regards when the club would open, and that was 29 August 1959."

You saw the first public appearance of John, George and Paul as The Quarry Men.
"It was the re-emergence of them. They actually got together to open the Casbah. [They] didn't have a drummer but it was John,

George, Paul and Ken Brown. If it hadn't of been for the opening of the Casbah, maybe they'd never have got together again. There's been a lot of misconceptions about that because there were The Quarry Men before that but it was a totally different line-up but this was the particular line-up that had the essence to go on to become The Beatles. I watched them avidly. I'd heard them practicing, because they'd had a couple of rehearsals before that particular opening night and they'd helped decorate the club, so it was very much their club. John had painted the Aztec ceiling. Paul painted the rainbow ceiling. George painted the stars in the coffee bar along with myself and Ken Brown. The beauty of it is, the Casbah still stands with all those things as it closed its doors forty years ago. I actually stood in the audience that opening night and I was as mesmerized as the rest of the kids in there. The atmosphere was fantastic. The banter . . . The rapport they had with the crowd. And the type of music they were playing, the harmonies they were singing, the choice of material. It was something even then, I thought to myself, 'There's something special about that'. I felt it along with a lot of other people. There was a spark there. It was a diamond which hadn't been polished. It was there. It was waiting to be discovered. All the elements were there. It just needed to be picked up and kindled. It was all guitars. They weren't expensive guitars. They were electric, but they went through one amplifier and it wasn't the biggest of amplifiers, but regardless of that they still managed to put on this incredible show. That is what sticks in my mind. With the advent of other bands coming down – every major band in Liverpool played the Casbah on a regular basis – and you saw the different class of equipment that other people were using, 'Look at the equipment that the other people have got – yet they still sound as good as that'."

It's said that the Casbah had a capacity of 1,000 people, so your house must have been huge?
"By today's regulations, it would hold 300 max. We had 800 people in – they were like sardines – but the overspill of the people would end up in the courtyard, outside the club. They'd be sitting in the garden. As long as they could hear the music and enjoy the atmosphere. There'd be nights we'd have 1,500 people there. It stands in an acre of ground."

Does this mean you were from a quite well-to-do background?
"It was a case of working your way up the market. My mother was always infatuated with big houses. But it wasn't a case of, 'We're middle class so we're gonna live in a big house'. We worked hard for what we got."

In a way the Casbah Club seems to have had more potential than The Cavern because it could hold more people and it opened eighteen months before The Beatles made their first Cavern appearance. Is there any reason it didn't take off like The Cavern?
"It was The Cavern before The Cavern. The Casbah was the catalyst in Liverpool. We had music seven nights. In its hey-day there was seven bands on a week and every major band and every up-and-coming band played the Casbah. It was the Casbah which was the catalyst for the Mersey sound. Due to circumstance of events, unfortunately the club closed in June of '62. As we closed our doors, their doors were starting to open as regards the rock 'n' roll industry. Where before it was the Casbah which was the catalyst for music, The Cavern became the catalyst for music."

It was situated in West Derby. Where's that?
"It is a suburb. It's about four miles out from town centre. If she'd have continued to keep it going, maybe the Casbah would have eclipsed The Cavern."

How did you come to join The Beatles?
"By this time Stu had actually been approached to join the band and played bass. The funny thing was, that took place in the Casbah. That was something which I was privy to. John was on one side, Paul was on the other. They were persuading Stu to spend his money which he won from the John Moores exhibition to buy a bass 'cos they needed a bass player. By the time Paul phoned me to go to Germany because they needed a drummer – Tommy Moore had left them after a tour of Scotland – Stu was well ensconced in the band."

What did you think of Stuart Sutcliffe as musician?
"A lot of people tend to think of Stu, he could plunk the bass but that was about all. I think he was a better musician than

what people give him credit for. It's only when you play with other bass players afterwards that you realize there are better bass players around but what he gave was two hundred per cent."

Can you describe your style of drumming?
"I felt the engine room was lacking a little bit as regards drive and consequently I started to do things. I had a pretty big sound anyway as a drummer from copying Kupra and a lot of tom-tom work and when I went out to Germany I just felt that I needed to enhance it a bit more: we had to push the beat a bit more, we had to make it a bigger sound, so I started to do things on the drums which people nicknamed afterwards when I brought it back to Liverpool the Atom Beat. It was something which I just felt was required to actually push the band forward, tighten the sound, make if fuller, make it fiercer, make it more forceful. [In Germany] it developed six, seven hours a night. We just did exactly the same thing which we'd done in Germany but it just blew people away and the type of style that I was playing drumming, to the other drummers in Liverpool, it was like, 'What the hell is he playing?' and they tried to copy that style."

So what was the exact technique behind the Atom Beat?
"There was a very strong bass drum beat in it, which was my way of holding the rhythm down. I used to do a lot of bass drum work. One thing which people noticed as regards the sound of The Beatles was the bass drum. The bass drum cut through. This was something which hadn't been done before. That big sound. Other drummers had been pretty lightweight. I was doubling up on the snare drum, so instead of just playing off-shots, single shots, I was playing exactly the same with my left hand as what I was doing with the right."

Who were you closest to in the band?
"Out of all of them I was closest to John because we laughed at the same things. John and I spent the nights together propping the bars in Hamburg and chewing the fat and discovering one another and when we came back to Liverpool, he spent a lot of time at my house, I spent a lot of time at his."

Would it be fair to say that in those days John was actually quite a disturbed and unstable young man?
"I wouldn't say disturbed. I'd say there were two characters of John. When I got to know him, I thought it was a self-defence mechanism. It was his way of keeping the public at large [away]: 'Okay, that's as close as you get to me, that's the image I'm going to be portray'. Very caustic-witted, funny, hard-edged person. I realized that behind that façade there was a very tender and a very loving person but there was only a chosen few who actually get to see that particular side. The rest of the world saw what John wanted them to see."

Can you remember when John and Paul first started trying to work up some songs together?
"Middle of '61. The reason for it was, when we came back to Liverpool, most of the bands in Liverpool had been pretty light-weight, they'd been playing top twenty stuff: The Shadows, Cliff Richard and all this type of stuff. We came back with a repertoire which was totally different to everyone else's and, as a result of that, many of the bands in Liverpool changed the type of music they were playing and copied The Beatles. To be different from everyone else, they suddenly decided to introduce material which they had written themselves. And it was great. For them to actually turn round and say, 'Okay, here's a song which we've written ourselves' to the kids in the audience, it's like: wow. The funny thing was the calibre of the material was excellent. I'm talking about 'Like Dreamers Do', 'Love Of The Loved', the very early ones which were recorded and became gigantic hits for people afterwards."

What was the dynamic like between Paul and John?
"They were mates. They had been for quite some time. They played off one another. I watched that on stage. It was very much a case of one-upmanship between the two of them. It was great for the band and it was great for the audience watching it. They were perfect foils to one another. If one made a remark, the other would counteract with a remark just as quick. Forget the audience: they just happened to be there."

Were The Beatles the first Liverpool band to use harmonies?
"I wouldn't say they were the first. But they were doing three-part harmonies in 1959 and it became so expert. Afterwards people realized that if they could sing harmonies, that was the way to go. You had Paul who had this fantastic range. John was the grit and gravel – he had that little growl in his voice. George could pitch at any level. You put the three of those together and you've just got natural born harmonies."

What do you remember about Tony Sheridan?
"Tony deserves a lot of credit. I think he improved everyone's musicianship. We looked up to him as musicians. Playing with him, his musicianship, his choice of chords, his delivery, the way he involved himself with the band. He became another person on stage who was a Beatle. If I can quote Tony, Tony said when he played with The Beatles at the Top Ten, he never played with another band like it: it was like being Elvis Presley backed by The Jordinaires."

Everybody in Liverpool says you were by far the most popular Beatle. It must have done your ego a lot of good to find all the girls swarming around you?
"The funny thing is, I was never consciously aware of the fact that I was supposed to be the 'heartthrob' of the band. It was only after the dismissal, I suddenly realized with the reaction from the fans that I'd been that popular. It was very heart-warming but it was too late to do anything."

Some people have said that George Martin never managed to capture the power The Beatles had live, even the version of "Twist And Shout" he recorded. Would you agree with that?
"Forty years ago, recording techniques were completely different to what they are now. You had good records but you'd never get that stage sound on record, not at that time. They were more raucous than that."

Would you say that the recording of "Twist And Shout" was the closest anyone came to capturing The Beatles' live power?
"Yes."

When Brian Epstein signed you, presumably there were quire a few people taking the mick out of the band and implying it was because he was gay?

"I've heard so many different things: Brian signed us because he liked leather . . . Brian propositioned me – that's true, happened on the way to Blackpool but it was a flat rejection and no more was said about it. We realized that Brian was gay but it was fine as long as he was working for us and getting the results we wanted."

Was it an exciting time when you went down to EMI to talk about recording?

"When we went down to EMI the first time, we desperately needed an English recording contract. We were going down to meet George Martin to let him listen to our own material. It was very important. We'd been turned down by Decca. We'd had our releases with Polydor. But we suddenly realized in view of the fact that Decca had turned us down – it was the biggest company in England at that time – this was a very, very important thing for us. Yeah, we had the contract but we had to make sure that the material we did on that first release was something which we wanted to do. We'd rejected other material which had been sent down to us because we believed in our own material and that was the strength of the band."

If you read Spencer Leigh's book Drummed Out! *many, many Liverpool musicians are adamant that you were sacked because the others were jealous of the female attention you attracted. Is that your suspicion?*

"There's so many assumptions. I don't know to this day what the real reason is but they range from hairstyle to being anti-social to wouldn't speak to not being a good drummer, jealousy – you name it. Every conceivable angle has been developed but some of the basic ones which came out initially – the hairstyle – never got asked. If you look at me, I've gone into leathers, I've gone into suits, wore cowboy boots, I've grown my hair down the back of me neck: I've done everything they wanted me to do. We all had Tony Curtis/Elvis Presley/James Dean hair-cuts when we were younger. They changed. If they'd have asked me, I'd have changed. It was as simple as that. Why would I stop? I'd been doing what they wanted me to do for two years. Not being a good enough drummer: I've always turned round and rejected that one quite vociferously simply because of the fact that I was reputed to be one of the best drummers in Liverpool. And anti-social? Well, I can talk the hind legs off a donkey if I want to. So a lot of the things don't add up, but I wasn't there, I didn't know what the true allegations behind the dismissal were. Maybe I never will. There's only a few people now who are still alive who know those reasons."

Did Anthology 1 *change your perspective on The Beatles?*
"I've never thought that it was a bad thing that I was in The Beatles. There was one incident which changed my life, but I'd never said that the period that I was with them was a bad period. I've always looked back on that regardless of what happened as being two very exciting years. We conquered frontiers, we grew in musicianship. It was a privilege to be part of the band. The fact that they became the phenomena . . . I chased them as hard and as fast as I could but I couldn't get there. They were on the Concorde and I was still on the cargo plane. I led a very normal life. I went back into showbusiness in 1988. I thought it was going to be a one-off concert. Lo and behold here I am nearly fifteen years down the line touring with my own band. Touring the world and enjoying myself, right back in showbusiness again."

GEORGE MARTIN

The 1982 BBC Radio One series The Record Producers *was a landmark in the way it gave the men behind the studio consoles an extended turn in the spotlight. Researched and written by John Tobler and Stuart Grundy, it was staggering in its comprehensiveness: of all the major producers in rock history, only Phil Spector declined to be interviewed by them (although that didn't stop them putting together a programme on him). Naturally, George Martin was one of the producers profiled. Martin gave a highly articulate and engaging account of his time working with The Beatles and others.*

Tobler and Grundy issued a book of the same name, a book borne out of their frustration at having to prune down their vast quantity of fascinating material on the subject "to the simple, easily-assimilated morsels of information that radio is best suited to communicate". Published the same year, the book remains a cornerstone of the study of the record producer, though is now, outrageously, out of print.

The material below constitutes the first part of the George Martin chapter, covering his formative years and his time spent helming the sessions of the Far Four. In it, Martin reveals details – still largely unknown to this day – about his memories of the sacking of Pete Best, the recording of several of the group's famous songs and the circumstances surrounding the Get Back/Let It Be *sessions.*

Interview with George Martin

by John Tobler and Stuart Grundy

In much the same way as Jerry Leiber and Mike Stoller were the first American record producers, that accolade in Britain belongs to the man whose name was arguably the first to be widely accepted as such, George Martin. Almost everyone with any kind of interest in popular music knows that Martin produced the vast majority of records made by The Beatles, and was the man responsible for first presenting that unstoppable phenomenon to the world, but it's often forgotten that he had produced a wide variety of successful records prior to his involvement with The Beatles and many of their friends and contemporaries from Liverpool, and continues to produce other acts with some success today.

Martin was born on 3 January 1926, in London, and became interested in the piano at an early age. Having served his country in the Royal Air Force at the end of the Second World War, he studied for three years at the Guildhall School of Music, before working for a short time as a freelance oboe player, which was followed by a brief spell at the BBC in a clerical post, albeit one which demanded some musical expertise. Then came the invitation which certainly changed George Martin's life, although perhaps it would be overstating the case to suggest that it profoundly influenced the course of popular music – one of the professors at the Guildhall had suggested to the head of the Parlophone record label (one of the smaller labels within the giant EMI organization), that he should employ Martin as his assistant, and the latter gratefully accepted the position when it was offered to him.

"I joined EMI as assistant to Oscar Preuss, head of Parlophone Records, in November 1950. Parlophone was a very small label, very much junior to the big brothers, HMV and Columbia, and unlike them, had no American input. So Oscar did virtually everything himself, from light orchestral music through to Scottish country dance and the pop music of the day to Victor Silvester and people like that, and I came along to help him. He also used to do classical music, and as I was classically trained, I was given the job of producing classical music for the label, although the word 'producer' was never used at that time, basically because it was a bit like a factory business anyway – the guy who did the record production was an overseer who used to take charge of the sessions and organize them in the first place. His title was A & R manager, which didn't stand for 'Artistes & Repertoire' in 1950, it stood for 'Artistes & Recording'. He was the guy who actually signed the artists, so he had to know something about contracts, had to authorize payment to musicians and book them, book the studios, and go along to make sure that everything was all right. Inevitably, because someone had to exert some critical assessment of the whole thing, he was the guy who said, 'Well, I think we should take the tempo a bit faster, chaps', and that kind of thing, and gradually, his influence became a bit more marked, to the point where he was taking a very creative part in the building of the music, by which time he had become known as a record producer. I kind of evolved along with that process, as the years passed, but before that, Oscar Preuss had taught me everything he knew, and I gradually took over his job, so that by the time he retired in 1955, I was to all intents and purposes running the label, and was given the job of Head of Parlophone."

To elaborate a little on one of the items mentioned by George, the question of "American input" was fairly crucial in the first half of the 1950s – for the early part of that period, American CBS records were released in Britain on the Columbia label owned by EMI, which brought artists like Guy Mitchell, Frankie Laine, Doris Day and Johnnie Ray to the label, while HMV were fortunate enough to be able to release Elvis Presley's first dozen hits in Britain, these examples merely being the cream on the cake. Parlophone had no such licensing agreements, so that all its output was the result of Preuss, and later Martin, discovering and recording the talent which was available in Great Britain. This inevitably meant that a great deal of time was spent in the recording studio. "Yes, on an average day about fifty per cent of my time was studio work, but it was a very much more leisurely process than it is now. For a start, the Parlophone office was actually in the same building as Abbey Road Studios, so I just had to walk down the corridor to be in the studio. And of course, there weren't the pressures of modern-day recording – things were much cheaper, and it was all very friendly. You didn't sell many records either – if you sold fifteen hundred, that was about the break-even figure, and if you sold three thousand, you were on to a big seller.

"The EMI Studios were also not particularly well-equipped technically, and things were pretty primitive, although that's not to say that good records weren't made there, because they certainly were. The sound we got out of Number One Studio at Abbey Road was beautiful – I remember some of the early records I made with the London Baroque Ensemble, which were obviously mono in those days, where we used a very small number of microphones, maybe even a single Altec for a woodwind group, but the ambience of the studio was so good that we got beautiful sounds which still hold up and are heard today. Gimmickry was another matter, of course, and we found that American recording techniques were very much in advance of ours by the time 1955 came along, which was the beginning of the rock 'n' roll period. We listened to sounds coming out of America which would horrify most English people because they were so blatant and coarse, and things were being done to records technically which caused many a raised eyebrow among the legitimate engineers at Abbey Road, but the only way to fight them was to join them, so we started breeding a new kind of engineer and chucked away all the old conventions. Not that I necessarily liked all of the music coming out of America – some of it was very exciting, but I don't like pigeonholing things. I don't like calling myself a rock 'n' roll producer or a classical producer, because I've produced all sorts of records and enjoyed them all, I like being versatile and hate just doing one thing, because I think it wrong to be confined in that way."

An excellent illustration of what Martin means by versatility can be discerned from the curious fact that his first significant fame arguably came as a result of production of comedy records during the 1950s and early 1960s. "That was kind of an act of desperation really, because when Oscar retired in 1955, and I took over Parlophone, I was left with this tiny label which didn't mean much, and because HMV and Columbia had the benefit of all these strong American catalogues, their producers actually heard a lot of new American material before anyone else, and could play it to their artists. I envied this advantage, although I couldn't compete with them on their own level, so I had to find something between the cracks, something which other people weren't doing. One of the things they weren't doing was comedy records, and that was because most people thought they wouldn't sell. But I think my producing career really started with those comedy records, because I was getting very involved on the floor instead of just being in the control room saying, 'Yes, that's nice' or 'You're singing a bit flat.' It became a matter of going through material and saying, 'Let's not do this. If we put a bit of music behind this, or have the sound of a band saw coming in from the left, it'll make it much better.' It was creating before we got into the studio at that stage, and really that's what a producer is up to – he's sort of masterminding the concept of it what it's going to sound like before it actually happens, and the comedy records were tremendous training for me in that."

Probably the first notable comedy record made by Martin featured Peter Ustinov. "I'd met him through the London Baroque Ensemble, because he was very keen on classical music, and the original record we did, 'Phoney Folk Lore' and 'Mock Mozart', was a multi-track job where he sang four different times over all the different things. We didn't have multitrack machines in those days, so it had to be sound on sound, and of course everybody knows that when you put sound on sound you get horrendous quality after about three times, so we had to be awfully careful with our signal to noise ratios and things. In those days, it was considered to be not only adventurous but downright stupid to go to that extreme merely to get one person singing with himself, but it worked, and that record turned out to be a success, luckily for me. So I got the reputation for being an oddball, and I was quite friendly with Spike Milligan and Peter Sellers – this was in the early Goon days, before Peter became an international star – and when I made the first Peter Sellers album, my bosses had so little faith in it that they said I couldn't make a twelve-inch album, because it wouldn't sell at that price, and I was only allowed to make a ten-inch LP. So I arrogantly called it *The Best of Sellers,* and fortunately for me, it turned out to be that, so I was able to go on and do more things."

"Other things" included more work with The Goons, and in particular Peter Sellers and Spike Milligan (Harry Secombe, who was also a conventional singer, signed to another record label, seems not to have taken part too often), for albums like *Songs For Swinging Sellers* and *Bridge Over The River Wye,* respectively, *An Evening Of British Rubbish,* a highly bizarre live recording of a West End show which must have been completely meaningless to those unversed in certain peculiar aspects of British humour, a pair of hit singles in "Right Said Fred" and "Hole In The Ground" performed by Bernard Cribbins, four hit singles with the Temperance Seven, a nine-piece (of course) band who played pre-war styled music, and who topped the British charts with "You're Driving Me Crazy" in 1961, work with Rolf Harris, and another hit with "Goodness, Gracious Me", performed by Peter Sellers and Sophia Loren. Added to that, during the same early 1960s period, were live albums of *That Was The Week That Was,* the television programme fronted by David Frost and also starring many of the leading University comedians, *Beyond The Fringe,* which launched Peter Cook and Dudley Moore to fame, and *At The Drop Of A Hat,* a famous entertainment of its time, performed by Michael Flanders and Donald Swann.

"They were such charming people, and that was just a question of my going along to hear them at a little place in Notting Hill Gate, loving what I heard, and suggesting that we made it into an album. They were delighted and came into London, it was a big success and all was well, but it was good experience too. I recorded five different shows and edited it down to one – it's really the kind of thing people do on radio all the time now. You can't have any control over what people are doing, you just have to make the best of what's there, and it's good useful experience, knowing about acoustics and editing facilities. *Beyond The Fringe* was even more difficult in a way – they were up at Cambridge when we first got to them, and they were a success at the Edinburgh Festival before they came to London. Of course, their humour was very zany, and they never did the same thing twice in the same direction. By this time we were recording stereo, and with a live stereo recording, we had to be awfully careful with our editing, because sometimes Jonathan Miller would be jumping forty feet in the space of half a second."

Comedy was only one facet of the Parlophone success story under George Martin. One of the acts on the label which George produced was Jimmy Shand, who would apparently record one year's worth of Scottish country dance music in one lengthy session, this amounting to as many as eighty-four different tracks during one week which would be issued during the following year. Somewhat more acceptable to a less ethnic audience was the label's jazz output, which included work by such notable names as Johnny Dankworth (whose wife, Cleo Laine, George produced later in his career), and Humphrey Lyttleton, whose hit single, "Bad Penny Blues", was later quoted as being partially inspirational to "Lady Madonna" by The Beatles.

"John Dankworth actually hadn't had any big hits, although he'd had a lot of good selling records – Parlophone had always been pretty strong on jazz with Jack Parnell and His Band, Joe Daniels and His Hotshots and Johnny Dankworth and His Seven, and they were all fairly consistent sellers. Then John had this idea for a little nursery tale using the idea of big bands illustrating how they would play 'Three Blind Mice'. It was a kind of musical cartoon really, which he called 'Experiments With Mice', and when he played it to me, I thought it was very good, so we made a record of it and it sold, but I can't really take much credit for that except that we issued the record. As for 'Bad Penny Blues' and 'Lady Madonna', there's no connection at all, except that the piano sounds similar. That kind of piano work is pretty commonplace among your genuine rhythm and blues players, and I think Johnny Parker, the pianist with Humph's band at that time, had the idea of a sort of mixture of beats, a slow beat and the rolling barrel piano."

Such a wide variety of work was later to become a great advantage to Martin when it came to his more celebrated productions during the 1960s and beyond, as he himself confirms. "It was all a good training ground for what happened later, and I was able to experiment at playing with tapes and making 'Musique concrete' noises and so on – I've said it before, but I don't think I would have done what I did on *Sgt. Pepper* . . . unless I'd done the Peter Sellers albums in the first place. Another thing was that I wanted to have better technical facilities to enable me to do things like that Peter Ustinov record without having all the awful disadvantages – it wasn't until multi-tracking came along that we were able to enjoy that."

In 1962, George Martin met and was impressed by The Beatles, a quartet from Liverpool who had already been turned down by several record companies including the other two EMI labels, HMV and Columbia. Martin had made an impact on the history of The Beatles almost from the first day, when he decided that the group's drummer of the time, Pete Best, was not satisfactory. "I decided not to use Pete Best. When I first heard The Beatles in the studio, number three studio at Abbey Road, in June 1962, I think it was, I liked them very much, but I did think their drummer was weak, and afterwards when I signed them to a contract, I told Brian [Epstein] that I obviously didn't really want to change the group or get in anyone's hair, but I didn't want to use the drummer, and I would use a session drummer instead, and the world wouldn't know the difference. The guitar players and singers were okay, but the drummer, in my estimation, didn't have the beat and the drive and the regularity and the pace that I needed to get an exciting record – he was jolly good-looking, and he didn't say much, but that was it. I didn't know until afterwards that they'd made up their own minds anyway to give him the boot, so it was a kind of joint decision, but taken without any collusion, and so when the session came along, Pete wasn't there. I had a session drummer named Andy White ready, and they brought along this fellow called Ringo Starr, who I treated with a great deal of suspicion, because I didn't know what he was like either, so I kept him at arm's length for a while. He's never forgiven me for it."

Following a top twenty entry with their first single, "Love Me Do", and a top three hit with the follow-up "Please Please Me", George Martin found himself in the position of having to make an album with The Beatles which would bear the same title as the second hit, and would cater for the demand created by "Please Please Me". The fact that the album was completely recorded and mixed in thirteen hours says much for the direct-ness and unsophistication of the early 1960s . . . "Well, there was a reason for that. I was very excited about the boys and I thought we had a big group on our hands, and the first record didn't do all that well, getting to number seventeen. I was convinced that if I had the right song, I would have a real hit with them, and we got it with 'Please Please Me', which I knew was a number one when we made it, and it certainly turned out that way". (Note: This was true of some charts, although not of others. In the *Record Retailer* chart, which is generally regarded as the Bible in chart terms, "Please Please Me" peaked at number two). "So obviously, in order to consolidate their success, I had to have an album out on the market very quickly, and the thing to do was to record as many numbers as I could from their existing repertoire. I'd been to The Cavern, and I knew what they did, so I said, 'Look, just come into the studio and let's just go through the best songs in your act, and we'll just put them down, like a live performance, and take a little bit of trouble over it'. So they came into the studio one morning, and we worked right through until ten or eleven at night, and recorded ten tracks, and we put both the singles on as well. It was just like recording a live album in a way, because it was all done straight on to two-track – we didn't have four-track then – but it was done as two-track, not as stereo, because I kept the rhythm separated from the voices so that I was able to compress the two together and make a harder sound.

"That boomeranged on me later, because after I had left EMI, that record was issued as stereo. I was appalled! How they could get out these original tapes with all the rock 'n' roll backing on one side, and all the voices on the other, and when the voices stopped singing, you had all the terrible background pickup from the studio still vacant on that track – it was just horrendous, and they were actually putting them out like that. When I found out about it, I raised the roof, and they said, 'We're not allowed to touch those records, because The Beatles said they must go out as they originally were.' I said, 'They're not as they originally were – you're making a terrible mistake,' but there you are . . . I did the remix in Los Angeles for the American version of the record, but I didn't know what had happened to the English issue, and I actually got a letter from a guy in Poland who had listened to a Beatles record, and wrote 'Well, it's a very good record, but where are the voices?' He'd got a pressing where there was nothing at all on one side – the first instrumental Beatles!"

Many of the early recordings by The Beatles were accomplished fairly quickly, something which seemed to indicate that Martin, as producer, was concentrating more on capturing a performance than the niceties of an arrangement. "That's not really true, because the way it went was that I would always listen to the song first of all, invariably performed by its basic writer, John or Paul, strumming away on acoustic guitar. Then we'd consider what we were going to do with it, although the permutations weren't very difficult – you had two guitars, bass guitar and drums, and if anyone played keyboards, it was generally me, which meant there was very little to arrange, as we didn't have a symphony orchestra or anything like that. So my main role there was picking out introductions, choosing a place for the solo, and its length and its ending; because the rest of the song was already there. So I'd say, 'Okay chaps, this is what we do for an opening, and this is where George does something on his guitar, and don't make it longer than two minutes forty-five seconds because we won't get it on the air'. It was as simple as that, and that's how it worked out."

The Beatles became enormously famous in Britain in a remarkably short time, and by the end of 1963 had amassed three straight number one singles on top of their comparatively modest beginnings with "Love Me Do" and "Please Please Me", yet in America their records were almost totally ignored until the start of 1964, something which must have been of great concern to their producer and the head of their record label. "It was because their early records weren't issued by the right people in the United States. After our first success with 'Please Please Me', we sent the tapes to Capitol Records, which was one of our subsidiaries. Sir Joe Lockwood had bought Capitol Records some time before, and it was our own label, so I thought it would be a good idea for us to issue our success in America. So I was rather disappointed when the reply came back 'It may be all right for Britain, but "Please Please Me" is not the kind of record that will sell in our country. Thank you very much. Goodbye.' And I shrugged my shoulders and said that they ought to know their business, because it was their market. And when 'From Me To You' came along, we did the same thing – 'Look, this group is building, and it's very big in this country, and you really ought to take a listen,' and nothing happened again. So, very frustrated, we got on to a guy who worked for us in New York, Roland Rennie, I think it was, and told him that we'd been turned down by Capitol, and asking if he could get the records out on any other label. So the early Beatle records were sold for no money at all to very small labels like Tollie, Swan and Vee Jay, who were each given a title to work on. And then the third record came out, which was 'She Loves You', and again Capitol turned it down – it was like St Peter and the cock crowing three times. And when the fourth record, 'I Want To Hold Your Hand', came out, the thing had grown so much in England by that time that it was beginning to have repercussions in the States, and the records that had already been put out by the small labels were beginning to make a little bit of a dent. Capitol realized that they had to do something about it, which coincided with The Beatles going over there, and that time, the dam eventually broke, and Capitol agreed on 'I Want To Hold Your Hand'. Their story was that at long last they'd found the song that could really break them in the States. Rubbish! So they issued 'I Want To Hold Your Hand', and it coincided with the build-up, and as the little labels had the earlier ones on the market as well, the airwaves were being swamped with the Beatle sound, which in effect made the impact that much greater."

Having established themselves as a potent musical force, The

Beatles, unlike many of their contemporaries, were unwilling to retread an already proven format, something which Martin was at pains to avoid. "That was something I'd always said from the word 'Go', that we shouldn't just make formula things, we should try to be different as much as possible, and we tried very hard to do that. Sometimes I thought we'd been too risky and gone too far, but it paid off – Brian Epstein and I had this plan, that we would issue a single every three months and an album twice a year. That was the kind of general idea, the broad basis of what we worked out, although we didn't stick to it religiously. I wanted every album that came out to be different from the one before, and as soon as The Beatles realized their creative abilities in the studio, they got hooked into this thing of really building something new each one. They were more adventurous than I was, and they were coming to me asking what new sounds they could use, and what instruments I knew about that they didn't.

"'Yesterday' was the first time we used any other musicians than The Beatles or myself on a record, apart from the original session drummer, of course. It came about purely and simply because Paul had had this lovely song for a while – actually, our memories differ on this, because we were talking about it the other day and Paul said he didn't have it all that long, it wasn't 'scrambled eggs' for ever, and that he had the tune, which he called 'scrambled eggs', for about a month before he came up with the lyric. I thought it was longer than that – so I said when recording this, that the best thing for him to do was just to sing it and play guitar, and we'd decide what to put on it afterwards. I didn't think we could put Ringo on, because it would be too heavy. So that's what we did, and I still felt that drums wouldn't be appropriate, and told Paul that the only thing I could honestly think of to add to it would be strings, but Paul said, 'Oh, I don't think I want Mantovani and Norrie Paramor very much' – I think he'd probably heard what I'd done to Gerry and the Pacemakers with 'You'll Never Walk Alone'. But that was one of Gerry's favourites, and it had always been part of his act as a tear-jerking ballad in the rock 'n' roll style, and I thought it demanded a bit of syrup, so I put some strings on it which I thought would be fairly effective. That was all – I just thought it needed something a bit different from what we'd done before, and I had the freedom to do it, and it seemed to work out all right.

"So I told Paul that I didn't really mean strings like there were on Gerry's record, and Paul confirmed that he wanted something different. I suggested a small amount of strings, perhaps a classical string quartet, and he liked that idea, because he was living with Jane Asher at the time, and hers was a very classical family. So that's the way it happened, and he worked with me on the score – we actually sat down at the piano and said 'We'll put a cello on this note'."

The 1966 Beatles LP, *Revolver*, is generally considered to be the prologue to the group's greatest work, the *Sgt. Pepper* . . . album, and two tracks on *Revolver*, "Eleanor Rigby" and "Tomorrow Never Knows", seemed to be particular signposts to a future where The Beatles would be exploring uncharted territory. "They learned exceptionally quickly in their different ways, although John was inclined to leave things to us and do his rock 'n' roll bits, and his beautiful words, while the music side was basically Paul, and George to a lesser extent. 'Eleanor Rigby' was just an extension of 'Yesterday' in a way in the use of strings – I've always been very keen on the scoring of people like Bernard Herrmann, the old Bernard Herrmann who did all Hitchcock's scores. 'Eleanor Rigby' is very much based on a score he did for a film called *Fahrenheit 451*, with all these spiky strings. Then 'Tomorrow Never Knows' was certainly the beginning of a new era, and it was a kind of surrealistic look at building up sound pictures, which I thought was great, and was again harking back to the Peter Sellers stuff.

"Going into *Sgt. Pepper* . . . , there was a kind of development through 'Tomorrow Never Knows' and through 'Strawberry Fields Forever' and 'Penny Lane', which was a single that was the beginning of the *Pepper* album, although it wasn't on the album because we wanted a single out. You can see the connections between 'Tomorrow Never Knows', 'Strawberry Fields . . . ', right through to 'A Day In The Life'. It's all there, and that was the changing of direction. 'Strawberry Fields . . . ' is one of my favourites, actually – it started out with John, as always, playing the song to me sitting on a stool in front of me strumming an acoustic guitar, and it was a very gentle song, a beautiful song full of this wonderful word imagery, and I loved it. When we came to do the actual track, there was Ringo bashing away and John on his electric guitar, and it became very much heavier than I'd thought, but that was the way John wanted it and the way it evolved, so we did the track that way and finished it. John came back to me afterwards, a couple of days after the session, and said, 'Well, it wasn't really quite what I had in mind when I wrote the song, so could we do it again?', and this was the first time any of The Beatles had ever asked me to recut a track. So I said 'Okay, if you feel like it, but what do you want to do with it this time?', and he said he wanted me to do a score for it, and that he wanted to use some cellos and horns, so we worked out a score and did a completely new track, and that was fine too. But again he came back to me, and this time said he liked the new one, but he liked the first one again as well, so I said he couldn't have them both. And he said, 'Why not? Let's take the beginning of one and the end of the other one,' so I told him that there were two things wrong with that, the first being that they were in completely different keys, and the second that they were at completely different tempos, and he said, 'You can fix it. You know what I like,' and left me to it. Fortunately, I was able to mix it – God was on my side, because the difference in pitch, which was a semi-tone, was the right way, so that by slowing one down and speeding up the other, they would be brought more or less into line. So the two did go together, and that was the way it was issued – see if you can spot the join!"

On 1 June 1967, *Sgt. Pepper's Lonely Hearts Club Band* was released in Britain, and immediately set the world on its ear with its incredible selection of songs and production techniques. There was a great deal of experimentation, for example the sound of the barrel organ on "Being For The Benefit Of Mr Kite". "I wanted to have the sound of a calliope, a steam organ, that is very characteristic of fairgrounds, and there wasn't a machine that could play what we wanted, because it was a new tune, and there was no way we could actually dictate the tune, arrange it and put it on a steam organ – it's like a pianola, player piano, where you have to have rolls printed and so on, so it would be too cumbersome a process. In any case, I didn't really want a tune, I wanted a kind of miasma of sound, a background whirly-hurly-burly – I always think of things in visual terms, and this to me was the background wash giving me the colour in the background which set the scene and then the detail came up in front. So I cut up some tapes, and made a messy sound in the background which sounded like a fairground, and the only tapes I could use were those of existing recordings of steam organs which were playing things like 'Stars And Stripes Forever' and that kind of thing, which I had to disguise, because I couldn't have that going on in the background. So, by cutting them up, chopping them to pieces and turning them back to front, I got the necessary noise. I tried lots of experiments like that which didn't work out, but of course, I don't talk about those!"

In retrospect, one of the most interesting aspects of the recording of *Sgt. Pepper* relates to the fact that it was recorded on a four-track machine. "Well, that was all we had. I would have recorded on more tracks if I'd had the machines, but it's like anything else – if you're making a new sideboard and you've only got a hammer and chisel, you work with that, but if you've got a nice automated workshop, you'll obviously use that."

Things had obviously improved, at least technically, by the time that The Beatles recorded their two final group albums, *Let It Be* and *Abbey* Road, which, curiously, were released in reverse order. "*Let It Be* was a very unhappy album, and when we were recording that, I thought it was the end of everything, because everybody was at each other's throats, the boys were all warring amongst each other, nobody would make any decisions, and for the first time, the engineer wasn't my engineer. Up until the album before, we'd used Geoff Emerick, who had worked on *Sgt. Pepper*, and there had been a succession of engineers after that. For *Let It Be*, they brought in Glyn Johns, who was kind of a producer/engineer, and although we got on fine, there was a certain conflict of interests there, so that I don't think anyone was particularly happy during those recordings.

"It ended up being a very unsatisfactory record because John Lennon, of all people, had said, 'I don't want this album to have any production gimmicks on it at all, I want it to be an honest album.' I asked him what he meant, because I thought our recordings had been honest, and he said, 'I won't want any overdubbing of voices, or any editing. It's got to be like it is, man, a real honest live recording, so let's do it that way'. Now the original idea for this was a good one, because we were talking about making a live recording of a new album, and the idea was that we would have a lot of songs written by the boys and rehearsed *ad nauseam*, and then they would have a marvellous performance in front of a live audience, which would be recorded like a live album, like Flanders and Swann, if you like, which would be their new album. Nobody would have heard the material before, and it would have all the atmosphere and so on. But we couldn't get a large enough audience – The Beatles by this time were too famous to go into the Hammersmith Odeon, and we thought about going to the Forum in Los Angeles, but that would have cost too much because of the royalties in America. And then we thought of taking it to Tunisia, but then it would have been difficult to get the crowds there – it was in the middle of winter, by the way – and we couldn't do it in England in the open air, so we finished up in Twickenham Film Studios, with no audience because it was the only place. Abbey Road was booked, and the boys wanted to record in their own studios at Apple, which had been ill-conceived by the chap they employed to work on them, so that there was no equipment there, and to use their studios, I had to import mobile equipment from EMI before we started making tracks down there. Then they decided to film it all, so we had camera teams looking over our shoulders all the time – it was an awful mess. And so the only way I could make the album in the end was to make it an honest record and have all the burps and starts and false takes and, 'Can you 'ear me muther?' in the middle of it, almost like a documentary, and that was the way I finished it up with Glyn. There were some good songs on it, but I wasn't crazy about it, although it was what John wanted, and I thought that was the end of it.

"A few months afterwards, Paul rang me up and said, 'Look, I'm a bit fed up with the way things have been going. Will you come back and produce an album like you used to?' I said, 'Well,

Paul, I don't know whether it will work. I'd love to if I'm able to, but in order for me to be able to do that, you've got to agree to be produced, and you've got to do what I say' . . . And he said they'd do that, so I said I wanted my own engineer, Geoff Emerick, back, who had worked on *Sgt. Pepper* . . . , and he agreed to that, and I said I wanted to do it at Abbey Road, which he also agreed to. So I said, 'Well, I don't believe it, but we'll do it,' and it was a very happy album. We tried to put aside all the differences, and although it wasn't an integrated album, because everybody was writing their own material, and tended to be working mainly on their own songs, for which the others would reluctantly come in, it was a much happier album than I really expected. Paul and I worked very solidly on the second side – John didn't want the production things, which he'd never liked, and the concept things bored him to tears because he liked good old rock 'n' roll, so we compromised and had his rock 'n' roll things on one side, and our long-winded concept on the other, which was the way it worked out. I knew it was the end of the road, but it was a happy end, and I'm glad it worked out like that. I was considerably shaken when *Let It Be* was issued after that in the format it was, with Phil Spector's work on it."

To backtrack briefly on The Beatles' career, another world-famous recording which George Martin produced for the group was "All You Need Is Love", which was used as part of the first satellite television broadcast in a programme called *Our World*. "The specification for that song was pretty rigid. It had to be a new song, and it was going to be the English contribution to this programme which would be seen by two hundred million viewers – that was what they told us, and it was enough to terrify the pants off anyone, and they wanted it to be a live performance in the studio. But the boys never thought twice about this awe-inspiring thing they were faced with, and they just said they'd do it anyway, so they came to me and asked me to do a score for it and try to wrap it up for them. John wrote the song, and I said, 'Let's hedge our bets and do a backing track first,' so we went into the studio and did a basic rhythm track on John's song, and I wrote the introduction and the tag ending. And we got a band in the studio; and the boys performed it live, actually sung it in the studio live, with an audience there. Mike Vickers conducted the band in the studio, and I was in the control room with Geoff – it was a ludicrous day, because we had the television team there, who had their van in the courtyard in front of Abbey Road studios, and of course they couldn't see into the studio where it was being televised – and don't forget it was live television, it wasn't taped, and we were standing by during the countdown with someone saying, 'You're going to be on the air in front of two hundred million people, thirty seconds to go.' And at that point, the producer said, 'I've lost contact with the studio – George, you'll have to relay instructions to the floor man there. Can you do that?' And there was a camera looking at me and watching me on television as well, and I just giggled. I thought it was too ridiculous for words, the pressure of making a record under those circumstances. But it worked out all right, and when we'd finished the broadcast, I said, 'Well, we're obviously going to issue this record, so let's work on it now.' So the broadcast went out as one thing, but then I overdubbed John's voice again, and double tracked it and put extra voices on, and the record was issued in that form. It wasn't quite what was on television, but most people remember it that way."

To have dealt so successfully with such a potentially volatile group as The Beatles says much for George Martin's ability in dealing with people. "It's no good bullying people, because they dig their heels in and do the opposite – you have to lead rather than drive, and in fact, tact is one of the absolute requirements of a record producer. You've got to make the guy think that he thought of whatever it was in the first place, and you can't go around in a studio saying, 'What a clever chap I am for thinking of this,' because that immediately destroys the ego of the person with whom you're working. I still say that the artist is much more important than the producer, and he's your spearhead, so you've got to build him up, and thus, if you have a good idea, try to make him think of it. I'd far rather do that and get a really good record than end up with a rotten record for which I can take the credit."

It seems difficult to believe in retrospect, but George Martin did not receive credit as producer on the earliest Beatle records, including the *Please Please Me* album. "It was a tussle with EMI, because they didn't like producers getting too important – they were a pretty straight-laced company, and they didn't really think it would be a good idea for producers to get too much credit, because they might get too big for their boots, and being considered rather suspect people anyway, it was strongly resisted. It was only after a great deal of pressure from me, mainly, that we actually got credits on labels, so there are an awful lot of records I've made which people would never connect with me."

However, during the Merseybeat boom of the mid-1960s, it was well known that Martin was involved with nearly all the acts which composed Brian Epstein's stable of stars, many of whom were signed to Parlophone, including The Beatles, Billy J. Kramer and the Dakotas, and Cilla Black, while Gerry and the Pacemakers were on the by now similarly sized Columbia label. It was as though Brian Epstein was feeding George artists, and expecting their records to boast a little added Martin magic. "Yes, he was always looking for magic, and he got it to a certain extent, but at the end of that year, 1963, I was so worn out that I wanted some magic myself. I was in the studios right round the clock, and Brian was supplying me with an unending list of new artists, some of whom weren't all that good. Gerry was great, and Cilla [Black] was marvellous, and Billy [J. Kramer] was pretty good, but they got progressively less interesting as time went by. But in 1963, I was leapfrogging myself with all the records I was making – The Beatles, Gerry, Billy J. Kramer and Cilla Black were actually having records coming out in sequence, passing the baton of the number one spot from one to the other. I think we held the number one position for thirty-seven weeks out of fifty-two, and I really was working every day of the week, including the weekend, and every night, and not seeing anything except the inside of a studio, and killing myself in the process."

PAUL McCARTNEY

This interview was conducted in November 2001, just before the release of Paul McCartney's album Driving Rain.

Interview with Paul McCartney

by Sean Egan

You release one album every three years or so now. Is that your choice?
"We used to stick out an album every year because I suppose we just used to say to people, 'When do you want an album?' We used to be told, 'The market demands you do one a year' and, like, four singles a year. Now's it's more leisurely, really. I think because we were touring a lot you used to always want fresh material every year. I think when I'm not touring much – I haven't toured now for nearly ten years – there's not such a demand to come up with material so you just do it at a more relaxed pace. That's really why. I would actually be quite happy to do one a year but it's just I don't have to so I just do it whenever I fancy it."

Do you think that also brings a certain pressure with people saying if you've taken three years to do this album it should be three times better than if you'd taken one year?
"I don't know. It may be true. I don't think that about people's albums. I never bother how long it took them to make it normally, it's just whether I like the artist and whether I like the album they've produced."

Of course, although it's been a few years since your last album, you actually made this one quickly in terms of recording time.
"With some early Beatles albums like *Rubber Soul* and *Revolver*, even though they were put together quickly, they were pretty

cool albums. So I did this really to kind of echo that technique and I'm really pleased the way the tracks turned out. Most of the people who've heard it seem to agree with me that it's a pretty cool album – he said modestly."

There's sixteen tracks on the album. In the old vinyl days it would be something like ten.
"No it wasn't. In the old days it was exactly fourteen every time. Nowadays most people do about ten or eleven but we always used to do about fourteen. Seven a side on the vinyl. This was going to be fifteen. We just had that many songs that we liked and they all seemed to fit, and then suddenly after the Madison Square concert – after September 11 – we also had this 'Freedom' thing that everyone was interested in, so we put that on the end of the album, so it's now ended up sixteen. It's pretty good value for money!"

You seem to have gone for musicians who aren't that well known.
"In actual fact the producer suggested them. Because I knew I was going to go out to LA. I was just gonna go out there on a slightly experimental thing to see if I enjoyed working with the producer because I'd never worked with him. I'd met him personally and liked him but it didn't mean I was gonna enjoy working with him or that it would work out. He rang me about ten days beforehand and said, 'Well if we're gonna be that loose on it, isn't it a good idea if I ring a couple of guys to be just ready in case we want to work kind of live-ish?' So I said, 'Yeah, great.' And he happened to have in mind three people, so those are the guys that showed up on the Monday morning. The idea was if it worked out, we'd keep to it like that, if it didn't then I might go to multi-tracking and layering the things with me playing drums, bass and stuff. But in actual fact we really enjoyed playing together and got through a lot of work quite quickly."

How old are the musicians?
"The real young guy, the keyboard player, is twenty-three. The other two were slightly older, I would estimate – ooh, I don't know – about twenty-seven, thirty."

So part of a generation that grew up worshipping The Beatles. Are they able to not be intimidated by a living legend and to tell you if they think you're doing something wrong musically?
"People always think that with me. I try and make it clear to everyone that I don't want to be treated like that. Personally, when I'm just hanging out with people, there's no question of that. It's really people who don't know me or haven't met me tend to think, 'Well, he did do that' or 'He's a bit of a legend.' But really when we sit down and we have a cup of tea and we start talking about the songs, everyone speaks their mind. And of course the real person who's going to make those kind of decisions – the tough ones – is the producer, and he is very honest so if ever we did anything that we didn't really like, he'd say, 'Oh I don't really think that's too cool,' or whatever. A kind of nice way of putting it but what he meant is, 'It's crap.' I encourage people to do that knowing there is a possibility that they might get intimidated."

How did you find working with David Kahne as a producer instead of producing yourself?
"There's a sort of co-producing element that comes in because inevitably I'm going to do the bassline, I'm going to probably say how I want the drums to go and if I don't like the sound on a thing, I'm going to say, 'You know, I think that could be better if we did it that way.' It's really just to have a degree of freedom where I can actually 'switch off' and just say, 'Okay now I'm the bass player and I'm the singer.' But having said that, really, in truth, everybody in the band becomes a little bit of producer because they just get to throw in suggestions: 'What about if I tried this?' But no, it was kind of nice for me to hand over to a producer. I don't always do that. Just gives me a little bit more space really."

Speaking of being the bass player, I read that you're using the Hoffner violin bass that you made famous in the 1960s. Is this exactly the same instrument you were using back then?
"Yeah."

I've heard musicians say that was a fairly sub-standard bass?
"They were. It was like thirty pound it cost, so it's not exactly the world's most expensive, but the one I happen to have has got a really beautiful tone on it. They're not all great. I'll tell you why most bass players would think it's a little bit naff: there's a tuning problem on them, which I used to have but I used to just live with it. You could tune the bass strings and then when you hit the third fret, it can be a little bit sharp. I actually had it done by these people called the Mandolin Brothers in New York and they put it through the computer and the whole thing – or whatever they put it through – and did some real fine work in it and now it's spot on. It's really in tune. I think it's a really great instrument, actually. You've got to know how to play it. The trouble is, if you play it a bit too hard, it farts and it hits the pick-ups, so there's an art to playing it. I think if you play it okay, it sounds pretty good. I mean, it sounded pretty good on most of The Beatles' records. I think it sounds good on this record. Have you listened for it? Check it out. Listen to 'From A Lover To A Friend'. That's played in it. Sounds pretty good."

On the album, the opening track "Lonely Road" seems like a message from you to Linda.
"No, I don't write like that. I was just discussing that with someone. What happens is, I kind of write a bit more from the subconscious so I don't actually know what I'm trying to say so much when I write – it's more when I look back on it. I wish I could invent these really glorious meanings for everything but I tend to just sit down with a guitar and start going, 'I tried to get over you . . . ' It probably is to do with Linda but it could be to do with anyone. What I like about writing songs is that I have my meaning and I have my interpretation but obviously anyone who is just trying to get over someone, then it should relate to them too. I write things for me but I hope that if I'm writing a song where I have a particular kind of heartbreak in it, everyone knows about heartbreak of one form or another so I write these things hoping there's a kind of universal message but obviously it's probably about me but I wasn't too conscious of that. [In the song] I'm talking about 'Don't want to walk a

lonely road.' It's just about 'Don't want to get brought down' really. I think that's quite an international thought, that any girl who's just lost a boyfriend, anyone who's just got dumped, or whatever, the song can apply to them too."

And the track "Heather" came about apparently because Heather, your fiancée, doesn't know many Beatles songs?
"That's right. She was brought up on classical music so she knows more about Wagner then she does about The Beatles."

Is that weird for you?
"It is, actually. It's quite interesting though. It's quite refreshing. Her younger sister knows a lot about The Beatles and is more into it so it's not just a sort of ageist thing. I said to her, 'How is that?' Because a lot of people know, you know, 'Get Back'. And she said it was because she was raised mainly on classical stuff. She knows all about 'The Valkyrie', whereas I don't. So it's good, it's refreshing, and the song 'Heather' came about because of that, because I was just jamming and she said, 'Which one is that?' I said, 'What do you mean? I'm just making it up.' She didn't actually say, 'Which Beatles hit?', she said 'Which one is that?' She thought it was part of my past repertoire, one way or another. So it was quite cool. I was just jamming and I was ready to throw it away. She said, 'No, no, that's good.' So that made me keep it. I thought, I better call it 'Heather' in that case."

The song "Freedom", inspired by the terrorist attack on the world trade centre, reminds me of another song you wrote after an emotive event: "Give Ireland Back To The Irish". Do you think there's a danger that if you rush "into print" with your reaction to an event like that, a few years down the line it might seem a very naive song?
"Yeah, sure but I wrote it to be that. This is custom-made. I wrote it for one reason only, which was that at the Madison Square Garden concert I had the alternative of playing all the old songs like pretty much everyone was going to do – and so making the whole thing an oldies evening – or try and get a little bit interesting, maybe, and try and work something out. Pete Townshend said to me, 'Fucking hell, Paul – you are brave.

You're gonna workshop a song in front of 100 million people.' But the thing is I wanted to do it so I wrote it very simply as a kind of anthemic thing. Sure, there's a risk in anything you do, but I'm glad I wrote 'Give Ireland Back To The Irish'."

But that song never turns up on the compilation albums.
"It didn't [appear] on the Wings compilation [*Wingspan*], you mean. It's never been up for consideration on anything else. It didn't [go] on the Wings thing because it maybe wasn't the best bit of work, but it was number one in Ireland. And Spain, interestingly enough."

Some people have suggested that those on the West Bank might say, "Well hold on a minute, the reason this attack seems to have happened is because there's a lot of people here who don't have 'Freedom'?"
"Yeah sure, but the thing is if you look at any sort of attack like that, you have to then say, What could America have said? 'Okay, guys, fair enough, but just don't do it again'? I mean, are you kidding? This was not just a little stone's throw. This was taking out the two most important buildings in New York and attacking the Pentagon. That's an act of war, whichever way you look at it. It's easy – in print, particularly – to just say, 'Oh, this shouldn't have had a response,' but I think that's like not having a response to a Hitler attack. If we'd had no response to that, you and I probably wouldn't be here right now. There are certain things that overstep the mark. Hey listen, I agree with the IRA's aims to get a united Ireland – I just don't agree with the methods, that's all, and this was a method which was a particularly war-like act. Are you kidding? You've got to expect a war-like response, I would think. You bomb Pearl Harbor, you've got to pretty much understand you're saying something. You bomb New York, you're pretty much saying something. What should New Yorkers do or [the] US say – 'Well, okay guys, we'll let you off this time'? There may be a point: American policy is not all we would wish it to be, but that's not the point. So then go to the UN or discuss it. There are peace talks – get in the peace talks. But you just don't do a thing like this and expect no response. You're taking out innocent people. I'm a pacifist, but this was like a major attack on a major country."

After your last few albums, people have been talking about a Paul McCartney artistic renaissance. Do you feel that on the last few albums you've been doing something that's re-captured a past quality?
"I don't know. I always think that whatever albums I'm doing, I'm doing my best thing. I think on this album I'm playing good bass, I think there are some really cool songs on it and I think I'm singing well and I think the musicians who play with me are really good and I like it as an album. I think it's got strength. It's an album that I can play. So I'm proud of it. I think it's a decent album and if that adds up to me being reborn then so be it. I don't really see it as that because I never thought I'd died."

You've been going four decades as a recording artist so you're going to have your peaks and troughs in that time.
"You can't totally peak all the time: Sinatra, Elvis, the greatest all have moments. I think it's just impossible to just keep it up. You'd be God, wouldn't you, if every single thing you did was fantastic."

But are you aware when you're doing something really special?
"I think so. I think that happens kind of song by song really. I think you write a song and you go, 'Wow, there's something this one's got.' And on this album I personally think this is a special album because of the joy I had recording it and now the joy I have actually listening to it. The interesting thing about this album is I think the more you listen to it the better it gets."

How much overdubbing was there?
"There was some overdubbing, a small degree. It was mainly done live-ish and then we just made a record of it. There's a track called 'She's Given Up Talking' and that goes into like a voice effect but there's nothing really that unusual in the effects."

Does this mean you'll never have an orchestra behind you again?
"No, probably the opposite, it probably means next time out I'll do that. In actual fact there were a couple of quite smoochy ballads which were up for consideration on this album but this turned out to have its own kind of vibe. I think *Driving Rain*'s got its own sort of feel and the songs we picked we picked

especially because the those were ones that fitted into the *Driving Rain* bag. There were a couple of other songs that we'd done that will fit into another bag. Those have orchestra but we just decided that [the] slightly more raw edge thing was the direction we wanted to go on this so that was the way we chose [tracks]. Probably means next time I'll go another way just so as not to get bored."

The last couple of years a lot of people from your generation have reached the milestone of sixty: Dylan's there and Eric Burdon's there. Does a milestone like that approaching make you think deeper about things?
"No, not really, I don't think so. To me, each decade is like a milestone – and to most people. It depends how you approach that. To some people, thirty is really scary. I know a lot of people [who are] really dreading it. Then forty is: forget it, it's all over. I don't really think like that."

I'm thinking in terms of "I'd better put another album out because I don't know how many more I'll be able to put out".
"No, I don't think like that actually. I never have. There's people dying at sixteen. There's people in the hospital right now who won't get past the age of three. It's not my philosophy, that. I'll go when the time comes. I don't have that kind of a mind that thinks, 'Better do a couple of albums'. I mean, how would that benefit me anyway? Financially? Bung out a couple more albums so I can, what, spend it in heaven? That doesn't occur to me, that kind of thing. The only reason I do this stuff is because I love it. I love making songs and I love making music and that's why I do it, so it's not to do with trying to squeeze something in or worry about whether there's any time. I just don't think like that. I was never worried at thirty, forty, fifty and I'm not worried at sixty. And I hope I won't be worried at seventy, eighty, ninety, a hundred and a hundred-and-ten. Inevitably, before then the great reaper might decide my time's up but that's for him to decide or her to decide, not me. I don't really worry about that kind of stuff. I just get on with it. I like making music. You check out my bass playing on this album and you let me know if you think I'm playing well."

You're really into the bass now, aren't you!
"It's fucking great, man! Fucking good. Come back to me when you're playing bass as good as I am on this album and I'll give you a big kiss."

I think John Entwistle slightly beat you in terms of the first bass solo but "Michelle" has got a bass solo hasn't it?
"Well it depends what you call a bass solo. It's not a solo, no. I don't actually believe I've ever played a bass solo. I think that is John's territory. Mine are just bass lines supporting the band but they're somewhat melodic because that's the way I like to play. I was influenced by people like James Jamison from Motown and he's very melodic and I am too and I like that style."

What do you think about a bassist like Mark King, who seems a bit too "busy" in his style?
"The thing is, I never slag off anyone unless I really hate them and I don't mind him at all. He seems pretty good. It's not my style. It's that sort of Stanley Clarke slap-it-out kind of bass. I kind of admire it. It's nothing I'd want to play but I think it's pretty good. I probably wouldn't go out and buy his record but I can admire the skill he displays. It's pretty cool."

Last question is a Beatles question. Up to and including 1967, the mono mix was always more important and the stereo mix of an album was an afterthought which was done quickly and all the intricacies of the mono mix would be lost in it. So really, when we hear the CD versions of Help!, Rubber Soul, Revolver *and* Sgt. Pepper *..., because they are in stereo, we're not hearing them the way you intended us to hear them. This seems a glaring oversight.*
"People have certainly talked about doing that and we've considered it and it may be something that happens one day. What happened was, in the debate, it was decided that people with stereo equipment would not be too happy to have it coming out mono. You get these old black and white movies – or people might want to make a black and white movie now – but then everyone says, 'Well excuse me, everyone's got colour TVs and they want to see colour'. So it's really that kind of reason and we were a bit nervous about it at first – the record company

was keen to do them in stereo because they release stereo records – and we said, 'Well, let's hear them' and actually I thought on one they really sounded cool in stereo. No, it wasn't as we intended them – in fact I'd heard stuff that we'd made and was on there but the original mix didn't show up because it was mono. So I think it's six of one and half a dozen of the other. I think you're right in as much as this is a kind of omission but you've got to sort of weigh it against how many people would want mono records."

But there's a way round it now
"What's that?"

Well, there's space on a CD for both mono and stereo versions of 1960s albums. People who have bought the stereo already won't bother with them but the ones who especially want the mono version will pay for them all over again. I'm trying to persuade you here! "Yeah, I can see! Hey man, I'm with you. We made them in mono so I'm always happy to listen to them in mono. It's the old debate. If I go on tour, I really want to play a place with 500 people, because that's the buzz, so you see the whites of their eyes. I get to, let's say, Glasgow and five hundred people get in and five thousand people are left waiting outside, shouting angrily. So I do a five-thousander. Now, I go to New York and I say I'm going to do a five-thousander, then 20,000 people are angry and say 'We wanted to see Paul on his only visit to our town' so it's always a debate. You don't always do the thing that would be the favourite, most ideal thing to do. You sometimes make a compromise and I think that's what happened on all this mono stuff. But as you say, they can do both in the future, that maybe's the way to go. You're just opening the can of worms to allow even more Beatles releases. And if we ever do it, you can say, 'I told them to do that!' "

BILL HARRY

Bill Harry is the Forrest Gump or Zelig of The Beatles' story. A fellow attendee of Liverpool College of Art with John Lennon and friend of the band in general, he was eyewitness to, and even instigator of, many momentous events in their career. He also unwittingly gave a type of music a name with the paper he founded to celebrate Liverpool's vibrant music scene, Mersey Beat, *a publication which almost certainly – and contrary to the legend of "Raymond Jones" – first brought The Beatles to the attention of Brian Epstein.*

Epstein later persuaded Harry to turn Mersey Beat *into a national music paper,* Music Echo, *after he became convinced the Merseybeat boom was over. Harry resigned from the new paper over interference from Epstein and began working in PR, at the same time as continuing to write on music for various publications, including* The Beatles Book *when it was resurrected in the late 1970s. The Kinks, The Hollies and Led Zeppelin are just some of the three dozen-plus acts for whom Harry handled publicity before tiring of that profession in 1984. After launching magazines* Tracks *and* Idols, *he turned to writing books. He already has more than two dozen under his belt and is currently working on a book on sixty years of Liverpool music and another on the story of the* Mersey Beat *paper.*

He granted an exclusive interview for this book.

Interview with Bill Harry

by Sean Egan

What was the earliest gig you saw played by the future members of The Beatles?
"The first time I saw them was in the late 1950s at the art college. I introduced Stuart to John Lennon when we were together at the Ye Cracke pub. Stuart and I were members, along with Rod Murray, of the students' union there. So we booked them for our college dances because Paul and George were next door to us at the Liverpool Institute and they used to come into the college and practice in our life rooms. They used to be on the same bill as, say, the Merseysippi Jazz Band. Stuart joined them in January 1960. Me and Stuart proposed and seconded that we use our art college student union funds to buy a PA system for the dances which the group could use. At the time I referred [to] them as 'The college group' 'cos they were still trying to fiddle around trying to find a decent name. That was basically just John, Stuart, Paul and George. They didn't have a drummer at the time."

You disagree that the most difficult relationship in The Beatles was between Paul and George?
"Paul and George had always been together right at the beginning, even on the bus to school and trying to create music together and Paul was determined to get him in the band. John didn't want him in the band. John was against it. He thought he was a kid and he didn't particularly like George all that much."

It's said that Stuart couldn't really play.
"That's completely wrong. That myth came from Allan Williams'
book [*The Man Who Gave The Beatles Away*]. He made up so
many things, it was incredible and one of them was when they
were appearing at the audition for Larry Parnes at the Wyvern
Club, he kept going, 'Oh Stuart had his back to the audience
because he couldn't play.' They had this picture of Stuart doing
that and that's the picture that was mainly used everywhere,
but in fact the other pictures from the same session showed
him playing from the front. That built up and over the period
of time people'd write about, 'Oh he couldn't play this that and
the other.' Parnes was to say that he had no problem with Stuart.
That his objection was to [the] drummer Tommy Moore who
turned up late for the audition, was dressed differently from
the other members and was a lot older than them."

*There's an incident in Williams' book where The Beatles in Hamburg
are alleged to have urinated on nuns from a balcony. Did that
actually happen?*
"It's been a bit exaggerated but I believe it did happen . . .
Allan Williams' book was mainly written by Bill Marshall, who
was a *Daily Mirror* writer . . . who I was with years later when
I was [PR-ing] Kim Wilde and he told me he'd made most of
the book up. He said, 'This is my book rather than Allan's.'
For instance, he starts Allan Williams' book, 'I was their first
manager, I still have their contracts . . . ' Well he never actually
managed them and those contracts weren't management
contracts, they were the contracts for the Kaiserkeller Club as
an agent."

*They always seemed in the early days to have trouble keeping a
regular drummer. Why was that?*
" 'Cos when they first started playing at the first residency at
the Casbah Club, they never had a drummer around then and
as The Quarry Men initially didn't have a drummer I suppose
they initially felt they could do without one. It's strange but
that's the way it went. They didn't get one till 1960. They'd
perform without a drummer."

Did that work sonically?

"It seemed to. Nobody seemed to mind. Casey Jones told them they had to have a drummer. In fact I talked to the daughter of the one that they got to play drums with them initially [Norman Chapman]. He did a few gigs with them, then he was called up for National Service."

John Lennon must have been the most literate Teddy Boy ever?

"When I first asked him, I said I heard you wrote poetry, he was a bit embarrassed. He mustn't have thought it was a macho thing to do. I said, 'Well no, we like these San Francisco poets like Ginsberg and all those people. Poetry's a good thing.' So he showed me a poem he'd written. I thought it was fantastic. That's why I got him to write for *Mersey Beat*. I knew all his influences. He was very influenced by [comedian] Stanley Unwin with the fractured English, the radio guy. That's how he used to twist all his words. I think he was more influenced by Stan Unwin than anybody else. And of course *Through The Looking-Glass* was his favourite book. And he loved the Just William books. He'd always been a bit of a reader."

Did he harbour any ambition in the early days to be a published poet?

"No, no. I had to encourage him. He'd been writing for years and when he was at Quarry Bank School he used to do his *Daily Howl*. He used to write poems about the teachers, used to draw the teachers. He was always very active. I thought he was a very good wordsmith when I saw his stuff and I wanted him to write and encouraged him to go on. It was strange when I published his first work. He just gave me a couple of scraps of paper when I asked him for a biography of The Beatles. It was like a biography that nobody would ever conceive of. He did this thing about the man came down in the flying pie. I called it *Being A Short Diversion On The Dubious Origins Of Beatles Translated From The John Lennon*. John didn't think I'd publish it. I don't think he had confidence in it. When he gave it to me he was a bit hesitant, as if I'd say what a load of rubbish. When I published it, he was delighted and enthusiastic. He brought me virtually everything he'd written – about 250 songs, drawings, poems, everything – and said, 'They're yours, keep 'em, do whatever you want with 'em.' Obviously he wanted me to publish. So I started publishing a column with his stuff in called 'Beatcomber', which he liked, so that gave him a lot of confidence in his writing."

Where did the name The Beatles come from?
"When Stuart and John were trying to think of the name, they were thinking of all these ridiculous names similar to Johnny And The Moondogs: Long John Silver and something and all these kind of weird names. When they were at [the] Gambia Terrace [flat shared by Lennon, Sutcliffe and art student Rod Murray in 1960, prior to The Beatles' first trip to Hamburg], Stuart said, 'We've done a lot of Buddy Holly numbers – why not have a name like Buddy Holly's backing group, The Crickets? Well let's think of some insect' – and then they thought of Beetles. Now I was there, but so was [writer] Royston Ellis. Now Royston said that they had Beetles and he suggested the 'a', because he'd just done a book about the Beat Generation. But in fact they didn't put the 'a' in then. They went out one time it was the Silver Beets, then it was The Beatles – b-e-a-t-l-e-s – then it was The Beatals – b-e-a-t-a-l-s – then they went out once as The Silver Beets, then it was The Silver Beetles with two 'e's, and then Silver Beatles with the 'e' and the 'a', and finally they just stripped it down to just The Beatles in August 1960 just prior to going to Germany."

Was John as violent as has been suggested?
"He was never physically violent. The history is he ran away from fights. He'd flee. There's only two occasions. One outside Latham Halls: these guys threatened Stuart Sutcliffe and Pete Best, and John got involved with them and John broke his finger. The only other time was when he hit Bob Wooler. Before that when they were playing in Roseberry Street on the back of a lorry and some blokes threatened them, John ran into a house and he had to call the police and the police had to escort him to the bus stop. Then when they were at Wilson Hall in Garston, a couple of Teddy Boys said they'd beat him up, so he ran for the bus. I think Colin Hanton with him had left their stuff in

the road. So I don't know of any real incident when John was violent. What it is, he had this sort of overpowering charisma of being ready to pull you to pieces [with] words. At the art college, he'd come along the corridor and a group of girls would all stop and be quiet and be shaking in case he said something nasty to them. He even used to pull it with Stuart. Try to put him down. When you'd meet John in those early days, he tried to put you down and insult you and things and you had to stand up to him and tell him where to go. Once you did that, it was fine. If he could browbeat you and keep you down, he'd do that."

Was the relationship between Paul and John a real friendship or a professional relationship?
"I think it was more a professional relationship because they were two quite different sort of people really. John was the real rebel type and against everything and Paul was the opposite. John would be insulting and he'd get mixed with scallywags and getting drunk and things, whereas Paul was always polite. He'd been brought up to have particular manners and that Protestant work ethic from his father and [was] a perfect PR man. He liked Broadway musicals and Fred Astaire and everything and John was the rocker, into Elvis and everything, so they were two different type of personalities which was the good which complemented each other and this helped to make it a great songwriting team."

They finally found a drummer with Pete Best.
"They had got this booking to go to Germany and Tommy Moore, their drummer, wouldn't go. He'd had enough and his girlfriend said he's not having anything to do with them. They were due to do a gig at the Grosvenor Ballroom in Birkenhead but it's been cancelled by the corporation because all the fights and the roughness there, so since they didn't have anything to do that night with the gig cancelled they happened to go along to the Casbah and they saw that Pete had this brand new drum kit which looked fantastic. He was with the group The Blackjacks. They asked him would he be willing? In fact The Blackjacks were about to break up 'cos Chas Newby, the bass guitarist,

was going to go to university. So he auditioned with them and they got on well and that was that."

Some say Pete was a very influential drummer?
"He created what was called the Atom Beat. He developed this in Germany which helped to give The Beatles this big sound which they never had before. When they came back and people heard . . . the Atom Beat, most of the other drummers tried to start copying it and it made a tremendous impact. He had a certain way of playing."

If others were copying him, that seems to indicate he wasn't considered a technically deficient drummer?
"Well, he wasn't at all. He was considered very good."

When they went over to Hamburg for the first time in August 1960, how did you feel about such a step into the unknown?
"We thought, 'This is good. A Liverpool group going to Germany, it's fantastic,' because this was a time when people were rooted to where they lived. In fact most people round those times were born in a place and lived their entire life and died in the same place. It was just prior to the Spanish holidays and cheap travel. People used to go to Butlin's holiday camps or Blackpool and that was it, people of a certain working class economy."

What changes did you notice in them as people and as a band when they came back?
"The way they dressed, the black leather. The confidence they had. They used to come in the *Mersey Beat* office and help out. They used to come and answer the phone and things like that. I said it was their baptism of fire musically . . . They were tremendous when they came back from Hamburg . . . It also gave them something else apart from the music: this amazing confidence and belief in themselves."

How long were they over the first time?
"About three months."

They did their first Cavern gig in February 1961, a lunchtime session. How did the lunchtime sessions come about?
"That's what changed the entire Cavern persona and perception with people, and that's what made The Cavern the club. The Cavern was jazz-only. Ray McFall when he bought it noticed that the kids were going to all these halls and other places round Liverpool so he decided to start booking the rock groups in 1961. When he decided to do lunchtime sessions, it was a great idea. They hadn't been done at all anywhere in Liverpool, and of course being right in the city centre that means all the kids who worked all round the city centre could go at lunchtime to The Cavern. The problem was getting groups who'd be able to play because the kids who were in the groups weren't professional. They were either going to school or college or were apprentices or whatever and not that many could do lunchtime sessions. The Beatles could because none of them worked. That was a turning point in The Cavern and to some extent with The Beatles."

Do you remember the first time you heard a Beatles or Lennon/McCartney original?
"It would be at The Cavern. I remember them doing their own numbers at The Cavern and we were all excited by it."

The Beatles went back to Hamburg. Did you think that might be a bit unwise, insofar as they were leaving behind the following they were picking up in Liverpool?
"Not really because when they came back from Hamburg they were virtually penniless and had no bookings. The first booking they had was at the Casbah Club. Then Bob Wooler got them on Litherland Town Hall where people started taking notice of them, but they still didn't have much work. Brian Kelly started booking them for Litherland Town Hall and Aintree Institute but Mona Best began to do extra bookings to try to give them work and she increased the money that they were being [paid] for gigs. She was even booking places like Notty Ash Village Hall for them. They were applying to get back to Hamburg because they'd done the appearances at the Top Ten briefly and they'd been offered the season at the Top Ten by Peter Eckhorn

and they wanted to go there and play again with Tony Sheridan and that. Straightaway, Pete Best was negotiating to get them back at the Top Ten Club. Pete was like the manager of the group when they came back. He did all the bookings. Neil Aspinall lived with them. They already had the Casbah bouncer drive them round to gigs but they got Neil to be their full-time driving roadie. Pete and his mum were virtually managing the group at the time."

How long were they over there for a second time?
"It was just a short season. A matter of several weeks."
What kind of personality was Pete?
"The girls particularly liked him. Bob Wooler referred to him as mean, moody and magnificent. Girls used to sleep overnight in his garden just to be near him. They liked the moody atmosphere he had and the fact that he hardly ever spoke and everything. Bob Wooler thought he was the most important member of the group with popularity, so he did the unprecedented thing and he suggested that they put the drummer out in front and the three guitarists behind him. The first time they ever did that at a gig, all the girls rushed forward and dragged him off the stage, so they couldn't do that again. It never happened with any of the other Beatles. The girls didn't rush up and drag the others off the stage."

Was he close to any of the others?
"Only John. They were a bit tougher than the others and they liked to have a drink together. It's like in Hamburg. Pete was the only who agreed to go out with John to try and mug somebody. They were the only two who really wanted to keep in the black leathers. It was John who said they were cowards by sacking him. He felt a bit ashamed of that."

You started Mersey Beat *in July 1961. People assume it refers to the beat of the music?*
"No. Because 'beat' wasn't used in relation to music at the time. Beat was used at that time in relation to the Beat Generation, to beatniks, to Kerouac, and it has no relation or relevance to the rock 'n' roll music the groups were playing. Our local groups

were called rock groups . . . *Mersey Beat*, when I thought of the title, it was like a policeman's beat: it was the area I was gonna cover . . . After we'd been going for a while, people began to refer to the groups as beat groups. It was just the area: this is my beat, this is my Mersey Beat."

When they came back to Liverpool after that second time in Hamburg, were they able to pick up from before?
"Oh sure, because people were interested, because from the Litherland Town Hall gig they had a completely different sound. The one they developed in Hamburg and Pete, all the drummers came to listen. They were getting bigger and bigger locally."

As far as you're concerned, it was you who turned Brian Epstein on to The Beatles, not Raymond Jones, who is reputed to have gone into NEMS, Epstein's record shop, to ask for "My Bonnie"?
"The actual fact is, when I did the first issue of *Mersey Beat*, I went into NEMS and asked to see the manager. He didn't sell any music papers at all. Brian Epstein came down. He was all nicely dressed. I showed him the paper and asked if he could take some. So he ordered a dozen. Then he phoned me and he wanted some more: he was surprised, he'd sold out. Then he ordered more. And with the next issue, he ordered twelve dozen copies. People used to queue up outside the shop waiting for the latest issue. So he'd invite me into the office and go over every page: 'Oh, is all this happening?' Now with the cover of issue number two, the entire cover is The Beatles. And Brian says, 'This is fantastic, I can't believe this is happening in Liverpool.' He invited me for lunch. We had nice lamb chops. He wanted to talk. He was all excited. He'd never been aware that all this was happening in the city. He asked to be record reviewer and his record reviews appear in issue number three in August and he provided us our top ten charts. Then the next issue there was the entire full page article by Bob Wooler about The Beatles saying nothing like it will never happen again, rock revolutionaries. The only other thing on the page is a NEMS advert. And this is all well before this thing in the shop. Paul McCartney had brought me back a copy of the record and he gave one to

Bob Wooler and he began playing it locally. I was promoting them virtually every issue. Bob Wooler came up and says all the groups are complaining that you're writing so much about The Beatles, they say you should call the paper the Mersey Beatle. So I introduced a section of the paper called the Mersey Beatle. Brian invited me to [lunch] again and then he phoned me up and asked me if I could arrange for him to go to The Cavern. I phoned up Ray McFall and says, 'Brian Epstein of NEMS would like to come to The Cavern one lunchtime session.' He says, 'Oh alright, if he just walks in you can phone Paddy Delaney at the door.' Because of course Brian didn't want to go and stand with a bunch of kids at the lunchtime queue and pay a shilling to get in. When his book came out, he said. 'This guy Raymond Jones . . . ' I thought, 'What's happening here?' but I didn't care by then because I was doing all other things. Raymond Jones does exist. Raymond Jones was one of many people who had heard about the record and went in to ask about it at NEMS. Obviously with me promoting The Beatles and saying they were recording 'My Bonnie' and with NEMS selling 144 copies every issue, obviously people are gonna ask about it. But on top of that, when they were playing the lunchtime session at The Cavern, after they'd finished they'd go round the corner to NEMS, go into the record booths to play the records. Brian used to come down and [say] 'Who are they?' So he knew all about them. It's a good thing for him to start his book with."

The $64,000 question is would Epstein have decided to manage The Beatles if he hadn't been gay?
"Yes, because [of] the excitement that they generated, because he could actually see the exciting things that were happening the whole of Merseyside and that it was something for him to do. Because he'd been basically a failure in his other things. The family had been very dissatisfied with the incidents in his life."

But "My Bonnie" was a hoary old chestnut?
"It was awful [but it was] unique in those days for a Liverpool band to make a record."

They had the Decca audition in January 1962. Dick Rowe swore he never rejected them because "Bands with guitars are on the way out". What do you think?

"He didn't at all. Dick told me. It's a pity Dick died before he got his book published. I've talked to his son. Dick told me he never, ever said that. It's another Brian Epstein thing. Dick Rowe had been made the head of A&R at Decca to search out new bands, 'cos at that time A&R men never moved at all outside London. Groups had to go down there. But he wanted to find exciting new bands. In fact, when they got approached about The Beatles, every other record company [had] turned them down. People were making jokes about Brian Epstein that he couldn't even get them on the Woolworth's label. Yet Decca sent Mike Smith up to Liverpool to see them. That was unprecedented. Then they gave them a recording audition. So they did the recording audition and Mike Smith was very, very pleased and he contacted them and said, 'Yes, we're gonna sign you up, it's great.' They were all excited. Dick Rowe never turned them down. What happened was, Mike Smith had only just joined the department and he'd recorded two auditions on the same day, The Beatles and Brian Poole and The Tremeloes. Dick Rowe said to Mike Smith, 'You can have one of the groups.' Now at the time we had the 'A' roads, not the motorways, and it took over eight hours to get down to London from Liverpool, whereas Brian Poole and the Tremeloes were nearby in Aldershot, so if Decca were making a record and something's wrong and they wanted them back in the studio quick, it's easier to get a local group. So he chose Brian Poole and the Tremeloes. But Dick Rowe didn't turn them down. He left the decision to Mike. George Martin didn't really want to sign The Beatles. It was by accident and pressure from EMI Music. Alistair Taylor [of NEMS said], 'Brian Epstein used to come to the table and almost cry because George Martin wouldn't answer his calls' and all the rest of it. So then he told EMI that if they didn't go ahead with this Beatles audition, he'd stop stocking all the EMI records at all the stores. Brian kept phoning. He was supposed to give him them the audition and he could never get George Martin on the phone. It was just going nowhere. It could have gone on for years until he did the threat to EMI . . . George wasn't a rock guy. The only two rock people he had was Paul

Gadd and Shane Fenton. [Parlophone] was a mixture of classical, comedy records, all middle-of-the-road stuff. They did no rock. They weren't interested, and in fact George Martin wasn't interested. Brian Epstein had to virtually blackmail to get them to record for Parlophone. When they were recording, George Martin's assistant, who was the one who did the rock records, Ron Richards, was given The Beatles and on the first sheet of their recording audition, he's down as their recording manager. And that's how it was supposed to be. While they were doing the recording audition, when they began to play one of their own original numbers, the engineer went down to George Martin in the canteen and brought them up and then George Martin took over the session."

On 4 January 1962, there was a now famous headline in Mersey Beat: *"Beatles Top Poll", meaning they'd been voted Liverpool's best band. Some people have suggested the bands voted for themselves.*
"Everybody did. That's why me and [colleague] Virginia had to be very careful about what was happening. You're aware of things when you're counting and looking at the things, the handwriting and all the rest of it. Plus reports you got from people. We had a newsagent who said one guy came and got his entire stock. That was Joe Flannery, manager of Lee Curtis. When we came to do the poll, Rory Storm and the Hurricanes had the most votes and then looking through it again to make sure all is okay I notice that one big wad had all come in from the same postal [district] and they were all written in green ink in the same handwriting – forty of them. So I cancelled those and they were all for Rory Storm and the Hurricanes, and that made The Beatles number one and the Hurricanes numbers four."

You spelt Paul's name wrong on that front cover?
"That's John's fault. When I asked him to do the piece on The Beatles in the first issue, he put Paul's name down as 'Paul McArtrey'. I don't know whether he was doing a piss-take but when I came to do the copy, I copied John's spelling. When you're friends like that, sometimes you forget their second names. That's how I got Cilla Black her name: making it 'Black' when her name was 'White'."

In March that year, they got their first radio appearance on Teenager's Turn. *Was that a big deal for them?*
"It was. Mona Best had written to them."

Stuart Sutcliffe died at around this time. There's a dark rumour about this, namely that it was a delayed reaction to a kicking he got from John. Did John or anybody else say anything to you about this that made you think it might be true?
"The rubbish of this is absolutely incredible. Albert Goldman put that in his book – pure fantasy. Then Pauline Sutcliffe was doing an interview in one of the Beatles fanzines – *Beatles Unlimited* – and she was asked about this and she said, 'How dare he? What a complete loads of nonsense. This never happened.' Then when she does her third book, she's put that story down. I was in close touch with [Stuart's mother] Millie Sutcliffe. She phoned me every single month for fifteen years 'till she died. She'd always keep in touch with me about Stuart in Hamburg and she said, 'Oh God, I'm so worried.' He had the attic room in Astrid's house and there was a narrow stair coming down. She got onto me because he'd fallen down and hurt himself and started having headaches. And Astrid's mother said that the cause of his death was really this, when he fell down the attic steps. She found him at the bottom of the steps in a terrible state and so she put him to bed downstairs. Then he went to the hospitals and that."

He was fine before that?
"Yes he was. No problem at all. All the rumours and stupid things have come from Allan Williams' book in which it says there was a fight outside Litherland Town Hall. Well, it's a bit funny because Stuart didn't appear at Litherland Town Hall. The first time The Beatles appeared at Litherland Town Hall was 28 December 1960 and they had to get Chas Newby to play bass because Stuart was in Hamburg. And then Paul played bass. And then Stuart came back to Liverpool for a couple of days to see if he could get on the art course at Liverpool Art College but they wouldn't take him, presumably because the Beatles had taken the PA equipment and never returned it. He appeared with them at The Cavern and Latham Hall and that.

So the Allan Williams' story's ridiculous. He wasn't involved in a fight. I've got the direct quotes from Pete Best and also Neil Aspinall about a fight that occurred at Latham Hall but they said Stuart wasn't injured at all. It was John got his finger broke. People were following up this Allan Williams thing, all the myths in his book. Philip Norman, when he did his *Shout!*, I arranged for him to interview Millie Sutcliffe and he put the thing in his book which wasn't from Millie, 'When Millie heard that Stuart had died, her mind went back three years to Litherland Town Hall'. He put that in. That wasn't an actual fact."

What changes did you notice about the group when Stuart decided not to come back from that second trip to Hamburg?
"Paul was happier playing the bass. I suppose they were all tighter and all the rest of it."

George Martin has said he signed them not for musical reasons but because when they were together there was this incredible group charisma. Was this a quality you were aware of from knowing them?
"They always had it. As soon as I was at the Art College, '58, the first time I noticed John Lennon, he had the charisma about him and Stuart always had this intensity and emotion about him."

Controversy is going to rage forever about why Pete Best was sacked. Had you had any intimation before the sacking that the others weren't happy with him for whatever reason?
"None at all. I thought everything was fine. In fact, when I was told about the recording contract – Brian Epstein sent me a telegram: he sent one to the Beatles and one to me – about the Parlophone recording deal, I used it as the front cover story, but I only used a photograph of Pete Best with it."

For what reason do you personally think he was sacked?
"It's several. Paul and George basically wanted him out, not necessarily John. They may have had their own reasons. And George was a good friend of Ringo Starr. He really liked Ringo. And actually I had a story in *Mersey Beat* saying that George

had gone to Ringo's house to ask if he could join them, so maybe that's why [a fan] gave George his black eye at The Cavern. I just think they wanted somebody else in. There was a difference in character. I remember when we used to be sitting in the Jacaranda, everyone chatting, and Pete'd just sit there hardly saying a word. Didn't communicate like the others. Didn't have that sense of humour. That was one of the things. And I think they may have resented the fact that in Liverpool he was the most popular member of The Beatles with the girls and everyone acknowledges that. Then there was the fact that he and his mother were virtually managing them. His mother was quite a strong personality and I think they resented that a bit and they didn't want his mother to manage them and they thought that with his mother there all the time, she'd be interfering even if they had other managers. That was her son in the group and she'd be on people's backs all the time. It was a combination of all these different things."

But as far as you're concerned nothing whatsoever to do with drumming?
"No. In fact, Paul in his *Wingspan* documentary put an end to that. After all these years Paul actually admitted it in the documentary it wasn't his drumming. They used it as an excuse. Also, George Martin has a thing of changing his mind, looking at things with hindsight, because at the time when they went for the recording audition, generally in those days A&R men usually liked session musicians in the studio. Clem Cattini, Andy White, all the different sessions drummers were regularly in the studios. This was normal. When they did the session, George Martin told them – he actually told Mona Best – 'I think he's one of the biggest assets with the group, it's just that, in the studio, guitars and voice and thing's all right but it's a different sound you need for the drums. It can be fine on stage, we have a different thing in the studio.' That's what he said at the time. The Beatles used this as an excuse to sack Pete. Now, when he was sacked and Ringo went down, Ron Richards was doing the recording session and he thought Ringo was no good. Paul McCartney says Ringo was awful, he was no good at the session. and then George Martin came and said, 'No, this is no good,

Ringo, he just can't do it.' So they got Andy White because of Ringo Starr, not because of Pete Best."

Some Merseysiders say that The Beatles' raw power was never captured in the studio, apart from maybe "Twist And Shout". Do you agree with that?
"That's true. That's why John said, 'We were at our best when we played in Liverpool and Hamburg and we sold [out] after that.' They were a savage rock 'n' roll group. He was so upset when the image of The Beatles was changed. They became the loveable moptops. Andrew Loog Oldham was asked to become the press officer with The Beatles by Brian and he thought, 'They're so big that what you need now is an opposite,' so he created the image for The Rolling Stones. Now there you are having Brian Jones from Cheltenham and Mick Jagger from the London School of Economics and there you've got this swearing bunch of roughos from Liverpool playing in Hamburg before gangsters and prostitutes, taking pills and everything all the time and playing rough R&B and suddenly you get all these people, 'Oh, we like The Rolling Stones, not those moptops The Beatles, they're a sort of sissy-ish group.' John was furious at that: 'The Rolling Stones compared to us? We'd have blown The Rolling Stones ten miles off the stage.' John always felt The Rolling Stones had stolen his image, but of course Brian Epstein had changed the group from John's group into Paul's group. He knew he was losing John with all these image changes which John didn't agree with. It's like when he made them get rid of the black leather and put the mohair suits on. John, as a bit of a rebel, would undo the top button of the shirt but Paul'd come and tie that button up for him again. All these things were more to Paul's liking. Even when they were at The Cavern: 'Don't speak to the fans,' 'Don't take requests from the fans,' 'Don't smoke on stage,' and all this business. John absolutely hated that, all this regimen of notes and things that they had to do and they had to behave but he had to go along with to make some sort of success . . . That's the image that Brian Epstein cultivated and in some ways he had no option because at the time the whole media was run by a generation above us. You know what the BBC was like and the accent of the BBC at the time. Unless

they were well-dressed and conformed to what the radio and TV people and the producers expected, then it would have been very difficult and it was only because of The Beatles and the pathway they made that there was a Rolling Stones. There couldn't have been a Rolling Stones without The Beatles . . ."

They were your friends so you wanted to believe in them, but were you surprised that The Beatles proceeded to have genuine hit singles? "Not really, because the momentum had started. Even before I started doing *Mersey Beat*, I'd been writing to papers like the *Daily Mail* saying what was happening in Liverpool was unique. It was like New Orleans at the turn of the century, but rock 'n' roll instead of jazz. It seemed to be growing and I think it was ready to explode. With me being at the first radio show with them, with me being at the TV shows with them, I could see the almost mass hysteria starting, beginning of Beatlemania, so I felt then that it was inevitable. I felt probably by the end of '62, that they were gonna be massive. I didn't think massive in terms of the world but massive in terms of Britain."

The only good thing about "Love Me Do" seems to be John's wonderful bluesy harmonica. "John had always been involved with the harmonica since he was a kid because at his aunt Mimi's place, she took in lodgers and one of them used to play harmonica and showed John. Then when his cousin Stan Parkes used to take him to Scotland by bus, the conductor saw he was playing the mouth organ and took an interest in him and said somebody has left this really good harmonica on the bus and that if he'd come the next day he'd give it to him, which he did. I think the one that he played on 'Love Me Do' was one he stole in Arnhem, because when they stopped in Arnhem [on the first trip over to Hamburg] he went and stole a harmonica. Years later, a fan found the shop and went and paid for it. So he'd known about the harmonica but it wasn't really part of their stage act."

At the time of their early success, The Beatles did say they would never leave Liverpool. What happened? "This is the difficult situation and it was creating lot of controversy in *Mersey Beat* and things like that. Allan Williams – I came to London – he called me a plastic scouser. There was a certain amount of attitude in Liverpool. Yet one had to go to London because everything was based there. We had hoped that because of the success of The Beatles and Brian Epstein's other groups something would come to Liverpool, maybe a recording studio, a branch of a music publisher or something, because there was still nothing in Liverpool – only the groups and the artists."

Did Liverpool benefit from the success of The Beatles?
"Disaster in some ways. It helped to kill the scene. It ruined any knowledge of the true diversity of the music and the artists who were there."

Because people were only interested in bands that sounded like The Beatles?
"That's right."

Were you able to maintain your friendship as they became more successful?
"Oh sure, because initially I used to go to the radio shows and the gigs and be backstage with them on the concerts and then go travel up to the shows or go to the television shows with them, things like that. Then when I moved down to London, I used to go to the clubs, be chatting with them there. Then I took over the PR for clubs like the Speakeasy, Blaises, the Revolution and I used to see them regularly down there. And I always used to go Apple. Derek Taylor would have me round listening to all the previews of the coming records and I used to take people round, like The Beach Boys."

If you speak to people who lived through the 1960s today, they feel that The Beatles were more than just a pop group, that they changed the world. Was that your feeling then, or is it now?
"It wasn't just the music. They were trailblazers. They changed the whole concept of major concerts in the big stadiums in America and everything like that. They were the pathfinders of record covers. They were the pathfinders of the music video. It was their clothes, the style . . . I think people looked on The

Beatles more than just music. They looked on The Beatles almost as an exciting lifestyle . . . It seemed to me that they had certain sort of talents which put them heads and shoulders above everyone else. There were lots and lots and lots and lots of groups and artists who had hits and things and they never seemed to develop and evolve."

You apparently encouraged George in his songwriting?
"When I did the second issue of *Mersey Beat,* the entire front cover was 'The Beatles record in Germany'. I mentioned that George was the first Beatle to have an original number on a record in a professional studio because that's when they were backing Tony Sheridan for Bert Kaempfert and they asked if they could record one of their own original songs, so Kaempfert listened to their numbers and instead of picking one by Paul or John he picked the George Harrison one, 'Cry For A Shadow'. And I found that the first number they actually recorded of their own in the Kensington studio, Percy Phillips' studio, that was 'In Spite Of All The Danger', which is mainly George's. A couple of years later when it was only Lennon/McCartney numbers, I used to meet George regularly in the local clubs and I used to say, 'You were the first member of The Beatles to be mentioned as a songwriter on the cover of the *Mersey Beat.* What's happened? Why can't you write again? If you don't feel complete confidence, why don't you team up and write with Ringo?' So he did. He told me. He wrote a number with Ringo. I don't know what happened to it. I said, 'You must keep on writing'. When I was in Blackpool with them, George came up to me and said, 'I want to thank you. I was coming out one night to meet you again, you're gonna hassle me about songs so I thought I'd write a song called "Don't Bother Me". Thanks very much – I've made over £7,000 out of it so far.'"

Were you surprised that they split up when still so successful?
"No. Somehow I felt with time that the split was inevitable. The era of the 1960s had come to an end and that was fantastic and the future didn't bode well. One thing after another started happening, the rise of oil prices and all kinds of things."

People have always looked for the next Beatles.
"It'll never happen. The whole thing's changed. Every single newspaper has a rock columnist. The amount of radio shows is unbelievable. There were only one or two music books in the whole of the 1960s. One of the great things was that this belonged to us, this was ours because it wasn't on the radio, it wasn't in the media. This music belonged to us. I think that's part of what the kids in Liverpool felt when The Beatles left them, they felt they were part of this creation. Nowadays [there's] music wherever you [look]. It's not the same. It means less. The intensity that we had – you'd go to The Cavern and the hair would stand on the back of my neck when The Beatles came on – but the whole thing, the love of the music and the musicians and the people was all-enveloping and it's not the same now."

George seems to have changed the most, from happy-go-lucky to philosophical?
"This is it. He was the Beatle who was the one who was most stretched. His experiences stretched him into all these exciting things and the people he mixed with, the Monty Python crowd and all the rest of it, the Eastern people and Ravi Shankar and everything like that. This was a fantastic learning experience from the creative thing. It didn't happen with Ringo. I think Ringo's mentality still remained in the Dingle. With George, who hadn't had the best of educations, who hated school, it was like the School Of Life: he was learning and absorbing all these exciting things from others which he didn't want to do at school and things."

How spiritual was he?
"I think it's contradictory. George was the one completely obsessed by money. He was the one who wrote 'Taxman'. He was the one who'd go want to look at accounts. He was really fanatical about the money he earned and where it went. He was very material. Also, sexually, even when he was married, he did the wife-swapping thing with Ronnie Wood's wife. He used to smoke a lot. There was infidelity, smoking, drug-taking and avid for money, so quite contradictory to what Eastern philosophy basically is. He goes in a car and he's travelling to Spain or

somewhere and he's chanting for eight or nine hours 'Hare Krishna' and then he's sitting with one of his best mates Ringo Starr and his wife and in front of his own wife, he turns round and has to tell them that he's in love with Maureen, Ringo's wife, and he has an affair with Maureen. Patti runs and hides in the toilet. So you think, 'Is this a spiritual man?'"

What about the others?
"Paul is about the only one who stayed about the same. That's because of the upbringing with his father Jim, the way he was brought up: courtesy, good manners, consider other people. He was an ideal PR man and he knows how to manipulate the press."

Why didn't them both falling in love with women despised by the world in the late 1960s engender solidarity between John and Paul?
"Because I think John felt that all of the others resented Yoko. They thought she was exploiting him and things."

Some have suggested that Yoko was the austere figure of authority that Mimi had been to John.
"I think that was it. John had to have strong women. The Stanley sisters, I always thought there should have been a play or something about these five strong sisters who ruled the roost. They were married and everything but all you hear about is the women: 'My aunties this, my aunties that.' The five Stanley sisters were a fairly strong clan and he was brought up in a matriarchal environment and with Mimi being a strong woman and all his aunts being strong women, that's how he was reared. I think he was always looking for a very strong woman because he treated girls as doormats, and with Yoko being strong, I think that's what he'd been looking for all along."

Ringo's drumming has been much maligned. Do you think Ringo now regrets being so self-deprecating?
"No, because that was Ringo. Mind you, it's different in Liverpool. I was up there about a month ago for the premiere of the movie of *Love*. We were watching it and suddenly when Ringo came on, this fella shouts out 'Cunt!' Every time Ringo appeared,

he shouted it out, so they had to get the ushers and throw him out the place. [This is because of the comments about Liverpool] he made on *The Jonathan Ross Show*. They cut his head off that sculpture they made in Liverpool out of bushes. You've got to be careful of some Liverpudlians."

You've had a successful career in journalism and PR but do you feel like your life is inextricably bound up with The Beatles?
"Well it is. I can't escape it. I resented it a bit in that for sixteen years I was handling some of the world's leading bands – to me, Led Zeppelin were the biggest band in the world – but people [act like] I've done nothing else in my life but go to school with John Lennon. Lots of creative things and avenues I've wanted to go into seem blocked up because with publishers it's just another Beatle book they want. I have another big Beatle concept which is so big that I cannot do it unless there's a decent advance. It would be a mind-blowing thing, a definitive Beatles thing. Mark Lewisohn's been paid a million quid advance to do his one, which will be brilliant: three books of 900 pages each. Mine would be as long as that if not longer. Mine would be in ten books. But I can't do it for peanuts like some of these publishers offer. I wouldn't do it without an agent."
    See: www.merseybeat.co.uk

PART SIX: AND IN THE END . . .

To wrap it all up, an article by a renowned DJ and rock writer that summarizes and celebrates The Beatles' brilliant career with impressive economy of style.

AND IN THE END . . .

In 1981, Paul Gambaccini wrote and narrated a series for the BBC's Radio 1 called Masters of Rock. It examined the careers and music of the titans of popular music. Naturally, it included an edition about The Beatles.

Gambaccini also authored a book containing the transcripts of the series' programmes, albeit amended slightly to compensate for the grammatical liberties taken for the purposes of the broadcast medium. The latter fact and the fact that the Beatles programme transcript, stripped of the music that accompanied the words on the radio, ran to a mere eight pages hardly augured well for its quality.

Remarkably, though, it is one of the best pieces of writing ever published on the group. What it necessarily lacks in depth or originality it more than makes up for in conciseness and comprehensiveness: Gambo's tour of the most remarkable recording career of all time might be whistlestop, but it also touches every single base. For that reason, it seems an appropriate way to conclude this book.

The piece has dated only very slightly. It was written before the Anthology CDs/Threetles records. It also, in groping for a potential modern day media equivalent of The Beatles phenomenon, contains a reference to home video – then all the rage – that has been disproven by time. Otherwise, this writer would unhesitatingly show it to a Martian who wished to have The Beatles and what they stood for explained to him. Gambaccini himself says, "That's how I wrote it at the time! I figured there were a million pieces about The Beatles and I only had an hour [broadcast time], so I couldn't expand . . . I could only try to capture the essence for an alien who knew nothing about it. Spooky!"

Masters Of Rock: The Beatles

by Paul Gambaccini

I think of The Beatles whenever I hear John Lennon's song "Number Nine Dream". I think of The Beatles many times, but always when I hear John sing of something so long ago and ask himself whether it was just a dream: "Seemed so real to me."

That's how anyone who lived through the Beatle era must feel facing the distant but still vivid memory of a Liverpudlian quartet who revolutionized popular music and popular culture so profoundly it now seems impossible. But the wonderful thing about this dream is that it was genuinely real.

The Beatles were the most important and best musical entertainers of the twentieth century. That is quite a claim, but if we're going to consider a historical subject we might as well take the long view and look at our era as academics of the far future will. The five massively popular singers of this century, each associated with a breakthrough in style, have been Al Jolson, Bing Crosby, Frank Sinatra, Elvis Presley and The Beatles. The Fab Four have the edge over the other four because they wrote their own material, and several of their compositions seem certain to survive as has the music which is now called classical.

Of course, this judgment is possible through hindsight. No one would have predicted it just over twenty-five years ago, when John Lennon first played in The Quarry Men, named after the Quarry Bank High School he attended. Nor was the young rowdy's initial meeting with Paul McCartney particularly auspicious. Brought to see The Quarry Men by mutual friend

Ivan Vaughan in 1957, McCartney thought, "He's good. That's a good band there." Taken backstage, Paul thought the sixteen-year-old John smelled a bit drunk . . . but they got along fine. The Eddie Cochran number that brought them together was "Twenty Flight Rock". Paul was impressed that John also liked it, and Lennon was knocked out that McCartney could write out all the words. A week later, Paul joined The Quarry Men. He soon introduced them to his friend, George Harrison, a guitar buff who liked rock 'n' roll so much that he drew on a false moustache so he could look old enough to get in to see *The Blackboard Jungle*, the film that featured Bill Haley's "Rock Around The Clock". The evolution of The Quarry Men into Johnny And the Moondogs, The Silver Beatles, and finally The Beatles, complete with several personnel changes, is best told in Philip Norman's book *Shout!* It's a goldmine for Beatle buffs – their first hit doesn't make the top fifty until page 159!

"Love Me Do" entered the British charts in October 1962, and ultimately reached number seventeen. Two versions were recorded, one with the recently acquired drummer Ringo Starr and the other with safe session man Andy White. When White drummed, Ringo shook a tambourine. "Love Me Do" also featured a harmonica solo by John Lennon that had been directly inspired by the playing of Delbert McClinton on Bruce Channel's "Hey Baby". They'd been on a concert bill together earlier in the year. The song chosen for the next single had also been inspired by a current hitmaker. "Please Please Me" had been written in the slow dramatic style of Roy Orbison, but producer George Martin had suggested the group speed it up. When they did play the faster version, Martin agreed to scrap the Mitch Murray composition "How Do You Do It" which he and publisher Dick James had wanted The Beatles to release. They lengthened the song by repeating the first verse. The producer was so pleased he accepted the first take, saying "Gentlemen, you have just made your first number one."

He was right – or almost right, depending on which chart you went by in those days before the British Market Research Bureau. "Please Please Me" got to either one or two, certainly well enough to call for an album, which was named after the single.

Please Please Me showed The Beatles in transition, beginning to write their own material but still doing American rock 'n' roll favourites. They were not copyists: the original versions hadn't charted in Britain, and The Beatles had needed material to fill the hours of playing they had to do in The Cavern in Liverpool and in German club residencies. They were not revivalists: The Quarry Men had started at the beginning of the rock 'n' roll era, and the voice of John Lennon singing "Twist And Shout" or "Money" or the voice of Paul McCartney singing *à la* Little Richard is the voice of authentic rock 'n' roll at its best.

Not many singers of any kind could vocalize with the commitment and frightening energy John Lennon gave "Twist And Shout". Rock historians won't find the track in books of hit singles because it came out on an EP and EPs had their own lists in 1963. On that table, "Twist And Shout" did extremely well, and even more importantly, the album it came from, *Please Please Me*, dominated the LP chart that year, spending thirty weeks at number one, eventually eclipsed only by the next Beatles' set.

Here was the revolution of a form of entertainment. Before The Beatles, the best-selling albums were predominantly film soundtracks or original Broadway cast recordings. True, Elvis Presley did break through occasionally, and so did Ricky Nelson in the States and Cliff Richard and The Shadows in Britain. But it was the Beatle blockbusters that brought money to the album share of the market as no rock records had before. Almost overnight, young people bought LPs as they had previously purchased singles. To this day, rock music still rules the LP roost.

The Beatles achieved their massive album sales without hurting their singles figures. Indeed, every piece of plastic fed what quickly became a phenomenon. They began 1963 with "Please Please Me" and then had a seven-week run at number one with "From Me To You", the first single to sell a million-and-a-half copies in Britain ("She Loves You'), and the Christmas number one ("I Want To Hold Your Hand'). No artist has dominated British popular music in a single year as The Beatles did in 1963. Yet they were more than pop stars. They were news, regularly appearing in newspapers, magazines and newsreels.

They were a mass cult, subjects of hysterical carryings-on by young women that earned the phrase "Beatlemania". And they were cutters of class and age barriers, genuinely appealing to both sexes and all age groups and within the first three years of their success being named Members Of The British Empire and lunching with the Prime Minister, Harold Wilson. In a class-conscious society like Britain's, this was a precedent-setting penetration of the Establishment.

The Beatles feared that they might not succeed in the United States. No British rock singer had. They were also scared that if one act of the Beat Boom they led was going to cross the Atlantic, it might be fellow Liverpudlians Gerry and the Pacemakers, who had also scored three number ones in 1963, indeed, with their first three releases. The Beatles needn't have worried.

Everything they had released in the United States had been dismissed before "I Want To Hold Your Hand". A couple of singles actually had received an odd play on radio and the televized *American Bandstand* but none had sold. The only chart version of a Beatle tune had been Del Shannon's cover of "From Me To You" and that had only crept to number seventy-seven.

The American breakthrough was probably inevitable strictly on the merits of the music. But the form it took was undoubtedly shaped in part by the assassination of President John Kennedy on 22 November 1963. This traumatic tragedy, a constant possibility for world leaders today, was unthinkable then, and the nation's grief was genuine. As if by a gesture of repentance, the Singing Nun became number one for a month. Come the New Year, it was time to shake off the sadness. It is said that one extreme feeling can only be replaced by another. America substituted for its deep sense of loss a passion for The Beatles. "I Want To Hold Your Hand" made its chart debut in January. Within the month it was number one. Their first February appearance on *The Ed Sullivan Show* drew record viewing figures. What had happened in the UK in 1963 took place in the US in 1964: The Beatles became a national obsession.

Not just a chart craze – although re-releases of their previous discs did give them the top five singles in the United States one week in April, a feat which has never been duplicated. There was merchandizing on a scale hitherto unknown, with a range of products never before associated with any showbusiness sensation. Manager Brian Epstein has since been criticized for not winning better deals than he did, but the simple truth is that he could not have foreseen the unforeseeable, and was lucky to get the piece of the action he got.

There were more fundamental changes effected by The Beatles. Men had previously worn their hair short, perhaps in a crew cut. Now the male sex of the Western world let their hair grow, influenced by or in direct emulation of the Beatle haircut that came over the forehead.

There was another major move in 1964. The Beatles became the first rock stars to appear in a critically acclaimed motion picture.

"The new film with those incredible chaps, The Beatles, is a whale of a comedy," the movie critic of *The New York Times* wrote. "I wouldn't believe it either if I hadn't seen it with my own astonished eyes." *A Hard Day's Night*, a black-and-white film made on a limited budget, was an international critical and commercial success less than two years after "Love Me Do" had crawled into the British chart. The Beatle phenomenon was far-reaching and fast-moving.

One talent they had kept them going when other performers might have been stymied: they wrote their own material, so at least they knew from where the next song was coming. The Beatles were the first fully self-contained rock group: they wrote, sang and played their own material. Other rock 'n' rollers had required writers, as in the case of Elvis Presley, or a backing band, as with Chuck Berry. The Beatles provided the complete package. But the writing: that was crucial. After The Beatles, the power of Tin Pan Alley was drastically diminished, as it became assumed top artists would compose as well as sing. The solo singer, previously the norm in pop, had to make room for the group, as legions of rockers joined together in guitar-bass and drum ensembles modelled on The Beatles. Even the most contemporary of pop bands are working on a variation of The Beatles' line-up, allowing for the keyboards which Lennon, McCartney or even Billy Preston would sometimes play.

Lennon and McCartney were the outstanding songwriters

of the 1960s, providing themselves with a flow of first-rate material. "The greatest composers since Beethoven," *The Sunday Times* enthused. "The best songwriters since Schubert," said another critic.

Those were opinions; this is a statistic: "Yesterday", penned by McCartney, is the most recorded song in history. The melody of "Yesterday" occurred to Paul McCartney first thing one morning. He got out of bed and worked out the melody, using the temporary words "Scrambled egg, how I love a scrambled egg." It's now had well over a thousand versions, though none under the title "Scrambled Egg". It originally appeared as an album cut to fill out the soundtrack to the second film, *Help!* Only The Beatles had enough quality material to use a song like "Yesterday" as an album track. Almost every Beatle track received radio exposure in its time, especially in America. Artists queued to record Lennon and McCartney songs, both when they were writing together and, later, separately. To this day John Lennon has written more British number one hits than anyone else, Paul McCartney the most American number ones. But it must never be assumed that John and Paul were The Beatles, regardless of their great individual talents. George and Ringo added elements of personality which helped give The Beatles all aspects of young manhood in one group.

The Beatles – the unit – was greater than the sum of its parts. They were John, Paul, George *and* Ringo – not *or* – the first and, to this day, the only rock group whose Christian names were all known to all society.

There were other names important in The Beatles story, too, especially Brian Epstein and George Martin. Epstein was the Liverpool record store owner who made several brilliant strokes as their manager, particularly putting them in matching suits and haircuts, to tone down the rebellious streak that might have alienated part of the mass audience. The Rolling Stones, Bob Dylan, The Who – they all had their audience, but The Beatles belonged to everybody, thanks in no small measure to Brian Epstein. George Martin made his contributions in the studio, embellishing the Beatle compositions with the sounds they told him they wanted to hear but couldn't make themselves. Consider the haunting backing on "Eleanor Rigby", which remains one of the most astonishing tracks in all of pop, establishing an intense mood and telling a full story in just over two minutes. McCartney had originally called the woman "Daisy McKenzie", but changed it when he saw a clothing shop named "Rigby's" in Bristol. McKenzie became the name of the priest.

"Eleanor Rigby" first appeared on the 1966 album *Revolver*, one of the two consecutive masterpieces of The Beatles' so-called "middle period". The other was *Rubber Soul*, issued the previous year. They are both showcases for the possibilities of pop: John's reflective memoir, "In My Life", Paul's beautiful ballad, "Here There And Everywhere", the universally appealing children's song "Yellow Submarine", John's anticipation of psychedelia, "Tomorrow Never Knows", and Paul's ultra-commercial "Michelle". It is certainly impossible to single out one Beatles' album by chart position reached, since every studio LP they ever made was a number one. No other major act that made more than one record can make that claim. But these two packages are certainly peerless celebrations of rock music, The Beatles' greatness indicated by their seemingly effortless mastery of several styles.

In 1967 The Beatles released what are generally considered the finest single and the best album of all-time. The 45 was issued in February to placate the fans who were waiting for the next LP. There had not been a gap between Beatle albums as long as the ten months that separated *Revolver* and its successor.

By now McCartney and Lennon were writing many of their songs alone. On the single they each sang about Liverpool in a vastly different but equally brilliant way. Paul remembered "Penny Lane"; John longed for "Strawberry Fields Forever".

The two numbers each made perfectly ordinary parts of Liverpool seem to be magical places of wonder, proof that the feeling that goes into a song is more vital to its impact than its actual subject. Both tracks gave evidence of the experimentation the two men favoured. McCartney tended to go for new musical sounds, as he had with "Yesterday", "Eleanor Rigby", and "For No One". Lennon went for studio effects – the feedback at the start of "I Feel Fine", the first use of guitar feedback by a major artist, the reversed tape that served as the end of "Rain", the varispeed vocal on "Strawberry Fields Forever", which came courtesy of George Martin. Then there was George Harrison's idea of ending "She Loves You" on a sixth chord, and the unusual intervals used in the highly segmented "Paperback Writer". The Beatles made some radically experimental music, but people weren't conscious of it at the time because it was also incredibly commercial. They made the studio an instrument, inspiring countless others to try to make the most of its possibilities.

They certainly did so with their 1967 magnum opus, *Sgt. Pepper's Lonely Hearts Club Band.* As befitted The Beatles, it was the ultimate offering of the Summer Of Love. The title tune began and almost ended the work and because much of the subject matter seemed inspired by music hall and carnival characters, *Sgt. Pepper* . . . became known as the first "concept album". Many followed, quite a few lacking their model's wit and variety, and all without the dramatic power of "A Day In The Life", *Sgt. Pepper* . . . 's last track. It wasn't a coda or an afterthought, it was simply too daring and distinct to put anywhere but the end.

Ten years after it was issued, *Sgt. Pepper* . . . was voted the best rock album of all time by an international panel of critics. In another sense, too, it was The Beatles' peak. *Sgt. Pepper* . . . and the single that followed it, "All You Need Is Love", marked the last occasions The Beatles took the world with them as a unit. Millions hopped on the psychedelic bandwagon the Fab Four were simultaneously riding and leading.

The advocacy of peace and love, the rather obvious use of drugs, the donning of colourful costumes, the incorporation of Indian music meditation – young people around the world sampled them all. Some reined themselves in, some delved further into the fields. So it was with The Beatles. Without the restraining influence of Brian Epstein, who died that summer, the now grown men led their own lives.

John concentrated on his highly publicized personal and musical partnership with Yoko Ono. George won attention for his student-teacher relationship with Ravi Shankar, and praise for his work with Eric Clapton. It wasn't easy for him to revert to being the young one in a group dominated by Paul, who more than anyone else was desperately trying to save the world's most popular attraction.

The Beatles' 1968 work is clearly divisible into the efforts of individual members. The eponymous double LP, which became known as The White Album, had many marvellous moments, but they were obviously John's or Paul's or George's. Similarly, that autumn's single, which launched the group's Apple Label, is in retrospect one side John's "Revolution", and the A-side Paul's, "Hey Jude", originally conceived as a song for Julian Lennon, John's son, with the "Hey Jules" changed to "Hey Jude". The gesture showed that even though working separately the men were still friends, and Paul was pleased that John and Yoko considered the song wonderfully avant garde. At the time, it was: the words are often opaque or nonsensical, the song ends on a chant, and it was the longest number one ever. "Hey Jude" was number one in America for nine weeks, The Beatles' longest chart-topping run. It was one of the group's seventeen UK and twenty US number ones (more tracks were released as singles in the States). No act has ever had more number ones in either country.

The lasting memory of "Hey Jude" is the promotional clip, shown on *The David Frost Show* in Britain and *The Smothers Brothers* in America. The group are surrounded by a motley group of everyday Britons, almost a cross-section of society, all of them singing along. That image sums up The Beatles better than any other film or photograph.

Certainly better than this next feature film. *Get Back* was to be the title of an album that would return The Beatles to their roots. Instead, it was a half-hearted effort filmed for a documentary that turned out to be the record of their disintegration. The album and motion picture were called *Let It Be*; "Get Back" survived as a single which revealed that even in their death throes The Beatles could still cut it. *Let It Be* was the last album put out by The Beatles. Between its recording and release, held up to await editing of the movie, *Abbey Road* was made and issued.

It was a glorious goodbye. They pretty much knew it: the last song listed on the label was "The End". But John Lennon agreed not to speak of his decision to leave the group, and it wasn't until the spring of 1970 that Paul McCartney told the world press The Beatles had disbanded.

Those who have maintained a vigil ever since waiting patiently for "The next Beatles" are probably looking in the wrong direction. There will certainly again be consistently excellent songwriters and perhaps even an artist who will have seventeen number ones to match The Beatles and Elvis Presley. But that act will not be a rock group. It won't be because it can't be. The Beatles drew the boundaries they worked within; no one staying inside those boundaries can possibly duplicate their impact. The next "big thing" will have to be inventive in a new area, perhaps video.

It is only someone working in the most popular field of the moment turning out quality work quickly who can affect society as The Beatles did. The work of any major artist has a context. The Beatles' context was the 1960s, not the 1970s. They were part of a time when youth had just discovered a voice in rock 'n' roll. A whole culture shaped by economic affluence and political circumstances built up around that voice, which The Beatles spoke with the greatest clarity. They came to stand for the very world they were part of, and thus became personally vital to millions.

The Beatles were creatures of the 1960s, four men together, not part of the 1970s, a decade of self-analysis and self-fulfilment. The Beatles flourished in good economic times, not depression. They were part of an era where it was thought music and love could make anything possible, not a decade with a punk philosophy. The Beatles could not have been part of a world that said, "No". The Beatles said, "Yeah yeah yeah".

APPENDIX

THE BEATLES AND SOLO BEATLES COMPREHENSIVE UK DISCOGRAPHY

Compiled by Graham Calkin

Just about every Beatles book ever published has included a discography of some sort. This one, though, is something special. Beatles enthusiast Graham Calkin has compiled on his website a catalogue of every disc ever released in the UK bearing the names of The Beatles and the ex-members of the group. The discography also includes interview discs. Graham has granted permission for the reproduction of this extraordinary work here.

Though invaluable to the Beatle scholar and even the merely casually interested, the simple listing possible in the medium of print cannot convey the wealth of material available on the website, with its endless links to cover scans, full tracklistings, statistics and fascinating trivia and the reader is very much encouraged to check it out: http://www.jpgr.co.uk/i_all_date.html.

Graham adds this caveat about a discography that has been growing and evolving over a number of years: "Although I believe I have produced the most accurate and complete UK Beatles discography, I'm not suggesting I'm infallible . . ."

NOTES:

For reasons of simplicity, no attempt has been made to reflect different credits for records by Beatles members outside the band (e.g., Paul's albums are all credited to him, not "Wings" or "Paul and Linda McCartney", all of John's are credited to him and not "Plastic Ono Band" or "John Lennon and Yoko Ono".

The exception to this is where the member was recording under a *nom de guerre* (e.g. The Country Hams, The Fireman).

Records merely written by Beatle members are not included except in the case of projects that the relevant Beatle was helming artistically (e.g. *The Family Way, Wonderwall Music, Working Classical*). Similarly, guest appearances are not listed except where the Beatle was integral to the whole project (i.e. Traveling Wilburys). And then there are some projects with no Beatle involvement but whose omission would somehow feel wrong (e.g., *John Lennon's Jukebox*).

Imports are included in the case of new material that did not obtain a UK release.

Cassette and digital download releases are not included.

KEY: 7" = 7-inch vinyl single; 10" = 10-inch vinyl single; 12" = 12-inch vinyl single; LP = vinyl album; EP = Extended Play 7-inch vinyl record; CD = compact disc; DVD-A = DVD-Audio disc.

RELEASE DATE	ARTIST	FORMAT	LABEL	CAT NO.	TITLE	NOTES
05/01/1962	The Beatles	7"	Polydor	NH 66833	My Bonnie	Both sides credited to "Tony Sheridan & The Beatles"
05/10/1962	The Beatles	7"	Parlophone	R 4949	Love Me Do	
11/01/1963	The Beatles	7"	Parlophone	R 4983	Please Please Me	
22/03/1963	The Beatles	LP	Parlophone	PMC 1202	Please Please Me (MONO)	Sole occasion of a mono version of a Beatles album issued before a stereo version
12/04/1963	The Beatles	7"	Parlophone	R 5015	From Me To You	
26/04/1963	The Beatles	LP	Parlophone	PCS 3042	Please Please Me	
12/07/1963	The Beatles	EP	Polydor	EPH 21610	My Bonnie	Three tracks feature Beatles backing Tony Sheridan. Fourth is Lennon/Harrison-written instrumental "Cry For A Shadow"
12/07/1963	The Beatles	EP	Parlophone	GEP 8882	Twist and Shout	
23/08/1963	The Beatles	7"	Parlophone	R 5055	She Loves You	
06/09/1963	The Beatles	EP	Parlophone	GEP 8880	The Beatles Hits	
01/11/1963	The Beatles	EP	Parlophone	GEP 8883	The Beatles No.1	
22/11/1963	The Beatles	LP	Parlophone	PCS 3045	With the Beatles	
22/11/1963	The Beatles	LP	Parlophone	PMC 1206	With the Beatles (MONO)	
29/11/1963	The Beatles	7"	Parlophone	R 5084	I Want To Hold Your Hand	
06/12/1963	The Beatles	7"	Lyntone	LYN 492	The Beatles Christmas Record	Distributed to Beatles fan club members only
31/01/1964	The Beatles	7"	Polydor	NH 52906	Sweet Georgia Brown	Both sides credited to "Tony Sheridan & The Beatles"
07/02/1964	The Beatles	EP	Parlophone	GEP 8891	All My Loving	
28/02/1964	The Beatles	7"	Polydor	NH 52275	Cry For A Shadow	B-side credited to "The Beatles with Tony Sheridan vocal"
20/03/1964	The Beatles	7"	Parlophone	R 5114	Can't Buy Me Love	

RELEASE DATE	ARTIST	FORMAT	LABEL	CAT NO.	TITLE	NOTES
29/05/1964	The Beatles	7"	Polydor	NH 52317	Ain't She Sweet	B-side credited to "The Beatles with Tony Sheridan vocal"
19/06/1964	The Beatles	LP	Polydor	236 201	The Beatles First	German import. Tony Sheridan and Beatles recordings
19/06/1964	The Beatles	EP	Parlophone	GEP 8913	Long Tall Sally	
10/07/1964	The Beatles	LP	Parlophone	PCS 3058	A Hard Day's Night	
10/07/1964	The Beatles	LP	Parlophone	PMC 1230	A Hard Day's Night (MONO)	
10/07/1964	The Beatles	7"	Parlophone	R 5160	A Hard Day's Night	
04/11/1964	The Beatles	EP	Parlophone	GEP 8920	A Hard Day's Night (Extracts from the Film)	
06/11/1964	The Beatles	EP	Parlophone	GEP 8924	A Hard Day's Night (Extracts from the Album)	
27/11/1964	The Beatles	7"	Parlophone	R 5200	I Feel Fine	
04/12/1964	The Beatles	LP	Parlophone	PCS 3062	Beatles For Sale	
04/12/1964	The Beatles	LP	Parlophone	PMC 1240	Beatles For Sale (MONO)	
18/12/1964	The Beatles	7"	Lyntone	LYN 757	Another Beatles Christmas Record	Distributed to Beatles fan club members only
06/04/1965	The Beatles	EP	Parlophone	GEP 8931	Beatles For Sale	
09/04/1965	The Beatles	7"	Parlophone	R 5265	Ticket To Ride	
04/06/1965	The Beatles	EP	Parlophone	GEP 8938	Beatles For Sale No.2	
23/07/1965	The Beatles	7"	Parlophone	R 5305	Help!	
06/08/1965	The Beatles	LP	Parlophone	PCS 3071	Help!	
06/08/1965	The Beatles	LP	Parlophone	PMC 1255	Help! (MONO)	
03/12/1965	The Beatles	7"	Parlophone	R 5389	Day Tripper/ We Can Work It Out	
03/12/1965	The Beatles	LP	Parlophone	PCS 3075	Rubber Soul	
03/12/1965	The Beatles	LP	Parlophone	PMC 1267	Rubber Soul (MONO)	
06/12/1965	The Beatles	EP	Parlophone	GEP 8946	The Beatles' Million Sellers	

RELEASE DATE	ARTIST	FORMAT	LABEL	CAT NO.	TITLE	NOTES
17/12/1965	The Beatles	7"	Lyntone	LYN 948	The Beatles Third Christmas Record	Distributed to Beatles fan club members only
04/03/1966	The Beatles	EP	Parlophone	GEP 8948	Yesterday	
10/06/1966	The Beatles	7"	Parlophone	R 5452	Paperback Writer	
08/07/1966	The Beatles	EP	Parlophone	GEP 8952	Nowhere Man	
05/08/1966	The Beatles	LP	Parlophone	PCS 7009	Revolver	
05/08/1966	The Beatles	LP	Parlophone	PMC 7009	Revolver (MONO)	
05/08/1966	The Beatles	7"	Parlophone	R 5493	Eleanor Rigby/ Yellow Submarine	
06/12/1966	Paul McCartney	7"	Decca	F12536	Love In The Open Air	Written by McCartney but he does not appear; both sides credited to "The Tudor Minstrels"; re-recordings of tracks from soundtrack of The Family Way
10/12/1966	The Beatles	LP	Parlophone	PCS 7016	A Collection of Beatles Oldies	
10/12/1966	The Beatles	LP	Parlophone	PMC 7016	A Collection of Beatles Oldies (MONO)	
16/12/1966	The Beatles	7"	Lyntone	LYN 1145	Pantomime: Everywhere It's Christmas	Distributed to Beatles fan club members only
06/01/1967	Paul McCartney	7"	United Artists	UP 1165	Love in the Open Air	Written by McCartney but he does not appear; credited to "The George Martin Orchestra"; re-recordings of tracks from soundtrack of The Family Way
06/01/1967	Paul McCartney	LP	Decca	SKL 4847	The Family Way	Written by McCartney but he does not appear; credited to "The George Martin Orchestra"
17/02/1967	The Beatles	7"	Parlophone	R 5570	Penny Lane/ Strawberry Fields Forever	

RELEASE DATE	ARTIST	FORMAT	LABEL	CAT NO.	TITLE	NOTES
01/06/1967	The Beatles	LP	Parlophone	PCS 7027	Sgt. Pepper's Lonely Hearts Club Band	
01/06/1967	The Beatles	LP	Parlophone	PMC 7027	Sgt. Pepper's Lonely Hearts Club Band (MONO)	
07/07/1967	The Beatles	7"	Parlophone	R 5620	All You Need Is Love	
24/11/1967	The Beatles	7"	Parlophone	R 5655	Hello, Goodbye	
08/12/1967	The Beatles	EP	Parlophone	SMMT 1	Magical Mystery Tour	
08/12/1967	The Beatles	EP	Parlophone	MMT 1	Magical Mystery Tour (MONO)	
15/12/1967	The Beatles	7"	Lyntone	LYN 1360	Christmas Time (Is Here Again)	Distributed to Beatles fan club members only
15/03/1968	The Beatles	7"	Parlophone	R 5675	Lady Madonna	
30/08/1968	The Beatles	7"	Apple	R 5722	Hey Jude	
01/11/1968	George Harrison	LP	Apple	SAPCOR 1	Wonderwall Music	Written by Harrison but he does not appear
01/11/1968	George Harrison	LP	Apple	APCOR 1	Wonderwall Music (MONO)	Written by Harrison but he does not appear
22/11/1968	The Beatles	LP	Apple	PCS 7067/8	The Beatles	Informally called "The White Album"
22/11/1968	The Beatles	LP	Apple	PMC 7067/8	The Beatles (MONO)	Informally called "The White Album"
29/11/1968	John Lennon	LP	Apple	SAPCOR 2	Unfinished Music No.1 - Two Virgins	
29/11/1968	John Lennon	LP	Apple	APCOR 2	Unfinished Music No.1 - Two Virgins (MONO)	
20/12/1968	The Beatles	7"	Lyntone	LYN 1743/4	The Beatles Sixth Christmas Record	Distributed to Beatles fan club members only
17/01/1969	The Beatles	LP	Parlophone	PCS 7070	Yellow Submarine	
17/01/1969	The Beatles	LP	Parlophone	PMC 7070	Yellow Submarine (MONO)	
11/04/1969	The Beatles	7"	Apple	R 5777	Get Back	Both sides credited to "The Beatles with Billy Preston"

RELEASE DATE	ARTIST	FORMAT	LABEL	CAT NO.	TITLE	NOTES
09/05/1969	John Lennon	LP	Apple	ZAPPLE 01	Unfinished Music No.2 – Life With The Lions	
09/05/1969	George Harrison	LP	Apple	ZAPPLE 02	Electronic Sound	
30/05/1969	The Beatles	7"	Apple	R 5786	The Ballad Of John And Yoko	First Beatles stereo single
04/07/1969	John Lennon	7"	Apple	APPLE 13	Give Peace A Chance	
26/09/1969	The Beatles	LP	Parlophone	PCS 7088	Abbey Road	First Beatles album not issued in mono
24/10/1969	John Lennon	7"	Apple	APPLES 1001	Cold Turkey	
31/10/1969	The Beatles	7"	Apple	R 5814	Something	
07/11/1969	John Lennon	LP	Apple	SAPCOR 11	The Wedding Album	
12/12/1969	John Lennon	LP	Apple	CORE 2001	Live Peace in Toronto 1969	
19/12/1969	The Beatles	7"	Lyntone	LYN 1970/1	The Beatles Seventh Christmas Record	Distributed to Beatles fan club members only
06/02/1970	John Lennon	7"	Apple	APPLES 1003	Instant Karma	
06/03/1970	The Beatles	7"	Apple	R 5833	Let It Be	
27/03/1970	Ringo Starr	LP	Apple	PCS 7101	Sentimental Journey	
17/04/1970	Paul McCartney	LP	Apple	PCS 7102	McCartney	
08/05/1970	The Beatles	LP	Apple	PXS 1	Let it Be	Original boxed release with accompanying book
25/09/1970	Ringo Starr	LP	Apple	PAS 10002	Beaucoups Of Blues	
06/11/1970	The Beatles	LP	Apple	PCS 7096	Let it Be	First release of album in standard, non-boxed format
30/11/1970	George Harrison	LP	Apple	STCH 639	All Things Must Pass	
11/12/1970	John Lennon	LP	Apple	PCS 7124	John Lennon/Plastic Ono Band	
18/12/1970	The Beatles	LP	Lyntone	LYN 2154	From Then To You	Distributed to Beatles fan club members only
15/01/1971	George Harrison	7"	Apple	R 5884	My Sweet Lord	
19/02/1971	Paul McCartney	7"	Apple	R 5889	Another Day	
12/03/1971	John Lennon	7"	Apple	R 5892	Power To The People	

RELEASE DATE	ARTIST	FORMAT	LABEL	CAT NO.	TITLE	NOTES
09/04/1971	Ringo Starr	7"	Apple	R 5898	It Don't Come Easy	
28/05/1971	Paul McCartney	LP	Apple	PAS 10003	Ram	
30/07/1971	George Harrison	7"	Apple	R 5912	Bangla-desh	
13/08/1971	Paul McCartney	7"	Apple	R 5914	Back Seat Of My Car	
08/10/1971	John Lennon	LP	Apple	PAS 10004	Imagine	
07/12/1971	Paul McCartney	LP	Apple	PCS 7142	Wild Life	
10/01/1972	George Harrison	LP	Apple	STCX 3385	Concert For Bangla Desh	By various artists; Harrison and Starr play on much of the album.
25/02/1972	Paul McCartney	7"	Apple	R 5936	Give Ireland Back To The Irish	
17/03/1972	Ringo Starr	7"	Apple	R 5944	Back Off Boogaloo	
12/05/1972	Paul McCartney	7"	Apple	R 5949	Mary Had A Little Lamb	
15/09/1972	John Lennon	LP	Apple	PCSP 716	Some Time in New York City	
24/11/1972	John Lennon	7"	Apple	R 5970	Happy Xmas (War Is Over)	
01/12/1972	Paul McCartney	7"	Apple	R 5973	Hi Hi Hi	
23/03/1973	Paul McCartney	7"	Apple	R 5985	My Love	
19/04/1973	The Beatles	LP	Parlophone	PCSP 717	1962–1966	Informally called "The Red Album"
19/04/1973	The Beatles	LP	Parlophone	PCSP 718	1967–1970	Informally called "The Blue Album"
04/05/1973	Paul McCartney	LP	Apple	PCTC 251	Red Rose Speedway	
25/05/1973	George Harrison	7"	Apple	R 5988	Give Me Love (Give Me Peace On Earth)	
01/06/1973	Paul McCartney	7"	Apple	R 5987	Live And Let Die	
22/06/1973	George Harrison	LP	Apple	PAS 10006	Living in the Material World	
19/10/1973	Ringo Starr	7"	Apple	R 5992	Photograph	
26/10/1973	Paul McCartney	7"	Apple	R 5993	Helen Wheels	
16/11/1973	John Lennon	LP	Apple	PCS 7165	Mind Games	
16/11/1973	John Lennon	7"	Apple	R 5994	Mind Games	

RELEASE DATE	ARTIST	FORMAT	LABEL	CAT NO.	TITLE	NOTES
23/11/1973	Ringo Starr	LP	Apple	PCTC 252	Ringo	
07/12/1973	Paul McCartney	LP	Apple	PAS 10007	Band On The Run	
08/02/1974	Ringo Starr	7"	Apple	R 5995	You're Sixteen	
15/02/1974	Paul McCartney	7"	Apple	R 5996	Jet	
28/06/1974	Paul McCartney	7"	Apple	R 5997	Band On The Run	
04/10/1974	John Lennon	7"	Apple	R 5998	Whatever Gets You Thru The Night	
04/10/1974	John Lennon	LP	Apple	PCTC 253	Walls and Bridges	
18/10/1974	Paul McCartney	7"	EMI	EMI 2220	Walking In The Park With Eloise	Both sides credited to "The Country Hams"
25/10/1974	Paul McCartney	7"	Apple	R 5999	Junior's Farm	
15/11/1974	Ringo Starr	LP	Apple	PCS 7168	Goodnight Vienna	
15/11/1974	Ringo Starr	7"	Apple	R 6000	Only You	
06/12/1974	George Harrison	7"	Apple	R 6002	Ding Dong	
20/12/1974	George Harrison	LP	Apple	PAS 10008	Dark Horse	
31/01/1975	John Lennon	7"	Apple	R 6003	No. 9 Dream	
21/02/1975	John Lennon	LP	Apple	PCS 7169	Rock 'n' Roll	
21/02/1975	Ringo Starr	7"	Apple	R 6004	Snookeroo	
28/02/1975	George Harrison	7"	Apple	R 6001	Dark Horse	
18/04/1975	John Lennon	7"	Apple	R 6005	Stand By Me	
16/05/1975	Paul McCartney	7"	Capitol	R 6006	Listen To What The Man Said	
30/05/1975	Paul McCartney	LP	Capitol	PCTC 254	Venus and Mars	
05/09/1975	Paul McCartney	7"	Capitol	R 6008	Letting Go	
12/09/1975	George Harrison	7"	Apple	R 6007	You	
03/10/1975	George Harrison	LP	Apple	PAS 10009	Extra Texture – Read All About It	
24/10/1975	John Lennon	LP	Apple	PCS 7173	Shaved Fish	
24/10/1975	John Lennon	7"	Apple	R 6009	Imagine	
28/11/1975	Paul McCartney	7"	Capitol	R 6010	Venus And Mars/Rock Show	
12/12/1975	Ringo Starr	LP	Apple	PCS 7170	Blast from your Past	

RELEASE DATE	ARTIST	FORMAT	LABEL	CAT NO.	TITLE	NOTES
09/01/1976	Ringo Starr	7"	Apple	R 6011	Oh My My	
06/02/1976	George Harrison	7"	Apple	R 6012	This Guitar (Can't Keep From Crying)	
06/03/1976	The Beatles	7"	EMI	BS 24	Complete Singles Collection reissued	
08/03/1976	The Beatles	7"	Parlophone	R 6013	Yesterday	
09/04/1976	Paul McCartney	LP	Parlophone	PAS 10010	Wings At The Speed of Sound	
30/04/1976	Paul McCartney	7"	Parlophone	R 6014	Silly Love Songs	
10/06/1976	The Beatles	LP	Parlophone	PCSP 719	Rock 'n' Roll Music	
25/06/1976	The Beatles	7"	Parlophone	R 6016	Back In The U.S.S.R.	
23/07/1976	Paul McCartney	7"	Parlophone	R 6015	Let 'em In	
30/07/1976	The Beatles	LP	Polydor	2683 068	The Beatles Tapes From The David Wigg Interviews	Interview disc
17/09/1976	Ringo Starr	LP	Polydor	2302 040	Rotogravure	
15/10/1976	Ringo Starr	7"	Polydor	2001 694	A Dose Of Rock 'n' Roll	
19/11/1976	The Beatles	LP	Parlophone	PCTC 255	Magical Mystery Tour	
19/11/1976	George Harrison	LP	Dark Horse	K 56319	Thirty Three & 1/3	
19/11/1976	George Harrison	7"	Dark Horse	K 16856	This Song	
20/11/1976	George Harrison	LP	Parlophone	PAS 10011	Best of George Harrison	
29/11/1976	Ringo Starr	7"	Polydor	2001 699	Hey Baby	
10/12/1976	Paul McCartney	LP	Parlophone	PCSP 720	Wings Over America	
04/02/1977	Paul McCartney	7"	Parlophone	R 6017	Maybe I'm Amazed	
11/02/1977	George Harrison	7"	Dark Horse	K 16896	True Love	
29/04/1977	Paul McCartney	LP	Regal Zonophone	EMC 3175	Thrillington	Written by McCartney, who does not perform
02/05/1977	The Beatles	LP	Lingasong	LNL 1	Live! At the Star-Club in Hamburg, Germany; 1962	First release of Star-Club material
06/05/1977	The Beatles	LP	Parlophone	EMTV 4	Live at the Hollywood Bowl	
31/05/1977	George Harrison	7"	Dark Horse	K 16967	It's What You Value	

RELEASE DATE	ARTIST	FORMAT	LABEL	CAT NO.	TITLE	NOTES
24/06/1977	The Beatles	7"	Lingasong	NB 1	Twist And Shout	Both sides from the Live At The Star-Club album
16/09/1977	Ringo Starr	7"	Polydor	2001 734	Drowning In The Sea Of Love	
20/09/1977	Ringo Starr	LP	Polydor	2310 556	Ringo The 4th	
11/11/1977	Paul McCartney	7"	Capitol	R 6018	Mull Of Kintyre	
19/11/1977	The Beatles	LP	Parlophone	PCSP 721	Love Songs	
23/03/1978	Paul McCartney	7"	Parlophone	R 6019	With A Little Luck	
31/03/1978	Paul McCartney	LP	Parlophone	PAS 10012	London Town	
21/04/1978	Ringo Starr	LP	Polydor	2310 599	Bad Boy	
01/06/1978	Ringo Starr	7"	Polydor	2001 782	Lipstick Traces	
16/06/1978	Paul McCartney	7"	Parlophone	R 6020	I've Had Enough	
21/07/1978	Ringo Starr	7"	Polydor	2001 795	Tonight	
26/08/1978	Paul McCartney	7"	Parlophone	R 6021	London Town	
30/09/1978	The Beatles	LP	Parlophone	PCSPR 717	1962–1966 (Red Vinyl)	
30/09/1978	The Beatles	LP	Parlophone	PCSPR 718	1967–1970 (Blue Vinyl)	
30/09/1978	The Beatles	7"	Parlophone	R 6022	Sgt. Pepper's Lonely Hearts Club Band/ With A Little Help From My Friends	
01/12/1978	Paul McCartney	LP	Parlophone	PCTC 256	Wings Greatest	
02/12/1978	The Beatles	LP	EMI	BC-13	The Beatles Collection	
02/12/1978	The Beatles	LP	Parlophone	PSLP 261	Rarities	Bonus LP with Beatles Collection box set
16/01/1979	The Beatles	LP	Parlophone	PHO 7027	Sgt. Pepper's Lonely Hearts Club Band	Picture disc
16/01/1979	The Beatles	LP	Parlophone	PHO 7088	Abbey Road	Picture disc
16/02/1979	George Harrison	LP	Dark Horse	K 56562	George Harrison	
16/02/1979	George Harrison	7"	Dark Horse	K 17327	Blow Away	
23/03/1979	Paul McCartney	7"	Parlophone	R 6023	Goodnight Tonight	

RELEASE DATE	ARTIST	FORMAT	LABEL	CAT NO.	TITLE	NOTES
03/04/1979	Paul McCartney	12"	Parlophone	12 YR 6023	Goodnight Tonight	
20/04/1979	George Harrison	7"	Dark Horse	K 17284	Love Comes to Everyone	
11/05/1979	The Beatles	LP	Parlophone	PCS 7184	Hey Jude	
01/06/1979	Paul McCartney	7"	Parlophone	R 6026	Old Siam Sir	
08/06/1979	Paul McCartney	LP	Parlophone	PCTC 257	Back to the Egg	
30/07/1979	George Harrison	7"	Dark Horse	K 17423 P	Faster	
16/08/1979	Paul McCartney	7"	Parlophone	R 6027	Getting Closer	
12/10/1979	The Beatles	LP	Parlophone	PCM 1001	Rarities	First separate issue
16/11/1979	Paul McCartney	7"	Parlophone	R 6029	Wonderful Christmastime	
11/04/1980	Paul McCartney	7"	Parlophone	R 6035	Coming Up	
16/05/1980	Paul McCartney	LP	Parlophone	PCTC 258	McCartney II	
13/06/1980	Paul McCartney	7"	Parlophone	R 6037	Waterfalls	
19/09/1980	Paul McCartney	12"	Parlophone	12 R 6039	Temporary Secretary	
13/10/1980	The Beatles	LP	Parlophone	PCS 7214	The Beatles Ballads	
24/10/1980	The Beatles	LP	Music For Pleasure	MFP 50506	Rock 'n' Roll Music Vol. 1	
24/10/1980	The Beatles	LP	Music For Pleasure	MFP 50507	Rock 'n' Roll Music Vol. 2	
24/10/1980	John Lennon	7"	Geffen	K 79186	(Just Like) Starting Over	
03/11/1980	The Beatles	LP	World Records	SM 701/8	The Beatles Box	
17/11/1980	John Lennon	LP	Geffen	K 99131	Double Fantasy	
16/01/1981	John Lennon	7"	Geffen	K 79195	Woman	
20/02/1981	The Beatles	LP	Charly	CRV 202	Hear The Beatles Tell All (1964)	Interview disc
23/02/1981	Paul McCartney	LP	Parlophone	CHAT 1	The McCartney Interview	Interview disc
27/03/1981	John Lennon	7"	Geffen	K 79207	Watching The Wheels	
15/05/1981	George Harrison	7"	Dark Horse	K 17807	All Those Years Ago	
05/06/1981	George Harrison	LP	Dark Horse	K 56870	Somewhere In England	
15/06/1981	John Lennon	LP	Parlophone	JLB 8	John Lennon (Box Set)	

RELEASE DATE	ARTIST	FORMAT	LABEL	CAT NO.	TITLE	NOTES
17/07/1981	The Beatles	LP	Phoenix	PHX 1004	The Early Years Vol.1	10 Star-Club tracks
17/07/1981	The Beatles	LP	Phoenix	PHX 1005	The Early Years Vol.2	10 Star-Club tracks
31/07/1981	George Harrison	7"	Dark Horse	K 17837	Teardrops	
25/09/1981	The Beatles	LP	Audiofidelity	AFELD 1018	Historic Sessions	24 Star-Club tracks
13/11/1981	Ringo Starr	7"	RCA	RCA 166	Wrack My Brain	
20/11/1981	Ringo Starr	LP	RCA	RCALP 6022	Stop And Smell The Roses	
07/12/1981	The Beatles	EP	Parlophone	BEP 14	EP Collection	Box set
07/12/1981	The Beatles	EP	Parlophone	SGE 1	Rarities	
22/01/1982	The Beatles	LP	Phoenix	PHX 1011	Rare Beatles	10 Star-Club tracks
29/03/1982	The Beatles	LP	Parlophone	PCS 7218	Reel Music	
29/03/1982	Paul McCartney	7"	Parlophone	R 6054	Ebony And Ivory	
29/03/1982	Paul McCartney	12"	Parlophone	12 R 6054	Ebony and Ivory	
26/04/1982	Paul McCartney	LP	Parlophone	PCTC 259	Tug of War	
01/05/1982	The Beatles	LP	Goughsound	GP 5001	The Beatles Talk Downunder (1964)	Interview disc
24/05/1982	The Beatles	7"	Parlophone	R 6055	Movie Medley	7 Beatles tracks segued
21/06/1982	Paul McCartney	7"	Parlophone	R 6056	Take It Away	
25/06/1982	The Beatles	LP	Everest	CBR 1008	Beatles Interviews (1964/1966)	Interview disc
05/07/1982	Paul McCartney	12"	Parlophone	12 R 6056	Take it Away	
10/09/1982	The Beatles	LP	AudioFidelity	AFELP 1047	The Complete Silver Beatles	First release of material from the Decca audition
20/09/1982	Paul McCartney	7"	Parlophone	R 6057	Tug Of War	
??/10/1982	The Beatles	LP	EMI	BMC 13	The Beatles Mono Collection	Box set of 10 mono LPs from Please Please Me through to Yellow Submarine (omitting A Collection of Beatles Oldies) for export only
04/10/1982	The Beatles	7"	Parlophone	RP 4949	Love Me Do	
18/10/1982	The Beatles	LP	Parlophone	PCTC 260	20 Greatest Hits	
29/10/1982	The Beatles	7"	Audiofidelity	AFS 1	Searchin'	From Decca audition

RELEASE DATE	ARTIST	FORMAT	LABEL	CAT NO.	TITLE	NOTES
29/10/1982	Paul McCartney	7"	Epic	EPC A2729	The Girl Is Mine	Credited to "Michael Jackson/Paul McCartney"
01/11/1982	John Lennon	LP	Parlophone	EMTV 37	The John Lennon Collection	
01/11/1982	The Beatles	12"	Parlophone	12 R 4949	Love Me Do	
08/11/1982	George Harrison	LP	Dark Horse	923734-1	Gone Troppo	
08/11/1982	George Harrison	7"	Dark Horse	929864-7	Wake Up My Love	
15/11/1982	John Lennon	7"	Parlophone	R 6059	Love	
06/12/1982	The Beatles	7"	World Records	BSC 1	The Beatles Singles Collection box set	All the original Beatles singles, plus singles released since 1976
10/01/1983	The Beatles	7"	Parlophone	RP 4983	Please Please Me	
11/04/1983	The Beatles	7"	Parlophone	RP 5015	From Me To You	
16/06/1983	Ringo Starr	LP	Bellaphon	* NOT UK *	Old Wave	German Import. No UK release
22/08/1983	The Beatles	7"	Parlophone	RP 5055	She Loves You	
10/09/1983	The Beatles	LP	Audiofidelity	AFEP 20623	20 Greatest Hits	12 Decca audition tracks; 8 Polydor recordings (with Tony Sheridan)
10/09/1983	The Beatles	LP	Audiofidelity	AFEP 20629	20 Great Hits	20 Star-Club tracks
03/10/1983	Paul McCartney	7"	Parlophone	R 6062	Say Say Say	Credited to "Paul McCartney and Michael Jackson"
03/10/1983	Paul McCartney	12"	Parlophone	12 R 6062	Say Say Say	Credited to "Paul McCartney and Michael Jackson"
17/10/1983	Paul McCartney	LP	Parlophone	PCTC 1652301	Pipes of Peace	
28/11/1983	The Beatles	7"	Parlophone	RP 5084	I Want To Hold Your Hand	
05/12/1983	Paul McCartney	7"	Parlophone	R 6064	Pipes Of Peace	
16/12/1983	John Lennon	LP	Polydor	817238-1	Heart Play – Unfinshed Dialogue	
19/12/1983	The Beatles	LP	Breakaway	BWY 72	The Audition Tapes	12 Decca audition tracks
30/12/1983	The Beatles	LP	Breakaway	BWY 85	The Hamburg Tapes Vol.1	10 Star-Club tracks

RELEASE DATE	ARTIST	FORMAT	LABEL	CAT NO.	TITLE	NOTES
30/12/1983	The Beatles	LP	Breakaway	BWY 86	The Hamburg Tapes Vol.2	10 Star-Club tracks
30/12/1983	The Beatles	LP	Breakaway	BWY 87	The Hamburg Tapes Vol.3	10 Star-Club tracks
06/01/1984	The Beatles	LP	Phoenix	PHX 3-1	The Beatles Historic Sessions	Triple LP set; 12 Decca audition tracks; 30 Star-Club tracks
09/01/1984	John Lennon	7"	Polydor	POSP 700	Nobody Told Me	
23/01/1984	John Lennon	LP	Polydor	POLH 5	Milk and Honey	
27/01/1984	John Lennon	CD	Polydor	8171 602	Milk and Honey	
01/02/1984	The Beatles	LP	Goughsound	PGP 5001	Beatles Talk Downunder (1964)	Interview disc; picture disc
29/02/1984	Paul McCartney	CD	Parlophone	CDP 7 46018 2	Pipes of Peace	
09/03/1984	John Lennon	7"	Polydor	POSP 701	Borrowed Time	
09/03/1984	John Lennon	12"	Polydor	POSPX 701	Borrowed Time	
19/03/1984	The Beatles	7"	Parlophone	RP 5114	Can't Buy Me Love	
??/06/1984	John Lennon	LP	Silhouette	SM 10014	Reflections And Poetry	Interview disc
09/07/1984	The Beatles	7"	Parlophone	RP 5160	A Hard Day's Night	
15/07/1984	John Lennon	7"	Polydor	POSP 702	I'm Stepping Out	
15/07/1984	John Lennon	12"	Polydor	POSPX 702	I'm Stepping Out	
21/09/1984	John Lennon	LP	Polydor	POLH 13	Every Man Has A Woman	Various artists, one track by Lennon
24/09/1984	Paul McCartney	7"	Parlophone	R 6080	No More Lonely Nights (Ballad)	
24/09/1984	Paul McCartney	12"	Parlophone	12 R 6080	No More Lonely Nights	
22/10/1984	Paul McCartney	LP	Parlophone	PCTC 2	Give my Regards to Broad Street	
22/10/1984	Paul McCartney	CD	Parlophone	CDP 7 46043 2	Give my Regards to Broad Street	
12/11/1984	Paul McCartney	7"	Parlophone	R 6086	We All Stand Together	
16/11/1984	John Lennon	7"	Polydor	POSP 712	Every Man Has A Woman Who Loves Him	

RELEASE DATE	ARTIST	FORMAT	LABEL	CAT NO.	TITLE	NOTES
16/11/1984	John Lennon	CD	Polydor	8234 902	Every Man Has A Woman	Various artists, one track by Lennon
26/11/1984	The Beatles	7"	Parlophone	RP 5200	I Feel Fine	
04/02/1985	Paul McCartney	CD	Parlophone	CDP 7 46055 2	Band On The Run	
04/02/1985	Paul McCartney	CD	Parlophone	CDP 7 46056 2	Wings Greatest Hits	
04/02/1985	Paul McCartney	CD	Parlophone	CDP 7 46057 2	Tug Of War	
17/03/1985	The Beatles	LP	Cambra	CR 5149	Words And Music	Interviews plus tracks from Decca audition and Star-Club
09/04/1985	The Beatles	7"	Parlophone	RP 5265	Ticket To Ride	
16/06/1985	The Beatles	LP	Castle Showcase	SHLP 130	Live at the Star-club Vol.1	15 Star-Club tracks
16/06/1985	The Beatles	LP	Castle Showcase	SHLP 131	Live at the Star-club Vol.2	15 Star-Club tracks
23/07/1985	The Beatles	7"	Parlophone	RP 5305	Help!	
18/11/1985	John Lennon	7"	Parlophone	R 6117	Jealous Guy	
18/11/1985	Paul McCartney	7"	Parlophone	R 6118	Spies Like Us	
18/11/1985	John Lennon	12"	Parlophone	12 R 6117	Jealous Guy	
18/11/1985	Paul McCartney	12"	Parlophone	12 R 6118	Spies Like Us	
02/12/1985	The Beatles	7"	Parlophone	RP 5389	Day Tripper/ We Can Work It Out	
16/12/1985	The Beatles	CD	Overseas	38CP-44	Live at the Star-Club	First CD release of the 30 Star-Club tracks
24/02/1986	John Lennon	LP	Parlophone	PCS 7301	Live In New York City	
24/02/1986	John Lennon	CD	Parlophone	CDP 7 46196 2	Live In New York City	
06/06/1986	The Beatles	??	Lyntone	LYN 17148	The Beatles Live! The First Radio Interview	Disc issued free with book The Beatles Live! Contains first known recorded interview with The Beatles, taped 27/10/62 backstage at Hulme Hall, Cheshire
09/06/1986	The Beatles	7"	Parlophone	RP 5452	Paperback Writer	
14/07/1986	Paul McCartney	7"	Parlophone	R 6133	Press	A-side replaced by "Video Edit" after first week
14/07/1986	Paul McCartney	12"	Parlophone	12 R 6133	Press (Original Edition)	

RELEASE DATE	ARTIST	FORMAT	LABEL	CAT NO.	TITLE	NOTES
16/07/1986	The Beatles	CD	Overseas	30CT-55	The Silver Beatles	First CD release of the 12 Decca audition tracks.
01/08/1986	The Beatles	LP	Shanghai	GP 5001	Beatles Talk Downunder (1964)	Interview disc; picture disc
05/08/1986	The Beatles	7"	Parlophone	RP 5493	Eleanor Rigby/Yellow Submarine	
14/08/1986	Paul McCartney	10"	Parlophone	10 R 6133	Press	Includes both 7" mixes of Press
01/09/1986	Paul McCartney	LP	Parlophone	PCSD 103	Press to Play	
01/09/1986	Paul McCartney	CD	Parlophone	CZ 28	Press to Play	
10/10/1986	John Lennon	CD	Geffen	299 131	Double Fantasy	
27/10/1986	Paul McCartney	7"	Parlophone	R 6145	Pretty Little Head	
27/10/1986	Paul McCartney	12"	Parlophone	12 R 6145	Pretty Little Head	
03/11/1986	John Lennon	LP	Parlophone	PCS 7308	Menlove Avenue	
01/12/1986	Paul McCartney	7"	Parlophone	R 6148	Only Love Remains	
01/12/1986	Paul McCartney	12"	Parlophone	12 R 6148	Only Love Remains	
??/01/1987	Paul McCartney	LP	Baktabak	BAK 2003	Paul McCartney Interview	Interview disc
16/02/1987	The Beatles	7"	Parlophone	RP 5570	Penny Lane/Strawberry Fields Forever	
25/02/1987	The Beatles	LP	Premier	CBR 1047	Beatles Interviews Volume 2	Interview disc
26/02/1987	The Beatles	CD	Parlophone	CDP 7 46435 2	Please Please Me	
26/02/1987	The Beatles	CD	Parlophone	CDP 7 46436 2	With The Beatles	
26/02/1987	The Beatles	CD	Parlophone	CDP 7 46437 2	A Hard Day's Night	Album
26/02/1987	The Beatles	CD	Parlophone	CDP 7 46438 2	Beatles For Sale	
26/02/1987	The Beatles	CD	HMV	BEA CD25	4 CD Box Set	Contains first 4 Beatles albums
13/04/1987	John Lennon	CD	Parlophone	CDPCS 7308	Menlove Avenue	
24/04/1987	Paul McCartney	7"	A & M	FREE 21	Long Tall Sally	Issued free with album The Prince's Trust Tenth Anniversary Birthday Party
27/04/1987	Paul McCartney	CD	Parlophone	CDP 7 46611 2	McCartney	
27/04/1987	Paul McCartney	CD	Parlophone	CZ 29	Ram	

RELEASE DATE	ARTIST	FORMAT	LABEL	CAT NO.	TITLE	NOTES
30/04/1987	The Beatles	CD	Parlophone	CDP 7 46439 2	Help !	Album
30/04/1987	The Beatles	CD	Parlophone	CDP 7 46440 2	Rubber Soul	
30/04/1987	The Beatles	CD	Parlophone	CDP 7 46441 2	Revolver	
30/04/1987	The Beatles	CD	HMV	BEA CD25/2	3 CD Box Set	Contains Beatles albums 5–7
18/05/1987	George Harrison	CD	Apple	CDS 7 46688 2	All Things Must Pass	
18/05/1987	George Harrison	CD	Parlophone	CDPAS 10011	Best of George Harrison	
26/05/1987	John Lennon	CD	Apple	CDP 7 46641 2	Imagine	
26/05/1987	John Lennon	CD	Parlophone	CDP 7 46707 2	Rock 'n' Roll	
26/05/1987	John Lennon	CD	Parlophone	CDP 7 46642 2	Shaved Fish	
26/05/1987	Paul McCartney	CD	Parlophone	CDPCSP 720	Wings Over America	
26/05/1987	Ringo Starr	CD	Parlophone	CDP 7 46663 2	Blast from your Past	
01/06/1987	The Beatles	CD	Parlophone	CDP 7 46442 2	Sgt. Pepper's Lonely Hearts Club Band	
01/06/1987	The Beatles	CD	HMV	BEA CD25/3	Sgt. Pepper's Lonely Hearts Club Band	Box set with free gifts
06/07/1987	The Beatles	7"	Parlophone	RP 5620	All You Need Is Love	
06/07/1987	The Beatles	12"	Parlophone	12 R 5620	All You Need Is Love	
20/07/1987	John Lennon	CD	Parlophone	CDP 7 46768 2	Walls And Bridges	
03/08/1987	John Lennon	CD	Parlophone	CDP 7 46769 2	Mind Games	
10/08/1987	John Lennon	CD	Parlophone	CDP 7 46782 8	Some Time in New York City	
10/08/1987	John Lennon	CD	Parlophone	CDP 7 46783 2	Live Jam	
24/08/1987	The Beatles	CD	Apple	CDP 7 46443 8	The Beatles	Informally called "The White Album"
24/08/1987	The Beatles	CD	Parlophone	CDP 7 46445 2	Yellow Submarine	
24/08/1987	The Beatles	CD	HMV	BEA CD25/4	The Beatles	Informally called "The White Album"; Box set with free gifts
24/08/1987	The Beatles	CD	HMV	BEA CD25/5	Yellow Submarine	Box set with free gifts
21/09/1987	The Beatles	CD	Apple	CDP 7 48062 2	Magical Mystery Tour	
21/09/1987	The Beatles	CD	HMV	BEA CD25/6	Magical Mystery Tour	Box set with free gifts
05/10/1987	Paul McCartney	CD	Fame	CD-FA 3101	Wild Life	
05/10/1987	Paul McCartney	CD	Fame	CD-FA 3191	McCartney II	

RELEASE DATE	ARTIST	FORMAT	LABEL	CAT NO.	TITLE	NOTES
05/10/1987	Paul McCartney	CD	Fame	CD-FA 3193	Red Rose Speedway	
12/10/1987	George Harrison	7"	Dark Horse	W 8178	Got My Mind Set On You	
12/10/1987	George Harrison	12"	Dark Horse	W 8178 T	Got My Mind Set On You	
12/10/1987	The Beatles	LP	Raven	RVLP 1012	Downunder Vol.1	Interview disc
12/10/1987	The Beatles	LP	Raven	RVLP 1013	Downunder Vol.2	Interview disc
19/10/1987	The Beatles	CD	Apple	CDP 7 46446 2	Abbey Road	Album
19/10/1987	The Beatles	CD	Apple	CDP 7 46447 2	Let It Be	
19/10/1987	The Beatles	CD	HMV	BEA CD25/7	Abbey Road	Box set with free gifts
19/10/1987	The Beatles	CD	HMV	BEA CD25/8	Let It Be	Box set with free gifts
19/10/1987	Paul McCartney	CD	Fame	CD-FA 3213	Venus And Mars	
19/10/1987	The Beatles	CD	Charly Topline	TOPCD 523	Decca Sessions	12 Decca audition tracks
19/10/1987	The Beatles	LP	Charly Topline	TOP 181	Decca Sessions	12 Decca audition tracks
02/11/1987	George Harrison	LP	Dark Horse	WX 123	Cloud Nine	
02/11/1987	George Harrison	CD	Dark Horse	9 25643-2	Cloud Nine	
02/11/1987	Paul McCartney	LP	Parlophone	PMTV 1	All The Best	
02/11/1987	Paul McCartney	CD	Parlophone	CDPMTV 1	All The Best	
16/11/1987	Paul McCartney	7"	Parlophone	R 6170	Once Upon A Long Ago	
16/11/1987	Paul McCartney	12"	Parlophone	12 R 6170	Once Upon a Long Ago	
23/11/1987	The Beatles	7"	Parlophone	RP 5655	Hello, Goodbye	
25/01/1988	George Harrison	7"	Dark Horse	W 8131	When We Was Fab	
25/01/1988	George Harrison	12"	Dark Horse	W 8131 T	When We Was Fab	
29/01/1988	The Beatles	7"	Baktabak	BAKPAK 1004	A Rare Interview With The Beatles	Four 7" picture discs
01/02/1988	George Harrison	7"	Dark Horse	W 8131	When We Was Fab (Box Set Edition)	
06/02/1988	The Beatles	CD	Baktabak	CBAK 4001	Interview Picture Disc	Interview disc
06/02/1988	The Beatles	LP	Baktabak	CBAK 4001	The Beatles Conquer The U.S.A.	Interview disc
08/03/1988	The Beatles	CD	Parlophone	CDBPM 1	Past Masters Volume One	

RELEASE DATE	ARTIST	FORMAT	LABEL	CAT NO.	TITLE	NOTES
08/03/1988	The Beatles	CD	Parlophone	CDBPM 2	Past Masters Volume Two	
09/03/1988	The Beatles	CD	HMV	BEA CD25/9	Past Masters Volume One	Box set with free gifts
09/03/1988	The Beatles	CD	HMV	BEA CD25/10	Past Masters Volume Two	Box set with free gifts
14/03/1988	The Beatles	7"	Parlophone	RP 5675	Lady Madonna	
05/04/1988	John Lennon	CD	Parlophone	CDP 7 46770 2	John Lennon/Plastic Ono Band	
14/04/1988	The Beatles	CD	Baktabak	CBAK 4009	Interview Picture Disc Vol. 2	Interview disc
13/06/1988	George Harrison	7"	Dark Horse	W 7913	This Is Love	
13/06/1988	George Harrison	12"	Dark Horse	W 7913 T	This Is Love	
11/07/1988	John Lennon	LP	Baktabak	BAK 2096	The Last Word	Interview disc
04/08/1988	The Beatles	LP	Baktabak	BAK 2108	The Gospel According to . . . (1964–1966)	
04/08/1988	The Beatles	LP	Baktabak	BAK 2108	Beatles Interview Picture Disc Vol.2	Interview disc; picture disc
30/08/1988	The Beatles	7"	Apple	RP 5722	Hey Jude	
30/08/1988	The Beatles	12"	Apple	12 R 5722	Hey Jude	
10/10/1988	John Lennon	LP	Parlophone	PCSP 722	Imagine: John Lennon (Music from the Film)	
10/10/1988	John Lennon	CD	Parlophone	CDPCSP 722	Imagine: John Lennon (Music from the Film)	
17/10/1988	George Harrison	7"	Wilbury Records	W 7732	Handle With Care	Credited to "The Traveling Wilburys"; Harrison + Jeff Lynne, Tom Petty, Roy Orbison, Bob Dylan
17/10/1988	George Harrison	7"	Wilbury Records	W 7732W	Handle With Care	Credited to "The Traveling Wilburys"; Harrison + Jeff Lynne, Tom Petty, Roy Orbison, Bob Dylan; Special edition with picture sleeve and peel-off sticker

RELEASE DATE	ARTIST	FORMAT	LABEL	CAT NO.	TITLE	NOTES
17/10/1988	George Harrison	10"	Wilbury Records	W 7732TE	Handle With Care	Credited to "The Traveling Wilburys"; Harrison + Jeff Lynne, Tom Petty, Roy Orbison, Bob Dylan
17/10/1988	George Harrison	12"	Wilbury Records	W 7732T	Handle With Care	Credited to "The Traveling Wilburys"; Harrison + Jeff Lynne, Tom Petty, Roy Orbison, Bob Dylan
17/10/1988	George Harrison	CD	Wilbury Records	W 7732CD	Handle With Care	Credited to "The Traveling Wilburys"; Harrison + Jeff Lynne, Tom Petty, Roy Orbison, Bob Dylan; 3" CD single
24/10/1988	The Beatles	LP	Parlophone	BPM 1	Past Masters Volumes One & Two	
24/10/1988	George Harrison	LP	Wilbury Records	WX 224	Traveling Wilburys	Credited to "The Traveling Wilburys"; Harrison + Jeff Lynne, Tom Petty, Roy Orbison, Bob Dylan
24/10/1988	George Harrison	CD	Wilbury Records	9 25796-2	Traveling Wilburys	Credited to "The Traveling Wilburys"; Harrison + Jeff Lynne, Tom Petty, Roy Orbison, Bob Dylan
31/10/1988	The Beatles	LP	EMI	BBX 1	The Beatles (Box set))	Original 12 Beatles studio albums, plus Magical Mystery Tour and Past Masters (double LP)
31/10/1988	The Beatles	CD	EMI	CDS 7 91302 2	The Beatles (Box set))	Original 12 Beatles studio albums, plus Magical Mystery Tour and Past Masters (single CD)
31/10/1988	The Beatles	LP	Baktabak	BAK 2108	The Gospel According to The Beatles	Possibly the same as Beatles Interview Picture Disc Vol.2 (above)

RELEASE DATE	ARTIST	FORMAT	LABEL	CAT NO.	TITLE	NOTES
13/11/1988	The Beatles	LP	Baktabak	BAK 2114	Beatles Conquer The U.S.A.	Interview disc
21/11/1988	The Beatles	CD	Baktabak	CTAB 5001	Beatles at the Star-Club	30 Star-Club tracks
21/11/1988	The Beatles	LP	Baktabak	LTAB 5001	Beatles at the Star-Club	30 Star-Club tracks
28/11/1988	John Lennon	7"	Parlophone	R 6199	Imagine	
28/11/1988	John Lennon	12"	Parlophone	12 R 6199	Imagine	
11/12/1988	The Beatles	CD	Spectrum	SPEC 85025	Live at the Star-Club	30 Star-Club tracks
12/12/1988	The Beatles	CD	ABCD	ABCD 005	The Conversation Disc Series (1963–1965)	Interview disc
30/01/1989	John Lennon	CD	Capitol	CDP 7 91425 2 * NOT UK *	Double Fantasy	US Import. No UK release
14/02/1989	Ringo Starr	LP	Rhino	RP 5722	Starr Struck	
10/04/1989	The Beatles	7"	Apple	R 6213	Get Back	
08/05/1989	Paul McCartney	7"	Parlophone	R 6213	My Brave Face	
08/05/1989	Paul McCartney	12"	Parlophone	12 R 6213	My Brave Face	
30/05/1989	The Beatles	7"	Apple	RP 5786	The Ballad Of John And Yoko	
05/06/1989	Paul McCartney	LP	Parlophone	PCSD 106	Flowers in the Dirt	
05/06/1989	Paul McCartney	CD	Parlophone	CDPCSD 106	Flowers in the Dirt	
10/07/1989	Paul McCartney	CD	Parlophone	CDPAS 10010	Wings At The Speed Of Sound	
17/07/1989	Paul McCartney	7"	Parlophone	R 6223	This One	
17/07/1989	Paul McCartney	CD	Parlophone	CD R 6223	This One	
17/07/1989	Paul McCartney	12"	Parlophone	12 R 6223	This One	
24/07/1989	Paul McCartney	7"	Parlophone	RX 6223	This One	Single box set with new B-side
24/07/1989	Paul McCartney	CD	Parlophone	CDPCTC 257	Back To The Egg	
31/07/1989	Paul McCartney	12"	Parlophone	12RX 6223	This One	Additional track
29/08/1989	Paul McCartney	CD	Fame	CD-FA 3223	London Town	
07/10/1989	The Beatles	LP	Baktabak	VBAK 3004	Beatles Talk	
23/10/1989	John Lennon	CD	Parlophone	CDP 7 91516 2	Downunder Vol.1 (1964) The John Lennon Collection	

RELEASE DATE	ARTIST	FORMAT	LABEL	CAT NO.	TITLE	NOTES
23/10/1989	George Harrison	LP	Dark Horse	WX 312	The Best of Dark Horse: 1976–1989	
23/10/1989	George Harrison	CD	Dark Horse	9 25726-2	The Best of Dark Horse: 1976–1989	
30/10/1989	The Beatles	7"	Apple	RP 5814	Something	
06/11/1989	The Beatles	CD	EMI	CD BSC 1	Box set	Box set of 3" CD versions of 22 original Beatles singles released individually during the preceding year
13/11/1989	Paul McCartney	7"	Parlophone	R 6235	Figure Of Eight	
13/11/1989	Paul McCartney	12"	Parlophone	12 R 6235	Figure Of Eight	
17/11/1989	The Beatles	LP	Baktabak	VBAK 3006	Beatles Talk Downunder (and All Over) Vol.2 (1964)	Interview disc
23/11/1989	Paul McCartney	7"	Parlophone	R 6238	Party Party	
23/11/1989	Paul McCartney	CD	Parlophone	PCSDX 106	Flowers in the Dirt (World Tour Pack)	
27/11/1989	George Harrison	7"	Dark Horse	W 2696	Cheer Down	
27/11/1989	George Harrison	12"	Dark Horse	W 2696 T	Cheer Down	
12/01/1990	The Beatles	CD	Baktabak	CBAK 4024	Beatles Talk Downunder Vol.1 (1964)	Interview disc
22/01/1990	Paul McCartney	LP	Wax	BANDONTHE 1	London and Rome Press Conferences	Interview disc
05/02/1990	Paul McCartney	7"	Parlophone	R 6246	Put It There	
05/02/1990	Paul McCartney	12"	Parlophone	12 RS 6246	Put It There	
05/03/1990	The Beatles	7"	Apple	RP 5833	Let It Be	
05/03/1990	The Beatles	EP	Wax	FAB 7-1	Adelaide Press Conference (1964)	Interview disc
04/06/1990	The Beatles	EP	Wax	FAB 7-2	Vancouver Press Conference/Interviews 64	Interview disc

RELEASE DATE	ARTIST	FORMAT	LABEL	CAT NO.	TITLE	NOTES
18/06/1990	George Harrison	7"	Wilbury Records	W 9773	Nobody's Child	Credited to "The Traveling Wilburys"; Harrison + Jeff Lynne, Tom Petty, Bob Dylan (A-side only)
18/06/1990	George/Ringo	12"	Wilbury Records	W 9773T	Nobody's Child	A-side credited to "The Traveling Wilburys" (Harrison + Jeff Lynne, Tom Petty, Bob Dylan); extra track on B-side is Ringo Starr
18/06/1990	George/Ringo	CD	Wilbury Records	W 9773CD	Nobody's Child	Title track credited to "The Traveling Wilburys" (Harrison + Jeff Lynne, Tom Petty, Bob Dylan); extra track is Ringo Starr; CD single
??/07/1990	Paul McCartney	LP	Wax	TUGA 4	Press Conferences: Los Angeles and Madrid (and Detroit)	Interview disc
23/07/1990	George Harrison	LP	Wilbury Records	WEA WX 353	Nobody's Child	Title track credited to "The Traveling Wilburys" (Harrison + Jeff Lynne, Tom Petty, Bob Dylan)
??/08/1990	Paul McCartney	LP	Wax	PM 10	Rotterdam Press Conference	Interview disc
06/08/1990	The Beatles	EP	Wax	FAB 7-3	Seattle Press Conference	Interview disc
06/08/1990	The Beatles	LP	Discussion	STUD 10	George Martin Talks about The Beatles	Interview disc
06/08/1990	The Beatles	EP	Wax	FAB 7-3	Seattle Press Conference	Interview disc
10/09/1990	The Beatles	EP	Wax	FAB 7-4	Tokyo Interviews	Interview disc
19/09/1990	The Beatles	CD	Baktabak	CBAK 4034	Beatles Talk Downunder Vol.2 (1964)	Interview disc
08/10/1990	Paul McCartney	7"	Parlophone	R 6271	Birthday	
08/10/1990	Paul McCartney	12"	Parlophone	12 R 6271	Birthday	

RELEASE DATE	ARTIST	FORMAT	LABEL	CAT NO.	TITLE	NOTES
08/10/1990	Ringo Starr	LP	EMI	EMS 1375	Ringo and His All-Starr Band	
08/10/1990	Ringo Starr	CD	EMI	CZ 353	Ringo and His All-Starr Band	
29/10/1990	George Harrison	LP	Wilbury Records	WX 384	Traveling Wilburys Volume 3	Credited to "The Traveling Wilburys"; Harrison + Jeff Lynne, Tom Petty, Bob Dylan
29/10/1990	George Harrison	CD	Wilbury Records	7599 26324-2	Traveling Wilburys Volume 3	Credited to "The Traveling Wilburys"; Harrison + Jeff Lynne, Tom Petty, Bob Dylan
29/10/1990	The Beatles	EP	Wax	FAB 7-5	Dallas Press Conference	Interview disc
29/10/1990	The Beatles	EP	Wax	FAB 7-5	Dallas Press Conference	Interview disc
30/10/1990	John Lennon	CD	EMI	CDS 7 95220 2	Lennon (4CD Box Set)	
05/11/1990	Paul McCartney	LP	Parlophone	PCST 7346	Tripping the Live Fantastic	
05/11/1990	Paul McCartney	CD	Parlophone	CDPCST 73461	Tripping the Live Fantastic	
05/11/1990	George Harrison	7"	Wilbury Records	W 9523	She's My Baby	Credited to "The Traveling Wilburys"; Harrison + Jeff Lynne, Tom Petty, Bob Dylan
05/11/1990	George Harrison	12"	Wilbury Records	W 9523T	She's My Baby	Credited to "The Traveling Wilburys"; Harrison + Jeff Lynne, Tom Petty, Bob Dylan; additional track
05/11/1990	George Harrison	CD	Wilbury Records	W 9523CD	She's My Baby	Credited to "The Traveling Wilburys"; Harrison + Jeff Lynne, Tom Petty, Bob Dylan; CD single; additional track
12/11/1990	John Lennon	CD	BBC	BBCCD 6002	John and Yoko – The Interview	Interview disc

RELEASE DATE	ARTIST	FORMAT	LABEL	CAT NO.	TITLE	NOTES
19/11/1990	Paul McCartney	CD	Parlophone	CDPCSD 114	Tripping the Live Fantastic (Highlights)	
26/11/1990	Paul McCartney	7"	Parlophone	R 6278	All My Trials	
26/11/1990	Paul McCartney	12"	Parlophone	12 R 6278	All My Trials	
14/12/1990	John Lennon	CD	Thunderbolt	CDTB 095	Testimony	Interview disc
14/12/1990	Paul McCartney	CD	Wax	FORNO 1	Liverpool Press Conference	Interview disc
04/03/1991	Ringo Starr	CD	EMI	CDEMS 1386	Ringo	
11/03/1991	George/Ringo	CD	Discussion	YOURE 016	George and Ringo – 1980s Interviews	Interview disc
25/03/1991	George Harrison	7"	Wilbury Records	W 0018	Wilbury Twist	Credited to "The Traveling Wilburys"; Harrison + Jeff Lynne, Tom Petty, Bob Dylan
25/03/1991	George Harrison	7"	Wilbury Records	W 0018W	Wilbury Twist	Credited to "The Traveling Wilburys"; Harrison + Jeff Lynne, Tom Petty, Bob Dylan; special edition with free postcards
25/03/1991	George Harrison	12"	Wilbury Records	W 0018T	Wilbury Twist	Credited to "The Traveling Wilburys"; Harrison + Jeff Lynne, Tom Petty, Bob Dylan; additional track
25/03/1991	George Harrison	CD	Wilbury Records	W 0018CD	Wilbury Twist	Credited to "The Traveling Wilburys"; Harrison + Jeff Lynne, Tom Petty, Bob Dylan; CD single; additional track
20/05/1991	Paul McCartney	CD	Parlophone	CDPCSD 116	Unplugged - The Official Bootleg	
03/06/1991	The Beatles	CD	Baktabak	CBAK 4024	Beatles Talk Downunder (1964)	Interview disc re-release
03/06/1991	The Beatles	CD	Baktabak	CBAK 4034	Beatles Talk Downunder Vol.2	Interview disc re-release

RELEASE DATE	ARTIST	FORMAT	LABEL	CAT NO.	TITLE	NOTES
19/08/1991	George Harrison	CD	Epic	468835-2	Concert For Bangla Desh	
26/08/1991	The Beatles	LP	Baktabak	LINT 5004	Introspective	Interviews plus six live tracks of unknown origin: Twist And Shout, I Saw Her Standing There, Till There Was You, Roll Over Beethoven, Hippy Hippy Shake, Taste Of Honey
26/08/1991	The Beatles	CD	Baktabak	CINT 5004	Introspective	Interviews plus six live tracks of unknown origin: Twist And Shout, I Saw Her Standing There, Till There Was You, Roll Over Beethoven, Hippy Hippy Shake, Taste Of Honey
30/09/1991	Paul McCartney	CD	Parlophone	CDPCSD 117	Choba B CCCP	
07/10/1991	Paul McCartney	CD	EMI Classics	PAUL 1	Liverpool Oratorio	Written by McCartney but he does not appear
11/11/1991	The Beatles	LP	Discussion	REVOL 4	Press Conferences (1964–1966)	Interview disc
??/12/1991	Paul McCartney	CD	Discussion	LMW 281F	Press Conferences: Tokyo/Chicago 1990	Interview disc
27/01/1992	George Harrison	CD	Apple	CDPAS 10006	Living in the Material World	
27/01/1992	George Harrison	CD	Apple	CDPAS 10008	Dark Horse	
27/01/1992	George Harrison	CD	Apple	CDPAS 10009	Extra Texture - Read All About It	
04/05/1992	Ringo Starr	7"	Private Music	115 392	Weight Of The World	
16/05/1992	The Beatles	CD	Columbia	4689502	Rockin' at the Star-Club 1962	30 Star-Club tracks.
22/05/1992	Ringo Starr	CD	Private Music	262 902	Time Takes Time	
15/06/1992	The Beatles	CD	Parlophone	CD BEP 14	EP Collection	Box set
15/06/1992	The Beatles	CD	Parlophone	CDGEP 8880	The Beatles Hits	CD release of original EP

RELEASE DATE	ARTIST	FORMAT	LABEL	CAT NO.	TITLE	NOTES
15/06/1992	The Beatles	CD	Parlophone	CDGEP 8882	Twist and Shout	CD release of original EP
15/06/1992	The Beatles	CD	Parlophone	CDGEP 8883	The Beatles No.1	CD release of original EP
15/06/1992	The Beatles	CD	Parlophone	CDGEP 8891	All My Loving	CD release of original EP
15/06/1992	The Beatles	CD	Parlophone	CDGEP 8913	Long Tall Sally	CD release of original EP
15/06/1992	The Beatles	CD	Parlophone	CDGEP 8920	A Hard Day's Night (Extracts from the Film)	CD release of original EP
15/06/1992	The Beatles	CD	Parlophone	CDGEP 8924	A Hard Day's Night (Extracts from the Album)	CD release of original EP
15/06/1992	The Beatles	CD	Parlophone	CDGEP 8931	Beatles For Sale	CD release of original EP
15/06/1992	The Beatles	CD	Parlophone	CDGEP 8938	Beatles For Sale No.2	CD release of original EP
15/06/1992	The Beatles	CD	Parlophone	CDGEP 8946	The Beatles Million Sellers	CD release of original EP
15/06/1992	The Beatles	CD	Parlophone	CDGEP 8948	Yesterday	CD release of original EP
15/06/1992	The Beatles	CD	Parlophone	CDGEP 8952	Nowhere Man	CD release of original EP
15/06/1992	The Beatles	CD	Parlophone	CDMAG 1	Magical Mystery Tour	CD release of original EP
15/06/1992	The Beatles	CD	Parlophone	CDSGE 1	Rarities	CD release of original EP
29/06/1992	George Harrison	CD	Apple	CDSAPCOR 1	Wonderwall Music	
??/07/1992	Paul McCartney	CD	Discussion	BROADS 003	Press Conferences: London and New York	Interview disc
13/07/1992	George Harrison	CD	Dark Horse	7599 2 69642	Live In Japan	
??/10/1992	Paul McCartney	CD	EMI Classics	CDC 7 54642 2	Selections from Liverpool Oratorio	Written by McCartney but he does not appear
02/11/1992	The Beatles	CD	Parlophone	CD BSCP 1	CD Singles Collection	Box set
02/11/1992	The Beatles	CD	Parlophone	CDR 4949	Love Me Do	
02/11/1992	The Beatles	CD	Parlophone	CDR 4983	Please Please Me	
02/11/1992	The Beatles	CD	Parlophone	CDR 5015	From Me To You	
02/11/1992	The Beatles	CD	Parlophone	CDR 5055	She Loves You	
02/11/1992	The Beatles	CD	Parlophone	CDR 5084	I Want To Hold Your Hand	
02/11/1992	The Beatles	CD	Parlophone	CDR 5114	Can't Buy Me Love	
02/11/1992	The Beatles	CD	Parlophone	CDR 5160	A Hard Day's Night	Single

RELEASE DATE	ARTIST	FORMAT	LABEL	CAT NO.	TITLE	NOTES
02/11/1992	The Beatles	CD	Parlophone	CDR 5200	I Feel Fine	
02/11/1992	The Beatles	CD	Parlophone	CDR 5265	Ticket To Ride	
02/11/1992	The Beatles	CD	Parlophone	CDR 5305	Help!	Single
02/11/1992	The Beatles	CD	Parlophone	CDR 5389	Day Tripper/ We Can Work It Out	
02/11/1992	The Beatles	CD	Parlophone	CDR 5452	Paperback Writer	
02/11/1992	The Beatles	CD	Parlophone	CDR 5493	Eleanor Rigby/ Yellow Submarine	
02/11/1992	The Beatles	CD	Parlophone	CDR 5570	Penny Lane/Strawberry Fields Forever	
02/11/1992	The Beatles	CD	Parlophone	CDR 5620	All You Need Is Love	
02/11/1992	The Beatles	CD	Parlophone	CDR 5655	Hello, Goodbye	
02/11/1992	The Beatles	CD	Parlophone	CDR 5675	Lady Madonna	
02/11/1992	The Beatles	CD	Apple	CDR 5722	Hey Jude	
02/11/1992	The Beatles	CD	Apple	CDR 5777	Get Back	
02/11/1992	The Beatles	CD	Apple	CDR 5786	The Ballad Of John And Yoko	
02/11/1992	The Beatles	CD	Apple	CDR 5814	Something	
02/11/1992	The Beatles	CD	Apple	CDR 5833	Let It Be	Single
?/12/1992	Ringo Starr	CD	EMI	CDEMS 1467	Goodnight Vienna	
28/12/1992	Paul McCartney	7"	Parlophone	R 6330	Hope Of Deliverance	
?/01/1993	John Lennon	CD	Rock Classics	SSI 9999	Unfinished Music No.1 – Two Virgins	
05/01/1993	Paul McCartney	12"	Parlophone	12 R 6330	Deliverance	
02/02/1993	Paul McCartney	LP	Parlophone	PCSD 125	Off the Ground	
02/02/1993	Paul McCartney	CD	Parlophone	CDPCSD 125	Off the Ground	
28/02/1993	Paul McCartney	7"	Parlophone	R 6338	C'mon People	
?/04/1993	Paul McCartney	CD	Parlophone	CDPMCOL 1	McCartney	
?/04/1993	Paul McCartney	CD	Parlophone	CDPMCOL 2	Ram	
?/04/1993	Paul McCartney	CD	Parlophone	CDPMCOL 3	Wild Life	
?/04/1993	Paul McCartney	CD	Parlophone	CDPMCOL 4	Red Rose Speedway	
?/04/1993	Paul McCartney	CD	Parlophone	CDPMCOL 5	Band On The Run	

RELEASE DATE	ARTIST	FORMAT	LABEL	CAT NO.	TITLE	NOTES
??/04/1993	Paul McCartney	CD	Parlophone	CDPMCOL 6	Venus And Mars	
??/04/1993	Paul McCartney	CD	Parlophone	CDPMCOL 7	Wings At The Speed Of Sound	
??/04/1993	Paul McCartney	CD	Parlophone	CDPMCOL 8	London Town	
??/06/1993	The Beatles	CD	Holoview	3D 002	Ask You Once Again	Interview disc
07/06/1993	Paul McCartney	CD	Parlophone	CDPMCOL 9	Wings Greatest	
07/06/1993	Paul McCartney	CD	Parlophone	CDPMCOL 10	Back To The Egg	
07/06/1993	Paul McCartney	CD	Parlophone	CDPMCOL 11	McCartney II	
07/06/1993	Paul McCartney	CD	Parlophone	CDPMCOL 12	Tug Of War	
07/06/1993	Paul McCartney	CD	Parlophone	CDPMCOL 13	Pipes Of Peace	
07/06/1993	Paul McCartney	CD	Parlophone	CDPMCOL 14	Give My Regards To Broad Street	
07/06/1993	Paul McCartney	CD	Parlophone	CDPMCOL 15	Press To Play	
07/06/1993	Paul McCartney	CD	Parlophone	CDPMCOL 16	Flowers In The Dirt	
14/09/1993	Ringo Starr	CD	Rykodisc	RCD 20264	Ringo and His All-Starr Band Volume 2 – Live From Montreux	
15/11/1993	Paul McCartney	CD	Parlophone	CDPCSD 145	Strawberries Oceans Ships Forest	Credited to "The Fireman"
15/11/1993	Paul McCartney	LP	Parlophone	PCSD 145	Strawberries Oceans Ships Forest	Credited to "The Fireman"
15/11/1993	Paul McCartney	LP	Parlophone	PCSD 147	Paul Is Live	
15/11/1993	Paul McCartney	CD	Parlophone	CDPCSD 147	Paul Is Live	
04/09/1994	The Beatles	CD	Charly	CDCD 1185	Hear The Beatles Tell All	Interview disc
30/11/1994	The Beatles	LP	Apple	PCSP 726	Live at the BBC	
30/11/1994	The Beatles	CD	Apple	CDPCSP 726	Live at the BBC	
20/03/1995	The Beatles	EP	Apple	R 6406	Baby It's You	
20/03/1995	The Beatles	EP	Apple	RP 6406	Baby It's You	
20/03/1995	The Beatles	CD	Apple	CDR 6406	Baby It's You	
01/05/1995	Ringo Starr	CD	Parlophone	RP 6406	Sentimental Journey	
01/05/1995	Ringo Starr	CD	Apple	CDR 6406	Beaucoup Of Blues	Picture disc

RELEASE DATE	ARTIST	FORMAT	LABEL	CAT NO.	TITLE	NOTES
??/07/1995	The Beatles	CD	Sound and Media	SAM 7001	Interview Disc And Fully Illustrated Book	Interview disc
??/07/1995	The Beatles	CD	Thunderbolt	CDTB 506	Quote Unquote	Interview disc. No details in catalogue
??/08/1995	The Beatles	CD	MasterTone	JG 001-2	Rare Photos and Interview CD Vol.1	Interview disc
??/08/1995	The Beatles	CD	MasterTone	JG 002-2	Rare Photos and Interview CD Vol.2	Interview disc
??/08/1995	The Beatles	CD	MasterTone	JG 003-2	Rare Photos and Interview CD Vol.3	Interview disc
21/11/1995	The Beatles	LP	Apple	PCSP 727	Anthology 1	
21/11/1995	The Beatles	CD	Apple	CDPCSP 727	Anthology 1	
04/12/1995	The Beatles	7"	Apple	R 6422	Free As A Bird	Picture disc
04/12/1995	The Beatles	7"	Apple	RP 6422	Free As A Bird	Additional tracks
04/12/1995	The Beatles	CD	Apple	CDR 6422	Free As A Bird	
04/12/1995	The Beatles	CD	Laserlight	12591	Rockumentary No.1 – The Lost Beatles Interviews	Interview disc
04/12/1995	The Beatles	CD	Laserlight	12592	Rockumentary No.2 – Things We Said Today	Interview disc
04/12/1995	The Beatles	CD	Laserlight	15968	Rockumentary – In Their Own Words	Interview disc. 5-CD box set
04/12/1995	The Beatles	CD	Laserlight	12593	Rockumentary No. 3 Things We Said Today	Interview disc
04/12/1995	George Harrison	CD	Laserlight	12594	Rockumentary No. 4 The Secret Life of George Harrison	Interview disc
04/12/1995	John Lennon	CD	Laserlight	12595	Rockumentary No. 5 John Lennon Forever	Interview disc
04/03/1996	The Beatles	7"	Apple	R 6425	Real Love	
04/03/1996	The Beatles	7"	Apple	RP 6425(?)	Real Love	Picture disc; cat no stated same as non-picture 7" disc

RELEASE DATE	ARTIST	FORMAT	LABEL	CAT NO.	TITLE	NOTES
04/03/1996	The Beatles	CD	Apple	CDR 6425	Real Love	Interview disc
04/03/1996	The Beatles	CD	Laserlight	15981	Inside Interviews	Interview disc
04/03/1996	The Beatles	CD	Laserlight	12676	Inside Interviews No. 1 / In My Life	Interview disc
04/03/1996	The Beatles	CD	Laserlight	12677	Inside Interviews No. 2 / All Together Now	Interview disc
04/03/1996	The Beatles	CD	Laserlight	12678	Inside Interviews No. 3 / Beatlemania	Interview disc
04/03/1996	The Beatles	CD	Laserlight	12679	Inside Interviews No. 4 / Talk Downunder – Australia Beatlemania	Interview disc
04/03/1996	The Beatles	CD	Laserlight	12680	Inside Interviews No. 5 / Talk Downunder – Sydney to Seattle	Interview disc
18/03/1996	The Beatles	LP	Apple	PCSP 728	Anthology 2	
18/03/1996	The Beatles	CD	Apple	CDPCSP 728	Anthology 2	
??/04/1996	The Beatles	CD	Wax	DISSCD 1	Press Conferences 1964–1966	Interview disc
20/05/1996	The Beatles	CD	Wax	BEAT 1	Interview Disc 1	Interview disc
20/05/1996	The Beatles	CD	Wax	BEAT 2	Interview Disc 2	Interview disc
20/05/1996	The Beatles	CD	Wax	BEAT 3	Interview Disc 3	Interview disc
20/05/1996	The Beatles	CD	Wax	BEAT 4	Interview Disc 4	Interview disc
01/06/1996	John Lennon	LP	UFO	JOHN 1	John Lennon Interview	Interview disc
01/06/1996	Paul McCartney	LP	UFO	PAUL 1	Paul McCartney Interview	Interview disc
01/06/1996	George Harrison	LP	UFO	GEORGE 1	George Harrison Interview	Interview disc
01/06/1996	Ringo Starr	LP	UFO	RINGO 1	Ringo Starr Interview	Interview disc
31/07/1996	The Beatles	??	MagMid	MM 002	Quote Unquote Vol. 1	Interview disc. No details in catalogue
31/07/1996	The Beatles	??	MagMid	MM 009	Quote Unquote Vol. 2	Interview disc. No details in catalogue

RELEASE DATE	ARTIST	FORMAT	LABEL	CAT NO.	TITLE	NOTES
??/08/1996	The Beatles	??	Fab Four	FABFOUR 1	Interview Disc	Interview disc. No details in catalogue
??/08/1996	The Beatles	??	Fab Four	FABFOUR 2	Interview Disc	Interview disc. No details in catalogue
??/08/1996	The Beatles	??	Fab Four	FABFOUR 3	Interview Disc	Interview disc. No details in catalogue
??/08/1996	The Beatles	??	Fab Four	FABFOUR 4	Interview Disc	Interview disc. No details in catalogue
28/10/1996	The Beatles	LP	Apple	PCSP 729	Anthology 3	
28/10/1996	The Beatles	CD	Apple	CDPCSP 729	Anthology 3	
??/12/1996	George Harrison	CD	Apple	CDZAPPLE 02	Electronic Sound	
01/01/1997	Paul McCartney	CD	MPL	OOBU #5	Oobu Joobu – Ecology	Promotional CD of one of McCartney's performances as a DJ for his American radio Oobu Joobu series
28/04/1997	Paul McCartney	7"	Parlophone	RP 6462	Young Boy	
28/04/1997	Paul McCartney	CD	Parlophone	CD R 6462	Young Boy	
28/04/1997	Paul McCartney	CD	Parlophone	CD RS6462	Young Boy	Different additional tracks
05/05/1997	Paul McCartney	LP	Parlophone	PCSD 171	Flaming Pie	
05/05/1997	Paul McCartney	CD	Parlophone	CDPCSD 171	Flaming Pie	
??/06/1997	The Beatles	??	Fab Four	FABFOUR 5	Interview 1980	Interview disc. No details in catalogue
09/06/1997	John Lennon	CD	Rykodisc	RCD 10411	Unfinished Music No.1 – Two Virgins	
09/06/1997	John Lennon	CD	Rykodisc	RCD 10412	Unfinished Music No.2 – Life With The Lions	
09/06/1997	John Lennon	CD	Rykodisc	RCD 10413	The Wedding Album	
07/07/1997	Paul McCartney	7"	Parlophone	RP 6472	The World Tonight	
07/07/1997	Paul McCartney	CD	Parlophone	CD RS6472	The World Tonight	
07/07/1997	Paul McCartney	CD	Parlophone	CD R 6472	The World Tonight	Different additional tracks
12/08/1997	Ringo Starr	CD	Blockbuster	* NOT UK *	Ringo and His Third All-Starr Band – Volume 1	US Import. No UK release

RELEASE DATE	ARTIST	FORMAT	LABEL	CAT NO.	TITLE	NOTES
29/09/1997	Paul McCartney	CD	EMI Classics	CDC 5 56484 2	Standing Stone	Written by McCartney but he does not appear
27/10/1997	John Lennon	CD	Parlophone	8219542	Lennon Legend	
??/11/1997	The Beatles	??	Network	3D 002	Ask You Once Again	Interview disc. No details in catalogue. Possibly re-release of June 1993 Holoview CD
03/11/1997	The Beatles	??	Metro Independent	10026	Biography Series	Interview disc. No details in catalogue
15/12/1997	Paul McCartney	7"	Parlophone	RP 6489	Beautiful Night	
15/12/1997	Paul McCartney	7"	Parlophone	CD RS 6489	Beautiful Night	
15/12/1997	Paul McCartney	7"	Parlophone	CD R 6489	Beautiful Night	
03/08/1998	Ringo Starr	CD	Mercury	558 598-2	Vertical Man	
21/09/1998	Paul McCartney	LP	Hydra	HYDRA 4 97055 1	Rushes	Credited to "The Fireman"
19/10/1998	Ringo Starr	CD	Mercury	538 118-2	VH1 Storytellers	
29/10/1998	Paul McCartney	12"	Hydra	HYDRA 007	Fluid	Credited to "The Fireman"
02/11/1998	John Lennon	CD	Capitol	830 6142	Anthology	
02/11/1998	John Lennon	CD	Capitol	497 6392	Wonsaponatime	
02/11/1998	The Beatles	7"	Baktabak	TABOKS 1001	Live Recordings 1962	30 Star-Club tracks on a set of 15 singles
27/11/1998	The Beatles	CD	Thunderbolt	CDTB 194	East Coast Invasion	Interview disc. No details in catalogue
18/01/1999	The Beatles	CD	Oz It Records	OZIT CD0033	Magical And Mystical Words	Interview disc
22/03/1999	Paul McCartney	CD	Parlophone	499 1762	Band On The Run (25th Anniversary)	
13/09/1999	The Beatles	LP	Apple	521 4811	Yellow Submarine – Songtrack	
13/09/1999	The Beatles	CD	Apple	521 4812	Yellow Submarine – Songtrack	
04/10/1999	Paul McCartney	CD	Parlophone	523 3042	Run Devil Run	
19/10/1999	Ringo Starr	CD	Mercury	546 668-2	I Wanna Be Santa Claus	

RELEASE DATE	ARTIST	FORMAT	LABEL	CAT NO.	TITLE	NOTES
24/10/1999	Paul McCartney	7"	Parlophone	R 6527	No Other Baby	
24/10/1999	Paul McCartney	CD	Parlophone	CD R 627	No Other Baby	
24/10/1999	Paul McCartney	CD	Parlophone	CDRS 6527	No Other Baby	Mono CD
02/11/1999	Paul McCartney	CD	EMI Classics	CDC 5 56897 2	Working Classical	Written by McCartney but he does not appear
23/12/1999	John Lennon	CD	Parlophone	CDR 6534	Imagine	
25/12/1999	Paul McCartney	7"	Parlophone	523 2291	Run Devil Run	7" Box set
??/??/1999	Paul McCartney	12"	Hydra	HYDRA 008	Fluid – Nitin Sawhney Remixes	Credited to "The Fireman"
14/02/2000	John Lennon	CD	Parlophone	524 8582	Imagine	
14/02/2000	Paul McCartney	CD	EMI Classics	CDC 5 56961 2	A Garland For Linda	Various artists, one track written by McCartney
26/05/2000	The Beatles	CD	Thunderbolt	CDTB 208	Not For A Second Time	Interview disc. No details in catalogue.
28/07/2000	The Beatles	CD	Thunderbolt	CDTB 209	Things We Said Today	Interview disc
21/08/2000	Paul McCartney	CD	Hydra	HYDRA 5 28817 2	Liverpool Sound Collage	Various artists, "Paul McCartney" and/or "The Beatles" credited on three tracks
11/09/2000	The Beatles	??	Rock On ROM	STPROM 1	Interview Disc	Interview disc. No details in catalogue
02/10/2000	The Beatles	CD	Thunderbolt	CDTB 195	West Coast Invasion	Interview disc. No details in catalogue
09/10/2000	John Lennon	CD	Capitol	528 7392	Double Fantasy	
09/10/2000	John Lennon	CD	EMI	528 7402	John Lennon/ Plastic Ono Band	
09/10/2000	The Beatles	CD	Chrome Dreams	ABCD 067	As It Happened	Interview disc. No details in catalogue. Possibly cat. No. CIS 2001
13/11/2000	The Beatles	LP	Apple	529 3251	1	
13/11/2000	The Beatles	CD	Apple	529 9702	1	
13/11/2000	The Beatles	??	Walters	BDR 80012	1962 Live At The Star-Club	Star-Club tracks; no detail listed in catalogue.

RELEASE DATE	ARTIST	FORMAT	LABEL	CAT NO.	TITLE	NOTES
22/01/2001	George Harrison	CD	GN Records	530 4742	All Things Must Pass (Remastered)	
05/02/2001	Ringo Starr	CD	E.M.G.	EMG 12003-2	The Anthology . . . So Far	
07/05/2001	Paul McCartney	CD	Parlophone	532 8762	Wingspan	
27/09/2001	John Lennon	CD	EMI	535 9592	Milk and Honey	
29/09/2001	The Beatles	CD	Thunderbolt	CDTB 220	From Britain With Beat	Interview disc. No details in catalogue
29/10/2001	Paul McCartney	7"	Parlophone	R 6567	From A Lover To A Friend	
29/10/2001	Paul McCartney	CD	Parlophone	CDR 6567	From A Lover To A Friend	
05/11/2001	Paul McCartney	7"	Parlophone	RS 6567	Freedom	
05/11/2001	Paul McCartney	CD	Parlophone	CDRS 6567	Freedom	
12/11/2001	Paul McCartney	CD	Parlophone	535 5102	Driving Rain	
14/01/2002	George Harrison	CD	Parlophone	CDR 6571	My Sweet Lord	
28/01/2002	George Harrison	CD	Epic	468835-2	Concert For Bangla Desh (Remastered)	
11/02/2002	The Beatles	CD	Chrome Dreams	CDTY 001	Talkology Vol. 1	Interview disc. No details in catalogue
11/02/2002	The Beatles	CD	Chrome Dreams	CDTY 002	Talkology Vol. 2	Interview disc. No details in catalogue
11/02/2002	The Beatles	CD	Chrome Dreams	CDTY 003	Talkology Vol. 3	Interview disc. No details in catalogue
06/08/2002	Ringo Starr	CD	King Biscuit	* NOT U.K. *	Ringo and His New All-Starr Band	US Import. No UK release
21/10/2002	John Lennon	CD	EMI	542 4252	Mind Games	
18/11/2002	George Harrison	CD	Dark Horse/Parlophone	543 2462	Brainwashed	
??/??/2002	The Beatles	CD	Musicbank	APWCD 1200	Interviews	Interview disc
17/03/2003	Paul McCartney	CD	Parlophone	583 0052	Back In The World	
25/03/2003	Ringo Starr	CD	Koch Records	* NOT U.K. *	Ringo Rama	US Import. No UK release

RELEASE DATE	ARTIST	FORMAT	LABEL	CAT NO.	TITLE	NOTES
12/05/2003	George Harrison	7"	Parlophone	R 6601	Any Road	
27/10/2003	John Lennon	CD	EMI	595 0672	Lennon Legend	
17/11/2003	The Beatles	LP	Apple	595 7132	Let It Be . . . Naked	
17/11/2003	Paul/Ringo	CD	WSM	8122 74546 2	Concert For George	Various artists concert in tribute to Harrison. Starr and/or McCartney appear on several tracks
17/11/2003	The Beatles	CD	Apple	595 4380	Let It Be . . . Naked	
08/12/2003	John Lennon	CD	Apple	CDR 6627	Happy Xmas (War Is Over)	
01/03/2004	George Harrison	CD	Dark Horse/ Parlophone	GHBOX 1	The Dark Horse Years 1976–1992 (Boxset)	
01/03/2004	George Harrison	CD	Dark Horse/ Parlophone	594 0862	Thirty Three & 1/3	
01/03/2004	George Harrison	CD	Dark Horse/ Parlophone	594 0872	George Harrison	
01/03/2004	George Harrison	CD	Dark Horse/ Parlophone	594 0882	Somewhere In England	
01/03/2004	George Harrison	CD	Dark Horse/ Parlophone	594 0892	Gone Troppo	
01/03/2004	George Harrison	CD	Dark Horse/ Parlophone	594 0902	Cloud Nine	
01/03/2004	George Harrison	CD	Dark Horse/ Parlophone	594 6652	Live In Japan	
08/03/2004	John Lennon	CD	Virgin	VTDCD 698 2004 07	John Lennon's Jukebox	Various artists; no Lennon tracks
14/06/2004	Paul McCartney	CD	Uncut	UNCUT 2004 07	Something For The Weekend	Free various artists CD given away with the July 2004 edition of Uncut Magazine. Two tracks by McCartney
13/09/2004	John Lennon	CD	EMI	EBX 23	Double Fantasy/ Milk and Honey	

RELEASE DATE	ARTIST	FORMAT	LABEL	CAT NO.	TITLE	NOTES
20/09/2004	Paul McCartney	7"	EMI	R 6649	Tropic Island Hum	
20/09/2004	Paul McCartney	CD	EMI	CDR 6649	Tropic Island Hum	
27/09/2004	John Lennon	CD	Capitol	CDR 6649	Rock 'n' Roll	
01/11/2004	John Lennon	CD	Capitol	874 4282	Acoustic	
15/11/2004	The Beatles	CD	EMI	875 4002	The Capitol Albums Vol. 1	
31/05/2005	Paul McCartney	12"	Graze	GRAZE 010	Really Love You	One-sided single; Credited to "Twin Freaks"; mash-up mixes of previously released McCartney recordings
06/06/2005	Paul McCartney	12"	Graze	GRAZE 012	Really Love You	Credited to "Twin Freaks"; mash-up mixes of previously released McCartney recordings
14/06/2005	Paul McCartney	LP	Parlophone	311 3001	Twin Freaks	Credited to "Twin Freaks"; mash-up mixes of previously released McCartney recordings; manufactured to order
25/07/2005	Ringo Starr	CD	CNR Records	22 998798	Choose Love	
29/08/2005	Paul McCartney	7"	Parlophone	R 6673	Fine Line	
29/08/2005	Paul McCartney	CD	Parlophone	CDR 6673	Fine Line	
12/09/2005	Paul McCartney	CD	Parlophone	337 9612	Chaos And Creation In The Backyard	
12/09/2005	Paul McCartney	LP	Parlophone	337 9581	Chaos And Creation In The Backyard	
03/10/2005	John Lennon	CD	Parlophone	340 0802	Working Class Hero – The Definitive Lennon	
21/11/2005	Paul McCartney	7"	Parlophone	R 6678	Jenny Wren	
21/11/2005	Paul McCartney	CD	Parlophone	CDR 6678	Jenny Wren	Two-track CD
21/11/2005	Paul McCartney	CD	Parlophone	CDRS 6678	Jenny Wren	Three-track CD
03/04/2006	The Beatles	CD	EMI	360 3352	The Capitol Albums Vol. 2	

RELEASE DATE	ARTIST	FORMAT	LABEL	CAT NO.	TITLE	NOTES
25/09/2006	George Harrison	LP	Parlophone	366 9002	Living in the Material World (limited edition "digi-pack in a box")	
25/09/2006	Paul McCartney	CD	EMI Classics	370 4242	Ecce Cor Meum [Behold My Heart]	Written by McCartney but he does not appear
20/11/2006	The Beatles	CD	Parlophone/Apple	379 8082	Love	
20/11/2006	The Beatles	DVD-A	Parlophone/Apple	379 8102	Love	Special 2-disc edition with CD and audio-only DVD containing slightly extended version in 5.1 surroundsound
30/04/2007	The Beatles	LP	Parlophone/Apple	379 8081	Love	
04/06/2007	Paul McCartney	LP	Hearmusic	723 0383	Memory Almost Full	
04/06/2007	Paul McCartney	CD	Hearmusic	723 0348	Memory Almost Full	Also given away free with Mail On Sunday on 18/05/08
04/06/2007	Paul McCartney	CD	Hearmusic	723 0358	Memory Almost Full	Two-disc digipack
04/06/2007	Paul McCartney	CD	Hearmusic	723 0357	Memory Almost Full	CD with special packaging
11/06/2007	George Harrison	CD	Wilbury Records	R2 167804	Traveling Wilburys Collection	Box set of two CDs and one DVD. Harrison + Jeff Lynne, Tom Petty, Roy Orbison, Bob Dylan
18/06/2007	Paul McCartney	CD	Hearmusic	723 0384	Dance Tonight	Picture disc
27/08/2007	Ringo Starr	CD	Capitol	504 9332	Photograph: The Very Best Of Ringo	
05/11/2007	Paul McCartney	CD	Hearmusic	723 0620	Ever Present Past	
05/11/2007	Paul McCartney	7"	Hearmusic	723 0621	Ever Present Past	
13/11/2007	Paul McCartney	12"	Hearmusic	* NOT UK *	Amoeba's Secret	US Import. No UK release
07/01/2008	Ringo Starr	CD	Capitol	CDLIV 8	Liverpool 8	Single
14/01/2008	Ringo Starr	CD	Capitol	517 3882	Liverpool 8	
04/03/2008	Ringo Starr	DVD-A	Koch Records	* NOT UK *	Ringo 5.1	US Import. No UK release
02/06/2008	George Harrison	CD	Rhino	8122799180	Traveling Wilburys	Credited to "The Traveling Wilburys"; Harrison + Jeff Lynne, Tom Petty, Roy Orbison, Bob Dylan; Expanded edition

RELEASE DATE	ARTIST	FORMAT	LABEL	CAT NO.	TITLE	NOTES
02/06/2008	George Harrison	CD	Rhino	8122799179	Traveling Wilburys Volume 3	Credited to "The Traveling Wilburys"; Harrison + Jeff Lynne, Tom Petty, Bob Dylan; Expanded edition
04/08/2008	Ringo Starr	CD	Koch Records	* NOT UK *	Ringo & His All Starr Band Live 2006	US Import. No UK release
24/11/2008	Paul McCartney	LP	One Little Indian	TPLP1003	Electric Arguments	Credited to "The Fireman"; includes bonus CD
24/11/2008	Paul McCartney	CD	Pinnacle	TPLP1003CD	Electric Arguments	Credited to "The Fireman"